PP 0306125 6

D1362985

UNIVERSITY OF
PORTSMOUTH LIBRARY

LEGAL METHOD
& REASONING

UNIVERSITY OF PORTSMOUTH LIBRARY

CLASS NUMBER

340.0941   HAN

LOCATION

FOUR WEEK LOAN   06/05

To be returned by the last date or time stamped below, or
when recalled by the Librarian.

THE DUE DATE MAY CHANGE
IF THIS BOOK IS RESERVED

1 4 APR 2010

	1 4 APR 2010	
- 3 FEB 2006		
- 4 DEC 2006		
6 OCT 2008		

Loans remain the responsibility of the borrower until cancelled at the loans desk.

LEGAL METHOD & REASONING

Second Edition

Sharon Hanson, LLB, MA

Director of the Legal Studies Programme and Theology Diploma
Birkbeck College, University of London

WITHDRAWN
UNIVERSITY OF
PORTSMOUTH LIBRARY

Cavendish
Publishing
Limited

London • Sydney • Portland, Oregon

UNIVERSITY OF
PORTSMOUTH
LIBRARY

0306125

Second edition first published in Great Britain 2003 by
Cavendish Publishing Limited, The Glass House,
Wharton Street, London WC1X 9PX, United Kingdom
Telephone: + 44 (0)20 7278 8000   Facsimile: + 44 (0)20 7278 8080
Email: info@cavendishpublishing.com
Website: www.cavendishpublishing.com

Published in the United States by Cavendish Publishing
c/o International Specialized Book Services,
5824 NE Hassalo Street, Portland,
Oregon 97213-3644, USA

Published in Australia by Cavendish Publishing (Australia) Pty Ltd
45 Beach Street, Coogee, NSW 2034, Australia
Telephone: + 61 (2)9664 0909   Facsimile: +61 (2)9664 5420
Email: info@cavendishpublishing.com.au
Website: www.cavendishpublishing.com.au

© Hanson, S   2003
First edition   1999
Second edition   2003

All rights reserved. No part of this publication may be reproduced, stored in a retrieval system, or
transmitted, in any form or by any means, electronic, mechanical, photocopying, recording,
scanning or otherwise, without the prior permission in writing of Cavendish Publishing Limited,
or as expressly permitted by law, or under the terms agreed with the appropriate reprographics
rights organisation. Enquiries concerning reproduction outside the scope of the above should be
sent to the Rights Department, Cavendish Publishing Limited, at the address above.

You must not circulate this book in any other binding or cover
and you must impose the same condition on any acquirer.

British Library Cataloguing in Publication Data
Hanson, Sharon
Legal Method – 2nd ed
1 Law – Great Britain 2 Lawyers – Training of – Great Britain
I Title
349.4'1

Library of Congress Cataloguing in Publication Data
Data available

ISBN 1-85941-783-3
1 3 5 7 9 10 8 6 4 2
Printed and bound in Great Britain

To Victoria and Elizabeth Welch – two very special women.

WITHDRAWN
UNIVERSITY OF
PORTSMOUTH LIBRARY

PREFACE

The first edition of this book was written in the belief that a practical manual approach to issues of legal method would assist students in the development of their skills in legal study and practice. I was pleased at the positive responses from both staff and students and the helpful suggestions for development. This second edition is the result of listening to the readership and the development of my own ideas in this area. The changes made have in fact led to a change in the name of the book from *Legal Method* to *Legal Method & Reasoning*. This reflects the fact that the chapters on practical legal reasoning have been completely rewritten and extended to give a detailed account of argument construction.

Structurally the book has been streamlined into 10 chapters, each chapter containing an introduction, learning outcomes (to allow students to see more clearly the type of skill development that the chapter is seeking to encourage) and a summary.

The book also includes several completely revised chapters and the insertion of much new material. Major changes cover the rewriting and extension of the section on the the European Union and European Community law which is now found in Chapter 5. In addition, this chapter now includes two new discrete sections on treaties (what they are and how to handle them) and the law relating to human rights including the Human Rights Act 1998. The substantive law textbooks most correctly state that human rights is distinct from European and Community law but I have decided to place them within the context of the UK government's response to European treaties. This gives students a firm foundation in the reasons for the differences, rather than a command not to muddle the two areas by keeping them (somewhat unrealistically) distinct.

A second major change is the complete revision of the way in which the core skill of argument construction has been approached. This is dealt with in Chapter 7 and amalgamates work in several of the chapters in the first edition presenting it in a more user-friendly and structured manner. The material on reading secondary texts has been revised and can be found in Chapter 6. A new Chapter 8 deals with writing essays and answers to problem questions. The *Factortame* case study has been retained but placed into a separate chapter (Chapter 9) and is used to put together all of the skills discussed in this book.

The book is structured as follows.

Chapter 1: this chapter discusses how to use this text and introduces the clusters of skills involved in successful legal study.

Chapter 2: in this chapter, time is taken to consider the power that users of language can exert at the level of language itself. It introduces readers to the residual and hidden power that language has and the way in which it can pre-determine ways of seeing and understanding the world. These 'taken for granted' assumptions are not questioned; they have 'always been there', therefore they are considered to be 'true', or 'right' or the only way of thinking about the world. It is assumed by their very familiarity that these assumptions reflect reality without distortion. Yet all too often these 'taken for granted' assumptions facilitate discrimination, block reform and always exert power. The main argument of Chapter 2 is that language is never neutral.

Chapters 3–5: these deal with the issue of reading primary legal texts, both UK and European. They discuss ways of breaking into legislation (Chapter 3), law reports (Chapter 4) and European Community law, treaties and human rights law (Chapter 5).

Chapter 6: this chapter concerns itself with reading secondary texts. Central to the chapter is a reading exercise to demonstrate approaches to reading secondary texts.

Chapter 7: this is a core chapter of the book and discusses the definition of argument, the constituent parts of argument and the type of reasoning method preferred in the English legal system. It also discusses the relationship between argument and evidence, and how these go together. This chapter relies upon a firm grasp of the matters discussed in Chapters 2–5.

Chapter 8: this is a new chapter aiming to assist in the construction of essays and answers to legal problem questions. Having spent time looking at the mechanics of argument construction in Chapter 7, this chapter turns to the issue of developing confidence and competency in producing written work.

Chapter 9: this chapter draws together all of the skills referred to in this book through a case study of the *Factortame* litigation (frozen at one point in time).

Chapter 10: the final chapter is an extremely brief conclusion but useful nonetheless. It points in many respects to the next stages of competency in legal method, which is engagement with the study of legal theory and philosophy.

Many aspects of this book will seem difficult at first. As far as possible, issues are initially presented as simply as possible and then complexity is slowly introduced.

I have a belief in the value of diagrams to show a range of connections that are not always apparent to the student when narrative is read. Indeed, the number of diagrams used is one of the unique aspects of this text. Please attempt to engage with them, study them, think about them and refer to the text describing and placing them in context.

This book provides a large number of original legal texts as support materials for the exercises. These can be found in Appendices 1–3. At the end of the text you will also find a small bibliography. Further reading is not automatically given at the end of each chapter. However, it is included where such reading seems useful, for example, in Chapter 7, where other texts allowing students to develop their skills in argument construction are specifically referenced.

I believe that this second edition represents a useful development of the text from the first edition. I hope that students will continue to find the book challenging and enjoyable.

Sharon Hanson
London
June 2003

CONTENTS

CHAPTER 1

INTRODUCTION

1.1   HOW TO USE THIS TEXT

Successful legal study depends upon the simultaneous development of the following different but complimentary skills:

- excellent language skills;
- knowledge of the relevant area of law;
- highly competent argument identification, construction and evaluation skills.

The primary focus of this legal method book will be the legal text. Texts of the law (statutes, law reports) and texts about the law (textbooks, journals, articles) will be the objects of analysis. They will be studied in order to understand the construction of legal rules, to acquire skills of argument construction, analysis and critique, to appreciate links between and within the texts, to use this knowledge to solve practical and theoretical legal problems and to aid legal reasoning.

Too often, students are not clearly informed at the beginning of studies of the full extent of the skills required. Even when they are informed, students seem to forget; they are too busy memorising the obviously relevant to waste time trying to understand as well! Frequently, memorising becomes a comfortable tranquilliser protecting the student from the productive pain of fighting with incomprehension to reach a place of partial understanding. Sadly, within the discipline of law, successful memorising often merely ensures failure as the student knows it all and yet understands nothing.

The majority of books on the market that deal with method that is, the way in which legal rules are used to resolve certain types of disputes do so in the context of legal process or legal theory. Inevitably, many of these books tend to be weighted in favour of explaining the English legal system, its processes, personnel and doctrines. They do not give time to an appreciation of how to break into texts, often tending to veer between English legal system and legal theory, with some study skills and library usage information.

Although this text acknowledges the complexities of legal rules, the importance of critique and the construction of arguments, it also attempts, in a user-friendly manner, to make interrelationships clear and to allow the commencement of the task of understanding and reading the law, seeing arguments and using them.

Essentially, this is a book about practical thinking and the acquisition of skills and, as such, relies on reader reflection and activity.

My objective in writing this book was to provide a usable manual: the text draws a map to enable students to reach a place of understanding where they can recall relevant memorised knowledge and then apply it, or interpret it confidently with a clear comprehension of the interrelationships between rules, arguments and language, in the search for plausible solutions to real or imaginary problems.

This text is not a philosophical enquiry that asks why English law prefers the methods of reasoning it has adopted. Although such texts are of the utmost importance, they will mean more to the student who has first acquired a thorough competency in a narrow field of practical legal method and practical reason. Then, a philosophical argument will be appreciated, considered, evaluated and either accepted or rejected. This is not a theoretical text designed to discuss in detail the importance of a range of legal doctrines such as precedent and the crucial importance of case authority. Other texts deal with these pivotal matters and students must also carefully study these. Further, this is not a book that critiques itself or engages in a post-modern reminder that what we know and see is only a chosen, constructed fragment of what may be the truth. Although self-critique is a valid enterprise, a fragmentary understanding of 'the whole' is all that can ever be grasped.

This is a 'how to do' text; a practical manual. As such, it concerns itself primarily with the issues set out below:

How to ...

(a) develop an awareness of the importance of understanding the influence and power of language;

(b) read and understand texts talking about the law;

(c) read and understand texts of law (law cases; legislation (in the form of primary legislation or secondary, statutory instruments, bye-laws, etc), European Community legislation (in the form of regulations, directives));

(d) identify, construct and evaluate legal arguments;

(e) use texts *about* the law and texts *of* the law to construct arguments to produce plausible solutions to problems (real or hypothetical, in the form of essays, case studies, questions, practical problems);

(f) make comprehensible the interrelationships between cases and statutes, disputes and legal rules, primary and secondary texts;

(g) search for intertextual pathways to lay bare the first steps in argument identification;

(h) identify the relationship of the text being read to those texts produced before or after it;

(i) write legal essays and answer problem questions;

(j) deal with European influence on English law.

The chapters are intended to be read, initially, in order as material in earlier chapters will be used to reinforce points made later. Indeed, all the chapters are leading to the final two chapters which concentrate on piecing together a range of skills and offering solutions to legal problems. See Figure 1.1, below, which details the structure of the book.

There is often more than one solution to a legal problem. Judges make choices when attempting to apply the law. *The study of law is about critiquing the choices made, as well as critiquing the rules themselves.*

However, individual chapters can also be looked at in isolation by readers seeking to understand specific issues such as how to read a law report (Chapter 4) or how to begin to construct an argument (Chapter 7). The material in this book has been used by access to law students, LLB students and at Masters level to explain and reinforce connections between texts in the construction of argument to non-law students beginning study of law subjects.

The text as a whole will introduce students to the value of alternatives to purely textual explanations. An ability to comprehend diagrammatic explanations will be encouraged. Diagrams present another way of seeing, and the sheer novelty value of seeing the interconnections in a diagram can sometimes be enough to change confusion into comprehension. It is hoped that students will begin to draw them for themselves.

The numerous diagrams used in this text are integral to the successful understanding of legal method as presented here.

They have been specifically designed to:

- provide a way of taking students to deeper levels of understanding;
- give a basic description or blueprint for an area;
- demonstrate interconnections between seemingly disconnected areas/texts/skills.

To emphasise the value of diagrams, Figure 1.1, below, sets out the disarmingly simple, broad structure of this text.

Where specific materials are required to be read, these will be found in Appendices 1–3.

Patient study will be rewarded by clear progress in substantive law areas. If students work through the text methodically, they *will* reach a place of understanding where they know how to competently present arguments. They can then develop these skills during the course of their studies.

1.1.1 The structure of the book

Careful thought has gone into the structure of this book. If it is approached in order, students will obtain a systematic introduction to the skills vital to the academic stage of legal education. If students already possess some knowledge and wish to look at specific skills, then discrete chapters do stand alone. This book is, however, no substitute for English legal texts or texts in substantive areas such as European Community law. The book draws on a range of areas of law to demonstrate skill development, and to alert students to some of the confusions and mistakes easily made by new law students. It is a book that bridges the gap between substantive legal subjects and the skill base that needs to be acquired in relation to reading law, writing legal answers competently and engaging in competent argument construction. It will be of use within certain parts of legal method programmes. However, its overall practical approach will require supplementing with critical texts in the area of legal method.

1.2 LEARNING OUTCOMES

By the end of this chapter, readers should:

- be aware of how to use this book;
- understand the range of skills required for competent legal study.

Figure 1.1: overall structure of the book

STRUCTURE OF THE BOOK	CHAPTERS
SET UP	• Preface • Chapter 1: Introduction
LANGUAGE MATTERS	• Chapter 2: The Power of Language
READING THE LAW	• Chapter 3: Reading and Understanding Legislation • Chapter 4: Reading and Understanding Law Reports • Chapter 5: Reading English Law – The European Dimension • Chapter 6: Reading Books About Law – A Reading Strategy
ARGUMENT CONSTRUCTION	• Chapter 7: Legal Argument Construction
WRITING THE LAW	• Chapter 8: Writing Essays and Answers to Problem Questions
PUTTING IT ALL TOGETHER	• Chapter 9: A Demonstration: Using Primary and Secondary Legal Texts to Construct Arguments in Answer to One Particular Question
CONCLUSION	• Chapter 10: Conclusion
SUPPORT MATERIALS	• Appendix 1 – English Primary Legal Texts • Appendix 2 – European Dimension (1) • Appendix 3 – European Dimension (2)

1.3   SKILLS REQUIRED FOR COMPETENT LEGAL STUDY

This text is about legal method. However, as noted in the introduction, a number of skills are necessary for successful legal study. This section identifies these skills.

Studying is about learning: learning about self, academic subject areas and how to learn; new information about subjects, ideas, ways of seeing, arguing and thinking have to be understood, evaluated and used.

The *Shorter Oxford English Dictionary* defines 'learning' as the obtaining of knowledge about a skill or an art through study, experience or teaching. In fact, study is defined in several ways, although perhaps the definition that sums up the view of many students is as follows:

... a state of mental perplexity or anxious thought.

A more standard definition is also given as:

... mental application for the acquisition of some kind of learning.

Studying is also referred to as an act or as action. This is a particularly important definition which makes the point that studying is not passive, it is dynamic, ie, interactive.

> SO –
>
> studying is not a passive thing;
>
> it is dynamic and interactive.

Yet too many students do see studying as passive, as a process of soaking up and memorising what is, hopefully, just handed out by the teacher. It is, therefore, not seen as an engaged active process of searching for other ideas, weighing up possibilities and alternatives, criticising and evaluating.

The following pages will highlight the range of skills needed and as you progress through this text many of these skills will be developed.

One overarching skill is critical thinking which will be discussed in more detail in Chapter 7. It is essential for law students to utilise a critical approach to studies, because this ensures that they:

- search for hidden assumptions;
- justify assumptions;
- judge the rationality of those assumptions;
- test the accuracy of those assumptions.

In this way, law students ensure proper coverage for each area of their study.

1.3.1 Range of skills required for legal studies and their interrelationships

That a wide range of skills is needed for the study of law should by now be quite clear.

The required skills can be generically grouped into:

(a) general study skills;

(b) language skills;

(c) legal method skills;

(d) substantive legal knowledge skills,

and then sub-divided into specifics – this is the best way of discussing them.

1.3.1.1 General study skills

This text is *not* concerned with the detail of general study skills; there are excellent books on the market that cover them, and these can be found in the bibliography. However, it is vital to be alert to the core need for highly competent study skills. Skills under this heading include:

- how study time is managed, 'pre-planning the week';
- knowledge of course organisation;
- knowledge of the lecture role, small groups timetable; class contact based; or knowledge of distance learning guides if you are taking a distance learning course or a self-study scheme;
- the development of powers of concentration.

   Some students find it physically or emotionally impossible to sit down for two hours or even less and read in a useful, meaningful manner. Concentration is a skill acquired over time; it is a process;
- organising a *place* to study;
- setting up filing systems for:
  - ○ handouts;
  - ○ notes made from books, articles or lectures;
  - ○ subject specific problem questions, essay questions and past examination papers;
- learning to be a highly competent user of the library facilities (real or 'virtual');
- developing computing skills;
- developing writing and reading skills (also comes under language and legal method skills);
- developing the ability to answer questions (also comes under language and legal method skills).

1.3.1.2 *Language usage skills*

Students need to be competent language users. This involves demonstrating a competency in the following areas:

- grammar;
- punctuation;
- spelling;
- vocabulary;
- reading (primary texts *of* law and secondary texts *about* law);
- writing (notes, summaries and extended academic writing);
- interpretation of arguments by the analysis of the language in which the arguments are presented.

Again, not all of these areas are specifically dealt with in this text but the bibliography makes useful suggestions for further reading.

1.3.1.3 *Legal method skills*

These are skills concerning formal ways of understanding and analysing issues relating to the law. Much of this book is concerned with a *few* aspects of practical legal method; there are many more.

Legal method skills include:

- handling, applying and interpreting law reports;
- handling, applying and interpreting UK legislation and delegated legislation;
- handling, applying and interpreting European Community legislation, treaties generally, and human rights law;
- argument construction and deconstruction;
- answering legal questions, both problems and essays;
- legal reading and writing skills;
- oral argument skills.

1.3.1.4 *Substantive legal knowledge skills (for example, criminal law and tort – which, of course, are dealt with in your discrete courses)*

So, as you can see, there are many skills to be acquired and these are set out in diagrammatic form in Figure 1.2, below, to give another way of seeing the interrelationships between the range of skills. Deficiency in one group of skills can affect performance in all areas. It is possible to divide sub-skills into even smaller constituent parts and the diagram does this merely to illustrate the complex nature of the undertaking of such studies.

This complexity is not peculiar to the law either. If the course being undertaken was life sciences, again one would need similar generic skills of:

- general study skills;
- language usage skills (and perhaps foreign language skills);
- scientific method skills;
- understanding of substantive science subjects.

Students who think that it is enough to memorise chunks of their substantive law subjects are unsuccessful. They do not understand the need for the skills required in the other main areas of general study skills: English language skills, method skills, critical thinking and the balance of expertise required among them.

All of these skills need to be identified; students need to know which skills they have a basic competency in, which skills they are deficient in and which skills they are good at. Then, each skill needs to be developed to the student's highest possible competency.

> Legal study and intellectual discipline come with a cost. It is often a costly struggle to reach a place of understanding. However, to demonstrate a good level of competency in legal study is within the grasp of everyone.

Figure 1.2: diagrammatic representation of skills involved in the study of law

CHAPTER 2

THE POWER OF LANGUAGE

2.1   INTRODUCTION

Language, like the air we breathe, surrounds us and, also like the air we breathe, rarely do we question it. However, at the outset of legal studies it is vital to take an opportunity to consider the potential language has for both the exertion of power and the shaping of ideas. It is important to realise that language is the mediating and shaping structure of law, which is in turn mediated and shaped by users and interpreters of the law.

Desire, goals, experience, raw emotions, pain, happiness, fear and pleasure are all internally processed through language and outwardly communicated through language. Language is a key vehicle through which a person internalises life experiences, thinks about them, tries out alternatives, conceptualises a future and strives towards future goals.

Often people agree that they 'come to know themselves' through language. Through language someone can succinctly put into words the feelings of another. That other relates to that description and takes it for his or her own, usually increasing regard for the speaker. People can be explained through language. A person, using language, can make what is not present seem present and describe the past as today.

2.2   LEARNING OUTCOMES

By the end of this chapter, readers should:
- be able to explain why attention to the power of language is an important skill to develop for competent legal study;
- be able to state the ways in which it has been proposed that language shapes the social world;
- be able to list some of the characteristics of legal language;
- be able to explain the persuasive power of rhetoric and its place in legal documents;
- be able to discuss the ways in which language and its form can shape legal argument;
- be aware at a basic level of methods to use to explore language usage as an aid to understanding arguments.

2.3   LANGUAGE AND WORD CONSTRUCTION

To make an unusual comparison, both law and religion share a striking similarity; both contain rules in verbal form which are formal, authoritative, to be obeyed and of the highest authority; both deal in rules and stories which shape world views. Law finds its sources in legal cases decided by the judges over time, in Acts of a Parliament that has inherited its power from the monarch, and in the body of the monarch itself which contains the promises of both God and people. Today, law also finds its sources in the legislative acts of the European Community and the decisions of the European Court of Justice and the European Court of Human Rights (religion will often refer to a sacred text).

All our understanding is reducible to the ability to comprehend the expansiveness and limits of our language and the cultural boundedness of our language. It was Edward Sapir who most poignantly maintained that the limits of our language are the limits of our world.

Over the years of socialisation, 'ways of seeing' are developed that are socially constructed by the limits of a particular language. Yet, as language is all around, there is a temptation to see it as a neutral tool, a mirror that tells it 'like it is'. All language does is to give someone else's interpretation of *their* belief, or *their* experience. It is no more, and no less, than a guide to social reality. What is seen as, or believed to be, the real world may be no more than the language habits of the group. It is, therefore, often a biased view.

Languages also have their limits: if language does not have a word for something or some concept then that 'something' will not be seen nor that 'concept' thought. All language is, however, responsive to what linguists call the 'felt needs' of its speakers. Indeed, it is more likely that not only are thoughts expressed *in* words but that thoughts themselves are *shaped* by language.

An example of felt needs can be given from the vocabulary of weather. Although the English are often said to enjoy talking about the weather, for many decades our essentially mild climate has provided us with the need for only one word for 'snow' (that word is 'snow'!). In English there are several words for cold, but only one word for ice. By contrast, the Aztecs living in the tropics have only one word to cover 'snow', 'ice' and 'cold' as separate words were unlikely to be used. As English speakers, it is impossible to state that 'cold' is synonymous with snow. Coldness is a characteristic of snow, but there can be 'cold' without 'snow'. We would not be able to understand how snow and ice could be interchangeable. In English it is not possible for these two words to become synonyms.

However, Inuits have many different words for 'snow'. Words describe it falling, lying, drifting, packing, as well as the language containing many words for wind, ice and cold because much of their year is spent living with snow, ice, wind and cold.

The above is one small illustration of the relationship between living, seeing, naming, language and thought. Language habits predispose certain choices of word. Words we use daily reflect our cultural understanding and at the same time transmit it to others, even to the next generation. Words by themselves are not oppressive or pejorative, but they acquire a morality or subliminal meaning of their own. A sensitivity to language usage therefore can be most revealing of the views of the speaker.

For example, when parents or teachers tell a boy not to cry because it is not manly, or praise a girl for her feminine way of dressing, they are using the words for manly and feminine to reinforce attitudes and categories that English culture has assigned to males and females. Innocent repetition of such language as 'everyday, taken-for-granted' knowledge reinforces sexism in language and in society. In this way language determines social behaviour. Language, as a means of communication, becomes not only the expression of culture but a part of it. The feminine, masculine vocabulary is rarely questioned, yet its usage creates expectations that determine male as the norm, female as the secondary. Verbal descriptions of sex and gender *construct*, not merely describe.

Such construction of belief can be found transmitted through dictionaries. When defining 'manly' *Webster's Dictionary* says that manly means:

> ... having qualities appropriate to a man:
>> open in conduct
>>
>> bold
>>
>> resolute
>>
>> not effeminate or timorous
>>
>> gallant
>>
>> brave
>>
>> undaunted
>>
>> drinks beer. [Give me a break!!!]

For 'womanly' one finds:

> ... marked by qualities characteristic of a woman, belonging to attitudes of a woman not a man.

Female is defined by the negative of the other, of the male. In this way, sexism pervades the 'objective' nature of the dictionary, surbordinating the female to the male.

Sexist language pervades a range of sacred texts and legal texts and processes. Religion can be and is one of the most powerful ideologies operating within society, and many religions and religious groupings are hierarchically male oriented. The law maintains that the male term encompasses the female. Many religions maintain that man is made in the image of God; woman in the image of man. The female is once removed in both law and religion.

Even in the 19th century, English law continued to maintain that the Christian cleaving of male and female meant the subjugation of the female and the loss of her property and identity to the male. English family law was based upon Christian attitudes to family and accounted for the late introduction of flexible divorce laws in the 1950s. Both law and Christianity reflect a dualism in Western society. The power of language is illustrated here. A pervasive sexism is made possible and manifest through language which, therefore, easily carries discrimination.

So far, the discussion has centred on the construction of the world by, and through, language as written word. There are different ways of speaking and writing. People use the modes of speaking and writing experience and education notes as the most appropriate. However, language exerts power, too, through a hierarchy given to 'ways of speaking'; through a hierarchy based on accent as well as choice of, or access to, vocabulary.

People often change the way they speak, their accent and/or vocabulary. Such change may be from the informality of family communication to the formality of work. It may be to 'fit in': the artificial playing with 'upper class', 'middle class', 'working class', 'northern' or 'Irish' accents. Sometimes presentation to a person perceived by the speaker as important may occasion an accent and even a vocabulary change. Speakers wish to be thought well of. Therefore, they address the other in the way it is thought that the other wishes or expects to be addressed.

It has been said that Britain in the 1940s and 1950s was the only place in the world that a person's social status could be noted within seconds by accent alone. Oral communication and vocabulary was status laden. Accent revealed education, economic position and class. Today, particularly in certain professions (including law), regional accents can often be a source of discrimination. Such discrimination is not spoken of to those whose speech habits are different; only to those whose speech habits are acceptable, creating an elite.

Given the variety of oral communication, accent, tone and vocabulary, it is clear that it is not just the language that is important but how it is communicated and the attitude of the speaker. Does it include or exclude?

Written expressions of language are used to judge the ultimate worth of academic work but also it is used to judge job applicants. Letters of complaint that are well presented are far more likely to be dealt with positively. The observation of protocols concerning appropriate letter writing can affect the decision to interview a job applicant.

So, language is extremely powerful both in terms of its structure and vocabulary and in terms of the way it is used in both writing and speaking.

Rightly or wrongly, it is used to label one as worthy or unworthy, educated or uneducated, rich or poor, rational or non-rational. Language can be used to invest aspects of character about which it cannot really speak. An aristocratic, well spoken, English accent with a rich vocabulary leads to the assumption that the speaker is well educated, of noble birth and character and is rich; a superficial rationale for nobleness, education and wealth that is quite often found to be baseless.

2.4   CASE STUDY: THE RELATIONSHIP BETWEEN LANGUAGE, LAW AND RELIGION

Religion, politics and, of course, law find power in the written and spoken word. Many aspects of English law remain influenced by Christianity.

The language of English law, steeped in the language of Christianity, speaks of the 'immemorial' aspects of English law (although the law artificially sets 1189 as the date for 'immemoriality'!).

In many ways the Christian story is built into the foundation of English law. Theories of law describe the word of the Sovereign as law; that what is spoken is authority and power, actively creating law based on analogy just as God spoke Christ into creation.

Since the 16th century, when Henry VIII's dispute with the Holy Roman Catholic Church caused England to move away from an acceptance of the religious and political authority of the Pope, English monarchs have been charged with the role of 'Defender of the Faith'. As an acknowledgment of modern pluralist society, there have recently been suggestions that the Prince of Wales, if he becomes King, should perhaps consider being 'Defender of Faith', leaving it open which faith; although the role is tied at present to Anglicanism, that Christian denomination 'established by law'.

English law recognises the Sovereign as the fountain of justice, exercising mercy traceable back to powers given by the Christian God. Indeed, this aspect of the monarch's power, delegated to the Lord Chancellor, gave rise to a stream of English law known as equity, that area of law which rectifies the cruelties and injustices of the common law. An area of law where would-be litigants must prove their moral worth prior to the hearing of the case.

It can be seen that it is the body of the sovereign that tacitly unites religion, law and politics. It is, of course, the Government that has acquired these powers in reality; the monarch is merely the symbol of their existence. English monarchs still retain, by law, the power to heal.

The English system of secular justice, in terms of personnel, processes and rules, is steeped in the Judaeo-Christian justice as interpreted and mediated through English translations of the Greek translations of the Hebrew and Aramaic of the Bible. A Greek language whose vocabulary is shot through with the philosophy of dualism – light/dark, good/bad, good/evil, male/female, slave/free, gods/humans – a dualism not that apparent in Hebrew and Aramaic. This dualism has entered the law through language.

So language is powerful, it enables the manifestation of the past in the present and the projection of the future into the present. Language, thus, facilitates easy discussion of complexities like time.

Lawyers too, in a similar manner, have tried to prove that the integrity of the judge and/or legislator is carried in the words. A key problem in relation to the integrity of law is the maintenance of certainty *despite* the variability of language.

Some legal doctrines relating to the interpretation of law deny that language has a flexibility, fearing that this would be a sign of its weakness and lack of certainty; others acknowledge the flexibility of language and look to the legislators intention. This, too, is a search for the mythical as legislation is changed for a variety of reasons during its drafting and creation stages. If language is seen to be too flexible, the law begins to look less certain.

The root problem here is the language, not the law, yet the two are intimately connected, for the law is *carried* by the language; so is it not true that the law is the language?

The following illustration of linguistic difficulties that concern translation, interpretation and application initially draws quite deliberately from religion to attempt to break preconceptions about language, and to illustrate the problems arising from the necessarily close relationship between language and law. There will be a return to law shortly.

The Christian religion, rather than any other religion, is being considered because it is the religion that remains today at the core of English law. This is one reason why English law can have, and has had, difficulty with concepts from differing religious traditions that have presented themselves before the courts demanding acceptance and equality.

Whilst English law states that it maintains neutrality in matters of religion and yet fails to resolve major tensions within it in relation to Christianity, discrimination remains at the heart of English law. The law's understanding of Christianity has come from the collected texts that make up the Bible: texts that different Christian groups in England, Scotland and Wales went to war over in the 16th and 17th centuries. The wars were initiated and supported by differing political factions established after Henry VIII made his break with the authority, but not the theology, of Rome in the early 16th century. Henry VIII took for himself the title 'Defender of the Faith' and it has remained as a title of English monarchs since.

Christianity has played an influential role within English politics since the 8th century. The laws of Alfred the Great are prefaced by the Decalogue, the basic ten commandments to which Alfred added a range of laws from the Mosaic code found in the old testament. So, even at this stage there was a strong Judeo-Christian stamp on the law. But it was the close connection between Crown and Church which developed after Henry's break from Rome that allowed English law to be greatly influenced by Christianity. This has led to the situation that now prevails in contemporary England that there is a close interdependency between the norms of Christianity, the law and the constitution. In the coronation oath, the monarch promises to uphold the Christian religion by law established. The Archbishop of Canterbury asks the monarch 'Will you to the utmost of your power maintain the laws of God, the true profession of the Gospel and the Protestant reformed religion established by law?' To which the Monarch responds 'All this I promise to do'. No monarch can take the throne without making the oath.

The next section brings together the issue of language, Christianity and law to draw out some of the problems of language.

2.4.1   Sacred texts, English law and the problem of language

The sacred texts of the Old Testament and the New Testament collected in the Bible have been translated into numerous languages. Many misunderstandings of texts can be caused by mistranslations.

English translations of the Bible are translations of translations. The Aramaic of the original speakers of the Christian message was written in Greek during the first century and from there translated into other languages. The historical Jesus did not, so far as we know, speak to people in Greek; he most likely spoke Aramaic. A few fragments were written in Aramaic, yet the English translations are made from the 'original' Greek!

The Old Testament was written in Hebrew. However, the English translation is from an 'original Greek translation' of the Hebrew. To suggest why the source of translation might matter is also to illustrate the importance of other readings, other interpretations. Other readings and other interpretations are core issues for lawyers: what do these words mean for this situation rather than what do these words mean for ever.

To illustrate this point within religion the first phrase in the first sentence from a Christian prayer known as the 'Our Father' or 'The Lord's Prayer' will be considered. The English translation found in the 'King James Version' from the 'original' Greek will be compared to an English translation from an Aramaic version dating from 200 AD. The King James version is authorised by law for use by the Anglican church established by law.

The King James Version of the Bible was developed after much bloodshed in the 17th century, and the Aramaic comparison is derived from Douglas Koltz who tried a reconstitution of the Aramaic from the Greek. This latter translation is, therefore, a little suspect as Aramaic is far more open textured than Greek (or indeed English) as will be discovered. However, the exercise provides a useful illustration of the flexibility of language, as well as the manipulation of language users!

The King James translation from the Greek is as follows:

Our Father which art in heaven. [The Gospel of Matthew, Chapter 6, verse 9.]

The translation from the Aramaic into English is startlingly different:

O Birther! Father-Mother of the Universe.

Suddenly, potential nuances inherent in the words of the suggested original source language, Aramaic, become apparent.

The power of translators to choose words is often not thought of or not seen. Those who rely on translations often do not realise the enormous power they entrust to others to mediate language for them. Even less do readers realise the power entrusted to those who interpret texts. In Aramaic, the sex of God is opened out into male/female; in the Greek version, upon which the English translation depends, the choice is made male/Father.

Koltz has an agenda which is outside the present discussion. However, the potential paradigm shift involved in considering an English translation from the Aramaic is tremendous and shows the power of language, and the importance of understanding its cultural situation.

The mundane English concept of Father, as God in heaven, in the translation from Greek, opens out in the Aramaic translation into 'Birther', potentially, 'Mother/Father'. One of the greatest conflicts of interpretation concerns the relationship between male and female.

The concept 'Heaven', chosen for the Greek and hence the English translation, is taken to be that particular place of God. In Aramaic, it opens out into 'Universe', a cosmology of infinite size and one in which we and the universe are in an osmotic relationship with all that is created and all that is the creator God. There are, therefore, vastly differing conceptions of creator and heaven depending upon language and translation.

Figure 2.1: diagrammatic representation of the shades of meaning attributed to 'Our father who art in heaven' in the Aramaic rendering of the sentence Abwoon d'bwashmaya

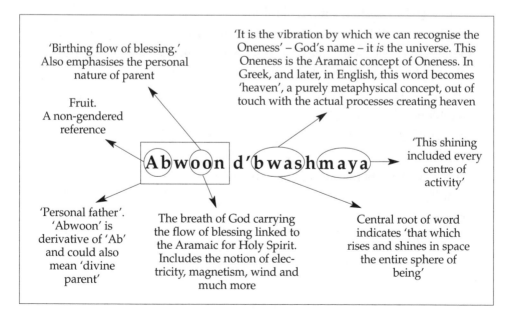

The impoverishment of the English text is shocking by comparison and even the latest amplified version of the New Testament, 'The message' (1996) from the Greek reads:

> Father, reveal who you are. Set the world right.

Lawyers and legal theorists, like priests and theologians, put interpretations upon the meaning of words and phrases. Both professions engage in a creativity that is unimaginable in the traditional explanations of what they are doing and English law purports to pronounce on matters both religious and legal. It is the law of England through parliamentary legislation that regulates major aspects of the Church of England and it is the law of England that makes lawful or unlawful any revisions to the Anglican Book of Common Prayer. The rituals of the Anglican Church also underpin vital aspects of the ceremonial establishing the legitimacy of constitutional arrangements.

2.5   LANGUAGE AND THE LAW

Lawyers work with language all the time. They have been described as wordsmiths, people whose craft, trade, is the highly competent use of both oral and written language.

Lawyers work with legal rules that come in two major forms – UK domestic legislation and European Community law (where it is said that the legal rule is in a 'fixed verbal form'), and case law or common law. At common law, the judgments of the judges contain the rules of law, but these rules have to be extracted from the personal communication of the decision in a case given by the judge. Although written, as the judgment is always taken down verbatim by the court stenographer, it is therefore said that such rules are *not* in a 'fixed verbal form'. In fact just the reverse is true. These contain rules in an unfixed verbal format. Both forms give a certain latitude to interpreters.

Lawyers when dealing with legal rules:

(a) determine their likely application to the facts of a case;

(b) predict the application of the rules and therefore the outcome of the case;

(c) interpret the language of rules.

This gives the law:

(a) credibility;

(b) respectability;

(c) intelligibility.

The major functions of the lawyer are therefore:

(a) analysis;

(b) critique;

(c) interpretation.

The language of the law is also entwined with history. Often, the justification of a rule can be by history, by age, alone.

Edward Coke, a lawyer of much influence in the 17th century, gave the following explanation for the importance of history in relation to law:

> We are but of yesterday ... our days upon the earth are but as a shadow in respect of the old ancient days and times past, wherein the laws have been the wisdom of the most excellent men, in many successions of age, by long and continued experience, (the trial of light and truth) fined and refined.

Coke, *Calvin's Case*, 7 Coke's Reports.

Our common law is said to be the collective wisdom of the ages. This is a powerful *myth*, not a powerful *truth*!

A key doctrine of English common law is the doctrine of precedent. This is the doctrine that states when deciding cases in court judges must have regard to whether the same issue has come before the courts in the past. If it has then the same decision must be reached. This doctrine is of immense importance because it determines the development of the law. Not only is precedent important to the language of the law, defining the relevant and the irrelevant, but the language of the law taken together with precedent defines appropriate argument strategies and vocabulary.

2.5.1   Characteristics of legal language

It is often said that law has its own language; it does not, but the language of law does have its distinctive characteristics.

For example, those social actors engaged in creating law tend to use linguistic terms dealing with generalisations and categories that have to be applied to individual specific circumstances.

It is necessary to begin to understand the processes involved in legal reasoning, and particularly to begin to understand how lawyers are taught to think. English law deals in terms of broad principles, rules and standards. The guardians, enforcers, creators and interpreters of the law will state that the law is objective, that these legal rules and standards are objective. Yet they had their origins in the subjective analysis of one or more judges or other social actor.

Other characteristics of legal language are formality, precision and the existence of a technical vocabulary. Often everyday words are used, but given a different, specialised meaning. Figure 2.2, below, gives a fuller indication of the characteristics of legal language.

Figure 2.2: characteristics of legal language

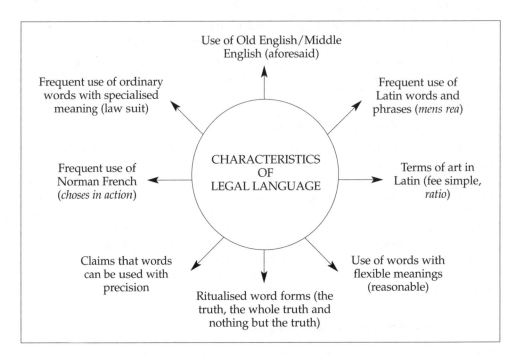

Many characteristics of legal language have their roots in the historical origins of legal procedure and it is now difficult to provide rational justification for them. They have become fossils, indicators of historical development. Other characteristics remain as justifiable attempts to reach precision in language usage.

Lawyers want to be able to use a distinctive language that is precise, brief, intelligible and durable, but of course, they fail. Failure is inevitable. Lawyers are particularly reliant on being able to persuade by argument. Argumentation will be considered in Chapter 7. It is useful now, however, to spend a little time considering language as used for the purposes of persuasion.

2.5.2   The persuasive power of language: political and legal rhetoric

Rhetoric was defined by Aristotle as the universal art of persuasion and, before him, Plato called it in typically sexist form:

... winning men's minds by words.

A specialised form of rhetoric was identified by Aristotle as belonging to the law, and this was forensic rhetoric. In English law, the principle persuasive device is the appeal to legal authority, to previous decisions of the court or of a higher court pointing to similar situations and reasoning connected to those situations. This has already been identified as the doctrine of precedent.

It is instructive to consider the potential for persuasive power that exists in the use of poetic language or, more appropriately, figurative language. Therefore, three extracts from two different types of oral communication that have been noted verbatim will be considered in order to explore poetic language, its function and its existence. The first extract in Figure 2.3, below, is from a speech by a civil rights activist committed to peaceful protest in 1960s America, the second and third extracts are from the summing up in an English libel case in 1983.

2.5.2.1 Extract 1: 'I have a dream': Martin Luther King (28 August 1963)

Read Figure 2.3, below. This is a political speech, using religious imagery, poetic and emotional language to construct an argument challenging the American Government, calling upon it to honour the promises made in the Declaration of Independence. Obviously this speech has a particular context, ie, geography. Its immediate context is with American civil rights canvassing for race and sex equality laws. With regard to geography, many students may not properly take in the importance of the place where the speech is made. It is made at the Lincoln memorial. This is the memorial to Abraham Lincoln who went to war in the 19th century on the issue of slavery, won and secured the freedom of slaves in the Emancipation Declaration.

So, the opening sentence most importantly draws attention to Lincoln:

Five score years ago, a great American, in whose symbolic shadow we stand signed the Emancipation Proclamation.

The raw poetic quality of this speech comes from its original orality. One can understand the use of dramatic imagery in speeches as it assists in recall for the hearer. Not only was this style more popular in the 1950s and 1960s, but it was a particular hallmark in the speaking and writing of Martin Luther King. A range of images is used to communicate to the listener, and later the reader, the feelings of the speaker. This is laid out in Figures 2.4 and Figure 2.5, below, demonstrate the imagery in diagrammatic format.

This extract is full of poetic, emotional language. Feelings and conditions are described by reference to a range of metaphors and similes.

The major figurative devices (lines 17–18) are the likening of the Declaration of Independence to a promissory note to all Americans, and the concept of the Negro (term used in the speech) coming to 'cash a check' (line 28) (cheque) which they feel has been returned marked 'insufficient funds' (lines 28–29) and have come incredulous to cash it again refusing to believe that 'there are insufficient funds in the great vaults of opportunity' (lines 30–31). The hearer would easily recall these major similes, and be able to classify the honourable behaviour of a government keeping promises and contrasting it to a dishonourable government breaking major promises. They also remain vivid to the reader.

The argument links follow from the setting up of these images of cheques to be cashed and the dishonouring of cheques which consequentially require re-presenting. In the third and fourth paragraphs, the argument is set up using the poetic. These two paragraphs are broken down on p 22.

Figure 2.3: extract 1 – 'I have a dream', Dr Martin Luther King on the steps of the Lincoln Memorial in Washington DC, 28 August 1963

(Each line of the extract has been numbered for ease of reference.)

1	Five score years ago, a great American, in whose symbolic	
2	shadow we stand, signed the Emancipation Proclamation. This	
3	momentous decree came as a great beacon light of hope to	Paragraph 1
4	millions of Negro slaves who had been seared in the flames	
5	of withering injustice. It came as a joyous daybreak to end	
6	the long night of captivity.	
7	But one hundred years later, we must face the tragic fact	
8	that the Negro is still not free. One hundred years later,	
9	the life of the Negro is still sadly crippled by the	
10	manacles of segregation and the chains of discrimination.	
11	One hundred years later, the Negro lives on a lonely island	Paragraph 2
12	of poverty in a vast ocean of material prosperity. One	
13	hundred years later, the Negro is still languishing in the	
14	corners of American society and finds himself an exile in	
15	his own land. So we have come here today to dramatise an	
16	appalling condition.	
17	In a sense we have come to our nation's capital to cash a	
18	check. When the architects of our Republic wrote the	
19	magnificent words of the constitution and the Declaration	
20	of Independence, they were signing a promissory note to	Paragraph 3
21	which every American was to fall heir. The note was a	
22	promise that all men would be guaranteed the inalienable	
23	rights of life, liberty, and the pursuit of happiness.	
24	It is obvious today that America has defaulted on this	
25	promissory note insofar as her citizens of colour are	
26	concerned. Instead of honouring this sacred obligation,	
27	America has given the Negro people a bad check which has	
28	come back marked 'insufficient funds'. But we refuse to	
29	believe that the bank of justice is bankrupt. We refuse to	
30	believe that there are insufficient funds in the great	
31	vaults of opportunity of this nation. So we have come to	
32	cash this check – a check that will give us upon demand the	
33	riches of freedom and the security of justice. We have come	Paragraph 4
34	to this hallowed spot to remind America of the fierce	
35	urgency now. This is no time to engage in the luxury of	
36	cooling off or take the tranquillising drug of gradualism.	
37	Now is the time to rise from the dark and desolate valley	
38	of segregation to the sunlit path of racial justice. Now is	
39	the time to open the doors of opportunity to all of God's	
40	children. Now is the time to lift our nation from the	
41	quicksand of racial injustice to the solid rock of	
42	brotherhood.	

Figure 2.4: imagery used in extract 1: 'I have a dream'

Light

'great beacon light of hope'	Line 3
'joyous daybreak'	Line 5
'the sunlit path of racial justice'	Line 38

Fire

'seared in the flames of withering injustice'	Lines 4–5

Darkness

'the long night of captivity'	Line 6
'the dark and desolate valley of segregation'	Lines 37–38

Captivity

'the Negro is still not free'	Line 8
'manacles of segregation'	Line 10
'chains of discrimination'	Line 10
'an exile in his own land'	Lines 14–15

Money

'cash a check'	Lines 17–18
'promissory note'	Line 25
'insufficient funds'	Line 28
'bank of justice'	Line 29
'great vaults of opportunity'	Lines 30–31

Drugs

'the tranquillising drug of gradualism'	Line 36

Geology

'quicksand of racial injustice'	Line 41
'solid rock of brotherhood'	Lines 41–42

Geography

'lonely island of poverty'	Lines 11–12
'vast ocean of material prosperity'	Line 12

Religion

'to all of God's children'	Lines 39–40
'this hallowed spot'	Line 34
'honouring this sacred obligation'	Line 26

Building

'architects of our republic'	Line 18

Infirmity/sickness

'crippled by the manacles of segregation'	Line 9
'languishing in the corners of American society'	Lines 13–14

Third paragraph

(1) '... to cash a check'

(2) '... the architects of our Republic'

(3) '... were signing a promissory note'

(4) '... every American was to fall heir'

(5) '... a promise that all men would be'

(6) '... guaranteed the inalienable rights of life, liberty, and the pursuit of happiness'

The idea could be expressed in non-poetic terms as follows:

> Non-poetic summary of third paragraph:
>
> When the Declaration of Independence was signed, all Americans were promised inalienable rights.

Fourth paragraph

(1) '... America has defaulted on this promissory note ... Instead of honouring'

(2) '... America has given the Negro people a bad check'

(3) '... which has come back marked insufficient funds'

(4) '... we refuse to believe that there are insufficient funds'

(5) '... we have come to cash this check'

(6) '... give us upon demand the riches of freedom and the security of justice.'

These non-poetic summaries are not as compelling as the poetic language

> Non-poetic summary of fourth paragraph:
>
> America has not kept this promise, but we refuse to believe it will not keep its promise.

In addition to metaphor and simile the text also provides many examples of repetition. As a figurative device utilised in the text, it tends to add emphasis, to thicken the impact, aid the memory in recalling the argument or illustration, yet nothing is added except momentum which is poetic. Repetition which concerns calls for justice is also given a momentum that is emotionally charged, for example, in the fourth paragraph the following clusters of repetition occur:

1	'... we refuse to believe' '... we refuse to believe'	Lines 28–29
2	'... we have come' '... we have come'	Lines 31–33
3	'... now is the time' [to rise from ...] '... now is the time' [to open the door of opportunity] '... now is the time' [to move from the quicksand]	Lines 37–40

Another device used is particular to the Greek dualism favoured by the West, that of a range of illustrations based on opposites (set out in Figure 2.5, below).

Figure 2.5: illustrations based on opposites

line 5	(joyous)	day (break) ◄––► night	(long)		line 6
line 38	(sun)	light ◄––► dark	(desolate)		line 37
line 26	(instead of)	honour(ing) ◄––► fraud	(bad check)		line 27
line 33	(riches of)	freedom ◄––► captivity	(long night of)		line 6
lines 29 & 33	(security/bank of)	justice ◄––► injustice	(withering)		line 5
line 41	(quicksand)	not solid ◄––► solid	(rock)		line 41

Several devices carry the message of this speech, for example:

- the emotive, poetic language;
- the imagery of the opposites;
- the image of the cheque and the fraud.

All these build up to stating the core argument: that the emancipation agreement and the Declaration of Independence assured all Americans that they had rights that could never be taken away. Negroes had asked for those rights and had not been given them. America had unjustifiably denied these rights.

Figure 2.6: imagery used in extract 1

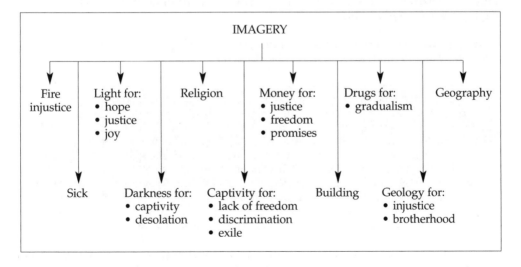

This is a forceful argument made far more immediately forceful and poignant by the use of the poetic and emotive, passionate language. People may acknowledge the logic of an argument without agreeing to concede to demands. Persuasion can therefore be an essential device to encourage people to move from concept to action. Figurative language is drawn from a range of sources (see Figures 2.4 and 2.5, above) and given a new target domain. But it is the hearer/reader who makes the ultimate connections.

That such language is used in politics is not surprising. Politicians seek to persuade by all means possible and, as Aristotle remarked, persuasive language is used to effect by the introduction of figurative language. Such language is only one aspect of rhetoric, but, as this extract demonstrates, it is a powerful aspect.

Lawyers and the judiciary will always state that emotional and poetic language has no place in the courtroom, in the language of law. Part of the rationale for this is that poetic and emotional language can exercise much power and in matters of innocence and guilt it is surely more just to rely on rationality not emotion. This view can be particularly traced back to the insistence by Francis Bacon who, in the 17th century, insisted that law must be seen to have an objective, scientific, rational methodology. However, it is impossible for there to be a pure science of law given its necessary reliance on language, and the imprecision of language. Therefore, often it is the appeal to the rational neutrality of the science of legal decision making that is misleading. Figurative language is often used in the courtroom despite the view that it is inappropriate, as extracts 2 and 3 illustrate (in Figures 2.7 and 2.9, below, respectively).

2.5.2.2 Extracts 2 and 3: Lord Justice Comyn in Orme v Associated Newspapers Group Inc (1981)

Figure 2.7: extract 2 – Lord Justice Comyn summing up in Orme v Associated Newspapers Group Inc (1981)

(This case was a defamation case involving membership of the Unification Church. Orme is the UK Director of the church.)

> This is not a battle between the freedom of religion and the freedom of the press; two freedoms which we treasure greatly. This is rather a battle of right and wrong. Has the Daily Mail infringed the plaintiff's right to a good, clean reputation, or has the plaintiff Mr Orme in all the circumstances no right to any reputation at all in this case because of what he and his organisation have done and do? Was the Daily Mail wrong about its allegations in its article? Was it wrong about its allegations during this case? Or was the plaintiff wrong; was the plaintiff giving a false picture? That is what it is, members of the jury, not a battle between freedom of the press and freedom of religion, but a battle of right and wrong.

This extract is useful as an illustration of language techniques, repetition, figurative language (particularly, metaphor) in action; as well providing the basis for a necessarily limited discussion of what the function of these techniques may be.

It is set out again below, with phrases and sentences numbered for discussion purposes.

Figure 2.8: numbered format of extract 2

1	This is not a battle between the freedom of religion
2	and the freedom of the press;
3	two freedoms which we treasure greatly.
4	This is rather a battle of right and wrong.
5	Has the Daily Mail infringed the plaintiff's right to a good, clean reputation,
6	or has the plaintiff Mr Orme in all the circumstances no right to any reputation at all in this case because of what he and his organisation have done and do?
7	Was the Daily Mail wrong about its allegations in its article?
8	Was it wrong about its allegations during this case?
9	Or was the plaintiff wrong;
10	was the plaintiff giving a false picture?
11	That is what it is, members of the jury, not a battle between freedom of the press and freedom of religion,
12	but a battle of right and wrong.

Looking at Figure 2.8, above, the first two and last two sentences of the extract (lines 1, 2, 11 and 12) form a 'sandwich' comprising repetition of the main assertion that the case is not a battle between freedom of the press and freedom of religion. It is as if he is saying that the argument is so because 'I say so, twice!'.

Another example of repetition is found in the structure of the run of three rhetorical questions, both in terms of length and the use of amplification through alliteration: 'was juxtaposed with wrong' in lines 7, 8 and 9.

The structure of the extract also demonstrates that the judge has the authority to impose that reading of events. For he says, in line 11, 'This is what it is, members of the jury'.

Who is the 'we' found in line 3?

(a) Is it the royal 'we', symbolising the ultimate authority of the court?

(b) Is it merely the judge?

(c) Does it include judge and jury?

'We' is undeniably an inclusive term. It is suggested that, in this instance, the judge is talking in relation to the court and the law, as an official spokesman of the law.

The choice of the word 'battle', as part of what turns out to be a continuing war metaphor which runs throughout the entire summing up, as a major organising theme that argument is war, is interesting. The word 'fight' or 'skirmish' is not chosen, but 'battle'. The reference to battle puts the case 'high up' in a hierarchy of modes of physical fighting – for example skirmish, scrap, fight, battle. Battle denotes that opposing armies gather together with their greatest degree of strength to fight for as long as it takes for a clear victor.

Of course, it is not unusual to find 'fighting' metaphors used to describe English trials. Because of their accusatorial nature ('He did it judge.' 'No, he did it judge.'). Early in the history of English dispute resolution, trial by battle (a physical fight) was used to determine guilt and innocence as a perfectly acceptable *alternative* to trial by law.

There were also other alternatives such as blood feud (speaks for itself) and trial by ordeal. At the latter, the Church was in attendance to oversee a range of tests that, to an observer, would look like the infliction of punishment after guilt had been determined. If the test was successfully passed – and it could only be 'won' if the Christian God intervened – the person taking the test was innocent. For example, in one form of trial by ordeal the person claiming innocence would plunge a hand into boiling water. If there was no blistering after a few days (highly unlikely, it was believed at the time, without supernatural intervention), the person was judged to be innocent.

For those who feel adventurous, trial by battle remains on the statute books. Relief may be felt that trial by ordeal is no longer an option.

Gradually, royal justice as trial by law took over through a combination of efficiency and threat by the crown. Later in his summing up, Comyn J refers to the battle as a 'Battle Royal'. This connection could be taken as a reminder that the majority of battles from the 16th century onwards involving the monarch were indeed battles concerning religious differences. A serious event about right and wrong. The notion of 'right' suggesting ideas of 'good' and the notion of wrong suggesting ideas of 'evil'. The text also discusses Christian cosmology and the existence of Satan. Throughout the text, the discussion of the battle between 'good' and 'evil' shadows here the religious. 'Right' and 'wrong' are also suggestive of the moral dimensions of the case.

Whilst the English adversarial system lends itself to the use of such war imagery, the judge reserves the right to say what the battle is about and he clearly rules out the possibility that it is a battle between individual freedoms of expression (religious freedom and the freedom of the press). This is a classic example of setting boundaries by stating what is *not* legitimately involved and a classic illustration of an everyday activity in the court.

No rationale is given for the boundaries and exclusion. Indeed the elaborate explanations given for exclusion could be evidence that strongly suggest that, insofar as the judge is concerned, the dispute before him is indeed a battle concerning religious freedom.

Comyn J defines the area of dispute. He draws its boundaries without the slightest recognition of another interpretation of events. It is good to realise at the beginning of legal studies that the court has the power to draw boundaries without explanation, in this way. It is part of its exercise of power.

In Figure 2.9, below, extract 3: *Orme v Associated Newspapers Group Inc* (1981) is set out.

It contains 16 examples drawn from the totality of the summing up which runs to over 200 pages. They give the flavour of the summing up but have been chosen particularly to illustrate the use of repetition and alliteration.

Figure 2.9: extract 3 – *Orme v Associated Newspapers Group Inc* **(1981)**

1   'Are the **m**oonies a **m**alevolent **m**enace?'
2   'has the *Daily Mail* behaved **dis**honestly and **dis**gracefully?'
3   'that **poor** man, his **poor** wife, his **poor** son'
4   '**searching**, perhaps more than we did, **searching searching searching** for the truth and for reason'
5   'Decide it **fairly, squarely,** and **truly**'
6   '**m**ean, **m**erciless, **m**aterialistic and **m**oney-grabbing'
7   '**b**ad press, **b**ad deal, **b**ad treatment'
8   '**m**atching, **m**atching and **m**ating'
9   '**r**amp and **r**acket'
10 '**d**evious and **d**eceitful'
11 '**chanting, cheering** and giggling'
12 'A **fraud**, a **fake** , a **hoax**'
13 'Is this a **m**ad **man** or a bad **man** ... **or** a **m**egalomaniac'
14 '**hum**an and **hum**ane people'
15 '**inherent** badness, **inherent** greed'
16 '*Is he* an old **h**umbug, *is he* a **h**ypocrite or *is he* a decent **h**onourable man standing up manfully for an **h**onourable *bona fide* religion?'

Even from the disconnected statements in Figure 2.9, above, it can be gathered that the dispute revolves around the character of a man or group and it is noticeable from the figurative language that there are more references to 'bad' qualities than to 'good' in relation to the qualities of this man or group – a characteristic feature of the entire summing up. It is clear that some authority needs to decide whether the individual or group is, therefore, good or bad.

The examples illustrate quite clearly Comyns J's preference for alliteration and repetition and the instances have been highlighted in bold. In addition, examples 12 and 13 are framed according to a classic argument within Christian theology concerning the claims of Jesus Christ to be the son of God. 'Is he mad, or bad or who he says he is?' However, the two examples cited only allow for pejorative choices. Example 15 instills a sense of balance in that the third choice is 'an honourable' choice and, in that sense, correctly mirrors the theological argument referred to above.

The summing up in *Orme* contains in excess of 162 metaphors. In many instances, there are several to a page, often repeated up to 50 pages later and expanded to become organising thematic metaphors for the text, the predominant themes relating to nature or war. Elaborate metaphors are repeated much later in the text in shorter format. However, the immediate effect is to recall the vividness of the original format.

These three examples of figurative language interwoven with persuasion give an illustration of poetic language in action:

• enhancing argument making it appear stronger (without cause);

• thickening it without adding substance;

• adding effect;

- carrying weak substantive arguments;
- making weak arguments appear strong.

Later, when the mechanics of argument construction have been identified, it will be useful to return to these extracts and read them again with an eye on argument connected to figurative language.

2.6   SUMMARY

This chapter has considered a range of issues to underline the importance of language in the study of law:

- religion and language;
- law and language;
- the power of language to limit, express and shape the world;
- law and figurative language.

Law is carried by words: excellent English language skills are the beginning of basic competency in handling legal rules that are either derived from the common law, statutory activity or the European Community. Sophisticated language skills, coupled with meticulous attention to detail and a thorough understanding of the substantive field of law, ensures appropriate levels of analysis; for the skills of handling complex legal rules, communicated through language, constitute the major practical and intellectual skill of the lawyer.

2.7   FURTHER READING

For those of you who have found the links between language and law, and the basic introduction to the power of language interesting, you may enjoy reading the following book which takes yet another perspective on the issue of language and law: Goodrich, P, *The Languages of Law from the Logics of Memory to Nomadic Masks*, 1990, London: Weidenfeld & Nicolson.

> The important message to be taken from this chapter is that, as the rules of law are learned, and the methods of making law discerned, it is essential to be aware of the power of language in order not only to analyse the rules themselves, but to ascertain in what way, if any, language is exerting a powerful influence on the constructors, applicators and interpreters of the law.

CHAPTER 3

READING AND UNDERSTANDING LEGISLATION

3.1   INTRODUCTION

This chapter introduces 'legislation': the first of four sources of English legal rules discussed in detail in this book. The others are common law/case law (see Chapter 4), the law relating to European human rights and fundamental freedoms, and European Community law (see Chapter 5). The chapter begins with a general introduction to these areas and then turns to the in-depth consideration of legislation. The chapter uses both text and diagrams to explain the standard layout of legislation and the need to concentrate on English language skills in order to understand the fundamental importance of prepositional words in legislation. Legislation at the macro-level of a whole statute, and at the micro-level of individual elements of legislation (sections, sub-sections) are discussed and issues of interpretation and rule handling raised. The relationship between common law/case law and legislation is considered in detail in Chapter 4.

3.2   LEARNING OUTCOMES

By the end of this chapter, readers should:

- be able to competently handle legislative rules;
- understand the layout of a statute;
- be able to identify 'connectors' and use them to understand the internal language of sections in a statute;
- be able to explain the relationship between statutes and law cases;
- be able to distinguish between primary and secondary legislation;
- be able to competently use tree diagrams to ascertain interconnections between sections and schedules in a statute.

3.3   SOURCES OF ENGLISH LAW

There are three major sources of English law that need to be understood immediately: common law/case law, legislation and European Community law. A fourth area is the developing importance of the case decisions of the European Court of Human Rights since the Human Rights Act was enacted in 1998. There are other sources and classifications but for the purposes of this text these four will be concentrated upon and are set out in Figure 3.1, below.

Figure 3.1: main sources of English law

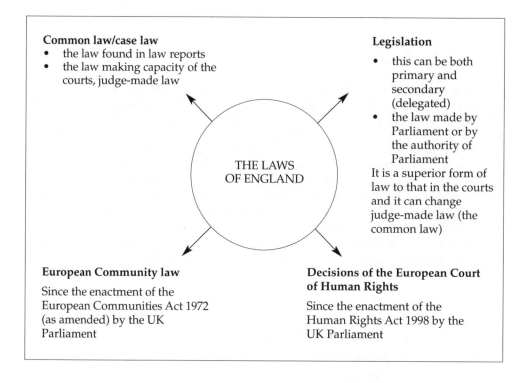

Common law/case law
- the law found in law reports
- the law making capacity of the courts, judge-made law

THE LAWS OF ENGLAND

Legislation
- this can be both primary and secondary (delegated)
- the law made by Parliament or by the authority of Parliament

It is a superior form of law to that in the courts and it can change judge-made law (the common law)

European Community law

Since the enactment of the European Communities Act 1972 (as amended) by the UK Parliament

Decisions of the European Court of Human Rights

Since the enactment of the Human Rights Act 1998 by the UK Parliament

One factor which may seem difficult at first is getting to grips with these various legal rules. To competently handle primary texts of law, there is a need to:

(a) locate and understand the various sources of the rules;

(b) learn how they can be used to provide a resolution to disputes of a legal nature;

(c) learn how to engage in applying and interpreting the rules;

(d) understand the interconnections between the main sources of English law and in particular the relationship between cases and legislation.

In order to give a context for the reading and analysing techniques that enable primary texts of law to be properly understood, it is necessary to describe briefly each of the main sources of law. These important sources of law are of course studied in more detail in courses on constitutional and administrative law (or public law), English legal system and European law and human rights.

3.3.1   The common law

The phrase 'common law' has several meanings which vary according to context but as used in *this* text it means no more and no less than:

> all the laws made by judges relating to
> England and Wales

There has been, and continues to be, much argument among legal philosophers as to whether judges actually make or create law out of nothing, or merely declare what the law has always been. Many judges state that they do not make the law, they discover it and thus *declare* what it has always been. This latter viewpoint is referred to as the *declaratory theory* of law making and these matters will be discussed in detail in other courses.

This is a practical book about *how to* analyse the *existing* common law as recorded in the law reports and how to understand UK and European legislation. It is, therefore for the reader to come to a conclusion about who is right over the issue of declaring or creating.

3.3.1.1   The doctrine of precedent

An English judge when deciding a case must refer to similar prior decisions of the higher courts and keep to the reasoning in those cases. If a previous case has dealt with similar facts and the same rules, then the present case has to be decided in the same way. This process is known as the doctrine of precedent.

The doctrine is referred to by the use of a Latin phrase which is usually shortened to:

Stare decisis = let the decision stand

Confusion can be caused to new students due to the range of similar phrases used to refer to the doctrine.

Often, the whole doctrine *and* the specific legal rule created in the case is referred to by an even more abbreviated Latin term, *ratio*.

- No *legal rule* exists to demand such adherence to previous cases.
- However, as a matter of custom and practice, the senior judiciary enforce it rigidly.

One of the most important questions when dealing with the doctrine of precedent is 'When is a court bound by a previous case?'

- Everything depends upon the court's position in the hierarchy of courts.
- As will be noted in Chapter 4, the English legal system is unique among *all* others because of the manner in which courts keep to the doctrine of precedent.

It is said that among the advantages of the doctrine are the following:

- it gives certainty to the law;
- it is a curb on arbitrary decisions;
- it is based on a notion of justice which maintains equality;
- it provides a rational base for decision making.

As is to be expected, many argue there are disadvantages of the doctrine:

- it makes the law inflexible;
- change is slow and convoluted;
- it encourages a tedious hairsplitting tendency in legal argument.

In addition, to understand the relationship between cases and legislation and the theory and practice of the doctrine of precedent it is also essential to understand the importance of accurate reporting of legal cases

The importance of cases and the extent of the legal rule developed only become apparent after the case, and one needs good reports. If you cannot trust the reporting, then you cannot trust the law.

3.3.2   Legislation

Legislation is the law made by Parliament or by individuals and groups acting on delegated parliamentary authority. The technically correct term for a piece of primary legislation is 'legislative Act'. It is the dominant form of law making.

In addition to creating legislation, Parliament can delegate, to another person or group, by an Act of Parliament, the power to create a limited range of laws for others. For example, powers can be delegated to:

- a local authority;
- a government minister;
- a professional body.

When this occurs, the legislation that is created is referred to as:

---

a statutory instrument

OR

delegated legislation

OR

secondary legislation
(for it is once removed from parliamentary power)

The legislation giving the power to make such secondary or delegated legislation is referred to as the *primary legislation,* or the *parent Act.*

3.3.3   Statutory interpretation: consideration of legislation by the courts

Quite often, the law created by Parliament, as well as that created by delegated parliamentary authority, is considered by judges in courts. Most commonly, judges will be called upon to decide the precise meaning of a phrase or a word. Given the discussion above concerning the flexibility of language and the problems of interpretation, the difficulties that such consideration can cause are obvious.

Issues of tremendous importance can be raised when a problem about the meaning of a statutory provision goes before a court. How do judges interpret statutes? The ability to have the final say in this manner gives judges, an undemocratic body, unprecedented power.

Judges have to:

- apply legislative rules to various fact situations;
- decide the meaning of words and phrases used in the statute (and of course words can mean many things, and can change over time);
- deal with judicial disagreement over the meaning of words.

A range of purported rules of interpretation has been developed over time for use by judges:

- there are three *known* rules of statutory interpretation, set out in Figure 3.2, below;
- there are probably *many unknown* rules. For example, the *'gut-feeling rule'*!

Figure 3.2: the three main rules of statutory interpretation

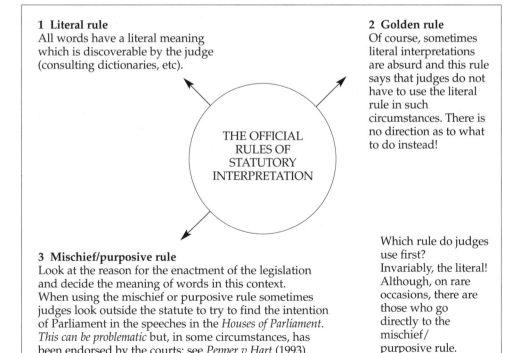

1 Literal rule
All words have a literal meaning which is discoverable by the judge (consulting dictionaries, etc).

2 Golden rule
Of course, sometimes literal interpretations are absurd and this rule says that judges do not have to use the literal rule in such circumstances. There is no direction as to what to do instead!

THE OFFICIAL RULES OF STATUTORY INTERPRETATION

3 Mischief/purposive rule
Look at the reason for the enactment of the legislation and decide the meaning of words in this context. When using the mischief or purposive rule sometimes judges look outside the statute to try to find the intention of Parliament in the speeches in the *Houses of Parliament*. *This can be problematic* but, in some circumstances, has been endorsed by the courts: see *Pepper v Hart* (1993).

Which rule do judges use first? Invariably, the literal! Although, on rare occasions, there are those who go directly to the mischief/ purposive rule.

> No legal rules exist that state which rules of interpretation
> can be used and the rules of interpretation that have been
> identified are not, themselves, legal rules.

3.3.4   The law of the European Community

The third major source of English law is the law of the European Community, which is dealt with in detail in Chapter 5.

In 1973, the UK joined the European Community. At the time legislation was enacted which said quite clearly that European Community law, created in the areas covered by the treaties signed by the UK Government, would have superiority over any conflicting UK legislation. So, in areas within the competence of the European Community, if there is a clash between national law and European Community law, European Community law must prevail.

Furthermore, the UK Government promised to legislate where necessary to ensure that Community law was observed in the UK.

There are several different types of law in the European Community with differing effects. Some European Community law is immediately incorporated in the body of English law, some has to be specially enacted by Act of Parliament.

Because of the initial complexities of the background, sources and classification of European Community law, these issues will be discussed in greater detail in Chapter 5.

Figure 3.3, below, sets out the various areas that need to be understood and interlinked to handle European Community law and relate it to the English legal system. It is important to note that the phrase European Union now tends to be used to cover all areas once referred to as European Community. This will also be discussed in detail in Chapter 5.

3.3.5   The law relating to human rights

Since the enactment of the Human Rights Act (HRA) 1998, English courts have to decide human rights cases by considering cases in the European Court of Human Rights. This area is discussed in more detail in Chapter 5.

3.3.6   Summary

Having briefly outlined the main types of English law that this text is primarily concerned with, it is also now possible to offer the following, more detailed diagram of the sources of English law.

Figure 3.3: areas of law to be understood in order to relate European Community law to English law

Figure 3.4: sources of law

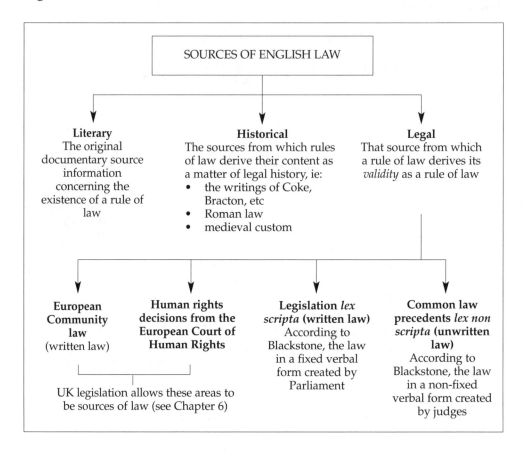

The successful comprehension of the literary, legal and historical sources and differences between the major sources of English law will give the student a firm grasp of how to use these primary texts. Such understanding is an indispensable foundation for competent legal studies.

It is now appropriate, after this brief overview of the three main types of law, to look at each area in detail. This chapter along with Chapters 4–5 consider the nature of the legal sources of law and strategies for reading and understanding them.

3.4   UNDERSTANDING THE FORMAT OF A STATUTE

3.4.1   Introduction

Having spent time discussing the power of language, considering issues of meaning and becoming alerted to the influence of figurative language, the importance of excellent language skills for the study of law should be clear.

In its legislative format, the language of the law will be found to be:

- in an unusual grammatical form;
- potentially confusing;
- tediously literal, dense text;
- exhibiting scant punctuation;
- liberally peppered with alphabetical and numerical dividers.

To read legislation and work to understand it involves the reader in the act of interpretation. Legislation is read for a range of different purposes but they all involve interpretation.

Interpreters of legal texts strive to ascertain what is being suggested at all levels of the text. Some interpret from a biased position, for example, the prosecution or defence. Others interpret from an open position, merely asking: what does this legislation provide for? How might these legal rules apply to this fact situation? What is the general social impact of this legislation? Does this legislation effectively address the issue?

It can be argued that an interpreter is creating something which is new by their act of interpretation: an interpretation which is triggered by the text but which, in reality, bears no resemblance to the writers' intention. This concept may be the basis of the school of art criticism which says: do not confuse the intellect of the artist with the beauty of the work created; do not expect the artist to know the meaning of the work!

Interpreters of legal texts have to adapt their methods according to the type of document they are dealing with, the myth of ascertaining the real meaning of words always being held out as an attainable and sensible goal. Much of the authority of English courts lies in their ability to know what the law means and to apply it.

This chapter will demonstrate the importance of students developing expertise in using various techniques for breaking into texts containing statutory legal rules, using a range of skills and methods in preparation for evaluating, analysing and critiquing them. All these skills require constant practice and reflection, and each type of legal text requires different methods of analysis. Practice steadily increases intellectual awareness, language appreciation, skills of prediction concerning interpretation difficulties and the ability to evaluate. Immediately the interconnections between a range of skills becomes apparent:

(a) skills of language analysis:

- sophisticated comprehension skills;
- vocabulary skills;
- grammar skills;
- excellent reading and writing skills;

(b) diagrammatic methods for organising texts:

- tree diagrams;
- flow charts;
- algorithms;
- Venn diagrams;

(c) textual methods for organising texts:

- tables;
- paragraph analysis, linking and summarising;

(d) identification of interrelationships between different types of legal rules;

(e) knowledge of substantive law, eg, the law of contract.

Many people do not know how to listen to, or read for, an argument. They hear or see words and do not know how to capture the potential meanings, arguments, truths and errors that they carry. They do not know how to split the text into its constituent parts to locate argument. Every skill that is necessary for the competent study of law is interconnected and most problems, whether purely theoretical (what is law?) or practical (what does this law mean for the defendant?) require the competent handling of interconnected skills of language use, legal rules and facts.

Figure 3.5, below, demonstrates some of the complexities and interrelationships referred to in this introduction. It is important to internalise these issues.

Figure 3.5: skills required for competent legal rule analysis

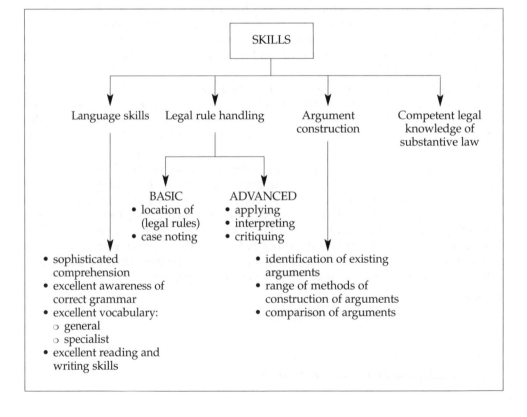

Those who grasp these interconnections and become competent handlers of rules and facts are successful interpreters of rules, assessors of situations and excellent problem solvers. They are, by definition, excellent lawyers.

3.4.2   Types of legislation: primary and secondary

Parliament authorises the creation of a range of different types of legal rule, as set out in Figure 3.6, below. They are all united by the fact that they are created in a fixed verbal form. Only *those* words were agreed by Parliament as containing the legal rule, not other words.

A characteristic of such rules is that they rarely come as single units – they are usually a collection of rules. They also come with attached definitions, defences, modes of interpretation and guidelines for operation.

Sometimes legislation is a reasonably well considered response to a particular issue such as:

- consumer protection;
- law and order;
- European Community obligations;
- family law.

Sometimes, legislation is quickly created as a reaction by parliament to a crisis or public outcry or a one off situation, for example, terrorism. Of course, in reality, it is the government of the day that determines what issues are put into the parliamentary law making machinery. Figure 3.7, below, illustrates the major procedure for the creation of legislation.

However, this text concentrates on the techniques for *understanding* such rules and the processes of *interpretation* that the courts, officials, ordinary people and law students follow in order to apply these rules.

Although each piece of legislation responds to particular issues, the finer details of the situations that the rules will have to be applied to will vary enormously. Therefore, another characteristic of legislation is that it is drafted in a general way, in order, it is hoped, to be applicable to the widest possible range of situations. This often presents a major challenge to those drafting the legislation and to those who are subsequently called upon to interpret it.

Another factor that must be borne in mind when considering the meaning and application of legislation is that it may have been changed in some way since enactment. For example, it may have been changed:

- by parliamentary authority, through legislation amending it (adding to or subtracting from it) or by repeal (abolishing it);
- by the House of Lords or the Court of Appeal determining the meaning of words and phrases used to make up the legal rule; UK courts have no power to amend or abolish legislation. But their power to interpret legislation can have a major impact on the application of the legislation;
- by European Community legal obligations directly entering English law and conflicting with the legal rule.

Figure 3.6: diagram indicating the range of direct and indirect legal rules created by Parliament

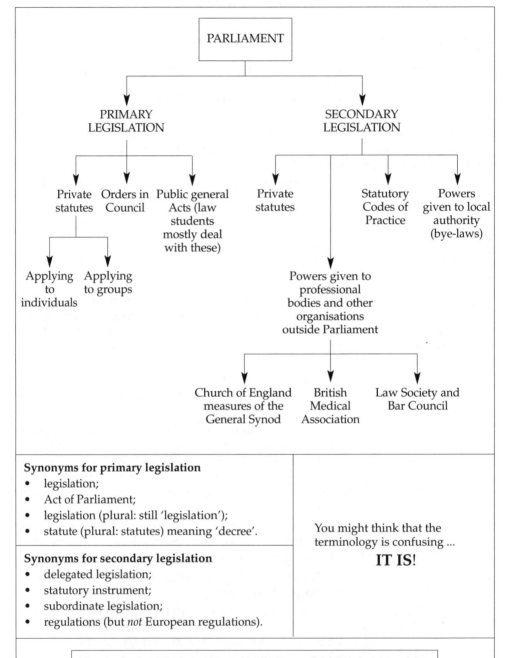

Synonyms for primary legislation
- legislation;
- Act of Parliament;
- legislation (plural: still 'legislation');
- statute (plural: statutes) meaning 'decree'.

Synonyms for secondary legislation
- delegated legislation;
- statutory instrument;
- subordinate legislation;
- regulations (but *not* European regulations).

You might think that the terminology is confusing ...

IT IS!

Note: the legislation currently in force has been created by Parliament over the past 700 years. Most legislation, however, has been created since 1850. There are surviving parchment rolls of legislation dating from about 1299. Statutes began to be printed towards the end of the 15th century.

Figure 3.7: Procedure for the creation of legislation (Parliament can also use fast-track law making processes. See in your English legal system course)

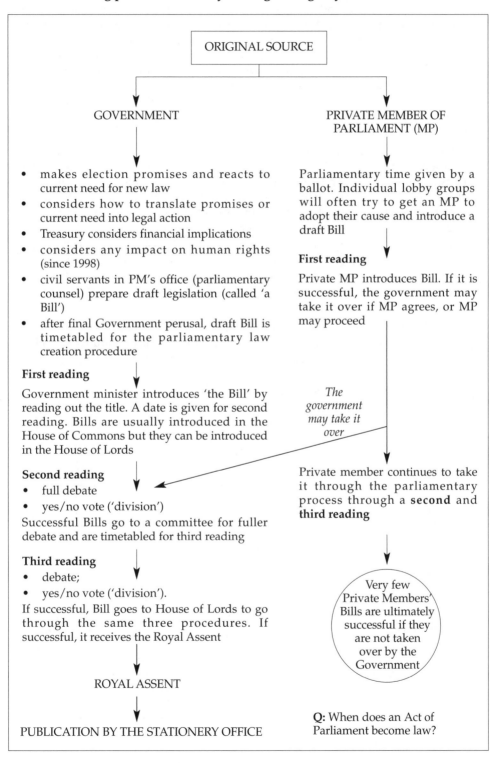

ORIGINAL SOURCE

GOVERNMENT

PRIVATE MEMBER OF PARLIAMENT (MP)

- makes election promises and reacts to current need for new law
- considers how to translate promises or current need into legal action
- Treasury considers financial implications
- considers any impact on human rights (since 1998)
- civil servants in PM's office (parliamentary counsel) prepare draft legislation (called 'a Bill')
- after final Government perusal, draft Bill is timetabled for the parliamentary law creation procedure

Parliamentary time given by a ballot. Individual lobby groups will often try to get an MP to adopt their cause and introduce a draft Bill

First reading

Private MP introduces Bill. If it is successful, the government may take it over if MP agrees, or MP may proceed

First reading

Government minister introduces 'the Bill' by reading out the title. A date is given for second reading. Bills are usually introduced in the House of Commons but they can be introduced in the House of Lords

The government may take it over

Second reading
- full debate
- yes/no vote ('division')

Successful Bills go to a committee for fuller debate and are timetabled for third reading

Private member continues to take it through the parliamentary process through a **second** and **third reading**

Third reading
- debate;
- yes/no vote ('division').

If successful, Bill goes to House of Lords to go through the same three procedures. If successful, it receives the Royal Assent

Very few Private Members' Bills are ultimately successful if they are not taken over by the Government

ROYAL ASSENT

PUBLICATION BY THE STATIONERY OFFICE

Q: When does an Act of Parliament become law?

3.4.3   The internal layout of legislation: a statute

There is a standard method of laying out statutes which, when recognised and understood, becomes a great help for analysis or evaluation. Most large statutes will be divided into parts for ease of reference. Each part will deal with different aspects of the overall collection of rules and their meanings. Each part contains sections which give more details in each area. Where appropriate, sections will deal with definitions. Sections can be further divided with the use of arabic numerals into sub-sections. Sub-sections are capable of further division, with the use of roman numerals, into paragraphs. Paragraphs can be further divided with alphabetical ordering into sub-paragraphs.

At the end of the statute, there will often be schedules and these are numerically divided as well. These deal further with matters raised in the various parts. Schedules can only relate to previous sections in the Act. They cannot create anything new without an anchoring in the main body of the statute. All statutes also contain marginal notes, headings and sub-headings. These organising devices, however, are said not to form part of the law.

Correct understanding of the relationship between parts, sections, sub-sections, paragraphs, sub-paragraphs, marginal notes, headings and schedules enables the general layout of the Act to be ascertained. Assistance is also obtained from the 'long title' of the Act, which looks more like a long sentence about what the statute is about!

Central to the analysis of statutes is the ability to understand these intratextual relationships. Figure 3.8, below, sets out the general layout of statutes and Figure 3.9, below, is an annotated first page of the Human Rights Act.

Figure 3.8: general layout of statutes

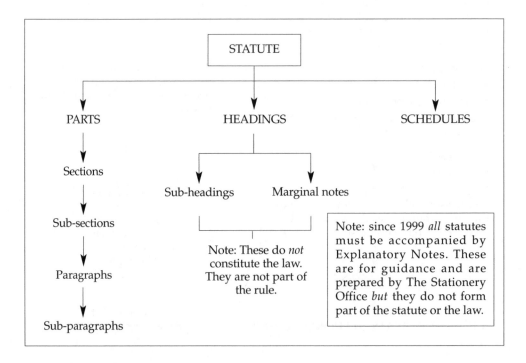

Figure 3.9: annotated first page of the Human Rights Act 1998

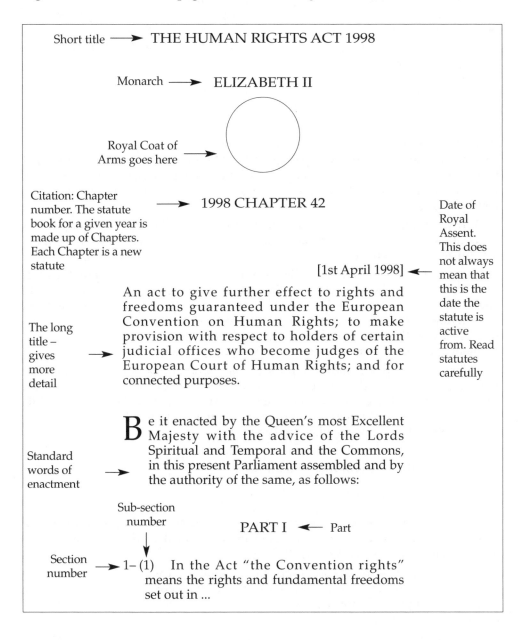

Short title ⟶ THE HUMAN RIGHTS ACT 1998

Monarch ⟶ ELIZABETH II

Royal Coat of
Arms goes here ⟶

Citation: Chapter
number. The statute   ⟶ 1998 CHAPTER 42
book for a given year is
made up of Chapters.
Each Chapter is a new
statute

Date of
Royal
Assent.
This does
not always

[1st April 1998] ⟵ mean that

this is the
date the
statute is
active
from. Read
statutes
carefully

The long
title –
gives   ⟶
more
detail

An act to give further effect to rights and
freedoms guaranteed under the European
Convention on Human Rights; to make
provision with respect to holders of certain
judicial offices who become judges of the
European Court of Human Rights; and for
connected purposes.

Standard
words of   ⟶
enactment

B e it enacted by the Queen's most Excellent
Majesty with the advice of the Lords
Spiritual and Temporal and the Commons,
in this present Parliament assembled and by
the authority of the same, as follows:

Sub-section
number

PART I ⟵ Part

Section
number   ⟶ 1– (1)   In the Act "the Convention rights"
means the rights and fundamental freedoms
set out in ...

A statute is divided into:	Vocabulary
<ul><li>sections;</li><li>sub-sections;</li><li>paragraphs;</li><li>sub-paragraphs;</li><li>Parts;</li><li>Schedules (at the end).</li></ul>	Repeal – abolition of all or part of a previous statute. Amend – changing part of a previous statute.

Parliament can enact laws about anything – but a law may prove impossible to enforce. Legend records that one particular King of England, Canute, was humbled when he attempted to demonstrate his sovereign power by seating his throne on the beach and ordering the tide not to come in! For come in it did, much to his embarrassment.

When approaching a statute as a new law student the most difficult task is understanding, at a basic macro- (wide) level, what the statute as a whole is striving to do and at the micro- (narrow) level what each section is saying.

As proficiency is gained in handling statutory rules it will be found that it is not usually necessary to deal with the entire statute. The overall statute can be briefly contextualised and only relevant sections need to be extracted for detailed consideration, analysis, or application. However, 'sections', those micro-elements of statutes, will be all the more confidently analysed because, at any given moment, it is known how to relate any aspect of the statute to its general layout.

Often, initial understanding eludes the law student. Doubts concerning the meaning of parts of the statute do not occur at the level of sophisticated analysis. They occur at the basic level of combining English language skills and legal skills to obtain foundational understanding. If doubts remain at this level, there can be no possibility of attaining sophisticated analysis!

3.4.4   Case study: breaking into statutes

3.4.4.1   Unfair Contract Terms Act 1977

To explore methods of breaking into statutes and understanding statutes at the macro- and micro-level the rest of this chapter will deal with a real statute, the Unfair Contract Terms Act (UCTA) 1977.

Figure 3.10, below, builds on the abstract general layout of Figure 3.8, above, by customising it to fit UCTA 1977. This statute will continue to be used for demonstration purposes for the rest of the chapter. The full text of the statute can be found in Appendix 1.

Study Figure 3.10, below, carefully. Note which parts are linked and which are not by following the lines and arrows. Reading the summarised headings constructs a basic overview of what the statute is about.

Before considering how to break into statutory language in such a way as to be able to confidently précis whole sections for the purposes of such a layout, it is important to study the layout until it is familiar and comprehensible. There are no shortcuts; this takes time.

Figure 3.10: general layout of the Unfair Contract Terms Act 1977 into its constituent parts and sections

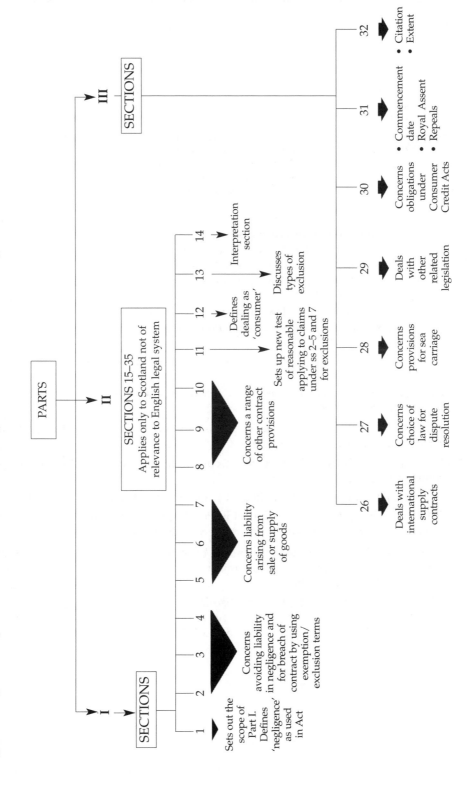

Figure 3.11: general layout of the Unfair Contract Terms Act 1977 – schedules

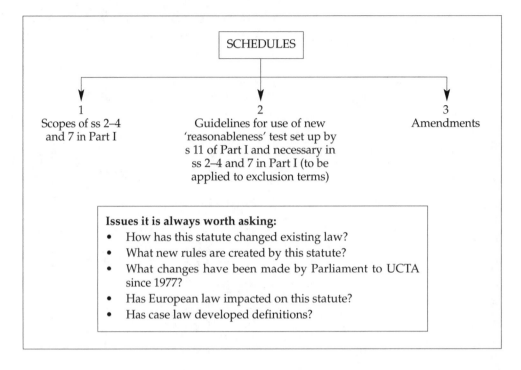

To test your comprehension, answer the following questions by recourse only to Figures 3.10 and 3.11, above:

(1) What areas of the statute need to be considered to find out if the exclusion terms in a contract are reasonable?

(2) What areas of the statute need to be considered to ascertain the repeals and amendments made by the statute?

(3) Where can the definition of dealing as a consumer be found?

(4) If I want to bring an action under s 4 in Part I of the statute, what other sections may be relevant and would, therefore, need to be considered?

This should have been a reasonably simple exercise and should also demonstrate both the use of such a layout and the importance of understanding how an entire piece of legislation fits together.

The next stage in building up expertise in the basics of handling statutes is to turn to the minute detail and consider how to break into the text as a piece of comprehension. Let us, therefore, consider s 3 of UCTA 1977:

3 – (1) This section applies as between contracting parties where one of them deals as consumer or on the other's written standard terms of business.

(2) As against that party, the other cannot by reference to any contract term:

(a) when himself in breach of contract, exclude or restrict any liability of his in respect of the breach; or

(b) claim to be entitled:

(i) to render a contractual performance substantially different from that which was reasonably expected of him, or

(ii) in respect of the whole or any part of his contractual obligation, to render no performance at all,

except in so far as (in any of the cases mentioned above in this sub-section) the contract term satisfies the requirement of reasonableness.

A glance back at the general layout of UCTA 1977 in Figure 3.10, above, will reveal that s 3 can be found in Part I of the statute and is one of three sections that are concerned with avoiding liability for breach of contract subject to the condition of reasonableness.

3.4.4.2 Using the language and grammar of s 3

An initial clue as to the relationship between the various parts of this section can be gathered from a consideration of:

(a) connectors. Connectors are words such as:

- 'or';
- 'and';
- 'on';
- 'but';
- 'if';
- 'for';

(b) punctuation;

(c) sentences;

(d) specialist vocabulary.

Section 3 of UCTA 1977 contains two sub-sections. Sub-sections are grouped together because they are intimately connected. Therefore, the first task is to look for connectors, those words that indicate what that intimate connection is.

3.4.4.3 Punctuation consideration

The second task is to consider the punctuation which although sparse is another clue as to which phrases belong together. Sub-sections are always connected to each other in some way. Paragraphs within sections and sub-paragraphs within sub-sections are intimately connected.

A diagram (Figure 3.12, below) can be constructed which gives relational indicators between s 3 and its sub-sections, paragraphs and sub-paragraphs. It can be seen to hang together like a two-dimensional mobile. The value of such a diagram is that the links are immediately apparent, simplifying the task of considering grammatical connections.

Figure 3.12: relational diagram of s 3

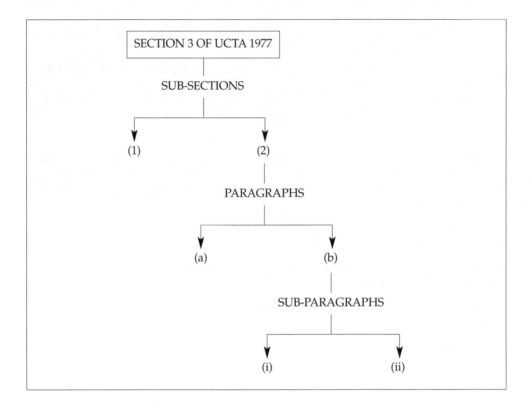

Look back to the text of s 3 and read it.

There are only two sentences in s 3. Sub-section (1) and sub-s (2) are both a sentence each. However the sentence making up sub-s (2) is 96 words long! The semi-colon in s 3(2)(a) suggests an appropriate end to a sentence but for the fact that the drafter presumably felt it that it would be misleading as the intimate idea-link desired with the rest of s 3(2) might not be made. Let us look at these two sentences in s 3(1) and s 3(2).

3.4.5   Subject search of sentences

3.4.5.1 Sentence 1: s 3(1)

> The subject of the sentence is the *'contracting parties'* to whom the *'section'* (that is, s 3 of UCTA) *'applies'*.

An immediate question to ask is when does the section apply to contracting parties? It applies, we are told in s 3(1) in two situations:

(a) 'where one of them deals as a consumer'; or

(b) 'on the other's written standard terms of business'.

The important connector word *'or'* connects (a) with (b). If the word 'or' is replaced by 'and', a different link would be made. Both situations (a) and (b) would need to occur together for s 3(1) to apply. The word, 'or', clarifies that in *either* situation, s 3(1) applies. So the key word for comprehension of the applicability of the rule is the connector word 'or'. It is now possible to state that s 3(1) makes it clear that s 3 as a whole applies when one of the parties to a contract is entering the contract as a consumer or agrees to contract on the other party's pre-prepared written standard terms.

Getting this far does not solve any difficulties but merely begins to limit the area covered by the section. It is at least now possible to exclude classes of contract which are not included in s 3. Take a moment to return to the text of s 3(1) and re-read it. We can now ask a question in the negative: 'what contracting parties are excluded from the operation of s 3?'. All contracts that are *not* consumer contracts, or not on the other party's written standard terms of business. Students often fail to notice the negative. It is important, however, in understanding the extent and the limits of s 3.

Looking at the original s 3(1), there are still phrases that may need explanation, for example, what do the following phrases mean:

(a) 'deals as a consumer'?

(b) 'written standard terms'?

(c) 'applies'?

> The answer to the meaning of (a) and (b) lies in definitional sections in other parts of the statute.
>
> Look at Figure 3.10, above. Can you find out where?
>
> (The answer to (c) lies in reading on!)

3.4.5.2 Sentence 2: s 3(2)

This section fleshes out the impact of s 3(1) in describing *what* it *is* that *applies*! The ordering is unusual to a first time reader. Surely it might be thought, one should first be told the rule and then told categories that need to comply with it?

Remember that sub-sections within a section are intimately linked so that just as sub-s (1) appears to refer forward by use of the phrase 'This section applies', then a reader of sub-s (2) may need to refer back to sub-s (1) – it may not stand alone. Sub-section (2) is no exception as this cross-referencing takes place immediately in the first words of sub-s (2), '*As against that party, the other*'. Some simple questions begin the process of clarification.

Q1:   (a)   Who is '*that party*'?

(b)   Who is the 'other'?

Answer: (a)   That party is the 'one' who is 'dealing as a consumer or on the other's standard terms of business' in s 3(1).

(b)   Therefore, by process of elimination, the 'other' is the one who is not 'dealing as a consumer or on the other's standard terms of business'.

Q2:   How can we know the answer to Question 1?

Answer: Because 'other' is specifically referred to in the first few words of sub-s (2). This other is:

(a)   first, the hidden 'other' party referred to by implication in sub-s 3(1) (that is, the one who is not dealing as a consumer);

(b)   secondly, there is the hidden 'other' party who actually writes the 'standard terms of business'.

There are, therefore, two categories of 'other'.

Q: So what is the subject of sub-s (2)?

A: It is the 'other'.

Q: How do we know this?

A: Because the person or company referred to as 'that party' has already been:

(a) identified; and

(b) defined in sub-s 1.

Sub-section 2, therefore, is concerned with what that '*other*' can and '*cannot*' do. That is outlined in paras (a) and (b).

It has taken time to explain the interconnections between sub-s (1) and the first seven words of sub-s (2) at a basic level. The full complexities of sub-s (2), paras (a) and (b) have not yet been touched. Luckily, once alerted to the types of issues to look out for, our minds are powerful tools and all of the foregoing discussion, questions and connectors will begin to be answered and noticed purely mentally and automatically whilst reading on and looking at s 3(2). A point will be reached later in your studies when only a few points would actually be noted down, as your familiarity with language and structure will enable ease of reading.

It is useful at this stage to turn again to the words of s 3 so far considered as laid out in Figure 3.13, below, and annotated.

Figure 3.13: annotation of s 3

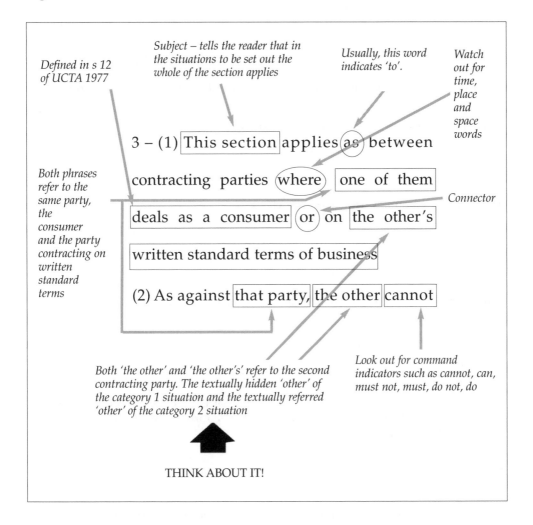

The discussion of 'breaking into' the text has been tedious because it is necessary to set out in minute detail what the experienced reader and analyst scans in seconds, virtually instantaneously, so that the process can be examined. Language skills (in terms of grammar and general/specialist vocabulary) are united with an understanding of drafting, structure and scope of the law.

Figure 3.15, below, sets out s 3 in full; study it carefully and be sure that textual intraconnections are understood. Note that, as in Figure 3.13, above, certain words have been outlined. This is to highlight the fact that the key to understanding statutory language and structure is to pay strict attention to grammatical clues as already indicated. In addition, it is vital consistently to look for the prepositional links. Words such as:

(a) to;

or;

and;

if;

so;

but;

therefore,

as these connect the words in the statute together like cement connects bricks in a building.

In addition consider the time and place words, such as:

(b) where;

when;

were,

as well as the command style words such as:

(c) cannot;

may not;

should not;

shall,

and beware of subject words which can also be overlooked:

(d) it;

other;

one;

part.

These little words in lists (a)–(d) are the very words that are often overlooked by the hasty reader. They are set out in diagrammatic form below. Reading in haste is a perilous thing for a lawyer to do.

Figure 3.14

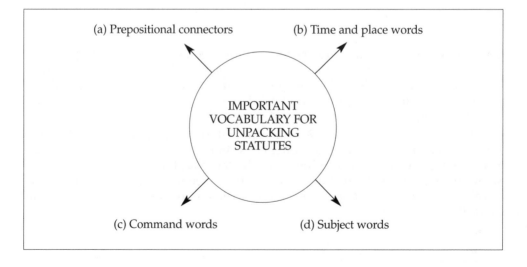

Figure 3.15: full text of s 3 set out as a tree diagram showing the internal connections

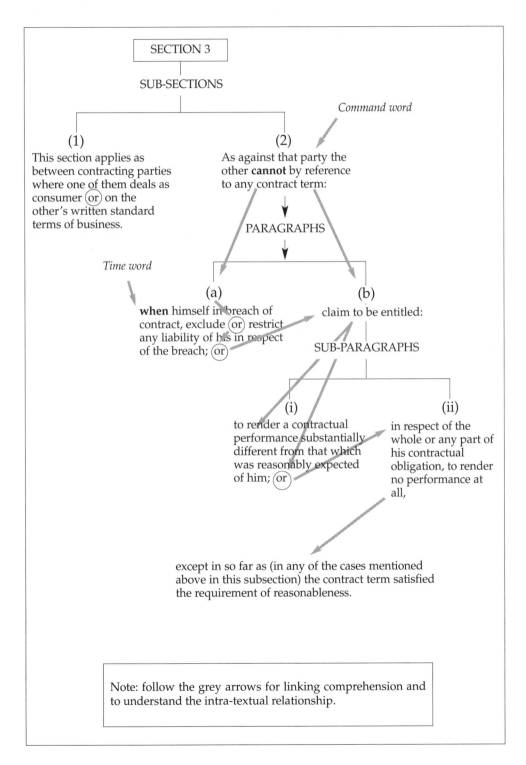

3.4.6   Section 11 task

Now try another difficult section: s 11 of UCTA 1977 (which sets up what has come to be called the *reasonableness test*) and start to put into practice what it is that you have learned. Figure 3.16, below, sets out s 11 and the guidelines for the application of the *reasonableness test* as set out in Schedule 2 of the Act.

Figure 3.16 is a complicated diagram and, as expertise develops in the reading of statutory material, much analysis is done mentally and summarised notes taken. Confidence can result in the ability to paraphrase main provisions in order to catch intratextual references alone.

Figure 3.17, below, is such a summarised version of s 11 together with Schedule 2 of UCTA 1977. Or, to put it another way, Figure 3.17 is a summarised version of Figure 3.16.

Given the relationship between law cases and statutes, it would also be useful to add, initially in list form only, to a 'section tree diagram' any cases dealing with aspects of the section – cases which may define the meaning of words or phrases or which apply aspects of the section. Figure 3.18, below, merely adds one case, the case that will be the subject of consideration in Chapter 4: *George Mitchell v Finney Lock Seeds* (1983).

First of all just read s 11 of UCTA 1977 set out in the box on p 55, below, followed by Schedule 2 to UCTA 1977 set out in the box immediately following. Take some time to digest the narrative. You could also try to turn s 11 and Schedule 2 into diagrams. When you have put the time in *then*, and only then, turn to the diagrams and follow them through.

Section 11 of UCTA 1977

Explanatory provisions

The 'reasonableness' test

11– (1)   In relation to a contract term, the requirement of reasonableness for the purposes of this Part of this Act, section 3 of the Misrepresentation Act 1967 and section 3 of the Misrepresentation Act (Northern Ireland) 1967 is that the term shall have been a fair and reasonable one to be included having regard to the circumstances which were, or ought reasonably to have been, known to or in the contemplation of the parties when the contract was made.

(2) In determining for the purposes of section 6 or 7 above whether a contract term satisfies the requirement of reasonableness, regard shall be had in particular to the matters specified in Schedule 2 to this Act; but this subsection does not prevent the court or arbitrator from holding, in accordance with any rule of law, that a term which purports to exclude or restrict any relevant liability is not a term of the contract.

(3) In relation to a notice (not being a notice having contractual effect), the requirement of reasonableness under this Act is that it should be fair and reasonable to allow reliance on it, having regard to all the circumstances obtaining when the liability arose or (but for the notice) would have arisen.

(4) Where by reference to a contract term or notice a person seeks to restrict liability to a specified sum of money, and the question arises (under this or any other Act) whether the term or notice satisfies the requirement of reasonableness, regard shall be had in particular (but without prejudice to subsection (2) above in the case of contract terms) to–

(a)   the resources which he could expect to be available to him for the purpose of meeting the liability should it arise; and

(b)   how far it was open to him to cover himself by insurance.

(5) It is for those claiming that a contract term or notice satisfies the requirement of reasonableness to show that it does.

Schedule 2 of UCTA 1977

'Guidelines' for Application of Reasonableness Test

The matters to which regard is to be had in particular for the purposes of sections 6(3), 7(3) and (4), 20 and 21 are any of the following which appear to be relevant–

(a) the strength of the bargaining positions of the parties relative to each other, taking into account (among other things) alternative means by which the customer's requirements could have been met;

(b) whether the customer received an inducement to agree to the term, or in accepting it had an opportunity of entering into a similar contract with other persons, but without having to accept a similar term;

(c) whether the customer knew or ought reasonably to have known of the existence and extent of the term (having regard, among other things, to any custom of the trade and any previous course of dealing between the parties);

(d) where the term excludes or restricts any relevant liability if some condition is not complied with, whether it was reasonable at the time of the contract to expect that compliance with that condition would be practicable;

(e) whether the goods were manufactured, processed or adapted to the special order of the customer.

Figure 3.16: layout of s 11 of UCTA 1977 including Schedule 2

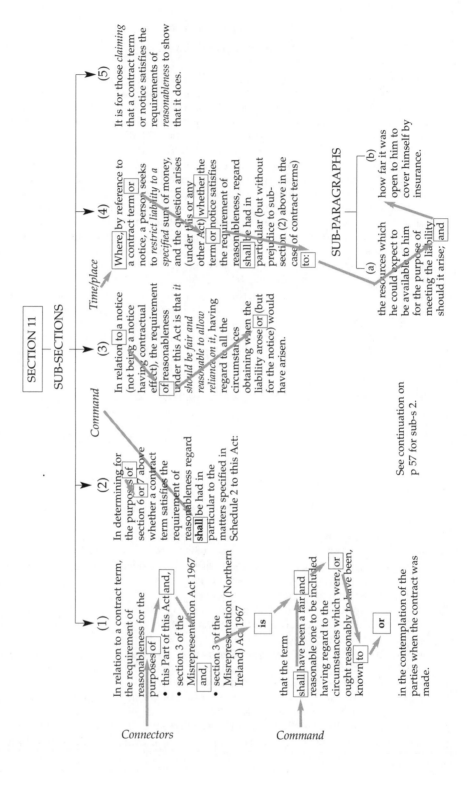

SECTION 11

SUB-SECTIONS

(1)

In relation to a contract term, the requirement of reasonableness for the purposes of—

- this Part of this Act and,
- section 3 of the Misrepresentation Act 1967 and,
- section 3 of the Misrepresentation (Northern Ireland) Act 1967

that the term

shall have been a fair and reasonable one to be included having regard to the circumstances which were, or ought reasonably to have been, known to

in the contemplation of the parties when the contract was made.

Connectors

is

Command

(2)

Command

In determining for the purposes of section 6 or 7 above whether a contract term satisfies the requirement of reasonableness regard **shall** be had in particular to the matters specified in Schedule 2 to this Act:

See continuation on p 57 for sub-s 2.

(3)

Time/place

In relation to a notice (not being a notice having contractual effect), the requirement of reasonableness under this Act is that *it should be fair and reasonable to allow reliance on it*, having regard to all the circumstances obtaining when the liability arose or (but for the notice) would have arisen.

(4)

Where, by reference to a contract term or notice, a person seeks *to restrict liability to a specified* sum of money, and the question arises (under this or any other Act) whether the term or notice satisfies the requirement of reasonableness, regard shall be had in particular (but without prejudice to sub-section (2) above in the case of contract terms) to:

SUB-PARAGRAPHS

(a)

the resources which he could expect to be available to him for the purpose of meeting the liability should it arise; and

(b)

how far it was open to him to cover himself by insurance.

(5)

It is for those claiming that a contract term or notice satisfies the requirements of *reasonableness* to show that it does.

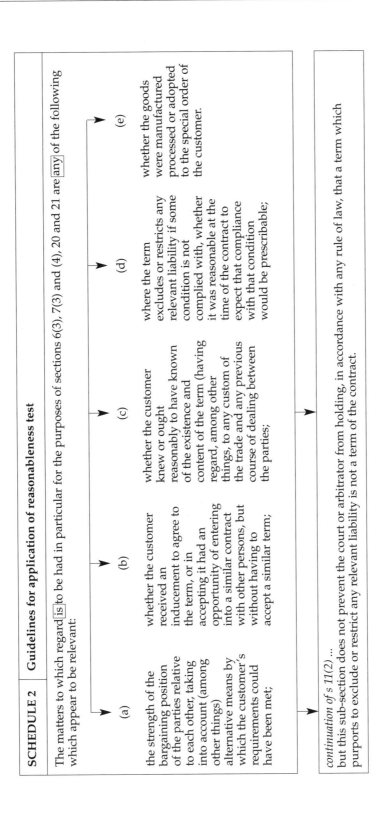

SCHEDULE 2 | **Guidelines for application of reasonableness test**

The matters to which regard is to be had in particular for the purposes of sections 6(3), 7(3) and (4), 20 and 21 are any of the following which appear to be relevant:

(a)

the strength of the bargaining position of the parties relative to each other, taking into account (among other things) alternative means by which the customer's requirements could have been met;

(b)

whether the customer received an inducement to agree to the term, or in accepting it had an opportunity of entering into a similar contract with other persons, but without having to accept a similar term;

(c)

whether the customer knew or ought reasonably to have known of the existence and content of the term (having regard, among other things, to any custom of the trade and any previous course of dealing between the parties;

(d)

where the term excludes or restricts any relevant liability if some condition is not complied with, whether it was reasonable at the time of the contract to expect that compliance with that condition would be prescribable;

(e)

whether the goods were manufactured processed or adopted to the special order of the customer.

continuation of s 11(2) …
but this sub-section does not prevent the court or arbitrator from holding, in accordance with any rule of law, that a term which purports to exclude or restrict any relevant liability is not a term of the contract.

Note: look now at the original text of s 11 in the full text of the statute in Appendix 1.

Figure 3.17: s 11 of UCTA 1977 (sets up new test of reasonableness for exclusion, exemption and limitation clauses)

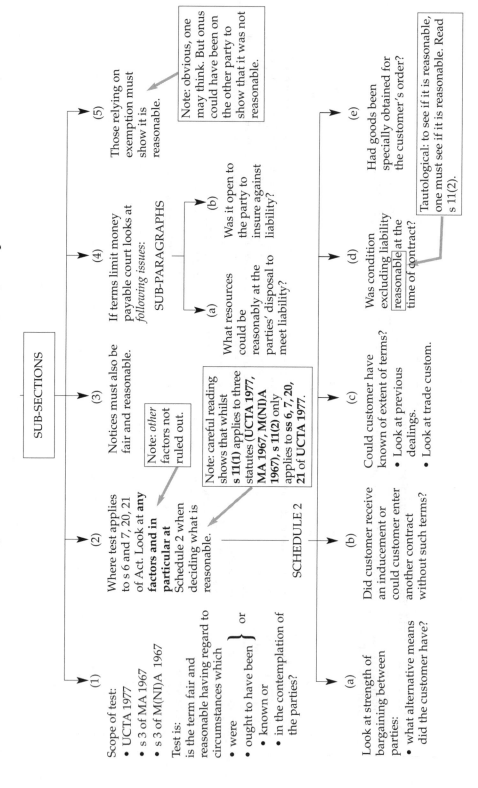

SUB-SECTIONS

(1)

Scope of test:
• UCTA 1977
• s 3 of MA 1967
• s 3 of M(NI)A 1967

Test is:
is the term fair and reasonable having regard to circumstances which
were
ought to have been } or
• known or
• in the contemplation of the parties?

(2)

Where test applies to s 6 and 7, 20, 21 of Act. Look at **any factors and in particular at** Schedule 2 when deciding what is reasonable.

Note: *other* factors not ruled out.

Note: careful reading shows that whilst **s 11(1)** applies to three statutes (**UCTA 1977, MA 1967, M(NI)A 1967), s 11(2)** only applies to **ss 6, 7, 20, 21 of UCTA 1977.**

SCHEDULE 2

(3)

Notices must also be fair and reasonable.

(4)

If terms limit money payable court looks at *following issues:*

SUB-PARAGRAPHS

(a)

What resources could be reasonably at the parties' disposal to meet liability?

(b)

Was it open to the party to insure against liability?

(5)

Those relying on exemption must show it is reasonable.

Note: obvious, one may think. But onus could have been on the other party to show that it was not reasonable.

(a)

Look at strength of bargaining between parties:
• what alternative means did the customer have?

(b)

Did customer receive an inducement or could customer enter another contract without such terms?

(c)

Could customer have known of extent of terms?
• Look at previous dealings.
• Look at trade custom.

(d)

Was condition excluding liability reasonable at the time of contract?

(e)

Had goods been specially obtained for the customer's order?

Tautological: to see if it is reasonable, one must see if it is reasonable. Read s 11(2).

Figure 3.18: s 11 of UCTA 1977 (sets up new test of reasonableness)

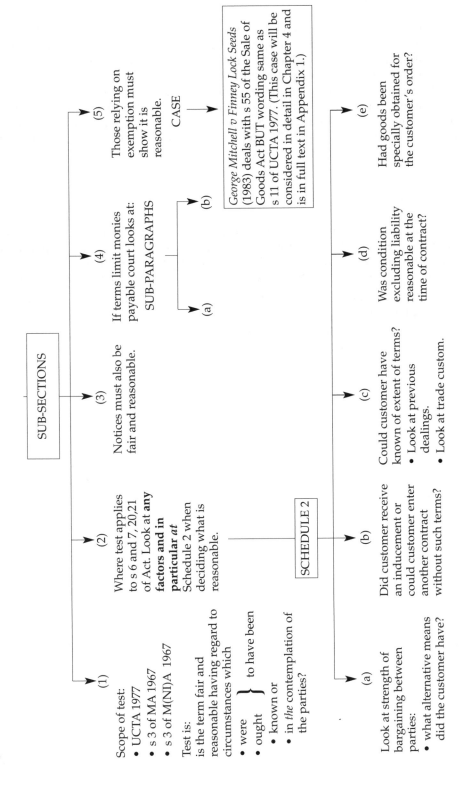

3.5   SUMMARY

This chapter has been concerned with giving a broad introduction to the layout, interpretation and methods of applying statutory rules. As such it has therefore concentrated on the issue of handling rules, and the areas where competent English language skills are an integral part of understanding the legislation. It has also introduced the systematic use of diagrammatic methods to break into legislation. This chapter provides a firm foundation for skills introduced later in the book concerning the interpretation of legislation by judges (Chapter 4), the European dimensions of law (Chapter 5) and the essentials of argument construction in Chapter 7.

3.6   FURTHER READING

If you are a law student you will be studying the areas covered in this chapter from different perspectives in English legal system and constitutional (or public) law courses. However, you may find the following texts useful reading. They are excellent texts relating to both the theoretical and practical aspects of legal method:

- Sychin, C, *Legal Method*, 1999 (3rd edn due 2003), London: Sweet & Maxwell, Chapters 7 and 8.
- Twining, W and Miers, D, *How To Do Things With Rules, a Primer of Interpretation*, 4th edn, 1999, London: Butterworths, Chapters 7 and 8.

CHAPTER 4

READING AND UNDERSTANDING LAW REPORTS

4.1   INTRODUCTION

The few legal disputes that cannot be resolved by negotiation between lawyers or last minute settlements outside the court are determined by the judges in the trial courts, and in even fewer cases, decided in the appellate courts by the senior judiciary.

The word 'few' must be stressed because a law student surrounded by law reports may think that the entire English legal system is composed of nothing but law reports. This is not the case: only about 4% of all formally commenced disputes reach a hearing in court and many of these settle at the doors of the court.

The decisions of judges are delivered orally in court, when the judge may read a pre-written judgment or speak from notes. The words spoken and recorded in writing constitute the words that contain any legally binding rules. At the time of delivery, they are also usually recorded verbatim by the court stenographer. In addition, official law reporters, as well as unofficial, are in court taking shorthand notes. The record of the judgment will be kept by the court, but some decisions, thought to be important to the development or understanding of the law, will be additionally published in one of the range of privately published series of reports of decisions in law cases in courts and tribunals. A case that is chosen for publication is called a law report. Each publisher will structure their reports differently, perhaps adding footnotes or summaries but the words attributed to the judge have to remain a true and accurate record of the words actually spoken. The reports given the highest regard are those that wait for the judge concerned to check the accuracy of their written record. Section 4.4, below, gives more detail.

Usually, judges in the civil courts and the appellate courts (both criminal and civil) will reflect upon the case before reaching a final decision; they therefore hold back (reserve) judgment until a later date. In criminal cases after the jury has reached a verdict in the trial court, the judge may sentence immediately or call for reports and sentence at a later date.

What judges say in their judgments is of immense importance, not only for the litigants, but for the development of the law. The English legal system is unique in its public insistence that cases must be decided in keeping with the reasoning process used by judges reaching decisions in similar previous cases of the same court or higher. This process of deciding a case in accordance with past judicial reasoning in similar cases is reasoning in accordance with the *doctrine of precedent*. The concept of keeping to past decisions is also tied to rules concerning the hierarchy of English courts. Trial courts (or courts of first instance) are at the bottom of the hierarchy and appeal courts at the top.

The House of Lords, as the highest court of appeal, and the most senior court in the English legal system is often referred to as the 'apex' of the court hierarchy. The further up the hierarchy one goes, the fewer cases the court deals with and the longer cases will last. This hierarchical relationship in relation to precedent is set out in Figure 4.1, below.

Many legal systems throughout the world have a rule of thumb adherence to the doctrine of precedent. However, few keep to the concept of binding precedent as rigidly as the English legal system. Indeed, it has been said that it is more difficult to get rid of an awkward decision in England than it is anywhere else in the world.

4.2   LEARNING OUTCOMES

By the end of this chapter, readers should:

- understand the basic rationale for the doctrine of precedent;
- be able to explain what the doctrine of precedent is;
- understand the difference between the theoretical dimension and the practical dimension of the doctrine of precedent;
- be able to competently read a case and prepare a case note;
- understand the relationship between reliable law reporting and the doctrine of precedent;
- understand the relationship between statutes and cases;
- be able to distinguish between year books, nominate reports, general and specialist series, and official reports;
- understand the constituent parts of the *ratio* of a case.

4.3   THE RELATIONSHIP BETWEEN LAW REPORTING AND THE DOCTRINE OF PRECEDENT

The only way of being able to keep successfully to the doctrine of binding precedent is to have a reliable system of law reporting. The competent production of volumes of reports of past cases is indispensable to the operation of the doctrine. Reliable law reports have only been available in England since 1865 although there are a range of fragmentary law reports going back to the 12th century, which are known as yearbooks. Reports existing in the *Yearbooks* cover the period from the late 12th century to the early 16th century. However, it is not always possible to discover if the report is of an actual case or a moot (an argument contest between lawyers). This makes them an unreliable source and also the detail that was given and the quality of the reports varies considerably. Some reports record outcome, but not facts, others record facts and outcome, but give no reasoning process. Reports also exist in the nominate (named) reports dating from the late 15th century to 1865. By the 19th century, a court-authorised reporter was attached to all higher courts and their reports were published in collected volumes again by name of reporter. By 1865, there were 16 reporters compiling and publishing authorised reports. They were amalgamated into the Incorporated Council of Law Reporting and the reports were published in volumes known as the *Law Reports*. These reports are checked by the judges of the relevant case prior to publication and a rule of citation has developed that if a case is reported in a range of publications, only that version printed in the *Law Reports* is cited in court. However, the accuracy of reports pre-dating the setting up of the Incorporated Council of Law Reporting in 1865 cannot be guaranteed.

Figure 4.1: hierarchical relationship of the courts

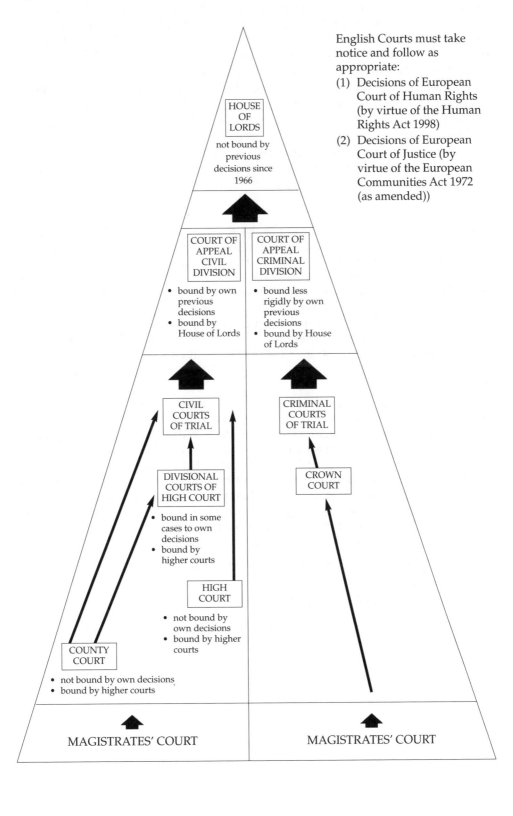

Surprisingly, there are no *official*, authoritative series of law reports in England to equate with the Queen's Printers copy of an Act of Parliament. The Stationery Office is responsible for publishing revenue, immigration and social security law cases. However, traditionally, law reports remain in the hands of private publishers. Today, there are numerous, often competitive, private publishers.

Although there are no official series of law reports, the courts do respect some reports more than others. A long established, conventional rule is that a law report, if it is to be accepted by the relevant court as an authority, must be prepared by and published under the name of a fully qualified barrister.

The greater accuracy of modern reporting, and the vetting by judges, necessitates longer delays before the cases are published. Also, the *Law Reports* only cover 7% of the cases in the higher courts in any given year. Interesting issues are:

(a) who selects which cases to report?

(b) how are they selected?

Editors select the cases for inclusion in the series of law reports. These are highly trained lawyers, well acquainted with precedent and the likely importance of cases. During the past 150 years publishers of law reports have been generalists or specialists. Some law reports are annotated, particularly for the use of practitioners, others left without annotations, introductions, etc. In addition to reported cases, the Supreme Court Library contains thousands of files of unreported cases. In 1940, the Lord Chancellor's Department prepared a report: *The Report of the Law Reporting Committee*. The Committee considered that, after editors had made their choices, 'What remains is less likely to be a treasure house than a rubbish heap in which a jewel will rarely, if ever, be discovered' (p 20). (Note the poetic language that forcefully carries the point.)

Of course, today, there is a vast range of electronic retrieval systems for accessing details of thousands of unreported cases. This has caused its own problems and there was a legitimate concern that courts would be inundated with cases that did not really contain any new law, but which had been retrieved from electronic sources. In the case of *Roberts Petroleum Ltd v Bernard Kenny Ltd* [1983] 2 AC 192, the House of Lords took the step of forbidding the citation of unreported cases of the civil division of the Court of Appeal without special leave. The rule remains, however, that to be an accepted version that can be quoted in court the report must have been prepared and published by a barrister.

When law students read law reports they must ask:

(a) is this report the most authoritative version available?

(b) are there fuller versions?

(c) if unreported, does this case add to the law?

Figure 4.2, below, sets out the types of reports available for the law student to consult.

Figure 4.2: range of available law reports

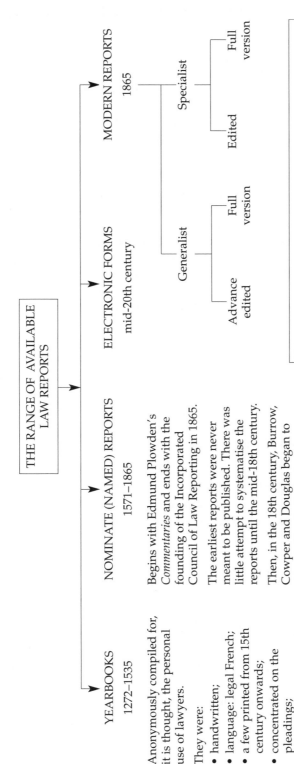

THE RANGE OF AVAILABLE LAW REPORTS

YEARBOOKS
1272–1535

Anonymously compiled for, it is thought, the personal use of lawyers.

They were:

• handwritten;
• language: legal French;
• a few printed from 15th century onwards;
• concentrated on the pleadings;
• often no judgment recorded.

They are rarely cited today.

Modern reprints include a series by the Selsdon Society.

NOMINATE (NAMED) REPORTS
1571–1865

Begins with Edmund Plowden's *Commentaries* and ends with the founding of the Incorporated Council of Law Reporting in 1865.

The earliest reports were never meant to be published. There was little attempt to systematise the reports until the mid-18th century.

Then, in the 18th century, Burrow, Cowper and Douglas began to standardise the layout.

In the late 18th century, judges began to review reports of their judgments or make written versions available to reporters. They also got involved in the appointment of reporters to courts.

Reports began to be published more quickly.

ELECTRONIC FORMS
mid-20th century

MODERN REPORTS
1865

Generalist   Specialist

Advance   Full   Edited   Full
edited   version   version

Notes:

• *Weekly Law Reports* (WLR) take five months to be published.
• *Law Reports* (LR) take 10–14 months to be published.
• Cases in appellate courts appear on LEXIS, an electronic database, within days.
• There are about 500 different publishers.
• *English Reports* 1771–1865 most comprehensive.
• *Revised Reports* 1785–1865.
• *All England Reports* (All ER) 1558–1993.

4.4   THE THEORETICAL DIMENSIONS OF THE DOCTRINE OF PRECEDENT

Many legal theorists and practitioners have attempted, over the years, to give precise definitions of the English doctrine of precedent. Unfortunately for law students, there are no simple shortcuts to understanding the *practical* everyday working of the doctrine of precedent.

However, a few theoretical ground rules can be established, which at least place the operation of the doctrine of precedent within a context:

(1) judges at all levels of the court hierarchy *must follow* decisions of the higher courts;

(2) judges in the higher courts *must follow* previous decisions of their own court – or that of a higher court if the case was similar, and does not fall into any allowed exceptions. It is accepted, however, that in the Court of Appeal, a more relaxed attitude can be taken in relation to criminal appeals;

(3) since a Practice Statement by the Lord Chancellor in 1966, judges in the House of Lords have the freedom to decline to follow their own previous decisions *(Practice Direction (Judicial Precedent)* [1966] 3 All ER 77). This freedom is exercised sparingly – but in a more relaxed way in its criminal jurisdiction than in its civil jurisdiction.

Much depends on the definition of similar. How similar must a previous case be before it becomes a precedent to be followed in a current case? Notice, again, how everything turns on language and the meaning of words.

The facts of cases usually vary in some way. Law is about life and life rarely replicates itself exactly, but trends and degrees of similarity can be noted. The following issues need to be dealt with:

(1) must the law be similar now as then?

(2) what happens if there are small fact differences?

(3) what if there are a range of small differences – is the case sufficiently similar?

There are no definitions of similar for the purposes of the doctrine and this is where the judge can bring subjective influences into the decision making processes. He or she can determine what 'similarity' is.

In addition, how can the *reason* for the case be extracted? Similar cases must be decided in accordance with the same reasoning process. The actual doctrine as it has developed refers to keeping to the reasons for deciding past cases. *How* does one find the reasoning?

Wambaugh, a theorist working in America in the late 19th century, suggests that one way of ascertaining the reason for the decision *(ratio decidendi)* is to look for a general rule of law in the judgments and test whether it is foundational for deciding the case by translating it into the negative form and seeing if the case would then have been decided differently.

In other words, he suggests locating the *ratio* by using a negative method as illustrated by the flow chart in Figure 4.3, below. Wambaugh emphasises the *search* for a rule.

Figure 4.3: Wambaugh's method for locating the *ratio*

EXTRACT A PROPOSITION OF LAW

CHANGE ITS FORMULATION TO THE NEGATIVE

APPLY THE NEGATIVE FORMULATION TO THE CASE

IF OUTCOME IS THE SAME: THE IDENTIFIED PROPOSITION OF LAW IS NOT THE *RATIO* OF THE CASE

IF OUTCOME IS NOT THE SAME: THE IDENTIFIED PROPOSITION OF LAW IS THE *RATIO* OF THE CASE

> Problem: this method is designed to work only with one proposition of law. Cases can have more than one proposition.

Another famous legal theorist, Goodhart, wrote an influential essay 'Determining the *ratio* of a case' which refers far more to the *'principle'* in the case than the *'ratio'* (1930) 40 Yale LJ 161. He emphasises facts:

(a) what are the material facts as found by the judge?

(b) what is the judge's decision?

(c) unless there is a new material fact (or there are some missing material facts) a future court, depending upon its place in the court hierarchy, and thus its obligations under the doctrine of precedent, must follow it.

Goodhart does consider the rule, or what he calls the principle of the case. He gives a thorough discussion of finding the principle of a case, which revolves around the tension between a range of issues and he also appears clearer about where he considers the principle *cannot* be found.

A major problem with Goodhart's suggested method, an aspect of which is set out in Figure 4.5, below, is that he places rather a lot of emphasis upon the facts.

Although it can be said that reading a judgment in the light of the facts of the case is a core requirement of the doctrine, there also needs to be attention given to the way that the case is:

(a) argued;

(b) pleaded (exactly how have the lawyers formally lodged the complaint?);

(c) reasoned,

in relation to other precedents. Every judgment has to be read in the light of previous and, if relevant, with a view as to how subsequent cases may be affected.

Even taking these two methods together, problems remain:

(a) what should an interpreter do when there is a decision without reasons? Can the *ratio* be inferred?

(b) what can be done with the diversity of forms of judgments?

While it is true to say that the *ratio decidendi* of a previous case comes from the language of a judge, the interpreter (as seen from Chapter 2) can bring new meanings.

In the appellate courts, depending upon the importance of the case, three, five or seven judges can sit. Each can give judgment, although often a judge says 'I concur with my learned colleague, Lord Bridge' or some such similar phrase. At times there may be one or more judgments disagreeing with the majority view that a certain litigant should win the case.

In such cases, there is no doubt that *each reasoned judgment* has a *ratio*. But can it be said that there is a *ratio of the court*?

There is, of course, no problem where it is clear that the majority agree with the same statements of the application of the law. But what if the different judges *agree* on outcome and *disagree* on reasons for the outcome? This can happen. Consider Figure 4.4, below.

Figure 4.4: same outcome for different reasons

For example:		
(a) Judge 1 states that given Facts X, Y, Z for reasons A, B, C, the conclusion is D	Given Because of Conclusion is	XYZ ABC D
BUT		
(b) Judge 2 states that given Facts X, Y for reasons A, D, E the conclusion is D	Given Because of Conclusion is	XY ADE D

How can these differences be reconciled?

There are therefore a range of situations which complicate statements about the bindingness or strength of a given precedent. Lack of agreement among judges in relation to the reasoning process can weaken the precedential value of the case, because judgments in cases can result in different scenarios:

For example:

(a) the majority of judges agree to dismiss/allow the appeal on one ground.

A minority of judges agree with the majority as to outcome, but base their decision on a different ground.

In this situation, the *ratio* of the majority is binding and strong. The *ratio* of the minority is entitled to weighty consideration in a future case;

(b) the majority agree to dismiss/allow the appeal but there is no common ground as to why the appeal has been dismissed or allowed.

In this situation, there is no clear majority in favour of any *ratio*. The case, therefore, lacks authority for the narrowest interpretation of the *ratio*. But it is impossible to state clearly how such a case is viewed other than to treat it as a weak authority.

When there is a strong original *ratio* that is wide, there is the most scope for later interpretation to mould the law. If, eg, case A has just been decided, the *ratio* for which the decision is binding being found in the actual opinion of the judge, in later cases (case E) which seek to interpret and apply case A, the judge may have to interpret case A in the light of the new set of facts before him and also interpretations given by subsequent case B, C and D.

What seems to happen is that, when a judge is considering Case E currently before the court:

(a) the judge states what is considered to be the *ratio* in the earlier Case A;

(b) the judge then considers that *ratio* in the light of the facts in Case A;

(c) the judge also considers the observations made by judges in later Cases B, C and D concerning Case A;

(d) ultimately, the judge formulates a rule of law based on a number of cases – the original Case A and Cases B, C and D – and applies this composite reasoning to Case E before the court.

Figure 4.5: Goodhart's method of locating the *ratio*

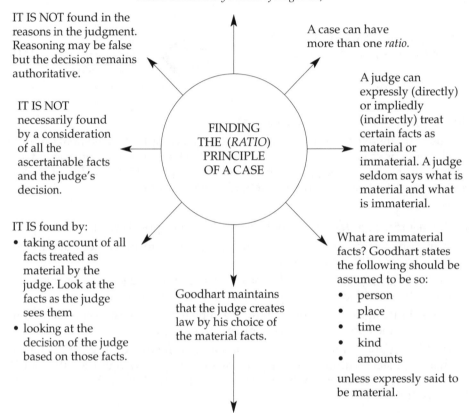

IT IS NOT found in the rule of law set out in the opinion.

(This view is the *opposite* of what is stated in *Halsbury's Laws of England*!)

IT IS NOT found in the reasons in the judgment. Reasoning may be false but the decision remains authoritative.

A case can have more than one *ratio*.

IT IS NOT necessarily found by a consideration of all the ascertainable facts and the judge's decision.

FINDING THE (*RATIO*) PRINCIPLE OF A CASE

A judge can expressly (directly) or impliedly (indirectly) treat certain facts as material or immaterial. A judge seldom says what is material and what is immaterial.

IT IS found by:
- taking account of all facts treated as material by the judge. Look at the facts as the judge sees them
- looking at the decision of the judge based on those facts.

Goodhart maintains that the judge creates law by his choice of the material facts.

What are immaterial facts? Goodhart states the following should be assumed to be so:
- person
- place
- time
- kind
- amounts

unless expressly said to be material.

Note: however, Rupert Cross has said that it can be impossible to formulate the *ratio* by reference to the facts regarded as material. You may need to know what legal rules the court was thinking of and also know why certain facts were seen as material.

However, before previous cases can be considered as potential *ratios*, they need to be located according to whether or not they are similar to the present case.

Sometimes, counsel for the litigants will strenuously argue that previous cases are not precedents because they can be distinguished on their facts. In other words, they are not similar; the court may agree out of persuasion or policy. In this way extremely subtle 'differences' are found between two cases.

It is difficult if not impossible to come up with a clear formula that will always work for ascertaining the *ratio* of a case. But a reasonable idea of the *difficulties* in ascertaining the *ratio* is a necessary and revealing step for any interpreter engaged in the search for a *ratio*.

Appreciation of the difficulties prevents simplistic case analysis which will ultimately lead to simplistic and inadequate construction of legal arguments. If an argument is being made on weak, tenuous or stretched grounds, it is better to know than be ignorant as to the basis of the case one is constructing.

One of the major difficulties involved concerns the different types of information and skills that have to be utilised in deciding whether a case is a precedent. To provide some light relief, work through the questions in the chart in Figure 4.6, below. It is an over-simplistic chart asking some of the necessary questions to decide if a previous case constitutes a precedent to be followed in a current case.

As mentioned above, the law tends to work through generalised rules which have to be applied to specific circumstances. This is why lawyers spend so much time comparing, contrasting and differentiating situations, for they are constructing arguments based upon similarity and difference. Legal rules are, by convention and necessity, expressed as general rules. Lawyers have to reason from the generality of the rule to the specificity of the situation.

At times, lawyers have to research previous cases meticulously to assist in predicting the outcome of the current case. After all, there is no point in going to court if the exact point the client wishes to make has already come before a court and been determined to his detriment. Part of the lawyer's particular expertise is knowing how to look quickly through past cases to find relevant decisions either supporting or opposing a client's case. The location of materials is relatively easy given the range of on-line databases available. Unfortunately, students often do not have unlimited access to training in how to use such databases. So, there is a need to rely on one of the citators to locate relevant cases.

Searches can be made, first, to pinpoint cases dealing with specific legal rules; secondly, a range of cases with similar facts can be located through analysing the first trawl of data. These cases then need to be carefully read and analysed. The lawyer has to construct an argument and predict the opponent's arguments. This is done by, initially, checking relevant cases. It must be evident by now that the ability to locate and subsequently analyse law reports is extremely important.

After careful reading, the lawyer has to construct detailed arguments concerning similarities with other cases that help the client's position, and arguments need to be constructed demolishing the potential precedential value of cases not helping the client. This latter skill is called *distinguishing*, and it is a particularly important skill for those who wish to ensure that a precedent is not followed.

Figure 4.6: chart for assistance in deciding whether a given case constitutes a binding precedent

START

Don't know → Is the case in the same court? — Yes → Are you in the Crown Court, county court or magistrates' court? — Yes → **OUTCOME 1. Doctrine of precedent does not apply**

Are you in the Crown Court, county court or magistrates' court? — No → Are you in the Court of Appeal? — No → Are you in the High Court? — Yes → Is court acting within its jurisdiction that attracts precedent — No → **OUTCOME 2. Doctrine of precedent does not apply**

Check citation and introduction and return to question

Is the case in the same court? — No → Is the case in a higher court?

Is the case in a higher court? — Yes → Are the facts of the case substantially similar?

Don't know → Check facts carefully and return to question

Are the facts of the case substantially similar? — Yes → Has the law applicable changed in any way since the case was decided?

Are the facts of the case substantially similar? — No → **OUTCOME 2. Doctrine of precedent does not apply**

Don't know → Check for change in citators or in electronic databases and return to question

Has the law applicable changed in any way since the case was decided? — Yes → **OUTCOME 2. Doctrine of precedent does not apply**

Has the law applicable changed in any way since the case was decided? — No → Were all relevant binding precedents considered by the court when the case was decided?

Don't know → Check cases judicially considered and textbooks and return to question

Were all relevant binding precedents considered by the court when the case was decided? — No → **OUTCOME 3. Doctrine of precedent applies. The case is a weak, binding precedent**

Were all relevant binding precedents considered by the court when the case was decided? — Yes → Did the majority of judges decide the outcome according to similar reasoning?

Don't know → Identify the *ratio* of each judge and compare and return to question

Did the majority of judges decide the outcome according to similar reasoning? — No → **OUTCOME 3. Doctrine of precedent applies. The case is a weak, binding precedent**

Did the majority of judges decide the outcome according to similar reasoning? — Yes → **OUTCOME 4. Doctrine of precedent applies. The case is a strong binding precedent**

Warning! The outcome of such a process is rarely as simple as following a chart!

A lawyer may need to argue convincingly that the part of the previous judgment that is being relied on by an opponent is not part of the reasoning process leading to judgment; that it was an 'aside' comment, based on a hypothetical situation (technically referred to as an *obiter dictum* comment).

On the other hand, perhaps the only argument a lawyer has to support the client's position is an aside comment. If the comment was made by a senior judge in the Court of Appeal or the House of Lords, and it is a relevant comment on the exact circumstances of the present case, then it could be argued that this is an important indicator of what that court would do if such a case came before it.

Cases in the higher appellate courts, the Court of Appeal and the House of Lords, contain more than one judgment. Usually, there are three in the Court of Appeal and five in the House of Lords, but there can be more in an important case. Here, the lawyer's task in ascertaining the strength of a precedent in a previous case may be more difficult. Often, there will be a dissenting judgment. This judgment can eventually, through a range of other cases, come to represent the majority view of an area of law. If the judge who is dissenting has a particular reputation for excellence, then the judgment will be seriously considered by those coming to read the case for the precedential value of the majority judgments. In time, the argument presented by the dissenting judge, the minority view, may be accepted as the more appropriate way forward.

English law, as created, developed and refined in the courts, does not resemble a straight line of development; rather, it is a winding road of distinctions, consideration of majority and minority views, determinations according to similarity, more judgments, then more distinctions. Change is slow but English law remains flexible.

4.5 THE DOCTRINE OF PRECEDENT IN PRACTICE: HANDLING LAW REPORTS

When law cases in any area are considered, it is important that the reader knows several things about the case for future usage. These are set out in Figure 4.7, below. Most importantly, law reports have a standard layout. Carefully consider Figures 4.8 and 4.9, below.

4.5.1 What happens if a judge does not like a precedent?

Some judges are better than others at 'dodging' precedent:

> If a judge of reasonable strength of mind thought a particular precedent was wrong he must be a great fool if he couldn't get round it.
>
> [Lord Radcliffe (House of Lords) in an interview with Alan Patterson (1984).]

Yet, contrast this with the following quotation:

> I am unable to adduce any reason to show that the decision which I am about to pronounce is right – but I am bound by authority which of course it is my duty to follow.
>
> [*Per* Buckley LJ, *Olympia Oil and Cake Co Ltd v Produce Brokers Ltd* (1915) 21 Com Cas 320.]

Figure 4.7: issues that must be understood in order to apply a case according to the doctrine of precedent

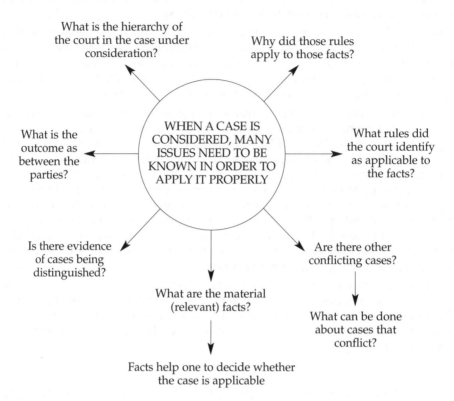

It is all a matter of interpretation! Perhaps the difficulties of this area are beginning to become apparent.

Figure 4.8: a typical English law report with its constituent parts labelled

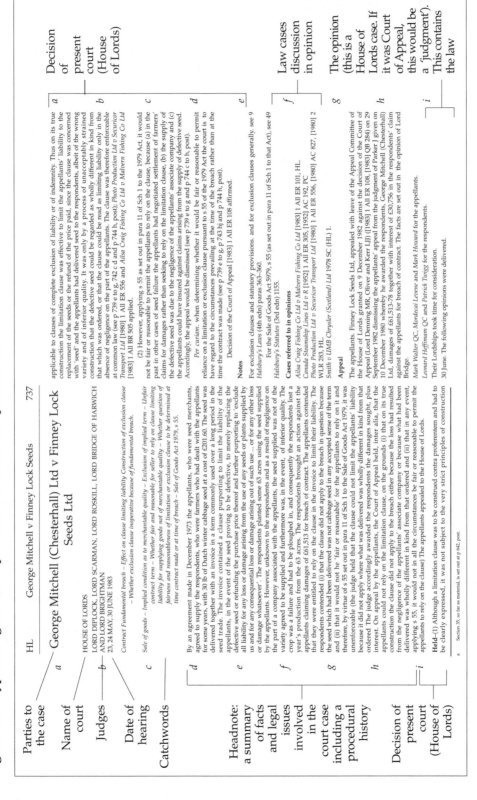

Parties to the case

Name of court

Judges

Date of hearing

Catchwords

Headnote: a summary of facts and legal issues involved in the court case including a procedural history

Decision of present court (House of Lords)

a — Decision of present court (House of Lords)

b

c

d

e

f — Law cases discussion in opinion

g — The opinion (this is a House of Lords case. If it was Court of Appeal, this would be a 'judgment'). This contains the law

h

i

HL   George Mitchell v Finney Lock Seeds   737

George Mitchell (Chesterhall) Ltd v Finney Lock Seeds Ltd

HOUSE OF LORDS

LORD DIPLOCK, LORD SCARMAN, LORD ROSKILL, LORD BRIDGE OF HARWICH AND LORD BRIGHTMAN

23, 24 MAY, 30 JUNE 1983

Contract Fundamental breach – Effect on clause limiting liability Construction of exclusion clause – Whether exclusion clause inoperative because of fundamental breach.

Sale of goods – Implied condition as to merchantable quality – Exclusion of implied term – Unfair contract term – Whether fair and reasonable for seller to rely on clause limiting liability for supplying goods not of merchantable quality – Whether question of fairness and reasonableness of limitation or exclusion clause to be determined at time contract made or at time of breach – Sale of Goods Act 1979, s 55.

By an agreement made in December 1973 the appellants, who were seed merchants, agreed to supply the respondents, who were farmers who had dealt with the appellants for some years, with 30 lb of Dutch winter cabbage seed at a cost of £201.60. The seed was delivered together with an invoice in a form commonly used over a long period in the seed trade. The invoice contained a clause purporting to limit the liability of the appellants, in the event of the seed proving to be defective, to merely replacing the defective seed or refunding the purchase price thereof and further purporting to exclude all liability for any loss or damage arising from the use of any seeds or plants supplied by us and for any consequential loss or damage arising out of such use ... or for any other loss or damage whatsoever'. The respondents planted some 63 acres using the seed supplied by the appellants. However, unknown to the respondents and as a result of negligence on the part of a company associated with the appellants, the seed supplied was not of the variety agreed to be supplied and furthermore was, in the event, of inferior quality. The crop was a failure and had to be ploughed in, and consequently the respondents lost a year's production from the 63 acres. The appellants brought an action against the appellants claiming damages of £61,513 for breach of contract. The appellants contended that they were entitled to rely on the clause in the invoice to limit their liability. The respondents contended (i) that the clause did not apply to the breach in question because the seed which had been delivered was not cabbage seed in any accepted sense of the term and (ii) that it would not be 'fair or reasonable' for the appellants to rely on it and therefore, by virtue of s 55 set out in para 11 of Sch 1 to the Sale of Goods Act 1979, it was unenforceable (the judge held that the clause could not limit the appellants' liability because it did not apply where what was delivered was wholly different in kind from that ordered The judge accordingly awarded the respondents the damages sought, plus interest. On appeal by the appellants, the Court of Appeal held, inter alia, that the appellants could not rely on the limitation clause, on the grounds (i) that on its true construction the clause did not apply to the breach either because the loss had resulted from the negligence of the appellants' associate company or because what had been delivered was wholly different in kind from that ordered and (ii) that in any event, applying s 55, it would not in all the circumstances be fair or reasonable to permit the appellants to rely on the clause) The appellants appealed to the House of Lords.

Held–(1) Although a limitation clause was to be construed contra proferentem and had to be clearly expressed, it was not subject to the very strict principles of construction

─────

applicable to clauses of complete exclusion of liability or of indemnity. Thus on its true construction the limitation clause was effective to limit the appellants' liability to the replacement of the seeds or the refund of the price paid, since the clause was concerned only with 'seed' and the appellants had delivered seed to the respondents, albeit of the wrong variety and of inferior quality. It was only by a process of unacceptably strained construction that the defective seed could be regarded as wholly different in kind from that which was ordered, or that the clause could be read as limiting liability only in the absence of negligence on the part of the appellants. The clause was therefore enforceable at common law (see p 739 e to g, 742 c d and p 744 h, post); *Photo Production Ltd v Securicor Transport Ltd* [1980] 1 All ER 556 and *Ailsa Craig Fishing Co Ltd v Malvern Fishing Co Ltd* [1983] 1 All BR 505 applied.

(2) However, applying s 55 as set out in para 11 of Sch 1 to the 1979 Act, it would not be fair or reasonable to permit the appellants to rely on the clause, because (a) in the past in other cases of seed failure the appellants had negotiated settlement of farmers' claims for damages rather than seeking to rely on the limitation clause, (b) the supply of the defective seed was due to the negligence of the appellants' associate company and (c) the appellants could have insured against claims arising from the supply of defective seed. Accordingly, the appeal would be dismissed (see p 739 e to g and p 744 c to h, post).

Per curiam. when determining whether it would be fair or reasonable to permit reliance on a limitation or exclusion clause pursuant to s 55 of the 1979 Act the court is to have regard to the circumstances prevailing at the time of the breach rather than at the time the contract was made (see p 739 e to g, p 743 hj and p 744 h, post).

Decision of the Court of Appeal [1983] 1 All ER 108 affirmed.

Notes

For exclusion clauses and statutory provisions. and for exclusion clauses generally; see 9 *Halsbury's Laws* (4th edn) paras 363–360.

For the Sale of Goods Act 5979, s 55 (as set out in para 11 of Sch 1 to that Act), see 49 *Halsbury's Statutes* (3rd edn) 1155.

Cases referred to in opinions

Ailsa Craig Fishing Co Ltd v Malvern Fishing Co Ltd [1983] 1 All ER 101, HL.
Canada Steamship Lines Ltd v R [1952] 1 All ER 305, [1952] AC 192, PC
Photo Production Ltd v Securicor Transport Ltd [1980] 1 All ER 556, [1980] AC 827, [1980] 2 WLR 283, HL.
Smith v UMB Chrysler (Scotland) Ltd 1978 SC (HL) 1.

Appeal

The appellants. Finney Lock Seeds Ltd, appealed with leave of the Appeal Committee of the House of Lords granted on 9 December 1982 against the decision of the Court of Appeal (Lord Denning MR, Oliver and Kerr LJJ) ([1983] 1 All ER 108, [1983] QB 284) on 29 September 1982 dismissing the appellants' appeal from the judgment of Parker J given on 10 December 1980 whereby he awarded the respondents, George Mitchell (Chesterhall) Ltd, damages of £61,513-78 together with interest of £30,756 in the respondents' claim against the appellants for breach of contract. The facts are set out in the opinion of Lord Bridge.

Mark Walter QC, Mordecai Levene and *Mark Howard* for the appellants.
Leonard Hoffmann QC and *Patrick Twigg* for the respondents.

Their Lordships took time for consideration.

30 June. The following opinions were delivered.

─────

a   Section. 35, so far as material, is set out at p 642. post.

Figure 4.9: the anatomy of a law report

As revealed by Figure 4.8, above, each law report is made up of a range of parts each doing different things which are as follows:

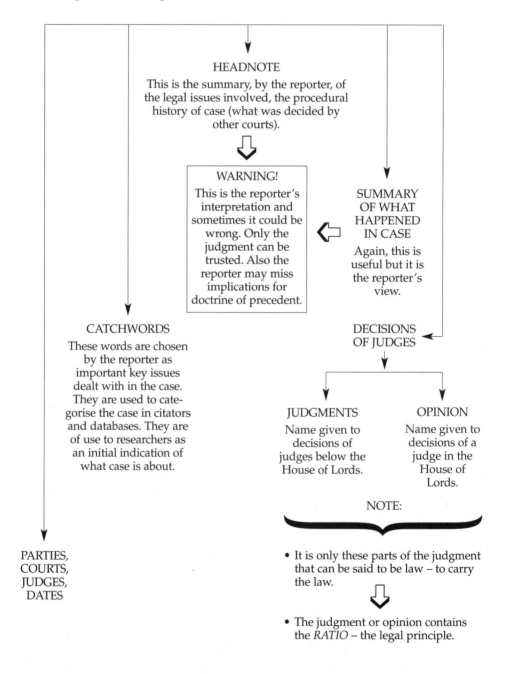

In the same way that religious texts can be said to be literature in terms of both prose and poetry, so the law report can also be considered as a literary text.

The illustrations and aside comments made by judges in their judgments may be complex, relating to politics, history, art, religion, literature and so on. Quotations may be given in different languages and reports can sometimes be liberally peppered with Latin legal maxims (see Figure 4.10, below, for some of the most common). Law reports are complex pieces of written English and, therefore, of double difficulty to students in terms of their legal content and, generally, in terms of their sophisticated English usage.

All judges have different ways of expressing themselves but they all share seniority within the English legal system. Unlike other jurisdictions there is no such concept as the career judge. Promotion to the 'bench' occurs as recognition of years of proven ability, usually, as a barrister. However, lower ranks of the judiciary are now appointed from successful solicitors.

Therefore, although law students are very new to the enterprise of law, they are called upon to engage in sophisticated evaluation of the highly competent analysis of the English legal system's most senior judges, who combine years of successful practice with excellent skills in language usage and technical substantive law ability. These judges may discuss several complex issues simultaneously, applying and interpreting the law to the facts of specific disputes.

The student is, therefore, confronted by excellent and sophisticated written texts. What is required is for the student to obtain:

- a good grasp of the relevant area of substantive law;
- an appreciation of issues relating to language usage;
- an understanding of the doctrine of precedent in practice;
- a familiarity with statute;
- a sound foundation in the mechanics of argument construction to make initial sense of the text.

Judges are social actors with their own preferences who attempt to act fairly in judgment despite themselves and their natural inclinations. However, at root a judgment is a subjective text and a student's or a lawyer's interpretation of that text is also subjective. Any interpretation should be tested against the text and evaluated to see if it is a plausible reading. As noted already in Chapter 2, the language of the law tries to be injected with scientific objectivity, but flounders because of the imprecision of language.

4.5.2   A case study of *George Mitchell (Chesterhall) Ltd v Finney Lock Seeds* [1983] 2 All ER 732–44

One law report will now be considered in depth in order to demonstrate one method of reading, note taking, evaluating and using a case to construct arguments.

It will, initially, be approached as a sophisticated English comprehension exercise. This will demonstrate how far one can get by meticulous reading in the absence of detailed knowledge of a particular area of law (in this case, the law of contract). No assumptions will be made concerning the reader's knowledge of the law of contract.

4.5.2.1 *The context of the case*

It is, of course, useful if a student *does* understand the legal context of a dispute! For this reason, the basic framework of the law of contract is set out in Figure 4.11, below. The events which occur in *George Mitchell* are signalled by the square.

Figure 4.10: some common Latin phrases used by judges in reports

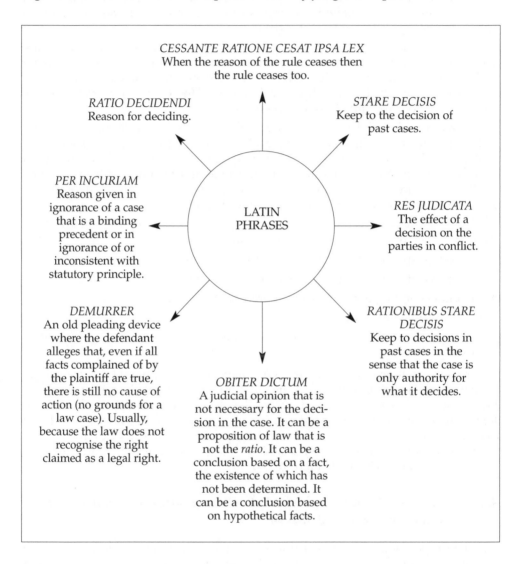

Figure 4.11: diagrammatic representation of the law of contract

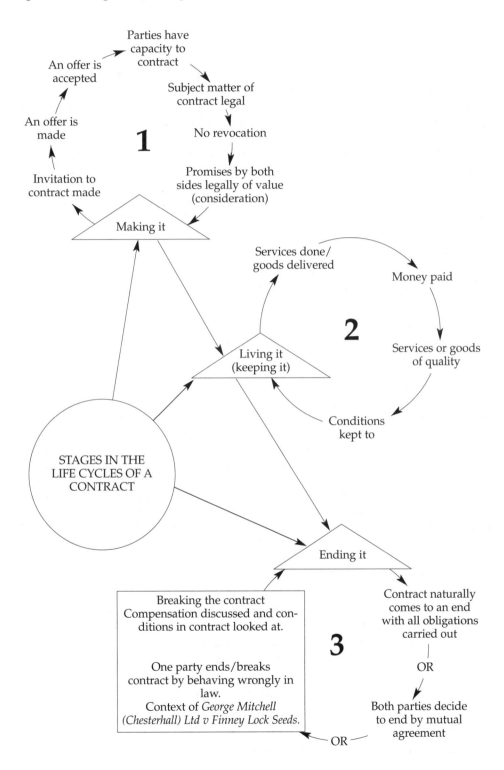

Of the three main areas of the law of contract identified in Figure 4.11, above:

(1) making it;

(2) living it (keeping it);

(3) ending it,

the case under consideration concerns 'ending it', and of the various ways noted, it concerns ending it by breaking it due to a wrongful act.

In other words, it is concerned with what should happen under the contract to compensate the claimant. (The claimant is the person or company complaining and bringing a case in the civil courts.) Usually, contracts contain provisions that lay down the compensation payable to one party if the other party breaks the contract by not doing what he or she says will be done. The contract in *George Mitchell (Chesterhall) Ltd v Finney Lock Seeds* is no exception.

However, to ascertain properly what the main issues are in the case it has to be broken into with some determination. This case has been specifically chosen for several reasons:

• it is short;

• there is only one main, agreed judgment by Lord Bridge;

• the issues discussed are highly complex;

• the case involves consideration of both common law rules and statutory rules operating side by side;

• it links into the work already discussed in Chapter 3;

• it links into Chapter 6.

4.5.2.2 Stage 1: the basic reading

Any student successfully breaking into this case and comprehending the methodology will be able to use methodology to break into other cases.

The case study requires the reader's active engagement and asks for certain tasks to be carried out. It is divided into four stages. Stage 1 involves skim reading, stage 2 involves checking the skim reading and making a first note of Lord Bridge's judgment, stage 3 spends time considering the issues in the case, stage 4 is concerned with a paragraph by paragraph summary of the judgment of Lord Bridge. This stage also involves a 'statutory diversion' looking at the statutory references brought up in the case. The final section of this chapter discusses case noting and uses *George Mitchell* as the case to be noted.

(1) Turn to Appendix 1.

(2) Read the case of *George Mitchell (Chesterhall) Ltd v Finney Lock Seeds* as quickly as you can. If this takes you more than 60 minutes you need to work on your reading strategies generally.

(3) As you read, note how paragraphs begin and end, as these are often indicators of the progression of discussion or argument.

(4) Carefully register differences in language as you move from the information packed first pages through to the different judgments.

    • Be aware of the use of any technical language.

    • Look up non-technical words you do not understand in a good dictionary.

(5) Give a summary, in no more than 200 words, of what this case is about.

Note:

- remember that the section of the law report that contains the law is the judgment;
- remember that the binding aspect of the judgment is the *ratio decidendi* ... 'the reason for deciding';
- knowledge of facts alone does not give you a clue as to the precedent;
- knowledge of the applicable rules alone does not give you the precedent;
- knowledge of rules and facts does not give you the precedent. Only the reasons why those rules applied to those facts gives you an understanding of the precedent created.

INTELLECTUAL HEALTH WARNING!

DO NOT PROCEED WITH THIS CHAPTER
UNTIL YOU HAVE QUICKLY READ THE CASE.

Do tasks (1)–(5), above. (Contrast your summary in (5) with the issues raised in the following discussion.)

Many students pick up that this case about a buyer of seeds wanting compensation because he was sold the wrong seeds. Furthermore, the buyer made it clear which seeds he wanted but the wrong seeds were accidentally sent. However, this is far too general a description of the issues in the case. On a first reading, with the help of the headnote, it may have been apparent that the buyer won this case which, incidentally, was won on appeal in the House of Lords. The House of Lords' decision between the parties was that the seller/supplier of seeds had to pay compensation to the buyer for the delivery of the wrong seeds, but this does not give you any useful information for future use. It certainly does not give the precedent of the case. If you only have the basic facts you will not get too far in being able to *use* this case. It is essential to understand *why* the buyer won the case.

4.5.2.3 Stage 2: checking the basics

(1) Look again at the case and check you have a clear idea of facts in this case. (Make a note.)

(2) Are any of the facts disputed by the parties or are they agreed? Write your answer.

(3) What are the specific issues in this case? State them in list form.

(4) What is the procedural history of the case? What other courts has this case been in and what did the previous courts decide?

(Answering questions (1)–(4) properly enables you to follow the development of arguments.)

(5) Go back and carefully read and make notes on:

(a) the headnote;

(b) the procedural history;

(c) the judgment of Lord Bridge;

(d) list words and phrases that you do not know, check them out in a dictionary
or in the text for sense,

and make a full summary of the judgment in no more than 300 words making
sure you include the discussion or issues.

> DO NOT CONTINUE OVER UNTIL YOU HAVE
> COMPLETED (1)–(5). WHEN YOU HAVE FINISHED,
> CONTINUE BELOW ...

- Did you find all the facts and issues?
- Did you correctly ascertain the procedural history?

Check your summary against the diagram in Figure 4.12, below. This diagram was
constructed by a careful reading of the headnote together with the introductory
summaries made by the law reporter of the decisions in the earlier courts and in
the court deciding the actual report being read. These explanations are the
reporter's summaries and do not form part of the law. Sometimes it has been
known for the headnote to actually be wrong. So it is always best to read the
judgment to double-check the facts, issues and procedural history.

> Do not forget that the only part of the law report
> containing the law is the judgment of each judge.

4.5.2.4 Stage 3: finding and beginning to understand the issues in the case

It is necessary to look in detail at the issues because these may seem extremely
complicated on a first reading. Did you find all the issues? The issues, according to
the judgment of Lord Bridge, are as follows.

(1) The first issue is whether the relevant condition, on its true construction in the context
of the contract as a whole, is effective to limit the appellant's liability to a refund of the
price of the seeds (the common law issue).

(2) The second issue is whether, if the common law issue is decided in the appellant's
favour, they should nevertheless be precluded from reliance on this limitation of
liability pursuant to the provisions of the modified s 55 of the Sale of Goods Act 1979
which is set out in para 11 of Schedule 1 to the Act and which applies to contracts
made between 18 May 1973 and 1 February 1978 (the statutory issue).

[Lord Bridge, see Appendix 1, p 310.]

Figure 4.12, below, states the issues, although finding and understanding what
these issues are as a matter of basic comprehension is not easy. It may not be too
difficult to locate sentences in a case where the judge says what the issues are.
Unfortunately, it does not necessarily follow that having found these sentences you
will also understand the issues just by reading the sentences. You may have to
work extremely hard to reach a place of understanding.

Figure 4.12: *George Mitchell (Chesterhall) Ltd v Finney Lock Seeds (1983)* – **facts, issues and procedural history**

FACTS

THE PLAINTIFF'S ARGUMENT AT THE TRIAL (THE RESPONDENTS IN CA/HL)

George Mitchell Ltd Farmers

A large crop failed because the wrong seeds were delivered. The Company has lost thousands of pounds: they want full compensation.

THE CONTRACT

Price: £201.60 **paid by plaintiffs**
Goods: 30lb **delivered by defendants**

'Winter Dutch Cabbage Seeds'

'THE PROBLEM CLAUSE'
the defendants limited their liability for negligence, etc, to the cost of replacing the seeds, or refunding cost of seeds

THE DEFENDANTS ARGUMENT AT THE TRIAL (THE APPELLANTS IN CA/HL)

Finney Lock Seeds Seed Merchants

We sold the wrong seeds. However, we can rely on the limitation clause (the problem clause) and we are only liable for replacement seeds. (Wrong seeds actually delivered by 'sister' company.)

ISSUES

(1) Whether, by application of the common law, the condition (the relevant clause) in the contract limiting liability of the defendants is effective, and could limit the defendants' liability.

(2) If the answer to (1) is 'YES' ... then whether the condition limiting liability is *fair and reasonable'* under applicable statutory rules in s 53 of the Sale of Goods Act 1979. If it is, the defendant can limit liability. If it is not, the defendant cannot limit liability. (Statutory rules always overrule common law rules)

PROCEDURAL HISTORY

(1) HIGH COURT: TRIAL COURT
- Plaintiffs win full compensation for lost crop.
- Judge states that condition not operative at common law.

(2) COURT OF APPEAL
- Defendants appeal from High Court.
- Court holds clause not operative at common law.
- Appeal dismissed.
(Denning LJ dissents from majority reasoning: says clause is operative *but* unfair *under statute*. He argues clause IS operative at common law)

(3) HOUSE OF LORDS
- Defendants appeal from Court of Appeal.
- Clause held operative at common law but unfair under statutory provisions. (Note: this agrees with Lord Denning's dissenting judgement in Court of Appeal.)
- Appeal dismissed.

So how can one begin to understand these issues? The immediate problems are:

- unfamiliar vocabulary;
- unfamiliar legal references;
- complex grammatical structure;
- dense (perhaps boring) text.

The first task is to annotate the above text from the judgment to reveal the areas of lack of understanding, words and phrases that need defining and the areas of interconnection. This is similar in method to the annotation of s 3 of the Unfair Contract Terms Act (UCTA) 1977 in Chapter 3. This is done in Figure 4.13, below. But remember that where a statute is concerned the actual words are *fixed* in law by the statute. It is the law in a fixed verbal form. When dealing with a judgment any common rules contained and constructed in the judgment are not fixing rules with specific words. It is said that decisions of judges state rules in an *unfixed* verbal format.

Figure 4.13: the two issues as set out by Lord Bridge – issue 1

Issue 1

What is 'the relevant condition'? It is the one mentioned by Lord Bridge on p 310. It is his label for the contentious clause that is the subject of case. On p 310, he divides the condition into two issues. See Figure 4.14, below, for issue 2.

'The first issue is whether the relevant condition, on its true construction in the context of the contract as a whole, is effective to limit the appellant's liability to a refund of ... the price of the seeds (the common law issue).' (Lord Bridge, Appendix 1, p 310, para 3.)

This relates to the law made through precedent in the courts. Contract is a creature of precedent not Parliament. But over the years, Parliament has intervened to protect parties. To protect them, for example, from cases such as this when the operation of the common law acts to the clear disadvantage of the wronged party.

This is crucial. The condition agreed by the buyers is that if there is a problem they can only claim back the cost of the seeds. But here the loss of the buyers is in the region of £60,000. The seeds cost a mere £201.60. So ... a straight refund means that the buyers' basic loss is £59,797.40!

Figure 4.14: the two issues as set out by Lord Bridge – issue 2

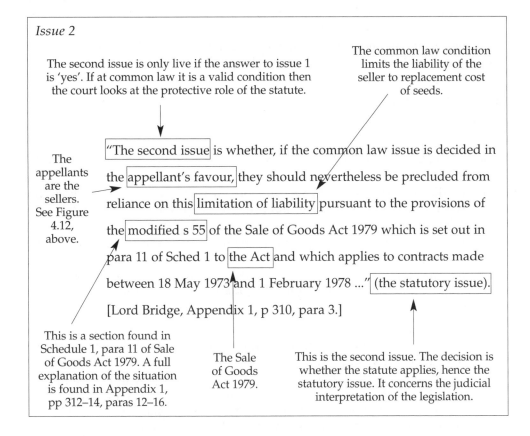

As can be seen, a number of matters needing to be clarified arise from the mere identification of two issues. Note that Bridge gives the two issues a short-hand label:

(1) the common law issue; and

(2) the statutory issue.

However, students often read and re-read without appreciating how to move from lack of understanding towards understanding. They do not notice how words can be clarified by an appreciation of the intertextual links and which words or phrases could be clarified by recourse to textbooks in the area. Again the two issues are found in a paragraph of Lord Bridge's judgment. Reading carefully paragraphs in the immediate vicinity can assist in understanding. The responsibility of the reader is to read *with* understanding, therefore stopping to clarify points along the way.

It is useful here to ensure that the procedural history of this case is understood. This will enable the student to obtain an appreciation of the differences in opinion by the various judges who have considered the case before its arrival in the House of Lords. Lord Bridge discusses the procedural history and it is set out in the headnote.

The case was won by the plaintiffs (the buyers) in the trial court (the High Court) and the defendants (the sellers) appealed to the Court of Appeal, where they are called the appellants, and again lost. They then appealed to the House of Lords, where they also lost. There was a lot of money at stake: the difference between the £201.60 that the seeds cost as awarded by the Court of Appeal or the £90,000+ that the trial judge awarded.

Consider, for a moment, what you have read and what you know so far. Does it seem fair to you that George Mitchell won? If so, why? If not, why not?

So far we have considered:

(a) Procedural history.

(b) Facts.

(c) The operative rules of law:

- It is known that both common law rules and statutory rules are relevant to the case.

- Further, it is known that if the common law rules are found to apply in the seller's favour he still has to jump the hurdle presented by the statutory rules.

- Recall, if there is a clash between common law rules and statutory rules, the statutory rules prevail.

(d) A verbatim account of the two issues in the case (however, these are probably not fully comprehended yet, despite Figures 4.13 and 4.14, above!):

- It is clear that Lord Bridge will argue through each of the issues.

- If the appellants succeed in issue 1 they may still fail overall if they fail over issue 2. (Can you understand why? The answer is in the first sentence of text setting out 'the second issue'. See Figure 4.14, above.)

- Logically, one would expect Lord Bridge to commence with the arguments over issue 1, the common law issue, as this is the gateway to an argument over issue 2 which will only take place if issue 1 is decided in the appellant's favour (and this is contentious limitation clause what he does).

(e) Understanding the clause. This is set out in Figure 4.15, below.

Until all of these matters are linked and understood it is not possible to fully comprehend the reasoning in the case.

Now take time to consolidate the information we have so far and return to the judgment of Lord Bridge, concentrating on his arguments concerning issue 1 (Appendix 1, p 310, para 3).

4.5.2.5 Stage 4: breaking into Lord Bridge's speech

You will have already read Lord Bridge's speech by now. It is also now appreciated that the arguments in this case are quite complex and the initial method of breaking into the text for understanding is to look at each paragraph.

Paragraphs are intended to convey a new idea. So each paragraph represents an idea or a cluster of ideas. Careful ordering of paragraphs is essential in a piece of writing if a sense of progression is to be maintained. Therefore when reading for understanding a précis of each paragraph begins the process of understanding.

Figure 4.15: diagrammatic text of the relevant condition

In Appendix 1, p 310, Lord Bridge says he will call the *condition* in the *contract* that limits liability the 'relevant condition'.

In the same paragraph, he stated that the condition was composed of three sentences, numbered 1, 2, 3. He states he will call each sentence a clause. The condition is set out below according to the structure imposed by judge.

'I will refer to the whole as "the relevant condition" and to the parts as "clauses [1], [2] and [3]" of the relevant condition.' (Lord Bridge, Appendix 1, p 310, para 2.)

Clause [1] (sentence 1)	Clause [2] (sentence 2)	Clause [3] (sentence 3)
'In the event of any seeds or plants sold or agreed to be sold by us not complying with the express terms of the contract of sale ... or any seeds or plants proving defective in variety or purity we will, at our option, replace the defective seeds or plants, free of charge to the buyer or will refund all payments made to us by the buyer in respect of the defective seeds or plants and this shall be the limit of our obligation.'	'We hereby exclude all liability for any loss or damage arising from the use of any seeds or plants supplied by us and for any consequential loss or damage arising out of such use or any failure in the performance of or any defect in any seeds or plants supplied by us or for any other loss or damage whatsoever save for, at our option, liability for any such replacement or refund as aforesaid.'	'In accordance with the established custom of the seed trade any express or implied condition, statement or warranty, statutory or otherwise, not located in these conditions is hereby excluded.'

Paragraphs must not be skipped over, as the task in hand is to ensure that *each* paragraph *is understood*. Each paragraph is a stepping stone, leading the reader to the end of the text and the conclusion of the argument. Yet often a student will read too quickly skipping over words and phrases that are not understood.

As paragraphs relate to each other, any points not understood in a paragraph should be able to be cleared up in earlier or later paragraphs, unless they contain information *assumed* to be known to the reader. So if you find references you do not understand cast your eyes back to see if this has already been clarified.

One of the most important connections in a text is the relationship between paragraphs. The paragraphs in the text of Lord Bridge's speech will be numbered and summarised. As expertise is acquired, such summaries will normally take place in the head of the student with only a few paragraphs noted in rough. The paragraphs in the full text of the case in Appendix 1 are also numbered in square brackets (eg, [1]). This allows you to easily access the full text of the paragraph and compare it with the summary. I suggest you keep a hand in Appendix 1, read the relevant paragraph from the original and then read the summary. Did you understand the original? If not – why not?

LORD BRIDGE'S SPEECH

START

PARA 1

- Facts. The seller delivered the wrong cabbage seed to the buyer who, as a consequence, had a failed crop with grave financial consequences. The contract of sale limited the seller's liability to a refund of the price of the seeds.

PARA 2

- Issues arise from three sentences in the conditions of sale.
- These are set out and identified.
- States he will call the contentious limitation clause 'the relevant condition', and will refer to each sentence as a clause, so clauses 1, 2, 3 (see Figure 4.15, above). If a student reads carelessly this important explanation will be overlooked then the phrase 'relevant condition' and 'clauses 1, 2, 3' will cause confusion when they are used later in the text to refer to his divisions of the contentious limitation clause.

PARA 3

- Sets out the two issues as the common law and the statutory issues.
- Gives details of relevant legislation.

PARA 4

- Discusses the finding of the trial judge that under the common law the 'relevant condition' could not be relied upon by the sellers. The reason being the seed delivered was 'wholly different'. (As we have already noted issue 2 (see Figure 4.14, above), the statutory issue, need only be dealt with if issue 1 (see Figure 4.13, above) is decided in favour of the sellers.)

PARA 5

- Discusses the finding of Denning LJ in the Court of Appeal. Denning LJ thought the common law issue should be decided in favour of the sellers. He said that the wording of the condition was sufficient to cover the situation. Kerr and Oliver LJJ decided the common law issue against the sellers.
- Kerr LJ's reasoning was that the condition would only cover them for *defects* in the *'correct'* named seeds. Not for delivery of the wrong seeds.
- Oliver LJ's reasoning was that the condition did not cover the breach because it only happened through the negligence of the seller.

PARA 6

- The Court of Appeal, however, was unanimous in deciding the statutory issue against the sellers.

PARA 7

- Lord Bridge discusses the way that Denning LJ traced the history of the court's approach to such conditions. The conditions being ones that 'limit' or totally 'exclude' a contractual party's liability for any damage caused.
- Lord Bridge picks out two relevant cases (*Photo Production Ltd v Securicor Transport Ltd* [1980] 1 All ER 101 and *Ailsa Craig Fishing Co Ltd v Malvern Fishing Co Ltd* [1983] 1 All ER 101) and uses these to explore the common law issue. Note that the judge is beginning to deal with cases decided previously and commenting upon them in relation to whether he is bound by the doctrine of precedent.

PARA 8

- Lord Bridge brings up the phrase 'fundamental breach'. Depending on the positioning of the student in a contract course, this phrase will be known or unknown. The word 'fundamental' suggests an important, core, foundation breach or break of the contract. The essence of the points made are that:
  - ○ the *Photo Production* case made it clear that, even if there is a finding of fundamental breach of contract by one party, like the seller here, this finding does not stop a party, the seller, relying on limiting or excluding conditions in the contract;
  - ○ the *Ailsa Craig* case drew distinctions between:
    limiting clauses;
    exclusion clauses.

Basically, limitation clauses should not be judged according to the strict principles applied to exclusion clauses, although they remain to be construed *contra proferentem* against the party claiming their protection (*contra proferentem* means construed strictly / against the party relying on it).

PARA 9

- Lord Bridge criticises the trial judge, Parker J, and the Court of Appeal judge, Oliver LJ, for trying to go back to the position.
- Before the *Photo Production* case, Lord Bridge said a fundamental breach *does not* stop a party relying on exclusions or limitation clauses.

PARA 10

- Lord Bridge points out that the condition applies to seeds sold and indeed seeds were sold!
- Lord Bridge says that the condition unambiguously applies to the present situation.

PARA 11

- Lord Bridge says that Kerr LJ (in the Court of Appeal) in finding for the seller had in fact misinterpreted what Lord Fraser had said about *The Canada Steamship v R* [1952] 1 All ER 303 in the *Ailsa Craig* case!
  - This is an excellent paragraph for demonstrating the way in which judges argue about other cases, following, distinguishing, overruling or stating the precedent or a case erroneously.
- Lord Bridge decides the common law point in favour of the sellers in agreement with Lord Denning in the Court of Appeal.

PARA 12

- Lord Bridge turns to discuss the 'statutory' issue.
  - We now begin to understand the reference to 'the Act' in issue (2) as set out by Lord Bridge at Appendix 1, p 310, para 2.
- The modified s 55 of the Sale of Goods Act 1979 is set out.
- The Sale of Goods Act 1979 was a statute that was pure consolidation. (This means that it merely collected together the existing law and put it in one place.)
- Modified s 55 preserves the law between 18 May 1973 (the date that the Supply of Goods (Implied Terms) Act came into force) *and 1 February 1977* (the date that the Unfair Contract Terms Act 1977 came into force).

PARA 13

- Section 55, sub-ss (1), (4), (5) and (9) are set out. Students need to study s 55 carefully to ensure that they understand what it is providing for and that they can follow the discussion of it by Lord Bridge.

So, let us stop here for a moment ...

for a statutory diversion.

4.6   STATUTORY DIVERSION: THE MODIFIED s 55 OF THE SALE OF GOODS ACT

This is an appropriate moment to look in more detail at s 55 of the Sale of Goods Act 1979 and to experiment with ways of breaking into it. To understand properly the development of the reasoning of the court on the statutory issue, it is vital to spend time understanding the basic layout, interconnections and effect of the provisions. Often, students do not pay sufficient attention to such matters and then wonder why they cannot understand discussions!

The purely textual explanation is complicated and needs to be read in conjunction with the statutory provision.

Two diagrams will follow: the first (Figure 4.16, below) sets out s 55 in its entirety according to the method used in Chapter 3 for s 11 of UCTA. This enables the parts to be seen as a whole and the interconnections are apparent. It will be similarly annotated.

> Can you notice any similarities between s 11 of UCTA 1977 and s 55 of the Sale of Goods Act 1979?

The second diagram, Figure 4.17, below, is a précis version of s 55, identifying the most relevant sections according to the facts of the case. This is done by indicating whether the relevant section applies to this case, does nor apply or whether it is unknown whether it applies.

Putting personal comprehension time in before the judge's deliberation enables readers to check their view against that of the judge and begins the process of evaluation.

Often, students continue reading text when it is clear to them that they do not understand what they are reading. The sensible thing to do is to return to that point in the text when understanding was last achieved and re-read, not continue past the part of the text that is not understood!

In texts discussing complex issues, tiny connectors, if missed, rob the reader of understanding. A paragraph by paragraph reconsideration will often restore comprehension.

> Ensure that you carefully consider these diagrams before moving on.

Figure 4.16: text of s 55 in diagrammatic format

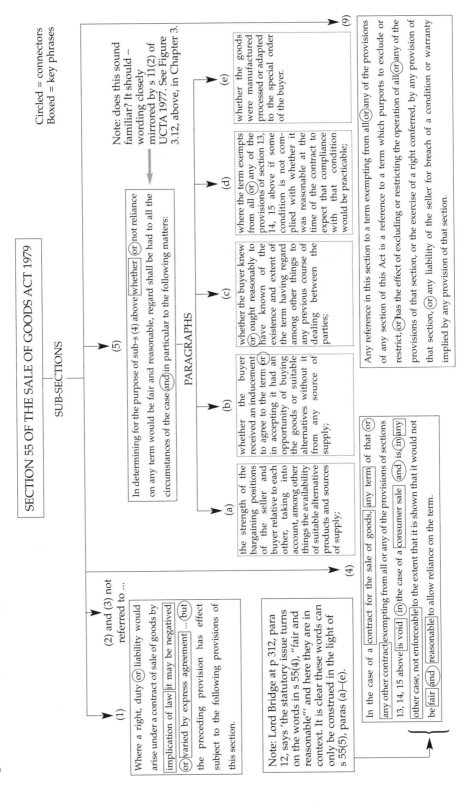

Figure 4.17: revised diagram of s 55 – summarised after careful first reading

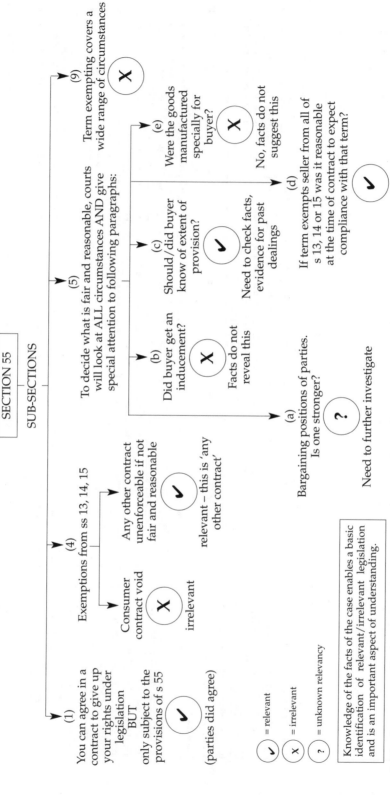

Q: What do ss 13, 14 and 15, say? If you were studying contract you would already know. However, from a comprehension perspective, Lord Bridge does discuss them – you can work it out as a matter of comprehension. At Appendix 1, p 313, para 14, he says, '... cl 3 of the relevant provision is to exclude, *inter alia*, the terms implied by ss 13, 14, 15. Statute law, while accepting that all common law parties can agree to any legal contract, provides that, in some areas, "protective" terms will be "read into" [implied into] the contract even if, in reality, they have not been written in or spoken'.

Now, the paragraph by paragraph consideration will recommence.

PARA 14

- Lord Bridge observes that the contract in question is not a consumer contract but 'any other contract':
  - This information is obtained by a careful reading of s 55(4) plus knowledge of what a consumer sale is; look back at Figure 4.16 *and* re-read s 55(4).
  - As for consumer contract recall the phrase as it was referred to in Chapter 3 when UCTA 1977 was dissected.
  - This contract is commercial not consumer and therefore falls under the second heading in s 55(4).
- Lord Bridge further observes that cl 3 of the relevant condition exempts the seller from liability for breach of ss 13 and 14 of the Sale of Goods Act.
  - This is a good example of the need to have an active dialogue with the text. Clause 3 is the third sentence of the relevant condition and the relevant condition is the condition limiting liability.
  - How is this known? Because on p 310 Lord Bridge states (para 2 (see précis above)): issues arise from three sentences in the conditions of sale. These are set out and identified. He states he will call this the relevant condition, and will call each sentence a clause, so cll 1, 2, 3. See also Figure 4.15, above.
- Lord Bridge goes on to say that ss 13 and 14 provide that:
  - items sold by description should correspond to the description;
  - items sold should be of merchantable quality,

  and that cll 1 and 2 substitute for the full protection of the legislation the limited obligation to replace seeds or refund price of seeds.
- Lord Bridge sums up that the statutory issue depends on whether cll 1 and 2 are 'fair and reasonable' according to the criteria as set out in s 55(4) and (5).

PARA 15

- Lord Bridge gives some general guidelines about how the judiciary should respond to the powers given to it in s 55.
  - Students may be tempted to skip over this paragraph, but valuable information is given concerning judicial interpretation of statutes.
  - One of the reasons that the case is important is that for the first time the House of Lords is being asked to consider a modern statutory provision that gives the court power to decide to override contractual provisions limiting or excluding liability that have been agreed between the parties at common law. This is a far reaching power to interfere with the freedom of individuals to contract. The court can say 'no', you cannot freely agree this, because, in our opinion, it is not fair and reasonable.

- o   The actual decision in this case specifically regarding s 55 is of limited importance (as we are told s 55 is protecting the contracts made between 18 May 1973 and 1 February 1978) and, as such, would soon outlive its usefulness.
- o   *However*, the wording of s 55 is substantially replicated in s 11 and Schedule 2 of UCTA 1977, which Bridge predicts will be of increasing importance (and he was correct).

- He discusses the fact that the exercise of any power to decide what is fair or reasonable will involve legitimate judicial differences and that the courts should refrain from interfering with the decision of the previous court unless they feel that there was a clearly wrong decision or that the case was decided on some clearly erroneous principle.

PARA 16

- Lord Bridge turns to a question of construction, of the meaning of words used in the statute.
- The onus is on the respondents to show that it would not be fair or reasonable to allow the appellant to rely on the relevant condition.
- Appellants said the court must look at the situation at the date of the contract, but Lord Bridge said that the true meaning of the phrase in s 55(5) 'regard shall be had to all the circumstances of the case' must mean that the situation at the time of breach *and* after breach must be taken into account.

PARA 17

- Lord Bridge discusses another issue of the meaning of words used in the statute. The meaning of the words 'to the extent' in s 55(4).
- Lord Bridge asks: 'Is it fair and reasonable to allow partial reliance on a limitation clause, to decide ... that the respondents should recover say, half their consequential damage?'
- Lord Bridge goes on to say that he considers that the meaning of the phrase 'to the extent ' is ' in so far as or in circumstances in which'.
- He suggests that the phrase does not 'permit the kind of judgment of Solomon illustrated by the example'.
  - o   The reference to Solomon is typical of the literary/religious referencing that one often finds in cases.
  - o   Solomon was an Old Testament king accredited with much wisdom in his judging. When confronted with a baby claimed by two mothers he suggested cutting it in half so each could have half. The false mother agreed, the real mother said no, the other mother could have the baby. Thus, he located the real mother.

PARA 18

- Lord Bridge goes on to say that his answer in relation to the question is not necessary for the outcome of this case and declines to answer one way or the other!
  - ○ It is interesting to note that if he *had* categorically answered the question, yes or no, it would be a clear example of an *obiter dictum* statement in a strong case by a senior judge and may well have been used in argument in a later case where this issue is at the core of the case.

PARA 19

- Eventually, Lord Bridge turns to the 'application of the statutory language' to the case.
- He states that only s 55(5)(a) and (c) are relevant. (This is the moment to re-read s 55(5)(a) and (c) in Figure 4.16, above, if you do not remember the provisions. Otherwise, one loses sight of the argument!)
- As to s 55(5)(c), he says of course the buyer knew of the condition as it was standard throughout the trade.

PARA 20

- As to s 55(5)(a), he states that there was evidence that similar limitations had never been negotiated with representative bodies.
- Witnesses for the appellant said that it had always been their practice in genuine justified claims to settle above the price of the seeds but that, in this case, settlement had not been possible. Lord Bridge said 'this evidence indicated a clear recognition ... that reliance on the limitation of liability imposed by the relevant condition would not be fair or reasonable'.

PARA 21

- Lord Bridge concluded, therefore, that wrong seed was supplied due to the negligence of the applicant's sister company. Seedsmen could insure against the risk of crop failure caused by the wrong supply without materially increasing the cost of seeds.

PARA 22

- Lord Bridge felt no doubts about the decision of the Court of Appeal over statute.
- Lord Bridge refers to an earlier point in para 15 that it is wise to 'refrain from interference' in matters of legitimate judicial difference (see Appendix 1, p 313, para 15).

PARA 23

- 'If I were making the original decision, I should conclude without hesitation that it would not be fair or reasonable to allow the appellants to rely on the contractual limitation of their liability.'

PARA 24

- Appeal dismissed.

A quick review of the paragraphs begins to show the patterns of argument delivery. Re-reading the paragraphs looking at the statutory diagrams (Figures 4.16 and 4.17, above) allows the argument to be reviewed whilst looking at the entire provision.

The paragraph approach has also allowed the common law issue and the statutory issue to be isolated. Reviewing Figure 4.12, above, dealing with the facts, issues and procedural history enables the appreciation of the differences between the reasoning in the Court of Appeal and the House of Lords, although both courts reached the same decision.

It should be possible at this stage to identify the precise rationale behind the court's view of the common law issue and the statutory issue. In relation to the statutory issue, it should be possible to pinpoint precisely the statutory areas of relevance and how the court dealt with the issue. A summary of this information has been put into diagrammatic form in Figure 4.18, below.

As proficiency is developed, it is possible to read carefully and move straight away to a diagrammatic representation, although, ultimately, a brief conventional textual note should be made to supplement the diagram. Brief, of course, as you will have seen, does not mean easy or simple!

Figure 4.18: issues in *George Mitchell (Chesterhall) Ltd v Finney Lock Seeds* and their resolution (references to 'paras' are to paragraphs in Lord Bridge's judgment as set out in this chapter and annotated in the full text in Appendix 1

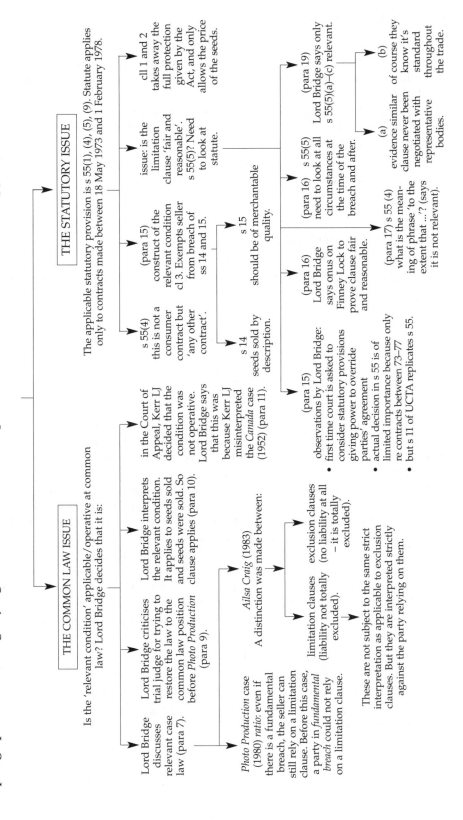

4.7   CASE NOTING

It is at this point that a case note can be made. The case note has to contain all of the information that enables the case to be used. One of the most important tasks of a law student or, indeed, a legal professional is the ability to read a case and make a usable record of it.

The cases that are reported are invariably important as non-important cases remain as court transcripts. The case note must note all of the important issues for the application of precedent, such as:

- date of court and formal citation;
- hierarchy of court, judges;
- facts;
- issues before the trial court;
- identification of applicable legal rules;
- issues, if different before appellate court(s);
- procedural history of the case (in what other courts has the matter been heard);
- judicial reasoning as to:

> *why those* rules applied
> to *those* facts
> in *that* way.

A case note cannot be used if it only records the facts and not the rationale for the outcome as everything in law depends upon the legal reasoning. A case can only be properly used in legal argument when the reasoning of the court is both known and understood.

Many students misunderstand the purpose of case noting and think that it is sufficient to have the facts of the case and know the rules concerned. This is a little like having the ingredients for a cake and knowing that, when heated, something changes, but not knowing what to do with the ingredients.

It is often not even necessary to rehearse the facts of a case in an argument in which the case is used. What is important is to know points of similarity and difference in facts so that adjustments can be made to the reasoning processes in applying the earlier case to the later situation.

If strenuous efforts have been made to understand a law report thoroughly, the following benefits will be achieved:

(1) the case note will contain all the ingredients to enable it to be competently applied to any problem question or incorporated into any relevant essay;

(2) understanding of the topic and arguing techniques will be increased;

(3) competent execution of assessments and examinations (*if* your analysis of the questions asked is not wrong!)

CASE NOTE *George Mitchell (Chesterhall) Ltd v Finney Lock Seeds* [1983] 2 All ER 737–44

COURT   HOUSE OF LORDS

JUDGES   Lords Diplock, Scarman, Roskill, Bridge of Harlow, Brightman

DATE   23, 24 May and 30 June 1983

FACTS

The respondents purchased 30lb seeds from the appellants for £201.60 in December 1973. The invoice contained a standard limitation clause stating that the only liability of the appellants was replacement of the seeds or a refund of the cost of the seeds. All other liability was excluded. The respondent's crop failed. The wrong seed and seed of an inferior quality had been delivered due to the negligence of the appellant's sister company.

ARGUMENT

The respondents argued that the limitation clause did not apply:

(1) at common law, because the wrong seed was delivered and it was not of merchantable quality;

(2) under statutory provisions, because the clause was not fair and reasonable under s 55 of the Sale of Goods Act 1979; the limitation clause in the contract was unenforceable at law according to s 55(4).

PROCEDURAL HISTORY

Trial

Parker J: The limitation clause was not operative at common law because of the negligence in delivering the wrong seed.

Court of Appeal

On appeal by Finney Lock Seeds: Denning, Kerr, Oliver LJJ.

Kerr and Oliver LJJ held the limitation clause could not be relied upon because:

(1) on its true construction the condition did not apply at common law because loss due to the negligence of sister company and the seed was wholly different than delivery of the wrong seed (Kerr and Oliver LJJ);

(2) also, applying s 55 it would not be fair and reasonable

(Note: comment by drafter of case note: Having said the clause did not apply at common law to negligence there was of course no relevance in dealing with the statutory issue which is only operative if the clause is deemed to apply at common law!);

(3) Denning LJ held, in the minority, that the limitation clause could apply at common law. However, it was not a fair and reasonable clause under s 55 of the Sale of Goods Act 1979.

DECISION IN CASE

House of Lords (all judges agreed with the opinion of Lord Bridge.)

Lord Bridge

(1) The common law issue

That the limitation clause was operative and could effectively limit liability. The wording of the condition was unambiguous in this regard. Limitation clauses do not have to adhere to the strict principles laid down for complete exclusion clauses (see *Ailsa Craig* (1983)), although they must be clearly expressed and must be strictly interpreted against the party relying on them (*contra proferentem*).

Decision partly supported by the following precedents

Photo Production Ltd (1980).

Even in cases of fundamental breach, (core) limitation clauses are available to be relied upon by one party.

Ailsa Craig (1983).

There is a difference of approach appropriate between limitation and exclusion clauses. Limitation clauses do not have to be so strictly interpreted.

(2) The statutory issue

Even though the clause was enforceable at common law, after considering s 55(4), (5)(a) and (c), Lord Bridge decided that the common law provision was overridden by the statutory obligation in s 55(4) for such clauses to be fair and reasonable otherwise. The clause was therefore unenforceable.

The grounds for deciding clause unfair and unreasonable were that:

(a) in applying s 55(5)(a), it was clear that in the past appellants had sought to negotiate a settlement that was higher than the price and had not relied on the limitation clause;

(b) supply of seed was due to the negligence of appellants sister company;

(c) appellant could easily have insured against loss.

Obiter dicta

(a) The phrase 'to the extent that' discussed and said to mean 'in so far as' or 'in the circumstances which'. Section 54(4). Although this is not relevant to this case it is possibly an important *obiter dictum*.

(b) There may be some mileage in discussion concerning whether there can be partial reliance on limitation clauses again. Although this is not relevant to this case, possible important *obiter dicta*.

(c) The phrase 'in all the circumstances' in s 55(5) means one should take account of circumstances at and after time of the breach.

(d) Appellate courts in a case like this, where there is room for legitimate judicial difference, should refrain from interfering unless it is considered that the decision reached was based on the application of wrong principles or the case is clearly wrongly decided.

Decision of court

Appeal dismissed.

4.8   STATUTORY INTERPRETATION: THE RELATIONSHIP BETWEEN CASE LAW AND LEGISLATION

4.8.1   Introduction

The discussion of *George Mitchell (Chesterhall) Ltd v Finney Lock Seeds* (1985) has indicated what happens when a problem about the meaning of a statutory provision goes before a court. In this section, attention will be given to statutory interpretation in court.

The courts and tribunals have, as one of their most important tasks, the application of legislative rules to various fact situations. They must decide whether these legislative rules apply to given situations.

Already in this text there have been several illustrations of words not meaning what they appear to mean. Despite the supposed certainty of statutory rules, rules in 'fixed verbal form'. Words can change over time, and courts will disagree over the meaning of words. Choices of meaning, not perceived by the drafters, may lie latent in the words and are drawn out in court in a manner defeating intention, narrowing, extending or making meaningless the ambit of the rule.

Many people need to apply statutory rules, often this application will be purely routine but sometimes doubts will arise. Such doubts may, or may not, reach court. How do judges set about deciding the meaning of words? Reference has already been made to the three rules of statutory interpretation. The literal, the mischief and the golden rules (see Figure 3.2, above, in the introduction to Chapter 3). These rules it should be remembered are rules of practice not rules of law.

Do judges really use the rules of statutory interpretation? If so, which rule do they use first? Judges rarely, if ever, volunteer the information that they are now applying a certain rule of interpretation. Often, judges look to see if there can be a literal meaning to the words used in the disputed statutory rule. However, there is no rule that states that they must use the literal rule first.

Holland and Webb (1994) quite correctly assert that interpretation is more a question of judicial style than the use of interpretational rules. Indeed, should a student attempt to use the rules of statutory interpretation as a guide in the interpretation of a statutory word or phrase, the uselessness of the rules as an interpretational tool becomes immediately apparent.

However, as a justificatory label they may have a function. As students gain experience in reading judgments they notice vast differences in judicial styles. Some judgments seem to be based on a blow by blow analysis of precedents and earlier usage of words, others seem based on tenuous common sense rationales.

Decisions based on the external context of the statute will be identified. This covers situations where judicial decision making appears to be based on issues of public policy, a particularly favoured device in the 1960s and 1970s. Reliance on public policy rationale can be referred to as the 'grand style' or the 'teleological' approach.

Cases may also turn on the *form of* the statute itself, that is, its *internal* context. Much of the analysis engaged in here is at the level of the internal. However, never forget the external world context. Judges who rigidly adopt the internal approach are often referred to as *formalists*. Such judges say that they do not create law, they find it. They find it by following the pathways of the rules of statutory interpretation by moving *within* the document this is the statute.

A closer consideration of the simplest definitions of the rules of statutory interpretation enables the classification of the literal rule as the *formalist* approach and the mischief rule as the *teleological* approach. The golden rule, of course, allows one to ignore the formalist approach of the literal rule. It is most likely to result in a teleological approach as the judge, through the golden rule, is released from formalism! (See Figure 3.2, above, in Chapter 3.)

4.8.2   Case study of *Mandla v Dowell Lee*

Read the extract from the judgment of Lord Fraser in the case of *Mandla v Dowell Lee* [1983] 1 All ER 118 in Appendix 1 and then read and reflect on the following discussion based upon the reading of the judgment as giving examples of formalism and a teleological approach.

The case of *Mandla v Dowell Lee* involved the interpretation of legislative provisions in the Race Relations Act 1976 and went through both appellate courts (the Court of Appeal and the House of Lords) surrounded by much publicity. The crux of the case concerned whether Sikhs constituted an ethnic group and could claim the protection of the Race Relations Act 1976. The Court of Appeal decided that Sikhs did not constitute a racial group and could not claim the protection of the Race Relations Act.

It was an unpopular decision, taken two days before Lord Denning MR's retirement as Master of the Rolls (the senior judge in the Court of Appeal) and caused rioting in the streets before a quick reversal of the Court of Appeal's decision by the House of Lords.

The particular legislative provisions were ss 1 and 3 of the Race Relations Act 1976. Section 3 was the gateway provision. If this section gave Sikhs protection, then the Act applied and the claim under s 1 could be made. More particularly, the entire case revolved around the interpretation of three words. The meaning of the word 'ethnic' in s 3 and the meaning of the words 'can' and 'justifiable' in s 1.

The case is a good example of the movement from theoretical rules to their interpretation and application in reality; a movement from rules in books, to the legal construction of reality. It is also a good illustration of the power of the appellate court to determine the meaning of legislation.

The facts of the case were that Mr Mandla, a Sikh, wanted his son to go to a private secondary school. The child was offered a place which was subsequently revoked when the father informed the school that the child would not remove his turban as school uniform rules required. The headmaster stated that the rules concerning uniform were rigid and that other Sikh pupils removed turbans during school hours. Mr Mandla reported the matter to the Commission for Racial

Equality (CRE) who took up the case. The CRE alleged that the son had been unlawfully discriminated against, either directly or indirectly, on racial grounds, in that he had been denied a place at the school because of his custom of wearing a turban.

4.8.3 The meaning of the word 'ethnic' in s 3 of the Race Relations Act 1976

The case raised a number of issues. The first issue, which was of tremendous importance to the *Sikh community*, was whether the Race Relations Act was the relevant statute to take action under. The Race Relations Act states that it is unlawful to discriminate against another on racial grounds in the areas covered by the Act. One of these areas is education. To bring an action, it had to be proved that Sikhs were a racial group.

Section 3 of the Act defines racial grounds as:

> ... a group of persons defined by reference to colour, race, nationality or ethnic or national origins.

The main argument centred around whether Sikhs fitted into the word 'ethnic' as other words and phrases in the list in s 3 were accepted as not applicable.

The trial court found that Sikhs were not a racial group and the appellant appealed to the Court of Appeal and came before Lord Denning. The Court of Appeal had two choices. It could take the teleological approach – looking at the wider context – considering the history behind the legislation, the mischief that it was designed to rectify; or it could choose a formalist approach, considering the text, the word or words, and their possible meanings in a more literal sense.

Lord Denning had always, in essence, taken a teleological approach. He had, for much of his legal career as a senior judge, fought against blind literalism. He had always fought for the right to 'fill in the gaps' left in legislation. Indeed, his career was often based on the right to take the broader teleological view rather than the narrow, literalist view.

Surprisingly, he chose, in this case, to take the formalist approach, to stand by the literal meaning of the words. He discussed the history of the word 'ethnic' (its etymology). Certainly, the etymology of the word is fascinating; however, why did the legislators put in the word 'ethnic'? Did they do so after scanning its etymology? Of course, it is not known. Yet, an interpretation based on the history of a word obviously presumes that, yes, the legislators did consider the etymology of the word. Otherwise, there is no point in the court doing so.

When constructing legal rules in fixed verbal form, language is of the utmost importance. Thought is given to the best words to be used to 'fix' or 'stick' the rule, so that contrary interpretations cannot be reached by courts; and so that the mischief to be tackled is tackled. However, as noted in Chapter 2, the flexibility of language will not allow it to be permanently fixed.

The choice of words is often determined by:

(1) a desire to make it impossible for judges to change the meaning;

(2) a desire to make a major policy change as uncontentious as possible;

(3) a desire to compromise, or a need to compromise, to ensure that major aspects of the draft statute get through the legislative process, and are not blocked by the opposition within, or external to, the government.

In the Court of Appeal in *Mandla v Dowell Lee*, Lord Denning looked at the history of the word 'ethnic', charting its meaning and usage through three editions of the *Oxford English Dictionary* (1890, 1934, 1972). However, he always argued that words do not and cannot have a literal meaning and yet, here, in a highly contentious case, he traced the history of words.

He noted that, in its original Greek form, 'ethnic' meant 'heathen' and was used by the translators of the Old Testament from Hebrew to Greek to mean non-Israelite, or gentile. Earlier in this text, in Chapter 2, we considered the issue of the use of the phrase 'the original Greek'. He identified the first use of 'ethnic' in English as describing people who were not Christian or Jewish.

Lord Denning referred to the 1890 edition of the *Oxford English Dictionary* to confirm this etymology. He then referred to the 1934 edition, stating that its meaning had, by then, changed to denote 'race, ethnological'. This is hardly surprising as the great anthropological expeditions of the 1920s and 1930s introduced the idea of ethnography as the descriptions of unknown groupings of people. His Lordship stated that the 1934 version indicated that 'ethnic' meant 'divisions of races' and, as far as he was concerned, this was right.

This is, of course, a highly dubious and subjective viewpoint. But a judge has the power, via language analysis, to make a choice between what is, and what is not, right. Indeed, this is the judge's task. The court has to decide.

Finally, he referred to the 1972 version of the dictionary, which gave a wider definition of 'ethnic'. It was this definition that was relied upon by the plaintiff's counsel. Here, 'ethnic' was defined as relating to:

> ... common racial, cultural, religious, or linguistic characteristics, especially designating a racial or other group within a larger system.

Lord Denning then turned to discuss 'origins' for, as used in s 3 of the Race Relations Act, 'ethnic' appears in a small phrase including the word 'origins' ('or ethnic or national origins'). Turning again to the dictionary, noting its usage with parentage he decides that it meant, as in previous case law, 'a connection arising at birth'.

'Origin', he said, therefore meant a group with a common racial characteristic. His Lordship reconsidered the entire phrase as used in s 3:

> ... a group of persons defined ... by reference to ... ethnic ... origins.

He concluded that the group must be distinguishable from another by a definable characteristic. Re-reading his judgment in the Court of Appeal, it is noticeable that he constantly used the words he is supposed to be defining in the definitions.

Yet, Lord Denning's normally preferred technique was the teleological, the mischief or the purposive rule. He may have reasoned in a manner more in keeping with the Race Relations Act if he had used his favourite technique of the purposive approach.

Having defined ethnic origin, the next task was to apply that definition to Sikhs to consider whether they could be said to be 'people defined ... by reference to ... ethnic origins'.

Lord Denning launched into a potted and largely inaccurate history of the word 'Sikh' and the people who follow the teaching of Guru Nanak. Again, in a subjective and arbitrary manner, Lord Denning decided that:

(a) Sikhs can only be distinguished by religion,   *and therefore*

(b) they are not defined by 'ethnic origins',   *and therefore*

(c) they are not a racial group,   *and therefore*

(d) it is not illegal to discriminate against Sikhs.

Lord Denning's entire reasoning process rests on dictionary definitions and homespun inaccurate conclusions. He went on to criticise the CRE for bringing the case, stating that schools should not be interfered with when they properly manage their affairs.

Oliver LJ in the same court said that the dictionary shows 'ethnic' to be a vague word and he doubts whether only the most general assistance can be obtained from dictionaries. Can one discern a community in a loose sense among Sikhs, he asked rhetorically? Without providing evidence, he says no, customs among Sikhs are so disparate they cannot be said to be members of an ethnic group. However, the essence of the discrimination legislation is that the 'man in the street' is the one to discriminate. The court concluded that Sikhs were not an ethnic group. The CRE appealed to the House of Lords.

The House of Lords reversed the decision of the Court of Appeal, allowing the appeal. The House of Lords found that, to be an ethnic group, a group must be regarded by itself and others as a distinct community with, for instance, a shared culture, history, language, common descent or geography, customs, religion. Not all of these factors need be present.

The main judgment given was by Lord Fraser. He discussed the views of Lord Denning and Oliver LJ in the Court of Appeal. He dispensed with the dictionary arguments and the suggestion that ethnic denotes race by saying, in favour of a teleological approach:

My Lords, I recognise that 'ethnic' conveys a flavour of race but it cannot, in my opinion, have been used in the Act of 1976 in a strictly racial or biological sense. For one thing, it would be absurd to suppose that Parliament can have intended that membership of a particular racial group should depend upon scientific proof of biological characteristics (if possible to prove). It is clear that Parliament must have used the word in a more popular sense. 'Racial' isn't a term of art, either legal or scientific. No, ethnic today has a wide populist meaning denoting common factors of shared history, etc. It would include converts, etc. So by birth or adherence one can have an ethnic origin.

He finds support for his views in a line of New Zealand cases which maintain that it is important how a group regards itself, and is regarded by others. He says that, not only does he like this definition, but:

> ... it is important that courts in English speaking countries should, if possible, construe the words which we are considering in the same way where they occur in the same context.

He concludes that, applying his broader definition of ethnic origin, Sikhs are a racial group on ethnic grounds.

This opens the gateway for the court to consider if indeed the boy had been unfairly discriminated against by the school which had refused to admit him unless he removed his turban.

The answer to this issue revolves around the meaning of two words in s 1(1)(b) of the Race Relations Act 1976. These words are 'can' in s 1(1)(b)(i) and 'justifiable' in s 1(1)(b)(iii).

Section 1(1)(b) is a potentially difficult section and is set out for consideration below:

1(1) A person discriminates against another in any circumstances relevant for the purposes or any provision of this Act if:

(a) ...

(b) he applies to that other a requirement or condition which he applies or would equally apply to persons not of the same racial group as that other but:

    (i) which is such that the proportion of persons of the same racial group as that other who can comply with it is considerably smaller than the proportion of persons not of that racial group who can comply with it; and

    (ii) which he cannot show to be justifiable irrespective of the colour, race, nationality or ethnic or national origins of the person to whom it is applied; and

    (iii) which is to the detriment of that other because he cannot comply with it.

Let us leave the judgment of Lord Fraser for a moment and consider s 1(1)(b).

Using the tree diagram method that is now quite familiar to you, Figure 4.19, below, shows the relationship between the various aspects of s 1(1)(b).

Figure 4.19: s 1 of the Race Relations Act 1976

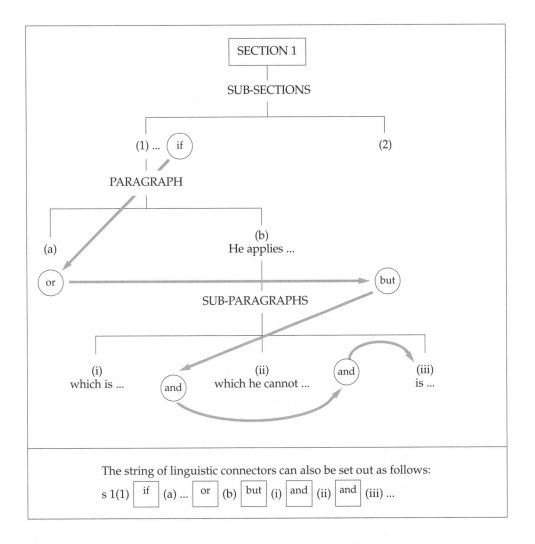

The first task is to break into this section and to search for connectors to see what sub-sections and paragraphs or sub-paragraphs are connected and which ones, if any, are not connected. This section again illustrates the fundamental importance of *connectors* to ascertain meaning of statutory phrases.

The connectors between the sections, sub-sections, paragraphs and sub-paragraphs reveal the type and function of the connection. For example, if the connector is '*or*' it is clear that the connector is indicating that *two* things are in the *alternative*.

If the connector is '*and*', it is equally clear that the connector is indicating that two things *both* have to be present.

There is a major difference between saying

- (i) *or* (ii); and saying
- (i) *and* (ii).

However, as has been mentioned above, students often do not read the connectors *'and'*, *'if'*, *'but'*.

Now consider the connectors between sections, sub-sections, paragraphs and sub-paragraphs in Figure 5.1, above. The following pattern is obtained:

```
s 1  (1)   ... if
     (a) ... or
     (b) ... but
            (i)   ... and
            (ii)  ... and
            (iii) is ...
```

What can be ascertained from this seemingly abstract pattern?

- Something in s 1(1) will be the case *if* something in para (a) *or* (b) is the case.
- Paragraph (b) is tied to sub-paras (i), (ii), and (iii) by the connector *'but'*.
- Sub-paragraphs (i), (ii) and (iii) are all tied together by the two connectors *'and'* which occur at the end of sub-paras (i) and (ii).

After the study of s 1, both in terms of connectors and substance, it is appropriate to return to the discussion of the meaning of the words 'can' and 'justifiable', which were the subject of deliberations in the House of Lords. Recall, we have only been considering the judgment of Lord Fraser.

4.8.4   The meaning of the word 'can' in s 1(1)(b)(i)

The school's argument was that 'can' simply meant that someone could do something physically. So, of course, it is always physically possible to remove a turban. However, the religious, conscientious, cultural, psychological dimensions of behaviour are thereby ignored. If the Race Relations Act is to have any impact, it cannot be the object of such simplistic interpretation. Lord Fraser stated that 'can' does not merely mean 'can physically comply'. 'Can' means 'can comply' in practice, given the constraints of ethnic origin. If restrictive interpretations were to be placed on a word as seemingly innocent as 'can', it would be possible to undermine the entire purpose of the Act. Herein lies the power of the interpreter of language which, at root, will always remain flexible.

4.8.5   The meaning of the word 'justifiable' in s 1(1)(b)(ii)

Sub-paragraph (ii) of sub-s (b) in s 1 maintains that a condition is discriminatory if it cannot be justified on grounds other than race. The school argued that it wanted total equality among its pupils in all areas including dress. Therefore, the 'no turban rule' was a necessary aspect of uniform, discipline and equality. The school insisted that it was non-sectarian yet the headmaster also maintained that the school wished to project 'a Christian image'. Therefore, by implication suggesting that the turban was also said to be a challenge to the Christian faith. The headmaster also objected because it was a manifestation of the appellant's ethnic origins.

Lord Fraser found that the school could not justify the condition on grounds other than on ethnic origin and that this was illegal under the Act. In addition, Lord Fraser stated that Lord Denning's criticism of the CRE was completely unjustified.

This brief discussion of one case reveals the different approaches to statutory interpretation. Context and perhaps judicial attitudes dictate the rules used. Rules of interpretations are not referred to. Perhaps the best indicator of what is going on is a careful consideration of what is being said and what 'styles' of interpretation seem represented by the tone of the judgment. Each judge does indeed have a personal style.

Interpretational problems can never be solved by the neat application of interpretational rules, even worse perhaps the rules do little or nothing to solve problems. At the risk of heresy, perhaps all that purported interpretational rules do is simply to justify solutions. As mentioned above, there is rarely one right answer, only a range of more plausible and less plausible outcomes, varying according to interpretational styles.

Judges use their creativity in working out a solution according to criteria which must be rational either in reality or in argument. They invariably go beyond the text when constructing answers. Lord Denning, for example, moved from dictionary definitions to subjective assertion. Often, judges say no more than 'this is the answer because I say so'.

Judges, as previously noted, can be classified as formalists or contextualists. It is possible to begin to guess as to which rules the judges think they are using. It is good also to accept that it is not always possible to understand what they are arguing, and to realise that, at times, judges themselves are wrong and not themselves too sure of the appropriate outcome. This is what makes comprehension of the methods of statutory interpretation, and the use of precedents, so difficult. It is essential to realise the limits of a supposed scientific approach and the limitless possibilities that open up when the illogical bridges from one set of rationale to the next are located and the power of language appreciated.

As the judges engage more with the European dimensions of interpretation they are being forced to engage more often with the teleological approach used in European cases. As discussed in Chapter 5, the Human Rights Act 1998 states that judges in deciding cases on the enforcement of European Convention rights *must* have regard to the case law and jurisprudence of the European Court of Human Rights. In addition by virtue of the European Communities Act 1972 (as amended) English courts are required to take notice of the decisions of the European Court of Justice. It is highly likely that this consistent engagement will result, over time, in a profound change to the tradition of statutory interpretation within the English legal system.

4.9   SUMMARY

This chapter has been concerned with introducing, in some depth, common law/case law, the second major source of English legal rules discussed in this book. The role of the judiciary in the development of English law has become apparent as the chapter has progressed. This chapter has also indicated the central importance of a careful dissection of the law reports to ensure that the correct aspects of the case are correctly summarised for a case note and further use. Taken together with Chapter 3, the foundations of an indispensable 'how to' approach have been laid. It is now appropriate in the next chapter to place this foundation in its European context looking at the law relating to European human rights and fundamental freedoms and the law relating to the European Community. In Chapter 9, three sources of English law (legislation, case law and European Community law) are further developed by being brought together in a case study.

4.10   FURTHER READING

As already mentioned in Chapter 3, if you are a law student the ground covered by this chapter will also be covered in English legal system courses and constitutional or public law courses.

Coverage of reading cases can be found in the following excellent texts relating to both the theoretical and practical aspects of legal method.

- Sychin, C, *Legal Method*, 1999, London: Sweet & Maxwell, Chapters 7 and 8.
- Twining, W and Miers, D, *How To Do Things With Rules*, 4th edn, 1999, London: Butterworths, Chapters 7 and 8.

CHAPTER 5

READING ENGLISH LAW –
THE EUROPEAN DIMENSION

5.1   INTRODUCTION

This chapter seeks to provide a clear foundation for the study of the European dimension of English law – that part of English law very much affected by some of the UK government's international agreements with other European Nation States contracted via treaties. A step by step approach is taken in this chapter introducing treaties generally and considering their definition, legal and political effects, and describing their standard format. If the concept of treaties is not basically understood, students can find themselves at a disadvantage studying the detail of the law relating to the European dimension of English law.

Having laid out treaties generally, the chapter then turns to look at each of the discrete areas of the European Convention on Human Rights (ECHR), the European Union (EU) and European Community (EC) law. European political co-operation, as well as conflicts between the Nation States of Europe, has always exerted a profound influence on the development of the UK and upon the law. At the broadest level of European influence much contemporary English law is the result of decision making at the level of law and policy within the institutions of the EC (established 1957), now contained within the much larger European Union (established 1992). At the narrow level of European influence, the ECHR (established 1951), whilst always giving rights to UK citizens to bring actions at the international level, has since 1998 profoundly changed aspects of English law relating to fundamental human rights by incorporating these European rights directly into English law.

The overall aim of this chapter is to ensure that you approach the detailed study of these areas with a competent understanding of the basic interrelationships, similarities and differences involved. The chapter, therefore, looks at the following issues.

- Defining treaties and describing their standard format.
- Describing the standard mechanisms used to make all, or part of an international treaty part of English law.
- Outlining the institutions and law in the area of European human rights, and discussing the effect of the domestic Human Rights Act (HRA) 1998 and its relationship with the ECHR.
- Explaining the creation of the EC.
- Outlining in brief some of the most important institutions of the EU and EC law.
- Explaining the creation of the EU and its relationship to the EC and the English legal system.
- Describing the effect and influence of these areas on English law.
- Considering appropriate approaches to European Court of Justice (ECJ) cases.

The overall aim of this chapter is to provide a commentary concerning the relationships and differences between the areas of the ECHR, EU, EC and EC law to assist in the management of the study of these complex areas in relation to English law and in their own right. The detailed study of these areas, for law students, will occur in your English legal system, public law and European law courses.

5.2   LEARNING OUTCOMES

By the end of this chapter and the associated reading, readers should:

- be able to understand the general consequences and standard format of a Treaty and how it is internally organised and subsequently amended;
- be able to explain the context within which European human rights operate and how it affects the English legal system;
- be able to place the English HRA 1998 in its appropriate context and explain how it relates to the ECHR;
- be able to describe the various types of secondary legislation produced by the EC;
- be able to distinguish between primary and secondary EC law;
- be able to discuss the similarities and differences between the EC and the EU;
- understand the difference between the European Court of Human Rights (ECtHR) and the ECJ;
- understand the role of the ECJ;
- understand the relationship between the English legal system, the EC and the EU;
- appreciate the difference in style and rationale between European legal judgments and legislation and English legal judgments and legislation.

5.3   READING AND UNDERSTANDING TREATIES

Many of the difficulties encountered by students of English law approaching its European dimension are the vast number of unfamiliar terms. Often students do not appreciate the international nature of treaties and their normal effect. Therefore when discussing the peculiarities of the English approach to international treaties made by the UK Government confusions creep in. This section of the chapter is therefore designed to give a brief introduction to the general purpose and format of treaties.

5.3.1   The definition of a treaty and its legal effects

5.3.1.1 Definition

A treaty is a political agreement between two or more States. Treaties, conventions, charters, codes and agreements are in fact all treaties as defined by the Vienna Convention (despite the differing terms used). The sole difference between a convention and an agreement is that an agreement is usually signed by Heads of Government with no intention that it should be subsequently ratified by the State (for the meaning of ratification and the significance of signing, see below). A bi-lateral treaty is between two States, a multi-lateral treaty is concluded between more than two States.

5.3.1.2 Legal effect

A treaty is only subject to international law and has no effect on the English legal system unless specific legislation is passed by the UK Parliament allowing the provisions of the Treaty to have such an effect. If there is the political will to translate any part of the treaty into English law this has to be specifically done by placing all, or part, of the treaty into legislation. Otherwise it merely remains a treaty at the international political level with *absolutely no legal effects* in the UK. It may, depending on its nature, be enforceable against Contracting States under international law.

5.3.1.3 Naming a treaty

Every treaty has a formal name (which is usually abbreviated) and in addition many treaties are by custom referred to by the place where the treaty was signed! This can be confusing; check out the examples below in Figure 5.1, below.

Figure 5.1: naming complexities

1   The Treaty on European Union 1992 (establishing the European Union)
    (a) Formal name: the Treaty on European Union 1992
    (b) Abbreviation: TEU 1992
    (c) Place of signing – Maastricht: It is therefore also called the Treaty of Maastricht.
(Note: there was a second Treaty on European Union in 1997 (TEU 1997). Place of signature: Amsterdam, and referred to as the Treaty of Amsterdam. These similar names have to be distinguished by date and place of signature.)
2   The European Convention on Human Rights and Fundamental Freedoms 1951
    (a) Formal name of treaty: The European Convention on Human Rights and Fundamental Freedoms.
    (b) Tends to be called The European Convention on Human Rights or the Convention.
    (c) Abbreviation: ECHR
    (d) Place of signature: London. But this is never used.
(Note: this is an example of another word for treaty – a convention.)

5.3.2   The subject matter of treaties

The potential subject matter of treaties is unlimited; they can be about anything over which the government has authority. Treaties tend to contain two types of propositions:

- specific obligations that States agree to follow and enforce;
- statements about ideals and expression of joint hopes, standing as statements of good intention.

An example would be the expressed desire of States to co-operate in co-ordinating developments in a specific area (for example, the treaties setting up the EU to co-operate in a range of areas).

5.3.3   The process of formalising agreement to be bound by a treaty

Once the matters to be included in the treaty are settled, it is drafted, approved by prospective States and then opened for signature by an authorised person from each State (the signatory). Sometimes it is not possible for everyone to be available to sign it at the same time in each other's presence. It is formally signed by the Head of Government or other authorised person (the signatory) or persons (signatories) in each State.

The signature is in an expression of interest by the relevant State and an additional process has to take place. The whole government, *or* legislature, *or* people, of each signatory State in the usual manner for that State has to agree to the treaty, allowing ratification of the treaty to take place. This marks the formal agreement by the State to be bound by the treaty as signed.

An example of this two stage process is Norway's application to join the EC in 1973. The government of Norway signed an accession treaty joining the EC. However, the people of Norway were not prepared to support joining and the government lost a referendum (a ballot put to the people). The government, therefore, could not ratify the treaty and Norway did not join the EC.

5.3.4   The methods to minimise dissent in the negotiation process

When a treaty is being negotiated by a group of nation States it may well be the case that whilst one State may be in favour of most of the treaty there are matters under discussion which they do not like, and cannot at that time agree to. Rather than risk the whole treaty failing to be negotiated, which could be an international political disaster, methods have been devised to get round these potential serious problems.

If the nation State agrees with the core of the treaty but does not wish to be bound by certain aspects of the treaty they can make this clear by entering what is called a *'derogation'*. They agree the treaty with the disliked item 'taken away': the State opts out of that aspect. A written record of the derogation is drawn up, signed by the State concerned, and attached to the treaty.

If the State is potentially sympathetic to an aspect of the treaty but for political reasons (perhaps lack of support in the nation as a whole for that particular item) does not wish to agree that aspect at that time the State can formally say that they want to think about the treaty or modify it slightly, and agree it at a later date. This is done by the State recording a written *'reservation'* in relation to the operation of that part of the treaty in that State. As with derogations a written record of the reservation is drawn up, signed by the State concerned and attached to the treaty.

5.3.5   Changing a treaty

Treaties can be changed in several ways as indicated in Figure 5.2, below.

Figure 5.2: ways of changing treaty

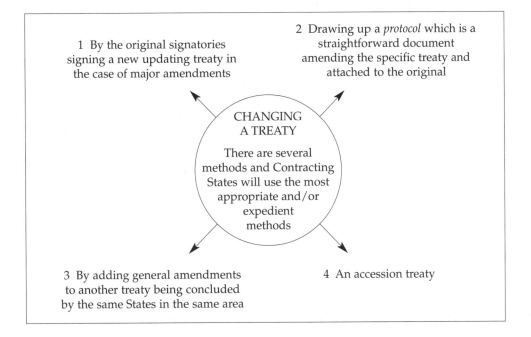

1 By the original signatories signing a new updating treaty in the case of major amendments

2 Drawing up a *protocol* which is a straightforward document amending the specific treaty and attached to the original

CHANGING A TREATY

There are several methods and Contracting States will use the most appropriate and/or expedient methods

3 By adding general amendments to another treaty being concluded by the same States in the same area

4 An accession treaty

5.3.6   Cancelling an agreement

If a State wishes to cease to be bound by a treaty, it may sign an instrument cancelling its agreement – this is an *abrogation* which is also attached to the original treaty.

5.3.7   Official records of treaties

The Secretary General of the Council of Europe (see below) is the depository for European conventions, agreements and treaties. The Secretary General keeps all of the originals and usually presides over their signatures. He also keeps the written records (instruments) of ratification, or accession (joining other States to a treaty that has already been negotiated and ratified). He also arranges registration of these European documents with the Secretary General of the United Nations.

5.3.8   The standard layout of a treaty

A treaty, like English legislation, has a standard format. At the beginning of the
treaty is a preamble setting out the main goals of the treaty and the aspirations of
the parties. It is divided into clusters of items dealing with similar matters. Each
cluster is called a title (which roughly equates with the division of an English
statute into parts). Titles contain numbered items called Articles, each one setting
out a basic rule or principle. Articles can be divided into paragraphs and sub-
paragraphs. The numbering system is Arabic and it not as dense and complex as
that used by English statutes.

Figure 5.3: standard layout of a treaty

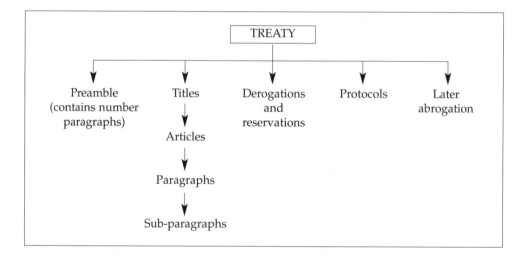

5.3.9   How do obligations entered into through treaties become part of
English law?

If the UK government wishes all, or part of a treaty, to become part of English law
it must *specifically incorporate* the treaty, or part of it, into the English legal system
via legislation. This legislation goes through the same procedures as any other
piece of legislation. If the government expects the treaty to give rise to a range of
other measures over time it will usually place sections in this legislation delegating
the authority to make later legal changes to others (such as the minister of
appropriate government departments). This saves time as there is no need for the
full legislative process in Parliament. Whilst it is still the subject of parliamentary
debate, it does have a *fast track procedure*.

    In relation to treaties becoming part of English law in this way, there is always
the possibility that Parliament may refuse to enact the legislation, which would
leave the government in an extremely difficult situation. However, the UK
Parliament is usually controlled by the political party forming the government and
the government would not risk the embarrassment of failure but would guage its
position in Parliament prior to signature of a relevant treaty.

Figure 5.4: matters to be taken into account when handling treaties

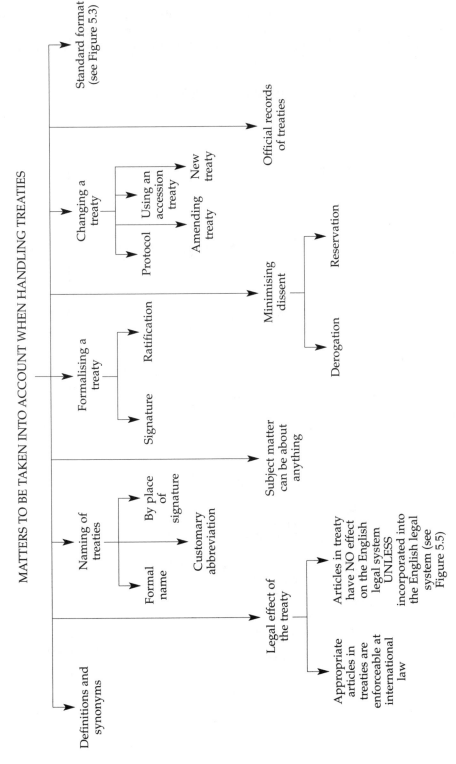

MATTERS TO BE TAKEN INTO ACCOUNT WHEN HANDLING TREATIES

5.3.10 Summary

This section has taken the opportunity to describe treaties, their standard layout, their naming systems, amendments and, where appropriate, their methods of incorporation into English law. It is useful to be familiar with these prior to discussing human rights, the EC and EU.

Figure 5.5: incorporation of treaties into English law

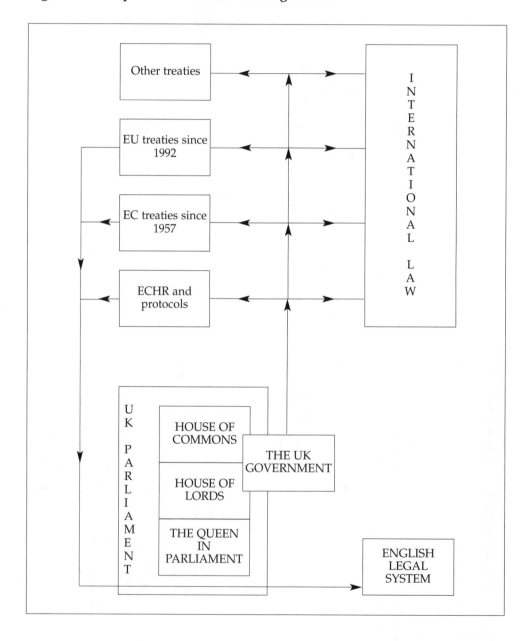

5.4   EUROPEAN CONVENTION ON HUMAN RIGHTS AND FUNDAMENTAL FREEDOMS

5.4.1   Background

The European Convention on Human Rights and Fundamental Freedoms 1951 (the ECHR) was one of many inter-state initiatives that took place in the years immediately after the Second World War. Several such initiatives are set out in Figure 5.6, below.

Figure 5.6: inter-state initiatives post-1949–57

---

(1) 1948: the United Nations was established.

(2) 1948: the Organisation for Economic Co-operation and Development (OECD) was established (with financial aid from the US) to restructure European economies devastated by war.

(3) 1949: the North Atlantic Treaty was signed forming the North Atlantic Treaty Organisation (NATO) a military alliance between US, Canada and Europe.

(4) 1949: 10 European States set up the Council of Europe specifically focussing on:
- the protection of human rights;
- social programmes;
- co-operation.

(5) 1951: the Treaty of Paris set up the European Coal and Steel Community (ECSC).

(6) 1957: the Treaty of Rome set up the European Atomic Energy Community (Euratom).

(7) 1957: the Treaty of Rome set up the European Economic Community (EEC).

5.4.1.1 The Council of Europe

The 10 founding members of the Council of Europe were Austria, Belgium, Denmark, France, Italy, Luxembourg, UK, Norway and Sweden, and over time have been joined by 11 others: Austria, Cyprus, West Germany, Greece, Iceland, Lichtenstein, Malta, Portugal, Switzerland and Turkey. Any European State can be a member of the Council of Europe if certain basic minimum standards of conduct, particularly in relation to the observation of human rights and fundamental freedoms, are observed. In 1951, the same 10 founding members of the Council of Europe drafted and agreed the ECHR. Today there are 21 European signatories to the Convention.

The rationale behind the Convention which is explored in detail in public law, human rights and English legal system courses, is the protection of a series of agreed rights considered core to life, such as the right to life, to a family, to privacy, and to freedom from slavery.

5.4.2   Institutions enforcing the Convention

The Council of Europe originally set up three institutions: the Committee of Members, the Commission of Human Rights and the ECtHR set out in Figure 5.7, below. The last two were merged in 1998 to create a more efficient system for dealing with cases.

Figure 5.7: the institutions of the Council of Europe

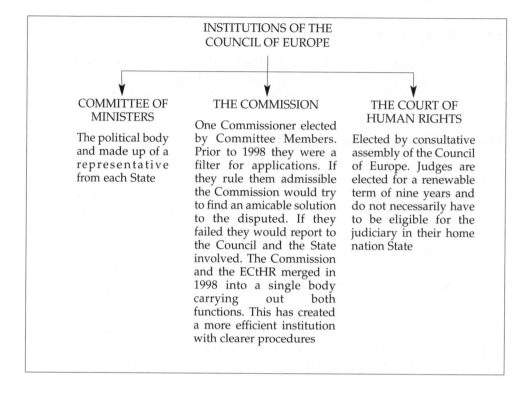

INSTITUTIONS OF THE
COUNCIL OF EUROPE

COMMITTEE OF MINISTERS

The political body and made up of a representative from each State

THE COMMISSION

One Commissioner elected by Committee Members. Prior to 1998 they were a filter for applications. If they rule them admissible the Commission would try to find an amicable solution to the disputed. If they failed they would report to the Council and the State involved. The Commission and the ECtHR merged in 1998 into a single body carrying out both functions. This has created a more efficient institution with clearer procedures

THE COURT OF HUMAN RIGHTS

Elected by consultative assembly of the Council of Europe. Judges are elected for a renewable term of nine years and do not necessarily have to be eligible for the judiciary in their home nation State

5.4.3   Relationship of the Convention with English law

The UK has had many cases brought against it by individuals, and its track record in relation to human rights has been demonstrated to be worrying. Between 1975 and 1990, 30 cases were brought against the UK and in 21 of these cases the ECtHR found that the government had violated the ECHR. By 1997, the number of successful applications against the UK had risen to 50. In 1997, when the Labour government came into power one of its election promises was to incorporate these Convention rights into English law.

5.4.3.1 1951–98

As an international treaty the Convention had no force within the English legal system, and Convention rights were not enforceable in English courts. However, the UK government could be taken to the ECtHR by individuals and, as noted above, it was. *But*, having said that, although the Convention had no force in the English legal system, it was not ignored over the course of almost 50 years between

1951 and 1998. English courts *were indeed influenced* by the Convention in a range of ways. Judges in the House of Lords stated that they would presume that Parliament did not intend to legislate contrary to the ECHR. Therefore, if during the course of statutory interpretation there were two possible interpretations, one in conformity with the Convention and one not in conformity with the Convention, the interpretation in conformity with the Convention should be preferred. The House of Lords, however, was careful to stress that it should not be assumed that such an interpretation *must* be applied. Judicial discretion remained.

5.4.3.2 Human Rights Act 1998

The relationship between the UK and the ECHR was changed in 1998 with the incorporation of the majority of the rights in the ECHR into English law. The enforcement procedures and processes in the Convention were *not* incorporated – *only* the majority of rights and this is potentially a problem. For example, Article 13 of the ECHR places a duty on every Member State to provide an effective remedy in national courts for infringement of the Convention. This has *not* been incorporated.

The HRA 1998 was enacted with an 'in force' date for the majority of its sections of October 2000. UK citizens can now bring actions under the ECHR in English courts under domestic law. The Act sets out the Convention rights incorporated into the English legal system in Schedule 1.

Consider the text of s 1, set out in Figure 5.8, below, and note the process used to lay out what is and what is not included in the Act. The long title of the Act gives an indication of the purpose of the Act.

The two rights not referred to relate to Article 2:

Everyone's right to life shall be protected by law. No one shall be deprived of his life intentionally save in the execution of a sentence of a court following his conviction of a crime for which this penalty is provided by law ...

and to Article 13 which requires every State to ensure that there are appropriate and effective remedies in the national courts.

At the level of the ECtHR, the procedure for bringing an action is generally as follows.

Figure 5.8: s 1 of the Human Rights Act 1998 (including long title and author notes)

Author notes	

Author notes

*This is the short hand term that will be used throughout the statute and is set out immediately and given a precise definition. In other States Convention rights mean **all** of the Convention rights but this statute narrows it to a specific meaning set out in paragraphs (a), (b) and (c) sub-section (1).* ——

Note Articles 1, and 13 and those post 14 are not referred to.

This list gives all the rights now to be claimed in UK courts. ——

Protocols are late additions and these related to education, property, elections and death penalties.

'Opt outs'.

Time out to consider.

Section 1(4) gives power to minister to make delegated legislation. ——

Finalised. ——

It is interesting that the minister has the power to create delegated legislation even if protocol NOT ratified (but this is qualified by s 1(6)).

An Act to give further effect to rights and freedoms guaranteed under the European Convention on Human Rights; to make provision with respect to holders of certain judicial offices who become judges of the European Court of Human Rights; and for connected purposes [9th November 1998].

1(1) In this Act 'the Convention rights' means the rights and fundamental freedoms set out in–

    (a) Articles 2 to 12 and 14 of the Convention,

    (b) Articles 1 to 3 of the First Protocol, and

    (c) Articles 1 and 2 of the Sixth Protocol, as read with Articles 16 to 18 of the Convention.

(2) Those Articles are to have effect for the purposes of this Act subject to any designated derogation or reservation (as to which see sections 14 and 15).

(3) The Articles are set out in Schedule 1.

(4) The Secretary of State may by order make such amendments to this Act as he considers appropriate to reflect the effect, in relation to the United Kingdom, of a protocol.

(5) In subsection (4) 'protocol' means a protocol to the Convention–

    (a) which the United Kingdom has ratified; or

    (b) which the United Kingdom has signed with a view to ratification.

(6) No amendment may be made by an order under subsection (4) so as to come into force before the protocol concerned is in force in relation to the United Kingdom.

Figure 5.9: procedure for bringing an action in the European Court of Human Rights

- Domestic remedies must have been exhausted (Article 35).
- Application to the ECtHR must be within six months of final hearing in the domestic court.
- It must be an admissible application.
- There can be a limited audience in a court of first instance (a chamber) relating to the matter.
- Within three months a party can ask for a Grandchamber hearing.
- Enforcement of the decision of the court is a matter for the Committee of Ministers. Here the matter reverts to the political level but a State who consistently abuses human rights can be expelled from the Council of Europe.

The remedies under the English legislation allow for the following.

Figure 5.10: remedies under the Human Rights Act 1998

- English courts and tribunals take account of cases in the ECtHR and other relevant courts and decide cases accordingly.
- English courts can note whether legislation is incompatible with the Convention and if so issue a declaration of incompatibility. They have no power to declare primary or secondary legislation invalid, although they do have a power to invalidate secondary legislation *if* the primary legislation that it is based on does not forbid it. This severely limits the power of the judges to enforce the Convention rights.
- *If* Parliament decides that the incompatibility should be dealt with there is a fast track procedure for delegated legislation to deal with the speedy removal of the incompatibility allowing a 'remedial' order to be enacted.
- Public authorities can be fined for contravention of the Act.
- Courts must act in a manner compatible with the Act.
- All statutes must carry a declaration of compatibility with the HRA 1998 signed by the minister responsible for the original Bill stating that the legislation is not incompatible or if it *is* incompatible that the government intends the legislation to be incompatible.

In keeping with the 'hands on' approach of this text, the HRA 1998 can be found in Appendix 2. Read it through quickly to get an idea of it and then carefully do the following exercise. You will also find two diagrams: the HRA 1998 sections and the HRA 1998 Schedules.

5.4.4   Human Rights Act 1998

(1) Turn to Appendix 2 which sets out the text of the HRA 1998 and set it out as a tree diagram according to the method demonstrated by Figure 3.10, above, in Chapter 3 for the Unfair Contract Terms Act 1977.

Note that you will have to decide how you wish to deal with the detail of the attached relevant articles of the ECHR and its protocols (found in the schedules to the Act).

You should also find a way of clearly indicating derogations and reservations noted in the ECHR and protocols. (Check you understand what these are.)

(2) Consider the statute as a whole.

(a) Do you find the text in written form more helpful, or your diagram? Or do both assist you in understanding the areas covered by the statute?

(b) If you find your diagram more useful why is that the case? What can you understand with your diagram that you did not understand with the text?

> If you wish to practise the legal skills of organising statues using diagrams, carry out tasks (1)–(4) before moving on.

(3) Now turn to Appendix 2, Figures A2.1 and A2.2, where you will find a tree diagram of the HRA 1998. Use the model diagram in Appendix 2 as a check that you have learnt the full range of necessary skills.

From your own diagram as well as the model diagrams in Appendix 2, Figures A2.1 and A2.2, you can begin to see the interconnections just from an appreciation of the basic headings of each section and schedule. One can immediately see that this statute has no parts (unlike the Unfair Contract Terms Act, which has many parts). It also has only a few sections (again, unlike the Unfair Contract Terms Act). However, it does contain four schedules, one of which lists all of the incorporated Convention rights.

(4) Remember that we discussed in Chapter 3 how matters referred to in schedules only have legal effect in so far as the content of the schedules is referred to in the sections of the statute. Look carefully to see what the relationship in this statute is between the schedules and the sections of the main body of the statute. Recall that the excerpt from s 1(1)(a)–(c) of the HRA 1998 set out in Figure 5.8, above, lists these rights.

In this particular statute you will find that one role of the schedules is to set out the articles in the Convention. Another role is to set out the protocols, derogations and reservations.

(a) Compare your diagram with Figures A2.1 and A2.2 in Appendix 2 and note any differences.

(b) Consider if you can understand why there are differences and where, if at all, Figures A2.1 and A2.2 are more useful diagrams.

(c) Amend your diagram as necessary.

5.4.5   Summary

This section has examined the ECHR and the HRA 1998 discussing briefly their effects on English law.

The mere incorporation of the Convention rights into English law without the enforcement machinery takes some of the power out of the Convention at the level of the English UK domestic courts. However, the incorporation of the rights does make far reaching changes to the way in which legislation is scrutinised in Parliament, and to the operation of precedent, as judges in court now have to take notice of cases in the ECtHR and other relevant cases. Much of the development of both the judicial review process of judges reviewing decisions by central, devolved and local government and common law will depend on whether English judges choose to vigorously support the Convention and uphold rights, using where necessary a purposive rather than a literal approach to interpretation. However, although they can declare that legislation is incompatible with the Convention they cannot invalidate that legislation.

The limit on their actions when they are faced with incompatible legislation seems problematic. This is a problem caused by the decision not to incorporate Article 13, specifying that there must be the provision of an effective remedy in national courts. This is a major area of national court weakness in the UK's chosen method of incorporating the ECHR.

The primary rationale for discussing these matters is to consider the European dimensions of English law with a view to issues of legal method, to obtain a basic grasp of how the ECHR as a treaty has operated at European level for 50 years and what changes may occur now that the Convention rights have been incorporated into the English legal system. In addition, students need to be familiar with the terminology used to discuss treaties, and be careful not to confuse the ECHR with the EC or EU, or both. Some of the reasons for the confusion can be found in the similar terminology.

Students consistently confuse the Council of Europe (which among other things was instrumental in ensuring the creation of the ECHR) with similarly named institutions in the EC and now the EU (eg, the European Council is now called the Council of the European Union). Part of the difficulty confronting the student lies in the close proximity between names (for example, the Council of Europe and the Council of the European Community). In addition the similar time scales when the Convention was signed in 1951 and the Treaty of Rome in 1957 (setting up the EC) can cause confusion.

Part of the difficulty is just the unfamiliarity of the area, the institutions and the vast array of new concepts and names. These problems will not just go away but they will lessen as understanding of differences and similarities increases. The European context of English law is becoming increasingly important. This second section of this chapter was designed to help students grasp the significance of the ECHR before and after its partial incorporation into English law. It is predicted that it will be a rapid growth area for the English legal system and it is important that it is not confused with anything else. Yet it is also important to note that the EC and EU make reference to the ECtHR. Therefore, it is not really sufficient to say that these areas are entirely separate as they do have interrelationships. With these distinctions in mind, it is now appropriate to turn to the EC, EC law and the EU.

A parting example of the increasing interconnections between human rights and the EU can be given. In 2000, the European Council (now beginning to be more currently referred to as the Council of the European Union) met. Irrespective of the name change this body remains the council of the heads of government of the Member States of the EU. They met as the Council with representatives from the Commission. It is this group that has authority to sign the treaties of the Union at political level. At the meeting in 2000 they agreed to set up a convention to draft a Charter of Fundamental Rights for the European Union. The Convention was composed of 15 Member State representatives, 30 MPs from national parliaments, 16 Members of the European Parliament, members of the Commission and members of the European Court of Justice and the Council of Europe. They drafted a charter of 50 rights. The latest EU treaty, the Treaty of Nice, which came into force in February 2003, declared support for the 50-right charter that has been drafted.

> Note: the point is that these areas of human rights and EU interact, and need to, in the real world so it is better to understand the interrelationships and the limits and boundaries!

Figure 5.11, below, attempts to place some of this narrative into an accessible diagram.

Figure 5.11: interrelationship between the European Convention, European Union and European Community

THE COUNCIL OF EUROPE

Founding members of the Council of Europe drafted and agreed the ECHR

ECHR

Most EC Member States are ALSO members of the Council of Europe

All EC Member States are signatories of the ECHR

EC

No State will be admitted to the EC if they are not a signatory of the ECHR. It is a precondition of membership

All EC Member States are automatically members of the EU set up in 1992. Membership of the EC is the **only** way of joining the EU

EU

TEU 1997, Article 6 states that the EU holds the ECHR in mind. The EU itself is not a signatory

5.5   THE EUROPEAN UNION AND THE EUROPEAN COMMUNITY

5.5.1   General introduction

Much difficulty can be encountered in approaching this area of study simply because some texts in the area are uncertain as to the most appropriate terms to be used to describe the EU, the EC and EC law. Some texts prefer the term Community and others Union. Some commentators are even confused themselves and use terms wrongly. In addition, there are many excellent texts on the market, as well as leading law reports from the ECJ, that were produced before the structural changes and name changes that occurred from 1992. These texts are still relevant, so it is necessary to understand that some treaties have changed their names over time, can be called by several names concurrently and have changed their article numbering systems. There have been changes to institutions: some have had name changes (such as the 'Assembly' to 'European Parliament'); some have had powers removed or added, and some have been relatively recently created (for example, the Committee of the Regions). It is therefore important to be clear about the construction of the EU, the place of the EC, its areas of legal competency and the extent and limits of EC law, name changes of institutions and treaties, and changes to the numbering of articles in the treaties.

This introduction sets out the approach taken, and the terms to be used in this section with the reasons for their use explained. The section will also give a historical and chronological review of the development of the Union and the current place of the Community. This should enable you to read most texts in the area with a reasonably clear map of your own of the interconnections between the EU, the EC, EC law and their effects on the English legal system.

For the rest of this section the following abbreviated terms will normally be used:

- 'Union' when referring to the European Union;
- 'Community' when referring to the European Community;
- 'Community law' or 'EC law' when referring to European Community law.

The relationship between the English legal system, the Union and the Community is complex. But then the very concept of the Union itself is complex. The Union was established in 1992 and currently there are 15 Member States, with 13 more candidate States waiting to join. There are three spheres of activity in the Union customarily referred to as the three 'pillars' of the Union.

Pillar 1: the three founding Communities established in the 1950s:

(a) the European Coal and Steel Community (ECSC);

(b) the European Atomic Energy Community (Euratom);

(c) European Economic Community (EEC), since 1992 called the European Community, which was set up by the EEC Treaty.

Pillar 2: agreed co-operation in the area of foreign affairs and security.

Pillar 3: agreed co-operation in the areas of home affairs and justice.

It is a Union that is joined together not as a federal system of States, such as the United States of America, nor as a range of States contracting at only the political level. The Union is a supra-national Union of States agreeing to be bound together in part politically, in part co-operatively and socially and in large part through a unique legal order – the *acquis communautaire* ('community patrimony') or 'Community law'. A legal order that has effect by being incorporated into the legal systems of every Member State, and the English legal system is no exception. The legal order of the Union remains rooted in that part of the Union that is the Community. It is the nature of the legal order that makes the Union unique. For although the Union is established by treaties, it is not just governed by international law and political relationships based on agreement at inter-governmental level. The founding treaties of the Union which date back to the inception of the Communities in the 1950s insist that the law of the Union (which technically remains Community law) becomes part of the legal systems of all of the States who are members of the Union.

The Union is the direct successor to the three communities that were set up in the 1950s by six European States. Just as over time the references to the three Communities became one reference to the 'European Community', now the supra-national organisation that is referred to has grown since 1992 and the general name by which it is known is no longer the European Community, but the European Union. Clearly the Union is a much larger entity than the Community, as can be seen from the list of the three areas covered by the Union set out above. But the idea of a large Union had always been within the documents setting up the European Community. The Community remains intact – but as one of three spheres of activity. However, concentrated within the Community are the law-making powers of the Union.

The Union was established by the Treaty of Maastricht 1992 and the Treaty of Amsterdam 1997 (both formally called the Treaty on European Union (TEU)). The same institutions that had served the three Communities were enlarged to serve the Union. The Treaty of Nice in 2000 made further steps towards altering aspects of the institutions of the Union to be ready for enlargement of the number of Member States who were to become part of the Union from 2004. In coming years, the nature of the Union will become increasingly streamlined as it grows in size. The Treaty of Nice reached major agreement on the simplification of the voting procedures for the enactment of secondary legislation, and declared adherence to the Union's proposed Charter on Fundamental Rights. The terms of reference for the next inter-governmental conference on the Union will consider the simplification of the founding treaties into one new treaty. There are therefore more changes ahead that will affect law students!

For all public intents and purposes, there is now only the Union. The official website http://europa.eu.int only refers to European Union and within its legal pages speaks of European Union law. However, it remains true to say that to use that term is technically incorrect. The Union has no law making powers outside those conferred by the founding treaties of the Community, so the appropriate phrase is Community law or European Community law (EC law), not Union law.

The next section will deal with the basic consideration of the historical development of the European Community and European Community law. It will lay out the treaties of importance and note the different types of law, and the mechanisms for Community law having an effect within the legal systems of Member States. The legal systems of the Member States are often referred to by the term 'domestic law', a metaphoric use of 'domestic' linking it to 'home'. The courts in Member States tend to be referred to by two phrases: 'domestic courts', or 'national courts'.

As already noted, whilst much smaller than the ever-growing Union, the Community contains the law making powers of the Union, and therefore it determines its legislative competency. The next section will also attempt to draw attention to areas where name changes have lead to confusion. Despite the wholesale use of the term 'European Union' it is useful to deal with name changes incrementally by going back to the creation of the Community and tracing its development into the Union.

Those matters chosen for discussion are those most likely to be problematic and necessary to properly understand from the perspective of legal method.

For example, what is often not made clear in the texts is the issue of *how* a State joins the Union and here its symbiotic relationship with the Community is made clear. You can only be a member of the Union if you are already a member of the Community. The Community is the gateway to the Union. But whereas the Community has legal competency to make law affecting Member States, the Union does not.

5.5.2   1951–92: the development of the European Community

The EC was established through the founding Treaty of Rome 1957 concluded between France, West Germany, Belgium, Italy, Netherlands and Luxembourg, five of whom were also members of the Council of Europe. At the time of its creation it was known as the European Economic Community (EEC for short) and the treaty establishing it became known as the EEC Treaty. In 1951 the same six States had established the European Coal and Steel Community (ECSC), and on the same day as the EC was established they also established the European Atomic Energy Community (Euratom) through a second Treaty of Rome. There were therefore three distinct Communities with some shared and some separate institutions. In 1965, a Merger Treaty merged the institutions of the three Communities, but the Communities themselves remained distinct.

The UK was not keen to join the Community in 1957, preferring to set up the European Free Trade Area (EFTA) with Austria, Denmark, Norway, Portugal, Sweden and Switzerland. (In part of course the EFTA could be seen as a defensive move by European States not in the EEC.) All of the original members of EFTA with the exception of Norway are now members of the EC. In fact, the UK changed its policy relatively quickly and applied for membership only four years later in 1961, but France blocked the application for just over 10 years. The UK finally signed and ratified a Treaty of Accession in 1972. The Treaty of Rome is unusual in that it insists on its provisions being enforced by the legal systems of Member States. The UK therefore had to incorporate large parts of the Treaty into English law through the enactment of the European Communities Act (ECA) 1972.

The founding States of the EC wished to use the fact of economic unity to forge greater political and social unity. There was a desire for a broader EU than that based on materials and movement of people and goods. This agenda was advanced by the Single European Act 1986 which paved the way for the single currency – the euro. Finally, the EU was created in 1992 by the Member States of the EC concluding the TEU 1992, also known as the Maastricht Treaty. This treaty, in so far as it relates to the Union, remains operative at the international level but has no effect on the legal systems of Member States. When the Union, through its institutions, operates within the legislative competence of the Community actions do have an effect on the legal systems of Member States. Should areas within the wider Union require embedding in the legal systems of the Community, then in fact what occurs is an appropriate agreement to move matters from the Union into the sphere of legal competency of the Community. For example, the agreement between Member States of the Union to co-operate on home affairs and justice (pillar 3, above) led to large areas of this 'pillar' being moved into the legal competency of the Community so that it could become the subject of law making that was effective within the legal systems of Member States.

Figures 5.12 and 5.13, below, attempt to show the way in which the Community remains the gateway to the Union, as at its core is the EC Treaty (the Treaty of Rome 1957 (as amended)) which gives all the rights, liabilities and obligations.

Figure 5.12: the European Community as the gateway to the European Union

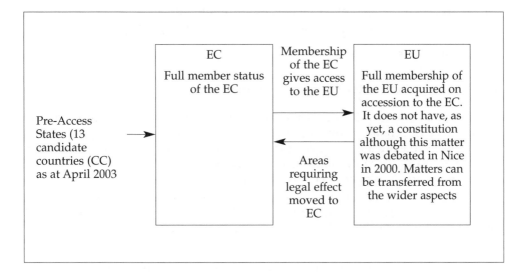

As can be seen, the EU is much broader than the EC.

Figure 5.13: the interrelationship between the EC and EU

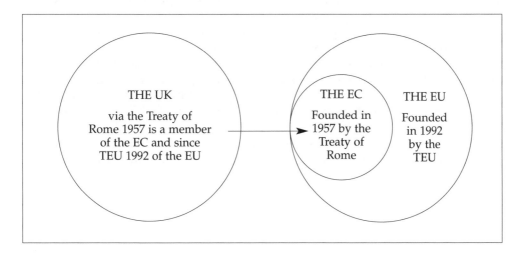

In order to understand the development of the Community and the development of the Union it is necessary to bear in mind several matters:

(a) The nature of the Union and the Community.

(b) The treaties setting up the Community and then the Union (included here are the founding treaties, the accession treaties, and the amending treaties).

(c) The institutions of the Community and latterly the Union.

(d) The sources, types and differing effects of Community law.

(e) The effect of Community law or EC law on the English legal system.

These areas will be considered next.

5.5.3   The nature of the European Community

The Treaty of Rome 1957 states the main principle of the Community as the maintenance of economic and social progress, and naturally flowing out of this primary principle are a number of other principles aiming to unite Member States for the purpose of social, economic and legal union. It specifically states it is aiming to lay 'the foundations of an ever closer union'.

Part of the difficulty that can occur in attempting to understand the Community perhaps lies in the fact that it was never a specific place but a way of trading and of relating financially, legally, politically, socially and culturally.

> The Community is a market place that cannot be seen, a community that cannot be visited, and a people who are united in their diversity.

Since 1992, the introduction of the EU and the idea of the European citizen has perhaps done more to 'ground' the idea of a geographic place. This will be looked at later.

Within its area of competency, as laid down in the Treaty of Rome and subsequently amended, the Community established a specific supra-national legal and political order that each Member State agrees to be part of and bound by. Of course in agreeing to be part of a supra-national legal order it is inevitable that some aspects of self rule need to be willingly delegated to the decisions of the European legal and political institutions. (This caused much difficulty as a concept in the UK.)

However, having said this, each State in the Community remains separate, and that separateness is still the case within the bigger grouping that is the European Union.

Figure 5.14: the EU and the EC

> The European Union now encompassing the Community IS NOT:
>
>   a state in its own right; OR
>
>   a federation of States with a federal government.
>
> The European Union now encompassing the Community IS:
>
>   an absolutely unique supra-national organisation.

The preamble to the Treaty of Rome invited other European States to join the founding six and has expanded to a total of 15 Member States at present: Austria, Belgium, Denmark, Finland, France, Germany, Greece, Ireland, Italy, Luxembourg, Netherlands, Portugal, Spain, Sweden and the UK. In addition, there are 13 States waiting to join. The EC has a special application procedure and States need to match a range of criteria judged against human rights records and economic stability prior to joining. The 13 States, which are formerly referred to as 'candidate countries' (CC) have been in pre-access preparation for a few years. The 13 candidate States are Bulgaria, Cyprus, Czech Republic, Estonia, Hungary, Latvia, Lithuania, Malta, Poland, Romania, Slovakia, Slovenia and Turkey and 10 of these are likely to join in 2004 with two in 2006 and the place of Malta and Turkey undecided.

These matters change, however, and for updated information you should use the European Union website: www.europa.eu.int.

5.5.4   The treaties setting up the Community and the Union

There are a number of treaties that are important for the setting up of the Community and the Union. They have been chronologically listed in Table 5.1, below, with their range of names, main purpose, and the type of treaty. This table should provide you with a useful and quick reference for future use. Following on from the table is a diagram (Figure 5.15, below) that sets out the treaties according to type and function rather than date. Considered together, Table 5.1 and the diagram in Figure 5.15 give a clear view of the main treaties establishing the Community and the Union.

Table 5.1: classification of internal treaties of the EC and their main provisions in chronological order

Year	Place of treaty	Formal title of treaty	EC provision	*Abbr	EU provision	Type of treaty
1951	Paris In force 27/7/52	Treaty establishing the European Coal and Steel Community	Sets up the European Coal and Steel Community	ECSC	Pre-dates Union	Founding treaty
1957	Rome In force 1/1/58	Treaty establishing the European Atomic Energy Community	Sets up the European Atomic Community	Euratom	Pre-dates Union	Founding treaty
1957	Rome In force 1/1/58	Treaty establishing the European Economic Community	Sets up the European Economic Community	EEC Treaty **now** EC Treaty	Pre-dates Union	Founding treaty
1965	Brussels In force 1/7/67	Treaty establishing a single Council and Commission of the European Communities	The institutions of the three Communities are merged but the Communities remain distinct	Merger Treaty	Pre-dates Union	Merger treaty
1973	– 22/1/72	Accession Treaty	Ireland, Denmark, UK join the three Communities	–	Pre-dates Union	Accession treaties
1980	Athens In force 1/1/81	Accession Treaty	Greece joins the three Communities	–	Pre-dates Union	Accession treaty
1985	–	Accession Treaty	Spain and Portugal join the three Communities	–	Pre-dates Union	Accession treaty

Year	Place of treaty	Formal title of treaty	EC provision	*Abbr	EU provision	Type of treaty
1986	London In force 1/2/87	Single European Act	Paves the way for a closer economic union for the single currency	SEA	Pre-dates Union	Amending treaty
1990	–	Accession Treaty	GDR joins the three Communities	–	Pre-dates Union	Accession treaty
1992	Maastricht In force	Treaty on European Union	Sets up the Court of Auditors	–	Establishes the EU and idea of the European citizen	Founding treaty of the EU and amends EC
1997	Amsterdam In force	Treaty on European Union	–	TEU	Continues the establishment of the EU	Amending treaty
2000	Nice	Treaty of Nice Amending the Treaty on European Union, the Treaties Establishing the European Communities and Certain Related Acts	–	–	Working towards establishing a charter of fundamental rights and paving way for the European constitution	Amending treaty

Figure 5.15: treaties establishing the European Community and the European Union

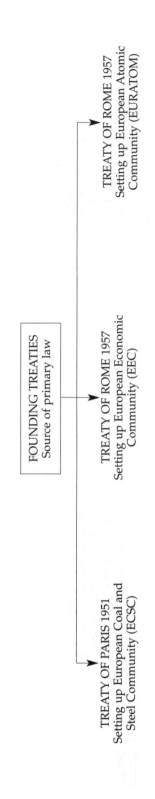

FOUNDING TREATIES
Source of primary law

TREATY OF PARIS 1951
Setting up European Coal and
Steel Community (ECSC)

TREATY OF ROME 1957
Setting up European Economic
Community (EEC)

TREATY OF ROME 1957
Setting up European Atomic
Community (EURATOM)

Notes:

The European Court, on a number of occasions, has stated that
one could consider the founding treaties as a constitution.

Founding members: France, West Germany, Italy, Belgium,
Holland, Luxembourg.

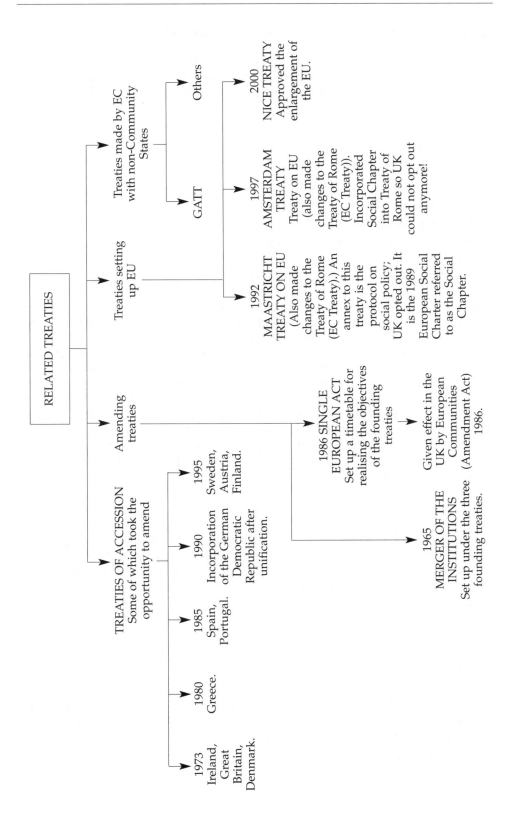

RELATED TREATIES

TREATIES OF ACCESSION
Some of which took the opportunity to amend

1973
Ireland, Great Britain, Denmark.

1980
Greece.

1985
Spain, Portugal.

1990
Incorporation of the German Democratic Republic after unification.

1995
Sweden, Austria, Finland.

Amending treaties

1986 SINGLE EUROPEAN ACT
Set up a timetable for realising the objectives of the founding treaties

Given effect in the UK by European Communities (Amendment Act) 1986.

1965
MERGER OF THE INSTITUTIONS
Set up under the three founding treaties.

Treaties setting up EU

1992
MAASTRICHT TREATY ON EU
(Also made changes to the Treaty of Rome (EC Treaty).) An annex to this treaty is the protocol on social policy; UK opted out. It is the 1989 European Social Charter referred to as the Social Chapter.

1997
AMSTERDAM TREATY
Treaty on EU (also made changes to the Treaty of Rome (EC Treaty)). Incorporated Social Chapter into Treaty of Rome so UK could not opt out anymore!

Treaties made by EC with non-Community States

GATT

Others

2000
NICE TREATY
Approved the enlargement of the EU.

5.5.5   The institutions of the European Community

The Treaty of Rome set up a range of institutions to make the European Community function. The number of institutions has steadily increased in the intervening decades and currently some of the most important and relevant for your purposes are:

- the European Parliament;
- the European Commission;
- the Council of Ministers;
- the European Court of Justice;
- the Court of Auditors;
- the European Central Bank (ECB);
- the European Investment Bank (EIB)

5.5.5.1 The European Council (now known as the Council of the European Union)

This is an important group and is often confused with the Council of Ministers (and of course the name makes it ripe for confusion with the Council of Europe discussed in 5.4.1.1, above, in relation to the ECHR). The Council of the European Union is made up of the heads of government of Member States with representatives from the Commission of the Union. Whilst such a group has been core in the idea of the Community from the beginning it is not part of the legal or executive institutions of the Union. It is purely composed of those with loyalty to the Member State but desiring to forward their own agenda alongside the Union. They meet twice a year or more if necessary and have the power to agree new treaties. What appears to be happening is that the Council of the European Union is exerting increasing power and influence on the policy of the Union whilst standing outside the institutions.

5.5.5.2 The important law making institutions

Several institutions within the EC have essential roles in the law making process either as initiators of legislation or with the authority to make law. You will, of course, learn about these in detail in English legal system, EU and public law courses. The main ones are as follows:

- the European Parliament;
- the European Commission;
- the Council of Ministers;
- the European Council;
- the ECB.

These areas will be covered in detail in specific subjects such as English legal system and constitutional law but they will be discussed briefly and sometimes illustrated with tables or diagrams for two reasons:

- to provide a quick overview that will hopefully aid reading set texts covering these areas; and

- to demonstrate the use of diagrams or tables to assist you in scanning a large amount of potentially complex information and beginning to understand the links between discrete areas of information. Often understanding develops as links between different areas of a topic become clear.

Try to carefully consider these diagrams rather than just skimming them.

Figure 5.16

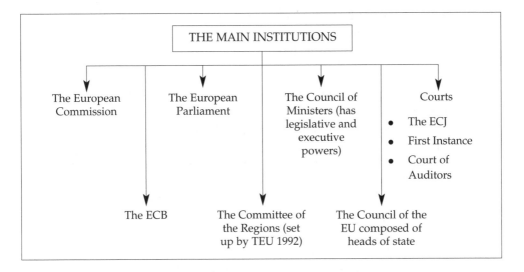

5.5.6 Sources of law in the European Community

European Community law

IS NOT

international law as NORMALLY understood or obligations between governments of states regulated by international law because Community law has the consequence that there is a limited transfer of sovereign rights from Member States to the Community, and the citizens of Member States also become citizens of the European Community.

European Community law

IS

- a distinct legal order that every Member of the Community is bound by on membership.
- a legal order known as the *'acquis communautaire'*.
- a legal order that is specifically referred to in the TEU 1997 (the Treaty of Amsterdam) which clearly states that the Union is committed to maintaining the full *acquis communautaire*.

5.5.7 Types of Community law (primary and secondary legislation and case law of the European Court of Justice)

There are several types of EC law each with *different* legal consequences. Some of the law that is developed in the Community immediately becomes part of the English legal system, other laws state a goal to be achieved within a timescale of years and the governments of the Member States are free to decide how best to comply with that law. Perhaps the choice of available types of law is one of the most difficult to understand when approaching the area for the first time. This chapter will run through the main issues and will be followed by a series of diagrams to assist your understanding.

Characteristics of EC law are as follows.

(1) It is of several types:

(a) Primary law – articles in treaties. The superior form of law.

(b) Secondary legislation:

- *Regulations*: addressed to all Member States.
- *Directives*: addressed to all Member States (which can appear as framework directives giving quite detailed guidance for changes to a large area).
- *Decisions*: addressed to named Member States and/or individuals and organisations.
- *Recommendations* (not legally binding).
- *Opinion* (not legally binding).

(c) Secondary law: decisions of the ECJ in individual cases and on matters referred to it as a preliminary reference with regard to interpretation of the Treaty of Rome. The legal authority for this power is found in Article 234 (formerly 177) of the Treaty of Rome.

(2) Community law is produced by different partnerships between the institutions: the Council, the Commission, the European Parliament; or by institutions with the authority acting alone: the Council, the Commission, the European Court. The Union website at www.europe.eu.int has guides to the creation of legislation and copies of all legislation and case law for the Union going back to the 1950s.

(3) Community law has varying degrees of:

- legal effect; and
- legal consequences,

depending on whether it is primary or secondary law. With regard to secondary legislation, it depends on what type of secondary legislation it is.

Some types of secondary legislation request that Member States ensure a goal is achieved within a timescale, leaving it up to the State to determine how the goal should be achieved. These types of legal rules are said to be binding as to 'outcome'.

Other types of secondary legislation immediately place legal obligations directly into the legal system of all Member States. These are *binding in their entirety* and said to be *directly applicable*. Still other types place legal obligations directly upon certain named States, individuals and organisations.

(4) The treaties, regulations and directives enacted by the Union do not directly state that they give individuals rights that they can enforce in their national courts. These legal rules are addressed in the first place to the Union and the Member State. Yet under the founding treaties Member States are expected to enforce the rights, liabilities and powers that are a consequence of membership in national courts. The ECJ has developed the concept of *direct effect* which describes EC primary or secondary law that give individuals rights that are enforceable in their national courts. Set criteria have to be present. Direct effect is easier to prove in relation to regulations than it is in relation to articles and directives.

The criteria demand that:

- the rule does not require any action from the State (and directives *do*); *and*

- that the right to be enforced is clear and precise and can be activated without recourse to the State (which is not the automatic case in relation to articles in a treaty concluded at State level or a directive issued to the State demanding certain outcomes within a timescale).

However, articles and directives considered on a case by case basis by the European and national courts *have* been held to give individuals rights. The case of *Van Gend en Loos* discussed later in this chapter deals with *direct applicability* and *direct effect* of articles.

(5) A major difficulty is caused by the lack of uniformity of terms in relation to '*directly applicable*' and '*direct effect*'.

'*Directly applicable*' is the phrase used in Article 249 (formerly 189) of the EC Treaty to refer to the process by which Community law of certain types is immediately and automatically part of the legal system of Member States as soon as it is created in the EC.

'*Direct effect*', which is not a phrase occurring in any of the treaties, is the phrase consistently used in the ECJ in two senses to refer to:

- the process by which individuals acquire rights they can enforce in national courts (against other individuals – horizontal direct effect, and against the State itself – vertical direct effect); *and*

- the process by which EC law is immediately and automatically part of the legal system of Member States as soon as it is created in the EC.

This *is* confusing, especially as some Community law that is created by Article 249 (formerly 177) of the EC Treaty is not said in the Treaty to be directly applicable in the sense of immediately and automatically becoming part of the legal system of Member States. Yet the ECJ has held that such law can, if certain criteria are present, have direct effect. In fact, they have gone one step further and constructed the concept of indirect effect. It is indirect precisely because the law is not directly applicable but somehow an individual can enforce it in a national court.

From a pragmatic point of view there is a need to accept this confusion, and seek to derive the meaning of the phrase from its context. Some legal academics advise forgetting the issue, which is like running away, and does create further confusion. The courts use the phrase synonymously. The EC Treaty, however, remains silent about individual rights in national courts and only uses the term 'direct applicability' to refer to the process by which EC law is immediately and automatically part of the legal system of Member States as soon as it is created in the EC.

For the purposes of explaining some of the issues surrounding EC law, this text will assume the artificial distinction between direct applicability and direct effect. It will assume therefore that 'directly applicable' applies to the process of automatic assimilation into the legal systems of Member States and that 'direct effect' refers to individuals deriving rights from Community law enforceable in national courts. Remember, however, that the terms tend to be conflated.

These matters will now be set out as a series of tables and diagrams to assist you in the development of understanding.

Table 5.2: main sources of secondary legislation, sources and effects

Primary	Source	Effect on Member State	Effect on individuals if criteria of precision, clarity, and lack of Member State action
Articles EC in treaties	Member States	Directly applicable	Direct effect
Secondary legislation	**Source institution**	**Effect on Member State**	**Effect on individuals if criteria of precision, clarity, and lack of Member State action**
Regulations	Council and Commission in consultation with the European Parliament	Article 249 (189) EC Treaty says regulations are directly applicable and binding in their entirety	Direct effect
Directives including framework directives	Council and Commission in consultation with the European Parliament	Article 249 (189) refers to directives but does not provide for them being directly applicable. Binding only as to outcome, with States given a certain timescale of 2–5 years	Capable of direct effect after the timescale for action by the Member State has been taken. This is referred to as indirect effect!
Decisions, including framework decisions	Commission	Article 249 (189) states they are directly applicable to those to whom they are addressed	Capable of direct effect
Recommendations	Commission	Article 249 (189) makes provision for them. Non-legally binding	No direct effect
Opinions	Commission	Article 249 (189) makes provision for them. Non-legally binding	No direct effect

Note: regulations, directives and decisions adopted under Article 234 (formerly 189) must be signed by the President of the European Parliament and the Council of Ministers or the European Commission and published in the *Official Journal*. Although they are published on the EU website, the published version is in the *Official Journal* (OJ). For an example drawn from a directive, see Figure 5.18, below, and note the signatories.

Figure 5.17: specimen directive for information as to layout

COUNCIL DIRECTIVE 2000/43/EC

of June 29th 2000

implementing the principle of equal treatment between persons irrespective of racial or ethnic origin

THE COUNCIL OF THE EUROPEAN UNION

Having regard to the Treaty establishing the European Community and in particular Article 13 thereof,

Having regard to the proposal from the Commission

Having regard to the opinion of the European Parliament

Having regard to the opinion of the Economic and Social Committee

Having regard to the opinion of the Committee of the Regions

Whereas

(1) The Treaty on European Union marks a new stage in the process of creating an ever closer union among the peoples of Europe

(2) In accordance with Article 6 of the Treaty on European Union, the European Union is founded on the principles of liberty, democracy, respect for human rights and fundamental freedoms, and the rule of law, principles which are common to the Member States, and should respect fundamental rights as guaranteed by the European Convention for the Protection of Human Rights and Fundamental Freedoms and as they result from the constitutional traditions common to Member States, as general principles of Community law.

[*Another 26 general paragraphs follow*]

CHAPTER 1

GENERAL PROVISIONS

Article 1   Purpose

The purpose of this Directive is to lay down a framework for combating discrimination on the grounds of racial or ethnic origin, with a view to putting into effect in the Member States the principle of equal treatment ...

Article 16   Implementation

Member States shall adopt the laws, regulations and administrative provisions necessary to comply with this Directive by July 19th 2003 or may entrust management and labour, at their joint request with the implementation of this Directive as regards provisions falling within the scope of collective agreements ...

Article 18   Entry into force

This Directive shall enter into force on the day of its publication in the Official Journal of the European Communities.

Article 19   Addressees

This Directive is addressed to the Member States.

Figure 5.18: the different types of secondary laws

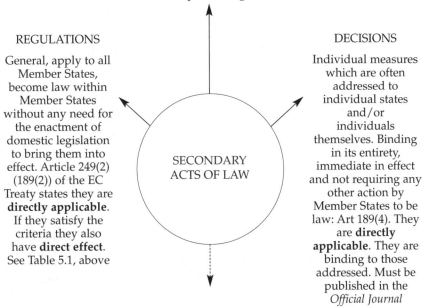

DIRECTIVES

Ask for a specific result within a timescale of one to three years. Addressed to **all**, **one** or **some** Member States. Member State has to take such action as it considers is necessary to ensure that the desired result is achieved. Binding in so far as it prescribes an outcome within a timescale. Not **directly applicable** (Art 249(3) (189(3)) of the EC Treaty). They can have **vertical direct effect** when timescale for government implementation has passed. TEU 1992 amended Art 191(2) of the EC Treaty and directives must now be published in the *Official Journal*. Article 169 of the EC Treaty allows Commission to commence enforcement proceedings for default

REGULATIONS

General, apply to all Member States, become law within Member States without any need for the enactment of domestic legislation to bring them into effect. Article 249(2) (189(2)) of the EC Treaty states they are **directly applicable**. If they satisfy the criteria they also have **direct effect**. See Table 5.1, above

SECONDARY ACTS OF LAW

DECISIONS

Individual measures which are often addressed to individual states and/or individuals themselves. Binding in its entirety, immediate in effect and not requiring any other action by Member States to be law: Art 189(4). They are **directly applicable**. They are binding to those addressed. Must be published in the *Official Journal*

RECOMMENDATIONS AND OPINIONS IN RELATION TO THE OPERATION OF COMMUNITY LAW

These have no immediate legal force. May be persuasive. The ECJ however has said that Member States should take them into account when deciding issues such as ambiguity in domestic law. Article 211C (formerly 155)

Note: Article 190 EC Treaty now requires that each legally binding Act contains a statement of reasons on which the law is based. It is possible for there to be inter-institutional disagreement on the basis of the law!

5.5.8 Principles of European Community law

Like all legal systems the legal order of the Community has developed certain principles that inform the interpretation and, to a certain extent, the creation of law. These principles are set out in diagrammatic form in Figure 5.20, below.

5.5.9 Legislative competency of European Community law

The legal order only has the power to make law in the areas given to it. This is its area of legal competency. Figure 5.20, below, sets these out in diagrammatic form.

Figure 5.19: legislative competency of the EC (now EU)

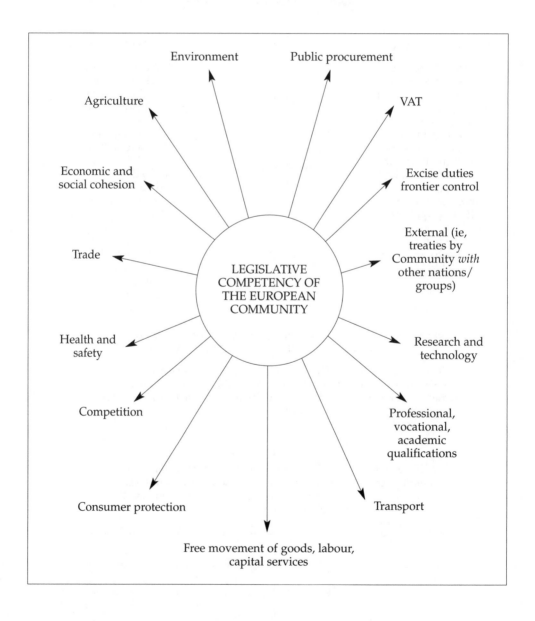

Figure 5.20: principles upon which law making takes place

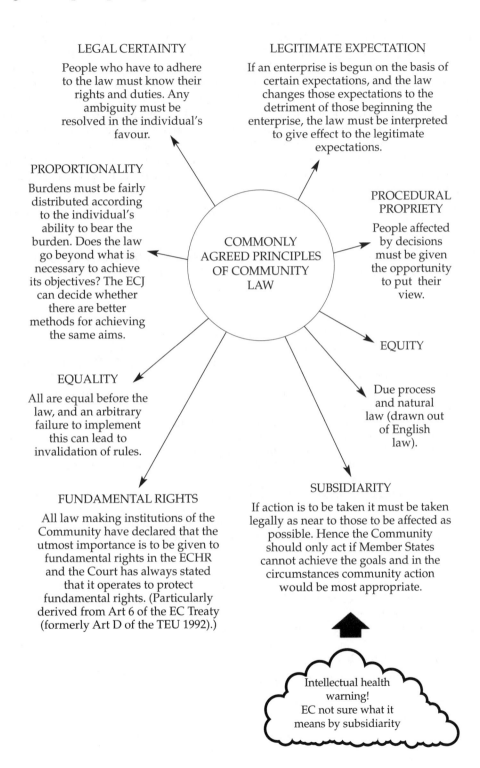

LEGAL CERTAINTY

People who have to adhere to the law must know their rights and duties. Any ambiguity must be resolved in the individual's favour.

LEGITIMATE EXPECTATION

If an enterprise is begun on the basis of certain expectations, and the law changes those expectations to the detriment of those beginning the enterprise, the law must be interpreted to give effect to the legitimate expectations.

PROPORTIONALITY

Burdens must be fairly distributed according to the individual's ability to bear the burden. Does the law go beyond what is necessary to achieve its objectives? The ECJ can decide whether there are better methods for achieving the same aims.

COMMONLY AGREED PRINCIPLES OF COMMUNITY LAW

PROCEDURAL PROPRIETY

People affected by decisions must be given the opportunity to put their view.

EQUITY

EQUALITY

All are equal before the law, and an arbitrary failure to implement this can lead to invalidation of rules.

Due process and natural law (drawn out of English law).

FUNDAMENTAL RIGHTS

All law making institutions of the Community have declared that the utmost importance is to be given to fundamental rights in the ECHR and the Court has always stated that it operates to protect fundamental rights. (Particularly derived from Art 6 of the EC Treaty (formerly Art D of the TEU 1992).)

SUBSIDIARITY

If action is to be taken it must be taken legally as near to those to be affected as possible. Hence the Community should only act if Member States cannot achieve the goals and in the circumstances community action would be most appropriate.

Intellectual health warning! EC not sure what it means by subsidiarity

5.5.10   Common confusions

As noted at the beginning of this section, from a technical point of view one of the main problems confronting students is getting a grip on the name changes that have occurred. In addition, the articles in the founding Treaty of Rome have had their numbering changed, as the Treaty of Amsterdam sought to regularise the changes brought about by various amendments (including alphabetical amendments made by the TEU 1992). This has impacted at the very basic level of textbooks. Books prior to 1993 will have a different set of names to those after and books between 1993 and 1997 will not reflect the number changes. At present books referring to the articles in the Treaty of Rome use the following method: the *new* number of the article in the newly named treaty is given, with the *old* article number in brackets immediately after. For example, Article 249 (189) EC Treaty and in some cases the texts will only refer to the EC Treaty as EC.

Figure 5.21, below, puts some of these confusions together to assist in defusing confusion!

Figure 5.21: name and numbering changes introduced by the Treaty of European Union (TEU 1992), also known as the Treaty of Maastricht

(1) The European Economic Community was renamed the European Community.
(2) The founding treaty of the EEC, the Treaty of Rome 1957 that had come to be called the European Economic Community Treaty (or EEC Treaty as customarily abbreviated) was renamed the European Community Treaty (or EC Treaty as it is now customarily abbreviated).
(3) Sometimes in texts you will find references to articles, however, as (10EC) when the author has dropped the word 'treaty'.
(4) TEU 1992 inserted articles in the Treaty of Rome. This was mainly effected by using alphabetical indicators A, B etc with subdivisions within the ALPHA runs. Textbooks prior to 1993 refer to the old numbering; textbooks since either refer to the new numbering with the old in brackets or to only the new numbering so do check the publication date of your text.
(5) Major numbering changes to the Treaty of Rome were introduced by the Treaty of European Union (TEU 1997), also know as the Treaty of Amsterdam 1997. The numbering of the articles of the Treaty of Rome was completely revised. Books and articles tend at present to use the new number with the old in brackets.

Demonstration
- 10EC (formerly 5) = Article 5 of the Treaty of Rome 1957 or the European Economic Community Treaty as amended by TEU 1992 (the name changes) and TEU 1997 (the number changes)!
- 10 (5) EC Treaty could also be used instead of 10EC (5).
(5) Confusion can be caused when reading cases in the ECJ and books prior to the number and name changes.

This demonstrates the importance of understanding changes and abbreviations.

Other common confusions – NAMES:

The Council of Europe, the European Council, the Council of the European Union and the Council of Ministers. Some confusions are just caused because names are so similar. These have to be learn and differentiated:

- The European Council:

  Now renamed

  Name given to the meetings of the HEADS of GOVERNMENT of members of the European Union. THE COUNCIL OF THE EUROPEAN UNION in 1992.

- The Council of Ministers:

  Name given to PERMANENT body of GOVERNMENT REPRESENTATIVES that changes according to the issues debated (eg, agriculture, free movement of workers, taxation).

- The Council of Europe:

  The body established to protect fundamental rights of peoples – it has NO connection to the European Community or the European Union. *However,* those States who are members of the Council of Europe are also members of the EC and the EU. However, there are also members of the Council of Europe who are NOT members of the EC and EU. ALL of the candidate countries, for example, are members of the Council of Europe.

In addition some names have been substituted by custom and practice rather than clear statement. For example, the institutions of the EU are the same as the institutions of the EC. Often they now refer to themselves as institutions of the EU carrying out their EU competency. So the recent Race Directive (due to be implemented by 2003) states it is commissioned by the Council of the European Union but it is secondary law with the legal competency of the EC. So the reference of the directive is Council 2000/43/EC.

Figure 5.22, below, shows how to break down an essential complex treaty. From the information given in this chapter try to construct two other diagrams: one for the Treaty on European Union 1997 (the Treaty of Amsterdam) and one for the Treaty of Nice 2000.

Figure 5.22: the Maastricht Treaty – changes

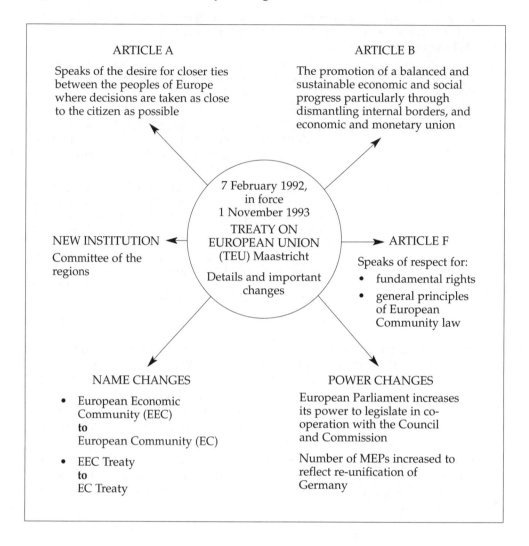

ARTICLE A

Speaks of the desire for closer ties between the peoples of Europe where decisions are taken as close to the citizen as possible

ARTICLE B

The promotion of a balanced and sustainable economic and social progress particularly through dismantling internal borders, and economic and monetary union

7 February 1992, in force 1 November 1993
TREATY ON EUROPEAN UNION (TEU) Maastricht
Details and important changes

NEW INSTITUTION

Committee of the regions

ARTICLE F

Speaks of respect for:

- fundamental rights
- general principles of European Community law

NAME CHANGES

- European Economic Community (EEC)
  to
  European Community (EC)

- EEC Treaty
  to
  EC Treaty

POWER CHANGES

European Parliament increases its power to legislate in co-operation with the Council and Commission

Number of MEPs increased to reflect re-unification of Germany

5.5.11 The issue of the supremacy of Community law over English law

Now that you have a reasonably secure but basic knowledge and understanding of the Community it is appropriate to turn to a discussion of the particular legal and constitutional changes to the English legal system and the English constitution caused by the political act of the UK joining the EC in 1973.

Article 10 of the EC Treaty (formerly Article 5), stated that Member States of the Community had to ensure compliance with Community law. Much of it was also intended to have an immediate effect in Member States as soon as it was created in the institutions of the Community (remember the same institutions now serve the Union). In other words, it should automatically enter the legal system of Member States.

Article 10 of the EC Treaty (formerly Article 5) provides that Member States:

take all appropriate measures, whether general or particular to ensure fulfilment of the obligations arising out of this treaty or resulting from action taken by the institutions of the Community. They shall facilitate the achievement of the Community's tasks [Article 10 (formerly Article 5)].

This Article was a major problem for the English legal system as there was no mechanism for ensuring this constitutionally.

The European Community's primary law was created by founding treaties and the source of all forms of secondary Community law is derived from these treaties. The European Court has stated that one could consider the founding treaties of the three Communities together with appropriate changes in the related treaties as a 'constitution', because these treaties represent the supreme internal source of primary law and the facilitation of secondary law making.

The EC Treaty provides that the breach of any article by a Member State can result in action brought in the ECJ either by any other Member State, or by the European Commission. *Costa v ENEL* (Case 6/64) (a landmark case) stated in no uncertain terms that:

The treaty has created its own legal system which, on entry into force of the treaty, became an integral part of the legal systems of the Member States and which their courts are bound to apply. [A phrase that is known as the 'Costa principle'.]

Furthermore in the leading EC case of the *Commission v Italy* (Case 48/71) the ECJ declared that:

if a national law is incompatible with European Law then all national bodies and national courts in the relevant Member State are to automatically cease to enforce that law.

The supremacy of European Community law has been established therefore from two perspectives:

(a) EC law is supreme over national law.

(b) Member States must have *processes* whereby the individual can claim the protection of EC law. (The right without the possibility of effective enforcement is useless!)

The issue of the Member State possessing effective process so that individuals can claim the protection of EC law was the core issue in another leading case that splintered into a range of cases with the same litigants dealing with the application and enforcement of EC law at national level. These cases are known collectively as the Factortame cases. These are discussed in more detail below.

In the *Commission v The UK relating to the case of R v Secretary of State for Transport ex p Factortame* (Case 213/89), the ECJ ruled that limited national remedies cannot be allowed to restrict the access to legal rights in EC law, meaning that national State's legal competence 'at home' is now limited by Community law. However, it is only limited in those areas of Community legal competence when domestic/national law conflicts with EC law (see Figure 5.19).

5.5.12　The relationship between Community law, the Union and the English legal system

The wording of Article 10 of the EC Treaty (formerly Article 5) is uncompromising and in order to comply with it the UK enacted the ECA 1972 to incorporate the Treaty of Rome into UK law. Again, these areas will be studied in detail in substantive subject areas, but in brief the key section is s 2 which among other things provides that:

> where Community treaties give rise to rights, powers, liabilities, and obligations these shall be recognised in UK courts along with any remedies and procedures provided by the treaties. Provision is made for the Queen by an Order in Council (or a minister by regulation) to make provisions for implementing Community obligations.

Note the delegation to a minister and the use of statutory delegated legislation signalled by the phrase 'Order in Council'. This means that Parliament does not have to be involved. No such fast track power is given in the area of taxation, delegated legislation, creation of new criminal offences with certain punishments, or retrospectivity (making lawful action unlawful and backdating the operation of the law). In these cases, Parliament itself must enact legislation.

Community law impinges in several ways on our reading of English law. It is expected, for example, that in certain situations an English court, or any domestic court, considering an important point of Community law will refer to the European Court for a preliminary ruling as to the correct interpretation of the treaty. Under Article 234 (formerly 177) of the EC Treaty, courts from which there is no recognised national appeal *have to ask* for a preliminary ruling from the ECJ. Other courts where there is an appeal *may ask* for a preliminary ruling. This gives an important power to the ECJ to ensure uniformity in the development of Community law and the official interpretation of the treaties.

The decisions of the ECJ have a real impact on the understanding and application of law. The ECJ has an overarching duty and right to have all matters relating to the legal interpretation of articles or protocols referred to it from the domestic courts of Member States. As the supreme court in the EC, its decisions determine how EC law is applied and interpreted in English courts dealing with EC issues.

In addition, it hears disputes concerning infringement of articles, protocols and law of the Community. Parties with the right to bring cases include the following:

(a) Institutions of the EC can bring cases between each other.

(b) The Commission can bring cases against Member States.

(c) Member States can bring cases against other Member States and institutions of the EC.

(d) Individual citizens of Member States who are also concurrently European Citizens can bring actions against the EC, its institutions, their own State or other Member States in areas where the law has given them this right.

The next part of this section explores the role of the ECJ in more detail through the reading of a case.

The following diagram explains the way in which Community law enters the English legal system. The detail of this will be explored in your substantive law course.

Figure 5.23: main types of EC law

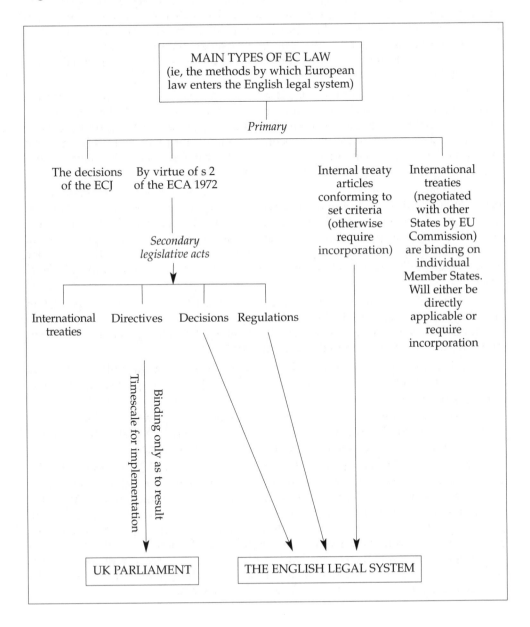

5.5.13   How to handle Community law reports

It is now important to sum this section up by looking at the issues surrounding the reading of Community law reports and reflecting on the development of reading skills. All legal systems have some appreciation and acknowledgment of precedent. The Community legal order is an artificially created legal system that draws on the legal systems of the Member States for the establishment of approaches to interpretation and law making in relevant areas. The majority of Member States operate from a Civil Code legal system unlike the UK's preference for a common law system. Because of the familiarity of most Member States with civil law systems and the fact that all of the founding members were nation States with civil law systems, the European Community's legal system is deeply embedded in the civil system.

In the English law's common law tradition, the legal theory underpinning the practical approach to decision making in the law courts is the declaratory theory. This states that when a judge in court is deciding a case he declares in his decision what the law *is*. The case can then become an important precedent, as it states the law and determines when other courts must follow it. One case can determine and preset the law within the limits of the doctrine of precedent.

In civil law systems codes are used to organise areas of law. All civil systems are based in different ways on Roman law where the legal theory position is that when a judge in a court makes a decision about the law, that decision is *evidence* of the law. The ECJ, not surprisingly, when setting up legal principles that apply across all cases, drew upon the legal experience of all Nation States, but the minority approach of the English legal system is not the approach in the Community legal order.

As you will remember from Chapter 3, in the English common law system decisions of the courts are the law, rather than evidence of what it is thought to be. Through the system of precedent in the English legal system, previous court cases and law cases are presented to the court as precedents.

But this is not the case in the ECJ where arguments consider other cases and other documents and practices in order to present what may seem appropriate principles of the law.

It should have been apparent from the previous chapter and the discussion in that chapter on the doctrine of precedent that English law, despite its theoretically rigid binding nature, is extremely flexible in the mouths of judges.

It may seem odd that there is a lack of precedent in the ECJ. But the ECJ has a determination to carefully develop and keep legal principles which do give a great deal of consistency and coherence to Community law. Commentators have noted that it has now become normal and accepted for courts to refer to earlier cases and use these earlier cases as the rationale for decisions, which begins to feel like precedent. However, even given these suggestions of openness to the concept of precedent there is no suggestion that the ECJ would ever reach a decision that it did not want to purely because of other cases deciding matters differently. The reverse could, however, occur in the English legal system.

5.5.14   Understanding law reports from the European Court of Justice

When you read ECJ reports – unless you are reading them in French – you will be reading a translation, for French is the working language of the court and the French judicial style is the commonly accepted model. You will find short sentences with facts, arguments and final conclusions. The language is formal and characterless in contrast to English judgments, which take on the linguistic style of the particular judge. There are no judgments disagreeing and only one judgment reflecting the opinion of the Court. Indeed, judges are sworn to secrecy over disagreements!

Instead of reading a judgment that is conducting a reasoned argument one tends to find the listing of ultimate conclusions as assertions.

Figure 5.24: layout of a Community case

Text:

Sets out in simple paragraphs the procedural background and the questions before the ECJ.

Judgment:
- Issues of fact and law are set out.
- Facts of the case: court sets out the facts.
- Arguments and observations: here the court gives a precis of the arguments presented by all involved parties.
- Grounds of judgment: the court begins its determination.
- Costs.
- Formal finding of the court.

5.6   TASK: THE CASE OF *VAN GEND EN LOOS v NEDERLANDSE TARIEFCOMMISSIE* (CASE 26/62) [1963] CMLR 105

5.6.1   The purpose of the task

The purpose of this task is to enable the development of confidence in reading EC law reports and to test how far you have understood the aspects of EC law discussed in this chapter. For example, the case uses the old names and numbering of the EC Treaty. Can you automatically 'translate' these or at least know what has changed even if you have to look it up. Are the words and phrases used familiar and understandable (for example, 'directly applicable', and 'direct effect')?

Part of the initial difficulty in reading a European law report is the necessity to read it being aware of, and sensitive to, a number of pieces of information:

(a) the status of the Community court and its jurisdiction;

(b) the authority of the ECJ within the English legal system.

(c) familiarity with the terminology for describing differing Community law (articles, regulations, directives, etc);

(d) the relationship between differing Community rights and obligations;

(e) following and considering the arguments put forward;

(f) a consideration of the impact of the case on Community law and the English legal system.

This reading gives you an opportunity to see where you are in your understanding of these matters. *Van Gend en Loos* was decided early in the development of Community law and remains a leading case on the potential legal effect of an article in one of the founding treaties in the legal system of Member States.

5.6.2   The initial reading

It is always a good idea to quickly read documents before a more considered reading, as long as you know why you are reading them. So, please now turn to Appendix 2 and read the case quickly (note that the numbers in brackets from (1)–(97) have been placed in the case to assist you with later work on it. Just ignore them for now). Once you have read the case quickly and have a general idea of what it is about, read it a second time, more slowly, and then answer the following questions:

(1) In no more than 50 words, state the facts of the case (the fewer words the better).

(2) What does *Vand Gend en Loos* want the court to allow?

(3) What has to be decided before *Vand Gend en Loos* can get what they want?

(4) What is the rationale behind the decision?

(5) What are the legal issues in the case?

(6) Do you find the language of the case difficult, or the case itself difficult to read? Give reasons for your answer.

5.6.3   The second reading: the tabulated micro-analysis of the case

What you may have noticed in your reading of the case and subsequent answering of the questions is that the language of the law report is very different in style to that of an English law report. You are reading a translation of the working language of the EU, which is French not English, although all languages have equal status within the Community. What you will have immediately noticed is that the report reads as a series of descriptions and assertions. You will not find the reasoned, illustrative argumentative techniques that are the more familiar to the common law lawyer. Think, for example, of the case of *Mandla v Dowell Lee* [1983] 1 All ER 162 or *George Mitchell (Chesterhall) Ltd v Finney Lock Seeds* [1983] 2 All ER 732–44.

To assist you to methodically engage with this case, it has been broken down into a table style format that takes you through each paragraph. The paragraphs have been numbered in the table according to the bracketed numbers that have been inserted into the text in Appendix 3 so that you can read the actual paragraph as well as its précis in the table. This should be useful as you can see a steady demonstration of summarising dense or technical text. In addition, a classification of the function of each paragraph is given under headings such as:

- descriptive;
- setting out facts;
- procedural;
- conclusion;
- proposition or point in an argument;
- inference,

because internally identifying the function of an argument is part of the way that one is able to start to organise a text in terms of its arguments and its proofs. The layout of the table is therefore as follows.

Heading	Para nos	Précis of paras	Classification of paras
eg facts	eg (1)	eg text summarising	eg procedural

You will be able to see how the text builds up to a final decision. You should be able to clearly see the arguments and have a view yourself on the outcome.

Work through this text slowly. Where necessary refer back to diagrams or tables in the rest of this chapter that may help you. You will find the task completes the purpose of this chapter by giving a firm basis for reading law reports resting on the complex issues discussed. You should be checking the original paragraph to see if you would have made a correct précis.

From the text, tables, diagrams and tasks in this chapter you should have been able to acquire a firm foundation for your analysis of this area in your other subjects.

> Note: it is important to realise that critique is only as good as your initial comprehension of the issues, rules, facts and arguments in the text (in other words, you cannot run before you can walk!).

Table 5.3: tabulated micro-analysis of *Van Gend en Loos*

Headings	Paragraph nos	Précis of paragraph	Classification of paragraph
Text	2–3	Reference for a preliminary ruling, ruling, under Art 177, para 1(a) and para 3 of the EEC Treaty from the Tariefcommissie, the final court of jurisdiction in revenue cases in the Netherlands. **NOTE:** the EEC Treaty refers to the Treaty of Rome 1957 setting up the European Community. Since the Treaty of Maastricht 1995, this Treaty is now referred to as the EC Treaty.	Descriptive: the legal basis of the case in the ECJ.
	4–6	States questions for preliminary ruling: (1) Is Art 12 of the EEC Treaty directly applicable and can individuals make a claim in their own domestic courts under Art 12? (2) If the answer to question (1) is 'yes', was the application of an import duty in breach of Art 12 or was it a reasonable alteration as allowed by Art 12?	Descriptive: issues to be determined by the ECJ.
The Court **Note how sentences flow into and out of headings.**	5	President Presidents of Chambers (2) Rapporteurs (2) Judges (2) Advocate General Registrar **NOTE:** the Advocate General is always asked to give an opinion in major cases. He operates as the *conscience* of the Court but does not have to be listened to. However, his opinion is published and can, on occasion, be seen as a type of dissenting opinion.	Descriptive: Court personnel.

Headings	Paragraph nos	Précis of paragraph	Classification of paragraph
Judgment, facts and procedure	6	9 September 1960 Van Gend en Loos imported urea-formaldehyde into the Netherlands from the Federal Republic of Germany describing it as 'Harnstoffharz (UF resin) 70, Aqueous emulsion of ureaformal-dehyde'. Customs declaration 8 September 1960.	Description: the facts.
	7	The Tariefbesluit in force since 1 March 1960 classified the product under 39.01-a-1, headed according to a protocol between Belgium and the Netherlands of 25 July 1958 and ratified in law, in the Netherlands, 16 December 1959.	Description: facts continued.
	8	Specifies the duty for emulsion at 8%.	Description: facts continued.
	9	8% charged.	Description: facts continued.
	10	20 September 1960 Van Gend en Loos lodges an objection with Inspector of Customs and Excise against application of the duty.	Description: procedure.
	11	Van Gend en Loos argues that on 1 January 1958 (the date in force of the EEC Treaty) the classification was 279-a-2 in the Tariefbesluit of 1947 and the duty 3%. The Tariefbesluit of 1 March 1960 heading 279-a-2 replaced by heading 39-01-a-1.	Point in argument to inspector.
	12	The Tariefbesluit created a sub-division in what was 279-a-2 for amino-plasts in aqueous emulsions of 8%. The rest were charged at 3%. So all is not the same.	Continuation of point to inspector.
	13	By increasing the import duty after the EEC Treaty in force the Dutch Government had infringed Art 12 which says that Member States cannot between themselves introduce any new customs duties or increase those already in existence.	Conclusion of argument to inspector.

Headings	Paragraph nos	Précis of paragraph	Classification of paragraph
	14	6 March 1961: objection of Van Gend en Loos dismissed by the inspector on grounds of inadmissibility. It was complaining not about *how* tariff *applied* but *how* it was *set*.	Point in argument and conclusion to inspector.
	15	4 April 1961: Van Gend appeals to the Tariefcommissie.	Procedure.
	16	Van Gend presents same arguments as in paras 11–13 above to Tariefcommissie. Netherland's argument was that when the EEC Treaty came into force, the product concerned was not under 279-a-2 but 332 and that was now charged at 10%, so there was no increase.	Argument of Van Gend en Loos. Argument of Netherlands.
	17	Tariefcommissie did not formally decide if product within 279-a-2 or 332 of the 1947 list. They said parties raised issues concerning the interpretation of the EEC Treaty and proceedings were suspended and the matter referred to the ECJ on 16 August 1962 under Art 177.	Procedure of Tariefcommissie in asking for a preliminary ruling.
	18	23 August 1962: decision of the Tariefcommissie given to the parties, the Member States and Commission of EEC.	Procedure: notification of interested and affected parties.
	19	Written observations were submitted by: • parties to the main action; • Belgium Government; • German Government; • Commission of EEC; • Government of the Netherlands. **NOTE:** any interested Member State can submit written observations.	Procedure.
	20	29 November 1962: oral submission of Van Gend en Loos heard and views of EEC Commission heard. Questions put to them by Court and written replies given.	Procedure in ECJ.

Headings	Paragraph nos	Précis of paragraph	Classification of paragraph
	21	12 December 1962: Advocate General gives his reasoned oral opinion, stating that the ECJ can only answer question (1) put to it by the Tariefcommissie and hold that Art 12 imposes a duty only on Member States. **NOTE:** see paras 4–6 above.	Procedure: opinion of Advocate General in ECJ.
Eleven arguments and obser-vation	22	Refers to the arguments in para 19 above and says summarised.	Information.
The first question: in issue admis-sibility	23	The government of the Netherlands and tax authority are in agreement and confirmed that the main complaint was that they had infringed Art 12.	Argument: agreement on the point.
	24	Dutch government states that an individual cannot have the right to bring an action concerning infringement of the treaty. Only Member States *or* the Commission can do this under Arts 169–70 and that individual cannot seek a preliminary ruling.	Point in argument of the Dutch government.
	25	Dutch government says ECJ cannot decide this issue because it is not about interpretation, but application.	Point in argument of the Dutch government.
	26	Belgian government says first question is a reference to the Court of a problem of constitutional law and therefore falls exclusively within the jurisdiction of Netherlands courts.	Point in argument of Belgian government.
	27	The Court states that it has two international treaties, both part of national law. It needs to decide under national law which treaty prevails if they conflict. Does the earlier prevail?	Court stating issues.
	28	Question is a typical question of national constitutional law within the exclusive jurisdiction of national law and has nothing to do with interpretation of the EEC Treaty.	Point in argument of Belgian government.

Headings	Paragraph nos	Précis of paragraph	Classification of paragraph
	29	Decision on first question unnecessary for Tariefcommissie to give judgment but cannot have any influence on the solution to the problem.	Point in argument of Belgian government.
	30	Whatever the ECJ says the Tarief-commissie has the same problem to solve. Can it ignore the law of 16 December 1959 ratifying protocol because it conflicts with the law of 5 December 1957 ratifying the EEC Treaty?	Point in argument of Belgian government.
	31	So, question raised is not appropriate for a preliminary ruling because the answer cannot enable the Tariefcommissie to make a final decision.	Conclusion of argument of Belgian government.
	32	EEC Commission observed that it is not up to the national court to determine the effect of the EEC Treaty. The problem is indeed one of interpretation.	Point in argument of EEC Commission.
	33	EEC Commission says if there is a finding of inadmissible then individuals would not be protected from infringement by Member States.	Point in argument of EEC Commission.
On the substance	34	Van Gend en Loos argues that Art 12 has direct applicability. It also has direct effect without the need for national law to give the right. Infringement of Art 12 affects fundamental principles of Community and individual also needs protection. Article 12 is well suited for direct application and national court must set aside custom duties in breach of it.	Argument and conclusion of Van Gend en Loos before the ECJ.
	35	EEC Commission says answer to question (1) is important and will affect interpretation and effect of Art 12 in the legal systems of other Member States and other clear articles regarding the principle of direct applicability.	Point in argument of Commission before ECJ.

Headings	Paragraph nos	Précis of paragraph	Classification of paragraph
	36	EEC Commission states that an analysis of the Treaty shows that there was an intention by Member States to create a legal system of Community law and that it should apply in national courts.	Point in argument of EEC Commission.
	37	Community law must be effectively and uniformly applied throughout the whole of the Community.	Point in argument of EEC Commission.
	38	Internal effect of Community law cannot be decided internally. Only Commission can do this and Community law must prevail.	Point in argument by EEC Commission.
	39	Just because Community law is directed to the State it does not mean that an individual with an interest cannot apply to the Court.	Point in argument by EEC Commission.
	40	Commission believes that Art 12 contains a rule of law capable of being the subject of an effective application to a national court.	Point in argument by EEC Commission.
	41	Provisions are clear – they create a specific, unambiguous obligation not affected by other articles. It is self-sufficient and does not require any Community action to make the obligation clear.	Point in argument by EEC Commission.
	42	Dutch Government draws a distinction between (1) internal effect (**NOTE:** what we now refer to as direct applicability) and (2) direct effect, Says (1) is a prerequisite for (2).	Point in argument of the Dutch government.
	43	Can only have internal effect (that is, direct applicability) if it is the intention of the contracting parties and terms and conditions allow it.	Point in argument of the Dutch government.
	44	Wording only puts obligation on Member States who are free to decide how they intend to fulfil obligations.	Point in argument of the Dutch government.
	45	It does not have internal effect, it can have direct effect.	Point in argument of the Dutch government.

Headings	Paragraph nos	Précis of paragraph	Classification of paragraph
	46	Even if it did have internal effect it cannot have direct effect.	Point in argument of the Dutch government.
	47	Alternatively, treaty does not differ from a standard international treaty. The conclusive factors remain intention of the parties and provisions of the treaty.	Point in argument of the Dutch government.
	48	Whether Art 12 is directly applicable is one of interpretation of Netherlands law and not in the jurisdiction of the ECJ.	Point in argument of the Dutch government.
	49	If it was held that Art 12 applied internally and had direct effect it would upset the system created by treaty – creating uncertainty in law and the responsibility of States could be put in issue by means of a procedure that was never intended.	Point in argument of the Dutch government.
	50	Article 12 is not an exception and does not have direct internal effect.	Conclusion of argument of Belgian government.
	51	Article 12 is not a rule of law of general applicability saying that any new duty is without effect. It says members should refrain from imposing new duties.	Point in argument of Belgian government.
	52	Article 12 does not create directly applicable rights for individuals. Government asked to obtain a goal. National courts cannot be asked to enforce it.	Point in argument of Belgian government.
	53	Article 12 is not directly applicable. It imposes international obligations which need to be nationally implemented.	Point in argument of German government.
	54	Customs duties only come from Nation States not EEC Treaty.	Point in argument of German government.
	55	Obligation only applies to other contracting Member States.	Point in argument of German government.
	56	In German law, a provision contrary to Art 12 would be valid.	Point in argument of German government.

Headings	Paragraph nos	Précis of paragraph	Classification of paragraph
	57	Only measures taken by the institutions protect nationals which are of direct or individual concern to nationals.	Point in argument of German government.
The second question: admissibility	58	Netherlands and Belgium Governments say second question is inadmissible.	Conclusion of argument of Belgian and the Dutch governments.
	59	Article 177 procedure inappropriate to explain issues raised in questions.	Argument of Belgian and Dutch governments.
	60	If a State can be brought before the ECJ outside Arts 169/170, the legal protection of States would be diminished.	Point in argument of Dutch government.
	61	Article only created state obligation so ECJ under Art 177 cannot decide issues of conflict.	Point in argument of German government.
	62	Van Gend en Loos says that the direct form of question (2) needs an examination of facts for which the Court has no jurisdiction under Art 177.	Conclusion of argument of Van Gend en Loos.
	63	The real question should be 'can it be said moving from rules before 1 March 1960 that it is not an increase even though it is an arithmetical increase'.	Point in argument of Van Gend en Loos.
Grounds of judgment Procedure	64	Tariefcommissie did not make objection to reference. And there are no grounds for the ECJ to do so.	Procedure: comment by ECJ.
The first question: raised by jurisdiction of the court	65	Discuss argument of Belgium and Netherlands Governments challenging the jurisdiction of ECJ to determine whether EEC Treaty prevails over Netherlands legislation. Only national courts can be subjected to application in accordance with Arts 169–70	Point in argument of ECJ dealing with issues Belgian and Dutch governments.

Headings	Paragraph nos	Précis of paragraph	Classification of paragraph
	66	ECJ is not asked to decide on applicability of Treaty according to national law. It is interpreting the scope of Art 12 within the context of Community law in conformity with Art 177. So the argument put forward by the two governments has no foundation.	Conclusion of argument of ECJ to point raised on jurisdiction by Belgian and Dutch governments.
	67	Belgium states that ECJ has no jurisdiction because no answer by ECJ would have a bearing on Tariefcommissie answer to the issues before it.	ECJ notes point in argument of Belgian government.
	68	Belgium further argues that to get jurisdiction the question raised has to be clearly interpretational. ECJ cannot review why question asked in certain ways.	Point in argument of ECJ in response to issues raised by Belgian government.
	69	Wording relates to the Treaty, therefore, there is jurisdiction. The argument concerning lack of jurisdiction is unfounded.	Conclusion of argument of ECJ.
On the substance of the case	70	The Court restates question (1). Has Art 12 direct applicability in national law in the sense that nationals may lay claim?	Information: restatement of first issue.
	71	Considers the spirit, schema and wording of the Article to find the answer.	Point in argument of ECJ.
	72	Objective of Treaty is a Common Market which implies Treaty is more than an agreement of mutual obligations. Preamble to the Treaty speaks of government and peoples. Institutions established who affect nationals.	Point in argument of ECJ.
	73	Article 177 confirms that States have acknowledged that Community law can be invoked by nationals in national courts.	Point in argument of ECJ.
	74	Community constitutes a new legal order. States have limited sovereignty in certain areas and nationals, independently of the legislation of Member States, have rights/ obligations granted by the treaty.	Conclusion of point argued by ECJ.

Headings	Paragraph nos	Précis of paragraph	Classification of paragraph
	75	Article 9 bases Community on a customs union, prohibits custom duties. It is at the beginning of defining the Community and is applied and explained by Art 12.	Description of relation ship between Art 9 and Art 12.
	76	Wording of Art 12 creates a clear and unconditional negative obligation. Nothing for States to do. Article is ideal for direct effect in relationship between Member States and their subjects.	Point in the argument of ECJ.
	77	Article 12 does not require any legislation by Member States. Nationals can benefit from a negative obligation.	Point in argument of ECJ.
	78	Argument put forward on Arts 169–70 by the governments giving observations was misconceived. Just because power is given for the Commission and Member States to raise issues before the ECJ it does not mean such issues *cannot* be raised in national courts in appropriate circumstances.	Point in argument of ECJ.
	79	If action under Art 12 were restricted to Arts 169–70 actions, this would deny direct legal protection of nationals. Also, Arts 169–70 action may be ineffective after national changes.	Point in argument of ECJ.
	80	Nationals having rights increases effectiveness of supervision in addition to Arts 169–70.	Point in argument of ECJ.
	81	According to the spirit, general scheme and wording of Treaty, Art 12 must be interpreted as having direct effect creating individual rights.	Conclusion of argument of ECJ.
The second question: the juris-diction of the court	82	Belgian and Dutch governments say look at classification of product. Van Gend en Loos and inspectors have different ideas.	Description.
	83	The Court has no jurisdiction to consider the reference made by the Tariefcommissie.	Conclusion of argument by ECJ.

Headings	Paragraph nos	Précis of paragraph	Classification of paragraph
	84	But the real meaning of the question by the Tariefcommissie is whether in law an effective increase in duties charged due to a new classification contravenes the prohibition in Art 12.	Point in argument by ECJ.
	85	This question does involve the interpretation of the Treaty and the meaning to be given to the concept of duties.	Point in the argument of the ECJ.
	86	Therefore, we do have jurisdiction.	Conclusion of point made by ECJ.
	87	Wording of Art 12 makes it clear that one must look at duties and charges applied at date of entry into force of Treaty.	Point in argument of ECJ.
	88	With regard to prohibition an illegal increase may arise by rearrangement and re-classification under a higher percentage duty.	Point in argument of ECJ.
	89	It does not matter how increase achieved, the fact of the increase is the important matter.	Point in the argument of the ECJ.
	90	Application of Art 12 with interpretation given above is within the jurisdiction of the national court. The courts must ask if product charged at a higher rate than on 1 January 1958.	Conclusion to second question.
	91	ECJ has no jurisdiction to check the validity of conflicting views, this is for national courts.	Conclusion by ECJ.
The costs	92	Costs by EEC and Member States not recoverable. This ruling is part of the case before the Tariefcommissie so decisions as to costs for them.	Decision regarding costs.
	93	On those grounds, after pleadings, reports, parties, opinions of Advocate General and with regard to Arts 9, 12, 14, 169, 170 and 177 of the Treaty.	Grounds.

Headings	Paragraph nos	Précis of paragraph	Classification of paragraph
The court rules *that*	94	*In* answer to the question: (1) Art 12 has direct effect and creates rights for nationals to be protected in national courts; (2) to determine whether there is an increase look at charges before and after 1 January 1958; (3) decision as to costs for the Tariefcommissie.	End.

Having persevered with the reading of the case and the notations, the differences between this Community case and common law reports is stark. The judges in the ECJ do not use analogy, poetic language, asides, stories, counter arguments.

There is a veneer of scientific detachment in the language of the Court. The style is unadorned description, technical language without explanation, assertion, the summarising without comment of a wide range of arguments by the parties, the Advocate General, and the governments wishing to make observations. When the ECJ turns to the decisions it will make, it dismisses arguments without explanation with phrases such as, 'this is misconceived', 'No, this is not right' and states 'this is the case' without giving reasons why.

The Court argues deductively without making any attempts to refer to policy. Yet, it must surely be aware of the policy dimensions of its decisions. If it had decided against Van Gend en Loos, then the power of the fledgling Community would have been severely diminished. In the view of the Advocate General, companies would follow the national customs tariffs and not be guided by the provisions of the treaty. The ECJ may well have been taking the opportunity to assert the power of the Community over the individual Member State. This is conjecture in the absence of any comment on policy from the Court itself.

Potentially powerful and persuasive arguments were put forward that the ECJ did not have the jurisdiction to hear the case; the Court merely replied that they did have jurisdiction. This was based on the grounds that the meaning behind the question raised an issue of interpretation within its jurisdiction.

The Court's simplistic decision following from this that any arithmetical change, even if it resulted from a re-classification within the existing order rather than a deliberate increase, would constitute an infringement of the treaty – is severe and open to question. In the face of arguments that would concentrate upon the intention of Member States concerning infringement, the ECJ says any arithmetical increase constitutes an infringement irrespective of intention.

Indeed, much policy has to be read into all judgments of the ECJ and this judgment is no exception. Perhaps given the tensions between Member States and their creation, the EC, this is a wise and deliberate policy. The Member States gave birth to something that, in many respects, is more powerful and can dictate terms to an individual Member State.

There is little usage of what may be described as the forensic skill of the English judge. The major part of the report concerns summaries of the arguments put forward by both parties, the Advocate General, other interested Member States, and the governments of affected Member States.

Given the detail of the summarised arguments, and the range of arguments presented, it is interesting to note that it is acceptable for the Court to dismiss arguments without reasons. Theoretically, of course, an English judge could do the same, but the entrenched method of reasoning by analogy based on precedent makes such a course of action unlikely.

5.7   SUMMARY

This chapter has attempted to give an outline description of the main areas where English law needs to be read and understood in its European dimension. These areas are the law relating to human rights, and the EU and its law making powers (EC law). The chapter began with a basic introduction to the idea of treaties in general as the main method of the British government making political agreements – agreements that are usually operative at the level of international law. The chapter then explained the ways in which the law relating to human rights and the legal aspects of the EU have become part of English law.

CHAPTER 6

READING BOOKS ABOUT LAW –
A READING STRATEGY

6.1   INTRODUCTION

This chapter briefly introduces a general reading strategy and demonstrates its use by applying it to the reading of a short article 'The European Union belongs to its citizens: three immodest proposals' (1997) 22 EL Rev 150–56.

At the beginning of this book, the distinction was made between primary books of law and secondary books about law.

For while the core of legal studies is, or should be, the primary legal text, it is also necessary to competently handle secondary legal texts – textbooks, journal articles, newspaper articles.

Books about law are consulted, in panic or at leisure, for a range of reasons:

- to obtain a general grasp of an area of law;
- to obtain a description of a topic;
- to obtain a range of different views about the same case/statute/area/theory/method;
- to obtain a sophisticated analysis of a topic or case.

Usually, this information is being sought to provide the raw material for use in answering an essay question, writing a project, or answering a problem question.

The ultimate piece of writing will only be as good as the student's ability to:

- understand the assessment task;
- competently undertake the research required;
- identify the arguments in the material read;
- understand the arguments in the material read;
- evaluate the arguments in the material read;
- compare the arguments in the material read;
- differentiate between information, description and argument;
- write a good conclusion to an assessment.

6.2   LEARNING OUTCOMES

By the end of this chapter and the relevant reading, readers should:

- be able to make competent notes of a secondary legal text;
- be able to identify the argument(s) in a secondary legal text;
- be able to explain the differences between articles;
- be able to explain competently the interrelationship between articles;
- be able to explain competently the views of articles in relation to common law and statutory rules;

- be able to apply a range of methods for breaking into secondary texts;
- gain confidence in reading secondary texts.

6.2.1   A reading strategy

For each text located, decisions have to be made.

- Is this text relevant?
- Is it necessary to skim read and/or scan, and/or close read?
- What is/are the argument(s) of the text?

Vital decisions have to be taken about the reading.

It is absolutely essential from the outset to have a plan for reading. Reading in the context of studying always implies reading for a purpose. The parameters of the problems before the reader have to be carefully thought out before commencing reading.

Students may be given a problem question to research, or an essay to write. With both types of assessment activity, it is vital that the limits of the question are correctly identified by looking for clues in the grammar used to construct the question. For example, the facts of problem cases are often set in the areas between decided cases where there is an area of 'unknown', an area that the student is expected to talk about confidently. Competent identification of the issues from the outset often determines the quality of the answer before any creative writing has begun. These matters are explored in greater detail in Chapter 8.

The care given to the reading of cases and statutory provisions has *also* to be brought to the reading of secondary explanatory, interpretative or evaluative texts. Reading with an idea of *why* the text is being read as well as with a view to *what it is hoped to do with the extracted information will* enable the student to read with a mixture of skimming strategies, detailed reading strategies and note-taking.

The 'why' can be as simple as 'I am reading to find out what this article is about' through to 'does this article support the argument that I am trying to construct?'. Many students, however, read blindly – 'This is on the reading list so I have to read it'. They do not fit their reading into a strategy: 'Am I reading this for description, information or analysis?' 'Am I seeking to find out basic things about the topic or am I trying to support propositions in my argument?'

It is essential to develop a reading strategy. There are some basic steps which will be set out below. However, the most important issue to grasp is that reading can never be a purely passive act, because a writer always seeks to engage the reader in active dialogue with the text. No one writes in order not to be read, and no one wishes to be read passively without thought entering into the reading process. It is necessary to become aware of an inner dialogue between self and text as reading progresses, or to acquire an inner dialogue if one is not present! The reader should be continually processing, reflecting, considering, agreeing or disagreeing as reading is in progress.

Readers should particularly note if other thoughts enter their head (like 'what's on TV?'!). If readers become frustrated with the text, the reading should stop and questions asked. Is the reader scared, threatened, annoyed with the text and, if so, why? Not allowing enough time to read a text can be fatal to understanding, which in turn causes stress.

There are four main stages to any reading enterprise:

(1) preparation prior to reading:

- locating texts;
- ascertaining purpose for reading;

(2) methods of reading;

(3) understanding what is being read;

(4) critically evaluating what is being read.

These are deceptively easy stages to set out but much harder to utilise for the first time, especially if readers have already established ill-disciplined approaches to reading.

Each of the above stages can be split into sub-stages; such analysis is necessary to obtain the fullest comprehension of the text. The following strategy for competent reading demonstrates this.

6.3   A STRATEGY FOR COMPETENT READING

STAGE 1

Preparation prior to reading

Reading intention:
- why am I reading this text?
- what do I hope to get out of it?

Reader prediction of use and content of text:
- this involves a consideration of what the writer is saying. This can be judged from the subject matter and the title;
- the very act of choosing a text involves prediction:
  - ○   that this text is relevant;
  - ○   that the text will begin to answer some of the questions that you have in your mind.

STAGE 2

Methods of reading

Skimming: read very quickly and generally through a text noting:

- publication date – for the study of law, it is particularly vital to know which edition you are reading; texts can go out of date due to changes in the law in a matter of months;
- index;
- foreword;
- any headings and sub-headings;
- author details;
- introductory paragraphs;
- the first sentence or two of paragraphs following introductions;
- look at concluding paragraphs.

This activity assists in deciding the potential relevance of the text.

Scanning:

- Unlike the general skim through, scanning involves quickly looking for specific words, phrases or information.

Detailed reading:

- Reading will allow attention to be given to secondary or subsidiary points in the text. Here, the reading is slower and careful. Check unfamiliar vocabulary. Some words and phrases become clear as more text is read.

Note the type of language used:

    technical;

    figurative;

    journalistic;

    academic;

    personal (you must ...);

    impersonal (one must or it is therefore);

    intimate;

    distanced.

Note how arguments are put together:
- are points backed up by reference to evidence?
- are points made left to stand alone without evidence?

Details on argument are found in Chapter 7.

STAGE 3

Understanding what is being read

Guessing words that you do not know:
- Do not expect to know all the words read. Even as a more extensive vocabulary is acquired, there will be words that are not known.

Identifying main ideas:
- Many main ideas will have been discovered on a first skimming. A second reading begins the process of identifying the main points made by the writer. This aids in the acquisition of a deeper understanding of the arguments presented in the text.

Identifying subsidiary ideas:
- As the main points are identified, it is possible to organise the information and classify secondary, subsidiary points.

Identifying overall text organisation:
- Every writer has a different way of organising, classifying and structuring their work. This needs to be ascertained by any reader who wishes to break into the text successfully.

An initial issue is to decide whether the writer is:
- outlining an area;
- discussing a specific problem;
- proposing a solution to a problem;
- comparing and contrasting ideas;
- speaking of the present, future or the past.

STAGE 4

Evaluating what you are reading

Ascertaining the purpose of the writer:
- This is crucial.
- Does the writer want to inform you about something or try to persuade you of the correctness of a particular point of view?
- Often a writer will seek to both inform and persuade.

Ascertaining the argument(s) of the writer:
- Some texts are said to be complex not because they use particularly difficult words or arguments but because, in order to understand the full detail of the writer's position, extensive knowledge of other areas within or outside the particular discipline will be required.

Ascertaining the attitude of the writer:
- Writers are usually biased towards a certain view in their writing, although on occasion a writer may be neutral.
- You must be able to gain skill in identifying a writer's attitude to the ideas he or she is discussing.
- You must at least know whether the writer is neutral or biased.

Each of the above four stages is interconnected and a good way of showing such interconnection is by using a diagram as in Figure 6.1, below.

Figure 6.1: diagrammatic summary of a reading plan

A READING STRATEGY

1 Preparation prior to reading

- Intention for reading: why am I reading? What am I reading?
- Choosing texts
- Prediction: what is this text likely to be about?

2 Methods of reading

- Skimming: read through quickly
  - What are the primary issues?
  - What are the secondary issues?
- Scanning: check for keywords
  - Lexicon? vocabulary?
  - Style?
- Close/detailed
  - What is argument?
  - Arguments?
    - How are arguments put together?
      - Are points backed by evidence?
      - Are points unsupported?

3 Understanding what is being read

- Identifying primary ideas
- Identifying secondary ideas
- Identifying overall text organisation

4 Critical evaluation of what is being read

- Writer
  - What is the writer's purpose?
  - What is the argument?
    - Attitude? (Is writer biased?)
- What do 'I' think? (Your critique)
  - Style?
  - Content?
  - Argument
    - Is it weak?
    - Is it strong?
      - Supported by evidence?
      - Not supported by evidence?

6.4   PRACTICAL DEMONSTRATION OF THE STRATEGY FOR READING: ANALYSIS OF AN ARTICLE

Applying the reading strategy demonstrates that reading appropriately is a highly disciplined, complex and skilled process. The strategy will be applied to an article, 'The European Union belongs to its citizens: three immodest proposals' by JHH Weiler; the full text can be found at the end of this chapter. Numbers in square brackets in the article refer to the paragraph numbers mentioned in the text of this chapter.

Task

The article to be read, 'The European Union belongs to its citizens: three immodest proposals', is a relatively uncomplicated article in terms of language usage and concepts introduced. This makes it ideal for current purposes to provide a short demonstration of the reading strategy and enable feedback.

The first task is for *you* the reader to participate.

You are asked to:

1   Study carefully the four stage reading strategy that has been set out above in both its narrative and diagrammatic forms. Make sure that you understand how each of the stages is interconnected. This may take any time from 20 minutes to an hour.

2   Then following each stage of the reading plan read the article. Make notes as appropriate.

3   Compare your notes of the reading with the demonstration of the reading strategy that follows immediately after this task.

   (i)   Were there any major differences between your version and the version in this text?

   (ii) How did this occur? Where you have any gaps go back to the text to see how you missed them.

6.4.1   The demonstration: the reading plan applied to the article

6.4.1.1 Stage 1: preparation prior to reading

Reading intention

- Why am I reading this text? It can be said that there are at least two reasons:
  - to learn *how* to read texts; or
  - this particular legal text happens to be the one chosen (by tutor or by self)!
- What do I hope to get out of it?
  - a strategy for competent reading;
  - some new knowledge from the article.

Reader prediction of use and content of text:

- this involves a consideration of what the writer is saying. This can be judged from the subject matter and the title. What does the title suggest?

It is about the European Union and is suggesting it 'belongs to its citizens'. The last phrase of the title is a deliberate play on words. Usually, an author would say 'I am making three *modest* proposals'. This author is being controversial and states 'three *immodest* proposals'. Usually, people will argue that they are only suggesting modest, small changes. Here the suggestion is that the changes are large and perhaps outrageous. The title also sounds like a political slogan, a call to arms maybe 'The European Union belongs to its citizens'. So the article is, or should be, about proposals relating to the concept of the Union belonging to its citizens.

6.4.1.2 Stage 2: methods of reading

Skimming

Read very quickly and generally through the text noting:

- **publication date**: 1997. The date gives a context to the article. You could be reading it years later when changes may have occurred. You need to know this.
- **headings and sub-headings**:
  - introduction;
  - proposal 1: the European Legislative Ballot;
  - proposal 2: Lexcalibur – the European Public Square;
  - proposal 3: limits to growth;
- **author details**:
  - Name: JHH Weiler.
  - Title: Professor of Law and Jean Monnet Chair, Harvard University.
  - Job: Co-director, Academy of European Law, European University Institute Florence.

> Note: Jean Monnet was one of the original architects of the European Community in 1957.

Figure 6.2: introductory paragraphs 2–8

Para 1	Asks the reader to recall days of the Maastricht Treaty. Notes who was for and who against and raises doubts about understanding.
Para 2	Talks of: – street reaction relating back to title; – disempowerment of the individual European citizen.
Para 3	Gives three 'roots' of disempowerment: (i) democratic deficit;
Para 4	states second root. (ii) ever-increasing remoteness, opaqueness and inaccessibility of European governance;
Para 5	third root: (iii) competencies of the Union.
Para 6	One sentence: don't be surprised by the alienation.
Para 7	Says proposals of IGC 'very modest', with those who gain being governments, and consumers losing out.
Para 8	Says the author will give three proposals that can make a difference without a political fuss.

The three proposals:
- proposal 1: the European Legislative Ballot;
- proposal 2: Lexcalibur – the European Public Square;
- proposal 3: limits to growth.

- Read the first sentence of two of the paragraphs following introductions.
- Look at concluding paragraphs on last page. Article does not have a signalled conclusion as it had a signalled introduction. But it does conclude with para 30 stating:

  'The IGC has proclaimed that the European Union belongs to its citizens. The proof of the pudding will be in the eating [p 343].'

  (IGC = Inter-Governmental Conference)
- Did you note the use of the figurative language?
- This activity has assisted in deciding the potential relevance of the text.
- If the work in hand concerned the European citizen, enough has been gained by the introduction, headings and last paragraph to conclude that the article is relevant.

Scanning

- Unlike the general skim through, scanning involves quickly looking for specific words, phrases or information.
- This would be used with this article if it was being scanned for potential relevancy.

Detailed reading

A detailed reading will allow attention to be given to identifying primary and secondary or subsidiary arguments properly in the text.

Here, the reading is slower and careful. Do make sure that you check out unfamiliar vocabulary. Also some words and phrases become clear as more text is read.

For example:

- what does the word 'Lexcalibur' mean? Where does this word come from?
- what does the phrase 'the European public square' mean?

Neither the word 'Lexcalibur' nor the phrase 'the European Public Square' can be found in a dictionary. However, their meaning unfolds in the article.

Note the type of language used.

Thinking closely about the text the most obvious language usage is *figurative*. The writer uses short sentences, slogans, rhetorical questions, poetic language, metaphor, invents words. Take a look at the demonstration of this in Figure 6.3, below.

Figure 6.3: figurative language

Political imagery	the Mandarins heralded
Mathematical imagery	'what's-in-it-for-me?' calculus
Architectural/geological	shaky foundation
Nature imagery	roots of disempowerment
Scientific imagery	the specific gravity of whom continues to decline
Nature imagery	the second root goes even deeper
Religious imagery	an apocryphal statement
Food imagery	it is End of Millennium Bread and Circus Governance
Elemental imagery	could be shielded behind firewalls
Grand teleological style	ours is a vision which tries to enhance human sovereignty, demystify technology and place it firmly as servant and not master
Food imagery	<ul><li>the European Court of Justice should welcome having this hot potato removed from its plate</li><li>the proof of the pudding will be in the eating</li></ul>

Scanning for argument: the argument was relatively well signalled by the introduction and the headings.

What is the main argument?

The following has been divided into proposition and evidence supporting it. Many readers do not differentiate the two which is a major error and leads to confusion and misunderstanding. A proposition is a statement being put forward as a point in argument construction. It can be given strength by evidence supporting it.

- **Proposition 1, para 2**:

  The Maastricht Treaty was not the remarkable diplomatic achievement it was claimed to be.

  Evidence: street reaction apathetic, confused, hostile, fearful:

  (i) Danes voted against it;

  (ii) French approved it marginally (1%);

  (iii) commentators at the time said that if there had been greater scrutiny in Great Britain and Germany the outcome would have been uncertain;

  (iv) even those supporting it were just plain greedy.

- **Proposition 2, para 3**:

  There was a 'growing disillusionment with the European construct as a whole'.

- **Proposition 3, para 3**:

  The *'moral and political legitimacy'* of the European construct is in decline.

  Evidence: There is 'a sense of disempowerment of the European citizen' which has many roots, but three stand out:

  (i) democratic deficit;

  (ii) remoteness;

  (iii) competencies of union.

- **Conclusion**: a package of three proposals (a limited ballot by citizens concerning legislation; internet access to European decision making; establishment of a constitutional council), taken from research, initiated by the European Parliament, can make a real difference to increase the power of the European citizen without creating a political drama.

The argument as set out in the introduction (in paras 1–3)

The Maastricht Treaty was not the diplomatic achievement it was claimed to be. The European citizen continues to be disempowered. There remains a growing disillusionment with the European construct as a whole which is suffering from a decline in its moral and political legitimacy. However, a package of three proposals (a limited ballot by citizens concerning legislation; internet access to European decision making; establishment of a constitutional council), taken from research, initiated by the European Parliament, can make a real difference to increase the power of the European citizen without creating a political drama.

6.4.1.3 Stage 3: understanding what you are reading

- Guessing words that you do not know.

  Do not expect to know all the words read. Even as a more extensive vocabulary is acquired, there will be words that are not known. You may even have singled the following out already: Lexcalibur, democratic 'deficit', 'competencies of the Union', 'specific gravity' and 'apocryphal statement'.

- Identifying main ideas.

  Here, the main idea is that a package of three proposals (a limited ballot by citizens concerning legislation; internet access to European decision making; establishment of a constitutional council), taken from research, initiated by the European Parliament, can make a real difference to increase the power of the European citizen without creating a political drama.

- Identifying subsidiary ideas.

  Here, that there could be potential clashes between the constitutional council and the function of the European Court of Justice.

- Identifying overall text organisation.

  Every writer has a different way of organising, classifying and structuring their work. This needs to be ascertained by any reader who wishes to break successfully into the text. Here the author has clearly indicated structure through the headings and has discussed points in the order indicated.

  The writer is:

  o   discussing a specific problem; and

  o   proposing a solution to that problem.

6.4.1.4 Stage 4: evaluating what you are reading

- Ascertaining the purpose of the writer.

  The writer wants to inform about something and indicate the correctness of a particular point of view.

- Evaluating the argument(s) of the writer.

  The argument here is relatively easy to extract because the article is written in a punchy, journalistic style while keeping to headings. What is clear, however, is that the detail given to setting out the three proposals is not given to indicating evidence to support propositions – perhaps because the writer feels that many of his propositions are self-evident.

  Having ascertained the arguments, then it is up to the reader to decide what is thought.

  A student's view of the argument of the writer is initially limited by their lack of knowledge of the issues spoken of. As research is continued in an area for an essay, more is learnt, more about competing views, and more about the area generally. Then, the student's view of the argument may change.

  Even if an argument is preferred, it can still be a weak or strong argument either theoretically or practically. It can be weak because no evidence to show support for important propositions or ultimate conclusion has been put forward.

Students may need far more information before they can evaluate the writer's proposals concerning problems and solutions. The student may not agree with the problem. If a problem has been misdiagnosed, then the solution will not work. If the problem has been correctly identified, but the wrong causes attributed then, again, the solution will not work.

Reading is, therefore, a dynamic act, not a purely passive thing.

In any text identifying problems and putting forward solutions in argument or description formats, the following questions need to be asked:

○　is it plausible to classify these circumstances as a problem?;

○　is it plausible to maintain that these are the causes of the problem?;

○　given the view on the above two questions, is it plausible to offer these solutions?

Then ask: 'OK, is this conclusion plausible?'

'Do I agree with the conclusion to the argument?'

'If I do not, how do I attack it?'

'Do I agree with all of the propositions that are the building blocks in this argument?'

'Are the propositions strong or weak?'

Ask these questions in relation to the article on the European citizen.

If there is any area of lack of understanding, ask 'why?'

○　are there problems with the vocabulary, or the concepts, or is there too much presupposed information, etc?

- Ascertaining the attitude of the writer.
  - Writers are usually biased towards a certain view in their writing, although on occasion a writer may be neutral.
  - You must be able to gain skill in identifying a writer's attitude to the ideas he or she is discussing.
  - You must at least know whether the writer is neutral or biased.

6.5　USING THE ARTICLE WITH OTHER TEXTS

Having read this article, it is possible to represent the argument in the article as a diagram which is a useful method of viewing all arguments unidimensionally which our brain cannot do with text. This is demonstrated in Figure 6.4, below.

Task: imagine that there are other articles about citizenship by authors X, Y and Z, the original article by Weiler could then be annotated according to whether X, Y or Z agree or disagree with Weiler's arguments and evidences. This is set out in Figure 6.5, below. Study these diagrams carefully and understanding will be gained in the area of the use of secondary texts.

Figure 6.4: diagram of arguments in article

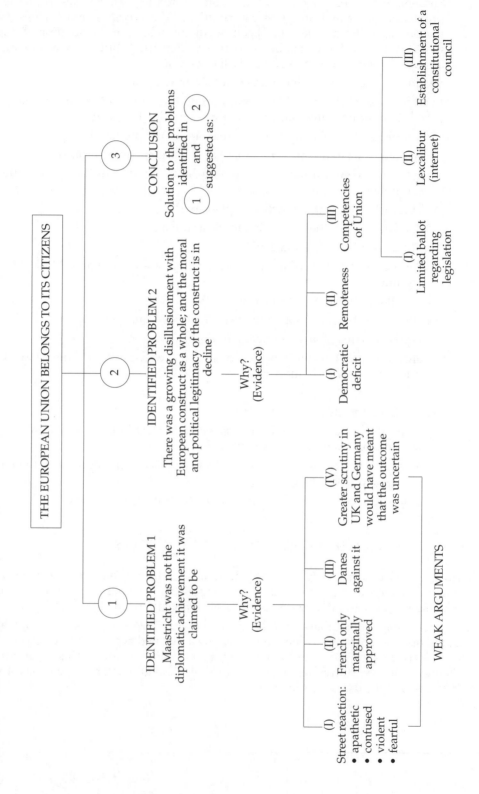

Figure 6.5: how to annotate a diagrammatic presentation of the argument of an article with other authors (X, Y and Z) who agree/disagree with the argument of the original article

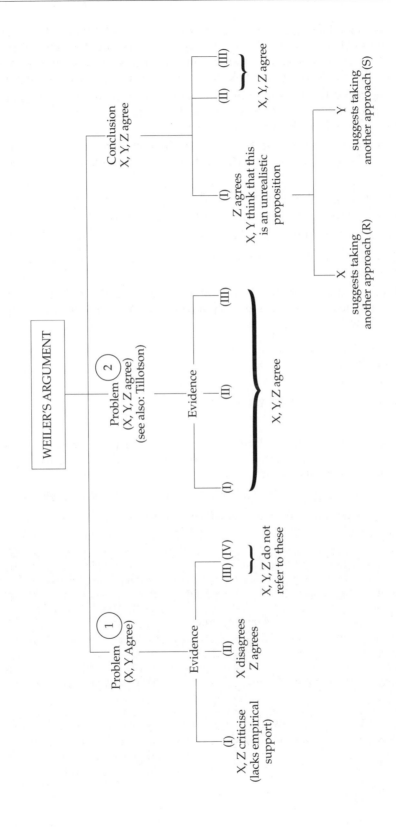

If one were marshalling evidence for an essay entitled 'Does the European Union belong to its citizens?', it would be possible to incorporate the views of Weiler, and authors X, Y and Z in such an essay by simply writing to the diagram. In addition, one would look in leading textbooks to see if those authors had anything to state.

Having noted the areas of agreement and disagreement on the diagram, a clear view emerges of strong and weak arguments. Then, it is possible for the student to come to a personal conclusion.

The student may feel that it is not possible to come to a clear conclusion. This feeling can be right or wrong, depending upon the answers to the following questions:

(a) is there enough information collected to properly cover the area?

(b) have all of the arguments put forward been understood?

(c) is there a lack of empirical/practical evidence to support theoretical positions?

It is vital to decide whether there is enough information and this is often a subjective matter.

A brief conclusion to the above suggested essay follows below. It centres on Weiler's articles and the imaginary authors X, Y, Z. Hopefully, it forcefully illustrates how:

- identification;

- organisation;

- classification;

- competent reading strategy and notes;

- diagrams,

can work together to bring clarity of thought and expression. Textbooks are not included in the conclusion but if a textbook did comment on a theory or give useful insights, these could also be incorporated.

'The European Union belongs to its citizens.' Discuss.

Conclusion

Weiler (1997) argues that at present the European citizen does not exert power over policy and law making within the European Union. This indicates that the European Union certainly does not belong to its citizens. However, as noted above, he convincingly argues that with very little change the situation could be rectified. X (1997), Y (1998) and Z (1998), in large part, agree with Weiler, both in terms of the problems and solutions presented by him.

It is suggested that Weiler's argument is well set out and is essentially backed by supporting evidence and attainable solutions. It is further suggested that the evidence presented concerning proposition 1, that Maastricht was not the diplomatic achievement it was claimed to be, is weak. A point also noted by X (1997) and Y (1998).

Proposition 2 is strongly supported by the available evidence. If the governments of the Member States and the institutions of the European Community seriously consider the issue of the European citizen in terms of Weiler's problems and solutions, it may well be that, in the opening years of the new millennium, it will be possible to maintain that the European Union does belong to its citizens.

6.6   'THE EUROPEAN UNION BELONGS TO ITS CITIZENS:
        THREE IMMODEST PROPOSALS' (1997) 22 EL REV 150–56

*JHH Weiler, Manley Hudson Professor of Law and Jean Monnet Chair, Harvard
University; Co-Director, Academy of European Law, European University Institute,
Florence*

[1]   'Despite its rhetorical commitment to a Union ... which belongs to its
        citizens', the recent Irish Presidency IGC draft has precious little in the way
        of empowering individual citizens of the Union. This essay presents three
        suggestions from a broader study presented to the European Parliament
        which are designed to increase the democratic and deliberative processes of
        Community and Union governance. The first, the European Legislative
        Ballot, proposes a form of limited 'direct democracy' appropriate for the
        Union. The second, the 'Lexcalibur initiative', proposes placing Community
        and Union decision making on the Internet to enhance accessibility and
        transparency of Community decision making. The last proposes the creation
        of a Constitutional Council, modelled on its French namesake, to adjudicate,
        ex ante, challenges to the legislative competencies of the Community
        legislator.

Introduction

[2]   Cast your mind back to the heady days of the Maastricht Treaty. The
        Mandarins heralded a remarkable diplomatic achievement: a new Treaty,
        new name, new pillars and above all a commitment to Economic and
        Monetary Union within the decade. Recall now the reaction in the European
        street ranging from fear and hostility through confusion and
        incomprehension to indifference and outright apathy. The Danes voted
        against that Treaty, the French approved it by a margin of barely 1% and
        most commentators agree that had it been put to public scrutiny in, say,
        Great Britain or even Germany the outcome would have been far from
        certain. Even those who supported it were motivated in large part by a
        'what's-in-it-for-me' calculus – a shaky foundation for long term civic
        loyalty.

[3]   The reaction in the street did not relate only or even primarily to the content
        of the Treaty; it was the expression of a growing disillusionment with the
        European construct as a whole the moral and political legitimacy of which
        were in decline. The reasons for this are many but clearly, on any reading, as
        the Community has grown in size, in scope, in reach and despite a high
        rhetoric including the very creation of 'European Citizenship', there has been
        a distinct disempowerment of the individual European citizen, the specific
        gravity of whom continues to decline as the Union grows.

[4]   The roots of disempowerment are many but three stand out.

        First, is the classic so called 'Democracy Deficit': the inability of the
        Community and Union to develop structures and processes which would
        adequately replicate at the Community level the habits of governmental
        control, parliamentary accountability and administrative responsibility

which are practised with different modalities in the various Member States. Further, as more and more functions move to Brussels, the democratic balances within the Member States have been disrupted by a strengthening of the ministerial and executive branches of government. The value of each individual in the political process has inevitably declined including the ability to play a meaningful civic role in European governance.

[5] The second root goes even deeper and concerns the ever increasing remoteness, opaqueness, and inaccessibility of European governance. An apocryphal statement usually attributed to Jacques Delors predicts that by the end of the decade 80% of social regulation will be issued from Brussels. We are on target. The drama lies in the fact that no accountable public authority has a handle on these regulatory processes. Not the European Parliament, not the Commission, not even the governments. The press and other media, a vital estate in our democracies are equally hampered. Consider that it is even impossible to get from any of the Community Institutions an authoritative and mutually agreed statement of the mere number of committees which inhabit that world of comitology. Once there were those who worried about the supranational features of European integration. It is time to worry about infranationalism – a complex network of middle level national administrators, Community administrators and an array of private bodies with unequal and unfair access to a process with huge social and economic consequences to everyday life – in matters of public safety, health, and all other dimensions of socio-economic regulation. Transparency and access to documents are often invoked as a possible remedy to this issue. But if you do not know what is going on, which documents will you ask to see? Neither strengthening the European Parliament nor national parliaments will do much to address this problem of post-modern governance which itself is but one manifestation of a general sense of political alienation in most western democracies.

[6] The final issue relates to the competencies of the Union and Community. In one of its most celebrated cases in the early 1960s, the European Court of Justice described the Community as a '... new legal order for the benefit of which the States have limited their sovereign rights, albeit in limited fields' (*Van Gend en Loos* Case 26/62 [1963] ECR 1). There is a widespread anxiety that these fields are limited no more. Indeed, not long ago a prominent European scholar and judge wrote that there simply is no nucleus of sovereignty that the Member States can invoke, as such, against the Community'. (Lenaerts, 'Constitutionalism and the many faces of Federalism' (1990) 38 AJ Com L 205, 220. The Court, too, has modified its rhetoric; in its more recent Opinion 1/91 it refers to the Member States as having limited their sovereign rights '... in ever wider fields': Opinion 1/91 [1991] ECR I-6079, para 21.)

[7] We should not, thus, be surprised by a continuing sense of alienation from the Union and its Institutions.

[8] In the Dublin Summit the present thinking of the IGC has been revealed in a document entitled 'The European Union Today and Tomorrow'. The opening phrase of the document reads: 'The European Union belongs to its Citizens'. But don't hold your breath when it comes to the actual proposals.

They are very modest. The second phrase of the new text reads: 'The Treaties establishing the Union should address their most direct concerns.' There is much rhetoric on a commitment to employment, there are a few significant proposals on free movement, elimination of gender discrimination and other rights. There are some meaningful proposals to increase the powers of the European Parliament and even to integrate formally, even if in limited fashion, national legislatures into the Community process. But overall, the net gainers are, again, the governments. At best, this is the ethos of benign paternalism. At worst, the proposals represent another symptom of the degradation of civic culture whereby the citizen is conceived as a consumer – a consumer who has lost faith in the Brand Name called Europe and who has to be bought off by all kind of social and economic goodies, a share holder who must be placated by a larger dividend. It is End-of-Millennium Bread and Circus governance.

[9]   What can be done? Here is a package of three proposals plucked from a recent study commissioned by the European Parliament which my collaborators and I believe can make a concrete and symbolic difference. (JHH Weiler, Alexander Ballmann, Ulrich Haltern, Herwig Hofmann, Franz Mayer, Sieglinde Schreiner-Linford, *Certain Rectangular Problems of European Integration, European Parliament*, 1996.) We also believe that they could be adopted without much political fuss. You decide.

Proposal 1: the European legislative ballot

[10]   The democratic tradition in most Member States is one of representative democracy. Our elected representatives legislate and govern in our name. If we are unsatisfied we can replace them at election time. Recourse to forms of direct democracy – such as referenda – are exceptional. Given the size of the Union, referenda are considered particularly inappropriate.

However, the basic condition of representative democracy is, indeed, that at election time the citizens '... can throw the scoundrels out' – that is replace the Government. This basic feature of representative democracy does not exist in the Community and Union. The form of European governance is – and will remain for considerable time – such that there is no 'Government' to throw out. Even dismissing the Commission by Parliament (or approving the appointment of the Commission President) is not the equivalent of throwing the Government out. There is no civic act of the European citizen where he or she can influence directly the outcome of any policy choice facing the Community and Union as citizens can when choosing between parties which offer sharply distinct programmes. Neither elections to the European Parliament nor elections to national Parliaments fulfil this function in Europe. This is among the reasons why turnout to European Parliamentary elections has been traditionally low and why these elections are most commonly seen as a mid-term judgment of the Member State Governments rather than a choice on European governance.

[11]   The proposal is to introduce some form of direct democracy at least until such time as one could speak of meaningful representative democracy at the European level. Our proposal is for a form of a Legislative Ballot Initiative coinciding with elections to the European Parliament. Our proposal is allow

the possibility, when enough signatures are collected in, say, more than five Member States to introduce legislative initiatives to be voted on by citizens when European elections take place (and, after a period of experimentation possibly at other intervals too). In addition to voting for their MEPs, the electorate will be able to vote on these legislative initiatives. Results would be binding on the Community institutions and on Member States. Initiatives would be, naturally, confined to the sphere of application of Community law – that is, in areas where the Community Institutions could have legislated themselves. Such legislation could be overturned by a similar procedure or by a particularly onerous legislative Community process. The Commission, Council, Parliament or a national parliament could refer a proposed initiative to the European Court of Justice to determine – in an expedited procedure – whether the proposed ballot initiative is within the competencies of the Community or is in any other way contrary to the Treaty. In areas where the Treaty provides for majority voting the Ballot initiative will be considered as adopted when it wins a majority of votes in the Union as a whole as well as within a majority of Member States. (Other formulae could be explored.) Where the Treaty provides for unanimity a majority of voters in the Union would be required as well as winning in all Member States.

[12]   Apart from enhancing symbolically and tangibly the voice of individuals qua citizens, this proposal would encourage the formation of true European parties as well as transnational mobilisation of political forces. It would give a much higher European political significance to Elections to the European Parliament. It would represent a first important step, practical and symbolic, to the notion of European citizenship and civic responsibility.

Proposal 2: *Lexcalibur* – **the European public square**

[13]   This would be the single most important and far reaching proposal which would have the most dramatic impact on European governance. It does not require a Treaty amendment and can be adopted by an Inter-Institutional Agreement among Commission, Council and Parliament. It could be put in place in phases after a short period of study and experimentation and be fully operational within, we estimate, two to three years. We believe that if adopted and implemented it will, in the medium and long term, have a greater impact on the democratisation and transparency of European governance than any other single proposal currently under consideration by the IGC.

[14]   Even if it does not require a Treaty amendment we recommend that it be part of the eventual IGC package as a central feature of those aspects designed to empower the individual citizen.

[15]   We are proposing that – with few exceptions – the entire decision-making process of the Community, especially but not only Comitology – be placed on the internet.

[16]   For convenience we have baptised the proposal: *Lexcalibur* – the European public square.

[17]   We should immediately emphasise that what we have in mind is a lot more than simply making certain laws or documents such as the *Official Journal* more accessible through electronic data bases.

[18]   We should equally emphasise that this proposal is without prejudice to the question of confidentiality of process and secrecy of documents. As shall transpire, under our proposal documents or deliberations which are considered too sensitive to be made public at any given time could be shielded behind 'fire-walls' and made inaccessible to the general public. Whatever policy of access to documentation is adopted could be implemented on *Lexcalibur*.

[19]   The key organisational principle would be that each Community decision making project intended to result in the eventual adoption of a Community norm would have a 'decisional web site' on the Internet within the general *Lexcalibur* 'Home Page' which would identify the scope and purpose of the legislative or regulatory measure(s); the Community and Member States persons or administrative departments or divisions responsible for the process; the proposed and actual timetable of the decisional process so that one would know at any given moment the progress of the process, access and view all non-confidential documents which are part of the process and under carefully designed procedures directly submit input into the specific decisional process. But it is important to emphasise that our vision is not one of 'Virtual Government' which will henceforth proceed electronically. The *primary* locus and mode of governance would and should remain intact: Political Institutions, meetings of elected representative and officials, Parliamentary debates, media reporting – as vigorous and active a public square as it is possible to maintain, and a European Civic Society of real human beings. The huge potential importance of *Lexcalibur* would be in its *secondary effect*: It would enhance the potential of all actors to play a much more informed, critical and involved role in the Primary Public Square. The most immediate direct beneficiaries of Euro governance on the Internet would in fact be the media, interested pressure groups, NGOs and the like. Of course, also 'ordinary citizens' would have a much more direct mode to interact with their process of government. Providing a greatly improved system of information would, however, only be a first step of a larger project. It would serve as the basis for a system that allows widespread participation in policy-making processes so that European democracy becomes an altogether more deliberative process through the posting of comments and the opening of a dialogue between the Community Institutions and interested private actors. The Commission already now sometimes invites e-mail comments on its initiatives. (See, for example, its draft notice on co-operation with national authorities in handling cases falling within Arts 85 or 86 [1996] OJ C262/5.) Such a system obviously needs a clear structure in order to allow a meaningful and effective processing of incoming information for Community Institutions. Conceivable would be, for example, a two-tier system, consisting of a forum with limited access for an interactive exchange between Community Institutions and certain private actors and an open forum where all interested actors can participate and discuss Community policies with each other. This would open the unique opportunity for deliberations of citizens and interest groups beyond the

traditional frontiers of the Nation State, without the burden of high entry costs for the individual actor.

[20]   Hugely important, in our view, will be the medium and long term impact on the young generation, our children. For this generation, the internet will be – in many cases already is – as natural a medium as to older generations were radio, television and the press. European Governance on the net will enable them to experience government at school and at home in ways which are barely imaginable to an older generation for whom this New Age 'stuff' is often threatening or, in itself, alien.

[21]   The idea of using the internet for improving the legitimacy of the European Union may seem to some revolutionary and in some respects it is. Therefore its introduction should be organic through a piecemeal process of experiment and re-evaluation but within an overall commitment towards more open and accessible government.

[22]   There are dimensions of the new Information Age which have all the scary aspects of a 'Brave New World' in which individual and group autonomy and privacy are lost, in which humanity is replaced by 'machinaty' and in which Government seems ever more remote and beyond comprehension and grasp the perfect setting for alienation captured most visibly by atomised individuals sitting in front of their screens and 'surfing the net'.

[23]   Ours is a vision which tries to enhance human sovereignty, demystify technology and place it firmly as servant and not master. The internet in our vision is to serve as the true starting point for the emergence of a functioning deliberative political community, in other words a European polity cum civic society.

[24]   For those who wish to see what this might look like we have prepared a simulation of *Lexcalibur*: www.iue.it/AEL/EP/Lex/index.html.

Proposal 3: limits to growth

[25]   The problem of competencies is, in our view, mostly one of perception. The perception has set in that the boundaries which were meant to circumscribe the areas in which the Community could operate have been irretrievably breached. Few perceptions have been more detrimental to the legitimacy of the Community in the eyes of its citizens. And not only its citizens. Governments and even courts, for example the German Constitutional Court, have rebelled against the Community constitutional order because, in part, of a profound dissatisfaction on this very issue. One can not afford to sweep this issue under the carpet. The crisis is already there. The main problem, then, is not one of moving the boundary lines but of restoring faith in the inviolability of the existing boundaries between Community and Member State competencies.

[26]   Any proposal which envisages the creation of a new Institution is doomed in the eyes of some. And yet we propose the creation of a Constitutional Council for the Community, modelled in some ways on its French namesake. The Constitutional Council would have jurisdiction only over issues of competencies (including subsidiarity) and would, like its French cousin, decide cases submitted to it after a law was adopted but before coming into

> force. It could be seized by the Commission, the Council, any Member State or by the European Parliament acting on a majority of its members. We think that serious consideration should be given to allowing Member State Parliaments to bring cases before the Constitutional Council.
>
> [27]   The composition of the Council is the key to its legitimacy. Its President would be the President of the European Court of Justice and its members would be sitting members of the constitutional courts or their equivalents in the Member States. Within the European Constitutional Council no single Member State would have a veto power. All its decisions would be by majority.
>
> [28]   The composition of the European Constitutional Council would, we believe, help restore confidence in the ability to have effective policing of the boundaries as well as underscore that the question of competencies is fundamentally also one of national constitutional norms but still subject to a binding and uniform solution by a Union Institution.
>
> [29]   We know that this proposal might be taken as an assault on the integrity of the European Court of Justice. That attitude would, in our view, be mistaken. The question of competencies has become so politicised that the European Court of Justice should welcome having this hot potato removed from its plate by an *ex ante* decision of that other body with a jurisdiction limited to that preliminary issue. Yes, there is potential for conflict of jurisprudence and all the rest – nothing that competent drafting cannot deal with.
>
> [30]   The IGC has proclaimed that the European Union belongs to its citizens. The proof of the pudding will be in the eating.

6.7   SUMMARY

This chapter has been designed to outline a method for approaching the reading of secondary texts. It continues to signal the importance of always reading with a purpose and of acquiring the ability to adopt different reading strategies according to the purpose of the reading.

The chapter has demonstrated the laid out method of reading secondary texts to assist students to develop their own reading skills. It is recognised, however, that reading and understanding arguments are linked. If students do not understand what an argument is and how it is constructed then reading a text may not be enough. With this in mind Chapter 7 concentrates upon the techniques of argument construction.

CHAPTER 7

LEGAL ARGUMENT CONSTRUCTION

7.1   INTRODUCTION

This chapter is an introduction to the construction of legal argument. The ability to engage in competent argument is seen as an essential skill in most areas of life. All academic disciplines place value on the competent construction of argument, and law is no exception. Law students tend to be taught law through a method that emphasises law cases and relies heavily on the development of argumentative strategies to apply the law and facts to simulated legal problems. Lawyers as professionals spend much of their time engaged in aspects of problem solving for clients which has, as a corollary, the ability to use excellent argumentative skills on behalf of their client.

The law as an institution has a vested interest in demonstrating that its trial procedures are fair and its legal rules are neutrally applied. In this context not only are pseudo-scientific approaches to decision making applied to the production of evidence but they are applied to the accepted methods of legal reasoning and legal argument construction. Emotion and passionate language from lawyers is not acceptable. Argument must be a dispassionate appeal to reason. An appeal based on argument constructed from the evidence (produced according to the rules of evidence) and applicable legal rules as applied to a set of facts. Of course, the majority of trials involve competing versions of the facts or of the meaning of words in legal rules (otherwise there would not be a contested trial). Argument therefore is a core skill for the theoretical study and practice of law.

Argument in fact pre-supposes competency in a number of complex skills groupings. For example:

- The ability to use various methods of legal reasoning (deductive, inductive and abductive) reasoning.
- An understanding of logic and its limits.
- An ability to handle language well.
- An ability to handle rules (to interpret and to apply them).
- An ability to understand the nature of problems, and the use of rules to solve them.
- An appreciation of the idea of problem solving, or problem analysis.
- An appreciation of the distinctions between fact analysis and legal analysis.
- An appreciation of various definitions of argument.
- An idea of argument as a process and as a structure.
- Knowledge of discrete terms such as propositions, evidence, inference which make up the constituent parts of argument.

This chapter will retain the practical 'how to' approach that is the determining characteristic of this text as it turns its attention to concentrate on issues connected to argument construction. The chapter will therefore consider in detail:

- Defining the nature of arguments, and of problems and rules as key concepts within the context of legal argument.

- Outlining methods of legal reasoning (such as the use of inductive, deductive and abductive reasoning and reasoning by analogy) and describe how these inform strategies for argument construction.
- Discussing in detail the relationship between propositions building an argument and proofs supporting propositions. (This is particularly accomplished by considering in detail a modified Wigmore Chart Method. A fact analysis process that is instructive at the level of argument construction.)

Argument concerns not only laying out facts and rules, it also involves aspects of persuasion, and determination of where the weight lies in opposing arguments. Assessors in the court, judges or jurors, decide whether an argument is strong or weak, proved or unproved. In the final analysis, how does the court, or how does anyone, decide the criteria for the *evaluation* of an argument? Evaluation cannot be solely guided by rules. Ultimately, argument construction is also a personal thing. Different people will take different routes to evidence, and relate the evidence differently to the issues. Much depends upon an individual's ability to both imagine and reason; to imagine doubts, as well as links in proof. Nothing exists in the realm of methods to tell anyone what a strong link may be. We may be excellent at the processes of transmitting, storing and retrieving facts and information but we do not have similarly developed skills of obtaining defensible conclusions from these facts and this information.

7.2   LEARNING OUTCOMES

By the end of this chapter, readers should:

- be able to define an argument and distinguish between the general meanings of argument and legal argument;
- understand the relationship between the diagnosis of problems and the construction of rules to solve problems;
- understand the difference between fact analysis and legal analysis and the connections between these activities;
- be able to basically define and then differentiate between inductive, deductive and abductive reasoning;
- be aware of the need to develop critical thinking;
- understand the way in which an argument relies on factual analysis, legal reasoning, persuasion and critical thinking;
- be able to note the connections between language and argument;
- be able to construct a modified Wigmore Chart and apply it. To be able to construct a competent argument in relation to a legal problem to be solved according to rules of legal reasoning acceptable within the English legal system;
- be able to construct a competent critical argument relating to theoretical aspects of the study of law.

7.3   LEGAL EDUCATION AND THE INTRODUCTION OF SKILLS OF ARGUMENT

At the academic stage of education the standard framework around which teaching takes place is that of legal analysis. Legal education is orientated towards the case method: how cases in courts are described and analysed. The student's skill in understanding cases, how they have been argued and how the law has been applied, is tested by asking the student to solve a hypothetical problem. The student is given the hypothetical facts. Often students are asked to present advice for one fictional party to a case. The student goes to the library (virtual or real) and searches in books and journals, and the law reports to find similar, analogous cases, noting how these have been decided and why. Then that student infers how the hypothetical case he or she has to argue will be decided, basing their inferences on the way applicable legal rules were applied in real cases. The legal analysis that students are trained to do, of course, involves basic analysis of the facts of the case. Which are the material facts? How can the facts as given be organised to make it clear that earlier cases apply? In the standard university problem question (see Chapter 8), the facts do not need to be ascertained, they are given as a neat logically ordered story. In real life, these stories are messier, the relevant facts more difficult to extract, and the doubts and solutions are not so clear.

At the vocational stage of legal training, the student is taught to engage in factual analysis and this provides the framework for the course. The student is also taught how to structure, organise and analyse a large amount of what we could call 'raw data'. They are taught to draw out the probable story from clients, the inferences in the data and see how available evidence can support the argument on the case to be proved. Evidence is correlated to the relevant facts, the facts in issue (eg, that Anna stole a book). The legal principles are assumed. Indeed this aspect of legal education reverses the process noted above in university education of drawing out legal analysis. The legal principles are for the present at least, not in issue, but a given. Theft is against the law. The test of development for the student is to see how skilled they are in deciding whether the factual data that has been made available can be put into a structure that makes it possible to construct a viable argument. An argument that proves Anna is guilty of theft, for example, because enough evidence exists to prove the elements of the unlawful act according to the relevant standard of proof.

In reality the good lawyer needs to be able to engage in competent legal analysis and factual analysis. Whilst the difference between the two is important the rigid demarcation between the two for the purpose of the academic/vocational divide is unnecessary and at the early stages of acquiring a legal education highly problematic. This demarcation is beginning to break down as the value of legal skills at the academic stage of training is being recognised in UK law schools.

Teaching legal analysis alongside factual analysis, and then subjecting the outcomes of both processes to critical analysis, gives a more holistic approach to the theoretical and the practical study of law. In addition, legal education does not only address factual analysis and legal analysis; it critically addresses macro issues relating to the law as an institution, interrogating the development of substantive law, personnel, methods of reform, underpinning ideologies and prevailing attitudes towards legal philosophy.

The common law model rests on assumptions that underlie both theory and practice and this will become clear as legal study is undertaken. It is said that in fact it rests on notions of the ideal type of rationalist tradition (Twining and Miers (1999))

This model involves *the pursuit of 'truth' through rational means*. Can you make accurate present judgements based on reasoning in cases occurring in the past on similar facts? This is certainly what the doctrine of precedent demands. The English legal system has developed principles designed to draw out that past reasoning and use it in the present and to obtain consistent decision making. Such a pursuit has as a high, but not overriding priority, the securing of justice under law. The model of adjudication is instrumentalist in that the pursuit of truth through reason is only a means to achieving a particular type of justice: the implementation of substantive law.

- The *mode* of decision making is rational not irrational, and because it is highly aspirational its practice is often critiqued.
- The *mode* of reasoning is inductive (to be explained below). Although there is room for constructing deductive argument (again to be explained below) proof always needs to be by inductive means, as will be described.

As you will have noted by now, argument requires careful attention to detail, planning and understanding that there is a close relationship between:

- cases of authority;
- language usage;
- logic and reasoning;
- planning;
- imagination; and above all
- excellent skills in critical thinking.

The phrases 'critical thinking', 'critical reasoning', 'critical reflection' come up often so it is important to be clear about what these mean.

7.4   CRITICAL THINKING

Central to the task of study is the cultivation of excellent critical thinking. Every day, all the time, information is received, processed, evaluated, ignored or acted upon by the human brain. This information is received via all the senses, hearing, seeing, touching, smelling. It is processed in micro seconds, and often without the person's conscious awareness of the process of:

- *receipt* of information;
- *evaluation* of information;
- *action* based on evaluation (do nothing/do something/store information for later use).

In our everyday life, if we refuse the information, or do not receive it, or fail to evaluate and act on it in some way, even if it is just to decide to ignore it, we would not be able to function as a human organism. In addition to the processes just described, it is also the case that often the action we take in everyday life is in part based on guesswork. What is often not appreciated is that the guesswork actually proceeds from a certain level of knowledge and experience.

Given that everyday life is a process of receipt of information, evaluation, guess work and action it is obvious that learning is not an exception to the normal rhythms of life seen in terms of receipt, evaluation and action; on the contrary it is merely a highly sophisticated and stylised part of life.

One important characteristic of highly competent people is that in many areas of their lives they have developed *a critical approach* to what they do, see and think. Not critical in the sense of 'fault finding' but critical in the sense of:

exercising

careful   judgments

based upon

careful   observation

careful   investigation

careful   consideration

of the issues relevant to the matter about which a judgment is to be made.

Most educators and senior managers would state that critical thinking, critical analysis and critical reflection are essential skills sought after in students and employees. Usually, these phrases are not defined and left as vague attributes. However, the skills involved are not vague. For they are identified by others looking for them!

There are many differing definitions of critical thinking.

It has been said to be:

- reasoning logically;
- the ability to locate underlying assumptions;

Or it has been described as clusters of skills and attitudes such as:

- analytic and argumentative skills.

Or it is described in terms of approaches to study or tasks, such as the ability to be:

- curious;
- flexible;
- sceptical.

Critical thinking is also usually thought of as an academic and/or intellectual skill but it also has crucial practical outworking in life. But what should be clear from the above discussion of what it may be is that is it not just a cerebral rational attribute and act. Critical thinking is equally informed by passion, emotion and imagination. Imagination can in fact be essential to leaps of creativity that are later identified as 'critical'. Being a critical thinker therefore is bigger than just cognitive acts of logical reasoning, and the careful consideration of argument. It also involves an ability to find assumptions behind beliefs, actions and behaviour, and bring creativity to the activity of thinking.

A critical thinker will be able to forward justification for their ideas and actions and those of others. They can compare and contrast, work through processes, subject justifications to a number of interpretations, and they can predict and test the accuracy of those predictions. They can work artificially by constructing models of the 'real' and recognise that is what has been constructed.

There is another dimension to critical thinking which is 'reflection'. Subjecting our learning to analysis based on comparing it with our experience of practice. Critical thinking involves the whole person and can be seen as a life enhancing necessary life:

> I argue that the ability to think critically is crucial to understanding our personal relationships, envisioning alternative and more productive ways of organising the workplace, and becoming politically literate. [Brookfield (1987:14).]

This takes us a long way beyond the discipline of law, legal method and studying law.

Critical thinkers are always searching for the hidden assumptions behind what others just call 'common sense', or 'everyday' accepted ways of acting or thinking. They are aware of diversity in values and behaviour. When critical thinkers locate underlying assumptions they know they have to ask if they fit in with current notions of social reality. These assumptions are carefully dissected and their accuracy, as well as their validity, questioned. At this point these competent individuals consider alternative ways of acting and alternative assumptions to back these new ways of acting.

This is the intellectual process that is foundational to studying. Each discipline may require slightly differing approaches that accord to its accepted practices and procedures, but the foundational importance of critical thinking remains intact within every part of the academic community. Each discipline will have developed its own beliefs practices and procedures, its own theory and methods and its own underlying assumptions. The study of law is no exception.

For critical thinkers nothing is closed, fixed, or certain. Everything is potentially flexible, open and possible. They are always asking what is it that lies behind the ideas, beliefs, actions that people hold or take?

This is not to say that critical thinkers hold no strong views or cannot believe in anything because they hold to the view that essentially everything is open to question. It is possible to hold the strongest convictions that something is right while accepting that all values, views, beliefs are open to question and that there can be alternative views. Critical thinkers can always imagine another plausible story, or explanation, or value. They are not going to believe in universal truths without thorough investigation and indeed will probably always remain healthily sceptical of universal views, truths and explanations.

Competency in critical thinking develops over time and no doubt all readers of this book will have developed it outside the study of law, although they may not have put a name to the process. This development can be transferred to your legal studies. But you may not have really considered the issue of critical thinking before.

In academic studies, critical thinking and a healthy scepticism of universality, are demonstrated by approaches to reasoning. Critical thinkers for example are aware that often arguments contain contradictions and these contradictions have to be looked for. They are also able to distinguish between differing types of statement, for example they can understand the difference between a statement of fact and an statement of opinion; this naturally affects the expertise of their reasoning processes. It makes a great deal of difference whether an argument is based on opinions or facts! The core of critical thinking is the constant considered identification and challenging of the accepted. It involves the evaluation of values and beliefs as well as competing truth explanations and of course texts; it involves both rationality/objectivity and emotions/subjectivity; it involves the questioning of the very categories of thought that are accepted as proper ways of proceeding and to ensure that one always:

- *searches* for hidden assumptions;
- *justifies* assumptions;
- *judges* the rationality of those assumptions;
- *tests* the accuracy of those assumptions.

In this way you will ensure the best levels of coverage for each area of your study. The next section covers each of the main clusters of skills.

The critical thinker has to engage not only with micro questions within the text, both at the superficial and the deep readings, but also with the macro-issues surrounding topics, courses and ultimately the legal system. Much of your degree study will revolve around working with legal primary or secondary texts, reconciling, distinguishing and/or following the arguments of others as well as the tentative construction of your own arguments. Much of your time may be spent explaining differences of interpretation that seem close.

When deciding what words mean in texts we make far reaching decisions and often engage with morals, religion, justice, ethics, in the search for meaning, for the truth of the text in this time.

Critical thinkers look for hidden assumptions underlying the face value explanations of the texts, they are not deceived by the theorists particularity dressed as neutrality, they are aware of the power of language and the value of argument. They know that all texts are not logical and do not necessarily feel that they have to be so. Texts will form the 'bare bones' of your studies. They are carried in language that has to be read, interpreted, questioned and seen in its fragmented contexts. It is vital to develop a critical approach.

7.5   THE DEFINITION OF ARGUMENT

> 'You did it!'
>
> 'No I didn't.'
>
> 'Yes you did.'
>
> 'No I didn't.'
>
> 'Prove it then!'
>
> 'Why should I? You prove I did.'
>
> 'No, why should I? You prove you didn't.'

What is clear by now is that lawyers must be competent argument constructors and dismantlers. An ability to construct a good argument is the core of successful study in any area. But what is an argument – let alone a good one? The word argument has a range of meanings, but all revolve around proving the validity of an assertion. Consider Figures 7.1 and 7.2, below, which illustrate the various meanings of 'argue' and 'argument'.

Figure 7.1: to argue

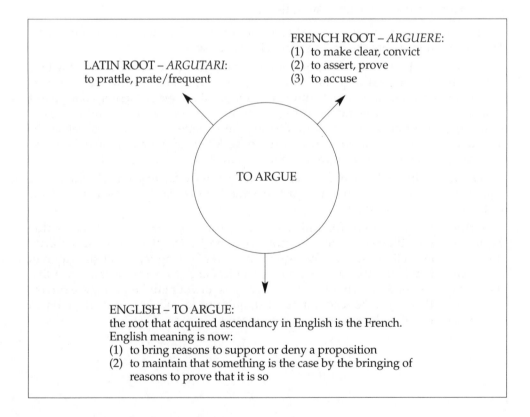

LATIN ROOT – *ARGUTARI*:
to prattle, prate/frequent

FRENCH ROOT – *ARGUERE*:
(1) to make clear, convict
(2) to assert, prove
(3) to accuse

TO ARGUE

ENGLISH – TO ARGUE:
the root that acquired ascendancy in English is the French.
English meaning is now:
(1) to bring reasons to support or deny a proposition
(2) to maintain that something is the case by the bringing of
     reasons to prove that it is so

Figure 7.2: argument

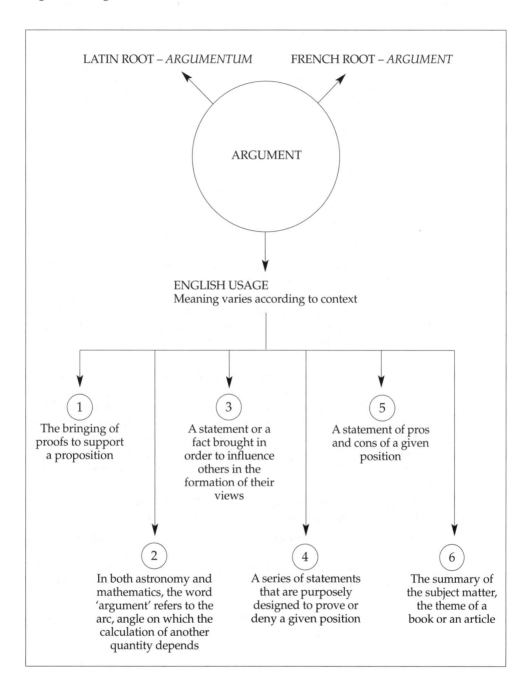

Various disciplines have differing approaches to argument and some of these are set out in Figure 7.2, above.

For our purposes, the following working definition of an argument will be used:

> An argument is a series of statements, some backed by evidence, some not, that are purposely presented in order to prove, or disprove, a given position.

Such *given positions* could be:

(a) Mary is guilty of theft contrary to the Theft Act 1968;

(b) Mary is not guilty of theft contrary to the Theft Act 1968;

(c) the European Union does not belong to its citizens;

(d) the European Union does belong to its citizens.

To engage then in the *process* of argumentation is to deploy methodically a *series* of arguments. Note the words *process* and *series*.

Legal arguments take place through the mediating influence of language both oral and written. As already noticed, language is a notoriously flexible and subjective medium of communication. The consideration already given to statutory, European and common law rules, and the discretion language injects into the process of interpretation demonstrates this flexibility. This is what moulds the law and determines outcomes. How perilously we hover on the brink of another explanation when we engage in the interpretation of words.

An argument can be viewed as a journey *from* problem *to* solution. In the case of legal problems, this journey is through the medium of the interpretation and application of legal rules to problems that have been pre-classified as legal problems. It is a journey that requires a map; a map others can follow that allows the argument crafter to take the other exactly to the desired destination; a map that eloquently explains why it is not a good idea to take that side road or that alternative route; a map that also explains how, if matters were different, another route could have been taken.

However, this journey cannot be undertaken without preparation and if the preparation is not properly carried out then the end may not be reached.

Many students hate the preparation and the journey and do not see it as a challenge during the course of which their developing study, research, legal and language skills are further refined. If the preparation and the journey can be enjoyed, and not just endured, then the road is set for lifelong successful learning, learning that has good results.

An argument is only as good as the ability to realise that a number of issues have to be balanced, as illustrated in Figure 7.3, below.

Figure 7.3: argument construction

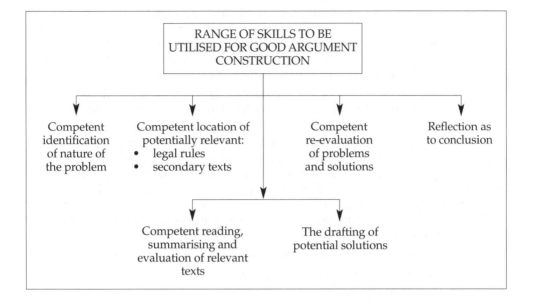

7.6   THE NATURE OF PROBLEMS AND RULES

Before continuing to discuss the detail of argument construction and the legal reasoning preferences of the English legal system it is useful to look briefly at the nature of problems and rules. A number of issues are raised by the activity of resolving problems by making rules and/or applying rules. Twining and Miers introduce the idea that much of law concerns rule handling and that an integral part of rule handling requires an understanding of the nature of problems. For the life of the law is equally connected with the human condition and the issue of problems as it is connected to the manipulation of legal rules.

The definition of a problem varies according to context and can be:

(a) a difficult question put forward for an answer in scholastic disputation;

(b) the question asked in the standard formal logic method of deductive reasoning;

(c) in mathematics and physics an inquiry or a question which, starting from a given position, investigates some fact, result or law.

Twining and Miers (1999:114) states that:

> A problem arises for an individual when she is faced with a puzzling question to answer, or a difficult choice to make, or some obstacle in the way of achieving a particular objective. A person is faced with a theoretical problem when she is confronted by a question calling for an answer that dissolves the puzzlement or solves the problem, without necessarily calling for action. A person is faced with a practical problem when there is some doubt about what to do. It is unwise to draw too sharp a line between theoretical and practical problems.

Of course it is not just individuals who have problems; problems can have a corporate or social impact requiring community or societal action.

The real issue is how you move from problem to solution. Students often do not know how to go on the journey. They cannot see the 'start' and they miscalculate the length of the journey. By correctly identifying, classifying, interpreting, one begins to journey from problem to solution but also solutions can involve *guessing* and *trying*. Solving problems with rules requires imagination.

Everything can be seen as a question awaiting an answer. Life itself could be described as a journey through questions and answers towards a solution. It is a risky business.

Solutions can be aimed at *dealing* with the problem, *or* making the problem solver *feel better*. Solutions aimed at making the problem solver feel better could include doing nothing, leaving, or it could include a reconciliation and extraction of a promise not to repeat the problematic behaviour. A parent who smacks a child for behaving in a manner unacceptable to the parent *may not have solved the problem* of the behaviour but the parent *may feel better*, thus, the problem of the parent feeling bad may have been solved.

Much depends on the role of the problem solver. Is the problem solver:

(a) a family member in a dysfunctional family;

(b) a teacher in a school;

(c) a defence lawyer in court;

(d) a judge in court;

(e) a politician in the cabinet;

(f) a scientist in a laboratory;

(g) a 'victim'?

Is the problem a purely paper issue or a personal issue? A seemingly simple problem can be complex for those seeking a solution. It has been said that no problems come as single units but as a series of interconnected issues and problems. Problems, like so many other issues, are *processes*, often *complex processes*.

If the nature of problems generally is not understood, it is difficult to understand the nature of legal rules, and the complexity of using legal rules as solutions to problems defined as legal.

Twining and Miers apply the concept of standpoint to problems and obtain some extremely interesting results because they point out that problems change their nature according to the perspective from which they are viewed.

Problem solving and problem management is a part of everyday life and the skills in these areas that have been developed automatically can assist students in turning their attention to a more methodical approach to dealing with complex legal problems.

To use knowledge, it is necessary to be aware that it is possessed. Often, people are not aware of the methods they have developed to solve problems. Some people develop bad problem solving techniques to deal with life (anger, fear, frustration, running away). It is equally possible to develop bad problem solving techniques for academic work (fear, running away, laziness, guilt, denial and frustration).

Problem solving involves accurately:

(a) seeing that there is a problem;

(b) deciding what type of problem it is (which determines much about the eventual solution);

(c) presenting (a) solution(s) to the problem.

What needs to be grasped immediately is that solutions are the *end product of a series of complicated interrelated operations.*

Teenage alcoholism, as a problem, is viewed very differently according to whether one is:

(a) a teenager who drinks moderately, heavily, or not at all;

(b) a police officer;

(c) a legislator;

(d) a parent of a teenage alcoholic;

(e) a parent of a teenager who drinks illegally but within their limits;

(f) a parent of a teenager who does not drink;

(g) a teacher;

(h) a youth worker;

(i) a seller of alcohol;

(j) a member of the medical profession;

(k) a social worker;

(l) a counsellor.

In many disciplines, professionals use problem solving models which enable users to check certain steps along the road to eventual solution. One of the best known and most useful problem solving methods within legal education is the model devised by Twining and Miers (1991), replicated in Twining and Miers (1999).

Seven steps from identification through diagnosis, prescription and implementation aimed at solution are given as follows.

7.6.1   Problem solving model

(1) **CLARIFICATION** of individual's standpoint, role, objectives, general position;

(2) **PERCEPTION** by individual of the facts constituting the situation;

(3) **EVALUATION** of one or more of the elements making the situation undesirable, obstructive, bad ... in other words, 'what's the problem?';

(4) **IDENTIFICATION** of a range of possible solutions to the perceived problem;

(5) **PREDICTION** of:

   (a) the cost of each option;

   (b) obstacles associated with each option;

(6) **PRESCRIPTION** choosing a solution to the problem; the construction of an effective policy for solving the problem;

(7) **IMPLEMENTATION** of that policy.

Things often go wrong because legislators, as well as problem solvers, often rather like impatient general practitioners:

- prescribe first; and
- diagnose later!

This course of action is a classic government response in a crisis, or student response when confronted with an essay.

Even when an attempt is made to follow a model or to try to cover all eventualities, solutions to problems often cause more problems. Because one searches deeper into a problem, it is usually observed to be a cluster of problems with a range of causes, and a range of potential solutions, each with a different set of obstacles and costs.

Much of a lawyer's job, like that of many other people, involves solving or managing such problems. They tend to be drawn into solving problems in a range of ways, mostly revolving around the application and meaning of legal rules. So, it is worthwhile paying some attention to what is meant by a rule.

Having opened the issue of 'argument' up by discussing the nature of problems it is now necessary to look at rules in a similar manner.

7.6.2   What is a rule?

There are many meanings to 'rule'. A rule can be a principle, a maxim governing individual or group conduct in life or in a game. It can be a system that creates a way of life. Within monastic life, the way of life according to rules can mean that the group itself is defined and described as the rule – the rule of St Benedict, for example. Some rules only have force within religious or social settings; others have effect within legal settings.

Some rules only have force within a given academic discipline, philosophy, law or indeed legal method. Language itself is subject to rule formation in its rules of grammar, rules that some literary stars have attempted to subvert. James Joyce in *Ulysses* or in *Finnegan's Wake*, for example.

Other rules constitute a standard against which correct behaviour is judged – religious rules, for example.

Figure 7.4: a basic definition of a legal rule

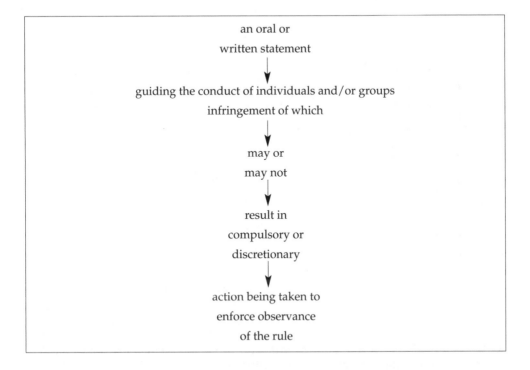

A rule often represents the view of a group concerning lawful, moral, social, acceptable, good action.

The same rule can carry out several functions. 'Do not kill' has a moral function, backed by a range of religious or philosophical groups worldwide. It also has a social function. To enable it to be enforced it has been given a legal base. Infringement can lead to severe penalties.

A rule that has not been created by the law making process or accepted by those empowered to create law is not deemed to be a legal rule.

Rules in general – and legal rules are no exception – are concerned with stating that people engage in certain activity either in thought, or word or deed.

Figure 7.5: The vocabulary of rules

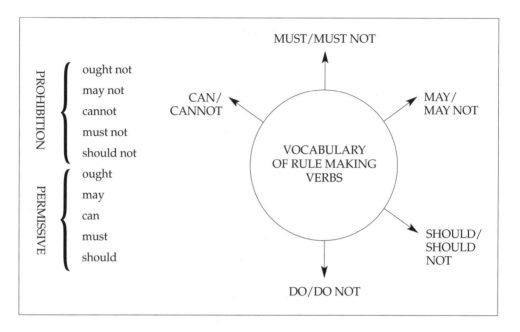

Rules often also contain statements about values. They are vehicles for communicating statements about justice, ethics, equality and fairness.

They stop   (they are **prescriptive**);

They guide   (they are **normative**);

They allow   (they are **facilitative**).

All legal rules are created by State authorised procedures and are enforced by the full force of the State. Often, the difficulty with legal rules is that they are general and need to be applied to specific situations. Rules need to be interpreted. That a rule seems applicable may be clear but the precise meaning of an important word or phrase may not be clear.

Statutory rules in our simple majority democracy often reflect the political values of the party in power. They can, therefore, be described as instruments of policy. Whatever the original intention of the political designers of the statutory rule, when users of these rules come to interpret them, defects in design are always apparent because words can, so often, be made to mean what the utterer did not intend them to mean: another reminder that language is flexible.

The judges in the courts have constructed rules of interpretation of statutes which have for nearly 100 years, taken as their predominant attitude the view that legal rules are to be interpreted without recourse to the reason, motive, or policy of the creator. The argument has a certain force, for a statutory rule can change its nature during its passage through the Houses of Parliament.

Figure 7.6: classification of rules according to their nature

7.7 CONSTRUCTING ARGUMENTS

So, now that a little thought has been given to:

(a) the meaning of argument;

(b) the nature of *problems* and *rules*;

(c) the mediating power of language,

it is hoped that the complexity of any attempt to solve problems by recourse to rules is better appreciated.

Despite the difficulties it is essential that lawyers are able to construct arguments, to fully engage in the process of effective reasoning. Without that core skill, a lawyer lacks competence.

Argument construction utilises a number of preparatory skills:

- summarising texts;
- choosing amongst appropriate texts for the most useful;
- research and organisation of texts;
- critique and analysis;
- the appropriate collection of materials in order to persuade the listener of the validity of the arguments presented.

Legal argument is often a delicate balance of facts and/or theories and the application of existing rules connected by reasoned comments to persuade of the validity of adopting the outcome suggested. In the court room, both parties put forward arguments and the judge chooses the argument that is either the most persuasive or that is the closest to the judge's own belief concerning the outcome of the case.

So far, in this text, there have been opportunities to read judgments and the judges have presented their decisions in the form of reasoned responses to the questions posed by the case. In the classroom, students are constantly called upon to practise and refine their skills in legal problem solving by engaging in reasoning processes leading to full scale argument construction.

For the practising lawyer, a valid argument is of the utmost importance. Decisions as to right action can only be made by people who are able to distinguish between competing arguments and determine that, in a given set of circumstances, one argument is more valid than another. Judges are, of course, the ultimate arbiters of the acceptable decision. Sometimes, this decision is quite subjective.

7.7.1   Logic

It is generally believed that academic and professional lawyers and, indeed, law students, are well skilled in the art of reasoning. Furthermore, it is believed that they are people who argue 'logically'.

To most, the term 'logical' indicates a person who can separate the relevant from the irrelevant, and come to an objective view, based often on supposedly objective formula. Colloquially, people accuse others, who change their mind or who are emotional in their arguing, of allowing their emotions to get the better of them, of 'not being logical'.

The dictionary defines logic as the science of reasoning, thinking, proof or inference. More than that, logic is defined as a science in its own right – a sub-section of philosophy dealing with scientific method in argument and the uses of inference. Hegel called logic the fundamental science of thought and its categories. It certainly claims to be an accurate form of reasoning: its root is found in the Greek word *logos* meaning reason.

Figure 7.7: a definition of logic

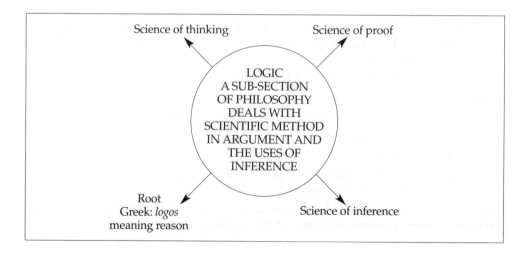

The lawyer, like a scientist, spends time considering the importance of supporting all statements with evidence and considers how one might weigh evidence on a scale of weak to strong. What is it that is actually proved by the evidence?

However, the lawyer deals in words, reports, reconstructions; the lawyer was not present observing the wrong, the accident, the incident. The scientist can always replay the event, observe the event. So, there is not a strict correlation between the lawyer and the scientist.

The logician, like the lawyer, deals in statements expressed in words and symbols called propositions. In the context of logic, the word 'proposition' only means making a statement or an assertion about something. Essentially, logic is the study of propositions and how conclusions may be correctly obtained from propositions in the process of reasoned argument.

There are two main types of logic: deductive and inductive. There is also a third process: abduction. Each of these processes will be briefly explained. In addition, 'analogic argument' (which is really a form of inductive reasoning) will be discussed, because analogic reasoning is the type of reasoning used within the English legal system where the courts argue from precedent to precedent. In fact analysis is a species of inductive reasoning.

Reasoning itself is analogous to a journey:

(a) prepare/collect information;

(b) order/organise information;

(c) start working through the information once the direction of travel is clear.

When people set out on a journey, they normally have an idea of where they are going. If they do not know where they are going, this is usually a matter of deliberate choice. When people begin to consider argument construction, they need to know where they are going: 'To begin with the end in mind.' Many students, however, do not know where they are going, hope they will know when they get there, and often give up exhausted and arbitrarily state 'Therefore, this is the end'!

It is not possible to craft a good argument by accident. Useful information to include as evidence for an argument may be uncovered accidentally; however, the argument *can never* be accidentally constructed.

7.8   TYPES OF LEGAL REASONING

7.8.1   Deduction

Reasoning can be described as a careful journey through various propositions. Movement being allowed by evidence leading to inference. In deductive reasoning, the argument has to follow a prescribed form.

A major premise – which tends to state a generality	This form of argument is called a *syllogism*
A minor premise – which tends to state a particularity	
Conclusion	

The subject in the major premise (or proposition) *becomes* the predicate in the minor premise and the conclusion is necessary, or compelled. There is no other conclusion possible in that form of reasoning. However, this form of reasoning leaves no space for examining the truth or otherwise of the premises, and is of limited use within legal reasoning for this very reason. Indeed, a logician would not be concerned about the verifiability of the premises only the purity of the form. So, an argument could be logically valid without being correct; that is, the premises could be mistaken but the form may be correct and lead therefore to the conclusion.

Figure 7.8: demonstration of deductive reasoning

Deductive reasoning

Main proposition: To steal is to act contrary to s 1 of the Theft Act 1978

Minor proposition: Anna has stolen a book

Conclusion: Anna has acted contrary to s 1 of the Theft Act 1978

1   As can be seen the MAIN proposition is a general comment that to steal is to act contrary to the law.
2   The MINOR proposition reduces it to a particular incident 'Anna stole a book'. The conclusion is compelled.
3   But ... does it get us anywhere in trying to ascertain Anna's guilt?

No!

Why not?

Because ... We need an argument to prove that Anna did indeed steal the book.

In fact, the example above with Anna stealing the book demonstrates the form well.

| The MAIN | premise MUST | be | GENERAL |
| The MINOR | premise OUGHT | to be | PARTICULAR |

Whilst the journey through the deductive form has been correct, we cannot say yet if the minor premise is true. Law is not just an intellectual exercise. Consequences flow if there is a conviction of a criminal offence. So in fact more needs to be done before a conviction can take place for this theft. The minor premise has to be proved. Anna stole the book which is outside the remit of deduction. It is this minor premise that would be the focus of a trial.

The reasoning most valued within law demonstrates a consistency of approach, and logic as consistency is highly valued. However, the law is not, and cannot be, a closed system that can be made the subject of a final software programme. Analytically there are always other possibilities, which makes a lot of legal decision making contingent. In a civil court confronted with the real litigant the law expects the contingent nature of legal decision making to turn *'on a balance of probabilities'*. In the criminal court it expects the contingent nature of legal decision to be based upon a jury or magistrate finding the minor premise *'proved beyond all reasonable doubt'*.

Deduction can be useful if a new legal rule is being tested to discover whether it is going to clash with any existing legal rule. It can also be useful when precedent is being teased out for the first time and logical consequences need to be tracked.

Logic distinguishes between deductive and inductive. An inductive argument can for example have as an inference a generalisation (eg, innocent people do not run away).

Figure 7.9: generalisations

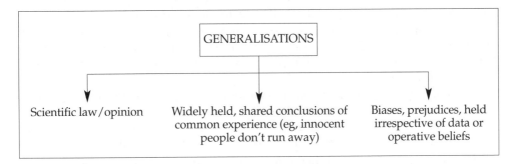

A generalisation can be quite easily attacked as it is usually constructed on flimsy arguments. But it is also worth remembering that no argument can ever be 100% sound. Remember our system requires less than perfect proof: balance of probabilities in the civil area and beyond reasonable doubt in the criminal law. So, accusing someone of not having a perfect 100% argument is not a good argument! No one has a 100% case.

7.8.2   Induction

There is another form of arguing which involves arguments that put forward some general proposition (the conclusion) from fact or facts that seem to provide some evidence for the general given proposition or group of propositions (the premises).

This is perhaps the closest to the everyday legal argument when decisions are made concerning which side of a dispute is accorded the privileging of their story in terms of the law's authority to provide an   declaration of right followed by sanction and/or compensation.

Inductive reasoning is similar to deductive reasoning in so far as the conclusions are based on premises. However, in inductive reasoning, the conclusion reached extends beyond the facts in the premise. The premise supports the conclusion, it makes it *probable*. Therefore, there is less certainty and it is possible that another conclusion exists. A sub-division of inductive reasoning is reasoning by analogy or analogous reasoning, this being the method best known to English legal method.

The difference between deductive and inductive reasoning is that deductive reasoning is a closed system of reasoning, from the general to the general or the particular, and includes cases where *the conclusion is drawn out; it is, therefore, analytical,* whereas inductive reasoning is an open system of reasoning. It involves finding a general rule from particular cases and is *inconclusive* which suggests the end processes of legal judgments are inconclusive. However, when it is, the courts ensure that inconclusive reasoning can be enforced!

Like deductive reasoning, the logic of inductive reasoning has no interest in the *actual truth* of the propositions that are the premises or the conclusion.

Just because a logical form is correctly constructed, it does not mean that the conclusion expressed is *true*. The truth of a conclusion depends upon whether the major and minor premises express statements that are *true*. The statements may be false.

Much time is spent by lawyers in court attempting to prove the truth of statements used as building blocks in the construction of arguments.

In an inductive argument, the premises only tend to support the conclusions, but they do not *compel* the conclusion. By tradition, the study of inductive logic was kept to arguments by way of analogy, or methods of generalisation, on the basis of a *finite* number of observations.

Argument by analogy is the most common form of argument in law. Such an argument begins by stating that two objects are observed to be similar by a number of attributes. It is concluded that the two objects are similar with respect to a third. The strength of such an argument depends upon the *degree* of relationship.

Lawyers are advisers and they offer predictive advice based on how previous similar cases have been dealt with. All advice is based on the lawyers' perception of what would happen in court; this is usually enough to ensure that, in the vast majority of civil cases, matters between disputants are settled. The lawyers' perception is based upon their experience of how judges reason.

Although deductive reasoning lends support to the Blackstonian theory that the law is always there to be found, there is room for the judge to exercise discretion. A judge will have to find the major premise. The judge may do this by looking at statutes or precedent. In the absence of statute, precedent or custom, he or she may need to create one by analogy or a process of induction. Once the judge has stated the major premise the judge will need to examine the facts of the case to ascertain if they are governed by the major premise. If this has been established, the conclusion will follow syllogistically.

In the vast majority of cases, the conclusion will simply be an application of existing law to the facts. Occasionally, the decision creates a new law which may or may not be stated as a proposition of law. To ascertain whether a new law has been stated may require a comparison between the material facts implied within the major premise and the facts which make up the minor premise.

To summarise, judges are involved in a type of inductive reasoning called reasoning by analogy. This is a process of reasoning by comparing examples. The purpose is to reach a conclusion in a novel situation. This process has been described as a three stage process:

(1) the similarity between the cases is observed;

(2) the rule of law (*ratio decidendi*) inherent in the first case is stated. Reasoning is from the particular to the general (deduction);

(3) that rule is applied to the case for decision. At this point, reasoning is from the general to the particular (induction).

Figure 7.10: progression of law cases

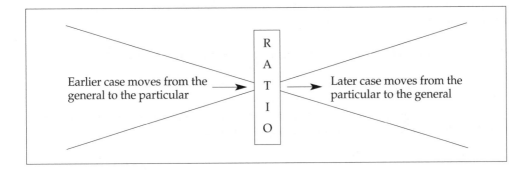

Inductive reasoning rests on implied law or assumption so it could lapse into deduction. A thesis is forwarded, which is, let us say, 'Anna has stolen a book'. Evidence is then brought forward and inferences drawn from that evidence that begins to suggest the likely outcomes.

We take a single isolated fact and upon it base immediately an inference as to the proposition in question. Of course if there are two or three inferences that we can draw upon all the better.

The thesis would be:

'Anna has stolen a book'

What inferences could we use to say it was her, to prove she did it, what is our evidence?

(1) An eyewitness saw Anna take a book from the shelf and leave the store. (Witness could be mistaken.)
(2) Anna was stopped outside the store with the book by the store detective.
(3) That particular book had not been noted out of the store by the computer sales system which still shows that it is on the shelf. (Has the system been operating well?)

Inferences 1–3 taken together seem to strongly indicate that Anna took the book out of the store. This appears enough to prove the physical act (*actus reus*) of theft at the level of evidence, that is, at the level of factual analysis. However, crimes usually require a mental element, the *mens rea*. This is a good moment to look at s 1 of the Theft Act 1978 and consider these issues of the *actus reus* and *mens rea*. The mental element required to prove theft is an intention to permanently deprive the true owner of the item stolen.

However, if Anna alleges that she did not intend to take the book, this is an argument stating that there was no intention to permanently deprive the *mens rea* remains unproved and theft cannot be proved. These issues can be more easily seen in Figure 7.11.

Figure: 7.11: the *actus reus* (act) and *mens rea* (mental intent) of theft

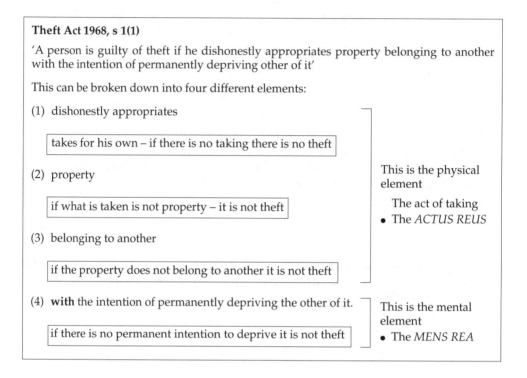

> **Theft Act 1968, s 1(1)**
>
> 'A person is guilty of theft if he dishonestly appropriates property belonging to another with the intention of permanently depriving other of it'
>
> This can be broken down into four different elements:
>
> (1) dishonestly appropriates
>
> > takes for his own – if there is no taking there is no theft
>
> (2) property   This is the physical element
>
> > if what is taken is not property – it is not theft   The act of taking
> >   • The *ACTUS REUS*
>
> (3) belonging to another
>
> > if the property does not belong to another it is not theft
>
> (4) **with** the intention of permanently depriving the other of it.   This is the mental element
>
> > if there is no permanent intention to deprive it is not theft   • The *MENS REA*

7.9   MAKING IT 'REAL' – *R v ANNA*

This chapter has given a brief explanation and has demonstrated the forms of, and the relationship between deductive and inductive reasoning. At the same time it has also introduced the two-part nature of most legal rules relating to criminal offences, the physical act (*actus reus*) and the mental act (*mens rea*). To make these distinctions come to life the rest of this section will deal with a fictitious criminal case of *R v Anna*. Anna has been accused of stealing a book from a shop.

The first relationship that *R v Anna* will be used to show is that between deductive and inductive reasoning. The two approaches to reasoning are set out in Figure 7.12. Both the inductive and the deductive forms are for the prosecution. Can you rephrase them to provide inductive and deductive forms in favour of the defence?

Figure 7.12: inductive and deductive reasoning

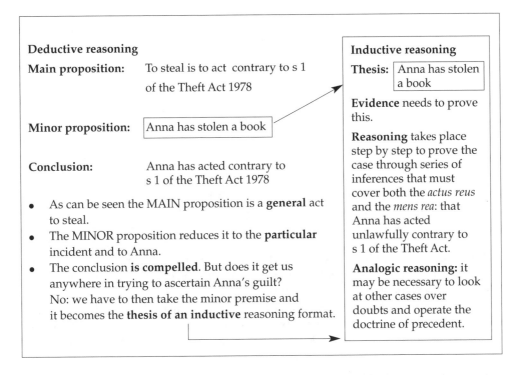

Deductive reasoning

Main proposition: To steal is to act contrary to s 1 of the Theft Act 1978

Minor proposition: Anna has stolen a book

Conclusion: Anna has acted contrary to s 1 of the Theft Act 1978

- As can be seen the MAIN proposition is a **general** act to steal.
- The MINOR proposition reduces it to the **particular** incident and to Anna.
- The conclusion **is compelled**. But does it get us anywhere in trying to ascertain Anna's guilt? No: we have to then take the minor premise and it becomes the **thesis of an inductive** reasoning format.

Inductive reasoning

Thesis: Anna has stolen a book

Evidence needs to prove this.

Reasoning takes place step by step to prove the case through series of inferences that must cover both the *actus reus* and the *mens rea*: that Anna has acted unlawfully contrary to s 1 of the Theft Act.

Analogic reasoning: it may be necessary to look at other cases over doubts and operate the doctrine of precedent.

It should not be overlooked that each inference placed by someone constructing an argument asserting Anna's guilt can provoke one of the following counter-responses:

(1) An explanation as to why the assertion is misguided. (Explain it away!)

(2) A straight denial. (Deny the validity or existence of the evidentiary fact backing your inference.)

(3) A rival evidential fact is set up and asserted.

In fact it is important when setting up an argument that the potential dangers of inference are considered. For there are loopholes for error and one of the most common is overlooking the fact that sometimes there is just a plurality of causes. There can be alternative explanations. The important task is to identify possible alternative conclusions and test them out. The question then becomes which are the stronger inferences? Does your favoured argument look strong or does a counter-argument stand up?

As noted above inductive reasoning is the closest to everyday legal reasons, as inductive reasoning involves putting forward a conclusion that seems strong, based on inferences that provide evidence in favour of one party.

So, your final argument will consist of a range of propositions or assertions that will invariably be backed by evidence. For some law problems, a cluster of arguments may need to be set up dealing with separate issues.

Figure 7.13: the constituent parts of argument

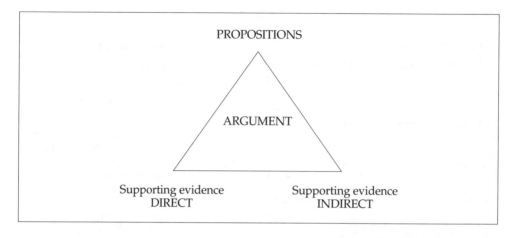

Whilst the diagram above looks simple it is necessary to bear in mind that the propositions may have alternative explanations and the evidence supporting these alternative explanations will need to be analysed.

So at the level of factual analysis it has been demonstrated that, in relation to law, deductive argument requires extension by tracking through the process of inductive reasoning, starting with the minor premise of the deductive argument.

7.9.1   Abductive reasoning

Lawyers inevitably look at possible inductive reasoning that counters their own argument, otherwise they could be caught by surprise. This involves constructing opposing hypothetical theses. The evidence a lawyer has may suggest alternatives, and perhaps even more plausible alternatives. This creative process which tends to argue around the data based on hypothetical matters, rather than on matters known, is called abductive reasoning.

However, legal argument does not just involve factual analysis. It also involves legal analysis. Over the next pages of this chapter using the fictitious case of *R v Anna* both factual and legal data will be considered.

Recall the definition of theft.

Theft Act 1968, s 1(1)

A person is guilty of theft if he dishonestly appropriates property belonging to another with the intention of permanently depriving that other.

We have referred to the minor premise in a deductive argument as forming the thesis of inductive reasoning. We have also indicated that the conclusion although logically valid may be wrong or untrue because either the major or the minor premise or both are wrong/untrue. The major way of attacking a deductive argument is through the premises. The conclusion is logically compelled and cannot be attacked. The major premise, however, may be targeted for argument.

The major premise of the deductive syllogism that has been considered in this chapter (see Figure 7.12, above) was expressed as:

- To steal is to act contrary to the Theft Act.

This can be expressed in a more specific manner and still remain general:

- It is contrary to s 1(1) of the Theft Act to dishonestly appropriate property belonging to another with the intention of permanently depriving that other.

The entire deductive argument can then be set out as shown in Figure 7.14, below.

Figure 7.14: a deductive argument

Major premise (general)
- It is contrary to s 1(1) of the Theft Act to dishonestly appropriate property belonging to another with the intention of permanently depriving that other.

Minor premise (particular)
- Anna dishonestly appropriated a book the property of X store with the intention of permanently depriving the store of it.

Conclusion (compelled)
- Anna has acted contrary to s 1(1) of the Theft Act.

We could still attack the minor premise by using it as the thesis of inductive reasoning. However, this time we want to attack the major premise. One way of doing this is to check the interpretation of the words and phrases in the major premise in so far as they replicate s 1(1) of the Theft Act.

What do you consider to be the meaning of the phrases:

- intention to permanently deprive (*mens rea*);
- dishonestly (*actus reus*);
- property (*actus reus*).

These are important words and phrases that may well become the focus of legal argument in the court. We will note later in this chapter how these words and phrases are of major importance in a theft case. In order to explore their meaning, it is necessary to consult other cases where these words and phrases in the Theft Act 1968 have been discussed.

Figure 7.15, below, sets out two opposing deductive arguments: one affirming the central deductive argument and one setting out to deny it. This type of structure is the skeleton of the majority of arguments revolving around the use of facts and legal authority to resolve legal dispute in a trial scenario.

Figure 7.15: deductive argument and two opposing inductive arguments

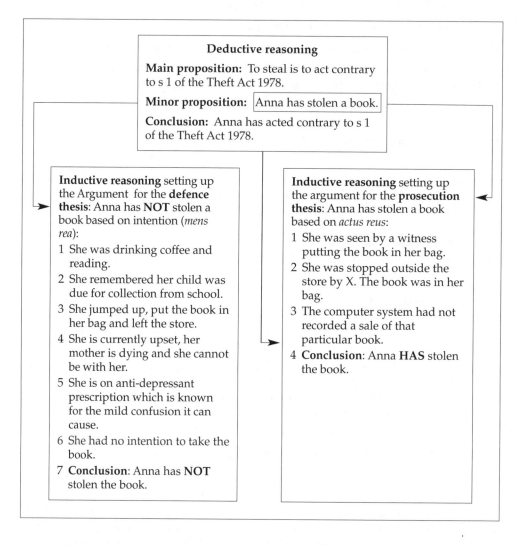

As can be seen, point 6 of the defence thesis in Figure 7.15, above, relates to the issue of intention, arguing that Anna did not have the necessary *mens rea*. Theft can only be proved if both the *actus reus* and the *mens rea* are present. The prosecution case argues that in fact Anna was seen instore taking the book by an eye witness and stopped and found with the book outside the store. This, argues the prosecution, demonstrates intention to permanently deprive (see points 1, 2 and 3 of the inductive thesis of the prosecution). The defence counter this argument by pointing to personal circumstances that negate intention (see points 2–6 of the prosecution thesis). As you are able to comprehend how the same information can give rise to differing arguments based upon evidence unknown to the other party at the time, you can appreciate the importance of careful construction of argument. In addition, of course, one needs to add the legal basis for the arguments found in the authority of decided cases. This will be considered later in the chapter. It is always a good idea to try and predict counter-arguments to your own. Then you can consider how you would deal with them.

The essential quality of a well structured argument is that it takes the reader/listener from the beginning to the end and makes them hold to the opinion that the argument is correct or the most plausible argument. Sometimes, the process of argument uses bridges from one fact to another that are not made of evidence but of inference.

It is not wrong to assert a proposition that is not backed by evidence, but an adjudicating body is not compelled to accept the validity of an unproved proposition. It is difficult to refute a proposition backed by strong evidence but of course evidence is not always strong, it may be tenuous, or medium strong, etc. So, there are many variables present in an argument. One has to look for the weak points. Most adjudicating bodies have elements of discretion and can accept the tenuous but plausible explanatory bridge from one proven fact to another as the argument progresses to conclusion. Much depends on the minor or major nature of the proposition asserted. If it is pivotal for the case, then it must be backed by evidence. Lawyers will tend to take the little jumps with plausibility and, hopefully, the big jumps with proven propositions!

At the everyday level of explanation, a legal argument tends to say:

- This happened.
- The following law states that this behaviour is illegal in certain circumstances.
- These witnesses, these official documents, this forensic evidence prove that it happened.
- It can be proved therefore that X did this.
- X, therefore, broke the law.

An essay may argue about theory, rather than fact, but the structures remain the same.

Argument construction is not difficult if there has been meticulous preparation of information. The argument will be basic or elegant depending upon the development of skills, understanding of the law, the level of preparation, thought and reflection that has gone into the argument construction. What one gets back is proportional to the quality of what has gone in. A strong argument may ultimately be rejected if there is a fair amount of discretion, but the person who has forwarded it will know it is good. Indeed, often an adjudicator, even when deciding against an argument, will compliment the argument constructor on the art with which it was done.

7.10   THE MODIFIED 'WIGMORE CHART METHOD'

Anderson and Twining (1991) brought the Wigmore Chart Method to the attention of legal educators. This is an interesting method using symbols, numbers and key lists to allow simultaneous consideration of evidence and facts to enhance factual analysis and ultimately impact legal analysis. The chart is set out in Figure 7.16, below, as a preview. The remainder of this section explains how such a chart is produced, what it says, and why it is indeed extremely useful as a teaching tool for argument construction.

Figure 7.16: a specimen Wigmore Chart

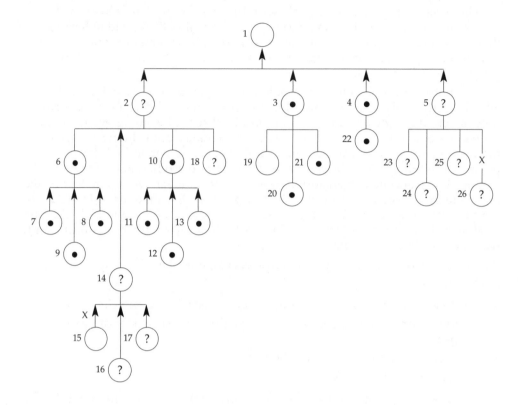

Ultimate probanda
1   Mary stole a £20 note contrary to section 1 of the Theft Act 1968

Penultimate probanda
2   Mary dishonestly appropriated
3   Property, £20 note,
4   Belonging to another (Andrew)
5   With the intention of permanently depriving Andrew of it

Key list
6   **Mary went into Andrew's room**
7   Statement of William supports 6
8   Statement of Andrew supports 6
9   Statement of Mary supports 6

Note: key list continues ... to number 26.

Do not be concerned by its appearance of complexity. It is a clear, manageable system of notation.

The best understanding of this method can be obtained from briefly discussing it from three perspectives:

1 The original Wigmore Chart Method dating from 1913.

2 Anderson and Twining's modification of the Wigmore Chart Method, from the mid-1980s.

3 Use of the modified method in this book as an aid for understanding argument construction. This will give a firm understanding of the discussions above through a practical demonstration.

This discussion will then be followed by a practical demonstration of the modified Chart Method (changed slightly for our use) looking at the fictional criminal case of *R v Mary*. This is a demonstration devised to continue the development of argumentative skills already discussed in this chapter. A second case, *R v Jack*, is provided at the end of the chapter to allow students to try out their developing skills by analysing and charting a new case and building an argument.

7.10.1   The original Wigmore Chart Method

John Wigmore wanted to restore an imbalance in the approach to evidence to be used in the trial. He first unveiled his views in an article published in the *Illinois Law Review* in 1913. He was concerned with issues surrounding the law of evidence. The law of evidence, as it is normally considered in university courses and in practice, is particularly concerned with the what type of evidence is admissible in court to prove the case of the parties. It is also concerned with the procedures that need to be followed to ensure that allowable evidence is not rendered inadmissible due to procedural and avoidable mistakes by those dealing with it before it reaches the court room. (This covers the field of forensic science as well as witness testimony.)

Wigmore, however, believed that while the admissibility of evidence and the following of procedures are important aspects of the law relating to evidence, there was another *more* important area that had been completely ignored. This was the aspect of proof itself. What is the *effect* of the admissible evidence? How does it build to a finding of case proved *for or against* one party? Can it be said that there is a science of proof? Here of course issues relating to evidence and the construction of argument begin to merge. Wigmore sees proof in terms of the proving of points in argument persuading judges and juries of the outcome of a case. He argued:

> ... there is, and there must be, a probative science – the principles of proof – independent of the artificial rules of procedure [Wigmore (1913:77)].

He forwarded the charting method shown in Figure 7.16, above, which was able to lay out and evaluate the individual and cumulative strength and likely *effect* of evidence on judges. It is a method based on logical principles of relationship between propositions asserted. He divided his research into a suitable method that could be trusted with such a purpose into three areas:

- the need for a clear object for the method ('the object');
- ensuring that the method constructed complied with a range of criteria set ('the necessary conditions');
- the structure ('the apparatus of the method').

7.10.1.1 The object

Wigmore believed that the object of the enquiry was to make sense of a mass of data presented as evidence, and to deal with it in a logical manner. The method has to allow all the data to be viewed simultaneously, ie, at the same time to allow for a more precise evaluation of the persuasive proof of that evidence. The interesting issue here is that the data included assertions (she had the motive, she stole the book), as well as evidence relating to the act of theft (the book was not logged as sold on the sales system, the coffee shop assistant saw Anna take the book). So, it was to be a method that was able to take on board different types of evidence and argumentative propositions.

Wigmore expressed his object as being able to:

> determine rationally the net persuasive effect of a mixed mass of evidence ... [Wigmore (1913: 78)].

and further comments that:

> knowledge in the highest perfection would consist in the simultaneous possession of facts. To comprehend a science perfectly, we should have every fact present with every other fact [Wigmore (1913:78)].

For we approach data in time, we read one fact and the next moment we read another fact in a sequence that is also moving through time. Wigmore aimed at producing a chart that allowed us to view data in one fixed moment by a sweep of the eyes. That is, to work sequentially at producing a structure that could be viewed simultaneously. Simultaneity also assists us in ordering our argument because the method is the evaluative means to the end of presenting a persuasive argument. Order is important and can affect outcome.

Wigmore was particularly vexed by the issue of persuasion, belief and outcome. For he noted that it was evidence as assembled that leads to a result. That result is conditioned by belief and belief is:

> purely mental. It is distinct from the external reality, or actual fact.

7.10.1.2 The necessary conditions

There are certain conditions and or criteria that have to be met in any method in order to attest to its efficiency. Wigmore identified those as:

- being able to deal with all *types* of evidence;
- being able to include all evidential data of relevance to an individual case;
- being able to show the relationship of *each* evidential fact in the case;
- having to present data in a simultaneous scheme;
- being capable of being full but not too complex;
- being able to distinguish between fact as alleged and fact as believed.

| Proposition | (a) Anna stole a book: | fact alleged |
| Proposition | (b) I believe Anna did steal the book: | fact as believed |

Between the two positions (a) and (b) there is a transitional point when the movement is from allegation to belief in the truth of the allegation or belief in the probable truth. Law is about probability: 'I believe beyond reasonable doubt Anna stole a book.' The transitional point between assertion and belief is often implicit inference.

It is important to remember that the chart can only show what the user now *believes* and how they got there. It *cannot* show what the user *ought* to believe.

7.10.1.3 The apparatus

Wigmore devised a chart that could deliver the objective and keep to the necessary conditions above. It was a chart that recorded symbols translated in a list of narrative. Each symbol stands for a type of evidentiary material, or a proposition of argument and is given a number. A key list briefly states in narrative form the proposition and/or evidentiary data the number stands for.

The symbols

The chart as devised by Wigmore contained a complex symbolic system which will not be used for our purposes now. However, some of the system will be explained as it assists greatly in understanding the modified form.

Wigmore gave two symbols for evidence. These are set out in Figure 7.17, below. A small horizontal line denotes defence, the symbol without a horizontal line denotes plaintiff or prosecution.

Figure 7.17: symbols for testimonial and circumstantial evidence

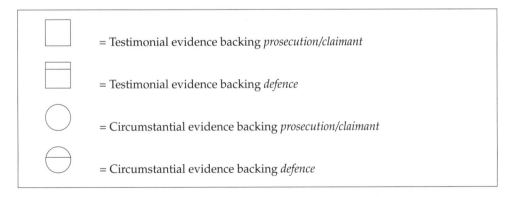

As you can see, the addition of the line indicates a proposition/evidentiary fact relating to the defence.

The removal of one line in the square and the opening of the circle represents the negative impact of testimonial or circumstantial evidence, as seen in Figure 7.18, below.

Figure 7.18: example of negative testimonial evidence

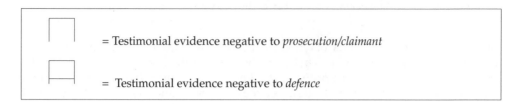

Ordering of information

This can be horizontal, vertical or diagonal. When information is vertical it is hierarchical.

Facts supporting other facts are placed below the fact to be supported and linked by a line.

Figure 7.19: testing understanding so far

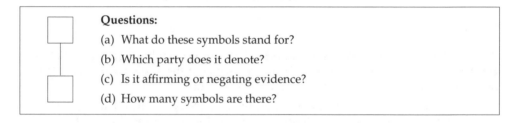

The probative weight of evidence. If one fact as explained corroborates another, it is connected by a line to the fact corroborated, etc. See the line in Figure 7.19. As soon as we believe the fact to be true the connecting line is changed to an arrow pointing in the direction of the proof (see Figure 7.20, below).

Figure 7.20: demonstration of belief and direction of proof

If we come to question the link we remove the arrow and place a question mark against the connecting line. If we come to doubt the truth of the testimonial evidence itself we place a question mark in the symbol (see Figure 7.21, below).

Figure 7.21: symbolic representation of doubts

We merely change the symbol. So a line can be represented in three ways as set out in Figure 7.22, below. This means that the chart is flexible to be a work in progress.

Figure 7.22: the three means of attaching a line

Wigmore also had closed dots and open dots placed inside symbols to denote belief of individual pieces of evidence.

Figure 7.23: symbols for belief and unbelief

Numbers

Each symbol on the chart is is numbered and relates to a list setting out brief narrative labels for the evidence represented by the symbol.

Figure 7.24: demonstration of joining symbols

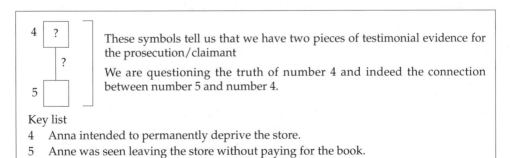

These symbols tell us that we have two pieces of testimonial evidence for the prosecution/claimant

We are questioning the truth of number 4 and indeed the connection between number 5 and number 4.

Key list
4   Anna intended to permanently deprive the store.
5   Anne was seen leaving the store without paying for the book.

Self-test: what do the following symbols in Figure 7.25, below, tell us? How many symbols are there?

Figure 7.25: self-test re: symbols

The analysis of the chart

The last stage is analysis, as the chart is only the means to the ends! As the full chart is considered links between propositions and evidence can be more clearly seen. The point of the chart is the juxtapositioning of the evidence, facts, assertions, etc in a way allowing simultaneous viewing so that they ultimately lead to a single finally believed outcome. The *process* of reaching the outcome *is the argument*. The *outcome is* the *conclusion* of the argument.

Wigmore had many symbols denoting explanation, weak and strong inferences, the movement from doubt to belief, unsupported and supported inferences. He had symbols denoting object as opposed to person testimony, symbols for denials, rival assertions, and for generalisations, etc. His charts were extremely complicated matters taking many hours to construct, which is probably why his methods were not widely taken on board in American law schools, although he himself used the method in his teaching for 40 years. In addition whilst the complex symbolic networks that he set up appeal to some students, many are perhaps fearful or completely alienated by what appear to be complex mathematical structures.

When Wigmore first set out his chart method in 1913 he said that it was not the symbols themselves that were important but the simultaneous juxtaposition of facts. Therefore the person constructing a chart could use their own symbols. Anderson and Twining did just that and made some changes to the charting method (that is, they modified it) for teaching. It is a good modification and is discussed below.

7.10.2 Anderson and Twining's modification of the Wigmore Chart Method

In an excellent book, *Analysis of Evidence* (1991), Anderson and Twining take the time to discuss the uses and limits of a Wigmore chart as a tool of legal education. They also note its use in other areas that require investigative tools. They recount an interesting story that demonstrates the far reaching applications of the method that Wigmore devised. They record David Schum presenting Wigmore's Chart method without revealing its source to a group of computer analysts in the 1980s. When he asked them to predict when the system was invented the earliest date given was 1970! The analysts said the sophisticated inference networks had not been developed prior to the 1970s. In the 1990s David Schum and others have effectively applied Wigmore's methodology to intelligence analysis, and other complex inferential systems such as weather forecasting. If Wigmore's method was to be able to cope it had to be able to deal with inference networks referring to the ways that evidence was dealt with in previously decided cases. All inference networks require chains of reasoning – links – and nothing is ever final, there is always a missing link. These factors constitute the complexity of inference networks. Wigmore's Chart was designed to take this into consideration. Therefore, as developed it allowed the construction of complex arguments, detailing chains of reasoning and linking evidence to matters to be proven, which is why it is a useful method to be applied to investigative and analytic tasks.

Technically a Wigmore Chart can be described as a form of Directed Acyclic Graph (DAG).

Figure 7.26: meaning of Directed Acyclic Graph

- It is – **Directed** if it shows the direction of reasoning via arrows (when belief in the connecting established).

- It is – **Acyclic** if you following any reasoning path or path of probabilistic inference you are NEVER led back to exactly where you started. This must never happen because if it does you are actually stuck in a probabilistic inferential loop from which there is no escape!

- It is a – **Graph** because it is a symbol based representation with translation.

Wigmore's Chart is most immediately concerned with the issue of the relevancy, credibility and the probative force of evidence. The linking of these issues in the mind of the student is essential. When joined to critical analysis the student will be placed in a position to construct the best argument that is available.

7.10.2.1 Uses and limitations of the Wigmore Chart Method

As has been indicated the chart in its full form is extremely time consuming to create and for that reason may be of extremely limited use to practitioners. However, it has great potential as a learning tool. Indeed, Wigmore used it for over 40 years with his own law students.

It was its educational value that caught the serious attention of Anderson and Twining. The chart method creates awareness about the nature and construction of argument and as a result students recognise how arguments are constructed using relations between propositions supported by proof. This awareness is not often directly encouraged within the parameters of legal education. The chart therefore brings argumentative structure out into the open as an object of consideration. Then judgements can be made about its *probative* and *persuasive* force.

Twining absolutely correctly says that if a student goes through the process of analysis in just one case in a disciplined way they gain an awareness of how easy it is to get argument wrong because they can see:

- reliance on unidentified generalisations;
- fallacies in argument;
- presentation of irrelevant material;
- gaps in reasoning and logical jumps being taken;
- shifting standpoints being left unacknowledged;
- propositions not supported.

If there is a gap or a doubt in your argument it is better to find it yourself and work on it. Then you can at least connect gaps in reasoning by propositions that are unsupported and *know* that you have done this and thus be in control of your argument.

Anderson and Twining suggest there are in fact seven stages to a chart:

(1) Clarification of standpoint (why is the chart being constructed).

(2) The formulation of UP (ultimate probanda).

(3) The formulation of PP (penultimate probanda).

(4) Formulation of theory/choice of propositions (interim probanda).

(5) Key list. ⎤
              ⎥ The chart and key list are the *means* not the *ends*
(6) Chart. ⎦

(7) Complete analysis.

Each of these will be briefly described.

7.10.2.2 Clarification of standpoint

We have noted the issue of standpoint. Schum noted that standpoint affects inference network construction. In addition how can an audience assess the chart created without a knowledge of the standpoint of the creator? The greater the detail that the charter goes into in relation to inference networks the greater the extraction and/or revelation of conditions of doubt. So, it is important to constantly ask oneself 'Where are we in the process?', 'What are my objectives?' and to be aware that one's standpoint can change in the execution of one project. Basically, we can say that standpoint is the function of three variables:

- Time and location (Wigmore had in mind the trial arena). We will have different times and locations depending on the exercise. Usually however it will be post trial. We will often be asking: was the court right on the evidence presented? Was there another story that was more probable? Although we may set exercises presenting as pre-trial.
- Objective purpose – organisation, evaluative, advocacy, educational.
- Role.

7.10.2.3 The formulation of the ultimate probanda

Probanda is the latin term for proposition but the latin is more flexible allowing a number of connections to be made. The term is therefore retained. The UP is the touchstone of relevancy controlling the relationship of *all* other propositions in the chart. It is the substantive law proposition – the elements of the crime or the civil wrong. It is also the matter to be proved. Once proved, there is no more to say on the point. This is the minor proposition (or premise) of an deductive argument that we have already noted as inevitably becoming the *thesis* of the necessary inductive argument.

Deductive argument

Main proposition: Theft is contrary to s 1 of the Theft Act 1968

Minor proposition: Anna stole a book   ⟶   *Thesis* of inductive argument

Conclusion: Anna is guilty of theft

7.10.2.4 The formulation of the penultimate probanda

Law prescribes the specific points, or elements that must be proven to a certain standard (standard of proof) to prove the UP. For example looking to the UP above let us remind ourselves of the definition of theft given above. Looking at the definition of theft again, and reminding ourselves how it is to be broken into its constituent elements we can see that our PP are those four elements.

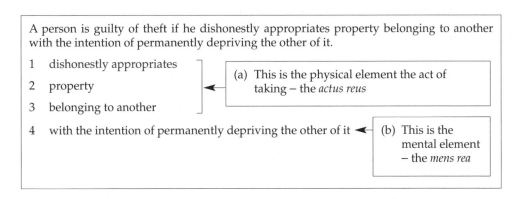

A person is guilty of theft if he dishonestly appropriates property belonging to another with the intention of permanently depriving the other of it.

1   dishonestly appropriates

2   property

3   belonging to another

(a) This is the physical element the act of taking – the *actus reus*

4   with the intention of permanently depriving the other of it

(b) This is the mental element – the *mens rea*

7.10.2.5 Formulation of the theory/theorem and choice of the interim probanda

At this point one comes to the main deviation in Anderson and Twining's presentation of the Wigmore Chart Method. They conclude most correctly that students, as well as practitioners, find the time required for a whole chart too much to be contemplated. They vastly simplify the range of symbols and aspects that will be included in the body of the chart. The propositions linking the evidence to the UP and PP are called interim probanda. These set up the inferences between evidence and UP. They can be assertions, generalisations, facts or other data. These provide the source of our claims about the strength of weakness of the final argument. If these are placed appropriately on the chart we can assess the argument, see gaps and doubts.

7.10.2.6 The construction of the list

As stated above the chart is a series of linked numbered symbols translated through a narrative key list: the chart records the propositions that define all evidence being considered and all interim, PP and UP. The synthetic element is the chart showing the link patterns.

7.10.2.7 The chart

The chart is constructed simultaneously with the key listing. We will look at this shortly.

7.10.2.8 Completion of the analysis

Again it is necessary to remember that the chart and key list are not the end of the process but the means of engaging in analysis. Nothing in this process should suggest that it is a mechanistic process. In so far as it allows the construction of argument it teaches how an argument is constructed, but it cannot decide how important evidence is. The user has to make this decision, evaluating strength, persuasive value, credibility, or positive or negative effect. It cannot tell the user if the evidence assembled is admissible. The chart orders material and shows relationship and gaps. The chart does not solve problems. If there is a gap the user has to decide how to deal with it at the moment of analysis and argument construction.

The human element in handling, locating, ordering, analysing evidence and constructing argument remains an act of knowledge, experience and imagination. Each inference requires an evaluation of its persuasive operation. Then the user needs to come to a view concerning the persuasive effect of the *total* mass of evidentiary facts.

Stephen Toulmin: 'Logic is concerned with the soundness of claims we make – with the solidity of the grounds we produce to support them, the firmness of the backing we provide for them.' What is the objective? For a process model it may be solving a diagnostic model or increasing understanding of complex things or for knowledge acquisition. Wigmore's analytic methods says Schum are 'a conceptual microscope that allowed me to examine many subtleties in evidence'.

The important point is to show alternative conclusions and test them out. Do they, or your counter-argument, stand up? Each inference can lead to the following processes:

As we noted earlier in the chapter, an assertion can be met by:

- explanation;
- denial;
- rival assertion.

All counter-responses to your argument fall into a category that either:

- explains it away;
- denies the existence of the evidentiary fact;
- offers a new rival evidential fact.

7.10.3 The modified chart as used in this book

This book uses aspects of Anderson and Twining's modification of the Wigmore Chart Method to demonstrate how propositions, evidence supporting propositions, and relationship between propositions work together with forms of deductive and inductive legal reasoning to allow outcomes to be reached in relation to factual and legal analysis. Further, it allows a demonstration of the ways in which critical thinking applied to the outcome of such factual and legal analysis allows competent and valid conclusions to be reached which can be on either side of an argument (for or against a specific party). This book has in fact narrowed the symbols used and the information placed on the chart. These changes are as follows:

(a) The chart is only constructed for one party at a time.

One symbol is used to denote all additions to the chart, a circle. ◯

(b) The chart therefore shows less information but remains useful.

The range of symbols used in this book for its adaptation of the Wigmore Chart Method are as set out in Figure 7.27, below.

Figure: 7.27: symbols used for the adapted and modified Wigmore Chart

Symbol		Meaning
◯	=	A circle indicates the placing of any proposition as an UP, PP or interim probandum on the chart
|	=	A line indicates a link between two propositions not yet finalised
| ?	=	A question mark beside a link indicates uncertainty of the link itself
⟶	=	Arrow indicates the direction of the supporting evidence. Tends to prove
—x⟶	=	Arrow with an X indicates direction of the evidence but also that it tends to disprove the probanda, or interim probanda
(?)	=	A question mark indicates the proposition uncertain
(●)	=	A solid dot indicates the proposition believed
(○)	=	An open dot indicates the proposition not believed
1, 2, 3	=	The numbers at the top left of circles indicate the numbers listed under the UP, PP and Key List narrative, eg 1 ◯

Turn back to Figure 7.16, above, and consider the meaning of the symbols using the explanations given in Figure 7.27, above.

7.11   THE DEMONSTRATION OF THE WIGMORE CHART
METHOD: THE FICTIONAL CASE OF *R v MARY*

To give students the experience of walking through the method to develop their understanding of how a legal argument is put together, a reasonably simple criminal law scenario has been created. However, the facts of the case are not laid out. They are to be found located in three statements made by two witnesses connected to the situation, and the statement of the defendant. From these statements the first task is to assemble the relevant facts, note the evidence available, note the elements of relevant law, identify any conditions of doubt at the factual level and construct a chart and key list for use by the prosecution.

Having constructed the Wigmore Chart, the factual analysis takes place which clears the ground for the legal analysis. This gives a demonstration at a simplified level of the relationship between factual and legal analysis and the need for both to construct arguments. At the academic level of legal education the problem is a given, it does not mean there is no value in an appreciation of fact analysis. On the contrary it can be used to assist us to see more clearly the issues to be teased out when engaged in the legal analysis.

7.11.1   The case of *R v Mary*

Mary has been charged with theft under s 1 of the Theft Act 1968.

Theft Act 1968, s 1

A person is guilty of theft if he dishonestly appropriates property belonging to another with the intention of permanently depriving that other.

The statements in the case of *R v Mary*

Statement 1: William

I share a flat with Andrew and Mary. I came home on Saturday afternoon and Mary asked me if she could borrow £20 because she wanted to buy a skirt. I didn't want to go out and get her money from the cash machine so I said No. She asked me if I thought Andrew would mind if she borrowed the £20 note in his emergency funds jar. Andrew was away. I said I couldn't speak for him. I didn't know. He is generous but can be difficult about his personal stuff. He wouldn't lend me his football shirt the other week. It just did not seem a good idea and I told her so. Mary said she was sure Andrew wouldn't mind her taking it. I saw her go into his room and she came out with the jar. She took out the £20 note which was all that was in it, and left a note in the jar saying she would pay it back Monday.

Statement 2: Andrew

I came home late on Sunday night to the flat I share with William and Mary two good friends. I was extremely tired. When I walked into the kitchen at about midnight I saw my emergency funds jar in the kitchen. There should have been a £20 note in it and it should have been in my bedroom. It had no money in it just a note from Mary which said 'Sorry – I had an emergency, need a skirt for my interview Monday, I'll put it back Monday night'. I was really angry – the money is mine for my emergencies. Mary knows that I don't like just anyone walking into my bedroom. As far as I am concerned she stole my money. I don't believe she can pay it back Monday or at all. She is unemployed and in debt. Perhaps if she had asked me personally I would have lent her the money to buy a skirt for her interview, but she didn't.

Statement 3: Mary

I share a flat with Andrew and William who are good friends with me. On Saturday I heard I had an interview for a clerical job on Monday. I have been unemployed for about six months and really needed a job. I thought it would be a good idea to get a new smart skirt for the interview. Andrew and William have been great about helping me out and even let me pay less rent. I was down to my last £10 on Saturday. I get unemployment money every Thursday. I thought that William might lend me some money but he wouldn't go down to the cash machine for me. Andrew is never like that, he has always lent me money when I have asked him. I knew that if he was here he would give me the money. I decided to take the £20 in Andrew's emergency fund jar. William did say it wasn't a good idea. I took it from Andrew's room and put a note in it saying, 'Sorry – I had an emergency, need a skirt for my interview Monday, I'll put it back Monday night'. I left it in the kitchen so he would know it was gone. I couldn't get anything. So I went to the cinema instead and brought home a take away meal and a rented video for me and William, which cheered us both up. When Andrew came home late Sunday he was unreasonable and shouted at me that I was a thief. He was furious I had gone into his room. But he goes into mine to get stuff he wants. I am really fed up with Andrew.

The basic issue surrounds whether the law has been broken. We have been told Mary has been charged with theft under s 1 of the Theft Act. We are to assume that the three statements provided containing all of the information in this scenario have been produced just for us to read and work on. For the purposes of this exercise we will assume that these statements were produced in ways not calling into doubt their admissibility or credibility. This means therefore that we only have to concentrate on their probative value. (What do they prove?)

The *seven* point approach of Twining and Miers will be used.

1   **Standpoint**: the standpoint of the Chart is that of the author of this book demonstrating the Wigmore Chart Method for the purposes of demonstrating the method and argument construction.

2   **Stages 2, 3 and 4**: relate to setting up the propositions and then key listing and charting. The impossibility of approaching each task in an isolated way is immediately perceived as we are going to work from statements. We have to find out the facts before we can draft the UP, PP, and interim probanda.

Task: so that you can appreciate the levels of analysis go back to the statements and highlight the key words and phrases that begin to allow you to break into them and locate the story, and the law. Then try to give answers to the following questions:

(1) What are the relevant facts?

(2) What key phrases in the statements give you clues as to the application of the law?

(3) Can you construct the deductive argument for the prosecution?

(4) Can you construct the inductive argument for the prosecution?

(5) Can you construct the opposing inductive argument for the defence?

(6) Are there any conditions of doubt in your mind surrounding the wording of s 1(1) of the Theft Act which may apply? (For example questions surrounding the presence of both *mens rea* and *actus reus*.)

DO NOT PROCEED UNTIL YOU HAVE ANSWERED QUESTIONS (1)–(6).

NOW ...

Consider the three statements of Andrew, William and Mary as they have been annotated opposite.

Check what you got right and what you missed. Ensure that you understand the issues and particularly ensure that you can follow the comments concerning the deductive and the inductive arguments.

THEN CONTINUE READING.

We will begin to construct the chart and key list. The figure above will have indicated the type of work that has to be put into reading documentation and sorting the issues. You may wish to flick back to Figure 7.16, above, to remind yourself of what it is that we are building! When considering laying out the chart it is useful to think in terms of levels.

Figure 7.28: annotated statements of the witnesses

We have already spent a lot of time dealing with the Theft Act and we will now use that knowledge in this demonstration. The statements on this page show the text that you should have noticed as indicating relevant issues above. The arrows here indicate the issues, the UP and PP. IF you were approaching this from scratch you would have to ascertain the PP. The facts: On Saturday Mary took a £20.00 belonging to Andrew from a jar in his bedroom. Andrew is away until Sunday night. She presumed he would have lent it to her if he had been there. She intends to pay the money back Monday. Andrew is angry, he accuses her of theft. Mary says she borrowed it. A fellow flatmate saw her take the money ...

Statement 1: William

I share a flat with Andrew and Mary. I came home on Saturday afternoon and Mary asked me if she could borrow £20 because she wanted to buy a skirt. I didn't want to go out and get her money from the cash machine so I said No. She asked me if I thought Andrew would mind if she borrowed the £20 note in his emergency funds jar. Andrew was away. I said I couldn't speak for him. I didn't know. He is generous but can be difficult about his personal stuff. He wouldn't lend me his football shirt the other week. It just did not seem a good idea and I told her so. Mary said she was sure Andrew wouldn't mind her taking it. I saw her go into his room and she came out with the jar. She took out the £20 note which was all that was in it, and left a note in the jar saying she would pay it back Monday.

Eye witness

If she has £10 until Thursday how can she pay back £20 Monday? Did she intend to pay it back?

This is where Mary casts doubt on *mens rea*. She thought Andrew would have given her permission which negates intention to permanently deprive.

This is where we see Mary's admission of an important element of the *actus reus*.

As you gain skills you will find that most of the linking done here in shading, arrows and text would be done as a mental process as you sift items for the task in hand.

Statement 2: Andrew

I came home late on Sunday night to the flat I share with William and Mary two good friends. I was extremely tired. When I walked into the kitchen at about midnight I saw my emergency funds jar in the kitchen. There should have been a £20 note in it and it should have been in my bedroom. It had no money in it just a note from Mary which said 'Sorry – I had an emergency, need a skirt for my interview Monday, I'll put it back Monday night'. I was really angry – the money is mine for my emergencies. Mary knows that I don't like just anyone walking into my bedroom. As far as I am concerned she stole my money. I don't believe she can pay it back Monday or at all. She is unemployed and in debt. Perhaps if she had asked me personally I would have lent her the money to buy a skirt for her interview, but she didn't.

Ultimate probanda: Mary stole £20 contrary to the Theft Act 1968

Penultimate probandum had permission
(1) *dishonestly appropriates (disputed)*
(2) *Property (no dispute, it was property)*
(3) *Belonging to another No dispute*
(4) *With the intention of permanently depriving that other (disputed).*

Ultimate probanda: Mary did not steal £20 contrary to the theft act 1968

Admission to taking but she says it was not theft, she thought she would have had permission

Statement 3: Mary

I share a flat with Andrew and William who are good friends with me. On Saturday I heard I had an interview for a clerical job on Monday. I have been unemployed for about six months and really needed a job. I thought it would be a good idea to get a new smart skirt for the interview. Andrew and William have been great about helping me out and even let me pay less rent. I was down to my last £10 on Saturday. I get unemployment money every Thursday. I thought that William might lend me some money but he wouldn't go down to the cash machine for me. Andrew is never like that, he has always lent me money when I have asked him. I knew that if he was here he would give me the money. I decided to take the £20 in Andrew's emergency fund jar. William did say it wasn't a good idea. I took it from Andrew's room and put a note in it saying, 'Sorry – I had an emergency, need a skirt for my interview Monday, I'll put it back Monday night' I left it in the kitchen so he would know it was gone. I couldn't get anything. So I went to the cinema instead and brought home a take away meal and a rented video for me and William, which cheered us both up. When Andrew came home late Sunday he was unreasonable and shouted at me that I was a thief. He was furious I had gone into his room. But he goes into mine to get stuff he wants. I am really fed up with Andrew.

7.11.2 The ultimate probanda

We begin with the end in mind which is the UP, which can also be said to be level 1. This is the matter to be proved to decide the issue. In this current case it is level 1: Mary stole a £20 note contrary to s 1 of the Theft Act 1968. This is expressed on the chart as:

Figure 7.29: the (UP), level 1

7.11.3 The penultimate probanda

The second level, as we are working backwards, is the PP, the elements that have to be proved to show that the UP is correct (in other words, the elements of the legal rule, in this case of s 1 of the Theft Act 1968). Again we have worked on this and know it.

LEVEL 2:	• Mary dishonestly appropriates
	• Property
	• Belonging to another
	• With the intention of permenantly depriving that other.

Which is set out as follows.

Figure 7.30: levels 1 and 2 of the chart

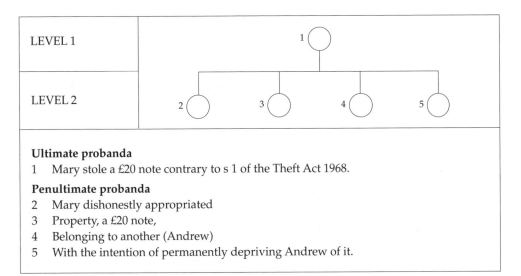

LEVEL 1	
LEVEL 2	

Ultimate probanda
1   Mary stole a £20 note contrary to s 1 of the Theft Act 1968.

Penultimate probanda
2   Mary dishonestly appropriated
3   Property, a £20 note,
4   Belonging to another (Andrew)
5   With the intention of permanently depriving Andrew of it.

Then we can insert arrows, and indicate the status of the testimony is it believed (●), disbelieved (○) or is its status doubted (?).

Figure 7.31: levels 1 and 2 with indicators of links, belief and doubt

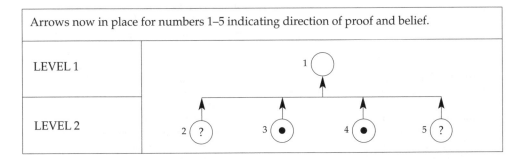

Arrows now in place for numbers 1–5 indicating direction of proof and belief.

LEVEL 1	
LEVEL 2	

7.11.4   The interim probanda

The next levels require you to have identified facts and evidence which has been selected from the statements. These were hinted at in Figure 7.28, above, which annotated the witness statements. Go back to the statements and remind yourself what they said. Do you already have a good idea of what is at issue at the level of fact and evidence? What should be put under item 5? This indicates the *mens rea*. What might you as a prosecutor be looking for? What might you as the defence be looking for? The arrows have now been placed on the chart and symbols for belief and uncertainty. Now look at Figure 7.32, below, which has a number of interim probanda (items 6–26). Did you notice most of these when you first checked the statements? As can be seen the main areas of uncertainty concern PP 2 and 5.

Figure 7.32: a more complete example of a Wigmore Chart

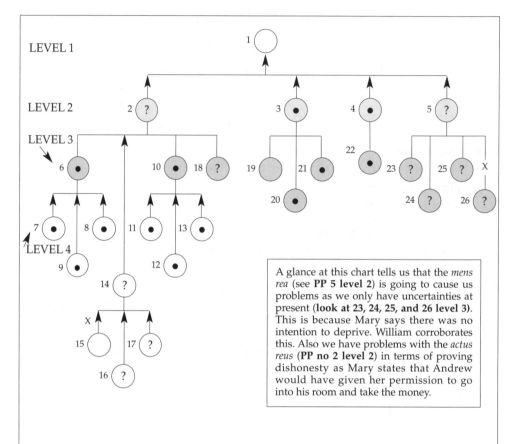

A glance at this chart tells us that the *mens rea* (see **PP 5 level 2**) is going to cause us problems as we only have uncertainties at present (**look at 23, 24, 25, and 26 level 3**). This is because Mary says there was no intention to deprive. William corroborates this. Also we have problems with the *actus reus* (**PP no 2 level 2**) in terms of proving dishonesty as Mary states that Andrew would have given her permission to go into his room and take the money.

Ultimate probanda

1   Mary stole a £20 note contrary to section 1 of the Theft Act 1968.

Penultimate probanda

2   Mary dishonestly appropriated
3   Property, a £20 note,
4   Belonging to another (Andrew)
5   With the intention of permanently depriving Andrew of it.

Key list

6   **Mary went into Andrew's room**
7   Statement of William supports 6
8   Statement of Andrew supports 6
9   Statement of Mary supports 6
10 **Mary took a £20 note from Andrew's room**
11 Mary's statement supports 10
12 Andrew's statement supports 10
13 William's statement supports 10
14 **Mary went into Andrew's room without permission**
15 Mary's statement denies 14
16 Andrew's statement supports 14
17 William's statement supports 14
18 **Mary was wilful about whether she had permission.**
19 Mary's statement supports 3
20 Andrew's statement supports 3
21 William's statement supports 3
22 Andrew's statement supports 4
23 Andrew's statement supports 5
24 William's statement denies 5
25 Mary's statement denies 5
26 **Mary only had £10 until Thursday so she had no ability to repay £20 on Monday**

7.11.5   The analysis

Having laid out the chart (and this chart will be left at this point although there is more that can be done), we can see two major problem areas, because the chart is structured to lead to the UP through the PP (that is, the elements of the legal rule concerned). We are able to notice at once where there is strength and where there is not.

Looking back at Figure 7.32, it can be seen that there are major queries relating to PP 5. This is the PP concerning intention which in s 1(1) is the only element of the *mens rea*. So, unless more certainty can be achieved in this area there is a problem. In addition, PP 2 has a question mark indicating uncertainty. This is the element of the *actus reus* requiring the dishonest appropriation but Mary alleges she acted in the certainty that Andrew would have lent her the money: in other words she had his permission. We can see that there are many elements of strength stacking up under PP 2 but a key issue is 14 – going into Andrew's room without permission. So clearly we are interested when we turn to the legal analysis in looking at case law dealing with this issue. Although we have tried to counter the problem with 14 by saying in 18 that Mary was wilful about whether she had permission or not, in the circumstances can we allege this?

So we should explore the following matters in the case authorities.

(a) *Actus reus*

   Re: PP 2

   • What is the legal meaning of dishonestly?
   • Does it include believing that you have permission to take something?
   • What is the test for a reasonable belief that you have permission? Is it according to what other reasonable people would think (an objective test) or is it according to whatever Mary thought – no matter how unreasonable? (A *very* subjective test.)
   • Can we argue she had conditional permission to take £20 for a skirt but she spent the money on something else? Does that matter? If she thought Andrew would give permission for the skirt does it matter that she went to the cinema and got a take away meal instead?

(b) *Mens rea*

   Re: PP 5

   Mary said that she did not intend to permanently deprive Andrew of his money.

   • However, she said she would pay Andrew back on Monday, yet she clearly would have no money until Thursday. Does this matter?
   • Does this suggest an intention to permanently deprive? Are there cases covering this?

As you can see whilst the chart is excellent at its task (factual analysis) it only highlights the areas for legal analysis. Which is why the charting process leads to legal analysis. This is the moment to look for answers at the level of statutory sources and case law which we will do briefly. We will just make a few explorations to indicate how this matter can be pursued.

7.11.5.1 The issue of the meaning of 'dishonestly appropriates'

Section 3(1) of the Theft Act 1968 defines appropriation as 'Any assumption by a person of the rights of an owner' which includes coming by property innocently but then assuming the rights of an owner. Importantly for Mary, in the case of *Anderton v Burnside* [1983] 3 All ER 288 HL, Lord Roskill commented (*obiter dictum*):

> In the context of s 3(1), the concept of appropriation involves not an act expressly or impliedly authorised by an owner but an act by way of adverse interference or usurpation of those rights.

However, it was an *obiter* comment not *ratio* and the facts are not similar, as Anderton involved the swapping of price labels. But Roskill's comments are highly relevant as Mary believes she has permission for her act. A permission based on past practice, being flatmates and being good friends. However, perhaps some doubt has been cast on the validity of this *dictum* by the House of Lords in *Gomez* [1992] AC 442. They held the *dictum* wrong, yet when considering the circumstances in *Gomez* the implied consent was not there. In *Gomez*, a taxi driver, when offered the wallet of a foreign passenger and told to take the fare, took too much. There was no implied consent to take money generally; the only implied consent was to take the fare. Importantly for Mary s 3(1) refers to the person who comes by property without stealing and later assumes the rights of an owner. Mary believes she has permission to take the money for a skirt. Does that cover her later use of the money for entertainment? Or was the implied consent conditional upon the precise use the money was put to?

Mary has told Andrew when she will pay him back, he has not asked for it yet. For the avoidance of doubt s 4 of the Theft Act defines property and money is included under the general heading of property.

Section 2 of the Theft Act also makes clear that implied consent can negate a claim of dishonest appropriation.

---

(1) A person's appropriation of property belonging to another is not to be regarded as dishonest

(a) ...

(b) if he appropriates the property in the belief that he would have the other's consent if the other knew of the appropriation and the circumstances of it.

'Dishonestly' has been held by the courts to be an ordinary word, to be interpreted by the jury or the judge as a matter of fact. It does not carry a technical legal meaning. The question is, was Mary as a matter of fact dishonest in the circumstances? In *Gilks* [1972] 3 All ER 280, the jury was asked to place themselves in the shoes of the defendant and then ask was the defendant dishonest? Was Mary dishonest in the circumstances of this case? The Court of Appeal thought that this was a reasonable question agreeing that if the defendant may have held the belief he claimed the prosecution had not established dishonesty. The defendant's belief applied, said the Court of Appeal 'not the standards of ordinary decent people, but the defendant's own standards, however deplorable'. In *Boggein v Williams* [1978] CLR 242, the court held the defendant's belief in his honesty was essential. In the leading case of *Ghosh* [1982] QB 1053; 2 All ER 689 a two point test was developed. Two questions had to be asked:

(1) Was what was done dishonest according to the ordinary standards of reasonable and honest people?

If the answer is 'no' the defendant is not guilty as there is no proved dishonesty and a vital element of the *actus reus* is unproved. If the answer is 'yes' then the second question has to be asked.

(2) Did the defendant realise that reasonable and honest people regard what he did as dishonest? If the answer is yes then the defendant is guilty. In our case Mary may well find that the answer to the first question would come in as 'no' and she escapes liability. Should it not, the second question should be answered in the negative and she still escapes liability. Most reasonable and honest people would regard the taking of the money in the precise circumstances reasonable and not dishonest.

The discussion of the issue of permanent deprivation as a core aspect of the *mens rea* would next be discussed. However, this demonstration is to indicate the relation ship between factual and legal analysis and the way in which factual analysis facilitates legal analysis and argument construction.

The standard legal problem question (which will be discussed in Chapter 8) is of course less obviously liable to give the information required for a full factual analysis. However, in terms of knowing what to look out for at the level of facts and evidence, it allows the map of potential areas to be developed.

7.12   TASK: THE CASE OF *R V JACK*

For those of you who would like to test your skills further there is another charting task with a set of witness statements in the fictitious case of *R v Jack*. The law applicable is again s 1(1) of the Theft Act.

(1) Construct your own Wigmore chart and keylist for the defence.

(2) Use your chart to determine the strengths and weaknesses of the prosecution case.

(3) What further evidence would be useful for either party.

(4) Write out an argument for the prosecution to prove that Jack is guilty.

(5) Write out an argument for the defence to prove that Jack is guilty.

There is no necessarily correct answer, and the statements are provided as an opportunity for developing your skills in the area of factual analysis and argument construction either in or out of a classroom setting.

7.12.1   Statements relating to the case of *R v Jack*

7.12.1.1 R v Jack

Statements for Wigmore Chart

Jack has been charged with theft (contrary to s 1(1) of the Theft Act 1968) of a shirt from the New Style Clothes Shop on 12 September.

Below, you will find witness statements. Read them carefully and construct a modified Wigmore Chart for the defence.

Witness statement no 1

Selina (owner of the New Style Clothes Shop): witness statement

I am the owner of the New Style Clothes Shop in Norbury. After cashing up on the night of Saturday 12 September, I found my stock to be down, a man's shirt was missing. I immediately checked the security cameras. At 12 o'clock midday, I saw a male that I now know to be Jack leaving a changing room. He was acting suspiciously and holding his arm under his jacket. He walked out of the shop without returning any clothes to the assistant. I have heard his name mentioned around here as a thief. I phoned the police who arrested Jack.

Witness statement no 2

Jack: statement given to defence solicitor

I did not steal the shirt, it is not my size or colour. Selina has a grudge against me and is trying to frame me. At 12 o'clock on Saturday, I was in the White Lies Pub with my friend, Frederick, who will support me on this. The first I knew about all this was when Constable Danger arrested me on Saturday evening. The search of my house did reveal a shirt but I had bought this a couple of days ago in the market, honestly. I admit I have a criminal record, but I have turned my back on all that now. I now have a steady job as a shop assistant in a charity book shop. But when they find out about this accusation, I will lose my job.

The ID parade was a fix, no one looked at all like me, so I stuck out as the tallest. I have brown hair, everyone else had black hair.

Witness statement no 3

PC Danger: police statement

On the evening of 12 September, I was on my beat in London Road, Norbury, South London when I received a radio message to proceed to the address of Jack to arrest him on a charge of theft. I knocked on the door and Jack opened it and said 'Oh no, not you lot trying it on'. I immediately told him he was being arrested on suspicion of stealing a shirt from New Style Clothes Shop, cautioned him, telling that he did not have to say anything but if he did it could be used against him. He said 'This is ridiculous. I know nothing about anything'. A subsequent search of the property revealed a shirt of the same design and make as that stolen from the New Style Clothes Shop.

Jack was taken to the Police Station where he refused to answer questions. He was charged with theft and released on bail.

Witness statement no 4

Mary (part time sales assistant, the New Style Clothes Shop): witness statement

I am a student, but I work in the New style Clothes Shop to supplement my grant. It is very convenient for me as I can travel to work one stop on the train and the shop is about three to five minutes from Norbury Railway Station. The first time I knew anything was wrong on Saturday 12 September, was when we were cashing up in the evening and Selina, my boss, started shouting that the tills didn't balance. She went into the back room to play back the security cameras. We saw a figure leaving a changing room at 12.15 pm. My boss became suspicious and she said that the man looked like Jack, a well known local thief who is always hanging around. She phoned the police.

I don't know Jack but, at an ID parade, I identified Jack as the man who was on the video. I am sure the figure on the camera is the thief.

Witness statement no 5

Frederick (best friend of Jack): witness statement

I was with Jack in the White Lies Pub on Saturday 12 September. I can't remember the time I met him, but it was around midday. I spent the afternoon with him and then he went home. The next thing I knew was that he had been nicked. I went with him to the ID parade, which was a fix. He stuck out like a sore thumb.

Witness statement no 6

Carl: owner of the White Lies Pub

I am the owner of the White Lies Public House, High Road, Norbury next door to the railway station. I recall seeing Jack and Frederick in the pub around 12.30 pm on Saturday 12 September.

7.13   SUMMARY

This chapter has introduced some extremely important issues relating to argument. You have been introduced to types of legal reasoning (deductive, inductive, abductive and analogic). You have been introduced to factual and legal analysis and the relationship between propositions in an argument. You have been introduced to the micro elements of argument and the relationships between evidence and propositions, and the way in which arguments are clusters of propositions. Finally, these issues have been embedded in one method for dealing with the management of facts: Wigmore Charts. The Wigmore Chart is a means to an end and does not replace legal analysis, but in many respects it rests on our knowledge of legal analysis as well as clearing the ground for us to engage in legal analysis and critical thinking.

7.14   FURTHER READING

Anderson, T and Twining, W, *Analysis of Evidence*, 1991, London: Butterworths.

Gold, N, Mackie, K and Twining, W, *Learning Lawyers Skills*, 1989, London: Butterworths.

Miers, D and Twining, W, *How To Do Things With Rules*, 1999, London: Butterworths.

Schum, DA, 'Alternative views of argument construction from a mass of evidence' 22 Cardozo Law Review 1461–502 (contains a valuable set of references within the discipline of law and in other disciplines concerning arguments).

Wigmore, H, 'The problem of proof' (1913–14) 8 Ilinois Law Rev 77.

CHAPTER 8

WRITING ESSAYS AND ANSWERS TO PROBLEM QUESTIONS

8.1 INTRODUCTION

This chapter considers the differences and similarities in approach required to produce written work in the form of essays and answers to legal problem questions. It is necessary to take the time to get in control of the information gathered for written work. It is appropriate for the student to consider the available material with a view to raising new issues for reflection. In doing this, the student begins to move beyond the texts: beyond summarising, identifying and classifying and even beyond predicting.

A competent approach to argument combined with a competent approach to writing allows students to produce a piece of work that demonstrates they understand and have made an area their own. Not all written work demands this, and not all students can thoroughly synthesise their skills on a consistent basis. Those who can, if they create argument rationally on the basis of existing theory, texts and practice, usually generate good results in the distinction category. Those who try to be creative but cannot demonstrate that they have any plausible evidence for their argument construct weak pieces of work that are at borderline, low grades. This group of students is not demonstrating understanding by careful application, interpretation, prediction and creativity. They are usually demonstrating incomprehension of the task they believe they have completed by handing in their work!

Often students for reasons of time, disorganisation or lack of understanding only engage in limited research for their written coursework, only trying to find articles that obviously answer the question set so that they can merely summarise them. They then precis the article, throw in a few quotes for good measure, and hope it will 'do'. It often does not 'just do' simply because the student has not put in the work to understand the question prior to writing the answer. Of course, there are times when it is necessary to take a pragmatic approach to essay preparation. But these planning decisions are one thing, not properly comprehending the dimensions of the task in hand is another matter.

This is probably a good moment to repeat the motto used elsewhere in this text that:

> There are no shortcuts to excellent work!

Writing, whether it is for a coursework essay or a problem question, or an extended dissertation, MPhil or even a PhD is a time-consuming task, and the time has to be knowingly used!

- It takes time to properly understand the basic issues.
- It takes time to appreciate the interconnectedness of the text.
- It takes time to determine your view.
- It takes time to compare texts, and to compare your view with the view of other writers, etc.

Once the student is in control of the texts, then the texts can be manipulated, alternative arguments can be constructed and student understanding of the relevant area or topic increased. Often, a student merely hands in a precis of a string of articles, texts and cases and calls it an essay. This is not an essay presenting a serious argument for consideration, supported by evidence and it will not attract a good mark. However, the precis, or summaries, if they are well prepared, can provide the basis of argument construction and good written work.

In an exam situation, as well as in coursework, students often take a lot of time discussing the facts and the outcomes of cases or the description of argument in texts, but often demonstrating little appreciation of the issues raised by the cases and little understanding of their relevance or application to the question. This is not because they are not capable of understanding but because they did not spend the proper time thinking about what the question was asking, preparing the texts to be used and constructing argument in written form.

8.2   LEARNING OUTCOMES

By the end of this chapter, readers should:

- be aware of the differences in approach that need to be adopted for essays and problem questions;
- have confidence preparing for both types of assessment;
- be able to structure work effectively;
- be able to bring together the skills of reading and argument construction and demonstrate competency in writing.

8.3   PREPARATION AND STRUCTURING OF ESSAYS

In answering a law essay question students are required to produced a piece of work offering a sustained argument concerning a particular question. Generally speaking, essay questions are set in the following formats:

(a) A question is set to be answered.

(b) A quotation is given with the bland request to discuss.

(c) A quotation is given and there is a request to extract issues.

Generally, an essay involves discussion in the formal sense of laying out an argument. In fact, the Latin stem of discuss is '*discutere*' which means to 'to dash to pieces', a rather forceful way of describing argument. The more usual way of describing the meaning of the word 'discuss' is 'to investigate or examine by argument, to sift, and to debate'. The word is often wrongly used and understood to mean just idly talking. Reading many student essays does lead one to suspect that students are idly and haphazardly just writing and wasting their hard work.

Each type of essay question requires a different approach, but the same general structure is required and the same store of information can be used. This also holds true in relation to problem questions, which are discussed at the end of this chapter.

The word essay means 'to lay out an argument'. All writing revolving around the laying out of argument in the form of an essay has a disarmingly simple structure:

(a) **An introduction** laying out the brief details of the argument, describing succinctly the issues the essay will discuss (and why) and hinting at the conclusion. It is important to 'begin with the end in mind'. The introduction can be thought of as the road map to the essay, detailing to the reader where they will be taken. Do, however, make sure that in your conclusion you have taken the reader to the place you said you were taking them to!

The introduction should be refined and finalised when the main body of the essay is finished and your conclusions are clearer.

(b) **The main part of the essay**, which is often referred to as the body of the text. Here, you will set out the propositions of your argument in a carefully pre-planned manner with each proposition supported by the evidence from the texts, cases, etc that you have consulted. (You should be clearer about argument structure having worked through Chapter 7.) It is absolutely essential to refer to case law, legislation, and textbooks and articles as appropriate in this main part of the essay or you will have nothing but unsupported claims that do not constitute an argument.

(c) **Your conclusion**. This is

- either – in answer to the specific question asked;

- or – finalises your own decisions concerning the critique and review of information you have been given 'to discuss';

- or – your final views on the issues you have been invited to extract for discussion.

Your conclusion should align with your introduction and contain a *brief* survey of your argument and evidence as laid out in the body of the text, detailing strengths and weaknesses and then moving to your specific concluding response to the essay task.

To obtain an idea of how essay tasks can differ in what they ask and the way they are presented read the following four sample essay tasks.

Essay Question 1

Critically assess the view that the Race Relations Act 1976, as amended, needs to be completely revised.

Essay Question 2

'Damages are meant to put a claimant, so far as money can do it, in the same position as if the contract had been performed.'

Explain and comment.

Essay Question 3

'The English legal system is like a house that is not only too small, it is in need of repair. The question is do we build another extension and repair as necessary or pull the whole thing down and start again?'

Discuss the issues arising from this quotation.

Essay Question 4

'In *R v Secretary of State ex p Factortame (No 1)* and *(No 2)* the English courts and the European Court of Justice made it clear that not only do English courts have the power to suspend Acts of Parliament conflicting with European Community law but that European Community law demands that the provisions of lawfully enacted Acts of the UK Parliament be overturned and the European Court can even dictate what national remedies should be available.'

Discuss solely by reference to the following texts:

(a) extracts from *R v Factortame (No 1)*;

(b) extracts from *R v Factortame (No 2)*;

(c) extracts from Tillotson, *European Community Law: Text, Cases and Materials.*

As you can see, the style in which questions can be set for an essay can differ enormously.

As a general rule an essay question tends to be set to test students' abilities in the following areas:

- current state of knowledge of the law or a law related issue;
- current state of ability to construct a sustained argument;
- current state of your ability to apply primary and secondary texts to an issue;
- knowledge of the grey areas of the law surrounding the cases decided in the given area under consideration;
- knowledge of available defences;
- knowledge of particular interpretational issues arising in the law under consideration;
- ability to engage in critical reasoning.

In addition to the standard structure of an essay (introduction, main body and conclusion), it is also possible to lay out a standard method for the preparation and construction of an essay question. This chapter uses a straightforward method containing eight stages. This is very similar to the four-stage model for approaching reading used in Chapter 6. This standard method can also inform the problem question process as will be noted later in this chapter. This process is now laid out in narrative form and as a quick reference diagram in Figure 8.1, below.

8.4   METHOD FOR THE PREPARATION AND CONSTRUCTION OF ESSAYS

(1)   *Stage 1: carefully reflect on the question*

- What is being asked?
- How many issues are raised?

This is an exercise in basic English comprehension. The question has to be deconstructed. It is very useful to convert it into a tree diagram that can be annotated as texts are collected.

The actual essay question must be constantly borne in mind as texts are read and research is conducted.

(2)   *Stage 2: search for relevant texts*

Locate:

(a) legal rules;

(b) legal discussion/decisions in:

- cases;
- textbooks;
- articles.

Once the issues raised by the question have been discovered and preliminary reading undertaken in the textbook, it is useful to scan the following: handouts from tutors, articles mentioned in the *footnotes* or *endnotes* in set textbooks, databases or relevant indices of law journals, databases or current law citator for up to date cases, legislation, etc.

(3)   *Stage 3: carefully read, note, organise and reflect on the material collected*

As you locate material that is relevant, photocopy it and highlight it, or make notes. Extract arguments presented and then *reconsider* the question.

The first task is reading, asking the basic questions detailed below, whilst at the same time recalling the actual issues detailed in the essay question you are doing the research for. Otherwise relevant details in your material could be overlooked.

Recall that you were introduced to the three reading techniques of skimming, scanning and detail in Chapter 6. Each of these techniques will be deployed as you approaching reading through your material. As you read texts you need to ask yourself questions which differ according to the text you are using. For example

(a) **Law cases**:

- What are the facts?
- What legal rules have been applied and why?
- What aspects of this case are relevant to my essay?
- How do the arguments presented assist in relation to the essay?

(b) **Textbooks**:

- What is being described?
- Do I understand?
- Does it fit with my understanding of the cases?
- Have I properly grasped the issues involved?
- What is of relevance to my essay?

(c) **Articles**:

- What is the writer's argument?
- Is it well supported by the evidence?
- Does the writer's argument support or deny my argument in the essay?

Is there a majority view developing in the texts concerning any of the issues raised by the question? Go back to the diagram of the essay question made under Stage 1. Note beside the various issues aspects of the texts that are of relevance to the issues identified as requiring discussion to answer the question. It is important to remain open to the possibility that personal ideas may change as more research is conducted and some texts present persuasive arguments that had not been previously considered.

(4)   *Stage 4: begin to form a view of possible arguments to be used to answer the question*

Add these to your diagram.

(5)   *Stage 5: consider the strength of your argument*

This stage is important. You should by now have a reasonably clear idea of how your argument may look. You will know what supporting evidence you have and where you lack support. Argument construction has been specifically dealt with in this text and can be located in Chapter 7. You do not have to throw out weak arguments if they serve to build a broader picture and support a broader argument.

(6)   *Stage 6: begin to write the essay plan*

Look at:

- the diagram of the question;
- the notes of cases and other texts;
- the notes of your personal ideas/argument.

(7)   *Stage 7: write the first draft of the essay*

Although you will have an idea of what you are doing and where you are going and indeed what your answer is to the question it is a good idea to start your detailed first draft in the body of the text.

Begin with the middle section:

- Review everything for your conclusion.

- Write the final introduction *last*, ensuring that the body of the text and your conclusion does what your introduction says they will do, and finalise your conclusion.

(8)   *Stage 8: write the final version of the essay*

During the review:

- consider whether there is a need to search for any more texts;
- pay particular attention to the conclusion and thoughts on the introduction;
- also review the argument. Is there evidence to back it up? Have opposing views been dealt with?

This method can also be more immediately represented as a flow chart (see Figure 8.1, below).

As you will have by now noted, writing is not a passive act. In Chapter 9, this method for writing an essay will be demonstrated by applying it to Question 4, above.

8.5   METHOD FOR THE PREPARATION AND CONSTRUCTION OF ANSWERS TO PROBLEM QUESTIONS

It is now appropriate to turn attention away from essay towards the other major type of written assessment that is found on a law programme – the problem question.

Problem questions can only be set around substantive law topics as they rely on the consideration of cases, common law, legislation and increasingly aspects of European Community law. These questions often also require knowledge of how an issue has been dealt with in another common law jurisdiction. Students are expected to competently handle rules and use the doctrine of precedent in practice. It is possible for some examination papers to be 50–75% problem questions, or perhaps even more. Even in courses that seem to be more discursive (such as English legal system) it is possible to construct some problem questions concerning police powers for example, and in constitutional and administrative law (now often called public law), there can be problem questions in relation to the administrative aspects of the course.

This section discusses in detail what the function behind problem questions may be and with that in mind looks at moving towards a strategy for answering problem questions.

Figure 8.1: a flow chart of the method for the preparation and construction of essays

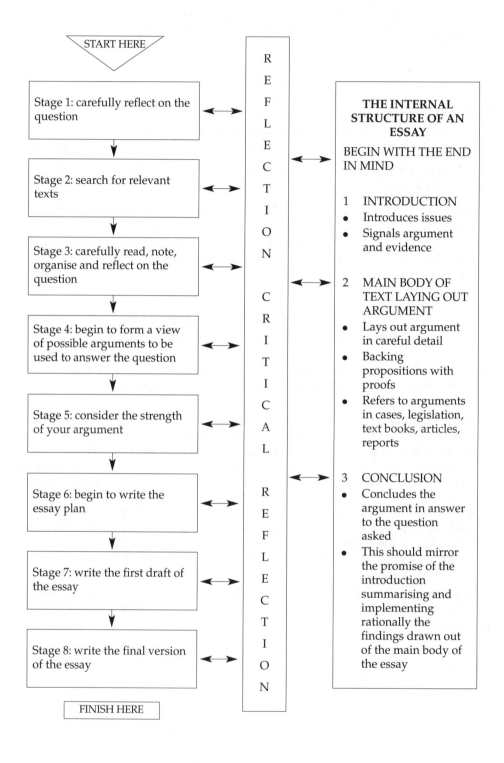

8.5.1   What is a problem question?

A problem question sets out a factual situation requiring the application of legal rules to move towards a solution. Look at the following selection of examples.

Problem Question 1

Baby Dream (BD) plc manufacture disposal baby nappies. 'Baby's Little Friend' (BLF) plc sent a telex to BD plc asking them to deliver 1,000 disposable nappies at a price of 8 pence per nappy. BD plc agree to do so by Telex. However, 30 minutes later they are offered 15p a nappy by another wholesaler who has run out and was in crisis trying to fill a big order. BD plc therefore send a telex to BLF revoking their acceptance and meets the other order at the higher price. The Managing Director of BLF plc receive the acceptance telex and the revocation telex at the same time. It is unclear which telex was read first.

Advise Baby Dream as to any legal liability they may have been incurred.

Problem Question 2

Frieda, an auctioneer, sold a collection of miniature oil portraits on enamel by auction. Each portrait was described in the auction catalogue. When Frieda invited bids for Lot 35 – described as 'Portrait, artist unknown', - her assistant Timmy held up Lot 25 by accident. Lot 25 was described in the catalogue as 'unknown girl', school of Bruett. However Jake immediately recognised it as a lost masterpiece by Bruett himself. No other bidders noticed Timmy's error and Jake's bid of £30 was accepted by Frieda. When Frieda realised what had happened she refused to let Jake have the painting, which has been valued at £6,500.

Advise Jake. Consider in particular whether a valid contract for the sale of the painting has been created.

Problem Question 3

Mary has worked for 'The project' one day a week as a volunteer researcher since 1995. In January 1998 she had a child and continued to do her volunteer research from home. In October 1999 the project offered her financial remuneration for the use of her own facilities and they offered weekly payments of £60. Mary told them that this was too much. She was told to keep the rest as a deserved reward. She is paid when she is sick and during holidays. In December 2000 when she has a second child they allow her three months payments without expecting work. In the period 2001–02 she is steadily pressured to extend her time to two days a week. She reluctantly agrees in December 2002. In April 2003, Mary sends the project a bill for £1,466 representing six months payments of an extra £60 a week for the extra day a week The project reply they have no contractual arrangement to pay her.

Advise the Project as to whether Mary has accrued any contractual rights and if so what type of contract she has entered into, and what their liability is.

Problem Question 4

Cedric, a 'coin' dealer, had a rare Roman coin for sale. He wrote to Dorothy, a collector who specialises in Roman coins, asking whether she would be interested in purchasing it. Dorothy wrote in reply, 'I am willing to pay £1,000 for the coin, I will consider it mine at that price unless I hear to the contrary from you and will collect it from your shop on Monday next week'.

Advise Dorothy as to the legal position:

(a) if Cedric ignored Dorothy's letter and sold the stamp to Timothy for £1,200;

(b) if Cedric put the coin aside in an envelope marked 'Sold to Dorothy' but Dorothy decided that she no longer wished to buy it.

8.5.2 Understanding the purpose of a problem question – what type of skills is it testing?

A problem question has a range of functions many of which are shared with the function of an essay. The distinctive aspect of a problem question however is the purported simulation of real legal problems requiring the application of the law in the light of the doctrine of precedent and in full appreciation of any legal gaps, or doubts in the law. More specifically, problem questions can be said to be testing the following areas:

* current state of your knowledge of the law in a given area;
* current state of your ability to use a factual situation and apply the law to it;
* current state of your ability to apply case law and legislation;
* current state of your memory (remembering the names, courts and dates of cases, and the sections, subsections and dates of legislation);
* current state of your understanding of the relationship between cases and statutes and the methods of arguing according to the doctrine of precedent;
* ability to organise the facts in a problem and systematically apply the law to those facts;
* ability to identify the legal issue or issues raised by the given factual scenario;
* knowledge of the grey areas of the law surrounding the cases decided in the given area under consideration;
* knowledge of available defences;
* knowledge of particular interpretational issues arising in the law under consideration;
* ability to construct an argument.

Above all, a problem question at the academic stage of education is looking for a highly competent ability to extract legal issues from fact situations and apply the law to them. Invariably you will be asked to discuss situations where there are conditions of doubt about facts, legal issues, or interpretation of the law.

(1)   *Stage 1: correct analysis of the constituent parts of the problem question*

(a) **Identify the FACTS given** – place on a tree diagram.

(b) **Identify the primary and secondary LEGAL ISSUES raised by the facts, available defences and doubts in the law**. Place on a tree diagram of the issues. List the issues under the facts.

(c) **Consider the LAW THAT MAY APPLY** (eg, legislation or common law and/or European Community law). The sources of law to be drawn on will vary according to the particular subject. Quickly list these under the issues on the tree diagram.

(2)   *Stage 2: Begin to work on discrete aspects of the problem question*

(a) Decide the order in which issues will be raised in your answer.

(b) Consider your view of uncertainties and gaps in the law in the area.

(c) Consider issues of interpretation and defence. A doubt about the interpretation of the law is not a defence, it is a doubt about the law. Make sure you do not make this mistake, as they require a different approach.

(3)   *Stage 3: Decide your view of the outcome of the specific questions asked in the problem question*

The facts in a problem question can give rise to many issues but all of these may not be necessary to resolve the specific question(s) set in your problem. Problem questions tend to ask you to do two main things:

(a) Discuss the issues raised in the problem scenario.

    OR

(b) Advise one of the parties.

Both types of problem question require the same knowledge to successfully answer them. However, your approach will be different. (In fact essay questions can be drawn from the same knowledge but also require a different approach.)

- In those drafted in response to a question in the style of (a) you raise all issues without privileging one party.

- In those drafted in response to a type (b) question you raise all issues but orientate to your argument to the effect of those issues on the party you are asked to advise. This includes discussing in detail the likely chances of the other party being the successful party.

8.5.3   Demonstration: beginning to answer a specific problem question

The key to successfully answering a problem question lies in spotting the 'clues' to the issues to be discussed. Many of these are purely linguistic. We will look at one particular problem, Problem Question 4, above, applying the stages outlined above.

(1)   *Stage 1: correct analysis of the constituent parts of the problem question*

(a) **Identify the FACTS given** – place on a tree diagram.

(b) **Identify the primary and secondary LEGAL ISSUES raised by the facts, available defences and doubts in the law**. Place on a tree diagram of the issues. List the issues under the facts.

(c) **Consider the LAW THAT MAY APPLY.**

The first task is to read the question and determine the topic. The problem chosen is contract. In an examination the speed with which a problem question is narrowed to a topic and then to issues within that topic can be of exceptional importance since time is of the essence. (Part of the technique is having engaged in consistent study techniques so you are up to date in your course study and your revision if an examination is involved.) You should have a clear idea of the areas of doubt where currently the law is unclear, as often this is the area in which problem questions will be located.

The first stage of analysis involves a combination of linguistic ability and legal knowledge. The problem question can be underlined and issues drawn out in a very simple first reading. This combination is demonstrated in Figure 8.2, below. The words that are the clues to the legal issues are boxed and arrows leading from these words begin to discuss the legal issues raised.

There are two things to note in a problem question like this one that comes with two labelled parts (a) and (b). You must answer *both* parts unless instructed clearly that candidates are to answer *either* (a) or (b). Many students can fall here and assume there is a choice. Do not exercise a choice unless this is clearly given otherwise you could lose half of the marks going for the problem question.

As can be seen a lot has been done to interrogate the question and divide it into its parts. It is important to break the question down into its constituent issues, so that the context of (a) and (b) can be appreciated.

(2)   *Stage 2: begin to work on discrete aspects of the problem question*

What should also be apparent is that you need to have a view as to whether a contract has been concluded between Cedric and Dorothy, and if so when, before (a) or (b) can be answered.

The issues to be considered can also be set out as a narrative. These are:

(1) What is the effect of Cedric writing to Dorothy to offer to sell the coin?

(2) What is the effect of Dorothy's letter?

(3) What is the effect of Cedric's two suggested responses:

   (a) that he ignored Dorothy's letter;

   (b) that he put a sticker on it saying sold but Dorothy did not collect it?

It should by now be apparent it was not the first time that the issue revolved around whether there has in fact been a contract concluded. The answer to this is dependent upon whether an offer and an acceptance can be located, and if so where they stand.

Figure 8.2: facts and legal issues

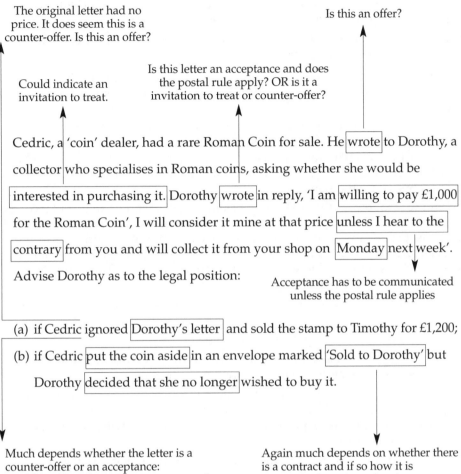

The original letter had no price. It does seem this is a counter-offer. Is this an offer?

Is this an offer?

Could indicate an invitation to treat.

Is this letter an acceptance and does the postal rule apply? OR is it a invitation to treat or counter-offer?

Cedric, a 'coin' dealer, had a rare Roman Coin for sale. He wrote to Dorothy, a collector who specialises in Roman coins, asking whether she would be interested in purchasing it. Dorothy wrote in reply, 'I am willing to pay £1,000 for the Roman Coin', I will consider it mine at that price unless I hear to the contrary from you and will collect it from your shop on Monday next week'.

Advise Dorothy as to the legal position:

Acceptance has to be communicated unless the postal rule applies

(a) if Cedric ignored Dorothy's letter and sold the stamp to Timothy for £1,200;

(b) if Cedric put the coin aside in an envelope marked 'Sold to Dorothy' but Dorothy decided that she no longer wished to buy it.

Much depends whether the letter is a counter-offer or an acceptance:
- If Dorothy's letter is an acceptance then the contract is concluded and Cedric is breaking it by selling the coin.
- If Dorothy's letter is a counter-offer there has been no acceptance. Acceptance must be communicated and this behaviour does not fall into any of the situations when silence can be construed as acceptance.

Again much depends on whether there is a contract and if so how it is constructed:
- If Dorothy's letter is an acceptance her desire to change her mind comes too late, she is bound.
- If Dorothy's letter is a counter-offer it may be the case that Cedric has accepted it by conduct. In which case her desire to change her mind has come too late.

Again, your approach should be to break down the question into its constituent parts:

(a) The effect of Cedric's letter – is it an offer or an invitation to treat?

(b) The effect of Dorothy's letter – is it an acceptance? Do the postal acceptance rules apply? Is Dorothy's letter a statement of intention?

(c) Is Dorothy's letter an offer? Can she waive the necessity for the communication of the acceptance if she so chooses?

The question therefore expects you to carefully consider the facts and the uncertainties, consulting case law and perhaps texts in areas touching on these matters.

As we have noted in our responses in Figure 8.2, above, with regard to part (a), if a contract has been formed, then Cedric is in breach of this contract when he sells the coin to Timothy. With regard to case law and commentators it does seem highly likely that, in these circumstances, no contract has been formed with Dorothy and Cedric is free to sell the stamp.

With regard to part (b), if Dorothy has made an offer, not an acceptance, then Cedric has possibly accepted the offer when he takes the step of setting aside the stamp, as it is possible to show acceptance by conduct. If this is the case, a contract has been formed and Dorothy is obliged to buy the stamp. It needs to be noted that there are flaws and weakness in this particular question. There are, however, significant weaknesses in reaching this conclusion.

It should also be noticed that at present we have suggested issues but as yet we have:

• No argument by way of linked propositions;

• No proofs (law cases) supporting or denying our propositions (or texts discussing areas where the law is unknown or uncertain).

Without a sustained argument backed by law cases there is no competent answer to the problem question! Yet often students stop at teasing out the issues in a haphazard way and maybe, just maybe throwing in one or two general cases. Can you begin to see the difficulty?

Having used the word identification to sort out the legal issues they come down to the following.

Is there a binding contract in existence between Cedric and Dorothy?

(a) Is Cedric's letter an offer or an invitation to treat?

(b) The answer to (a) determines the status of Dorothy's letter – it is either a counter-offer or an acceptance.

If yes how do we approach answering (a) and (b)? Much of the question revolves around the issue of communication.

An offer must be communicated and be certain

Cedric's letter uses the words 'interested' in buying. It mentions no price. It is hard to see how this could be an offer.

Because there was no offer Dorothy's letter cannot be said to be an acceptance. However, Dorothy is clearly interested and responds to the invitation to treat by putting in a counter-offer with a price and a method of acceptance. This counter-offer is clear and communicated and gives a price and constitutes an offer.

An acceptance of an offer must also be communicated

Communication can be construed from conduct.

(a) So if Cedric ignores the offer letter there is no contract.

(b) If Cedric puts the coin aside he can be said to communicate acceptance in the circumstances by his conduct.

We will not continue this demonstration as this is a legal method, not a contract text, and enough has been set out to demonstrate the strategy of approaching problem questions and how, with the aid of diagrams you can be reminded to lay out propositions, produce supporting case law and know where the doubts are. In an area of doubt, for example, on some occasions it may be enough to make a decision and back it by the state of uncertainty and any case support no matter how tenuous. What the reader who is also your marker is looking for is the skill of dealing with such legal issues with certainty and competency demonstrating knowledge of the area and the relevant cases. Each subject area will have its own areas of doubt and uncertainty and these are the areas to concentrate upon. The rules, the exceptions to the rules, the doubts.

(3)   *Stage 3: decide your view of the outcome of the specific questions asked in the problem question*

This is, of course, important. Figure 8.3, below, indicates a possible outcome to the problem question that allows all eventualities to be explored but also makes a choice about when a contract may have come into existence.

Finally Figure 8.4, below, sets out an approach to resolving problem questions.

Figure 8.3: locating the contract

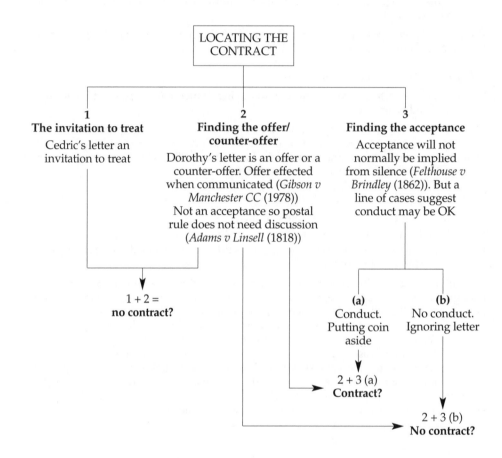

Figure 8.4: flow chart of the method for the preparation and construction of an answer to a problem question

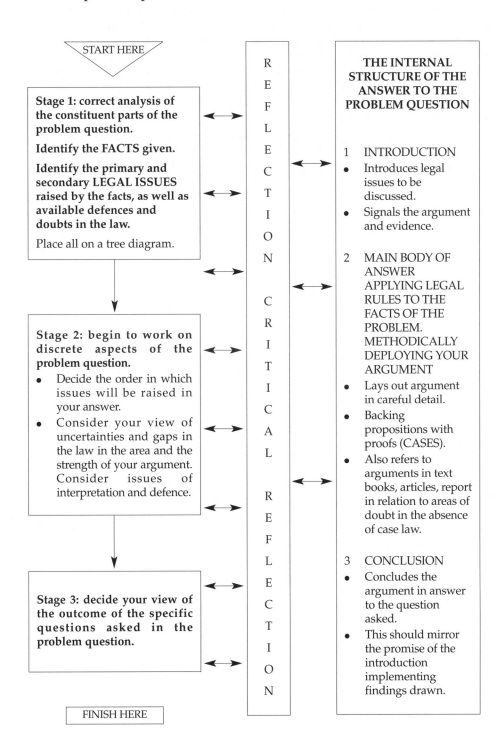

8.6   SUMMARY

This chapter has considered in detail ways of structuring approaches to written work in the area of law. It has highlighted the importance of being clear about the approaches required in the particular type of written work that you are doing. With this in mind the chapter has distinguished between various types of essay question and various types of problem question. The point, however, has also been made that the same type of information base is required for all questions. It is how this information, knowledge and understanding is drawn on to produce a particular written result that is important.

The next chapter brings together all of the skills and many of the discrete legal areas touched upon in this book to demonstrate how skills work together to produce one result, competent legal reading, argument construction and writing.

CHAPTER 9

A DEMONSTRATION: USING PRIMARY AND SECONDARY LEGAL TEXTS TO CONSTRUCT ARGUMENTS IN ANSWER TO ONE PARTICULAR QUESTION

9.1   INTRODUCTION

This chapter can be seen as the core of the book because it is designed to pull together and apply the strategies for reading, writing and argument construction laid out in the earlier chapters of this book. The purpose of this is twofold; to provide a practical demonstration of how these skills come together in essay writing and to enable the reader to transfer these skills to their work for their other law courses. In this way, the skills development that has taken place in this text can be used to develop understanding of law by informing learning, course assessment and examination performance.

The grounding of these strategies has been achieved by *simultaneously* applying them to the task of preparing to write an essay. The essay has been specifically drafted in a challenging area of law dealing with the relationship between European Community (EC) law and English law. The material to be drawn on for the essay question is confined to three quite difficult texts (two case reports and an extract from a relevant textbook). These three texts are set out in Appendix 3.

Working through this chapter, students will be able to gain a good understanding of their own skill development in these areas, and obtain a good grasp of how they can transfer these skills to the law courses they are studying. The decision to narrow the texts drawn upon and to put them in the Appendix was taken in order to ensure that the student's work as they progress through this chapter can be closely monitored to enable them to obtain the best check possible of their skills development.

This chapter is divided into six sections: 9.1–9.6. Section 9.3 is the core of the chapter and is concerned with applying the skills and strategies discussed in this book to an essay question. Section 9.3 acquires its structure from the writing strategy set out in Chapter 8 and is sub-divided into eight parts mirroring the stages in that strategy. Students are asked to engage in various tasks within writing these eight sections. The strategy taken is to approach the essay question and apply the eight stage method for writing laid out in Chapter 8, which is set out here as a reminder.

Strategy for writing an essay

1   Carefully reflect on the question.
2   Search for relevant texts.
3   Carefully read, note, organise and reflect on the materials collected.
4   Form a view of possible answers to the question.
5   Consider the strength of the argument being developed.
6   Finalise the essay plan.
7   Write a first draft of the essay.
8   Write the final version of the essay.

Whilst approaching the essay using the writing strategy, detailed reference is also made to the reading strategies set out in Chapter 6. The reading skills are noted at the relevant places within the writing strategy. In addition argument construction skills as set out in Chapter 7 are introduced into the writing strategy at appropriate places.

Section 9.3 is supported by section 9.4 as it contains reference material for section 9.3: summaries and diagrams. At various points in section 9.3, students will be specifically asked to refer to these. Through a comparison between their own work on the texts and the essay question and the diagrams and summaries in section 9.4, students will be able to chart progress.

This chapter seeks to make the importance of a simultaneous approach to skills development absolutely clear through its exposition of the interrelationship between:

• substantive legal subject knowledge, legal skills, general transferable skills (such as reading and writing skills);

• between factual analysis and legal analysis;

• between problems, rules and solutions;

• between reading, writing and argument construction.

9.2   LEARNING OUTCOMES

By the end of this chapter, readers should:

• know how to deconstruct an essay question;

• understand the inseparable relationship between reading, writing and argument construction skills for successful legal study;

• understand the different weights and values to be given to texts read for an essay;

• have a competent understanding of the constituent parts of an essay;

• have tested the development of understanding of the interrelationship between UK law and EC law;

- be able to apply knowledge of propositions and evidence to the process of argument construction directed to the answer of the essay question.

9.3   WRITING AN ESSAY

The essay question that is the vehicle for demonstrating 'putting it all together' is as follows.

> In *R v Secretary of State ex p Factortame (No 1) and (No 2)*, the English courts and the European Court of Justice made it clear that not only do English courts have the power to suspend Acts of Parliament conflicting with European Community law but that European Community law demands that the provisions of lawfully enacted Acts of the UK Parliament be overturned and the European Court can even dictate what national remedies should be available.
>
> Discuss solely by reference to the following texts:
> (1) extracts from *R v Factortame (No 1)*;
> (2) extracts from *R v Factortame (No 2)*;
> (3) extracts from Tillotson, J, *European Community Law: Text, Cases and Materials*, 2nd edn, 1996, London: Cavendish Publishing.
>
> (Note: texts (1), (2) and (3) can be located in Appendix 3.)

The question is slightly artificial in that it is limiting the choice of texts, and cutting out research. All texts referred to are supplied in Appendix 3 to allow a controlled demonstration of skills. It is now possible to carefully monitor the handling, interpretation and evaluation of the texts by the student, so that the following can be considered:

- What arguments were located in those texts?
- How were they found?
- What arguments in the given texts were missed?
- Why were they missed?
- How were arguments finally constructed?
- Which lower order skills still need work (eg, summarising)?
- Which higher order skills still need work (analysis)?

The essay is set in the area of EC law as it touches upon UK law. As has already been discussed, the relationship between Community law and English law is a complex matter and can involve the side by side consideration of all or some of the following texts:

- UK statutes;
- UK delegated legislation;
- UK case law;
- articles in EC treaties;

- EC legislation;
- opinions of the European Court of Justice (ECJ);
- decisions by the domestic courts of Member States in similar areas;
- explanations in textbooks;
- arguments in specialist articles.

In addition, the student has to:

- keep the doctrines and principles of the two legal orders (the Community's and the UK's) in mind simultaneously,

and *still* remember to answer the *specific* question asked!

This can seem a daunting task, but if the lower order skills of:

- organisation;
- classification;
- identification; and
- summarising,

are methodically deployed, then the texts will be broken into and sifted and made ready for answering a specific question. The competent execution of the lower order skills allows the development of the higher level cognitive skills of:

- analysis;
- evaluation;
- critique; and
- argument construction.

Once the texts have been carefully prepared by ordering and summarising:

- potential arguments can be reflected upon;
- arguments can be compared;
- differences of opinion expressed by judges and academics considered.

At this point, the student can indeed begin to have a personal view and write about it.

The initial task is to:

- understand each text as much as possible in isolation;
- consider the interconnections between the texts.

Law cases and texts that conflict are as intimately interconnected as law cases that agree with each other. The student needs to be able to put together:

- cases and arguments that are the same;
- cases and arguments that are different;
- cases and arguments that are mixed in that in some areas they agree and in some areas they disagree.

Chapter 7 on identifying and constructing arguments demonstrates that no problem is ever a simple unitary matter; that problems come in bundles. Whilst questions posed may appear simple and unitary, they never are.

Not only is there no such thing as a simple question, there is no such thing as a simple answer. All questions are complex and, of necessity, all answers are complex. It is never sufficient to give as an answer a purely descriptive commentary. No questions posed to test understanding will require only description. They will require evaluation and critique as well.

The student has to make choices. Decide what issues are most relevant; and what can, and what cannot, be discussed in the answer to the question.

The method set out in Chapter 8 for the preparation and construction of essays is one suggestion for 'putting it all together'. That method will now be used for the preparation of the texts and for the construction of the arguments that can be used in answer to the given essay question. The method for approaching the essay is on p 255 and set out in diagram form in Figure 8.1, above, in Chapter 8.

9.3.1   Stage 1: carefully reflect on the question

9.3.1.1 What is being asked?

This is an exercise in basic English comprehension. The way forward is to *textually* deconstruct the question and then convert it into a tree diagram that can be annotated as other information and arguments are collected from the texts. Efficient use of textual notation without a diagram would be as useful at this stage. When the level of attention to detail is realised, the methodology finally adopted depends on the development of personal preference.

The actual essay question must be constantly borne in mind as texts are read and research is conducted.

The first task, therefore, is to set the question out and annotate it.

Figure 9.1: annotated essay question

More connectors:
- and
- but

You will note these are English cases. How is the ECJ involved?

In *R v Secretary of State ex p Factortame (No 1) and (No 2)*, the English courts and the ECJ made it clear that not only do English courts have the power to suspend Acts of Parliament conflicting with European Community law but that European Community law demands that the provisions of lawfully enacted Acts of the UK Parliament be overturned and the European Court can even dictate what national remedies should be available'.

Signals first issue (the power to suspend)

Signals second issue (EC law demands)

Signals third issue (ECJ can even dictate ...)

Discuss solely by reference to the following texts:

This is an open invitation to say something analytic. It is suggesting: locate issues and debate. See diagram for detail of word

When precise instructions are given, students get *no* credit for doing more. Command here is *not* to look at other texts

(1) extracts from *R v Factortame (No 1)*;

(2) extracts from *R v Factortame (No 2)*;

(3) extracts from Tillotson, J, *European Community Law Text, Cases and Materials*, 2nd edn, 1996, London: Cavendish Publishing.

Note: texts (1), (2) and (3) can be located in Appendix 3.

From the above annotation, several issues are beginning to emerge, as follows.

9.3.1.2 *How many issues are raised?*

The question seems to be suggesting that, in the *Factortame* cases:

- English and European courts made it clear that English courts can suspend Acts of Parliament;
- European law demands that conflicting UK legislation must be overturned;
- the ECJ can dictate what national remedies should be available.

These issues have been set out as assertions, it is left to the student to determine whether these assertions legitimately describe the views of the relevant courts as set out in the two cases.

9.3.1.3 Tree diagram of issues raised by the essay question

The next step in deconstructing the question is to look at the text of the question again, together with the annotations, and turn it into a tree diagram. This can be used to put page references, quotes and arguments onto a grid that will assist in mapping out the arguments of the essay.

Figure 9.2: diagram of issues in the essay question

ESSAY ISSUES

In the two *Factortame* cases referred to, the UK courts have the power to suspend Acts of Parliament conflicting with EC law

In the two *Factortame* cases referred to, the ECJ ASSERTED:

1
UK courts can suspend Acts of Parliament

2
ECJ can demand Acts of Parliament are suspended

3
ECJ can dictate what natural remedies are available

Issues identified

In relation to each issue, it is necessary to find out if the relevant court did make this assertion or if it can only be inferred that they did, or they did not make it at all. The conclusion to the essay will need to make decisions

Note: reflect on how much work has been done on the question before any reading has been engaged in. All that has happened so far is a careful deconstruction along purely linguistic lines. However, a lot is now known about the question.

9.3.2   Stage 2: search for relevant texts

The relevant texts have already been determined in this case. Normally, however, once the issues raised by the question have been discovered and preliminary reading undertaken in the textbooks, it is useful to scan the following:

- handouts from tutors;
- articles mentioned in the *footnotes* or *endnotes* in set textbooks;
- available databases or relevant indexes of law journals;
- available databases or *Current Law Citator* for up to date law cases, legislation and so on;
- one of the article databases (such as Igenta) or indexes to various journals in years that are thought to be salient.

9.3.3   Stage 3: carefully read, note, organise and reflect on the materials collected

- Precis them.
- Extract arguments presented.
- *Reconsider* the question.

Here, it is relevant to turn to the limited materials used for this essay – the extracts from the two cases and the textbook by Tillotson.

The first task is reading, asking the basic questions detailed below in relation to cases and texts, all the time recalling the actual issues detailed in the essay question, otherwise, relevant details could be missed. As you read texts, you need to ask yourself the following questions:

- **Law reports:**
  What are the facts?
  What legal rules have been applied and why?
  What aspects of this case are of relevance to my essay?
  How do the arguments presented assist me in my current essay?
- **Textbooks**:
  What is being described?
  Do I understand?
  Does it fit my understanding of the cases?
  Have I properly grasped the issues involved?
  What is of relevance to my essay?
- **Articles**:
  What is the writer's argument?
  Is it well supported by the evidence?
  Does the writer's argument support or deny my argument in the essay?

Is there a majority view developing in the texts concerning any of the issues raised by the question?

When you have done this go back to the diagram of the question. Note beside the various issues aspects of the texts that are of relevance to the issues identified as requiring discussion to answer the question. It is important to remain open to the possibility that personal ideas may change as more research is conducted and some texts present persuasive arguments that had not been previously considered.

9.3.3.1 Law reports

(1)   General discussion

The reports of the law cases given in Appendix 3 will appear extremely complex initially. However, it is worth remembering that basic skills have already begun to develop. Experience has been commenced in the following areas:

(a) reading English and EC law reports and making case notes;

(b) argument identification/organisation;

(c) argument deconstruction/construction;

(d) knowledge of the hierarchy of courts;

(e) knowledge of the relationship between UK (domestic) legislation and European law.

The basic questions that need to be answered to ensure a firm grasp of the law report are:

(a) What are the facts?

(b) What legal rules have been applied and why?

(c) What aspects of this case are of relevance to my essay?

(d) How do the arguments presented assist me in my current essay?

When you begin to read these law reports you may ask yourself 'How can one begin to break into these texts?'. They are complex, long, and a mixture of common law and civil law styles as case *(No 2)* includes the ECJ rulings under Article 177 (the preliminary reference). Such a daunting case will not come your way too often as an undergraduate and, when it does, it will be in the context of a substantive law subject such as constitutional law or community law.

The approach taken in the text here is like being thrown into the deep end, but with a lifebuoy in place. The purpose of choosing a difficult set of texts is to demonstrate that:

(a) utilising sophisticated comprehension skills;

(b) recognising textual intraconnections;

(c) being able to classify, identify, organise texts,

enables a relatively firm grasp of what is going on to be ascertained even by beginners. Indeed, beginners viewing this as a comprehension exercise with fresh eyes can often obtain a more secure grasp than many law students specialising in the area will ever be able to attempt because beginners are open to legal method skills.

In *George Mitchell* [1983] 2 All ER 732–44 in Chapter 4 and the *Van Gend en Loos* case (Case 26/62) in Chapter 5, paragraph markers were taken. This was relatively easy with the short case of *George Mitchell*, a little more tricky with the length of *Van Gend en Loos*, although a table format simplified matters. The *Factortame* cases also have non-bracketed numbering to assist with cross-references. But here, a paragraph précis would create a book and not be very helpful. Yet the markers are useful. Paragraph clusters can be considered dealing with particular issues. The approach taken to this series of cases will be to ask you to:

- skim read: literally imagine that you have a pile of papers and are flicking them through your hands. But skim read a little more slowly than this! Do not stop to read in detail. Look out for:
    - ○ headings;
    - ○ courts, to find out the procedural history;
    - ○ dates, get a feel for the chronology of events;
    - ○ what are the issues in the case?

The skim reading will be followed by more detailed readings involving casenoting.

(2)   First skim reading of Factortame cases

The extracts from the two law cases are set out in Appendix 3; turn to them now and read through them. Be warned, however, that these are long cases; therefore, if you take one minute to read a page – which is quite fast – it would take 75 minutes to read it all. This puts the task into context. So make sure that you have enough time to do this task.

The cases are also of invaluable assistance for the micro-analysis of legal method – how to break into a highly complex set of cases giving vast amounts of information running to hundreds of pages.

The length of the report is daunting and the language and content of the text formidable. However, persistence will allow the refinement of your developing skills of organising, comparing, describing, classifying and identifying facts and legal rules.

Do not proceed until you have skim read the cases and taken notes according to the above guidance: Note how long it takes you to do so. Read the cases with your deconstruction of the question to hand so that you can ensure that you are constantly reading with a view also to the question.

Having looked at the cases and made notes answer the following questions:

(1) Describe *your* immediate reactions to the texts, to the issues, to the things you understood and to the things that you did not understand (you may relate to Figure 9.3, below).

(2) What you think the cases were about?

Figure 9.3: reaction to texts

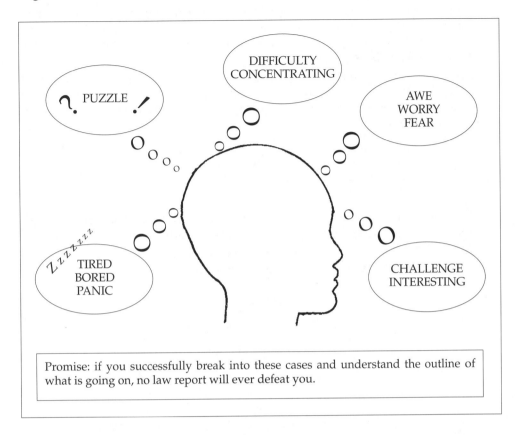

Promise: if you successfully break into these cases and understand the outline of what is going on, no law report will ever defeat you.

(3) Detailed reading of Factortame cases – and making a case note

Now re-read the cases in detail for the purposes of making a case note. You may need to re-read the section on case noting in Chapter 4.

Whilst a number of matters need to be dealt with there are four important areas that must be included in a case note.

(1) a meticulous precis of the facts of the case;

(2) careful ascertainment of the issues involved; what questions are before the relevant courts;

(3) careful listing of legal rules of relevance to the case;

(4) the decision of the court and the reasoning for that decision.

Taken together (1)–(4) will allow understanding of the case to develop which is essential.

Each of these four areas will now be considered in a little detail.

- *A meticulous precis of the facts of the case*

  In an English case, the facts are usually presented early on in the first judgment. Consider *Factortame (No 1)*. From the skim reading of the extracts from the cases, and from reading Tillotson, it should be clear that *all* the cases revolve around the same facts.

  If you missed this point, then you are not yet reading with the proper attention to detail. Retrace your steps by skim reading again. Find out why you missed it – although, in the end, the reason is always the same: reading with insufficient care and attention.

  > Reading words but not reading for sense.

  If you ascertained that all the cases involve the same facts, what are the facts? Turn back to the extract of *Factortame (No 1)*. Where are the facts to be found?

  Look at p 371, below: is there anything about the information on this page that strikes you as odd, unusual, unexpected, confusing?

THINK CAREFULLY!

  The case is called *R v Secretary of State for Transport ex p Factortame Limited and Others* and it is being heard in the Court of Appeal. It is on appeal from the first instance court, the Queen's Bench Divisional Court, and it is an action for judicial review. The Secretary of State for Transport has powers that will result in the ending of the applicant's ability to apply for a licence to fish. The applicants want the legislation and the power of the Secretary of State reviewed in the light of their assertion that the action is based on the authority of domestic legislation that conflicts with EC law. After stating this the next 81 paragraphs of the Court of Appeal report set out the judgment in the Divisional Court of the Queen's Bench by Neill LJ. This is in the High Court and, from this information, it is realised that this must be the report of the judgment in the original hearing. A student who is not properly reading, and thinking about, the heading could miss this and think that they are reading the Court of Appeal judgment. This judgment in the Queen's Bench Division is going to be where the initial recounting of the facts is to be found. This is an excellent lesson in reading for detail.

> Note: it is worth remembering that this version of the facts is the judge's version. This is the official, influential version. In this case, as it turned out, the facts were not disputed. In cases where the facts are disputed, the judge decides which is the 'true' version. An exercise of power.

- *Practical exercise before moving on*

  Now locate the facts, read them, underline any points, make notes and write a concise summary of the facts. No more than 25 lines. Now check your summary of the facts against the summary at the end of this chapter in section 9.5.1, below:

  ○ Have you missed out any facts? If so how did that happen?

  ○ Have you more facts than in the summary? Why did you add in facts not in the summary?

  ○ Is your summary longer than 25 lines? Why is this the case?

  Look at your extra facts again. Are they really facts? Or have you misidentified, or misclassified. For example, the following matters, although relevant, do not constitute facts:

  ○ political background: talking about the UK government's view of the Common Fisheries Policy? This is background context which is useful but *not facts* of the case;

  ○ the procedural history: which courts the case has been in;

  ○ the legal issues: both UK law and EC law.

  All of the above matters are highly relevant but they are not facts.

  If facts are missed out, check to see why this is the case. Was the mistake due to inattention during reading or confusion as to the difference between facts, issues and procedural history? Rectify and make sure that it does not happen again.

Q: Why does it matter that only the facts are put into this part of the summary?

A: It matters because clarity of understanding will never be achieved if separate matters are confused and intertwined. How can issues raised, or legal rules, be applied to the facts if the student has confused issues or history *as* facts.

- *Careful ascertainment of the legal issues involved*

  What questions are before the relevant courts?

- *Careful listing of legal rules of relevance to the case*

  The following explanation incorporates items (2) and (3) above. In order to properly appreciate the nature of the legal issues raised in an appeal, it is essential to understand the nature of the legal issues raised at the original trial, as the appeal is a consequence of the trial! As an appeal progresses, there may be changes to the grounds of the appeal. If the developmental history of the appeal is not properly understood, important changes may even be missed.

(a) Go back to the judgment of Neill LJ and show as concisely as you can on a tree diagram the following information:

- Who were the applicants?
- Why did the applicants appeal?
- What exactly did the applicants want the court to do?
- What legal rules were being relied on by the applicants?

(b) Read the Court of Appeal judgment and set out as concisely as you can on a tree diagram the answers to the following questions:

- Who were the appellants?
- Why did the appellants appeal?
- What exactly did the appellants want the court to do?
- What legal rules were being relied on by the appellants?

(c) Now read the House of Lords' judgment, and again on a tree diagram set out the answers to the following questions:

- Who were the appellants?
- Why did the appellants appeal?
- Why is there an opinion by the ECJ in this judgment?

> Note: Lord Goff refers to an interim order by the European Court in another action brought against the UK by the European Commission under Art 169 of the Treaty of Rome (the plot thickens). This required the UK to suspend the *nationality* requirements in the Merchant Shipping Act 1988.
>
> The UK Parliament amended s 14 to bring it in line with the interim order by regulations ratified 2 November 1989. This made the appellants appeal as stated unnecessary.
>
> So ... *why* did the applicants in this case still proceed with their appeal?

- What exactly did the appellants want the court to do?
- What legal rules were being relied on by the appellants?

As this is such a complex case, further clarification can be obtained by methodically listing on a separate page, preferably in chronological order, all UK and EC law involved. Just go through the High Court judgments and note down *all* references to legislative rules in both the UK and EC as well as all references to articles in treaties. (Do not get confused by the fact that subdivisions in a *regulation* are also referred to as articles.) This will include UK legislation and delegated legislation, EC Treaty articles and EC legislation created by the institutions. Once set out as *separate* lists, they can be converted into a composite diagram that also relates legal rules to relevant issues (see Figures 9.5 and 9.6, below).

The answers to the various questions asked concerning the cases in (a), (b) and (c) above should now be carefully considered and each set out as tree diagrams. When you have constructed a tree diagram using the questions asked of the cases as headings, a comparison of all three courts will encapsulate the most important aspects of the case. These diagrams are set out at the end of this chapter in Figures 9.7–9.11, below. They also include the information noted in response to (4), below.

Compare your tree diagrams relating to House of Lords, Court of Appeal and High Court with the ones prepared for this text (Figures 9.8–9.10, below). Did you miss anything? If you did – why was that?

Intellectual health warning!

Make the summaries and construct the diagrams before checking the diagrams in the text.

The diagrams are useful for broad, yet in depth, comparisons and for self-diagnosis:

- What was found?
- What was missed?
- What is now understood?

Note: the most important matters are:
- those that you did not see; or
- relevant matters that you decided were not relevant.

If you missed out issues, or thought relevant matters were irrelevant, you must ask yourself: *why did I do that?*

- *The decision of the court and the reasoning for that decision*

  Recall when issues relating to use of rules to solve problems were being discussed. It was stated that problems do not come in simple, single units, and neither do solutions. When the reasons for decisions are analysed, sometimes it is easy to forget this point. Judges sometimes present simple problems by their interpretation of the issues. However, in these cases, no one is pretending the outcome is simple.

  In sorting out:

  - the facts;
  - the applicants or appellants;
  - the issues in the main case;
  - the grounds of appeal,

much information will also have been assimilated concerning the reasoning of the court in response to the issues raised.

As students read judgments with the facts, issues and relationships between legal rules in place, then it becomes an easier task to isolate the text relating to the reasoning process. As the text is mentally ordered and classified, relevant aspects of the judgment in relation to reasoning can be identified, weak reasoning can also be considered. It is then less daunting to deal with a line of cases changing legal rules or the interpretation of legal rules.

If a statistical breakdown of the parts of any judgment was conducted, it would be found that a relatively small percentage of the judgment is related to reasoning. But, in an English law report knowledge of the reasoning process of the court is said to be the most vital element of the report.

In reading these judgments, much information can be gathered on the attitudes of the senior English judiciary concerning the relationship between EC law and UK law. For example, careful reading will have noted that all judges accept, without question, that, in cases of clear infringement of EC law by UK law, then UK law must be disapplied. Noting this will make the student question the interpretation of the case put forward by the essay question that they are essential about 'disapplying English statutes'.

An appreciation of the correct issue (can a court disapply as an interim measure before a rule has been held to conflict with EC law?) suggests the necessity for a vital yet subtle difference between what the essay question is suggesting and what the cluster of *Factortame* cases is about.

The reasoning of the courts can only be obtained by reading **all** judgments.

Go back over the information gathered in relation to the procedural history of these cases and, incorporating information in the cases, construct a diagram of the **actions** .

(4)   *Final consideration of the cases by reflecting on textual notes and diagrams*

The three diagrams 9.7–9.9 contain the basic reasoning behind the decision for you to check your findings against.

It is useful here to look at *all* the diagrams and tables:

Table 9.2:   the list of UK law and EC law;

Figures 9.4 and 9.5: UK and EC legal rules of relevance;

Figure 9.6:   provisions of the Treaty of Rome (EC Treaty) of relevance to the *Factortame* cases;

Figure 9.7:   the issues raised by the question;

Figures 9.8–9.10:   the three diagrams concerning the grounds of appeal, decision and reasoning in all three courts, including indication of grounds of preliminary ruling;

Figure 9.11:   the diagram of the actions in the case.

On only nine pages there is now an ordered summary of the essay question and the 72 page case extracts. Looking at these diagrams, it would be appropriate to write the case notes of the cases. Now that the case law has been read in its context it is necessary to broaden out and look at the secondary text.

9.3.3.2 Textbook and articles

Next read the extract from Tillotson, *European Community Law: Text, Cases and Materials*. Try to understand what he is describing and fit the cases into his commentary. There are other cases in the 'Factortame story'. As you read the text ask yourself the following preliminary questions:

- What is being described?
- Do I understand?
- Does it fit with my understanding of the cases?
- Have I properly grasped the issues involved?
- What is of relevance to my essay?

These questions represent important aspects of active reading. You approach this reading with a view. You are asking how the new material informs, changes, supports your view.

At the end of this stage, there will be an appreciation of how the textbook and the extracts from the law reports fit together. This is an appropriate time to ask if there is a majority view developing in the texts concerning any of the issues raised by the question?

Go back to the diagram of the essay question (Figure 9.2, above). Note beside the various issues aspects of the texts, with page references, that are of relevance to each issue that you have identified. It is now possible to begin to develop a view as to which parts of the texts deal with which issue, and move towards answering the essay question and clarifying your argument.

9.3.4   Stage 4: begin to form a view of possible answers to the question

The completion of the analysis of the cases and the textbook should have communicated a relatively strong grasp of the issues raised by these cases and the political background against which they were decided.

The work on the issues raised by the essay questions, together with the issues raised in the cases, should have revealed the subtle distinction that the cases revolve around the issue of the ability or otherwise of the UK courts to disapply a UK statute when it is only *suspected* of infringing European law. It is this point that had not been decided before by the courts. The cases are therefore about the viability of disapplying national legislation as an interim measure awaiting final determination. The urgency behind the application by *Factortame* and others is that irreparable damage will be done to their businesses even if they win the final case because:

- they could not get damages against the Crown as the law then stood;
- they would, therefore, go bankrupt before the matter was finally determined, as it would occur well after they had been unable to register.

Ascertaining these points allows much to be said in your essay.

The reading shows that, at a broad level, no English judge disputes the fact that EC law obliges English courts to disapply a national law if it conflicts with EC law. Neither does the UK government dispute this. That is why it is essential that the narrower issue is picked up: that the case concerns disapplying UK legislation by an English court as an *interim* measure awaiting final determination of the main issue concerning EC law and its infringement.

Look at the diagrammatic version of the essay question set out in Figure 9.6, below, and the way in which the limited knowledge so far obtained has been added to it. The diagrams of the cases in relation to issues, grounds and reasoning have been used to attach points to the issues raised by the question in Figure 9.6, below.

What judges say constitutes powerful evidence for an argument. It can be seen that the cases can be allocated to issues and arguments formed to agree or disagree, in part or in total.

Intellectual health warning!

Texts which deny your argument are not to be ignored, they are to be dealt with. You can argue that they are unreliable (for example, you may argue that the argument is pure theory with no evidence to back it up); you can argue that it is one possible plausible interpretation but that you are presenting another equally plausible interpretation. If you cannot explain away an argument denying your view, then perhaps you should reconsider your view. How strong is your argument?

9.3.5   Stage 5: consider the strength of your argument

Look at all the diagrams and the argument constructed. Refine the argument. Look back now to the deconstruction of the question and deal with *each* assertion.

9.3.5.1 Issues

The question seems to be suggesting that, in the 'Factortame cases':

- **Issue 1: English and European courts made it clear that English courts can suspend Acts of Parliament**

  Essay discussion (Precis form):

  This point was well established by the UK and EC courts *before* the case of *Factortame* was brought to court. The judges treat this point as uncontroversial and taken for granted in the case of *Factortame*. The courts did make it clear but only by re-stating the position already existing. The issue in this case was whether the court could order legislation to be disapplied as an interim measure when the main case concerned an application that there was a potential conflict with EC law. The sticking point being that at the time of the disapplication there was *no* conflict proved.

Evidence: quote from the cases briefly and summarise briefly the view of the judges. Refer to earlier cases deciding these points; refer to Tillotson.

- **Issue 2: European law demands that conflicting UK legislation must be overturned**

    Yes, it does; the courts accepted this before *Factortame* so this is stating the obvious.

    Evidence: s 2 of the European Community Act 1972.

    Quote from cases and Tillotson.

- **Issue 3: the ECJ can dictate what national remedies should be available**

    No, the case determined that the ECJ cannot. The ECJ stated in the preliminary ruling *requested* by the House of Lords that the absence of interim orders by way of a national remedy would be an injustice and would make the resort to European law non-viable in certain types of case. They did not say what remedies should be available. Indeed, the ECJ actually said that it was beyond its powers to say *what* remedies and *what* criteria should apply to them. They did, however, say that there should be remedies.

    Evidence: direct quotations and brief summaries from cases and Tillotson.

So, in brief, the argument of your essay is that the quotation is misleading for the reasons outlined. The word 'discuss' allows the essayist to expand or contract issues as is wished and armed with all the information the writer is in control!

Intellectual health warning!

In an exam situation and in an essay situation, many students would have merely spent pages discussing the facts and the outcomes, demonstrating, however, little appreciation of the issues raised by the cases and little understanding of the question. This is not because they are not capable of understanding, but because they did not spend enough time thinking about what the question was asking and preparing the texts to be used.

9.3.6   Stage 6: begin to write the essay plan

Look at:

- all the diagrams;
- notes of cases and other texts;
- notes of *your own ideas/argument*.

It is always worth taking the time to reflect on the plan and texts read.

9.3.7   Stage 7: begin to write the first draft of the essay

- Begin with the middle section.
- Review everything for the conclusion.
- Write the introduction last.
- Pay attention to the argument – does it clearly present itself?
- Pay particular attention to the conclusion and thoughts on the introduction.
- Also, review the argument. Is there evidence to back it up? Have opposing views been dealt with?

It is always worthwhile considering whether you need to search for any more texts. This is irrelevant here for the purposes of this exercise, but if the texts had not been pre-ordained it is highly likely that a first trawl through would demand further reading and/or research.

9.3.8   Stage 8: begin to write the final version of the essay

9.4   REFERENCE MATERIALS FOR SECTION 9.3 DIAGRAMS, SUMMARIES AND TABLES

9.4.1   Diagrams of UK and European legal rules of relevance (Figures 9.4–9.6)

Figure 9.4: UK legal rules of relevance in the *Factortame* cases (key law indicated by circles)

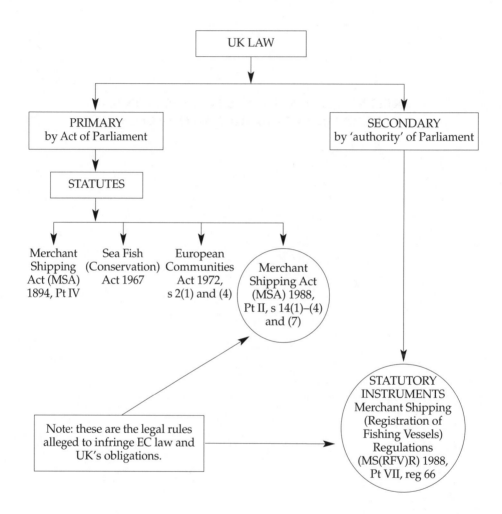

Figure 9.5: European Community legal rules of relevance in the *Factortame* cases (key law indicated by circles)

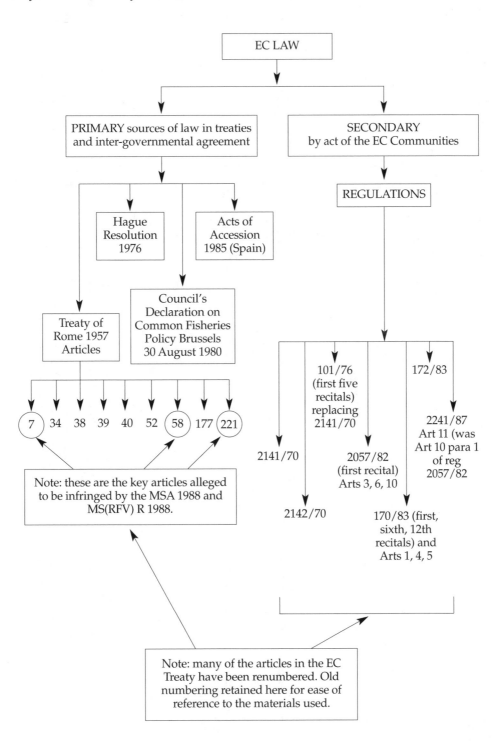

Figure 9.6: provisions in the Treaty of Rome 1957 of relevance to the *Factortame* cases (old numbers pre-1997 used to equate with cases

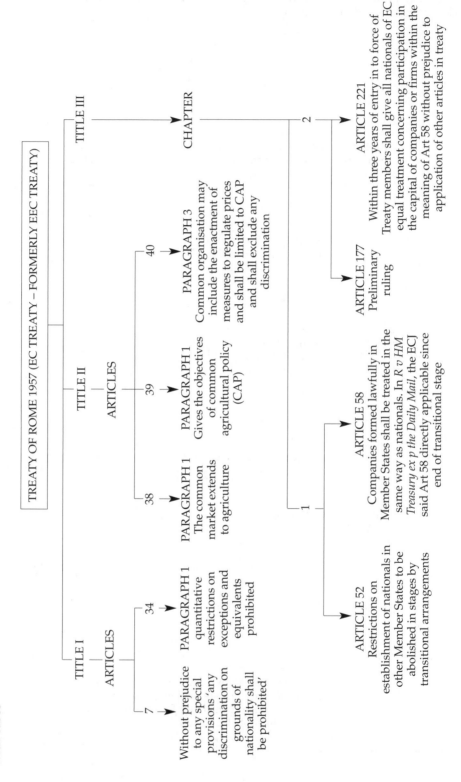

9.4.2 Diagrams of issues in the cases (Figures 9.7–9.10)

Figure 9.7: issues raised by the question with attached relevant references to cases

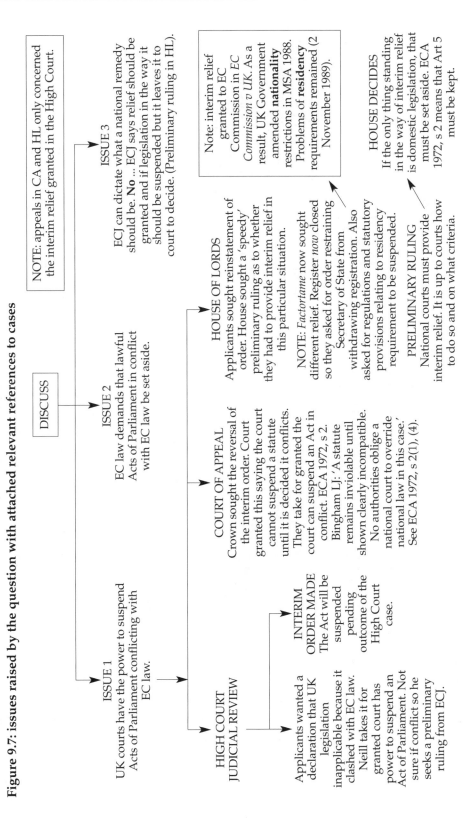

NOTE: appeals in CA and HL only concerned the interim relief granted in the High Court.

DISCUSS

ISSUE 1
UK courts have the power to suspend Acts of Parliament conflicting with EC law.

ISSUE 2
EC law demands that lawful Acts of Parliament in conflict with EC law be set aside.

ISSUE 3
ECJ can dictate what a national remedy should be. **No** ... ECJ says relief should be granted and if legislation in the way it should be suspended but it leaves it to court to decide. (Preliminary ruling in HL).

Note: interim relief granted to EC Commission in *EC Commission v UK*. As a result, UK Government amended **nationality** restrictions in MSA 1988. Problems of **residency** requirements remained (2 November 1989).

HOUSE OF LORDS
Applicants sought reinstatement of order. House sought a 'speedy' preliminary ruling as to whether they had to provide interim relief in this particular situation.

NOTE: *Factortame* now sought different relief. Register *now* closed so they asked for order restraining Secretary of State from withdrawing registration. Also asked for regulations and statutory provisions relating to residency requirement to be suspended.

PRELIMINARY RULING
National courts must provide interim relief. It is up to courts how to do so and on what criteria.

HOUSE DECIDES
If the only thing standing in the way of interim relief is domestic legislation, that must be set aside. ECA 1972, s 2 means that Art 5 must be kept.

COURT OF APPEAL
Crown sought the reversal of the interim order. Court granted this saying the court cannot suspend a statute until it is decided it conflicts. They take for granted the court can suspend an Act in conflict. ECA 1972, s 2. Bingham LJ: 'A statute remains inviolable until shown clearly incompatible. No authorities oblige a national court to override national law in this case.' See ECA 1972, s 2(1), (4).

INTERIM ORDER MADE
The Act will be suspended pending outcome of the High Court case.

HIGH COURT JUDICIAL REVIEW

Applicants wanted a declaration that UK legislation inapplicable because it clashed with EC law. Neill takes it for granted court has power to suspend an Act of Parliament. Not sure if conflict so he seeks a preliminary ruling from ECJ.

Figure 9.8: High Court decision in *Factortame*

HIGH COURT
FIRST HEARING

WHO WERE THE APPLICANTS?
Factortame

WHY DID THEY APPLY?
- New UK law meant they could not carry on in business.
- Alleged the UK law infringed EC law.

WHAT DID THEY WANT?
- Declaration.
  That the relevant UK law was not applicable to them because it contravened EC law.
- Order of Prohibition stopping Secretary of State treating their licence as having expired on 1 April 1989.
- Damages.

WHAT WERE THE RELEVANT LEGAL RULES?

UK

The disputed 'new law'
- MSA 1988, s 14.
- MS(RFV)R 1988.

Legislation giving supremacy to EC law
- ECA 1972.
- Sea Fishing (Conservation) Act 1967.

LEGAL FRAMEWORK
Treaty of Rome 1957 setting quotas:
- reg 170/83.
- Arts 1, 4, 5.
- reg 2057/82.
- Act of Accession 1985.

EC

Rules deemed contravened by UK new law
- Arts 7, 34, 38, 39, 40, 52, 58, 221.

THE DECISION

WHAT DID THE HIGH COURT DECIDE?
They needed a preliminary ruling under Art 177 of the Treaty of Rome to decide the issue.

WHY DID THEY SO DECIDE?
Can place common fisheries policy in wider context.
Can decide on s 5 view that Member State has absolute right to decide who flies UK flag.
Applicants argue UK acting excessively restrictively.
Authority allows them to grant relief. Now the House of Lords has duty to take account of and give effect to EC law.
EC law can give relief but takes time.
Loss to applicants and court satisfied it can exercise discretion. Currently, applicants cannot seek damages.
Local community benefits economically and so, on balance, more damage will be caused by not giving relief.

Figure 9.9: the Court of Appeal decision in relation to the injunction in *Factortame*

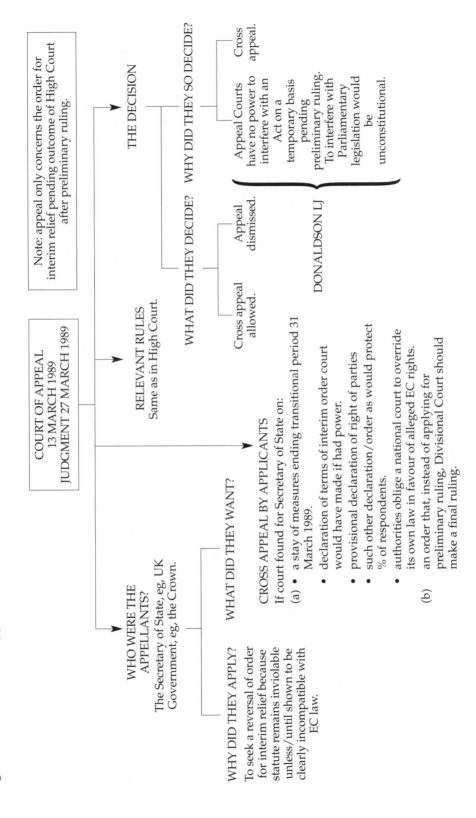

Figure 9.10: diagram of the House of Lords in relation to the granting of the injunction in *Factortame*

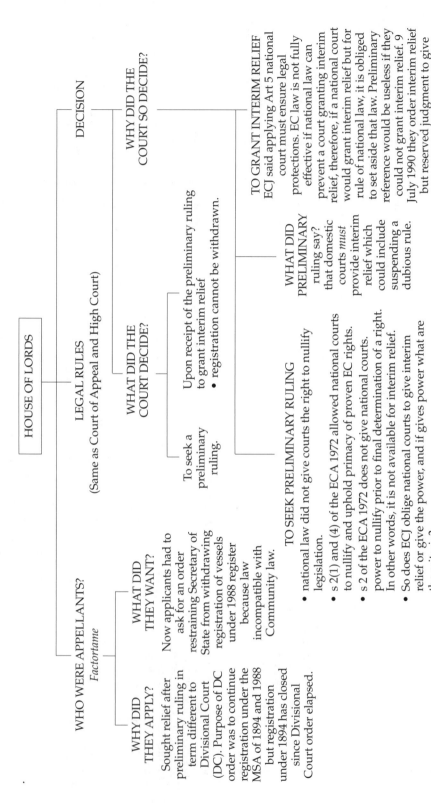

Notes to Figure 9.10

Preamble: reading the first few pages of this report, it becomes apparent that this House of Lords report is the second of a process. The case came before the House of Lords on 18 May 1989 and they decided it was appropriate to seek a preliminary ruling from ECJ on the issue of whether (given UK court had no power under UK law to grant type of interim relief required) a UK court is obliged to grant relief or whether EC law gave power to grant relief – and, if it gave power without obligations, what is the criteria to be applied in deciding whether or not to grant such interim relief protection.

Note: between order of Divisional Court, March 1989, and hearing in the House of Lords, 1990:

- there were two judgments by ECJ concerning the validity of certain conditions imposed by the Secretary of State on the granting of licences to fishing boats 18 October 1989;

- an Interim Order by President of ECJ (on application by European Commission) regarding nationality provisions, s 14 of the MSA 1988 EC action under Art 169 that ss 13–14 of the MSA 1988 contravened Arts 8, 52, 221. EC applied for order requiring UK to suspend application of national provisions regarding Member States, s 14 amended by MSA 1988 (Amendment) Order 1989 from 2 November 1989.

Applicants still pursued matters before the House of Lords relating to other aspects in s 14, especially domicile/residence in UK (shareholders/directors) made impossible to register.

Figure 9.11: actions/processes/issues/rules involved in *Factortame* and *Factortame* (No 2) (information solely derived from the cases and Tillotson)

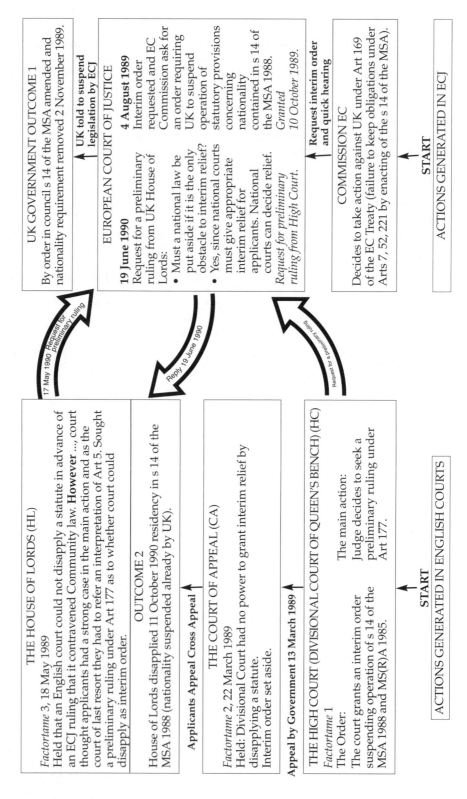

9.4.3   Summaries

9.4.3.1 Summary of the facts

The action revolved around a dispute between the British Government and Spanish companies legitimately registered to fish under the Merchant Shipping Act 1894 carrying on business in England. The majority of the directors and shareholders were Spanish and were resident outside the UK.

The UK introduced new conditions for granting licences in the Merchant Shipping Act 1988 which laid down that 75% of the directors and shareholders must be British nationals and reside in the UK. All vessels had to re-register as their existing licences expired on 31 March 1989.

The applicants could not comply with the new conditions for registration, their vessels would have to stop fishing and the companies would face financial disaster.

9.4.3.2 Summary of the political background as set out in the cases

If students had been searching for their own texts, they might have, quite legitimately, chosen to research the political background in more detail.

The UK joined the EC in 1973 and the powers of ministers regarding fishing contained in the Sea Fish (Conservation) Act 1967 became subject to the Common Fisheries Policy of the EC. Around the UK was a 200 mile European Community fishing zone.

The EC had introduced a system of fishing quotas for each Member State. For the purposes of calculating whether a quota had been exceeded, foreign vessels registered with Member States had their load calculated against the quotas of that State.

The British government had expressed concern that the full benefit of the quotas therefore was not going to British interests but to foreign economic interests. The British government was of the opinion that local fishing communities were suffering from such invasion of their waters and that they needed special protection. They therefore made major changes through legislation – the Merchant Shipping Act 1988.

9.4.3.3 Summary of the issue in the application for judicial review

The applicants alleged that the British Government, by stipulating that 75% of the shareholders and directors had to be of British nationality, were unnecessarily acting out of all proportion to the problem. Furthermore, the British Government had infringed their Community obligations by passing a statute that contained provisions in direct contravention of the Treaty of Rome 1957 – notably that Member States cannot discriminate against each other (see Articles 7, 52 and 221 of the Treaty of Rome).

9.4.3.4 Summary of procedural history

Factortame applied to the High Court for an order that the contravening sections of the Merchant Shipping Act 1988, together with parts of the accompanying regulations passed to implement the statute, should be disapplied pending a full hearing of the matter.

The High Court considered that the dispute raised a question requiring the interpretation of some of the articles in the EC Treaty and decided to operate their discretion to ask the European Court for a preliminary ruling under Article 177 to the question whether s 14 of the Merchant Shipping Act 1988 infringed Articles 7, 52 and 221 of the EEC Treaty.

This case commenced in December 1988 but the court decided to seek a preliminary ruling from the European Court and this was sent on 10 March 1989.

The High Court ordered the application of the statute to be suspended on the grounds:

- of changes brought about by entry into the EC and the UK obligations under the Treaty of Rome;
- of s 2(1) and (4) of the ECA 1972;
- that the applicants stood a good chance of winning the case and, if they had to await a ruling, the case could take two years. However, if they were unable to register and therefore unable to fish for two years they would be bankrupt;
- that this case for judicial review was not a case in which damages was a remedy on offer.

The government appealed against the High Court decision on the grounds that an English court cannot suspend an Act of the English Parliament before it has even been determined to be in conflict with European law. The Court of Appeal agreed with the government.

Factortame was forced to appeal to the House of Lords who said that, as far as the law as they saw it was concerned, the High Court could not suspend a statute. However, as the final court of appeal, they were obliged to seek a preliminary ruling on the matter from the ECJ under Article 177 (now Article 234), of the Treaty of Rome 1957 concerning whether a 'national court had to give relief pending a reference in a main action and, if it gave relief, did Community law give it the power to grant interim protection'? (See Chapter 5.)

The ECJ replied in the affirmative that a national court had to give relief. Furthermore, the ECJ stated that if a national law stood in the way of interim relief, that national law must be set aside. So, the House of Lords further ordered on 9

July 1990 that as the applicants' case was strong, interim relief, in the form of the suspension of s 14 of the Act, was granted.

By then, the Commission for the EC had commenced an action against the British government stating that s 14 of the Merchant Shipping Act 1988 infringed its treaty obligations under the founding Treaty of Rome 1957, Articles 7, 52 and 221. The Commission also applied to the ECJ for interim relief requiring the UK to suspend s 14 of the Merchant Shipping Act. The ECJ granted this on 10 October 1989. The UK complied by an Order in Council dated 2 November 1989. The range of actions in this rather complex litigation is set out in Figure 9.11, above.

9.5   TABLES

9.5.1   Table of the skim read of the cases

The skim reading should have revealed most of the following.

Table 9.1

Table 9.1	
Case 2 (yes, 2!) **An appeal against interim order made in** Case 1 **Case 2 is really an *interlocutory matter*** Court of Appeal	*R v Secretary of State for Transport ex p* *Factortame Limited and Others* Before the English Court of Appeal: On appeal from the English High Court: • Community law and national law; priority of Community law; European Court National Courts; Priority of Community law. Interim measure. • Constitutional law: UK Acts of Parliament; Priority of Community law.
Case 1: the trial **High Court** Printed in full prior to the judgments in the appeal on interlocutory matters.	Judgment of the Divisional Court. Neill LJ. The application for interim relief. Hodgson LJ.
OUTCOME	**Reference made to the European Court under Art 177.** **Interim order made suspending the operation of the contentious part of the Merchant Shipping Act 1988 and the accompanying regulations.**

Case 2
Court of Appeal
22 March 1989
	Appeal by Secretary of State against the
	interim order.
	Judgment of the Court of Appeal
	    The Master of the Rolls.
	    The application.
	    The appeal.
	    Reasons.
	Bingham LJ.

Outcome	**Appeal allowed.**
Case 3 **House of Lords** **Appeal on the interlocutory matter the** **subject of Case 2**	On appeal by the applicants from the Court of Appeal's decision to allow the appeal of the Secretary of State. *R v Secretary of State for Transport ex p* *Factortame Ltd and Others (No 2)*
11 May 1989	House of Lords I Background to the dispute. II The House of Lords judgment of 18 May 1989. III Course of the procedure.
4 August 1989	Commission of European Community takes the UK to the European Court under Art 169 of the EEC Treaty for a declaration that s 14 of the Merchant Shipping Act infringes the UK's obligations under Arts 7, 51 and 221 of the EEC Treaty.
4 August 1989	Commission seeks an interim order from the European Court to suspend the application of s 14 of the Merchant Shipping Act 1988.
2 November 1989	Order in Council by the UK Government comes into force amending s 14 to take account of the interim relief ordered by the European Court. IV Written observations Second question.
European Court **17 May 1990** **European Court** **19 June 1990**	**Reference under Art 177 to enable House of** **Lords to proceed to judgment** 17 May, Mr Advocate General Tesauro. 19 June, judgment delivered in Luxembourg.

House of Lords 11 October 1990	**Their Lordships took time for consideration.** 11 October, Lord Bridge of Harwich Lord Brandon of Oakbrook Lord Oliver of Aylmerton Lord Goff of Chieveley Lord Jauncey of Tullichettle (1) the threshold; (2) have the applicants crossed the threshold?; (3) balance of convenience.
Outcome	**Appeal allowed.**

9.5.2   Table of UK and European Community legislation

Table 9.2: UK legislation/delegated legislation and European Community Treaty articles and legislation of institutions

(a)   English legislation

    (i)   Primary legislation

- Part IV of the Merchant Shipping Act 1894 (Pt IV MCA 1894)
- Section 4 of the Sea Fish (Conservation) Act 1967, as amended
- European Communities Act 1972
- Parts II, s 14(1), (2), (3), (4), (7) of the Merchant Shipping Act 1988

    (ii)   English delegated legislation

- Merchant Shipping (Registration of Fishing Vessels) Regulations 1988
- Part VII, reg 66 of the Regulations 1988

(b)   Community law

    (i)   Treaties

- The Treaty of Rome 1957:
  - Art 7
  - Art 34, para 1

  Pt II

  Title II
  - Art 38, para 1
  - Art 39, para 1
  - Art 40, para 3

  Title III

  Chapter 1

Chapter 2
- ○   Art 52
- ○   Art 58, Chapter 3
- ○   Art 221
- ○   Art 177

(ii)   Resolutions

Hague Resolution, November 1976

(iii) Declarations

Council's Declaration on Common Fisheries Policy Brussels 30 May 1980

(iv)   Acts

Acts of Accession 1985

(v)   Regulations

Regulation 2141/70

2142/70

101/76 (replacing 2141/70 above)

First five recitals of 101/76

2057/82 First recital, Arts 3, 6, 10

170/83 First recital, sixth recital, twelfth recital, and Arts 1, 4 and 5 of that Regulation

172/83

2241/87 Art 11 (was Art 10, para 1 of reg 2057/82)

9.6   SUMMARY

The interrelationship of all of the skills required for successful legal study have been demonstrated in this chapter. While in many respects the chapter appears short, the materials that need to be worked through are long and complex. The work that you put in will be rewarded, however, and you can test yourself by taking the time to work through the diagrams and double check your work against the diagrams and summaries that function as both information and answers to tasks set in this chapter.

If you have slowly and methodically worked your way through the material and tasks in this chapter you will be well on the road to understanding the development of your skills in the area of reading, writing and argument construction.

CHAPTER 10

CONCLUSION

This text has attempted to provide a clearer view of the practicalities of reading legal texts, both primary and secondary, in order to engage in argument construction. Ways have been suggested of 'breaking into' texts to understand the flexibility and the inherent unreliability of language.

The power of 'the word' and of language generally were signalled at the beginning. This brief conclusion finishes by signalling – and no more, for this text is eminently a practical manual – that only a partial understanding is reached if one does not consider the power of the authority of law, attached to the flexibility of words; the power of law's context, of status; the power of the privileging of law over other institutions, and of its interpretation of words over other interpretation of those words. Law is applied, used or created by people acting in roles dealing with the memories of the law. 'The question of interpretation is that of whose memory, whose order of reference, does the law institute' (Goodrich (1990:253)).

Much time has been spent looking at mechanistic schemes for understanding legal words, legal texts, intertextual and intratextual links signalled as signposts along the way to that understanding, or even finding, the arguments for the outcome of the case. But, as Goodrich has stated, 'reading is never innocent' (Goodrich (1990:231)).

There are vast dimensions of analysis untouched, ready for the politician, the philosopher, feminist, criminologist, sociologist. There is a range of ever present yet buried motivational issues – why did the judge adopt that interpretation? Which rationale for adopting that interpretation do 'I' believe? (The rationale about political decision making or the rationale about the literal meaning or some other rationale.)

We have considered a few raw legal arguments and have noted the reasons given to support outcomes. Valuable issues can be raised by asking: 'OK, but why didn't the judge take another plausible interpretation?'

Judgments are the end result after parties and witnesses put their side, via official and tortuous questioning. In places where rules of evidence, magistrates and judges control what is and what is not said; by whom and how it is said. From the stilted collection of words, judgment is seamlessly created. Lawyers, judges, officials control definitions too – as well as choose interim and ultimate interpretations. And it is worth remembering here that only a small proportion of legal disputes come to trial. Many are not taken any further than a dispute between people.

Legal texts are never unambiguous representations of the law, they are the words from which interpretations flow. At the level of the obvious, the voice of consensus states '*we* all *know* what this means, *don't we*?' Equally, this can be said in a tone of incredulity, or of ridicule, '*we* all *know* what this means, don't we?'

In our texts, we build one story, one ending. The story could be different and so could the ending. Our bricks are words. After all this practicality – of study skills, English language skills, legal method skills and their interrelationship with substantive law and solving legal problems, all these little building bricks – there is the landscape that decides it all: the officials; the institutions; politics; the judiciary; the police; policy. Why one interpretation and not another?

The critical thinker has to remain engaged not only in micro questions within the text, both at the superficial and the deep readings, but also engage in macro questions at the level of law, politics and culture; at the level of text as social fact, as the product of a culture; continuing the search for underlying assumptions.

Much law degree study will revolve around 'fighting' with the language of and arguments in cases, reconciling, distinguishing and/or following them and explaining differences of interpretation where some might say there are no differences. Students learn an increasingly larger body of rules and, more and more, the overarching context of institutions and culture shrinks into the background. They are interesting from an academic perspective, but cultural legal content has no place in the everyday life of the law and its mediation of competing interests. It is in the interest of these legal institutional values that the legal 'story' is the one that covers all. There is a danger that the daily process of *doing* the law blinds the 'doers' who are on the street (the practitioners) to the motivational influences of some institutional creators of law.

When deciding what words mean in court, judges make far reaching decisions and maintain that they do not do so on grounds of morality, religion, justice or ethics, but purely as a true interpretation of the words. They support the view that one must believe in the ultimate good of the law and the ultimate ability of the law to determine what the law means. A problem can now be seen. As pointed out above, the law is not an autonomous neutral agent, it is used by people in a political and social role. Legal texts can be analysed as social texts created by social actors. Statutes are texts communicated via words created by politicians in compromise, interpreted by judges for a range of reasons, some explicit some not.

The orthodox view is that law is a neutral instrument to achieve a moral society. Law is objective, rational and logical. Can discussions about law ever be justifiably separated from discussions about power, from discussions of law maintaining society and its political ideology. Access to law making power is only available to players in the higher levels of the political machinery or professionals in the higher judiciary.

Law is not logical, nor does it have to be. There is social agreement that, for a range of reasons – political, social and moral – English law should be seen to be fair, and outrage when it is thought to be not fair. Statutory rules have attempted to engage in behaviour re-direction.

But to apply a rule to a problem requires the clarification of the problem and proof that the facts of the problem as presented are the facts that occurred. Rules have developed which state what must be proved by testimonial or forensic evidence and when evidence itself must be backed up.

Due to the developmental strategies of the common law, its orality of proceeding, the breaking away of the courts from the royal household, the ultimate ascendancy of statutory law and the complete reorganisation of the courts of England and Wales in 1875 and 1978, we now have a system of law which is based upon the reaction to arguments presented to those officials who decide which argument is legitimate, be they negotiators in offices, tribunals and juries, magistrates and appellate courts. This system is being challenged, stretched and changed by the new political and legal order of the European Union and European Community law, as well as changes to the law relating to human rights.

The English legal system has a concept of legal decision making that masks the use of discretion by judges. We only see their assertion of logical argument, objectivity and discriminatory 'common sense'.

The law as language is to be read, interpreted, questioned and seen in its fragmented contexts, to be the object of a healthy scepticism. It should not be invested with qualities it cannot control. Law is not justice – for indeed justice may demand that there be no law.

But that's another story!

APPENDIX 1

ENGLISH PRIMARY LEGAL TEXTS

(1) *GEORGE MITCHELL (CHESTERHALL) LTD v FINNEY LOCK SEEDS LTD*
[1983] 2 ALL ER 732–44

HOUSE OF LORDS

LORD DIPLOCK, LORD SCARMAN, LORD ROSKILL, LORD BRIDGE OF HARWICH
AND LORD BRIGHTMAN

23, 24 MAY, 30 JUNE 1983

…

Lord Diplock: My Lords, this is a case about an exemption clause contained in a contract for
the sale of goods (not being a consumer sale) to which the Supply of Goods (Implied Terms)
Act 1973 applied. In reliance on the exemption clause the sellers sought to limit their liability
to the buyers to a sum which represented only 0.33% of the damage that the buyers had
sustained as a result of an undisputed breach of contract by the sellers. The sellers failed
before the trial judge, Parker, who, by placing on the language of the exemption clause a
strained and artificial meaning, found himself able to hold that the breach of contract in
respect of which the buyers sued fell outside the clause. In the Court of Appeal both Oliver
LJ and Kerr LJ, by similar processes of strained interpretation, held that the breach was not
covered by the exemption clause; but they also held that if the breach had been covered it
would in all the circumstances of the case not have been fair or reasonable to allow reliance
on the clause, and that accordingly the clause would have been unenforceable under the
1973 Act. Lord Denning MR was alone in holding that the language of the exemption clause
was plain and unambiguous, that it would be apparent to anyone who read it that it covered
the breach in respect of which the buyers' action was brought, and that the passing of the
Supply of Goods (Implied Terms) Act 1973 and its successor, the Unfair Contract Terms Act
1977, had removed from judges the temptation to resort to the device of ascribing to the
words appearing in exemption clauses a tortured meaning so as to avoid giving effect to an
exclusion or limitation of liability when the judge thought that in the circumstances to do so
would be unfair. Lord Denning MR agreed with the other members of the court that the
appeal should be dismissed, but solely on the statutory ground under the 1973 Act that it
would not be fair and reasonable to allow reliance on the clause.

My Lords, I have had the advantage of reading in advance the speech to be delivered by
my noble and learned friend Lord Bridge in favour of dismissing this appeal on grounds
which reflect the reasoning although not the inimitable style of Lord Denning MR's
judgment in the Court of Appeal.

I agree entirely with Lord Bridge's speech and there is nothing that I could usefully add
to it; but I cannot refrain from noting with regret, which is, I am sure, shared by all members
of the Appellate Committee of this house, that Lord Denning MR's judgment in the instant
case, which was delivered on 29 September 1982, is probably the last in which your
Lordships will have the opportunity of enjoying his eminently readable style of exposition
and his stimulating and percipient approach to the continuing development of the common
law to which he has himself in his judicial lifetime made so outstanding a contribution.

Lord Scarman: My Lords, I have had the advantage of reading in draft the speech to be delivered by my noble and learned friend Lord Bridge. I agree with it, and for the reasons which he gives would dismiss the appeal.

Lord Roskill: My Lords, I have had the advantage of reading in draft the speech to be delivered by my noble and learned friend Lord Bridge. I agree with it, and for the reasons which he gives I would dismiss the appeal.

Lord Bridge of Harwich: [1] My Lords, the appellants are seedmerchants. The respondents are farmers in East Lothian. In December 1973 the respondents ordered from the appellants 30 lb of Dutch winter white cabbage seeds. The seeds supplied were invoiced as Finney's Late Dutch Special'. The price was £201.60. Finney's Late Dutch Special was the variety required by the respondents. It is a Dutch winter white cabbage which grows particularly well in the acres of East Lothian where the respondents farm, and can be harvested and sold at a favourable price in the spring. The respondents planted some 63 acres of their land with seedlings grown from the seeds supplied by the appellants to produce their cabbage crop for the spring of 1975. In the event, the crop proved to be worthless and had to be ploughed in. This was for two reasons. First, the seeds supplied were not Finney's Late Dutch Special or any other variety of Dutch winter white cabbage, but a variety of autumn cabbage. Second, even as autumn cabbage the seeds were of very inferior quality.

[2] The issues in the appeal arise from three sentences in the conditions of sale indorsed on the appellants' invoice and admittedly embodied in the terms on which the appellants contracted. For ease of reference it will be convenient to number the sentences. Omitting immaterial words they read as follows:

> [1] In the event of any seeds or plants sold or agreed to be sold by us not complying with the express terms of the contract of sale ... or any seeds or plants proving defective in varietal purity we will, at our option, replace the defective seeds or plants, free of charge to the buyer or will refund all payments made to us by the buyer in respect of the defective seeds or plants and this shall be the limit of our obligation. [2] We hereby exclude all liability for any loss or damage arising from the use of any seeds or plants supplied by us and for any consequential loss or damage arising out of such use or any failure in the performance of or any defect in any seeds or plants supplied by us or for any other loss or damage whatsoever save for, at our option, liability for any such replacement or refund as aforesaid. [3] In accordance with the established custom of the seed trade any express or implied condition, statement or warranty, statutory or otherwise, not stated in these Conditions is hereby excluded.

I will refer to the whole as 'the relevant condition' and to the parts as 'cll 1, 2, and 3' of the relevant condition.

[3] The first issue is whether the relevant condition, on its true construction in the context of the contract as a whole, is effective to limit the appellants' liability to a refund of £201.60, the price of the seeds (the common law issue).The second issue is whether, if the common law issue is decided in the appellants' favour, they should nevertheless be precluded from reliance on this limitation of liability pursuant to the provisions of the modified s 55 of the Sale of Goods Act 1979 which is set out in para 11 of Sched 1 to the Act and which applies to contracts made between 18 May 1973 and 1 February 1978 (the statutory issue).

[4] The trial judge, Parker J, on the basis of evidence that the seeds supplied were incapable of producing a commercially saleable crop, decided the common law issue against the appellants on the ground that:

> ... what was supplied... was in no commercial sense vegetable seed at all [but was] the delivery of something wholly different in kind from that which was ordered and which the defendants had agreed to supply.

He accordingly found it unnecessary to decide the statutory issue, but helpfully made some important findings of fact, which are very relevant if that issue falls to be decided. He gave judgment in favour of the respondents for £61,513.78 damages and £30,756 interest. Nothing now turns on these figures, but it is perhaps significant to point out that the damages awarded do not represent merely 'loss of anticipated profit', as was erroneously suggested in the appellants' printed case. The figure includes, as counsel for the appellants very properly accepted, all the costs incurred by the respondents in the cultivation of the worthless crop as well as the profit they would have expected to make from a successful crop if the proper seeds had been supplied.

[5] In the Court of Appeal, the common law issue was decided in favour of the appellants by Lord Denning MR, who said ([1983] 1 All ER 108, p 113; [1983] QB 284, p 296):

> On the natural interpretation, I think the condition is sufficient to limit the seed merchants to a refund of the price paid or replacement of the seeds.

Oliver LJ decided the common law issue against the appellants primarily on a ground akin to that of Parker J, albeit somewhat differently expressed. Fastening on the words 'agreed to be sold' in cl 1 of the relevant condition, he held that the clause could not be construed to mean 'in the event of the seeds sold or agreed to be sold by us not being the seed agreed to be sold by us'. Clause 2 of the relevant condition he held to be 'merely a supplement' to cl 1. He thus arrived at the conclusion that the appellants had only succeeded in limiting their liability arising from the supply of seeds which were correctly described as Finney's Late Dutch Special but were defective in quality. As the seeds supplied were not Finney's Late Dutch Special, the relevant condition gave them no protection. Kerr LJ, in whose reasoning Oliver LJ also concurred, decided the common a law issue against use appellants on the ground that the relevant condition was ineffective to limit appellants' liability for a breach of contract which could not have occurred without negligence on the appellants' part, and that the supply of the wrong variety of seeds was such a breach.

[6] The Court of Appeal, however, was unanimous in deciding the statutory issue against the appellants.

[7] In his judgment, Lord Denning MR traces, in his uniquely colourful and graphic style, the history of the courts' approach to contractual clauses excluding or limiting liability, culminating in the intervention of the legislature, first, by the Supply of Goods (Implied Terms) Act 1973, and second, by the Unfair Contract Term Act 1977. My Lords, in considering the common law issue, I will resist the temptation to follow that fascinating trail, but will content myself with references to the two recent decisions of your Lordship's House commonly called the two Securicor cases: *Photo Production Ltd v Securicor Transport Ltd* [1980] 1 All ER 996; [1980] AC 827 and *Ailsa Craig Fishing Co Ltd v Malvern Fishing Co Ltd* [1983] 1 All ER 101.

[8] The *Photo Production* case gave the final quietus to the doctrine that a 'fundamental breach' of contract deprived the party in breach of the benefit of clauses in the contract excluding or limiting his liability. The *Ailsa Craig* case drew an important distinction between exclusion and limitation clauses This is clearly stated by Lord Fraser ([1983] 1 All ER 101, p 105):

> There are later authorities which lay down very strict principles to be applied when considering the effect of clauses of exclusion or of indemnity: see particularly the Privy Council case of *Canada Steamship Lines Ltd v R* [1952] 1 All ER 305 at 310 [1952] AC 192, 208, where Lord Morton, delivering the advice of the Board, summarised the principles in terms which have recently been applied by this House in *Smith v UMB Chrysler (Scotland) Ltd* 1978 SC (HL) 1. In my opinion these principles are not applicable in their full rigour when considering the effect of conditions merely limiting liability. Such conditions will of course be read *contra proferentem*

and must be clearly expressed, but there is no reason why they should be judged by the specially exacting standards which are applied to exclusion and indemnity clauses.

[9] My Lords, it seems to me, with all due deference, that the judgments of the trial judge and of Oliver LJ on the common law issue come dangerously near to reintroducing by the back door the doctrine of 'fundamental breach' which this House in the *Photo Production* case had so forcibly evicted by the front. The judge discusses what I may call the 'peas and beans' or 'chalk and cheese' cases, ie, those in which it has been held that exemption clauses do not apply where there has been a contract to sell one thing, eg, a motor car, and the seller has supplied quite another thing, eg, a bicycle. I hasten to add that the judge can in no way be criticised for adopting this approach since counsel appearing for the appellants at the trial had conceded 'that, if what had been delivered had been beetroot seed or carrot seed, he would not be able to rely on the clause'. Different counsel appeared for the appellants in the Court of Appeal, where that concession was withdrawn.

[10] In my opinion, this is not a 'peas and beans' case at all. The relevant condition applies to 'seeds'. Clause 1 refers to 'seeds sold' and 'seeds agreed to be sold.' Clause 2 refers to 'seeds supplied'. As I have pointed out, Oliver LJ concentrated his attention on the phrase 'seeds agreed to be sold'. I can see no justification, with respect, for allowing this phrase alone to dictate the interpretation of the relevant condition, still less for treating cl 2 as 'merely a supplement' to cl 1. Clause 2 is perfectly clear and unambiguous. The reference to 'seeds agreed to be sold' as well as to 'seeds sold' in cl 1 reflects the same dichotomy as the definition of 'sale' in the Sale of Goods Act 1979 as including a bargain and sale as well as a sale and delivery. The defective seeds in this case were seeds sold and delivered, just as clearly as they were seeds supplied, by the appellants to the respondents. The relevant condition, read as a whole, unambiguously limits the appellants' liability to a replacement of the seeds or refund of the price. It is only possible to read an ambiguity into it by the process of strained construction which was deprecated by Lord Diplock in the *Photo Production* case [1980] 1 All ER 556, p 568, [1980] AC 82, p 851 and by Lord Wilberforce in the *Ailsa Craig* case [1983] 1 All ER 101, p 102.

[11] In holding that the relevant condition was ineffective to limit the appellants' liability for a breach of contract caused by their negligence, Kerr LJ applied the principles stated by Lord Morton giving the judgment of the Privy Council in *Canada Steamship Lines Ltd v R* [1952] 1 All ER 303, p 310; [1952] AC 192, p 208. Kerr LJ stated correctly that this case was also referred to by Lord Fraser in the *Ailsa Craig* case [1983] 1 All ER 101, p 105. He omitted, however, to notice that, as appears from the passage from Lord Fraser's speech which I have already cited, the whole point of Lord Fraser's reference was to express his opinion that the very strict principles laid down in the *Canada Steamship Lines* case as applicable to exclusion and indemnity clauses cannot be applied in their full rigour to limitation clauses. Lord Wilberforce's speech contains a passage to the like effect, and Lord Elwyn Jones, Lord Salmon and Lord Lowry agreed with both speeches. Having once reached a conclusion in the instant case that the relevant condition unambiguously limited the appellants' liability, I know of no principle of construction which can properly be applied to confine the effect of the limitation to breaches of contract arising without negligence on the part of the appellants. In agreement with Lord Denning MR, I would decide the common law issue in the appellants' favour.

[12] The statutory issue turns, as already indicated, on the application of the provisions of the modified s 55 of the Sale of Goods Act 1979, as set out in para 11 of Sched 1 to the Act. The 1979 Act is a pure consolidation. The purpose of the modified s 55 is to preserve the law as it stood from 18 May 1973 to 1 February 1978 in relation to contracts made between those two dates. The significance of the dates is that the first was the date when the Supply of Goods (Implied Terms) Act 1973 came into force containing the provision now re-enacted by

the modified s 55, the second was the date when the Unfair Contract Terms Act 1977 came into force and superseded the relevant provisions of the 1973 Act by more radical and far-reaching provisions in relation to contracts made thereafter.

[13] The relevant subsections of the modified s 55 provide as follows:

(1) Where a right, duty or liability would arise under a contract of sale of goods by implication of law, it may be negatived or varied by express agreement ..., but the preceding provision has effect subject to the following provisions of this section ...

(4) In the case of a contract of sale of goods, any term of that or any other contract exempting from all or any of the provisions of s 13, 14 or 15 above is void in the case of a consumer sale and is, in any other case, not enforceable to the extent that it is shown that it would not be fair or reasonable to allow reliance on the term.

(5) In determining for the purposes of sub-s (4) above whether or not reliance on any such term would be fair or reasonable regard shall be had to all the circumstances of the case and in particular to the following matters – (a) the strength of the bargaining positions of the seller and buyer relative to each other, taking into account, among other things, the availability of suitable alternative products and sources of supply; (b) whether the buyer received an inducement to agree to the term or in accepting it had an opportunity of buying, the goods or suitable alternatives without it from any source of supply; (c) whether the buyer knew or ought reasonably to have known of the existence and extent of the term (having regard, among other things, to any previous course of dealing between the parties); (d) where the term exempts from all or any of the provisions of s 13, 14 or 15 above if any condition is not complied with, whether it was reasonable at the time of the contract to expect that compliance with that condition would be practicable; (e) whether the goods were manufactured, processed, or adapted to the special order of the buyer ...

(9) Any reference in this section to a term exempting from all or any of the provisions of any section of this Act is a reference to a term which purports to exclude or restrict, or has the effect of excluding or restricting, the operation of all or any of the provisions of that section, or the exercise of a right conferred by any provision of that section, or any liability of the seller for breach of a condition or warranty implied by any provision of that section ...

[14] The contract between the appellants and the respondents was not a 'consumer sale', as defined for the purpose of these provisions. The effect of cl 3 of the relevant condition is to exclude, *inter alia*, the terms implied by ss 13 and 14 of the Act that the seeds sold by description should correspond to the description and be of merchantable quality and to substitute therefor the express but limited obligations undertaken by the appellants under cll 1 and 2. The statutory issue, therefore, turns on the words in s 55(4) 'to the extent that it is shown that it would not be fair or reasonable to allow reliance on this restriction of the appellants' liabilities, having regard to the matters referred to in sub-s (5).

[15] This is the first time your Lordships' House has had to consider a modern statutory provision giving the court power to override contractual terms excluding or restricting liability, which depends on the court's view of what is 'fair and reasonable'. The particular provision of the modified s 55 of the 1979 Act which applies in the instant case is of limited and diminishing importance. But the several provisions of the Unfair Contract Terms Act 1977 which depend on 'the requirement of reasonableness', defined in s 11 by reference to what is 'fair and reasonable', albeit in a different context, are likely to come before the courts with increasing frequency. It may, therefore, be appropriate to consider how an original decision what is 'fair and reasonable' made in the application of any of these provisions should be approached by an appellate court. It would not be accurate to describe such a decision as an exercise of discretion. But a decision under any of the provisions referred to will have this in common with the exercise of a discretion, that, in having regard to the various matters to which the modified s 55(5) of the 1979 Act, or s 11 of the 1977 Act direct attention, the court must entertain a whole range of considerations, put there in the scales on

one side or the other and decide at the end of the day on which side the balance comes down. There will sometimes be room for a legitimate difference of judicial opinion as to what the answer should be, where it will be impossible to say that one view is demonstrably wrong and the other demonstrably right. It must follow, in my view, that, when asked to review such a decision on appeal, the appellate court should treat the original decision with the utmost respect and refrain from interference with it unless satisfied that it proceeded on some erroneous principle or was plainly and obviously wrong.

[16] Turning back to the modified s 55 of the 1979 Act, it is common ground that the onus was on the respondents to show that it would not be fair or reasonable to allow the appellants to rely on the relevant condition as limiting their liability. It was argued for the appellants that the court must have regard to the circumstances as at the date of the contract, not after the breach. The basis of the argument was that this was the effect of s 11 of the 1977 Act and that it would be wrong to construe the modified s 55 of the Act as having a different effect. Assuming the premise is correct, the conclusion does not follow. The provisions of the 1977 Act cannot be considered in construing the prior enactments now embodied in the modified s 55 of the 1979 Act. But, in any event, the language of sub-ss (4) and (9) of that section is clear and unambiguous. The question whether it is fair or reasonable to allow reliance on a term excluding or limiting liability for breach of contract can only arise after the breach. The nature of the breach and the circumstances in which it occurred cannot possibly be excluded from 'all the circumstances of the case' to which regard must be had.

[17] The only other question of construction debated in the course of the argument was the meaning to be attached to the words 'to the extent that' in sub-s (4) and, in particular, whether they permit the court to hold that it would be fair and reasonable to allow partial reliance on a limitation clause and, for example, to decide in the instant case that the respondents should recover, say, half their consequential damage. I incline to the view that, in their context, the words are equivalent to 'in so far as' or 'in circumstances in which' and do not permit the kind of judgment of Solomon illustrated by the example.

[18] But for the purpose of deciding this appeal I find it unnecessary to express a concluded view on this question.

[19] My Lords, at long last I turn to the application of the statutory language to the circumstances of the case. Of the particular matters to which attention is directed by paras (a) to (e) of s 55(5) only those in paras (a) to (c) are relevant. As to para (c), the respondents admittedly knew of the relevant condition (they had dealt with the appellants for many years) and, if they had read it, particularly cl 2, they would, I think, as laymen rather than lawyers, have had no difficulty in understanding what it said. This and the magnitude of the damages claimed in proportion to the price of the seeds sold are factors which weigh in the scales in the appellants' favour.

[20] The question of relative bargaining strength under para (a) and of the opportunity to buy seeds without a limitation of the seedsman's liability under para (b) were interrelated. The evidence was that a similar limitation of liability was universally embodied in the terms of trade between seedsmen and farmers and had been so for very many years. The limitation had never been negotiated between representative bodies but, on the other hand, had not been the subject of any protest by the National Farmers' Union. These factors, if considered in isolation, might have been equivocal. The decisive factor, however, appears from the evidence of four witnesses called for the appellants, independent seedsmen, the chairman of the appellant company, and a director of a sister company (both being wholly-owned subsidiaries of the same parent). They said that it had always been their practice, unsuccessfully attempted in the instant case, to negotiate settlements of farmers claims for damages in excess of the price of the seeds, if they thought that the claims were 'genuine'

and 'justified'. This evidence indicated a clear recognition by seedsmen in general, and the appellants in particular, that reliance on the limitation of liability imposed by the relevant condition would not be fair or reasonable.

[21] Two further factors, if more were needed, weigh the scales in favour of the respondent. The supply of autumn, instead of winter cabbage seed was due to the negligence of the appellants' sister company. Irrespective of its quality, the autumn variety supplied could not, according to the appellants' own evidence, be grown commercially in East Lothian. Finally, as the trial judge found, seedsmen could insure against the risk of crop failure caused by supply of the wrong variety of seeds without materially increasing the price of seeds.

[22] My Lords, even if I felt doubts about the statutory issue, I should not, for the reasons explained earlier, think it right to interfere with the unanimous original decision of that issue by the Court of Appeal. As it is, I feel no such doubts. If I were making the original decision, I should conclude without hesitation that it would not be fair or reasonable to allow the appellants to rely on the contractual limitation of their liability.

I would dismiss the appeal.

Lord Brightman: My Lords, I would dismiss this appeal for the reasons given by my noble and learned friend Lord Bridge.

Appeal dismissed.

Solicitors: *Davidson Doughty & Co* (for the appellants); *McKenna & Co* (for the respondents).

Mary Rose Plummer, Barrister

(2) *MANDLA AND ANOTHER (APPELLANTS/PLAINTIFFS) v LEE AND OTHERS (RESPONDENTS/DEFENDANTS)* [1983] 1 ALL ER 162

THE JUDGMENT OF LORD FRASER OF TULLYBELTON IN THE HOUSE OF LORDS

Lord Fraser of Tullybelton: My Lords, the main question in this appeal is whether Sikhs are a racial group for the purposes of the Race Relations Act 1976 (the 1976 Act). For reasons that appear, the answer to this question depends on whether they are a group defined by reference to 'ethnic origins'.

The appellants are Sikhs. The first appellant is a solicitor in Birmingham and he is the father of the second appellant. The second appellant was, at the material date, a boy of school age. The first respondent (first defendant) is the headmaster of an independent school in Birmingham called Park Grove School. The second respondent is a company which owns the school, and in which the first respondent and his wife are principal shareholders. In what follows I shall refer to the first respondent as 'the respondent'. In July 1978 the first appellant wished to enter his son as a pupil at Park Grove School, and he brought the boy to an interview with the respondent. The first appellant explained that he wished his son to grow up as an orthodox Sikh, and that one of the rules which he had to observe was to wear a turban. That is because the turban is regarded by Sikhs as a sign of their communal identity. At the interview, the respondent said that wearing a turban would be against the school rules which required all pupils to wear school uniform, and he did not think he could allow it, but he promised to think the matter over. A few days later he wrote to the first appellant saying that he had decided he could not relax the school rules and thus, in effect, saying that he would not accept the boy if he insisted on wearing a turban. The second appellant was then sent to another school, where he was allowed to wear a turban, and, so far as the appellants as individuals are concerned, that is the end of the story.

The main purpose of the 1976 Act is to prohibit discrimination against people on racial grounds, and more generally, to make provision with respect to relations between people of different racial groups. So much appears from the long title. The scheme of the Act, so far as is relevant to this appeal, is to define in Part 1 what is meant by racial discrimination in various fields including employment, provision of goods, services and other things, and by s 17 in the field of education. There can be no doubt that, if there has been discrimination against the appellants in the present case, it was in the field of education, and was contrary to s 17(a) which makes it unlawful for the proprietor of an independent school to discriminate against a person in the terms on which the school offers to admit him as a pupil. The only question is whether any racial discrimination has occurred.

But the first appellant complained to the Commission for Racial Equality that the respondent had discriminated against him and his son on racial grounds. The Commission took up the case and they are the real appellants before your Lordships' House. The case clearly raises an important question of construction of the 1976 Act, on which the Commission wishes to have a decision, and they have undertaken, very properly, to pay the costs of the respondent in this House, whichever party succeeds in the appeal. In the county court Judge Gosling held that Sikhs were not a racial group, and therefore that there had been no discrimination contrary to the 1976 Act. The Court of Appeal (Lord Denning MR, Oliver and Kerr LJJ) agreed with that view. The Commission, using the name of the appellants, now appeals to this House.

The type of discrimination referred to in para (a) of that subsection is generally called 'direct' discrimination. When the present proceedings began in the county court, direct discrimination was alleged, but the learned judge held that there had been no direct discrimination, and his judgment on that point was not challenged in the Court of Appeal or before your Lordships' House. The appellant's case in this House was based entirely on 'indirect' discrimination, that is, discrimination contrary to para (b) of sub-s 1(1). When the proceedings began the appellants claimed damages, but that claim was pursued before this House. Having regard to s 57(3) of the 1976 Act, it would have been unlikely to succeed. They now seek only a declaration that there has been unlawful discrimination against them contrary to the Act.

Racial discrimination is defined in s 1(1) which provides as follows:

> A person discriminates against another in any circumstances relevant for the purposes of any provision of this Act if–
>
> (a) on racial grounds he treats that other less favourably than he treats or would treat other persons; or
>
> (b) he applies to that other a requirement or condition which he applies or would apply equally to persons not of the same racial group as that other but–
>
> (i) which is such that the proportion of persons of the same racial group as that other who can comply with it is considerably smaller than the proportion of persons not of that racial group who can comply with it; and
>
> (ii) which he cannot show to be justifiable irrespective of the colour, race, nationality or ethnic or national origins of the person to whom it applied; and
>
> (iii) which is to the detriment of that other because he cannot comply with it.

The case against the respondent under s 1(1)(b) is that he discriminated against the second appellant because he applied to him a requirement or condition (namely, the 'No turban' rule) which he applied equally to pupils not of the same racial group as the second respondent (that is, to pupils who were not Sikhs) but (i) which is such that the proportion of Sikhs who can comply with it is considerably smaller than in the proportion of non-Sikhs who can comply with it and (ii) which the respondent cannot show to be justifiable irrespective of the colour, etc of the second appellant, and (iii) which is to the detriment of the second appellant because he cannot comply with it. As I have already said, the first main question is whether the Sikhs are a racial group. If they are, then two further questions arise. Question two is what is the meaning of 'can' in para (i) of s 1(1)(b), and question three is, what is the meaning of 'justifiable' in para (iii) of that subsection?

'Ethnic origins'

Racial group is defined in s 3(1) of the Act which provides:

> 'racial group' means a group of persons defined by reference to colour, race, nationality or ethnic or national origins, and references to a person's racial group refer to any racial group into which he falls.

It is not suggested that Sikhs are a group defined by reference to colour, race, nationality or national origins. In none of these respects are they distinguishable from many other groups, especially those living, like most Sikhs, in the Punjab. The argument turns entirely upon whether they are a group defined by 'ethnic origins'. It is therefore necessary to ascertain the sense in which the word 'ethnic' is used in the Act of 1976. We were referred to various dictionary definitions. *The Oxford English Dictionary* (1897 edition) gives two meanings of 'ethnic'. The first is 'pertaining to nations not Christian or Jewish: gentile, heathen, pagan'. That clearly cannot be its meaning in the 1976 Act, because it is inconceivable that Parliament would have legislated against racial discrimination intending that the protection should not apply either to Christians or (above all) to Jews. Neither party contended that was the relevant meaning for the present purpose. The second meaning given in the *Oxford English Dictionary* (1897 edition) was 'pertaining to race: peculiar to a race or nation: ethnological'. A slighter shorter form of that meaning (omitting 'peculiar to a race or nation') was given by the *Concise Oxford Dictionary* in 1934 and was expressly accepted by Lord Denning MR as the correct meaning for the present purpose. Oliver and Kerr LJJ also accepted that meaning as being substantially correct, and Oliver LJ at [1983] IRLR 17 said that the word 'ethnic' in its popular meaning involved essentially a racial concept – the concept of something with which the members of the group are born; some fixed or inherited characteristic. The respondent, who appeared on his own behalf, submitted that that was the relevant meaning of 'ethnic' in the 1976 Act, and that it did not apply to Sikhs because they were essentially a religious group, and they shared their racial characteristics with other religious groups, including Hindus and Muslims, living in the Punjab.

For a group to constitute an ethnic group in the sense of the 1976 Act, it must, in my opinion, regard itself, and be regarded by others, as a distinct community by virtue of certain characteristics. Some of these characteristics are essential: others are not essential but one or more of them will commonly be found and will help to distinguish the group from the surrounding community. The conditions which appear to me to be essential are these: (1) a long shared history, of which the group is conscious as distinguishing it from other groups, and the memory of which it keeps alive; (2) a cultural tradition of its own, including family and social customs and manners, often but not necessarily associated with religious observance. In addition to those two essential characteristics, the following characteristics are, in my opinion, relevant; (3) either a common geographical origin, or descent from a small number of common ancestors; (4) a common language, not necessarily

peculiar to the group; (5) a common literature peculiar to the group; (6) a common religion different from that of neighbouring groups or from the general community surrounding it; (7) being a minority or being an oppressed or a dominant group within a larger community, for example, a conquered people (say, the inhabitants of England shortly after the Norman conquest) and their conquerors might both be ethnic groups.

My Lords, I have attempted so far to explain the reasons why, in my opinion, the word 'ethnic' in the 1976 Act should be construed relatively widely, in what was referred to by Mr Irvine as a broad, cultural/historic sense. The conclusion at which I have arrived by construction of the Act itself is greatly strengthened by consideration of the decision of the Court of Appeal in New Zealand (Richmond P, Woodhouse and Richardson JJ) in *King-Ansell v Police* [1979] 2 NZLR 531.

In that case, the appellant had been convicted by a magistrate of an offence under the New Zealand Race Relations Act 1971, the offence consisting of publishing a pamphlet with intent to incite ill will against Jews, 'on the ground of their ethnic origins'. The question of law arising on the appeal concerned the meaning to be given to the words 'ethnic ... origins of that group of persons' in s 25(1) of the Act. The decision of the Court of Appeal was that Jews in New Zealand did form a group with common ethnic origins within the meaning of the Act. The structure of the New Zealand Act differs considerably from that of the 1976 Act, but the offence created by s 25 of the New Zealand (viz inciting ill will against any group of persons on the ground of their colour, race, or ethnic or national origins) raises the same question of construction as the present appeal, in a context which is identical, except that the New Zealand Act does not mention 'nationality', and the 1976 Act does.

The reasoning of all members of the New Zealand court was substantially similar, and it can, I think, be sufficiently indicated by quoting the following short passages. The first is from the judgment of Woodhouse J, p 538, line 39 where, after referring to the meaning given by the 1972 Supplement to the *Oxford English Dictionary*, which I have already quoted, he says this:

> ... the distinguishing features of an ethnic group or of the ethnic origins of a group would usually depend upon a combination, present together, of characteristics of the kind indicated in the Supplement. In any case, it would be a mistake to regard this or any other dictionary meaning as though it had to be imported word for word into a statutory definition and construed accordingly. However, subject to those qualifications. I think that for the purposes of construing the expression 'ethnic origins' the 1972 Supplement is a helpful guide and I accept it.

Richardson J, p 542, line 51, said this:

> ... The real test is whether the individuals or the group regard themselves and are regarded by others in the community as having a particular historical identity in terms of their colour or their racial, national or ethnic origins. That must be based on a belief shared by the members of the group.

And at p 543, line 24, the same learned judge said this:

> ... a group is identifiable in terms of its ethnic origins if it is a segment of the population distinguished from others by a sufficient combination of shared customs, beliefs, traditions and characteristics derived from a common or presumed common past, even if not drawn from what in biological terms is a common racial stock. It is that combination which gives them a historically determined social identity in their own eyes and in the eyes of those outside the group. They have a distinct social identity based not simply on group cohesion and solidarity but also on their belief as to their historical antecedents.

My Lords, that last passage sums up in a way upon which I could not hope to improve the views which I have been endeavouring to express. It is important that courts in English speaking countries should, if possible, construe the words which we are considering in the same way where they occur in the same context, and I am happy to say that I find no difficulty at all in agreeing with the construction favoured by the New Zealand Court of Appeal.

The respondent admitted, rightly in my opinion, that if the proper construction of the word 'ethnic' in s 3 of the 1976 Act is a wide one, on lines such as I have suggested, the Sikhs would qualify as a group defined by ethnic origins for the purposes of the Act. It is, therefore, unnecessary to consider in any detail the relevant characteristics of the Sikhs. They were originally a religious community founded about the end of the fifteenth century in the Punjab by Guru Nanak, who was born in 1469. But the community is no longer purely religious in character. Their present position is summarised sufficiently for present purposes in the opinion of the learned county court judge in the following passage:

> The evidence in my judgment shows that Sikhs are a distinctive and self-conscious community. They have a history going back to the fifteenth century. They have a written language which a small proportion of Sikhs can read but which can be read by a much higher proportion of Sikhs than of Hindus. They were at one time politically supreme in the Punjab.

The result is, in my opinion, that Sikhs are a group defined by a reference to ethnic origins for the purpose of the 1976 Act, although they are not biologically distinguishable from the other peoples living in the Punjab. That is true whether one is considering the position before the partition of 1947, when the Sikhs lived mainly in that part of the Punjab which is now Pakistan, or after 1947, since when most of them have moved into India. It is, therefore, necessary to consider whether the respondent has indirectly discriminated against the appellants in the sense of s 1(1)(b) of the Act. That raises the two subsidiary questions I have already mentioned.

'Can comply'

It is obvious that Sikhs like anyone else, 'can' refrain from wearing a turban, if 'can' is construed literally. But if the broad cultural/historic meaning of ethnic is the appropriate meaning of the word in the 1976 Act, then a literal reading of the word 'can' would deprive Sikhs and members of other groups defined by reference to their ethnic origins of much of the protection which Parliament evidently intended the Act to afford to them. They 'can' comply with almost any requirement or condition if they are willing to give up their distinctive customs and cultural rules. On the other hand, if ethnic means inherited or unalterable, as the Court of Appeal thought it did, then 'can' ought logically to be read literally. The word 'can' is used with many shades of meaning. In the context of s 1(1)(b)(i) of the 1976 Act it must, in my opinion, have been intended by Parliament to be read not as meaning 'can physically', so as to indicate a theoretical possibility, but as meaning 'can in practice' or 'can consistently with the customs and cultural conditions of the racial group'. The latter meaning was attributed to the word by the Employment Appeal Tribunal in *Price v Civil Service Commission* [1977] IRLR 291, on a construction of the parallel provision in the Sex Discrimination Act 1975. I agree with their construction of the word in that context. Accordingly I am of opinion that the 'No turban' rule was not one with which the second appellant could, in the relevant sense, comply.

'Justifiable'

The word 'justifiable' occurs in s 1(1)(b)(ii). It raises a problem which is, in my opinion, more difficult than the problem of the word 'can'. But in the end I have reached a firm opinion that the respondent has not been able to show that the 'No turban' rule was justifiable in the relevant sense. Regarded purely from the point of view of the respondent, it was no doubt perfectly justifiable. He explained that he had no intention of discriminating against Sikhs. In 1978 the school had about 300 pupils (about 75% boys and 25% girls) of whom over 200 were English, five were Sikhs, 34 Hindus, 16 Persians, six Negroes, seven Chinese and 15 from European countries. The reasons for having a school uniform were largely reasons of practical convenience – to minimize external differences between races and social classes, to discourage the 'competitive fashions' which he said tend to exist in a teenage community, and to present a Christian image of the school to outsiders, including prospective parents. The respondent explained the difficulty for a headmaster of explaining to a non-Sikh pupil why the rules about wearing correct school uniform were enforced against him if they were relaxed in favour of a Sikh. In my view, these reasons could not, either individually or collectively, provide a sufficient justification for the respondent to apply a condition that is *prima facie* discriminatory under the Act.

An attempted justification of the 'No turban' rule, which requires more serious consideration, was that the respondent sought to run a Christian school, accepting pupils of all religions and races, and that he objected to the turban on the ground that it was an outward manifestation of a non-Christian faith. Indeed, he regarded it as amounting to a challenge to the faith. I have much sympathy with the respondent on this part of the case and I would have been glad to find that the rule was justifiable within the meaning of the statute, if I could have done so. But in my opinion that is impossible. The onus under para (ii) is on the respondent to show that the condition which he seeks to apply is not indeed a necessary condition, but that it is in all circumstances justifiable 'irrespective of the colour, race, nationality or ethnic or national origins of the person to whom it is applied': that is to say that it is justifiable without regard to the ethnic origins of that person. But in this case the principal justification on which the respondent relies is that the turban is objectionable just because it is a manifestation of the second appellant's ethnic origins.

That is not, in my view, a justification which is admissible under para (ii). That kind of justification that might fall within that provision would be one based on public health, as in *Panesar v The Nestles Company Ltd* [1980] IRLR 64, where the Court of Appeal held that a rule forbidding the wearing of beards in the respondent's chocolate factory was justifiable within the meaning of s 1(1)(b)(ii) on hygienic grounds, notwithstanding that the proportion of Sikhs who would [conscientiously] comply with it was considerably smaller than the proportion of non-Sikhs who could comply with it. Again, it might be possible for the school to show that a rule insisting upon a fixed diet, which included some dish (for example, pork) which some racial groups could not conscientiously eat was justifiable if the school proved that the cost of providing special meals for the particular group would be prohibitive. Questions of that sort would be questions of fact for the tribunal of fact, and if there was evidence on which it could find the condition to be justifiable its finding would not be liable to be disturbed on appeal.

But in the present case I am of opinion that the respondents have not been able to show that the 'No turban' rule was justifiable.

Before parting with the case I must refer to some observations by the Court of Appeal which suggest that the conduct of the Commission for Racial Equality in this case has been in some way unreasonable or oppressive. Lord Denning MR at p 21 merely expressed regret that the Commission had taken up the case. But Oliver LJ, p 23, used stronger language and suggested that the machinery of the Act had been operated against the respondent as 'an engine of oppression'. Kerr LJ, p 25, referred to notes of an interview between the respondent and an official of the Commission which he said read in part 'more like an inquisition than an interview' and which he regarded as harassment of the respondent.

My Lords, I must say that I regard these strictures on the Commission and its officials as entirely unjustified. The Commission has a difficult task, and no doubt its inquiries will be resented by some and are liable to be regarded as objectionable and inquisitive. But the respondent in this case, who conducted his appeal with restraint and skill, made no complaint of his treatment at the hands of the Commission. He was specifically asked by some of my noble and learned friends to point out any part of the notes of his interview with the Commission's official to which he objected, and he said there were none and that an objection of that sort formed no part of his case.

(3) UNFAIR CONTRACT TERMS ACT 1977

1977 CHAPTER 50

An Act to impose further limits on the extent to which under the law of England and Wales and Northern Ireland civil liability for breach of contract, or for negligence or other breach of duty, can be avoided by means of contract terms and otherwise, and under the law of Scotland civil liability can be avoided by means of contract terms.

[26 October 1977]

Be it enacted by the Queen's most Excellent Majesty by and with the advice and consent of the Lords Spiritual and Temporal, and Commons, in this present Parliament assembled, and by the authority of the same, as follows:

Part I
Amendment of Law for England and Wales and Northern Ireland

Scope of Part I   *Introductory*

1– (1) For the purposes of this Part of this Act, 'negligence' means the breach–

    (a) of any obligation, arising from the express or implied terms of a contract, to take reasonable care or exercise reasonable skill in the performance of the contract;

    (b) of any common law duty to take reasonable care or exercise reasonable skill (but not any stricter duty);

    (c) of the common duty of care imposed by the Occupiers' Liability Act 1957 or the Occupiers' Liability Act (Northern Ireland) 1957.

(2) This Part of this Act is subject to Part III; and in relation to contracts, the operation of sections 2 to 4 and 7 is subject to the exceptions made by Schedule 1.

(3) In the case of both contract and tort, sections 2 to 7 apply (except where the contrary is stated in section 6(4)) only to business liability, that is liability for breach of obligations or duties arising–

    (a) from things done or to be done by a person in the course of a business (whether his own business or another's); or

    (b) from the occupation of premises used for business purposes of the occupier,

and references to liability are to be read accordingly.

(4) In relation to any breach of duty or obligation, it is immaterial for any purpose of this Part of this Act whether the breach was inadvertent or intentional, or whether liability for it arises directly or vicariously.

Avoidance of liability for negligence, breach of contract, etc

Negligence liability

2– (1) A person cannot by reference to any contract term or to a notice given to persons generally or to particular persons exclude or restrict his liability for death or personal injury resulting from negligence.

(2) In the case of other loss or damage a person cannot so exclude or restrict his liability for negligence except in so far as the term or notice satisfies the requirement of reasonableness.

(3) Where a contract term or notice purports to exclude or restrict liability for negligence a person's agreement to or awareness of it is not of itself to be taken as indicating his voluntary acceptance of any risk.

Liability arising in contract

3– (1) This section applies as between contracting parties where one of them deals as consumer or on the other's written standard terms of business.

(2) As against that party, the other cannot by reference to any contract term–

(a) when himself in breach of contract, exclude or restrict any liability of his in respect of the breach; or

(b) claim to be entitled–

(i) to render a contractual performance substantially different from that which was reasonably expected of him, or

(ii) in respect of the whole or any part of his contractual obligation, to render no performance at all,

except in so far as (in any of the cases mentioned above in this subsection) the contract term satisfies the requirement of reasonableness.

Unreasonable indemnity clauses

4– (1) A person dealing as consumer cannot by reference to any contract term be made to indemnify another person (whether a party to the contract or not) in respect of liability that may be incurred by the other for negligence or breach of contract, except in so far as the contract term satisfies the requirement of reasonableness.

(2) This section applies whether the liability in question–

(a) is directly that of the person to be indemnified or is incurred by him vicariously;

(b) is to the person dealing as consumer or to someone else.

Liability arising from sale or supply of goods

'Guarantee' of consumer goods

5– (1) In the case of goods of a type ordinarily supplied for private use or consumption, where loss or damage–

(a) arises from the goods proving defective while in consumer use; and

(b) results from the negligence of a person concerned in the manufacture or distribution of the goods,

liability for the loss or damage cannot be excluded or restricted by reference to any contract term or notice contained in or operating by reference to a guarantee of the goods.

(2) For these purposes–

(a) goods are to be regarded as 'in consumer use' when a person is using them, or has them in his possession for use, otherwise than exclusively for the purposes of a business; and

(b) anything in writing is a guarantee if it contains or purports to contain some promise or assurance (however worded or presented) that defects will be made good by complete or partial replacement, or by repair, monetary compensation or otherwise.

(3) This section does not apply as between the parties to a contract under or in pursuance of which possession or ownership of the goods passed.

Sale and hire-purchase

6– (1) Liability for breach of the obligations arising from–

(a) section 12 of the Sale of Goods Act 1893 (seller's implied undertakings as to title, etc);

(b) section 8 of the Supply of Goods (Implied Terms) Act 1973 (the corresponding thing in relation to hire-purchase),

cannot be excluded or restricted by reference to any contract term.

(2) As against a person dealing as consumer, liability for breach of the obligations arising from–

(a) section 13, 14 or 15 of the 1893 Act (seller's implied undertakings as to conformity of goods with description or sample, or as to their quality or fitness for a particular purpose);

(b) section 9, 10 or 11 of the 1973 Act (the corresponding things in relation to hire-purchase), cannot be excluded or restricted by reference to any contract term.

(3) As against a person dealing otherwise than as consumer, the liability specified in subsection (2) above can be excluded or restricted by reference to a contract term, but only in so far as the term satisfies the requirement of reasonableness.

(4) The liabilities referred to in this section are not only the business liabilities defined by section 1(3), but include those arising under any contract of sale of goods or hire-purchase agreement.

Miscellaneous contracts under which goods pass

7– (1) Where the possession or ownership of goods passes under or in pursuance of a contract not governed by the law of sale of goods or hire purchase, subsections (2) to (4) below apply as regards the effect (if any) to be given to contract terms excluding or restricting liability for breach of obligation arising by implication of law from the nature of the contract.

(2) As against a person dealing as consumer, liability in respect of the goods' correspondence with description or sample, or their quality or fitness for any particular purpose, cannot be excluded or restricted by reference to any such term.

(3) As against a person dealing otherwise than as consumer, that liability can be excluded or restricted by reference to such a term, but only in so far as the term satisfies the requirement of reasonableness.

(4) Liability in respect of–

(a) the right to transfer ownership of the goods, or give possession; or

(b) the assurance of quiet possession to a person taking goods in pursuance of the contract,

cannot be excluded or restricted by reference to any such term except in so far as the term satisfies the requirement of reasonableness.

(5) This section does not apply in the case of goods passing on a redemption of trading stamps within the Trading Stamps Act 1964 or the Trading Stamps Act (Northern Ireland) 1965.

Other provisions about contracts

Misrepresentation

8– (1) In the Misrepresentation Act 1967, the following is substituted for section 3–

Avoidance of provision excluding liability for misrepresentation

3 If a contract contains a term which would exclude or restrict–

(a) any liability to which a party to a contract may be subject by reason of any misrepresentation made by him before the contract was made; or

(b) any remedy available to another party to the contract by reason of such a misrepresentation, that term shall be of no effect except in so far as it satisfies the requirement of reasonableness as stated in section 11(1) of the Unfair Contract Terms Act 1977: and it is for those claiming that the term satisfies that requirement to show that it does.

(2) The same section is substituted for section 3 of the Misrepresentation Act (Northern Ireland) 1967.

Effect of breach

9– (1) Where for reliance upon it a contract term has to satisfy the requirement of reasonableness, it may be found to do so and be given effect accordingly notwithstanding that the contact has been terminated either by breach or by a party electing to treat it as repudiated.

(2) Where on a breach the contract is nevertheless affirmed by a party entitled to treat it as repudiated, this does not of itself exclude the requirement of reasonableness in relation to any contract term.

Evasion by means of secondary contract

10– A person is not bound by any contract term prejudicing or taking away rights of his which arise under, or in connection with the performance of, another contract, so far as those rights extend to the enforcement of another's liability which this Part of this Act prevents that other from excluding or restricting.

Explanatory provisions

The 'reasonableness' test

11– (1) In relation to a contract term, the requirement of reasonableness for the purposes of this Part of this Act, section 3 of the Misrepresentation Act 1967 and section 3 of the Misrepresentation Act (Northern Ireland) 1967 is that the term shall have been a fair and reasonable one to be included having regard to the circumstances which were, or ought reasonably to have been, known to or in the contemplation of the parties when the contract was made.

(2) In determining for the purposes of section 6 or 7 above whether a contract term satisfies the requirement of reasonableness, regard shall be had in particular to the matters specified in Schedule 2 to this Act; but this subsection does not prevent the court or arbitrator from holding, in accordance with any rule of law, that a term which purports to exclude or restrict any relevant liability is not a term of the contract.

(3) In relation to a notice (not being a notice having contractual effect), the requirement of reasonableness under this Act is that it should be fair and reasonable to allow reliance on it, having regard to all the circumstances obtaining when the liability arose or (but for the notice) would have arisen.

(4) Where by reference to a contract term or notice a person seeks to restrict liability to a specified sum of money, and the question arises (under this or any other Act) whether the term or notice satisfies the requirement of reasonableness, regard shall be had in particular (but without prejudice to subsection (2) above in the case of contract terms) to–

    (a) the resources which he could expect to be available to him for the purpose of meeting the liability should it arise; and

    (b) how far it was open to him to cover himself by insurance.

(5) It is for those claiming that a contract term or notice satisfies the requirement of reasonableness to show that it does.

'Dealing as consumer'

12– (1) A party to a contract 'deals as consumer', in relation to another party if–

    (a) he neither makes the contract in the course of a business nor holds himself out as doing so; and

    (b) the other party does make the contract in the course of a business, and

    (c) in the case of a contract governed by the law of sale goods or hire-purchase, or by section 7 of this Act, the goods passing under or in pursuance of the contract are of a type ordinarily supplied for private use or consumption.

(2) But on a sale by auction or by competitive tender the buyer is not in any circumstances to be regarded as dealing as consumer.

(3) Subject to this, it is for those claiming that a party does not deal as consumer to show that he does not.

Varieties of exemption clause

13– (1) To the extent that this Part of this Act prevents the exclusion or restriction of any liability it also prevents–

(a) making the liability or its enforcement subject to restrictive or onerous conditions;

(b) excluding or restricting any right or remedy in respect of the liability, or subjecting a person to any prejudice in consequence of his pursuing any such right or remedy;

(c) excluding or restricting rules of evidence or procedure,

and (to that extent) sections 2 and 5 to 7 also prevent excluding or restricting liability by reference to terms and notices which exclude or restrict the relevant obligation or duty.

(2) But an agreement in writing to submit present or future differences to arbitration is not to be treated under this Part of this Act as excluding or restricting any liability.

Interpretation of Part I

14– In this Part of this Act–

'business' includes a profession and the activities of any government department or local or public authority;

'goods' has the same meaning as in the Sale of Goods Act 1893;

'hire purchase agreement' has the same meaning as in the Consumer Credit Act 1974;

'negligence' has the meaning given by section 1(1);

'notice' includes an announcement, whether or not in writing, and any other communication or pretended communication; and

'personal injury' includes any disease and any impairment of physical or mental condition.

Part II
Amendment of Law for Scotland

Scope of Part II

15– (1) This Part of this Act applies only to contracts, is subject to Part III of this Act and does not affect the validity of any discharge or indemnity given by a person in consideration of the receipt by him of compensation in settlement of any claim which he has.

(2) Subject to subsection (3) below, sections 16 to 18 of this Act apply to any contract only to the extent that the contract–

(a) relates to the transfer of the ownership or possession of goods from one person to another (with or without work having been done on them);

(b) constitutes a contract of service or apprenticeship;

(c) relates to services of whatever kind, including (without prejudice to the foregoing generality) carriage, deposit and pledge, care and custody, mandate, agency, loan and services relating to the use of land;

(d) relates to the liability of an occupier of land to persons entering upon or using that land;

(e) relates to a grant of any right or permission to enter upon or use land not amounting to an estate or interest in the land.

(3) Notwithstanding anything in subsection (2) above, sections 16 to 18–

   (a) do not apply to any contract to the extent that the contract–

      (i) is a contract of insurance (including a contract to pay an annuity on human life);

      (ii) relates to the formation, constitution or dissolution of any body corporate or unincorporated association or partnership;

   (b) apply to–

   a contract of marine salvage or towage;

   a charter party of a ship or hovercraft;

   a contract for the carriage of goods by ship or hovercraft; or,

   a contract to which subsection (4) below relates,

only to the extent that–

      (i) both parties deal or hold themselves out as dealing in the course of a business (and then only in so far as the contract purports to exclude or restrict liability for breach of duty in respect of death or personal injury); or

      (ii) the contract is a consumer contract (and then only in favour of the consumer).

(4) This subsection relates to a contract in pursuance of which goods are carried by ship or hovercraft and which either–

   (a) specifies ship or hovercraft as the means of carriage over part of the journey to be covered; or

   (b) makes no provision as to the means of carriage and does not exclude ship or hovercraft as that means, in so far as the contract operates for and in relation to the carriage of the goods by that means.

[Remainder of Part II omitted.]

SCHEDULES
Schedule 1
Scope of Sections 2 to 4 and 7

1   Sections 2 to 4 of this Act do not extend to–

   (a) any contract of insurance (including a contract to pay an annuity on human life);

   (b) any contract so far as it relates to the creation or transfer of an interest in land, or to the termination of such an interest, whether by extinction, merger, surrender, forfeiture or otherwise;

   (c) any contract so far as it relates to the creation or transfer of a right or interest in any patent, trade mark, copyright, registered design, technical or commercial information or other intellectual property, or relates to the termination of any such right or interest;

(d) any contract so far as it relates–

    (i) to the formation or dissolution of a company (which means any body corporate or unincorporated association and includes a partnership), or

    (ii) to its constitution or the rights or obligations of its corporators or members;

(e) any contract so far as it relates to the creation or transfer of securities or of any right or interest in securities.

2   Section 2(1) extends to–

(a) any contract of marine salvage or towage;

(b) any charter party of a ship or hovercraft; and

(c) any contract for the carriage of goods by ship or hovercraft,

but subject to this sections 2 to 4 and 7 do not extend to any such contract except in favour of a person dealing as consumer.

3   Where goods are carried by ship or hovercraft in pursuance or a contract which either–

(a) specifies that as the means of carriage over part of the journey to be covered; or

(b) makes no provision as to the means of carriage and does not exclude that means,

then sections 2(2), 3 and 4 do not, except in favour of a person dealing as consumer, extend to the contract as it operates for and in relation to the carriage of the goods by that means.

4   Section 2(1) and (2) do not extend to a contract of employment, except in favour of the employee.

5   Section 2(1) does not affect the validity of any discharge and indemnity given by a person, on or in connection with an award to him of compensation for pneumoconiosis attributable to employment in the coal industry, in respect of any further claim arising from his contracting that disease.

Schedule 2
'Guidelines' for Application of Reasonableness Test

The matters to which regard is to be had in particular for the purposes of sections 6(3), 7(3) and (4), 20 and 21 are any of the following which appear to be relevant–

(a) the strength of the bargaining positions of the parties relative to each other, taking into account (among other things) alternative means by which the customer's requirements could have been met;

(b) whether the customer received an inducement to agree to the term, or in accepting it had an opportunity of entering into a similar contract with other persons, but without having to accept a similar term;

(c) whether the customer knew or ought reasonably to have known of the existence and extent of the term (having regard, among other things, to any custom of the trade and any previous course of dealing between the parties);

(d) where the term excludes or restricts any relevant liability if some condition is not complied with, whether it was reasonable at the time of the contract to expect that compliance with that condition would be practicable;

(e) whether the goods were manufactured, processed or adapted to the special order of the customer.

Schedule 3
Amendment of Enactments

In the Sale of Goods Act 1893–

(a) in section 55(1), for the words 'the following provisions of this section' substitute 'the provisions of the Unfair Contract Terms Act 1977';

(b) in section 62(1), in the definition of 'business', for 'local authority or statutory undertaker' substitute 'or local or public authority'.

In the Supply of Goods (Implied Terms) Act 1973 (as originally enacted and as substituted by the Consumer Credit Act 1974–

(a) in section 14(1) for the words from 'conditional sale' to the end substitute 'a conditional sale agreement where the buyer deals as consumer within Part I of the Unfair Contract Terms Act 1977 or, in Scotland, the agreement is a consumer contract within Part II of that Act';

(b) in section 15(1), in the definition of 'business', for 'local authority or statutory undertaker' substitute 'or local or public authority'.

APPENDIX 2

THE EUROPEAN DIMENSION (1) PRIMARY AND SECONDARY TEXTS

(1) *VAN GEND EN LOOS* (CASE 26/62) [1963] CMLR 105

In Case 26/62

(1) Reference to the Court under sub-paragraph (a) of the first paragraph and under the third paragraph of Article 177 of the Treaty establishing the European Economic Community by the Tariefcommissie, a Netherlands administrative tribunal having final jurisdiction in revenue cases, for a preliminary ruling in the action pending before that court between

(2) NV Algemene Transport-En Expeditie Onderneming Van Gend en Loos, having its registered office at Utrecht, represented by HG Stibbe and LFD ter Kuile, both Advocates of Amsterdam, with an address for service in Luxemburg at the Consulate-General of the Kingdom of the Netherlands

AND

(3) Nederlandse Administratie Der Belastingen (Netherlands Inland Revenue Administration), represented by the Inspector of Customs and Excise at Zaandam, with an address for service in Luxemburg at the Netherlands Embassy

(4) on the following questions:

(1) whether Article 12 of the EEC Treaty has direct application within the territory of a Member State, in other words, whether nationals of such a State can, on the basis of the article in question, lay claim to individual rights which the courts must protect;

(2) in the event of an affirmative reply, whether the application of an import duty of 8% to the import into the Netherlands by the applicant in the main action of ureaformaldehyde originating in the Federal Republic of Germany represented an unlawful increase within the meaning of Article 12 of the EEC Treaty or whether it was in this case a reasonable alteration of the duty applicable before 1 March 1960, an alteration which, although amounting to an increase from the arithmetical point of view, is nevertheless not to be regarded as prohibited under the terms of Article 12.

(5) THE COURT

composed of: AM Donner (President), L Delvaux and R Rossi (Presidents of Chambers), O Riese, ch, L Hammes (Rapporteur), A Trabucchi and R Lecourt (Judges)

Advocate-General K Roemer

Registrar: A Van Houtte

gives the following

JUDGMENT

Issues of fact and of law

I   FACTS AND PROCEDURE

(6) The facts and the procedure may be summarised as follows:

1   On 9 September 1960 the Company NV Algemene Transport-en Expeditie Onderneming Van Gend en Loos (hereinafter called 'Van Gend en Loos'), according to a customs declaration of 8 September on form D.5061 imported into the Netherlands from the Federal Republic of Germany a quantity of ureaformaldehyde described in the import document as 'Harnstoffharz (UF resin) 70, aqueous emulsion of ureaformaldehyde'.

(7) 2   On the date of importation, the product in question was classified in heading 39.01-a-1 of the tariff of import duties listed in the 'Tariefbesluit' which entered into force on 1 March 1960. The nomenclature of the 'Tariefbesluit' is taken from the protocol concluded between the Kingdom of Belgium, the Grand Duchy of Luxemburg, and the Kingdom of the Netherlands at Brussels on 25 July 1958, ratified in the Netherlands by the Law of 16 December 1959.

(8) 3   The wording of heading 39.01-a-1 was as follows:

Product of condensation, poly-condensation, and poly-addition, whether modified or not, polymerized, or linear (phenoplasts, aminoplasts, alkyds, allylic polyesters and other non-saturated polyesters. silicones, etc ...):

(a) Liquid or paste products, including emulsions, dispersions, and solutions

	Duties applicable	
	gen %	spec %
1 Aminoplasts in aqueous emulsions, dispersions, or solutions	10%	8%

(9) 4   On this basis, the Dutch revenue authorities applied an ad valorem import duty of 8 per cent to the importation in question.

(10) 5   On 20 September 1960 Van Gend en Loos lodged an objection with the Inspector of Customs and Excise at Zaandam against the application of this duty in the present case. The company put forward in particular the following arguments:

(11) On 1 January 1958, the date on which the EEC Treaty entered into force, aminoplasts in emulsion were classified under heading 279-a-2 of the tariff in the 'Tariefbesluit' of 1947, and charged with an ad valorem import duty of 3%. In the 'Tariefbesluit' which entered into force on 1 March , heading 279-a-2 was replaced by heading 39.01-a.

(12) Instead of applying, in respect of intra-Community trade, an import duty of 3 per cent uniformly to all products under the old heading 279-a-2, a subdivision was created: 39.01-a-1, which contained only aminoplasts in aqueous emulsions, dispersions, or solutions, and in respect of which import duty was fixed at 8 per cent. For the other products in heading 39.01-a, which also had been included in the old heading 279-a-2, the import duty of 3% applied on 1 January 1958 was maintained.

(13) By thus increasing the import duty on the product in question after the entry into force of the EEC Treaty, the Dutch Government infringed Article 12 of that Treaty, which provides

that Member States shall refrain from introducing between themselves any new customs duties on imports or exports or any charges having equivalent effect, and from increasing those which they already apply in their trade with each other.

(14) 6   The objection of Van Gend en Loos was dismissed on 6 March 1961 by the Inspector of Customs and Excise at Zaandam on the ground of inadmissibility, because it was not directed against the actual application of the tariff but against the rate.

(15) 7   Van Gend en Loos appealed against this decision to the Tariefcommissie, Amsterdam, on 4 April 1961.

(16) 8   The case was heard by the Tariefcommissie on 21 May 1962. In support of its application for the annulment of the contested decision Van Gend en Loos put forward the arguments already submitted in its objection of 20 September 1960. The Nederlandse Administratie der Belastingen replied in particular that when the EEC Treaty entered into force the product in question was not charged under the heading 279-a-2 with a duty of only 3% but, because of its composition and intended application, was classified under heading 332 bis ('synthetic and other adhesives, not stated or included elsewhere') and charged with a duty of 10 per cent so that there had not in fact been any increase.

(17) 9   The Tariefcommissie, without giving a formal decision on the question whether the product in question fell within heading 332 bis or heading 279-a-2 of the 1947 'Tariefbesluit', took the view that the arguments of the parties raised questions concerning the interpretation of the EEC Treaty. It therefore suspended the proceedings and, in conformity with the third paragraph of Article 177 of the Treaty referred to the Court of Justice on 16 August 1962, for a preliminary ruling on the two questions set out above.

(18) 10   The decision of the Tariefcommissie was notified on 23 August 1962 by the Registrar of the Court to the parties to the action, to the Member States, and to the Commission of the EEC.

(19) 11   Pursuant to Article 20 of the Protocol on the Statute of the Court of Justice EEC written observations were submitted to the Court by the parties to the main action, by the Government of the Kingdom of Belgium, the Government of the Federal Republic of Germany the Commission of the EEC and the Kingdom of the Netherlands.

(20) 12   At the public hearing of the Court on 29 November 1962, the oral submissions of the plaintiff in the main action and of the Commission of the EEC were heard. At the same hearing questions were put to them by the Court. Written replies to these were supplied within the prescribed time.

(21) 13   The Advocate-General gave his reasoned oral opinion at the hearing on 12 December 1962, in which he proposed that the Court should in its judgment only answer the first question referred to it and hold that Article 12 of the EEC Treaty imposes a duty only on Member States.

II   ARGUMENTS AND OBSERVATIONS

(22) The arguments contained in the observations submitted in accordance with the second paragraph of Article 20 of the Protocol on the Statute of the Court of Justice of the European Economic Community by the parties to the main action, the Member States, and the Commission may be summarised as follows.

A THE FIRST QUESTION

Admissibility

(23) The Netherlands Government, the Belgian Government, and the Nederlandse Administratie der Belastingen (which in its statement of case declared that it was in complete agreement with the observations submitted by the Netherlands Government) confirm that the main complaint of Van Gend en Loos against the Government of the Benelux countries is that by the Brussels protocol of 25 July 1958 they infringed Article 12 of the EEC Treaty by increasing after its entry into force a customs duty applied in their trade with other Member States of the communities.

(24) The Netherlands Government disputes whether an alleged infringement of the Treaty by a Member State can be submitted to the judgment of the Court by a procedure other than that laid down by Articles 169 and 170, that is to say on the initiative of another Member State or of the Commission. It maintains in particular that the matter cannot be brought before the Court by means of the procedure of reference for a preliminary ruling under Article 177.

(25) The Court, according to the Netherlands Government, cannot, in the context of the present proceedings, decide a problem of this nature, since it does not relate to the interpretation but to the application of the Treaty in a specific case.

(26) The Belgian Government maintains that the first question is a reference to the Court of a problem of constitutional law, which falls exclusively within the jurisdiction of the Netherlands court.

(27) That court is confronted with two international treaties both of which are part of the national law. It must decide under national law – assuming that they are in fact contradictory – which treaty prevails over the other or more exactly whether a prior national law of ratification prevails over a subsequent one.

(28) This is a typical question of national constitutional law which has nothing to do with the interpretation of an Article of the EEC Treaty and is within the exclusive jurisdiction of the Netherlands court, because it can only be answered according the constitutional principles and jurisprudence of the national law of the Netherlands.

(29) The Belgian Government also points out that a decision on the first question referred to the Court is not only unnecessary to enable the Tariefcommissie to give its judgment but cannot even have any influence on the solution to the actual problem which it is asked to resolve.

(30) In fact, whatever answer the Court may give, the Tariefcommissie has to solve the same problem: has it the right to ignore the law of 16 December 1959 ratifying the Brussels Protocol, because it conflicts with an earlier law of 5 December 1957 ratifying the Treaty establishing the EEC?

(31) The question raised is not therefore an appropriate question for a preliminary ruling, since its answer cannot enable the court which has to adjudicate upon merits of the main action to make a final decision in the proceedings pending before it.

(32) The Commission of the EEC, on the other hand, observes that the effect of the provisions of the Treaty on the national law of Member States cannot be determined by the actual national law of each of them but by the Treaty itself. The problem is therefore without doubt one of interpretation of the Treaty.

(33) Further the Commission calls attention to the fact that a finding of inadmissible would have the paradoxical and shocking result that the rights of individuals would be protected in all cases of infringement of Community law except in the case of infringement by a Member State.

On the substance

(34) Van Gend en Loos answers in the affirmative the question whether the article has internal effect.

It maintains in particular that:

–   Article 12 is applicable without any preliminary incorporation in the national legislation of Member States, since it only imposes a negative obligation;
–   it has direct effect without any further measures of implementation under Community legislation, as all the customs duties applied by Member States in their trade with each other were bound on 1 January 1957 (Article 14 of the Treaty);
–   although the Article does not directly refer to the nationals of Member States but to the national authorities, infringement of it adversely affects the fundamental principles of the Community, and individuals as well as the Community must be protected against such infringements;
–   it is particularly well adapted for direct application by the national court which must set aside the application of customs duties introduced or increased in breach of its provisions.

(35) The Commission emphasises the importance of the Court's answer to the first question. It will have an effect not only on the interpretation of the provision at issue in a specific case and on the effect which will be attributed to it in the legal systems of Member States but also on certain other provisions of the Treaty which are as clear and complete as Article 12.

(36) According to the Commission an analysis of the legal structure of the Treaty and of the legal system which it establishes shows on the one hand that the Member States did not only intend to undertake mutual commitments but to establish a system of Community law, and on the other hand that they did not wish to withdraw the application of this law from the ordinary jurisdiction of the national courts of law.

(37) However, Community law must be effectively and uniformly applied throughout the whole of the Community.

(38) The result is first that the effect of Community law on the internal law of Member States cannot be determined by this internal law but only by Community law, further that the national courts are bound to apply directly the rules of Community law, and finally that the national court is bound to ensure that the rules of Community law prevail over conflicting national laws even if they are passed later.

(39) The Commission observes in this context that the fact that a community rule is, as regards its form, directed to the States does not of itself take away from individuals who have an interest in it the right to require it to be applied in the national courts.

(40) As regards more particularly the question referred to the Court, the Commission is of the opinion that Article 12 contains a rule of law capable of being effectively applied by the national court.

(41) It is a provision which is perfectly clear in the sense that it creates for Member States a specific unambiguous obligation relating to the extension of their internal law in a matter which directly affects their nationals and it is not affected or qualified by any other provision

of the Treaty. It is also a complete and self-sufficient provision in that it does not require on a Community level any new measure to give concrete form to the obligation which it defines.

(42) The Netherlands Government draws a distinction between the question of the internal effect and that of the direct effect (or direct applicability), the first, according to it, being a precondition of the second.

(43) It considers that the question whether a particular provision of the Treaty has an internal effect can only be answered in the affirmative if all the essential elements, namely the intention of the contracting parties and the material terms of the provision under consideration, allows such a conclusion.

(44) With regard to the intention of the parties to the Treaty the Netherlands Government maintains that an examination of the actual wording is sufficient to establish that Article 12 only places an obligation on Member States, who are free to decide how they intend to fulfil this obligation. A comparison with other provisions of the Treaty confirms this finding.

(45) As Article 12 does not have internal effect it cannot, *a fortiori*, have direct effect.

(46) Even if the fact that Article 12 places an obligation on Member States were to be considered as an internal effect, it cannot have direct effect in the sense that it permits the nationals of Member States to assert subjective rights which the courts must protect.

(47) Alternatively, the Netherlands Government argues that, so far as the necessary conditions for its direct application are concerned, the EEC Treaty does not differ from a standard international treaty. The conclusive factors in this respect are the intention of the parties and the provisions of the Treaty.

(48) However, the question whether under Netherlands constitutional law Article 12 is directly applicable is one concerning the interpretation of Netherlands law and does not come within the jurisdiction of the Court of Justice.

(49) Finally, the Netherlands Government indicates what the effect would be, in its view of an affirmative answer to the first question put by the Tariefcommissie:

- it would upset the system which the authors of the Treaty intended to establish;
- it would create, with regard to the many provisions in Community regulations which expressly impose obligations on Member States, an uncertainty in the law of a kind which could call in question the readiness of these States co-operation in the future;
- it would put in issue the responsibility of States by means of a procedure which was not designed for this purpose.

(50) The Belgian Government maintains that Article 12 is not one of the provisions:

- which are the exception in the Treaty;
- having direct internal effect.

(51) Article 12 does not constitute a rule of law of general application providing that any introduction of a new customs duty or any increase in an existing duty is automatically without effect or is absolutely void. It merely obliges Member States to refrain from taking such measures.

(52) It does not create therefore a directly applicable right which nationals could invoke and enforce. It requires from Governments action at a later date to attain the objective fixed by the Treaty. A national court cannot be asked to enforce compliance with this obligation.

(53) The German Government is also of the opinion that Article 12 of the EEC Treaty does not constitute a legal provision which is directly applicable in all Member States. It imposes on them an international obligation (in the field of customs policy) which must be implemented by national authorities endowed with legislative powers.

(54) Customs duties applicable to a citizen of a Member State of the Community, at least during the transitional period, thus do not derive from the EEC Treaty or the legal measures taken by the institutions, but from legal measures enacted by Member States. Article 12 only lays down the provisions with which they must comply in the customs legislation.

(55) Moreover the obligation laid down only applies to the other contracting Member States.

(56) In German law a legal provision which laid down a customs duty contrary to the provisions of Article 12 would be perfectly valid.

(57) Within the framework of the EEC Treaty the legal protection of nationals of Member States is secured, by provisions derogating from their national constitution system, only in respect of those measures taken by the institutions of the Community which are of direct and individual concern to such nationals.

B   THE SECOND QUESTION

Admissibility

(58) The Netherlands and Belgian Governments are of the opinion that the second as well as the first question is inadmissible.

(59) According to them the answer to the question whether in fact the Brussels Protocol of 1958 represents a failure by those states who are signatories to fulfil the obligations laid down in Article 12 of the EEC Treaty cannot be given in the context of a preliminary ruling, because the issue is the application of the Treaty and not its interpretation. Moreover such an answer presupposes a careful study and a specific evaluation of the facts and circumstances peculiar to a given situation, and this is also inadmissible under Article 177.

(60) The Netherlands Government emphasises, furthermore, that if a failure by a State to fulfil its Community obligations could be brought before the Court by a procedure other than those under Articles 169 and 170 the legal protection of that State would be considerably diminished.

(61) The German Government, without making a formal objection of inadmissibility, maintains that Article 12 only imposes an international obligation on States and that the question whether national rules enacted for its implementation do not comply with this obligation cannot depend upon a decision of the Court under Article 177 since it does not involve the interpretation of the Treaty.

(62) Van Gend en Loos also considers that the direct form of the second question would necessitate an examination of the facts for which the Court has no jurisdiction when it makes a ruling under Article 177. The real question for interpretation according to it [the firm] could be worded as follows:

(63) Is it possible for a derogation from the rules applied before 1 March 1960 (or more accurately, before 1 January 1958) not to be in the nature of an increase prohibited by Article 12 of the Treaty, even though this derogation arithmetically represents an increase?

Grounds of judgment

I PROCEDURE

(64) No objection has been raised concerning the procedural validity of the reference to the Court under Article 177 of the EEC Treaty by the Tariefcommissie, a court or tribunal within the meaning of that Article. Further, no grounds exist for the Court to raise the matter of its own motion.

II THE FIRST QUESTION

A JURISDICTION OF THE COURT

(65) The Government of the Netherlands and the Belgian Government challenge the jurisdiction of the Court on the ground that the reference relates not to the interpretation but to the application of the Treaty in the context of the constitutional law of the Netherlands, and that in particular the Court has no jurisdiction to decide, should the occasion arise, whether the provisions of the EEC Treaty prevail over Netherlands legislation or over other agreements entered into by the Netherlands and incorporated into Dutch national law. The solution of such a problem, it is claimed, falls within the exclusive jurisdiction or the national courts, subject to an application in accordance with the provisions laid down by Articles 169 and 170 of the Treaty.

(66) However in this case the Court is not asked to adjudicate upon the application of the Treaty according to the principles of the national law of the Netherlands, which remains the concern of the national courts, but is asked, in conformity with sub-paragraph (a) of the first paragraph of Article 177 of the Treaty, only to interpret the scope of Article 12 of the said Treaty within the context of Community law and with reference to its effect on individuals. This argument has therefore no legal foundation.

(67) The Belgian Government further argues that the Court has no jurisdiction on the ground that no answer which the Court could give to the first question of the Tariefcommissie would have any bearing on the result of the proceedings brought in that court.

(68) However, in order to confer jurisdiction on the Court in the present case it is necessary only that the question raised should clearly be concerned with the interpretation of the Treaty. The considerations which may have led a national court or tribunal to its choice of questions as well as the relevance which it attributes to such questions in the context of a case before it are excluded from review by the Court of Justice.

(69) It appears from the wording of the questions referred that they relate to the interpretation of the Treaty. The Court therefore has the jurisdiction to answer them. This argument, too, is therefore unfounded.

B ON THE SUBSTANCE OF THE CASE

(70) The first question of the Tariefcommissie is whether Article 12 of the Treaty has direct application in national law in the sense that nationals of Member States may on the basis of this article lay claim to rights which the national courts must protect.

(71) To ascertain whether the provisions of an international treaty extend so far in their effects it is necessary to consider the spirit, the general scheme, and the wording of those provisions.

(72) The objective of the EEC Treaty, which is to establish a Common Market, the functioning of which is of direct concern to interested parties in the Community, implies that this Treaty

is more than an agreement which merely creates mutual obligations between the contracting States. This view is confirmed by the preamble to the Treaty which refers not only to governments but to peoples. It is also confirmed more specifically by the establishment of institutions endowed by the sovereign rights, the exercise of which affects Member States and also their citizens. Furthermore, it must be noted that the nationals of the states brought together in the Community are called upon to co-operate in the functioning of this Community through the intermediary of the European Parliament and the Economic and Social Committee.

(73) In addition, the task assigned to the Court of Justice under Article 177, the object of which is to secure uniform interpretation of the Treaty by national courts and tribunals, confirms that the states have acknowledged that Community law has an authority which can be invoked by their nationals before those courts and tribunals.

(74) The conclusion to be drawn from this is that the Community constitutes a new legal order of international law for the benefit of which the States have limited their sovereign rights, albeit within limited fields, and the subjects of which comprise not only Member States but also their nationals. Independently of the legislation of Member States, Community law therefore not only imposes obligations on individuals but is also intended to confer upon them rights which become part of their legal heritage. These rights arise not only where they are expressly granted by the treaty, but also by reason of obligations which the Treaty imposes in a clearly defined way upon individuals as well as upon the Member States and upon the institutions of the Community.

(75) With regard to the general scheme of the Treaty as it relates to customs duties and charges having equivalent effect it must be emphasised that Article 9, which bases the Community upon a customs union, includes as an essential provision the prohibition of these customs duties and charges. This provision is found at the beginning of the part of the Treaty which defines the 'Foundations of the Community'. It is applied and explained by Article 12.

(76) The wording of Article 12 contains a clear and unconditional prohibition which is not a positive but a negative obligation. This obligation, moreover, is not qualified by any reservation on the part of States which would make its implementation conditional upon a positive legislative measure enacted under national law. The very nature of this prohibition makes it ideally adapted to produce direct effects in the legal relationship between Member States and their subjects.

(77) The implementation of Article 12 does not require any legislative intervention on the part of the States. The fact that under this article it is Member States who are made the subject of the negative obligation does not imply that their nationals cannot benefit from this obligation.

(78) In addition the argument based on Articles 169 and 170 of the Treaty put forward by the three Governments which have submitted observations to the Court in their statements of case is misconceived. The fact that these Articles of the Treaty enable the Commission and the Member States to bring before the Court a State which has not fulfilled its obligations does not mean that individuals cannot plead these obligations, should the occasion arise, before a national court, any more than the fact that the Treaty places at the disposal of the Commission ways of ensuring that obligations imposed upon those subject to the Treaty are observed, precludes the possibility, in actions between individuals before a national court, of pleading infringements of these obligations.

(79) A restriction of the guarantees against an infringement of Article 12 by Member States to the procedures under Articles 169 and 170 would remove all direct legal protection of the individual rights of their nationals. There is the risk that recourse to the procedure under these Articles would be ineffective if it were to occur after the implementation of a national decision taken contrary to the provisions of the Treaty.

(80) The vigilance of individuals concerned to protect their rights amounts to an effective supervision in addition to the supervision entrusted by Articles 169 and 170 to the diligence of the Commission and of the Member States.

(81) It follows from the foregoing considerations that, according to the spirit, the general scheme, and the wording of the Treaty, Article 12 must be interpreted as producing direct effects and creating individual rights which national courts must protect.

(82) III   THE SECOND QUESTION

A   THE JURISDICTION OF THE COURT

According to the observations of the Belgian and Netherlands Governments, the wording of this question appears to require, before it can be answered, an examination by the Court of the tariff classification of ureaformaldehyde imported into the Netherlands, a classification on which Van Gend en Loos and the Inspector of Customs and Excise at Zaandam hold different opinions with regard to the 'Tariefbesluit' of 1947. The question clearly does not call for an interpretation of the Treaty but concerns the application of Netherlands customs legislation to the classification of aminoplasts, which is outside the jurisdiction conferred upon the Court of Justice of the European Communities by sub-paragraph (a) of the first paragraph of Article 177.

(83) The Court has therefore no jurisdiction to consider the reference made by the Tariefcommissie.

(84) However, the real meaning of the question put by the Tariefcommissie is whether, in law, an effective increase in customs duties charged on a given product as a result not of an increase in the rate but of a new classification of the product arising from a change of its tariff description contravenes the prohibition in Article 12 of the Treaty.

(85) Viewed in this way the question put is concerned with an interpretation of this provision of the Treaty and more particularly of the meaning which should be given to the concept of duties applied before the treaty entered into force.

(86) Therefore, the Court has jurisdiction to give a ruling on this question.

B   ON THE SUBSTANCE

(87) It follows from the wording and the general scheme of Article 12 of the Treaty that, in order to ascertain whether customs duties of charges having equivalent effect have been increased contrary to the prohibition contained in the said Article, regard must be had to the customs duties and charges actually applied at the date of the entry into force of the Treaty.

(88) Further, with regard to the prohibition in Article 12 of the treaty such an illegal increase may arise from a rearrangement of the tariff resulting in the classification of the product under a more highly taxed heading and from an actual increase in the rate of customs duty.

(89) It is of little importance how the increase in customs duties occurred when, after the Treaty entered into force, the same product in the same Member State was subjected to a higher rate of duty.

(90) The application of Article 12, in accordance with the interpretation given above, comes within the jurisdiction of the national court which must enquire whether the dutiable product, in this case ureaformaldehyde originating in the Federal Republic of Germany, is charged under the customs measures brought into force in the Netherlands with an import duty higher than that with which it was charged on 1 January 1958.

(91) The Court has no jurisdiction to check the validity of the conflicting views on this subject which have been submitted to it during the proceedings but must leave them to be determined by the national courts.

IV COSTS

(92) The costs incurred by the Commission of the EEC and the Member States which have submitted their observations to the Court are not recoverable, and as these proceedings are, in so far as the parties to the main action are concerned, a step in the action pending before the Tariefcommissie, the decision as to costs is a matter for that court.

(93) On those grounds:

upon reading the pleadings;

upon hearing the report of the Judge-Rapporteur;

upon hearing the parties;

upon hearing the opinion of the Advocate-General;

having regard to Articles 9, 12, 14, 169, 170 and 177 of the Treaty establishing the European Economic Community;

having regard to the Protocol on the Statute of the Court of Justice of the European Economic Community;

having regard to the Rules of Procedure of the Court of Justice of the European Communities;

THE COURT

(94) in answer to the questions referred to it for a preliminary ruling by the Tariefcommissie by decision of 16 August 1962, hereby rules:

(95) 1   Article 12 of the Treaty establishing the European Economic Community produces direct effects and creates individual rights which national courts must protect.

(96) 2   In order to ascertain whether customs duties or charges having equivalent effect have been increased contrary to the prohibition contained in Article 12 of the Treaty, regard must be had to the duties and charges actually applied by the Member State in question at the date of the entry into force of the Treaty.

Such an increase can arise both from a rearrangement of the tariff resulting in the classification of the product under a more highly taxed heading and from an increase in the rate of customs duty applied.

(97) 3   The decision as to costs in these proceedings is a matter for the Tariefcommissie.

(2) HUMAN RIGHTS ACT 1998
1998 Chapter 42

ARRANGEMENT OF SECTIONS

Parliamentary procedure

19 Statements of compatibility.

Supplemental

20 Orders, etc under this Act.

21 Interpretation, etc.

22 Short title, commencement, application and extent.

SCHEDULES

Schedule 1   –   The Articles.

Part I   –   The Convention.

Part II   –   The First Protocol.

Part III   –   The Sixth Protocol.

Schedule 2   –   Remedial Orders.

Schedule 3   –   Derogation and Reservation.

Part I   –   Derogation.

Part II   –   Reservation.

Schedule 4   –   Judicial Pensions.

HUMAN RIGHTS ACT 1998
1998 CHAPTER 42

An Act to give further effect to rights and freedoms guaranteed under the European Convention on Human Rights; to make provision with respect to holders of certain judicial offices who become judges of the European Court of Human Rights; and for connected purposes.

[9th November 1998]

BE IT ENACTED by the Queen's most Excellent Majesty, by and with the advice and consent of the Lords Spiritual and Temporal, and Commons, in this present Parliament assembled, and by the authority of the same, as follows:

Introduction

The Convention rights

1– (1) In this Act 'the Convention rights' means the rights and fundamental freedoms set out in–

(a)   Articles 2 to 12 and 14 of the Convention,

(b)   Articles 1 to 3 of the First Protocol, and

(c)   Articles 1 and 2 of the Sixth Protocol,

as read with Articles 16 to 18 of the Convention.

(2)   Those Articles are to have effect for the purposes of this Act subject to any designated derogation or reservation (as to which see sections 14 and 15).

(3)   The Articles are set out in Schedule 1.

(4)   The Secretary of State may by order make such amendments to this Act as he considers appropriate to reflect the effect, in relation to the United Kingdom, of a protocol.

(5)   In subsection (4) 'protocol' means a protocol to the Convention–

(a)   which the United Kingdom has ratified; or

(b)   which the United Kingdom has signed with a view to ratification.

(6)   No amendment may be made by an order under subsection (4) so as to come into force before the protocol concerned is in force in relation to the United Kingdom.

Interpretation of Convention rights

2– (1)   A court or tribunal determining a question which has arisen in connection with a Convention right must take into account any–

(a)   judgment, decision, declaration or advisory opinion of the European Court of Human Rights,

(b)   opinion of the Commission given in a report adopted under Article 31 of the Convention,

(c)   decision of the Commission in connection with Article 26 or 27(2) of the Convention, or

(d)   decision of the Committee of Ministers taken under Article 46 of the Convention,

whenever made or given, so far as, in the opinion of the court or tribunal, it is relevant to the proceedings in which that question has arisen.

(2)   Evidence of any judgment, decision, declaration or opinion of which account may have to be taken under this section is to be given in proceedings before any court or tribunal in such manner as may be provided by rules.

(3)   In this section 'rules' means rules of court or, in the case of proceedings before a tribunal, rules made for the purposes of this section–

(a)   by the Lord Chancellor or the Secretary of State, in relation to any proceedings outside Scotland;

(b)   by the Secretary of State, in relation to proceedings in Scotland; or

(c)   by a Northern Ireland department, in relation to proceedings before a tribunal in Northern Ireland–

(i)   which deals with transferred matters; and

(ii)   for which no rules made under paragraph (a) are in force.

Legislation

Interpretation of legislation

3– (1) So far as it is possible to do so, primary legislation and subordinate legislation must be read and given effect in a way which is compatible with the Convention rights.

(2)   This section–

    (a)   applies to primary legislation and subordinate legislation whenever enacted;

    (b)   does not affect the validity, continuing operation or enforcement of any incompatible primary legislation; and

    (c)   does not affect the validity, continuing operation or enforcement of any incompatible subordinate legislation if (disregarding any possibility of revocation) primary legislation prevents removal of the incompatibility.

Declaration of incompatibility

4– (1) Subsection (2) applies in any proceedings in which a court determines whether a provision of primary legislation is compatible with a Convention right.

(2)   If the court is satisfied that the provision is incompatible with a Convention right, it may make a declaration of that incompatibility.

(3)   Subsection (4) applies in any proceedings in which a court determines whether a provision of subordinate legislation, made in the exercise of a power conferred by primary legislation, is compatible with a Convention right.

(4)   If the court is satisfied–

    (a)   that the provision is incompatible with a Convention right, and

    (b)   that (disregarding any possibility of revocation) the primary legislation concerned prevents removal of the incompatibility,

it may make a declaration of that incompatibility.

(5)   In this section 'court' means–

    (a)   the House of Lords;

    (b)   the Judicial Committee of the Privy Council;

    (c)   the Courts-Martial Appeal Court;

    (d)   in Scotland, the High Court of Justiciary sitting otherwise than as a trial court or the Court of Session;

    (e)   in England and Wales or Northern Ireland, the High Court or the Court of Appeal.

(6)   A declaration under this section ('a declaration of incompatibility')–

    (a)   does not affect the validity, continuing operation or enforcement of the provision in respect of which it is given; and

    (b)   is not binding on the parties to the proceedings in which it is made.

Right of Crown to intervene

5– (1) Where a court is considering whether to make a declaration of incompatibility, the Crown is entitled to notice in accordance with rules of court.

(2)   In any case to which subsection (1) applies–

       (a)   a Minister of the Crown (or a person nominated by him),

       (b)   a member of the Scottish Executive,

       (c)   a Northern Ireland Minister,

       (d)   a Northern Ireland department,

is entitled, on giving notice in accordance with rules of court, to be joined as a party to the proceedings.

(3)   Notice under subsection (2) may be given at any time during the proceedings.

(4)   A person who has been made a party to criminal proceedings (other than in Scotland) as the result of a notice under subsection (2) may, with leave, appeal to the House of Lords against any declaration of incompatibility made in the proceedings.

(5)   In subsection (4)–

       'criminal proceedings' includes all proceedings before the Courts-Martial Appeal Court; and

       'leave' means leave granted by the court making the declaration of incompatibility or by the House of Lords.

Public authorities

Acts of public authorities

6– (1) It is unlawful for a public authority to act in a way which is incompatible with a Convention right.

(2)   Subsection (1) does not apply to an act if–

       (a)   as the result of one or more provisions of primary legislation, the authority could not have acted differently; or

       (b)   in the case of one or more provisions of, or made under, primary legislation which cannot be read or given effect in a way which is compatible with the Convention rights, the authority was acting so as to give effect to or enforce those provisions.

(3)   In this section 'public authority' includes–

       (a)   a court or tribunal, and

       (b)   any person certain of whose functions are functions of a public nature,

but does not include either House of Parliament or a person exercising functions in connection with proceedings in Parliament.

(4)   In subsection (3) 'Parliament' does not include the House of Lords in its judicial capacity.

(5)   In relation to a particular act, a person is not a public authority by virtue only of subsection (3)(b) if the nature of the act is private.

(6)   'An act' includes a failure to act but does not include a failure to–

   (a)   introduce in, or lay before, Parliament a proposal for legislation; or

   (b)   make any primary legislation or remedial order.

Proceedings

7– (1) A person who claims that a public authority has acted (or proposes to act) in a way which is made unlawful by section 6(1) may–

   (a)   bring proceedings against the authority under this Act in the appropriate court or tribunal, or

   (b)   rely on the Convention right or rights concerned in any legal proceedings,

but only if he is (or would be) a victim of the unlawful act.

(2)   In subsection (1)(a) 'appropriate court or tribunal' means such court or tribunal as may be determined in accordance with rules; and proceedings against an authority include a counterclaim or similar proceeding.

(3)   If the proceedings are brought on an application for judicial review, the applicant is to be taken to have a sufficient interest in relation to the unlawful act only if he is, or would be, a victim of that act.

(4)   If the proceedings are made by way of a petition for judicial review in Scotland, the applicant shall be taken to have title and interest to sue in relation to the unlawful act only if he is, or would be, a victim of that act.

(5)   Proceedings under subsection (1)(a) must be brought before the end of–

   (a)   the period of one year beginning with the date on which the act complained of took place; or

   (b)   such longer period as the court or tribunal considers equitable having regard to all the circumstances,

but that is subject to any rule imposing a stricter time limit in relation to the procedure in question.

(6)   In subsection (1)(b) 'legal proceedings' includes–

   (a)   proceedings brought by or at the instigation of a public authority; and

   (b)   an appeal against the decision of a court or tribunal.

(7)   For the purposes of this section, a person is a victim of an unlawful act only if he would be a victim for the purposes of Article 34 of the Convention if proceedings were brought in the European Court of Human Rights in respect of that act.

(8)   Nothing in this Act creates a criminal offence.

(9)   In this section 'rules' means–

   (a)   in relation to proceedings before a court or tribunal outside Scotland, rules made by the Lord Chancellor or the Secretary of State for the purposes of this section or rules of court,

   (b)   in relation to proceedings before a court or tribunal in Scotland, rules made by the Secretary of State for those purposes,

(c)   in relation to proceedings before a tribunal in Northern Ireland–

   (i)   which deals with transferred matters; and

   (ii)   for which no rules made under paragraph (a) are in force,

rules made by a Northern Ireland department for those purposes,

and includes provision made by order under section 1 of the Courts and Legal Services Act 1990.

(10)   In making rules, regard must be had to section 9.

(11)   The Minister who has power to make rules in relation to a particular tribunal may, to the extent he considers it necessary to ensure that the tribunal can provide an appropriate remedy in relation to an act (or proposed act) of a public authority which is (or would be) unlawful as a result of section 6(1), by order add to–

   (a)   the relief or remedies which the tribunal may grant; or

   (b)   the grounds on which it may grant any of them.

(12)   An order made under subsection (11) may contain such incidental, supplemental, consequential or transitional provision as the Minister making it considers appropriate.

(13)   'The Minister' includes the Northern Ireland department concerned.

Judicial remedies

8– (1)   In relation to any act (or proposed act) of a public authority which the court finds is (or would be) unlawful, it may grant such relief or remedy, or make such order, within its powers as it considers just and appropriate.

(2)   But damages may be awarded only by a court which has power to award damages, or to order the payment of compensation, in civil proceedings.

(3)   No award of damages is to be made unless, taking account of all the circumstances of the case, including–

   (a)   any other relief or remedy granted, or order made, in relation to the act in question (by that or any other court), and

   (b)   the consequences of any decision (of that or any other court) in respect of that act,

the court is satisfied that the award is necessary to afford just satisfaction to the person in whose favour it is made.

(4)   In determining–

   (a)   whether to award damages, or

   (b)   the amount of an award,

the court must take into account the principles applied by the European Court of Human Rights in relation to the award of compensation under Article 41 of the Convention.

(5)   A public authority against which damages are awarded is to be treated–

   (a)   in Scotland, for the purposes of section 3 of the Law Reform (Miscellaneous Provisions) (Scotland) Act 1940 as if the award were made in an action of damages in which the authority has been found liable in respect of loss or damage to the person to whom the award is made;

(b)   for the purposes of the Civil Liability (Contribution) Act 1978 as liable in respect of damage suffered by the person to whom the award is made.

(6)   In this section–

'court' includes a tribunal;

'damages' means damages for an unlawful act of a public authority; and

'unlawful' means unlawful under section 6(1).

Judicial acts

9– (1) Proceedings under section 7(1)(a) in respect of a judicial act may be brought only-

(a)   by exercising a right of appeal;

(b)   on an application (in Scotland a petition) for judicial review; or

(c)   in such other forum as may be prescribed by rules.

(2)   That does not affect any rule of law which prevents a court from being the subject of judicial review.

(3)   In proceedings under this Act in respect of a judicial act done in good faith, damages may not be awarded otherwise than to compensate a person to the extent required by Article 5(5) of the Convention.

(4)   An award of damages permitted by subsection (3) is to be made against the Crown; but no award may be made unless the appropriate person, if not a party to the proceedings, is joined.

(5)   In this section–

'appropriate person' means the Minister responsible for the court concerned, or a person or government department nominated by him;

'court' includes a tribunal;

'judge' includes a member of a tribunal, a justice of the peace and a clerk or other officer entitled to exercise the jurisdiction of a court;

'judicial act' means a judicial act of a court and includes an act done on the instructions, or on behalf, of a judge; and

'rules' has the same meaning as in section 7(9).

Remedial action

Power to take remedial action

10– (1 This section applies if–

(a)   a provision of legislation has been declared under section 4 to be incompatible with a Convention right and, if an appeal lies–

(i)   all persons who may appeal have stated in writing that they do not intend to do so;

(ii)   the time for bringing an appeal has expired and no appeal has been brought within that time; or

(iii)   an appeal brought within that time has been determined or abandoned; or

    (b)   it appears to a Minister of the Crown or Her Majesty in Council that, having regard to a finding of the European Court of Human Rights made after the coming into force of this section in proceedings against the United Kingdom, a provision of legislation is incompatible with an obligation of the United Kingdom arising from the Convention.

(2)   If a Minister of the Crown considers that there are compelling reasons for proceeding under this section, he may by order make such amendments to the legislation as he considers necessary to remove the incompatibility.

(3)   If, in the case of subordinate legislation, a Minister of the Crown considers–

    (a)   that it is necessary to amend the primary legislation under which the subordinate legislation in question was made, in order to enable the incompatibility to be removed, and

    (b)   that there are compelling reasons for proceeding under this section,

he may by order make such amendments to the primary legislation as he considers necessary.

(4)   This section also applies where the provision in question is in subordinate legislation and has been quashed, or declared invalid, by reason of incompatibility with a Convention right and the Minister proposes to proceed under paragraph 2(b) of Schedule 2.

(5)   If the legislation is an Order in Council, the power conferred by subsection (2) or (3) is exercisable by Her Majesty in Council.

(6)   In this section 'legislation' does not include a Measure of the Church Assembly or of the General Synod of the Church of England.

(7)   Schedule 2 makes further provision about remedial orders.

Other rights and proceedings

Safeguard for existing human rights

11– A person's reliance on a Convention right does not restrict–

    (a)   any other right or freedom conferred on him by or under any law having effect in any part of the United Kingdom; or

    (b)   his right to make any claim or bring any proceedings which he could make or bring apart from sections 7 to 9.

Freedom of expression

12– (1) This section applies if a court is considering whether to grant any relief which, if granted, might affect the exercise of the Convention right to freedom of expression.

(2)   If the person against whom the application for relief is made ('the respondent') is neither present nor represented, no such relief is to be granted unless the court is satisfied–

    (a)   that the applicant has taken all practicable steps to notify the respondent; or

    (b)   that there are compelling reasons why the respondent should not be notified.

(3)   No such relief is to be granted so as to restrain publication before trial unless the court is satisfied that the applicant is likely to establish that publication should not be allowed.

(4)   The court must have particular regard to the importance of the Convention right to freedom of expression and, where the proceedings relate to material which the respondent claims, or which appears to the court, to be journalistic, literary or artistic material (or to conduct connected with such material), to–

    (a)   the extent to which–

        (i)   the material has, or is about to, become available to the public; or

        (ii)   it is, or would be, in the public interest for the material to be published;

    (b)   any relevant privacy code.

(5)   In this section–

    'court' includes a tribunal; and

    'relief' includes any remedy or order (other than in criminal proceedings).

Freedom of thought, conscience and religion

13– (1) If a court's determination of any question arising under this Act might affect the exercise by a religious organisation (itself or its members collectively) of the Convention right to freedom of thought, conscience and religion, it must have particular regard to the importance of that right.

(2)   In this section 'court' includes a tribunal.

Derogations and reservations

Derogations

14– (1) In this Act 'designated derogation' means–

    (a)   the United Kingdom's derogation from Article 5(3) of the Convention; and

    (b)   any derogation by the United Kingdom from an Article of the Convention, or of any protocol to the Convention, which is designated for the purposes of this Act in an order made by the Secretary of State.

(2)   The derogation referred to in subsection (1)(a) is set out in Part I of Schedule 3.

(3)   If a designated derogation is amended or replaced it ceases to be a designated derogation.

(4)   But subsection (3) does not prevent the Secretary of State from exercising his power under subsection (1)(b) to make a fresh designation order in respect of the Article concerned.

(5)   The Secretary of State must by order make such amendments to Schedule 3 as he considers appropriate to reflect–

    (a)   any designation order; or

    (b)   the effect of subsection (3).

(6)   A designation order may be made in anticipation of the making by the United Kingdom of a proposed derogation.

Reservations

15– (1) In this Act 'designated reservation' means–

    (a)   the United Kingdom's reservation to Article 2 of the First Protocol to the Convention; and

    (b)   any other reservation by the United Kingdom to an Article of the Convention, or of any protocol to the Convention, which is designated for the purposes of this Act in an order made by the Secretary of State.

(2)   The text of the reservation referred to in subsection (1)(a) is set out in Part II of Schedule 3.

(3)   If a designated reservation is withdrawn wholly or in part it ceases to be a designated reservation.

(4)   But subsection (3) does not prevent the Secretary of State from exercising his power under subsection (1)(b) to make a fresh designation order in respect of the Article concerned.

(5)   The Secretary of State must by order make such amendments to this Act as he considers appropriate to reflect–

    (a)   any designation order; or

    (b)   the effect of subsection (3).

Period for which designated derogations have effect

16– (1) If it has not already been withdrawn by the United Kingdom, a designated derogation ceases to have effect for the purposes of this Act–

    (a)   in the case of the derogation referred to in section 14(1)(a), at the end of the period of five years beginning with the date on which section 1(2) came into force;

    (b)   in the case of any other derogation, at the end of the period of five years beginning with the date on which the order designating it was made.

(2)   At any time before the period–

    (a)   fixed by subsection (1)(a) or (b), or

    (b)   extended by an order under this subsection,

comes to an end, the Secretary of State may by order extend it by a further period of five years.

(3)   An order under section 14(1)(b) ceases to have effect at the end of the period for consideration, unless a resolution has been passed by each House approving the order.

(4)   Subsection (3) does not affect–

    (a)   anything done in reliance on the order; or

    (b)   the power to make a fresh order under section 14(1)(b).

(5)   In subsection (3) 'period for consideration' means the period of forty days beginning with the day on which the order was made.

(6)   In calculating the period for consideration, no account is to be taken of any time during which–

> (a)   Parliament is dissolved or prorogued; or
>
> (b)   both Houses are adjourned for more than four days.

(7)   If a designated derogation is withdrawn by the United Kingdom, the Secretary of State must by order make such amendments to this Act as he considers are required to reflect that withdrawal.

Periodic review of designated reservations

17– (1) The appropriate Minister must review the designated reservation referred to in section 15(1)(a)–

> (a)   before the end of the period of five years beginning with the date on which section 1(2) came into force; and
>
> (b)   if that designation is still in force, before the end of the period of five years beginning with the date on which the last report relating to it was laid under subsection (3).

(2)   The appropriate Minister must review each of the other designated reservations (if any)–

> (a)   before the end of the period of five years beginning with the date on which the order designating the reservation first came into force; and
>
> (b)   if the designation is still in force, before the end of the period of five years beginning with the date on which the last report relating to it was laid under subsection (3).

(3)   The Minister conducting a review under this section must prepare a report on the result of the review and lay a copy of it before each House of Parliament.

Judges of the European Court of Human Rights

Appointment to European Court of Human Rights

18– (1) In this section 'judicial office' means the office of–

> (a)   Lord Justice of Appeal, Justice of the High Court or Circuit judge, in England and Wales;
>
> (b)   judge of the Court of Session or sheriff, in Scotland;
>
> (c)   Lord Justice of Appeal, judge of the High Court or county court judge, in Northern Ireland.

(2)   The holder of a judicial office may become a judge of the European Court of Human Rights ('the Court') without being required to relinquish his office.

(3)   But he is not required to perform the duties of his judicial office while he is a judge of the Court.

(4)   In respect of any period during which he is a judge of the Court–

> (a)   a Lord Justice of Appeal or Justice of the High Court is not to count as a judge of the relevant court for the purposes of section 2(1) or 4(1) of the Supreme Court Act 1981 (maximum number of judges) nor as a judge of the Supreme Court for the purposes of section 12(1) to (6) of that Act (salaries etc);

(b)   a judge of the Court of Session is not to count as a judge of that court for the purposes of section 1(1) of the Court of Session Act 1988 (maximum number of judges) or of section 9(1)(c) of the Administration of Justice Act 1973 ('the 1973 Act') (salaries etc);

(c)   a Lord Justice of Appeal or judge of the High Court in Northern Ireland is not to count as a judge of the relevant court for the purposes of section 2(1) or 3(1) of the Judicature (Northern Ireland) Act 1978 (maximum number of judges) nor as a judge of the Supreme Court of Northern Ireland for the purposes of section 9(1)(d) of the 1973 Act (salaries etc);

(d)   a Circuit judge is not to count as such for the purposes of section 18 of the Courts Act 1971 (salaries etc);

(e)   a sheriff is not to count as such for the purposes of section 14 of the Sheriff Courts (Scotland) Act 1907 (salaries etc);

(f)   a county court judge of Northern Ireland is not to count as such for the purposes of section 106 of the County Courts Act (Northern Ireland) 1959 (salaries etc).

(5)   If a sheriff principal is appointed a judge of the Court, section 11(1) of the Sheriff Courts (Scotland) Act 1971 (temporary appointment of sheriff principal) applies, while he holds that appointment, as if his office is vacant.

(6)   Schedule 4 makes provision about judicial pensions in relation to the holder of a judicial office who serves as a judge of the Court.

(7)   The Lord Chancellor or the Secretary of State may by order make such transitional provision (including, in particular, provision for a temporary increase in the maximum number of judges) as he considers appropriate in relation to any holder of a judicial office who has completed his service as a judge of the Court.

Parliamentary procedure

Statements of compatibility

19– (1) A Minister of the Crown in charge of a Bill in either House of Parliament must, before Second Reading of the Bill–

(a)   make a statement to the effect that in his view the provisions of the Bill are compatible with the Convention rights ('a statement of compatibility'); or

(b)   make a statement to the effect that although he is unable to make a statement of compatibility the government nevertheless wishes the House to proceed with the Bill.

(2)   The statement must be in writing and be published in such manner as the Minister making it considers appropriate.

Supplemental

Orders, etc under this Act

20– (1) Any power of a Minister of the Crown to make an order under this Act is exercisable by statutory instrument.

(2)   The power of the Lord Chancellor or the Secretary of State to make rules (other than rules of court) under section 2(3) or 7(9) is exercisable by statutory instrument.

(3)   Any statutory instrument made under section 14, 15 or 16(7) must be laid before Parliament.

(4)   No order may be made by the Lord Chancellor or the Secretary of State under section 1(4), 7(11) or 16(2) unless a draft of the order has been laid before, and approved by, each House of Parliament.

(5)   Any statutory instrument made under section 18(7) or Schedule 4, or to which subsection (2) applies, shall be subject to annulment in pursuance of a resolution of either House of Parliament.

(6)   The power of a Northern Ireland department to make–

>   (a)   rules under section 2(3)(c) or 7(9)(c), or

>   (b)   an order under section 7(11),

is exercisable by statutory rule for the purposes of the Statutory Rules (Northern Ireland) Order 1979.

(7)   Any rules made under section 2(3)(c) or 7(9)(c) shall be subject to negative resolution; and section 41(6) of the Interpretation Act Northern Ireland) 1954 (meaning of 'subject to negative resolution') shall apply as if the power to make the rules were conferred by an Act of the Northern Ireland Assembly.

(8)   No order may be made by a Northern Ireland department under section 7(11) unless a draft of the order has been laid before, and approved by, the Northern Ireland Assembly.

Interpretation, etc

21– (1) In this Act–

>   'amend' includes repeal and apply (with or without modifications);

>   'the appropriate Minister' means the Minister of the Crown having charge of the appropriate authorised government department (within the meaning of the Crown Proceedings Act 1947);

>   'the Commission' means the European Commission of Human Rights;

>   'the Convention' means the Convention for the Protection of Human Rights and Fundamental Freedoms, agreed by the Council of Europe at Rome on 4th November 1950 as it has effect for the time being in relation to the United Kingdom;

>   'declaration of incompatibility' means a declaration under section 4;

>   'Minister of the Crown' has the same meaning as in the Ministers of the Crown Act 1975;

>   'Northern Ireland Minister' includes the First Minister and the deputy First Minister in Northern Ireland;

>   'primary legislation' means any–

>   (a)   public general Act;

>   (b)   local and personal Act;

>   (c)   private Act;

>   (d)   Measure of the Church Assembly;

(e)   Measure of the General Synod of the Church of England;

(f)   Order in Council–

　　　(i)   made in exercise of Her Majesty's Royal Prerogative;

　　　(ii)   made under section 38(1)(a) of the Northern Ireland Constitution Act 1973 or the corresponding provision of the Northern Ireland Act 1998; or

　　　(iii)   amending an Act of a kind mentioned in paragraph (a), (b) or (c);

and includes an order or other instrument made under primary legislation (otherwise than by the National Assembly for Wales, a member of the Scottish Executive, a Northern Ireland Minister or a Northern Ireland department) to the extent to which it operates to bring one or more provisions of that legislation into force or amends any primary legislation;

'the First Protocol' means the protocol to the Convention agreed at Paris on 20th March 1952;

'the Sixth Protocol' means the protocol to the Convention agreed at Strasbourg on 28th April 1983;

'the Eleventh Protocol' means the protocol to the Convention (restructuring the control machinery established by the Convention) agreed at Strasbourg on 11th May 1994;

'remedial order' means an order under section 10;

'subordinate legislation' means any–

(a)   Order in Council other than one–

　　　(i)   made in exercise of Her Majesty's Royal Prerogative;

　　　(ii)   made under section 38(1)(a) of the Northern Ireland Constitution Act 1973 or the corresponding provision of the Northern Ireland Act 1998; or

　　　(iii)   amending an Act of a kind mentioned in the definition of primary legislation;

(b)   Act of the Scottish Parliament;

(c)   Act of the Parliament of Northern Ireland;

(d)   Measure of the Assembly established under section 1 of the Northern Ireland Assembly Act 1973;

(e)   Act of the Northern Ireland Assembly;

(f)   order, rules, regulations, scheme, warrant, byelaw or other instrument made under primary legislation (except to the extent to which it operates to bring one or more provisions of that legislation into force or amends any primary legislation);

(g)   order, rules, regulations, scheme, warrant, byelaw or other instrument made under legislation mentioned in paragraph (b), (c), (d) or (e) or made under an Order in Council applying only to Northern Ireland;

(h)   order, rules, regulations, scheme, warrant, byelaw or other instrument made by a member of the Scottish Executive, a Northern Ireland Minister or a Northern Ireland department in exercise of prerogative or other executive functions of Her Majesty which are exercisable by such a person on behalf of Her Majesty;

'transferred matters' has the same meaning as in the Northern Ireland Act 1998; and

'tribunal' means any tribunal in which legal proceedings may be brought.

(2)   The references in paragraphs (b) and (c) of section 2(1) to Articles are to Articles of the Convention as they had effect immediately before the coming into force of the Eleventh Protocol.

(3)   The reference in paragraph (d) of section 2(1) to Article 46 includes a reference to Articles 32 and 54 of the Convention as they had effect immediately before the coming into force of the Eleventh Protocol.

(4)   The references in section 2(1) to a report or decision of the Commission or a decision of the Committee of Ministers include references to a report or decision made as provided by paragraphs 3, 4 and 6 of Article 5 of the Eleventh Protocol (transitional provisions).

(5)   Any liability under the Army Act 1955, the Air Force Act 1955 or the Naval Discipline Act 1957 to suffer death for an offence is replaced by a liability to imprisonment for life or any less punishment authorised by those Acts; and those Acts shall accordingly have effect with the necessary modifications.

Short title, commencement, application and extent

22– (1) This Act may be cited as the Human Rights Act 1998.

(2)   Sections 18, 20 and 21(5) and this section come into force on the passing of this Act.

(3)   The other provisions of this Act come into force on such day as the Secretary of State may by order appoint; and different days may be appointed for different purposes.

(4)   Paragraph (b) of subsection (1) of section 7 applies to proceedings brought by or at the instigation of a public authority whenever the act in question took place; but otherwise that subsection does not apply to an act taking place before the coming into force of that section.

(5)   This Act binds the Crown.

(6)   This Act extends to Northern Ireland.

(7)   Section 21(5), so far as it relates to any provision contained in the Army Act 1955, the Air Force Act 1955 or the Naval Discipline Act 1957, extends to any place to which that provision extends.

SCHEDULES

SCHEDULE 1 THE ARTICLES
PART I THE CONVENTION

RIGHTS AND FREEDOMS

ARTICLE 2
RIGHT TO LIFE

1   Everyone's right to life shall be protected by law. No one shall be deprived of his life intentionally save in the execution of a sentence of a court following his conviction of a crime for which this penalty is provided by law.

2   Deprivation of life shall not be regarded as inflicted in contravention of this Article when it results from the use of force which is no more than absolutely necessary:

(a)   in defence of any person from unlawful violence;

(b)   in order to effect a lawful arrest or to prevent the escape of a person lawfully detained;

(c)   in action lawfully taken for the purpose of quelling a riot or insurrection.

ARTICLE 3
PROHIBITION OF TORTURE

No one shall be subjected to torture or to inhuman or degrading treatment or punishment.

ARTICLE 4
PROHIBITION OF SLAVERY AND FORCED LABOUR

1   No one shall be held in slavery or servitude.

2   No one shall be required to perform forced or compulsory labour.

3   For the purpose of this Article the term 'forced or compulsory labour' shall not include:

(a)   any work required to be done in the ordinary course of detention imposed according to the provisions of Article 5 of this Convention or during conditional release from such detention;

(b)   any service of a military character or, in case of conscientious objectors in countries where they are recognised, service exacted instead of compulsory military service;

(c)   any service exacted in case of an emergency or calamity threatening the life or well-being of the community;

(d)   any work or service which forms part of normal civic obligations.

ARTICLE 5
RIGHT TO LIBERTY AND SECURITY

1   Everyone has the right to liberty and security of person. No one shall be deprived of his liberty save in the following cases and in accordance with a procedure prescribed by law:

(a)   the lawful detention of a person after conviction by a competent court;

(b)   the lawful arrest or detention of a person for non-compliance with the lawful order of a court or in order to secure the fulfilment of any obligation prescribed by law;

(c)   the lawful arrest or detention of a person effected for the purpose of bringing him before the competent legal authority on reasonable suspicion of having committed an offence or when it is reasonably considered necessary to prevent his committing an offence or fleeing after having done so;

(d)   the detention of a minor by lawful order for the purpose of educational supervision or his lawful detention for the purpose of bringing him before the competent legal authority;

(e)   the lawful detention of persons for the prevention of the spreading of infectious diseases, of persons of unsound mind, alcoholics or drug addicts or vagrants;

(f)   the lawful arrest or detention of a person to prevent his effecting an unauthorised entry into the country or of a person against whom action is being taken with a view to deportation or extradition.

2   Everyone who is arrested shall be informed promptly, in a language which he understands, of the reasons for his arrest and of any charge against him.

3   Everyone arrested or detained in accordance with the provisions of paragraph 1(c) of this Article shall be brought promptly before a judge or other officer authorised by law to exercise judicial power and shall be entitled to trial within a reasonable time or to release pending trial. Release may be conditioned by guarantees to appear for trial.

4   Everyone who is deprived of his liberty by arrest or detention shall be entitled to take proceedings by which the lawfulness of his detention shall be decided speedily by a court and his release ordered if the detention is not lawful.

5   Everyone who has been the victim of arrest or detention in contravention of the provisions of this Article shall have an enforceable right to compensation.

ARTICLE 6
RIGHT TO A FAIR TRIAL

1   In the determination of his civil rights and obligations or of any criminal charge against him, everyone is entitled to a fair and public hearing within a reasonable time by an independent and impartial tribunal established by law. Judgment shall be pronounced publicly but the press and public may be excluded from all or part of the trial in the interest of morals, public order or national security in a democratic society, where the interests of juveniles or the protection of the private life of the parties so require, or to the extent strictly necessary in the opinion of the court in special circumstances where publicity would prejudice the interests of justice.

2   Everyone charged with a criminal offence shall be presumed innocent until proved guilty according to law.

3   Everyone charged with a criminal offence has the following minimum rights:

(a)   to be informed promptly, in a language which he understands and in detail, of the nature and cause of the accusation against him;

(b)   to have adequate time and facilities for the preparation of his defence;

(c)   to defend himself in person or through legal assistance of his own choosing or, if he has not sufficient means to pay for legal assistance, to be given it free when the interests of justice so require;

(d)   to examine or have examined witnesses against him and to obtain the attendance and examination of witnesses on his behalf under the same conditions as witnesses against him;

(e)   to have the free assistance of an interpreter if he cannot understand or speak the language used in court.

ARTICLE 7

NO PUNISHMENT WITHOUT LAW

1   No one shall be held guilty of any criminal offence on account of any act or omission which did not constitute a criminal offence under national or international law at the time when it was committed. Nor shall a heavier penalty be imposed than the one that was applicable at the time the criminal offence was committed.

2   This Article shall not prejudice the trial and punishment of any person for any act or omission which, at the time when it was committed, was criminal according to the general principles of law recognised by civilised nations.

ARTICLE 8

RIGHT TO RESPECT FOR PRIVATE AND FAMILY LIFE

1   Everyone has the right to respect for his private and family life, his home and his correspondence.

2   There shall be no interference by a public authority with the exercise of this right except such as is in accordance with the law and is necessary in a democratic society in the interests of national security, public safety or the economic well-being of the country, for the prevention of disorder or crime, for the protection of health or morals, or for the protection of the rights and freedoms of others.

ARTICLE 9

FREEDOM OF THOUGHT, CONSCIENCE AND RELIGION

1   Everyone has the right to freedom of thought, conscience and religion; this right includes freedom to change his religion or belief and freedom, either alone or in community with others and in public or private, to manifest his religion or belief, in worship, teaching, practice and observance.

2   Freedom to manifest one's religion or beliefs shall be subject only to such limitations as are prescribed by law and are necessary in a democratic society in the interests of public safety, for the protection of public order, health or morals, or for the protection of the rights and freedoms of others.

ARTICLE 10

FREEDOM OF EXPRESSION

1   Everyone has the right to freedom of expression. This right shall include freedom to hold opinions and to receive and impart information and ideas without interference by public authority and regardless of frontiers. This Article shall not prevent States from requiring the licensing of broadcasting, television or cinema enterprises.

2   The exercise of these freedoms, since it carries with it duties and responsibilities, may be subject to such formalities, conditions, restrictions or penalties as are prescribed by law and are necessary in a democratic society, in the interests of national security, territorial integrity or public safety, for the prevention of disorder or crime, for the protection of health or morals, for the protection of the reputation or rights of others, for preventing the disclosure of information received in confidence, or for maintaining the authority and impartiality of the judiciary.

ARTICLE 11

FREEDOM OF ASSEMBLY AND ASSOCIATION

1   Everyone has the right to freedom of peaceful assembly and to freedom of association with others, including the right to form and to join trade unions for the protection of his interests.

2   No restrictions shall be placed on the exercise of these rights other than such as are prescribed by law and are necessary in a democratic society in the interests of national security or public safety, for the prevention of disorder or crime, for the protection of health or morals or for the protection of the rights and freedoms of others. This Article shall not prevent the imposition of lawful restrictions on the exercise of these rights by members of the armed forces, of the police or of the administration of the State.

ARTICLE 12

RIGHT TO MARRY

Men and women of marriageable age have the right to marry and to found a family, according to the national laws governing the exercise of this right.

ARTICLE 14

PROHIBITION OF DISCRIMINATION

The enjoyment of the rights and freedoms set forth in this Convention shall be secured without discrimination on any ground such as sex, race, colour, language, religion, political or other opinion, national or social origin, association with a national minority, property, birth or other status.

ARTICLE 16

RESTRICTIONS ON POLITICAL ACTIVITY OF ALIENS

Nothing in Articles 10, 11 and 14 shall be regarded as preventing the High Contracting Parties from imposing restrictions on the political activity of aliens.

ARTICLE 17

PROHIBITION OF ABUSE OF RIGHTS

Nothing in this Convention may be interpreted as implying for any State, group or person any right to engage in any activity or perform any act aimed at the destruction of any of the rights and freedoms set forth herein or at their limitation to a greater extent than is provided for in the Convention.

ARTICLE 18

LIMITATION ON USE OF RESTRICTIONS ON RIGHTS

The restrictions permitted under this Convention to the said rights and freedoms shall not be applied for any purpose other than those for which they have been prescribed.

PART II THE FIRST PROTOCOL

ARTICLE 1

PROTECTION OF PROPERTY

Every natural or legal person is entitled to the peaceful enjoyment of his possessions. No one shall be deprived of his possessions except in the public interest and subject to the conditions provided for by law and by the general principles of international law.

The preceding provisions shall not, however, in any way impair the right of a State to enforce such laws as it deems necessary to control the use of property in accordance with the general interest or to secure the payment of taxes or other contributions or penalties.

ARTICLE 2

RIGHT TO EDUCATION

No person shall be denied the right to education. In the exercise of any functions which it assumes in relation to education and to teaching, the State shall respect the right of parents to ensure such education and teaching in conformity with their own religious and philosophical convictions.

ARTICLE 3

RIGHT TO FREE ELECTIONS

The High Contracting Parties undertake to hold free elections at reasonable intervals by secret ballot, under conditions which will ensure the free expression of the opinion of the people in the choice of the legislature.

PART III THE SIXTH PROTOCOL

ARTICLE 1

ABOLITION OF THE DEATH PENALTY

The death penalty shall be abolished. No one shall be condemned to such penalty or executed.

ARTICLE 2

DEATH PENALTY IN TIME OF WAR

A State may make provision in its law for the death penalty in respect of acts committed in time of war or of imminent threat of war; such penalty shall be applied only in the instances laid down in the law and in accordance with its provisions. The State shall communicate to the Secretary General of the Council of Europe the relevant provisions of that law.

SCHEDULE 2 REMEDIAL ORDERS

Orders

1– (1) A remedial order may–

- (a) contain such incidental, supplemental, consequential or transitional provision as the person making it considers appropriate;
- (b) be made so as to have effect from a date earlier than that on which it is made;
- (c) make provision for the delegation of specific functions;
- (d) make different provision for different cases.

(2) The power conferred by sub-paragraph (1)(a) includes–

- (a) power to amend primary legislation (including primary legislation other than that which contains the incompatible provision); and
- (b) power to amend or revoke subordinate legislation (including subordinate legislation other than that which contains the incompatible provision).

(3) A remedial order may be made so as to have the same extent as the legislation which it affects.

(4) No person is to be guilty of an offence solely as a result of the retrospective effect of a remedial order.

Procedure

2 No remedial order may be made unless–

- (a) a draft of the order has been approved by a resolution of each House of Parliament made after the end of the period of 60 days beginning with the day on which the draft was laid; or
- (b) it is declared in the order that it appears to the person making it that, because of the urgency of the matter, it is necessary to make the order without a draft being so approved.

Orders laid in draft

3– (1) No draft may be laid under paragraph 2(a) unless–

- (a) the person proposing to make the order has laid before Parliament a document which contains a draft of the proposed order and the required information; and
- (b) the period of 60 days, beginning with the day on which the document required by this sub-paragraph was laid, has ended.

(2) If representations have been made during that period, the draft laid under paragraph 2(a) must be accompanied by a statement containing–

- (a) a summary of the representations; and
- (b) if, as a result of the representations, the proposed order has been changed, details of the changes.

Urgent cases

4– (1) If a remedial order ('the original order') is made without being approved in draft, the person making it must lay it before Parliament, accompanied by the required information, after it is made.

(2)   If representations have been made during the period of 60 days beginning with the day on which the original order was made, the person making it must (after the end of that period) lay before Parliament a statement containing–

> (a)   a summary of the representations; and
>
> (b)   if, as a result of the representations, he considers it appropriate to make changes to the original order, details of the changes.

(3)   If sub-paragraph (2)(b) applies, the person making the statement must–

> (a)   make a further remedial order replacing the original order; and
>
> (b)   lay the replacement order before Parliament.

(4)   If, at the end of the period of 120 days beginning with the day on which the original order was made, a resolution has not been passed by each House approving the original or replacement order, the order ceases to have effect (but without that affecting anything previously done under either order or the power to make a fresh remedial order).

Definitions

5   In this Schedule–

> 'representations' means representations about a remedial order (or proposed remedial order) made to the person making (or proposing to make) it and includes any relevant Parliamentary report or resolution; and

> 'required information' means–

> (a)   an explanation of the incompatibility which the order (or proposed order) seeks to remove, including particulars of the relevant declaration, finding or order; and
>
> (b)   a statement of the reasons for proceeding under section 10 and for making an order in those terms.

Calculating periods

6   In calculating any period for the purposes of this Schedule, no account is to be taken of any time during which–

> (a)   Parliament is dissolved or prorogued; or
>
> (b)   both Houses are adjourned for more than four days.

SCHEDULE 3 DEROGATION AND RESERVATION
PART I DEROGATION

The 1988 notification

The United Kingdom Permanent Representative to the Council of Europe presents his compliments to the Secretary General of the Council, and has the honour to convey the following information in order to ensure compliance with the obligations of Her Majesty's Government in the United Kingdom under Article 15(3) of the Convention for the Protection of Human Rights and Fundamental Freedoms signed at Rome on 4 November 1950.

There have been in the United Kingdom in recent years campaigns of organised terrorism connected with the affairs of Northern Ireland which have manifested themselves in activities which have included repeated murder, attempted murder, maiming, intimidation and violent civil disturbance and in bombing and fire raising which have resulted in death, injury and widespread destruction of property. As a result, a public emergency within the meaning of Article 15(1) of the Convention exists in the United Kingdom.

The Government found it necessary in 1974 to introduce and since then, in cases concerning persons reasonably suspected of involvement in terrorism connected with the affairs of Northern Ireland, or of certain offences under the legislation, who have been detained for 48 hours, to exercise powers enabling further detention without charge, for periods of up to five days, on the authority of the Secretary of State. These powers are at present to be found in Section 12 of the Prevention of Terrorism (Temporary Provisions) Act 1984, Article 9 of the Prevention of Terrorism (Supplemental Temporary Provisions) Order 1984 and Article 10 of the Prevention of Terrorism (Supplemental Temporary Provisions) (Northern Ireland) Order 1984.

Section 12 of the Prevention of Terrorism (Temporary Provisions) Act 1984 provides for a person whom a constable has arrested on reasonable grounds of suspecting him to be guilty of an offence under Section 1, 9 or 10 of the Act, or to be or to have been involved in terrorism connected with the affairs of Northern Ireland, to be detained in right of the arrest for up to 48 hours and thereafter, where the Secretary of State extends the detention period, for up to a further five days. Section 12 substantially re-enacted Section 12 of the Prevention of Terrorism (Temporary Provisions) Act 1976 which, in turn, substantially re-enacted Section 7 of the Prevention of Terrorism (Temporary Provisions) Act 1974.

Article 10 of the Prevention of Terrorism (Supplemental Temporary Provisions) (Northern Ireland) Order 1984 (SI 1984/417) and Article 9 of the Prevention of Terrorism (Supplemental Temporary Provisions) Order 1984 (SI 1984/418) were both made under Sections 13 and 14 of and Schedule 3 to the 1984 Act and substantially re-enacted powers of detention in Orders made under the 1974 and 1976 Acts. A person who is being examined under Article 4 of either Order on his arrival in, or on seeking to leave, Northern Ireland or Great Britain for the purpose of determining whether he is or has been involved in terrorism connected with the affairs of Northern Ireland, or whether there are grounds for suspecting that he has committed an offence under Section 9 of the 1984 Act, may be detained under Article 9 or 10, as appropriate, pending the conclusion of his examination. The period of this examination may exceed 12 hours if an examining officer has reasonable grounds for suspecting him to be or to have been involved in acts of terrorism connected with the affairs of Northern Ireland.

Where such a person is detained under the said Article 9 or 10 he may be detained for up to 48 hours on the authority of an examining officer and thereafter, where the Secretary of State extends the detention period, for up to a further five days.

In its judgment of 29 November 1988 in the Case of Brogan and Others, the European Court of Human Rights held that there had been a violation of Article 5(3) in respect of each of the applicants, all of whom had been detained under Section 12 of the 1984 Act. The Court held that even the shortest of the four periods of detention concerned, namely four days and six hours, fell outside the constraints as to time permitted by the first part of Article 5(3). In addition, the Court held that there had been a violation of Article 5(5) in the case of each applicant.

Following this judgment, the Secretary of State for the Home Department informed Parliament on 6 December 1988 that, against the background of the terrorist campaign, and the over-riding need to bring terrorists to justice, the Government did not believe that the maximum period of detention should be reduced. He informed Parliament that the Government were examining the matter with a view to responding to the judgment. On 22 December 1988, the Secretary of State further informed Parliament that it remained the Government's wish, if it could be achieved, to find a judicial process under which extended detention might be reviewed and where appropriate authorised by a judge or other judicial officer. But a further period of reflection and consultation was necessary before the Government could bring forward a firm and final view.

Since the judgment of 29 November 1988 as well as previously, the Government have found it necessary to continue to exercise, in relation to terrorism connected with the affairs of Northern Ireland, the powers described above enabling further detention without charge for periods of up to 5 days, on the authority of the Secretary of State, to the extent strictly required by the exigencies of the situation to enable necessary enquiries and investigations properly to be completed in order to decide whether criminal proceedings should be instituted. To the extent that the exercise of these powers may be inconsistent with the obligations imposed by the Convention the Government has availed itself of the right of derogation conferred by Article 15(1) of the Convention and will continue to do so until further notice.

Dated 23 December 1988.

The 1989 notification

The United Kingdom Permanent Representative to the Council of Europe presents his compliments to the Secretary General of the Council, and has the honour to convey the following information.

In his communication to the Secretary General of 23 December 1988, reference was made to the introduction and exercise of certain powers under section 12 of the Prevention of Terrorism (Temporary Provisions) Act 1984, Article 9 of the Prevention of Terrorism (Supplemental Temporary Provisions) Order 1984 and Article 10 of the Prevention of Terrorism (Supplemental Temporary Provisions) (Northern Ireland) Order 1984.

These provisions have been replaced by section 14 of and paragraph 6 of Schedule 5 to the Prevention of Terrorism (Temporary Provisions) Act 1989, which make comparable provision. They came into force on 22 March 1989. A copy of these provisions is enclosed.

The United Kingdom Permanent Representative avails himself of this opportunity to renew to the Secretary General the assurance of his highest consideration.

23 March 1989.

SCHEDULE 3 DEROGATION AND RESERVATION – continued
PART II RESERVATION

At the time of signing the present (First) Protocol, I declare that, in view of certain provisions of the Education Acts in the United Kingdom, the principle affirmed in the second sentence of Article 2 is accepted by the United Kingdom only so far as it is compatible with the provision of efficient instruction and training, and the avoidance of unreasonable public expenditure.

Dated 20 March 1952

Made by the United Kingdom Permanent Representative to the Council of Europe.

SCHEDULE 4 JUDICIAL PENSIONS

Duty to make orders about pensions

1– (1) The appropriate Minister must by order make provision with respect to pensions payable to or in respect of any holder of a judicial office who serves as an ECHR judge.

(2)   A pensions order must include such provision as the Minister making it considers is necessary to secure that–

(a)   an ECHR judge who was, immediately before his appointment as an ECHR judge, a member of a judicial pension scheme is entitled to remain as a member of that scheme;

(b)   the terms on which he remains a member of the scheme are those which would have been applicable had he not been appointed as an ECHR judge; and

(c)   entitlement to benefits payable in accordance with the scheme continues to be determined as if, while serving as an ECHR judge, his salary was that which would (but for section 18(4)) have been payable to him in respect of his continuing service as the holder of his judicial office.

Contributions

2   A pensions order may, in particular, make provision–

(a)   for any contributions which are payable by a person who remains a member of a scheme as a result of the order, and which would otherwise be payable by deduction from his salary, to be made otherwise than by deduction from his salary as an ECHR judge; and

(b)   for such contributions to be collected in such manner as may be determined by the administrators of the scheme.

Amendments of other enactments

3   A pensions order may amend any provision of, or made under, a pensions Act in such manner and to such extent as the Minister making the order considers necessary or expedient to ensure the proper administration of any scheme to which it relates.

Definitions

4   In this Schedule–

'appropriate Minister' means–

(a)   in relation to any judicial office whose jurisdiction is exercisable exclusively in relation to Scotland, the Secretary of State; and

(b)   otherwise, the Lord Chancellor;

'ECHR judge' means the holder of a judicial office who is serving as a judge of the Court;

'judicial pension scheme' means a scheme established by and in accordance with a pensions Act;

'pensions Act' means–

(a)   the County Courts Act (Northern Ireland) 1959;

(b)   the Sheriffs' Pensions (Scotland) Act 1961;

(c)   the Judicial Pensions Act 1981; or

(d)   the Judicial Pensions and Retirement Act 1993; and

'pensions order' means an order made under paragraph 1.

Figure A2.1: Human Rights Act – sections

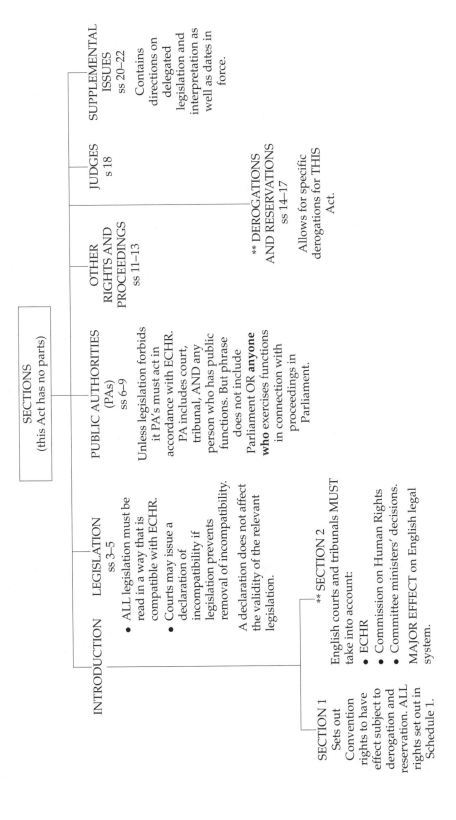

Figure A2.2: Human Rights Act 1998 – schedules

IMPORTANT ISSUES

1 Effect of s 2 of Act on English legal
   system and the Doctrine of
   Precedent.
2 Deliberate omission of Article 13 of
   ECHR on enforcement/remedies.
3 Extent and nature of
   derogations/reservations.
4 The way in which it will be used to
   extend laws.
5 Failure to set up Human Rights
   Commission.

APPENDIX 3

THE EUROPEAN DIMENSION (2): *FACTORTAME* CASE STUDY MATERIALS AND EXTRACTS FROM TILLOTSON

(1) *R v SECRETARY OF STATE FOR TRANSPORT EX P FACTORTAME LTD AND OTHERS* [1989] 2 CMLR 353

BEFORE THE ENGLISH COURT OF APPEAL

(Lord Donaldson MR; Lord Justice Bingham and Lord Justice Mann)

22 March 1989

[Gaz: GB890322]

ON APPEAL FROM THE ENGLISH HIGH COURT (QUEEN'S BENCH DIVISIONAL COURT)

(Lord Justice Neill and Mr Justice Hodgson)

10 March 1989

[Gaz: GB890310]

JUDGMENT (OF THE DIVISIONAL COURT)

Neill LJ: [1] The applicants in these proceedings comprise a number of companies incorporated under the laws of the United Kingdom and also the directors and shareholders of those companies. An amended list of these companies and individuals is now contained in Annex I to the application.

[2] Apart from three of the applicant companies, which carry on business as managers, the applicant companies are the owners of fishing vessels registered in the United Kingdom and authorised to fish under licence granted by the United Kingdom authorities. The applicants also now include Rawlings (Trawlings) Ltd and its directors and shareholders. Leave was given to join these additional parties as applicants at the outset of the hearing of the appeal on Monday 27 February 1989. At the same time, however, leave was given to Rawlings to be separately represented as the facts relating to this company are different in a number of respects from those relating to the other applicant companies.

[3] The relief sought by the applicants can be stated shortly as follows:

1 A declaration that the provisions of Part II of the Merchant Shipping Act 1988 (the 1988 Act) and the provisions of Part VII of the Merchant Shipping (Registration of Fishing Vessels) Regulations 1988 (the 1988 Regulations) may not be applied to the applicants on the grounds that such application is contrary to the law of the European Economic Community (EEC law) as given effect by the European Communities Act 1972.

2 An order of prohibition prohibiting the Secretary of State for Transport from treating the existing registration of the applicant vessels under Part IV of the Merchant Shipping Act 1894 as having ceased from 1 April 1989 unless the applicants satisfy the conditions of eligibility set out in Part II of the 1988 Act and Part VII of the 1988 Regulations.

[4] Part II of the 1988 act, which came into force on 1 December 1988, introduced a new system of registration of British fishing vessels. It also provided that any registration of a fishing vessel under the relevant provisions of the Merchant Shipping Act 1894 should not continue beyond the end of a period to be subsequently prescribed. By regulation 66 of the 1988 Regulations the end of this period has been prescribed as being 31 March 1989.

[5] The applicant companies between them own or manage 95 British fishing vessels, which are registered under the Merchant Shipping Act 1894. Fifty-three of these vessels were originally registered in Spain and flew the Spanish flag. Between 1980 and 1983 43 of these 53 vessels were registered as British fishing vessels under the Merchant Shipping Act 1894. Since 1983 the other 10 vessels, which were originally Spanish, have been similarly registered as British fishing vessels under the 1894 Act. The remaining 42 vessels have always been British fishing vessels. These vessels have been purchased by the applicants at various dates, mainly since 1983.

[6] It is common ground that, if the 1988 Act and the 1988 Regulations do apply to the applicants, it will not be possible for these vessels to remain registered or to be re-registered as British fishing vessels after 31 March 1989 so long as they remain in the ownership of the applicant owner companies as at present constituted. The reason is that most of the directors and shareholders of the applicant companies are Spanish citizens. None of the applicant Companies as at present constituted can satisfy the conditions required for a qualified company, as defined in section 14(7) of the 1988 Act. Nor do those directors or shareholders who are Spanish citizens, or who are resident or domiciled in Spain, satisfy the tests therein prescribed for a qualified person. Section 14 of the 1988 Act, so far as is material, provides as follows:

(1) Subject to subsections (3) and (4), a fishing vessel shall only be eligible to be registered as a British fishing vessel if–

    (a) the vessel is British-owned;

    (b) the vessel is managed, and its operations are directed and controlled, from within the United Kingdom; and

    (c) any charterer, manager or operator of the vessel is a qualified person or company.

(2) For the purposes of subsection (1)(a) a fishing vessel is British-owned if–

    (a) the legal title to the vessel is vested wholly in one or more qualified persons or companies; and

    (b) the vessel is beneficially owned–

        (i)   as to not less than the relevant percentage of the property in the vessel, by one or more qualified persons, or

        (ii) wholly by a qualified company or companies, or

        (iii) by one or more qualified companies and, as to not less than the relevant percentage of the remainder of the property in the vessel, by one or more qualified persons.

(3) The Secretary of State may by regulations specify further requirements which must be satisfied in order for a fishing vessel to be eligible to be registered as a British fishing vessel, being requirements imposed–

    (a) in connection with the implementation of any of the requirements specified in subsection (1)(a) to (c), or

    (b) in addition to the requirements so specified, and appearing to the Secretary of State to be appropriate for securing that such a vessel has a genuine and substantial connection with the United Kingdom.

(4) Where, in the case of any fishing vessel, the Secretary of State is satisfied that–

   (a) the vessel would be eligible to be registered as a British fishing vessel but for the fact that any particular individual, or (as the case may be) each of a number of particular individuals, is not a British citizen (and is accordingly not a qualified person), and

   (b) it would be appropriate to dispense with the requirement of British citizenship in the case of that individual or those individuals, in view of the length of time he has or they have resided in the United Kingdom and been involved in the fishing industry of the United Kingdom,

     the Secretary of State may determine that that requirement should be so dispensed with; and, if he does so, the vessel shall, so long as paragraph (a) above applies to it and any such determination remains in force, be treated for the purposes of this Part as eligible to be registered as a British fishing vessel.

Finally I should read subsection (7) of section 14. That provides as follows:

(7) In this section–

'qualified company' means a company which satisfies the following conditions, namely–

   (a) it is incorporated in the United Kingdom and has its principal place of business there;

   (b) at least the relevant percentage of its shares (taken as a whole), and of each class of its shares, is legally and beneficially owned by one or more qualified persons or companies; and

   (c) at least the relevant percentage of its directors are qualified persons;

'qualified person' means–

   (a) a person who is a British citizen resident and domiciled in the United Kingdom, or

   (b) a local authority in the United Kingdom; and

'the relevant percentage' means 75% or such greater percentage (which may be 100 per cent) as may for the time being be prescribed.

[7] The reasons why the British Government have thought it necessary to introduce this new system of registration were explained in the first affidavit sworn by Mr George William Noble on behalf of the Secretary of State on 3 February 1989 as follows, in paragraph 33:

First it is to ensure that the catch of all vessels on the United Kingdom Register, and consequently fishing against United Kingdom quotas, should enure to the benefit of the United Kingdom fishing industry in general and to local communities dependent on fishing in particular. Secondly, it will enable the United Kingdom authorities to exercise effective control over the activities of United Kingdom registered vessels from the point of view of safety. Thirdly the more effective policing which is now possible will help to achieve the EC conservation objectives and those of the [Common Fishing Policy] and maintain 'the relevant stability' of fishing operations throughout the Community.

It is clear that the Secretary of State relies primarily on the first of these reasons.

[8] The applicants' case is that the conditions imposed by section 14 of the 1988 Act, and the detailed provisions made thereunder in the 1988 Regulations, offend against the basic principles of the Treaty of Rome and against a number of specific articles of the Treaty.

[9] For the respondent Secretary of State it is argued, on the other hand:

1 That Community law does not in any way restrict a Member State's rights to decide who is entitled to be a national of that State, or who is entitled to fly its flag.

2 That, in any event, the new legislation is in conformity with Community law and, indeed, is designed to achieve the Community purposes enshrined in the Common Fisheries Policy.

[10] 1 shall have to look at these rival arguments again later, but first it is necessary to refer to the provisions in the Treaty of Rome on which the applicants rely and to trace, as shortly as possible, the history of the Common Fisheries Policy.

[11] The first Article to which our attention was particularly drawn is Article 7 of the Treaty, which is in these terms:

> Within the scope of application of this Treaty, and without prejudice to any special provisions contained therein, any discrimination on grounds of nationality shall be prohibited.

The applicants place great reliance on this article. Next I should refer to Article 34. Paragraph 1 of this Article reads:

> Quantitative restrictions on exports, and all measures having equivalent effect, shall be prohibited between Member States.

Title II, in Part Two of the Treaty of Rome, is concerned with agriculture, and we were referred to Articles 38, 39 and 40 in particular in that Title. Article 38 provides, in paragraph 1:

> The common market shall extend to agriculture and trade in agricultural products. 'Agricultural products' means the products of the soil, of stock-farming and of fisheries and products of first-stage processing directly related to these products.

In paragraph 1 of Article 39 are set out the objectives of the Common Agricultural Policy. They are important but, for the purposes of this judgment, I do not think it is necessary for me to set them out *in extenso*. Article 40 provides for the establishment of a common organisation and we were referred in particular to paragraph 3 of Article 40 which provides:

> The common organisation established in accordance with paragraph 2 [of Article 40] may include all measures required to attain the objectives set out in Article 39, in particular regulation of prices, aids for the production and marketing of the various products, storage and carry-over arrangements and common machinery for stabilising imports or exports.

> The common organisation shall be limited to pursuit of the objectives set out in Article 39 and shall exclude any discrimination between producers or consumers within the Community.

Title III of the Treaty is concerned with the free movement of persons, services and capital. Chapter 1 of this Title relates to workers, Chapter 2 is headed 'Right of Establishment', Chapter 3 is headed 'Services'. We were referred in particular to Articles 52 and 58 in Chapter 2. I should read those two articles:

> Article 52 Within the framework of the provisions set out below, restrictions on the freedom of establishment of nationals of a Member State in the territory of another Member State shall be abolished by progressive stages in the course of the transitional period. Such progressive abolition shall also apply to restrictions on the setting up of agencies, branches, or subsidiaries by nationals (of any Member State established in the territory of any Member State.

> Freedom of establishment shall include the right to take up and pursue activities as self-employed persons and to set up and manage undertakings, in particular companies or firms within the meaning of the second paragraph of Article 53, under the conditions laid down for its own nationals by the law of the country where such establishment is effected, subject to the provisions of the Chapter relating to capital.

Article 58, which deals with companies or firms, is in these terms:

> Companies or firms formed in accordance with the law of a Member State and having their registered office, central administration or principal place of business within the Community shall, for the purposes of this Chapter, be treated in the same way as natural persons who are nationals of Member States.

'Companies or firms' means companies or firms constituted under civil or commercial law, including co-operative societies, and other legal persons governed by public or private law, save for those which are non-profit making.

[12] Pausing there, it is relevant to note that in *R v Her Majesty's Treasury ex p the Daily Mail*, the European Court said this about Article 52:

> ... the Court must first point out, as it has done on numerous occasions, that freedom of establishment constitutes one of the fundamental principles of the Community and that the provisions of the Treaty guaranteeing that freedom have been directly applicable since the end of the transitional period. Those provisions secure the right of establishment in another Member State not merely for Community nationals but also for the companies referred to in Article 58.

[13] I come finally to Article 221, which is concerned with the participation in the capital of companies or firms. That article provides as follows:

> Within three years of the entry into force of this Treaty, Member States shall accord nationals of the other Member States the same treatment as their own nationals as regards participation in the capital of companies or firms within the meaning of Article 58, without prejudice to the application of the other provisions of this Treaty.

[14] On the basis of these articles it was argued on behalf of the applicants that they had a number of relevant rights under Community law, including the following:

  (a) the right not to be discriminated against on the grounds of nationality (Article 7);
  (b) the right in the case of the individuals to establish a business anywhere in the EEC (Article 52) (including the right to carry on fishing at sea) and, in the case of the companies (Article 58); and
  (c) the right in the case of the individual applicants to participate in the capital of the applicant companies (Article 221).

[15] It was further argued that these provisions of Community law were provisions which had direct effect and that the applicants' rights would be infringed by the application to them of the 1988 Act and the 1988 Regulations. It was submitted that these rights were fundamental rights which could not be swept away or submerged by the Common Fisheries Policy and that all provisions of the Common Fisheries Policy had to be read subject to these fundamental provisions.

[16] On behalf of the Secretary of State, on the other hand, it was argued that the provisions of the Treaty were of no direct relevance in this case because each Member State has a sovereign right to decide questions of nationality: that is, who are permitted to be nationals and who are permitted to fly the national flag. In the alternative, it was argued, the whole matter was governed by the Common Fisheries Policy, which was established to cope with the special problems in the fishing industry and which recognised the importance, and the need for protection, of national fishing fleets and national fishing communities, and that the legislation merely gave effect to the Common Fisheries Policy and was therefore wholly consistent with the Community law.

[17] It is therefore necessary to make some reference to the history and purpose of the Common Fisheries Policy. The Common Fisheries Policy was established in October 1970 before the United Kingdom acceded to the Common Market. We were referred to Regulation 2141/70 of 20 October 1970, which laid down a common structural policy for the fishing industry. We were also referred to Regulation 2142/70 of the same date in 1970, which established the common organisation of the market in fishery products. The recitals in these regulations are of importance but, as they are reflected in later regulations, for the sake of brevity I shall not refer to them in extenso in this judgment.

[18] The United Kingdom acceded to the EEC on 1 January 1973. Since that time the powers of Ministers contained in the Sea Fish (Conservation) Act 1967, as amended, to regulate fisheries has been subject to the provisions of the Common Fisheries Policy.

[19] In 1976 Regulation 2141/71 was repealed and replaced by Regulation 101/76. It will be convenient, to indicate the nature of the Common Fisheries Policy, to refer to the first five recitals in that 1976 Regulation:

> Whereas the establishment of a common organisation of the market in fishery products must be supplemented by the establishment of a common structural policy for the fishing industry;
>
> Whereas sea fisheries form the most important part of the fishing industry as a whole; whereas they have their own social structure and fish under special conditions;
>
> Whereas, subject to certain specific conditions concerning the flag or the registration of their ships, Community fishermen must have equal access to and use of fishing grounds in maritime waters coming under the sovereignty or within the jurisdiction of Member States;
>
> Whereas the Community must be able to adopt measures to safeguard the stocks of fish present in the waters in question;
>
> Whereas it is important that the fishing industry should develop along rational lines and that those who live by that industry should be assured of a fair standard of living; whereas, to that end, Member States should be authorised to grant financial aid so that these aims may be achieved in accordance with Community rules to be laid down; whereas, moreover, common action to achieve these aims may be financed by the Community, if it relates to the aims referred to in Article 39(1)(a) of the Treaty.

[20] When the Common Fisheries Policy was first established it was then contemplated that the vessels of all Member States should be free to fish up to the beaches of other Member States. In time, however, this policy was changed. By the Hague Resolution of November 1976 the Common Fisheries Policy was extended so as to create a two hundred mile fishing zone in the Community with effect from 1 January 1977. At the same time the Council was empowered to conduct negotiations with other countries outside the EEC with a view to reaching agreement about the use by these countries of their traditional fishing grounds, which fell within the new two hundred mile limit.

[21] The basic rules of the current Common Fisheries Policy are contained in Regulation 170/83, dated 25 January 1983. I shall have to refer to some of the provisions of this regulation in a moment. First, however, I should refer to the Council's declaration on the Common Fisheries Policy which was made in Brussels on 30 May 1980. That provides as follows:

1   The Council agrees that the completion of the common fisheries policy is a concomitant part in the solution of the problems with which the Community is confronted at present. To this end the Council undertakes to adopt, in parallel with the application of the decisions which will be taken in other areas, the decisions necessary to ensure that a common overall fisheries policy is put into effect at the latest on 1 January 1981.

2   In compliance with the Treaties and in conformity with the Council Resolution of 3 November 1976 (the 'Hague agreement'), this policy should be based on the following guidelines–

     (a) rational and non discriminatory Community measures for the management of resources, and conservation and reconstitution of stocks so as to ensure their exploitation on a lasting basis in appropriate social and economic conditions;

     (b) fair distribution of catches having regard most particularly to traditional fishing activities, to the special needs of regions where the local populations are particularly dependent upon fishing and industries allied thereto and to the loss of catch;

     (c) effective controls on the conditions applying to fisheries;

(d) adoption of structural measures which include a financial contribution by the Community;

(e) establishment of securely-based fisheries relations with third countries and implementation of agreements already negotiated. In addition, endeavours should be made to conclude further agreements on fishing possibilities, in which the Community – subject to the maintenance of stability on the Community market could also offer trade concessions.

I do not think it is necessary to read paragraphs 3 and 4 of that Regulation. I come back now to Regulation 170/83. The first recital was in these terms:

Whereas the Council of the European Communities has agreed that the Member States should act in concert to extend their fishing zones to 200 nautical miles with effect from 1 January 1977 along their North Sea and North Atlantic coastlines, without prejudice to action of the same kind in respect of other fishing zones within their jurisdiction, in particular in the Mediterranean; whereas, since that time and on this basis, the Member States concerned have also extended their fishing limits in certain areas of the West Atlantic, the Skagerrak and the Kattegat and the Baltic Sea; over-fishing of stocks of the main species, it is essential that the Community, in the interests of both fishermen and consumers, ensure by an appropriate policy for the protection of fishing grounds that stocks are conserved and reconstituted; whereas it is therefore desirable that the provisions of Council Regulation 101/76 of 19 January 1976 laying down a common structure policy for the fishing industry be supplemented by the establishment of a Community system for the conservation and management of fishery resources that will ensure balanced exploitation ...

Then there are further recitals which refer to provision about regulation of overall catches. The fourth recital says this:

Whereas the overall catch should be distributed among the Member States.

And the sixth recital says:

Whereas, in other respects, that stability, given the temporary biological situation of stocks, must safeguard the particular needs of regions where local populations are especially dependent on fisheries and related industries as decided by the Council in its resolution of 3 November 1976 and in particular Annex VII thereto.

The twelfth recital, which I think is the only other one that I need read for present purposes, provides:

Whereas the creation of a Community system for the conservation and management of fishery resources should be accompanied by the institution of an effective system of supervision of activities in the fishing grounds and on landing.

Three of the Articles of that regulation are relevant. Article 1 provides:

In order to ensure the protection of fishing grounds, the conservation of the biological resources of the sea and their balanced exploitation on a lasting basis and in appropriate economic and social conditions, a Community system for the conservation and management of fishery resources is hereby established.

For these purposes, the system will consist, in particular, of conservation measures, rules for the use and distribution of resources, special provisions for coastal fishing and supervisory measures.

Article 4 provides:

1   The volume of the catches available to the Community referred to in Article 3 shall be distributed between the Member States in a manner which assures each Member State relative stability of fishing activities for each of the stocks considered.

Article 5 provides:

> 1   Member States may exchange all or part of the quotas in respect of a species or group of species allocated to them under Article 4 provided that prior notice is given to the Commission.
>
> 2   Member States shall determine, in accordance with the applicable Community provisions, the detailed rules for the utilisation of the quotas allocated to them. Detailed rules for the application of this paragraph shall be adopted, if necessary, in accordance with the procedure laid down in Article 14.

In addition, we were referred to Regulation 2057/82, made in June 1982 to establish certain control measures for fishing activities for fishing vessels of the Member States. I draw attention to this regulation, because it refers to fishing vessels 'flying the flag' of a Member State. The first recital is in these terms:

> Whereas for catches by fishing vessels flying the flag of, or registered in, a Member State it is important to adopt rules for the control of catches in order to ensure that the limits fixed elsewhere for permissible levels of fishing are observed.

We were referred to a number of other recitals in that regulation, which I do not propose to read at this stage. Title I of the regulation was concerned with the inspection of fishing vessels and their activities and, by Article 1, each Member State was required, within ports situated within its territory and within its maritime waters, to inspect their fishing vessels 'flying the flag of, or registered' in a Member State. Our attention was also drawn to other references to 'fishing vessels flying the flag of or registered in a Member State' contained in Articles 3, 6 and 10 of Regulation 2057/82. Particular importance in this context was attached to paragraph 1 of Article 10 of this regulation, which has now been reproduced as Article 11 of Regulation 2241/87. These Articles are in these terms:

> All catches of a stock or group of stocks subject to quota made by fishing vessels flying the flag of a Member State or registered in a Member State shall be charged against the quota applicable to that State for the stock or group of stocks in question, irrespective of the place of landing.

Regulation 172/83 is also of importance. That regulation fixed the total allowable catches for 1982 and the share of those catches available to the Community, the allocation of that share between Member States and the conditions under which the total allowable catches might be fished. The recitals for this regulation refer to the interests of fishermen, to the fair allocation of total allowable catches among the Member States and, in the fourth recital, provided that particular account was to be taken of traditional fishing activities, the specific needs of areas particularly dependent on fishing and its dependent industries, and the loss of fishing potential in the waters of third countries.

[22] On the basis of these regulations, to which I have drawn attention, and later regulations including Regulation 2241/87, it was emphasised on behalf of the Secretary of State that these regulations repeatedly underlined the importance of the protection of traditional fishing activities, the special needs, of regions where local populations depended upon fishing and industries allied thereto, and the importance of distributing the available fish between the Member States in a manner which ensured each Member State relative stability of fishing activities for each of the stocks which was subject to protection. The regulations, as I have already noted, also made reference to fishing vessels 'flying the flag' of a Member State.

[23] The system adopted by the Council to ensure fair distribution was by the establishment of national quotas. These national quotas were directly linked to vessels flying the flag or registered in the individual Member State. As I have already observed, in Article 10 of the 1983 and Article 11 of the 1987 Regulations, all relevant fish caught by vessels flying the flag counted against the quota of that State. In order to decide how to share out the

available fish between Member States the Council took into account the quantities of fish which had been caught, on average, by the fishing fleets of the relevant State between 1973 and 1978.

[24] Once the area governed by the Common Fisheries Policy was extended as from January 1977 to a range of two hundred miles from the coastline of Member States, the Common Fisheries policy began to make an impact on areas of the Eastern Atlantic, including the Western Approaches, which had traditionally been fished by Spanish fishing vessels. Prior to the accession of Spain to the Community in 1986, the rights of Spain to fish in the waters of the Member States was governed by an agreement reached between the EEC and Spain in 1980. This agreement laid down strict limits on fishing by Spanish registered boats.

[25] The principle of national quotas was incorporated into the Act of Accession of 1985 whereby Spain and Portugal became members of the EEC. The Act of Accession prohibited more than 150 Spanish fishing vessels fishing in specified areas.

[26] From about 1980 onwards the applicants and others began to register vessels which had formerly been Spanish fishing vessels (that is, vessels which had formerly flown the flag of Spain) as British fishing vessels under the Merchant Shipping Act 1894. Some 53 of these vessels are those owned by the applicants. In addition, the applicants and others bought British fishing vessels with a view to using them for fishing in the area covered by the Common Fisheries Policy. The fish were, in the main, destined for the Spanish market.

[27] As time went by the United Kingdom Government became concerned at the growth of the practice whereby Spanish interests were either buying British fishing vessels or re-registering Spanish vessels under the Merchant Shipping Act 1894. The United Kingdom Government therefore decided to make use of the powers contained in section 4 of the Sea Fish (Conservation) Act 1967 to impose some additional conditions for the licences which are required before fishing for stocks which are subject to quotas under the Common Fisheries Policy by vessels ten metres length and over.

[28] These new conditions were announced on 6 December 1985. The conditions were of three kinds; operating, crewing and social security. The conditions were described by Mr Noble in his first affidavit in paragraph 22, and can be summarised as follows. The operating conditions were designed to ensure that the vessels concerned had a real economic link with the United Kingdom ports. That link was to be demonstrated in one of two ways; firstly, by selling a portion of the catch in the United Kingdom (the landing test) or, secondly, by making a specified number of visits to the United Kingdom (the visiting test). The crewing condition required that at least 75% of the crew should be made up of EEC nationals (excluding, for a period, nationals of Spain, Greece and Portugal) ordinarily resident in the United Kingdom. The social security condition required that all the crew should contribute to the United Kingdom's National Insurance Scheme. These conditions came into force in January 1986. They have been challenged by Spanish interests in the European Court in Luxembourg. It has been contended that they are contrary to Community law. The decision of the European Court in the two relevant references is now awaited. The cases have been brought respectively, at the suit of a company called Agegate Ltd and another company called Jaderow Ltd.

[29] In the course of the argument we were referred to the opinions in these two cases of Mischo AG in which he expressed views about the validity of the conditions. In summary, his opinion was this: that the crewing and social security conditions were valid, that the visiting test would be valid provided it did not interfere with exports, but that the landing test (included as part of the operating conditions) was in breach of Article 34 of the EEC Treaty. It should be remembered that earlier I referred to the terms of Article 34.

[30] It has been the contention of the Secretary of State that these conditions have not been observed by the applicants and that the further measures prescribed in the 1988 Act and the 1988 Regulations have been necessary to secure that the purposes of the Common Fisheries Policy are duly carried out, and also to ensure that proper policing and safety control are improved.

[31] Such then, in summary, is the background to this case and these are the relevant provisions both of the Treaty and of the Common Fisheries Policy to which our attention was particularly directed.

[32] In these circumstances, the first question for the consideration of this court is whether it would be right to try to resolve the issues between the parties ourselves or whether we should make a reference to the European Court in accordance with Article 177. In many cases it is right for a court of first instance to attempt to reach a conclusion itself and leave it to a higher court to make a reference to Luxembourg if that is thought appropriate. In the present case, however, I have no hesitation whatever in concluding that we should make a reference now. It is appropriate to look at the terms of Article 177, which provides as follows:

> The Court of Justice shall have jurisdiction to give preliminary rulings concerning:
> (a) the interpretation of this Treaty;
> (b) the validity and interpretation of acts of the institutions of the Community;
> (c) the interpretation of the statutes of bodies established by an act of the Council, where those statutes so provide.
>
> Where such a question is raised before any court or tribunal of a Member State, that court or tribunal may, if it considers that a decision on the question is necessary to enable it to give judgment, request the Court of Justice to give a ruling thereon.

It is apparent, therefore, that before a reference could be made two matters call for consideration. First, the court can only refer the matter to the European Court if it considers that a decision on the question is 'necessary to enable it to give judgment'. It is common ground in the present case that it is necessary to reach a decision on a question of Community law for the purpose of resolving the present case. Thus, it is necessary to determine the interrelation between Community law and the right of a Member State to determine nationality and the conditions which it can impose on those who wish to fly the national flag. It is also necessary to determine the interrelation between Community law as expressed in the Treaty and the special provisions of the Common Fisheries Policy.

[33] Once it has been established that a decision on the question is necessary, it is then for consideration whether the court in the exercise of its discretion should make the reference. The guidelines on the way in which this discretion should be exercised have been laid down in a number of cases, including in particular, *Bulmer v Bollinger* [1974]; *Customs & Excise Commissioners v Samex* [1983]; and *R v Pharmaceutical Society of Great Britain* [1987]. It will be convenient to refer to the judgment of Kerr LJ in the *Pharmaceutical Society* case at p 970, where he says this:

> Many factors may be relevant in considering the exercise of the discretion under the penultimate paragraph of Article 177. The judgment of Lord Denning MR, in *Bulmer Ltd v Bollinger SA* contains a useful list of guidelines which have stood the test of time. They were helpfully reviewed by Bingham J in the Commercial Court in *Customs and Excise Commissioners v Samex*. I do not find it necessary for present purposes to go through these. But I think that the following short extract from this valuable judgment is of considerable relevance to the present case. At p 1055G Bingham J said:
> Sitting as a judge in a national court, asked to decide questions of Community law, I am very conscious of the advantages enjoyed by the Court of Justice. It has a panoramic view of the

Community and its institutions, a detailed knowledge of the Treaties and of much subordinate legislation made under them, and an intimate familiarity with the functioning of the Community market which no national judge denied the collective experience of the Court of Justice could hope to achieve. Where questions of administrative intention and practice arise the Court of Justice can receive submissions from the Community institutions ... Where the interests of Member States are affected they can intervene to make their views known. That is a material consideration in this case since there is some slight evidence that the practice of different Member States is divergent.

Later Kerr LJ added this:

The English authorities show that our courts should exercise great caution in relying on the doctrine of 'acte clair' as a ground for declining to make a reference.

[34] In the present case the Court in Luxembourg is, in my view, in a much better position than any national court to place the provisions of the Common Fisheries Policy in the wider context of the Treaty provisions as a whole. It can also examine, from the point of view of the Community, the important and far-reaching submissions put forward on behalf of the Secretary of State that a Member State is free to determine who is to fly the national flag of a commercial fishing vessel irrespective of any restraints which might appear to be enshrined in the Treaty. I should record that on this aspect of the case the Solicitor General attaches great importance to paragraphs 7 and 9 of the opinion of the Advocate General in the *Jaderow* case, and to a passage in the judgment of *Pesca Valentia Ltd v Minister for Fisheries* [1988]. It is sufficient at this stage merely to cite the opening sentence of paragraph 7 of the Advocate General's opinion:

The Community law does not there restrict the power which each Member State has under public international law to determine the conditions on which it allows a vessel to fly its flag.

Furthermore, the European Court is much better placed than we are to consider the issue of proportionality. Thus the applicants seek to contend that, in any event, the desired objectives for protecting the fishing communities could be achieved by less restrictive measures. It is also to be assumed that in the present case other Member States, including perhaps Ireland and Spain, may wish to intervene.

[35] Having reached a clear and unambiguous conclusion on that aspect of the case, I must therefore turn to a question of greater difficulty; namely, whether this court has any jurisdiction to grant interim relief pending the determination of the reference. The question of interim relief is, it is said, of crucial importance in the present case because, according to the information which was given to us during the course of the hearing of the appeal, a decision may not be reached by the Court in Luxembourg until about the beginning of 1991.

The application for interim relief

[36] It is accepted on behalf of the Secretary of State that, at any rate in this court, there is binding authority for the proposition that in proceedings for judicial review interim relief by way of an injunction or stay of proceedings is available against the Crown. In *R v Licensing Authority ex p Smith Kline & French Laboratories (No 2)* [1989] the Court of Appeal by a majority approved the decision of my Lord, Hodgson J, in *R v Home Secretary ex p Herbage* [1987]. At p 393G Woolf LJ adopted the reasoning of Hodgson J in *Herbage* at p 886 of the Queen's Bench Report, and Taylor LJ expressed his concurrence at pages 395 to 396.

[37] I understand that the Secretary of State may seek to argue elsewhere that the decision on this matter in Herbage and the majority decision in *Smith, Kline & French (No 2)* are wrong. For present purposes, however, I must proceed on the basis that there is jurisdiction in an appropriate case to grant interim relief against the Crown.

[38] The submission on behalf of the Secretary of State is that, even if interim relief may be available in other cases, the court has no jurisdiction to grant such relief in the present case. In the alternative, it is submitted that as a matter of discretion such relief should not be granted.

[39] The submission on jurisdiction has been put forward on the following lines, which are conveniently summarised in paragraphs in Part 5 of the skeleton argument which has been put before us as follows:

> In the case of delegated legislation [that is the Regulations] it is a well established principle of English law that duly passed legislation is to be enforced unless and until it is declared invalid.
>
> The court cannot grant interim relief in respect of an Act of Parliament [the Merchant Shipping Act 1988].
>
> In any event the position in respect of an Act of Parliament must be stronger than the position in respect of delegated legislation.
>
> There is nothing in Community law which requires the granting of interim relief against a measure which is alleged to be contrary to the Treaty.

[40] The Solicitor General has referred us to the speeches in the House of Lords in *Hoffmann-La Roche v Secretary of State for Trade and Industry* [1975] AC 295 in support of the proposition that, unless and until a statutory instrument is declared to be invalid, it is effective and has the full force of law. This proposition must also apply, even more strongly, in the case of an Act of Parliament: unless and until an Act of Parliament has been disapplied the court cannot make any order which has the effect of preventing the law as declared by Parliament being enforced. It may be, it was said, that in certain circumstances the court will not grant an injunction to enforce a statutory instrument which is impugned as being contrary to Community law, but this does not mean that an English court can take some step by way of injunction or otherwise to prevent the enforcement of a statutory instrument, yet alone the enforcement of a statute.

[41] I should refer to the passages in *Hoffmann-La Roche* on which the Solicitor General placed particular reliance. Lord Reid said this:

> It must be borne in mind that an order made under statutory authority is as much the law of the land as an Act of Parliament unless and until it has been found to be *ultra vires*.

Lord Morris said:

> The order [one which has been affirmed by resolution both in the House of Commons and the House of Lords] then undoubtedly had the force of law. Obedience to it was just as obligatory as would be obedience to an Act of Parliament. There was only the difference that whereas the courts of law could not declare that an Act of Parliament was *ultra vires* it might be possible for courts of law to declare that the making of the order (even though affirmatively approved by Parliament) was not warranted within the terms of the statutory enactments from which it purported to derive its validity.

Finally, a passage in the speech of Lord Diplock where, under the heading 'The legal status of the order' he said this:

> My Lords, in constitutional law a clear distinction can be drawn between an Act of Parliament and subordinate legislation, even though the latter is contained in an order made by statutory instrument approved by resolutions of both Houses of Parliament. Despite this indication that the majority of members of both Houses of the contemporary Parliament regard the order as being for the common weal, I entertain no doubt that the courts have jurisdiction to declare it to be invalid if they are satisfied that in making it the Minister who did so acted outwith the legislative powers conferred upon him by the previous Act of Parliament under which the order purported to be made, and this is so whether the order is *ultra vires* by reason of its contents (patent defects) or by reason of defects in the procedure followed prior to its being

made (latent defects). In so far as there are passages in the judgment of Lord Denning MR in the instant case which may appear to suggest the contrary. I think that they are wrong. Under our legal system, however, the courts as the judicial arm of government do not act on their own initiative. Their jurisdiction to determine that a statutory instrument is *ultra vires* does not arise until its validity is challenged in proceedings inter partes either brought by one party to enforce the law declared by the instrument against another party or brought by a party whose interests are affected by the law so declared sufficiently directly to give him *locus standi* to initiate proceedings to challenge the validity of the instrument. Unless there is such a challenge and, if there is, until it has been upheld by judgment of the court, the validity of the statutory instrument and the legality of acts done pursuant to the law declared by it are presumed.

It followed, submitted the Solicitor General, that if the court referred the question of the validity of section 14 and the Regulations to the European Court and made no decision itself, the 1988 Act and the 1988 Regulations remained in full force and effect meanwhile.

[42] I find this a very formidable submission. I am not satisfied, however, that this approach takes sufficient account of the new state of affairs which came into being when the United Kingdom became a Member State of the European Community in January 1973. Twenty years ago the idea that the High Court could question the validity of an Act of Parliament or fail, having construed it, to give effect to it would have been unthinkable. But the High Court now has the duty to take account of and to give effect to European Community law and, where there is a conflict, to prefer the Community law to national law. The judgment of the European Court in *Simmenthal* 1978 is clear. At p 644 appears this passage:

> every national court must, in a case within its jurisdiction, apply Community law in its entirety and protect rights which the latter confers on individuals and must accordingly [disapply] any provision of national law which may conflict with it, whether prior or subsequent to the Community rule.

The reason for this is that since the European Communities Act 1972 came into force Community law has been part of English law; where it applies it takes precedence over both primary and secondary legislation. I should refer to part of section 2 of the European Communities Act 1972. Section 2(1) is in these terms:

> All such rights, powers. liabilities. obligations and restrictions from time to time created or arising by or under the Treaties, and all such remedies and procedures from time to time provided for by or under the Treaties, as in accordance with the Treaties are without further enactment to be given legal effect or used in the United Kingdom shall be recognised and available in law, and be enforced, allowed and followed accordingly; and the expression 'enforceable Community right' and similar expressions shall be read as referring to one to which this subsection applies.

I should read part of subsection 4:

> ... any enactment passed or to be passed, other than one contained in this Part of this Act, shall be construed and have effect subject to the foregoing provisions of this section; but, except as maybe provided by any Act passed after this Act, Schedule 2 shall have effect in connection with the powers conferred by this and the following sections of this Act to make Orders in Council and regulations.

The effect of that central part of subsection (4), together with section 2(1) is this, as I understand it: that directly applicable Community provisions are to prevail not only over existing but also over future Acts of Parliament (that is, Acts subsequent to 1972) in so far as those provisions may be inconsistent with such enactments.

[43] For my part, I do not propose to express even a tentative view of the likely result in the present reference, but neither side's arguments in my judgment can be described as

weak. They both merit the most careful scrutiny. The applicants' contentions invoke the support of fundamental principles of the Treaty of Rome. The Solicitor General relies on sovereign rights over nationality, and on the special provisions of the Common Fisheries Policy. In these circumstances I think it is right to look at the matter on the basis that the cogent and important arguments put forward on behalf of the applicants are to be set against arguments of a like weight urged with equal force on behalf of the Secretary of State.

[44] What follows from this? In my view, one cannot overemphasise the importance of the principle that, where applicable, Community law is part of the law of England. I should refer to a short passage in the judgment of Lord Denning MR in *Macarthys Ltd v Smith*. In that case the Court of Appeal referred certain questions to the European Court as to the effect of Article 119 of the Treaty on the provisions of the Equal Pay Act 1970. The European Court made a ruling in the matter. It came back to the Court of Appeal and Lord Denning said this:

> It is important now to declare – and it must be made plain – that the provisions of Article 119 of the EEC Treaty take priority over anything in our English statute on equal pay which is inconsistent with Article 119. That priority is given by our own law. It is given by the European Communities Act 1972 itself. Community law is now part of our law; and whenever there is any inconsistency Community law has priority. It is not supplanting English law. It is part of our law which overrides any other part which is inconsistent with it.

Then he turned to consider the facts of that case.

[45] At this stage no decision has been made. Is there some presumption in those circumstances in favour of the recent statute? The Solicitor General in the course of his argument placed reliance on a passage in the decision of the Court of Appeal in *Portsmouth City Council v Richards* which, as far as I know, is not reported but of which we have been provided with a transcript. Judgment was given on 16 November 1988. In the course of his judgment in that case Kerr LJ referred to a statement made by Lord Donaldson MR on the application which had come before the Court of Appeal earlier to adjourn the appeal. Kerr LJ said this:

> Secondly, I echo four sentences from the judgment of the Master of the Rolls on the application to adjourn the appeal in this case, which I have already read; but I repeat them for convenience:
> It is unarguably the case that the mere fact that [there is] a pending reference to the European Court is no ground for refusing interlocutory relief on the basis that the European Court of Justice may say that the Act is void. I can see no difference between the position of the European Court of Justice and the House of Lords. We must continue to enforce the law as it appears to us until we are informed otherwise.

On behalf of the applicants, on the other hand, reliance was placed on the decision in *Polydor Ltd v Harlequin Record Shops Ltd*, where the Court of Appeal refused to grant an injunction to enforce a prohibition on importation contained in section 16(2) of the Copyright Act 1956.

[46] From these cases I obtain this guidance. If the applicants for interim relief have only a weak case the court should not, and probably cannot, grant relief. In the words of the Master of the Rolls, as cited by Kerr LJ in the *Portsmouth* case, the court must enforce the law as it appears to the court to be. The decision in Polydor is really to the same effect. In that case the court took the view that Article 14 of the Portuguese Treaty was indistinguishable from Article 30 of the Treaty of Rome and that therefore, though the final decision rested with the European Court, the plaintiffs claim to have certain rights under the English statute should not be enforced. It appeared to the court that the law was that contained in the provisions of the Treaties.

[47] In the present case, however, I find myself unable at this stage to say what law ought to be enforced. Is section 14 to be applied *simpliciter* unless and until it is disapplied,

or should it be read provisionally as being subject to an unexpressed exception excluding those who may have superior rights by virtue of section 2 of the 1972 Act and the relevant articles the Treaty? The European Court itself can make interim orders, as is set out in Articles 185 and 186, but we were not referred to any authorities which show in what circumstances orders under these Articles are made. In any event, it would be some time before this case could come before the Court in Luxembourg, even on an interlocutory basis.

[48] In these circumstances I am satisfied that there is jurisdiction to grant interim relief. It exists in the national court to ensure that justice can be done. Moreover, it is to be remembered that the effect of any interim order in this case is only to suspend the coming into force of the time limit prescribed by statutory instrument. The court is not in a position at this stage to decide what the law is but, in my view, it can preserve the position for the time being if, in the exercise of its discretion, it considers it right to do so.

[49] I turn therefore to the issue of discretion. It is said on behalf of the applicants that if no interim relief is granted the financial consequences for them would be disastrous. The vessels would either have to be sold or laid up and substantial unemployment would be an inevitable consequence. It is stressed that the applicants have no alternative grounds in which they can fish. Moreover, as the law stands at present the applicants have no prospects – at any rate, in any court below the House of Lords recovering damages if they are ultimately successful before the European Court (see *Bourgoin SA v Ministry of Agriculture, Fisheries And Food*).

[50] It is further argued that in the case of certain ports, and, in particular, Milford Haven, the activities of some of the applicants bring substantial benefits to the local community. Details of this contention are set out in the supporting affidavits, including those of Mr John Couceiro, a director of Jaderow Ltd.

[51] At this stage I should also refer to the special position of Rawlings, which is explained by Mr Ramon Yllera, the Managing Director of that company, in his affidavit sworn on 20 February 1989. I should read some of the paragraphs of that affidavit to explain the facts relevant to that company:

3   Rawlings is a limited company incorporated in the UK in April 1980. Rawlings is the legal and beneficial owner of the fishing vessel 'Brisca' which is currently a British fishing boat within the meaning of the 1983 Act being registered under Part IV of the Merchant Shipping Act 1894.

4   Rawlings is a company the business of which is wholly carried on in the UK and which is controlled from the UK. It thus satisfies the first test of 'qualified company' in section 14(7)(a). However, although the two directors of Rawlings are both resident in the UK, the condition as to the relevant percentage of the director being of British nationality is not satisfied. This is because I am a Spanish citizen, though I have lived in Milford Haven with my wife and family since June 1986. The other director is John Edwin Crawford, a British citizen who resides in Neyland, Pembrokeshire and who satisfies, I believe, the test in the 1988 Act of a qualified person.

Then he sets out in paragraph 5 the fact that Rawlings employ 14 people, most of whom live in the Milford Haven area. He points out that the *Brisca* is the only vessel which, at the moment, Rawlings owns and operates. Then, in the subsequent paragraphs (particularly at paragraph 15) he sets out the operations of *Brisca* and the difficulties which would result if no interim relief were granted. He says that it would have serious and immediate financial consequences, and also draws attention to the fact that, because of the conditions attaching to the grants for the construction of the vessel, Rawlings cannot dispose of the vessel without the permission of the relevant authorities. Again, for the sake of brevity, I do not propose to read any other part of the affidavit; it can be referred to for the particular facts which are relevant to the case of that applicant.

[52] It is said on behalf of the Secretary of State, on the other hand, that the activities of the applicants are causing very considerable damage to what is described as 'the genuine British fleet', the concern of the Crown is more fully explained in the affidavits which have been sworn by Mr Noble, to which reference can be made. I merely summarise some of the contentions, which are as follows:

(1) the applicants are not part of the genuine British fleet;

(2) the activities of the applicants are hard to police;

(3) in the past (although, it is right to say, now to a lesser degree) fishing by the applicants and other Spanish owned vessels has led to the British quotas being exceeded, particularly in the case of Western Hake, which is a variety of fish which attracts a good price on the Spanish market;

(4) the suggested benefits to which reference was made on behalf of the applicants, to British ports (including, in particular, Milford Haven) are much exaggerated by the applicants and do little, it is said. to reduce the damage to the genuine fishing communities.

[53] In addition, it is submitted on behalf of the Secretary of State that, as this is a public law measure, the ordinary principles laid down in *American Cyanamid* have to be modified to take account of the public interest as expressed both in the Act and, as it is said, in the Common Fisheries Policy, which is specifically designed to protect national communities.

[54] There remain some issues of fact between the parties as to the extent to which the applicants are complying with conditions relating to visits and such matters its periodic surveys. The area of dispute has, however, now been much reduced and it seems that in broad terms the conditions which the Secretary of State seeks to impose are being observed to a substantial degree. The details are set out in schedules which have been put before the court, and to which reference has been made. It is also relevant to record that the applicants have stated that, in so far as any conditions which may be in dispute in the two pending references before the European Community are upheld as valid, they will comply with these conditions.

[55] I see the force of the argument that, if the Common Fisheries Policy is intended to protect traditional fishing communities of the Member States, great importance must be given to any measures which are designed for that purpose. In the present case, however, I am not in the end persuaded on the present evidence that there are identifiable persons or communities whose activities or livelihood are at present being so seriously damaged, or will be so seriously damaged, as to outweigh the very obvious and immediate damage which would be caused by these new provisions if no interim relief were granted to the applicants. The present state of affairs has continued for some time. The applicants are making efforts to comply with the conditions to which they have for the time being agreed, and they have expressed a willingness to comply with all such conditions as may be upheld in the two outstanding references. It is also relevant to note the opinion expressed by the Advocate General in paragraph 41 of his opinion in the *Jaderow* case: the condition that 75% of the fishermen fishing against the quotas of a Member State must ordinarily reside in that Member State and the rule requiring a vessel's periodic presence in a port of that country seems to me sufficient to ensure that the benefit of that Member State's quota actually goes to those truly forming part of that Member State's fishing Community.'

[56] I would therefore exercise my discretion in favour of granting some interim relief. The exact terms of this relief may require to be further considered. I would, however, make two further observations.

1   For my part, I would expect it to be very unusual for a court to exercise its discretion in favour of granting relief against the application of a statute or statutory instrument. In the present case, however, there is a European dimension of great importance, and the whole

matter has to be looked at in the context of a gradually developing problem of significance not only to this country but to other countries as well.

2   The continuance of any interim relief should, in my view, be dependent on the proper observance by the applicants of the condition of their licences which may from time to time be lawfully imposed.

[57] Subject to these matters, I would refer the case to the European Court in accordance with Article 177 of the Treaty and, in the meantime, would grant interim relief to the applicants.

Hodgson J: [58] The applicants, with leave, seek judicial review of two decisions of the respondent Secretary of State and of Part II of the Merchant Shipping Act 1988. The relief sought is a declaration backed by prohibition and damages. It is clear that if, now or hereafter, we grant relief the grant will involve holding that the provisions of an Act of Parliament which, in terms, apply to the applicants do not so apply because they contravene Community law.

[59] It is, I think, important to remember that the applicants are seeking a final order. These are not interlocutory proceedings. Were it not for the provisions of Article 177 we should be required today either to grant relief or dismiss the application. Article 177 however, uniquely in English law, gives the court a discretion to refer questions to another court, that of Europe. If we do refer that will mean that we cannot give the decision now which hereafter we shall have to give. By the court's own motion the parties' right to a decision will be delayed.

[60] The first question to which, therefore, we must address ourselves is whether or not at this stage to make a reference under Article 177. After several days of argument, and the citation of much European authority, we are as well equipped to resolve what is or may be in conflict between United Kingdom measures and directly effective provisions of EEC law as an English court could be. Nevertheless, I have no doubt that we ought to make a reference. I so conclude for these reasons:

(1)   Speaking entirely for myself, I realise that I am not well qualified 'to place in its context every provision of Community law nor to interpret it in the light of Community law as a whole'. I take that quotation from CILFIT, Case 283/81, paragraph 20. The whole paragraph is even more intimidating to an English judge. It reads:

> Finally, every provision of Community law must be placed in its context and interpreted in the light of the provisions of Community law as a whole, regard being had to the objectives thereof and to its state of evolution at the date on which the provision in question is to be applied.

The relationship between the Common Fisheries Policy and the articles of the Treaty of Rome, in particular Article 7 (discrimination on grounds of nationality), Article 52 (right of establishment) and Article 221, the extent to which the provisions of the Treaty affect the right a Member State to determine the conditions of eligibility for fishing vessels to have access to its flag and questions of proportionality seem to me to be matters much better left to the European Court's decision.

(2)   It is of great importance that decisions in the field of administrative law should be given as speedily as possible. It is abundantly clear that, sooner or later, there will be a reference to the European Court. It seems to me that the sooner it is done the better.

(3)   It seems to me also that most of the criteria referred to by Lord Denning MR in *HP Bulmer Ltd v J Bollinger SA*, which favour a reference, apply to this case. The answers to the questions to be asked will be conclusive, there have been no previous rulings on the points raised in the case, no one suggests they are *acte clair*, the facts are sufficiently decided and the questions can be formulated clearly. I do not think anyone underestimates the difficulty and importance of the issues raised.

[61] If we make a reference under Article 177 two things remain to be decided. First, do we have jurisdiction to make an interim order pending an answer to the questions referred? Second, if we have jurisdiction, should we in our discretion exercise it?

[62] The question whether a court has jurisdiction to make an interim order to retain the status quo pending a reference under Article 177 is, of course, one that would never have arisen before the United Kingdom's accession to the Treaty of Rome. Before that a court had no need to consider the question. It was obliged to give its decision there and then, and there was no room for the grant of interim relief. It is not, therefore, surprising that there is a lack of authority on the question.

[63] The respondents rely mainly of [sic] the decision of the House of Lords in *Hoffmann-La Roche v Secretary of State for Trade* to support their submission that the court had no jurisdiction to grant interim relief. I do not think that that decision addressed, or is more than marginally relevant to the question which faces us. It was decided at a time when it was unthinkable that there should be in an English court a higher authority than an Act of Parliament: but there is now in English law such a higher authority. My Lord, Neil LJ has cited the *dictum* of Lord Denning MR in *Macarthys v Smith* which explains the position with his habitual clarity. *Hoffmann-La Roche* was concerned not with primary but with delegated legislation, which can be struck down by the courts on limited grounds. The whole thrust of most of the argument was that while primary legislation is inviolable, delegated legislation is not (see in particular the passage from the speech of Lord Diplock to which my Lord has referred). Primary legislation is still inviolable, save that primacy over all other law is now given to the Treaty and Community law by the European Communities Act 1972.

[64] *In Polydor Ltd and RSO Records v Harlequin Record Shops Ltd*, the plaintiffs had obtained an interlocutory injunction restraining the defendants from importing gramophone records into the United Kingdom, on the grounds that they infringed section 16(2) of the Copyright Act 1956. The Court of Appeal referred the question whether section 16(2) was equivalent to a quantitative restriction on trade under Article 30 of the Treaty to the European Court, but refused to continue the injunction so that, in effect, the English statute was not enforced during the period between reference and decision. It is true that both Ormrod LJ and Templeman LJ (as he then was) thought, erroneously as it turned out, that the plaintiffs had no case and that there was no triable issue, and on that ground the case was distinguished by Kerr LJ in *Portsmouth City Council v Richards*, of which we have been provided with a transcript. But at paragraph 63 of *Polydor*, Templeman LJ said:

> In any event, it seems to me if there had been a triable issue I would have reached the conclusion that the balance of convenience requires no injunction.

[65] *Polydor* was, of course, the obverse of the problem which faces us. There, by not continuing the injunction, the court temporarily prevented an English statute being effected, whereas we are asked to bring about the same result by granting interim relief. But I would have thought that, if the respondents' contention is the correct one, the court in *Polydor* ought to have continued the injunction. The respondent seeks to distinguish *Polydor* on the ground that the litigation was between two private individuals. That is a distinction which in my judgment, since the decision of the Court of Appeal in *R v Licensing Authority ex p Smith Kline and French (No 2)*, we are not entitled to make.

[66] In any case I find it difficult to believe that a court which has jurisdiction to make a final order disapplying the provisions of an English statute does not also have jurisdiction in a proper case to make an interim order to the same temporary effect. If the court is not constrained by authority, and I believe it is not, it seems to me clear that to deny the court the power to make an interim order would be wrong.

[67] The final question, therefore, is whether the court should make an interim order to protect the applicants during the period between our reference and the answers to our questions. Not surprisingly, there is little guidance in the cases as to what guidelines should apply. The situation is novel in two ways: first, because the possibility of a final decision being delayed because of a reference under Article 177 only arose after the United Kingdom accession to the Treaty and the passing of the European Communities Act 1972; secondly, because, until my decision in *R v Home Secretary ex p Herbage* and its subsequent approval by the Court of Appeal in *Smith Kline and French*, it was not thought to be possible to obtain an interim injunction against a Minister.

[68] In parenthesis, I may say that I share Woolf LJ's difficulty, expressed in *Smith Kline and French*, in envisaging any good reason why (as recommended by the Law Commission) a court should not be entitled to make an interim declaration.

[69] In *Polydor*, which was a case between individuals, the Court of Appeal seems to have assumed that the principles laid down in *American Cyanamid v Ethicon* would guide the decision whether to grant interim relief in the period between reference and answer. But, in my judgment, the fact that here the interim relief is sought against a Minister greatly alters the situation. In *Herbage* I expressed the view that, in such cases, the principles governing interim injunctions in civil proceedings are not particularly helpful. I added that clearly the apparent strengths and weaknesses of the two opposing cases ought to be considered. I adhere to both those opinions.

[70] Some guidance may be obtained from two decisions of the Court of Appeal in cases where interlocutory injunctions were sought against local authorities. In *R v Westminster City Council ex p Sierbien*, Dillon LJ referred to the early authority. He said this:

> The position where there is a public element and an interlocutory injunction is sought was considered by the court in the case of *Smith v Inner London Education Authority* [1978] 1 All ER 411. That was concerned with the closure of the St Marylebone Grammar School. Certain parents were challenging the Education Authority's decision to close the school. They were doing so by action rather than by application for judicial review. In the state of the law at that time, that was a possible course. They had sought an interlocutory injunction. This court refused the injunction, primarily, I think, on the view of all the members of the court that the plaintiffs in that case had not shown a serious question to be tried within the straight *Cyanamid* test. But Lord Denning (as he then was) saw merit in the suggestion that the ordinary *Cyanamid* test could not really apply to cases against local authorities in public law, and Browne LJ agreed with that and took the view that the public aspect was of considerable importance. I myself feel that in a case where what is sought to be restrained is the act of a public authority in a matter of public law, the public interest is very important to be considered and the ordinary financial considerations in the *Cyanamid* case, though no doubt to some extent relevant, must be qualified by a recognition of the public interest.

> I think these principles apply equally when the relief sought is against a Minister.

[71] In my judgment, the first step is to consider the *prima facie* cases of each side and their respective strength. Unless the court is satisfied that an applicant has a strong *prima facie* case, I think it should hesitate long before granting interim relief in the form of an injunction or stay against a Minister.

[72] It seems to me that, doing the best I can with my inadequate qualifications, the applicants have a strong *prima facie* case on each of the three main areas of contention. In so far as the most extreme position taken by the respondent is concerned, I think it faces substantial difficulties. I confess that it was only at a late stage in the argument that I appreciated that it was being contended that, in laying down the flag conditions for fishing vessels, the United Kingdom's rights were completely untrammelled by any considerations

of discrimination, the right of establishment, or, indeed, any of the fundamental Articles in the Treaty.

[73] To test this submission in argument, I asked whether it would be permissible in Community law to add to the Act a fourth condition of eligibility for registration, that the crew of the vessel should at all times consist only of British citizens resident and domiciled in the United Kingdom. I did not, I think, receive any satisfactory answer to this question; perhaps because the answer is provided by the case of *EC Commission v France* (Case 167/73), and is 'No'.

[74] We have heard much argument as to the relationship between the Common Fisheries Policy and the main body of Community law. I consider, without elaboration, that on this part of the case also the applicants have *prima facie* strong arguments to advance.

[75] So far as the impact of the Community law principle of proportionality is concerned, I am of the same opinion. In my view the applicants can draw much comfort from the opinion of Mischo AG where he says, at paragraph 41 in the *Jaderow* reference that, first, the condition that 75% of the fishermen fishing against the quotas of the Member State must ordinarily reside in that Member State, and the rule requiring a vessel's periodic presence in a port of that county, seems to be sufficient to ensure that the benefit of that Member State's quota actually goes to those truly forming part of that Member State's fishing community.

[76] Next it is necessary to consider the public interest, which comprehends both the United Kingdom interests and the interests of the Community.

[77] I do not myself think that the impact of a standstill for some two years, which seems to be the most pessimistic forecast for an answer from the European Court, will seriously affect either interest if the respondents succeed on the reference. In the United Kingdom the only people who will suffer if the Spanish shareholders eventually assigned their shares to United Kingdom domiciled residents, are those unidentifiable United Kingdom nationals who, without a standstill, might have benefited earlier from a forced sale of Spanish owned shares. I do not see how the United Kingdom fishing interest itself would be affected.

[78] So far as Community interest is concerned, although the UK quota would continue, no doubt, to be fished to capacity, there are clearly already in place effective means both at national and Community level to ensure that it is not exceeded.

[79] Lastly one has, in my judgment, to look and balance against each other what the results will be if one or other of the conflicting arguments eventually prevails. If the applicants' argument eventually prevails but no standstill is provided, they will, unless they risk defying domestic United Kingdom law, suffer serious, irreversible and perhaps uncompensatable injury, I say perhaps uncompensatable because of the decision of the Court of Appeal in *Bourgoin*, Oliver LJ (as he then was) dissenting. If the answers from Europe are in the applicants' favour they will come back to this court and ask for declaratory relief, but they will want damages too which we should be constrained by authority from awarding.

[80] Against that, if the respondents' arguments prevail the UK fishing industry will only suffer the deferment for two years of the transfer of share capital from Spanish to United Kingdom nationals.

[81] In my judgment, the balance of fairness is really all one way and I would, without hesitation, make an interim order sufficient to maintain the status quo until the European Court answers the questions posed to it. [The order finally made is set out in the Court of Appeal judgment.]

JUDGMENT (OF THE COURT OF APPEAL)

The Master of the Rolls: [1] The background to this appeal is the Common Market Fishing Policy. If stocks of fish, or at all events stocks of some varieties of fish, are to continue to exist in the seas around Europe, some system has to be devised to prevent overfishing. This in turn involves the need for fixing quotas for national fishing fleets limiting the amount of fish which each may catch.

[2] Given a quota for the British fishing fleet, the Government has been concerned to ensure that all the vessels operating as part of this fleet can properly be regarded as British. To that end in 1985 new licence conditions were established under the Sea Fish (Conservation) Act 1967.

[3] Under that system certain conditions had to be fulfilled before a vessel registered as British under the Merchant Shipping Act 1894 could fish. These licence conditions related to such matters as the proportion of the catch which was landed in the United Kingdom, the frequency with which the vessel visited the United Kingdom, the proportion of the crew who were EEC nationals and the liability of the crew to contribute to the United Kingdom social security scheme.

[4] That 1985 licensing system has been the subject of a challenge in the European Court of Justice on the grounds that it contravenes European law. A decision on this is awaited.

[5] Last year the Government came to the conclusion that the 1985 licence conditions were not sufficiently restrictive for the protection of British fishing interests and it invited Parliament to enact, and Parliament did enact, the Merchant Shipping Act 1988 which, *inter alia*, empowered the Secretary of State to make regulations introducing a new register of British fishing vessels. The applicants are either unable, or would have great difficulty, to comply with the 1988 Scheme as formulated under the 1988 Act and the Merchant Shipping (Registration of Fishing Vessels) Regulations 1988, The obstacles which confront them arise out of the definitions of 'qualified company' and 'qualified person' in section 4 of the 1988 Act which import conditions relating to British citizenship and domicile. That Act and those regulations taken together wound up the register established by the 1894 Act and, if valid, might well force the applicants to sell or to reflag their vessels.

The application

[6] The applicants took the view that Part II of the 1988 Act which deals with the registration of British fishing vessels and those regulations conflicted with European law. They therefore applied for judicial review. The matter was, and is, of considerable urgency because section 13 of the Act read with the regulations will close the register established by the 1894 Act as from 31 March 1989. Thereafter, no vessel previously on that register and no other fishing vessel will be able to fish commercially unless they are qualified for entry in, and are entered in, the new register.

[7] The application was heard by Neill LJ and Hodgson J. In judgments of conspicuous clarity, they set out the facts, the relevant law, their conclusions and the reasons for those conclusions. Those conclusions were that:

   (a) it was necessary to enable [the court] to give judgment on the applications to seek certain preliminary rulings from the European Court of Justice; and

   (b) in the circumstances of this case the court was competent to grant and should grant interim relief in the form of orders that:

      1   Pending final judgment or further order herein, the operation of Part II of the Merchant Shipping Act 1988 and the Merchant Shipping (Registration of Fishing

Vessels) Regulations 1988 be disapplied, and the Secretary of State be restrained from enforcing the same, in respect of any of the applicants and any vessel now owned (in whole or in part), managed, operated or chartered by any of them, so as to enable registration of any such vessel under the Merchant Shipping Act 1894 and/or the Sea Fishing Boats (Scotland) Act 1886 to continue in being.

2   The Secretary of State does have liberty to apply to, the court in the event of non-compliance by any of the applicants' vessels with conditions of their fishing licenses, save that the enforcement of these conditions shall be subject where applicable to the provisions of the *Jaderow* Agreement and to any judgment or order made by the European Court of Justice in the *Agegate* and *Jaderow* cases.

3   Liberty to apply generally.

The appeal

[8] The Secretary of State appealed to this court seeking a reversal of the interim relief granted. The applicants' primary contention was that the decision of the Divisional Court was correct. However they served a notice of cross appeal to take effect if we were not prepared to uphold the Divisional Court's order. In this event they sought:

(a) (i) a stay of the measures bringing the transitional period referred to in section 13(3)(b) of the Merchant Shipping Act 1988 to an end on 31 March 1989 pursuant to Order 53 rule 3(10)(a) of the rules of the Supreme Court (in so far as the Order made by the Divisional Court does, not amount to an interim stay), or

(ii) a declaration of the terms of the interim Order which the court would have made if the court had had power to make such Order, or

(iii) a provisional declaration of the rights of the parties, or

(iv) such other declaration or Order as would protect the interests of the Respondents pending the judgment of the Court of justice; or

(b) an order that the Divisional Court instead of referring the questions to the Court of Justice under Article 177 give final judgment.

[9] In view of the urgency of the matter we announced our decision at the conclusion of the argument and said that we would put our reasons into writing for delivery at a later date. This we now do. Our decision was that the appeal should be allowed and the cross appeal dismissed, but that the applicants should have leave to appeal to the House of Lords. We declined to make any interim order pending such appeal.

Reasons

[10] It would unduly lengthen this judgment if I sought to summarise the reasons given by Neill LJ and Hodgson J for their decision on interim relief and I do not consider that such a summary would do them justice. Accordingly, I give my own reasons on the assumption that copies of their judgments will be available to the reader, notwithstanding that they have not yet been reported

[11] The Solicitor General appearing for the Secretary of State did not seek to urge us not to follow the decision of this court in *R v Licensing Authorities ex p Smith, Kline & French Laboratories (No 2)* that in proceedings for judicial review interim relief by way of an injunction, or stay or proceedings was available against the Crown. He indicated that in other circumstances he might have wished to argue that the decision was not binding on this court, because it was *obiter*, and that he might well wish to argue in the House of Lords that it was wrongly decided. So be it, but for our purposes we can accept this as a binding authority.

[12] The Solicitor General also accepted that the Divisional Court was in no position to dismiss the application for judicial review without first seeking a ruling from the European Court of Justice. In other words, it was not 'clear' that the applicants were wrong or wholly wrong in their contentions. For the applicants, Mr David Vaughan QC and Mr Nicholas Forwood QC made the same concession substituting 'right' for 'wrong' subject in each case to the qualification that if we concluded that interim relief could not be given, the potential hardship to their clients and, in particular, to Rawlings (Trawlings) Ltd for the reasons set out in the judgment of Neill LJ was such that the Divisional Court should have given a final ruling, preferably in favour of their clients, leaving it to an appellate court so make an application for a ruling from the European Court of Justice.

[13] The essential difference between the two parties on 'clarity' was that the Solicitor General was content to accept Neil LJ's formulation that 'I find myself unable at this stage to say what law ought to be enforced' and that for the applicants it was submitted that Hodgson J somewhat understated the position when he said that 'the applicants have a strong *prima facie* case on each of the three main areas' of contention'.

[14] Accepting, as I do, the extreme hardship which the applicants will suffer if they are required to give up fishing at the end of this month and accepting, as I also do, that the Government has some reason to claim that any failure to give effect to the 1988 Scheme would have adverse consequences for others engaged in, or who would wish to be engaged in, fishing against the British quota, I would have liked to have been able to give some degree of interim relief limited to maintaining the status quo for two or three months. This would have enabled the EC Commission to bring proceedings against the United Kingdom Government and to seek interim relief from the European Court of Justice. If the Commission failed to bring such proceedings or the European Court was unable or unwilling to grant interim relief, I would have been satisfied that European law had been given a reasonable opportunity of asserting itself and that the applicants would have had no reasonable cause for complaints against the British courts and British law for failing to assist them further.

[15] Underlying the whole of this problem is the unusual (to a British lawyer) nature of Community law, which is long on principle and short on specifics. This is intended as a statement of fact rather than a criticism. Indeed my own view is that Parliament would render a service to the nation if it moved slightly more in the direction of Community law and thus enabled the judiciary more easily and appropriately to apply the law to unusual or unforeseen circumstances. However. the result is often that the British courts are faced with an undoubted right or duty under British law and a claim that an inconsistent right or duty exists under Community law. If the British court can ascertain the nature and extent of this competing right or duty, there is little difficulty in resolving any inconsistency on the basis that Community law is paramount. This is the *'acte clair'* situation, but it is a comparative rarity. Much more commonly the British court cannot ascertain the nature and extent of the competing right or duty and it is to meet this problem that the right to seek a ruling by the European Court is provided under Article 177 of the Treaty of Rome. But it would be a mistake to think of that Court merely as having a greater expertise in Community law than a British court, although this is undoubtedly true, whatever the formal position its true function inappropriate cases is actually to make new law by the application of principle to specific factual situations. A challenge to national law based upon community law may, when properly analysed, amount to a submission not that the national law is inconsistent with Community law as it then exists, but that upon a reference being made to the European Court, that court will give a ruling creating new and inconsistent rights and duties: arising out of settled principles albeit with retroactive effect. In other words, national law is effective at present, but its life span is predictably short.

[16] Notwithstanding that I suspect that this is the position in the instant appeal. I would have been very willing to require the Secretary of State to hold his hand pending a ruling by the European Court (provided that this could be obtained within a reasonably short time). But this would only be possible if the 1988 legislation had called for any further action upon his part to enable the 1894 Act register to be wound up and the 1988 Scheme to come into force. But that is not the position. Part II of the 1988 Act and, in particular, section 3(2) and (3), is designed to produce an automatic ending of the 1894 register and an equally automatic creation of the 1988 Scheme, subject to a transitional period, the whole process being triggered by the making of regulations. Nothing happens before these regulations are made. Once they are made, that change is a *fait accompli*. The regulations concerned are SI 1988/1926 which were made on 2 November and came into force on 1 December 1988.

[17] We are thus faced with a situation in which positive action will have to be taken if the status quo is to be maintained after 31 March 1989. It was suggested that the Secretary of State could be required by the court to keep the 1894 register temporarily in force. However this would be contrary to principle, since the court would be requiring him to do an act for which he had no authority whatsoever. Furthermore, the mere maintenance of the register would not legalise fishing in the face of the provisions of the 1988 Act. I also considered whether it would be possible to quash the regulations which triggered the demise of the 1894 register and the birth of the 1988 Scheme which would undoubtedly have achieved the desired result. This is, however, impossible. The making of these regulations was not *ultra vires* unless the 1988 Act itself can be attacked. It was not *Wednesbury* unreasonable and there was no procedural irregularity.

[18] The ultimate question is thus whether the courts of this country have any power to interfere with the operation of the 1988 Act itself, either by modifying its operation or striking it down, and of doing so not on a permanent basis founded upon Community law or the British European Communities Act 1972 but on a temporary basis pending a ruling by the European Court of Justice. The answer to this question, I have no doubt, is in the negative, whether we base ourselves on national or on Community law or both.

[19] Looking at British national law without reference to the European Communities Act 1972, it is fundamental to our (unwritten) constitution that it is for Parliament to legislate and for the judiciary to interpret and apply the fruits of Parliament's labours. Any attempt to interfere with primary legislation would be wholly unconstitutional. That apart, there is a well settled principle of British national law that the validity of subordinate legislation and the legality of acts done pursuant to the law declared by it are presumed unless and until its validity has been challenged in the courts and the courts have fully determined its invalidity (see *Hoffmann-La Roche v Secretary of State for Trade*, per Lord Diplock). The position in relation to primary legislation must be the same. It appears that the European Court of Justice applying Community law reaches the same conclusion. Thus paragraph 4 of the Court's decision in the *Granaria* case (Case 101/781) states: 'Every regulation which is brought into force in accordance with the Treaty must be presumed to be valid so long as a competent court has not made a finding that it is invalid.'

[20] Accordingly, albeit with some reluctance, I have come to the conclusion that in the circumstances of this case there is no juridical basis upon which interim relief can be granted by the British courts. If the applicants have a remedy, it can only be provided by the European Court of Justice either in the form of a ruling in response to the reference made by the Divisional Court or in the form of interim relief in proceedings, not yet instituted by the Commission against the United Kingdom Government.

Bingham LJ: [21] The economic ideal upon which the European Community is founded is that there should within its frontiers be free competition not distorted by protective tariffs, quantitative restrictions, discriminatory practices or state subsidies but subject only to objectively justifiable constraints such as are to be found, for example, in Article 36 of the Treaty of Rome. To make this ideal effective in practice, a number of important and directly enforceable rights are conferred on the nationals or Member States by the Treaty, among their rights of equal and non-discriminatory treatment, rights of establishment, rights to provide services, rights of participation, and so on. It would, at first blush, seem inconsistent with this ideal that particular areas of economic activity should be reserved for the enjoyment of particular Member States to the exclusion of others, or that Member States should be free to discriminate in favour of their own nationals.

[22] A common structural policy for the fishing industry was first adopted in 1971. This was in accordance with the Treaty, which extended the common market to agriculture, including fisheries, and required establishment of a common agricultural policy. But the problem of fisheries acquired a new immediacy with the accession of the United Kingdom, Ireland and Denmark and the expected accession of Norway, all of them countries with long coast-lines and established fishing industries. Neill LJ has most helpfully and comprehensively identified the historical landmarks and legislative milestones leading to the Common Fisheries Policy which exists today, and I shall not attempt to repeat his summary. It is however, common knowledge that the achievement of a common fisheries policy has been more than ordinarily difficult. To this difficulty two factors, among others have contributed. The first was that fish are not an inexhaustible resource. At certain times some species have been over-fished to the verge of extinction. As was recognised in Article 102 of the Treaty of Accession, it was therefore necessary to take steps to conserve the biological resources of the sea. This could only be done by limiting the total allowable catches or the various species of fish. But how, within the overall total, should Member States compete? In the absence of some regulation a disorderly and potentially sanguinary free-for-all would have seemed likely. The second difficulty was that certain areas and communities within Member States, often in economically disadvantaged regions, were to an unusual degree dependent on the fishing industry. A sudden cessation, or sharp reduction, in activity would cause great hardship, both economically and socially.

[23] The solution adopted, as Neill LJ's summary makes clear, was based on total allowable catches for the different species and national quotas related to the level of past fishing activity. This solution is probably regarded as unsatisfactory by most of those involved in the fishing industry, but no doubt represents the best available compromise of an intractable problem. It does not, however, seem to accord closely with the prevailing free market philosophy of the Treaty.

[24] The problem of Community law at the heart of this case concerns the reconciliation of this free market philosophy, on which (and the directly enforceable rights expressed in the Treaty) the applicants rely, with the more regulatory framework of the common fisheries policy, on which the Secretary of State relies. More particularly, the question is whether, in the steps taken to ensure that its fishing quota is enjoyed beneficially and not merely nominally by British interests, the United Kingdom has contravened the prohibition of discrimination deeply embedded in Community law. Both judges in the Divisional Court thought this a difficult and important question on which a decision was necessary to enable them to give judgment. I agree, and no criticism has been addressed to that part of their judgments. Like Neill LJ I shall not express even a tentative view on the likely outcome of the reference to the European Court of Justice which the Divisional Court rightly ordered. Both sides accept that the answer to the Community law problem raised in the case is not *acte clair*. The major issue argued before us has accordingly been whether the Divisional Court was entitled, and if entitled right, to grant the applicants interim relief to protect their

interests during the period of perhaps two years which will elapse before the European Court answers the question to be referred to it.

[25] The Secretary of State challenges the existence of any power in the court to grant interim relief by way of injunction against the crown or any officer of the crown even in judicial review proceedings. The Solicitor General who appears for him accepts, however, that we in this court are bound by *R v Licensing Authority ex p Smith Kline & French Laboratories Ltd (No 2)* to reject that challenge. We accordingly heard no argument on the question and must for present purposes assume that in judicial review proceedings an interim injunction can generally be granted against the crown or one of its officers.

[26] The order made by the Divisional Court provided that 'the operation of Part II of the Merchant Shipping Act 1988 and the Merchant Shipping (Registration of Fishing Vessels) Regulations 1988 be disapplied, and the Secretary of State be restrained from enforcing the same ...' The Solicitor General's first submission is that there is no jurisdiction in the Court to disapply an Act of Parliament unless and until incompatibility with Community law has been established. The relief sought and obtained by the applicants, he submits, involves disapplication of the 1988 Act. That Act has not been shown to conflict with Community law. The court could not, therefore, disapply it.

[27] The Solicitor General's argument was launched from a secure base. Although in medieval times judges claimed and exercised a discretion to dispense with statutes if they thought fit, the supremacy of statute quickly became a cornerstone of British constitutional law. Coke said: 'Of the power and jurisdiction of the Parliament for making of laws, it is so transcendent and absolute as it cannot be confined either for causes or persons within any bounds.' The Bill of Rights 1688 declared unlawful the pretended power of dispensing with laws or the execution of laws by royal authority. According to Blackstone, 'True it is, that what the Parliament doth, no authority upon earth can undo'. Dicey stated that 'there is no power which, under the English constitution, can come into rivalry with the legislative sovereignty of Parliament' and listed as one of the three traits of parliamentary sovereignty as it exists in England 'the non-existence of any judicial or other authority having the right to nullify an Act of Parliament, or to treat it as void or unconstitutional'. The grant of relief such as the applicants obtained would not before 1973 have been thinkable, as I am sure they would accept.

[28] The applicants, however, contend that the European Communities Act 1972 implicitly confers jurisdiction on the court to grant such relief. Section 2(1) provides that all directly enforceable rights created or arising by or under the Treaties shall be given legal effect and enforced in the United Kingdom, and by section 2(4) any legal enactment is to take effect subject to the provisions of the section. The effect of the Act has been to incorporate the law of the Community into the law of the United Kingdom and to ensure that if any inconsistency arises between the domestic law of the United Kingdom and the law of the Community the latter shall prevail. This has been loyally and unreservedly accepted by the English courts. In *The Siskina*, Lord Hailsham said: 'it is the duty of the courts here and in other Member States to give effect to Community law as they interpret it in preference to the municipal law of their own country over which *ex hypothesi* Community law prevail'. Lord Denning MR in *Macarthys v Smith* was equally forthright:

> It is important now to declare – and it must be made plain – that the provisions of Article 119 of the EEC Treaty take priority over anything in our English statute on equal pay which is inconsistent with Article 119. That priority is given by our own law. It is given by the European Communities Act 1972 itself. Community law is now part of our law; and whenever there is any inconsistency, Community law has priority. It is not supplanting English law. It is part of our law which overrides any other part which is inconsistent with it.

As the European Court pointed out in *Van Gend en Loos v Nederlandse Administratie Der Belastingen*, 'the Community constitutes a new legal order of international law for the benefit of which the States have limited their sovereign rights, albeit within limited fields ...'. This reasoning was carried further in *Costa v ENEL* where the European Court said:

> By creating a Community of unlimited duration, having its own institutions, its own personality, its own legal capacity and capacity of representation on the international plane and, more particularly, real powers stemming from a limitation of sovereignty or a transfer of powers from the States to the Community, the Member States have limited their sovereign rights, albeit within limited fields, and have thus created a body of law which binds both their nationals and themselves.

> The integration into the laws of each Member State of provisions which derive from the Community, and more generally the terms and the spirit of the Treaty, make it impossible for the States, as a corollary, to accord precedence to a unilateral and subsequent measure over a legal system accepted by them on a basis of reciprocity. Such a measure cannot therefore be inconsistent with that legal system. The executive force of Community law cannot vary from one State to another in deference to subsequent domestic laws, without jeopardising the attainment of the objectives of the Treaty set out in Article 5(2) and giving rise to the discrimination prohibited by Article 7.

> The obligation undertaken under the Treaty establishing the Community would not be unconditional, but merely contingent if they could be called in question by subsequent legislative acts of the signatories. Wherever the Treaty grants States the rights to act unilaterally, it does this by clear and precise provisions (for example, Articles 15, 93(3), 223, 224 and 225). Applications by Member States for authority to derogate from the Treaty are subject to a special authorisation procedure (for example, Articles 8(4), 17(4), 25, 26, 73, the third sub-paragraph of Article 93(2), and 226) which would lose their purpose if the Member States could renounce their obligations by means of an ordinary law.

> The precedence of Community law is confirmed by Article 189, whereby a regulation 'shall be binding' and 'directly applicable in all Member States'. This provision, which, is subject to no reservation, would be quite meaningless if a State could unilaterally nullify its effects by means of a legislative measure which could prevail over Community law.

> It follows from all these observations that the law stemming from the Treaty, an independent source of law, could not, because of its special and original nature, be overridden by domestic legal provisions, however framed, without being deprived of its character as Community law and without the legal basis of the Community itself being called into question.

The matter could not be more clearly or authoritatively put than it was by the European Court in *Amministrazione delle Finanze dello Stato v Simmenthal SpA*:

> The main purpose of the *first question* is to ascertain what consequences flow from the direct applicability of a provision of Community law in the event of incompatibility with a subsequent legislative provision of a Member State. Direct applicability in such circumstances means that rules of Community law must be fully and uniformly applied in all the Member States from the date of their entry into force and for so long as they continue in force.

> These provisions are therefore a direct source of rights and duties for all those affected thereby whether Member States or individuals, who are parties to legal relationships under Community law.

> This consequence also concerns any national court whose task it is as an organ of a Member State to protect, in a case within its jurisdiction, the rights conferred upon individuals by Community law.

> Furthermore, in accordance with the principle of the precedence of Community law, the relationship between provisions of the Treaty and directly applicable measures of the institutions on the one hand and the national law of the Member States on the other is such that those provisions and measures not only by their entry into force render automatically inapplicable any conflicting provisions of current national law but – in so far as they are an

integral part of, and take precedence in the legal order applicable in the territory of each of the Member States – preclude the valid adoption of new national legislative measures to the extent to which they would be incompatible with Community provisions.

Indeed, any recognition that national legislative measures which encroach upon the field within which the Community exercises its legislative power or which are otherwise incompatible with the provisions of Community law had any legal effect would amount to a corresponding denial of the effectiveness of obligations undertaken unconditionally and irrevocably by Member States pursuant to the Treaty and would thus imperil the very foundations of the Community.

The same conclusion emerges from the structure of Article 177 of the Treaty which provides that any court or tribunal of a Member State is entitled to make a reference to the Court whenever it considers that a preliminary ruling on a question of interpretation or validity relating to Community law is necessary to enable it to give judgment.

The effectiveness of that provision would be impaired if the national court were prevented from forthwith applying Community law in accordance with the decision or the case law of the Court.

It follows from the foregoing that every national court must, in a case within its jurisdiction, apply Community law in its entirety and protect rights which the latter confers on individuals and must accordingly set aside any provision of national law which may conflict with it, whether prior or subsequent to the Community rule.

Accordingly any provision of a national legal system and any legislative, administrative or judicial practice which might impair the effectiveness of Community law by withholding from the national court having jurisdiction to apply such law the power to do everything necessary at the moment of its application to set aside national legislative provisions which might prevent Community rules having full force and effect are incompatible with those requirements which are the very essence of Community law.

This would be the case in the event of a conflict between a provision of community law and a subsequent national law if the solution of the conflict were to be reserved for an authority with a discretion of its own, other than the court called upon to apply Community law, even if such an impediment to the full effectiveness of Community law were only temporary.

The first question should therefore be answered to the effect that a national court which is called upon, within the limits of its jurisdiction, to apply provisions of Community law is under a duty to give full effect to those provisions, if necessary refusing of its own motion to apply any conflicting provision of national legislation, even if adopted subsequently, and it is not necessary for the court to request or await the prior setting aside of such provision by legislative or other constitutional means.

[24] [*sic*] In the face of this jurisprudence the Solicitor General was bound to accept, as he readily did, that if the answer given by the European Court to the question referred to it by the Divisional Court under Article 177 proves unfavourable to him, the Divisional Court will be obliged to give effect to that ruling by upholding any rights the applicants might be shown, in accordance with that ruling, to have, and this it will be obliged to do even though the 1988 Act had not been repealed and even though its decision involves dispensing with (or disapplying) express provisions of the statute.

[30] I have no doubt this is the law. Where the law of the Community is clear, whether as a result of a ruling given on an Article 177 reference or as a result of previous jurisprudence or on straightforward interpretation of Community instruments, the duty of the national court is to give effect to it in all circumstances. Any rule of domestic law which prevented the court from, or inhibited it in, giving effect to directly enforceable rights established in Community law would be bad. To that extent a United Kingdom statute is no longer inviolable as it once was. But the point upon which the Solicitor General takes his stand is that a statute remains inviolable unless or until it is shown to be incompatible with the higher law of the Community. A statute does not, he argues, lose its quality of inviolability

enshrined in our domestic law so long as it remains unclear, as it does in this case or in any other case which is, not *acte clair*, whether the statute is incompatible with Community law or not. I am persuaded, contrary to my initial view, that that argument is correct.

[31] We start from a position (before 1973) in which the court had no jurisdiction to dispense with the operation of a statute. If, therefore, the court now has such jurisdiction one must find the source of such additional jurisdiction. The authorities already cited not only entitle but oblige the court to give effect to Community rights, even if that means dispensing with the operation of a statute. But none of these authorities obliges a national court to override its own domestic law in favour of what is no more than an alleged or putative Community right, and if the English court is not obliged so to act it is not in my opinion, as the law now stands, entitled (under our own domestic law, which remains effective until displaced) to do so. I find no such obligation, expressly or impliedly, in the Treaty itself, or in the European Communities Act 1972, or in the jurisprudence of the European Court, or in any judgment of our own courts. If, of course, the European Court were to rule, as a matter of Community law, that the law obliged or entitled national courts to override national laws, whether statutory or otherwise, where to do so was judged necessary or desirable for the protection of claimed but unestablished Community rights, the situation would be quite different. But unless or until such ruling is given this court is in my view bound to hold that it has no jurisdiction to grant the interim relief which the applicants sought and the Divisional Court granted.

[32] Recognising the danger of this argument, the applicants contended that the interim relief sought involved not dispensing with the operation of the 1988 Act but staying the operation of regulation 66 of the 1988 Regulations. Statutory instruments, they pointed out, are subordinate legislation and have always (unlike statutes) been regarded as amenable to judicial review. This is of course so. It is not, however, suggested that regulation 66 or any other part of the Regulations is outside the powers conferred by the 1988 Act, nor is it suggested that the Regulations are invalidated by any procedural impropriety in their making. If the Act is unimpeachable there is no ground for impeaching the Regulations. The ground upon which the applicants sought and obtained interim relief was that the conditions imposed by section 13 on eligibility to be registered as a British fishing vessel are contrary to Community law. Interim relief could not be granted without temporarily dispensing with the operation of the Act, as the order of the Divisional Court in my view quite rightly recognised.

[33] I would for my part allow the Secretary of State's appeal on this jurisdictional ground alone. The applicants argued that if the Divisional Court could not grant the interim relief sought. then it should have ruled in the applicants' favour on the Community law point and dispensed with the operation of the Act and regulation 66 as part of a final judgment. This argument was not pressed and is in my view untenable. Hodgson J preferred the applicants' submissions on Community law, and may well have been right to do so. Neill LJ was neutral, regarding the arguments on both sides as formidable. Neither judge thought the answer to the Community law issue was obvious, and neither felt able to say what it was. It would have been quite wrong for the judges to leap sightless into the dark in order to protect rights which the applicants might turn out not to have.

[34] If, contrary to the view I have expressed, this court has jurisdiction to dispense with the operation of a statute to protect rights alleged but not established to exist in Community law, and assuming that there is jurisdiction to grant an interlocutory injunction against the Crown or one of its officers, the question remains whether (within the margin of appreciation accorded to it) the Divisional Court properly exercised its discretion to grant such relief.

[35] On a simple *American Cyanamid* approach to the problem the case for granting interlocutory relief was very strong, if not overwhelming. There was without doubt a serious issue to be determined and the applicants had a real prospect of success. If the Act and the Regulation took effect, the applicants stood to suffer very serious loss before the earliest date at which the European Court could, if they were right, rule in their favour. Such loss would, on existing English authority, be irreparable: *Bourgoin SA v Ministry of Agriculture, Fisheries and Food*. This would bear very hardly on all the applicants, and particularly hardly on Rawlings (Trawling) Ltd who are fully integrated with the United Kingdom fishing fleet, who have received grants from HMG, and from the Community as part of that fleet and whose activities form no part of the mischief (if it is mischief) at which the Act is directed. By contrast, the Secretary of State will himself suffer little or no detriment for two years or so, and an injury suffered by the United Kingdom fishing industry which he is concerned to protect will, because more diffused, be less acute than that suffered by the applicants. Maintenance of the status quo means continuing the current registration of the applicants' vessels until the legality of the statutory conditions making the applicants' vessels ineligible for registration is ruled upon.

[36] The Solicitor General contends that this simple and familiar approach is not the correct one because it fails to take account of the important principle that a law must be recognised and enforced as such unless and until it is overruled or invalidated. In support of this principle he referred us to *Hoffmann La-Roche & Co AG v Secretary of State for Trade and Industry* where the Secretary of State sought and obtained an injunction to enforce a statutory instrument the legality of which was challenged. Lord Reid said:

> It must be borne in mind that an order made under statutory authority is as much the law of the land as an Act of Parliament unless and until it has been found to be *ultra vires*. But I think it is for the person against whom the interim injunction is sought to show special reason why justice requires that the injunction should not be granted or should only be granted on terms.

Lord Morris said:

> ... the order then undoubtedly had the force of law. Obedience to it was just as obligatory as would be obedience to an Act of Parliament.

Lord Diplock said:

> Unless there is such challenge and, if there is, until it has been upheld by a judgment of the court the validity of the statutory instrument and the legality of acts done pursuant to the law declared by it are presumed.

These observations are, I think, fully consistent with familiar legal principles. An injunction may be wrongly granted, but until discharged it binds. A judgment may be wrongly given, but unless stayed it takes effect. In *Inland Revenue Commissioners v Rossminster Ltd* Lord Scarman gravely doubted the wisdom of interim relief against the Crown. 'The State's decisions must be respected unless and until they are shown to be wrong.' In *Nottinghamshire County Council v Secretary of State for the Environment* Lord Scarman elaborated these doubts, concluding:

> Judicial review is a great weapon in the hands of the judges; but the judges must observe the constitutional limits set by our parliamentary system upon their exercise of this beneficent power.

[37] There is some doubt how far the simple *American Cyanamid* approach is appropriate where the public interest is involved, and the existence of that interest is a very material consideration: *Smith v Inner London Education Authority*. In *R v Westminster City Council ex p Herbien*, Dillon LJ, referring to that decision, said:

But Lord Denning MR (as he then was) saw merit in the suggestion that the ordinary *Cyanamid* test could not really apply to cases against local authorities in public law, and Browne LJ agreed with that and took the view that the public aspect was of considerable importance. I myself feel that in a case where what is sought to be restrained is the act of a public authority in a matter of public law the public interest is very important to be considered and the ordinary financial considerations in the *Cyanamid* case, though no doubt to some extent relevant, must be qualified by a recognition or the public interest.

The applicants fairly urge that in a case such as this the public interest must embrace the Community interest. But they face the difficulty that whereas the national public interest (as seen by Parliament) is plain, the Community interest is as yet problematical.

[38] It would not be accurate or fair to suggest that these considerations were ignored by the Divisional Court. The authorities I have mentioned were referred to in the judgments and the same passages (more fully) cited. But I do, with respect, think that the Divisional Court erred in failing to direct itself that in all save the most exceptional case preponderant weight must be given to the rule that a statute, duly enacted, must be taken to represent the law unless or until displaced. I do not think the Divisional Court was correct to weigh equally in the scales an Act of Parliament, which might in future be held unlawful, and a Community right, which might in future be upheld. I do not think the Divisional Court acknowledged the constitutional enormity, as the law stands, of requiring a Secretary of State to act contrary to the clearly expressed will of Parliament when the unlawfulness of that expression has yet to be established. Nor do I think that the Divisional Court, in its references to *Simmenthal and Macarthys v Smith*, fully recognised that in those cases, unlike the present, the relevant Community law had been clearly and authoritatively established.

Article 155 of the Treaty provides that in order to ensure the proper functioning and development of the Common Market the Commission shall: ensure that the provisions of this Treatment and the measures taken by the institutions pursuant thereto are applied. Under Article 169 the Commission may, if it considers that a Member State has failed to fulfil an obligation under the Treaty, take the matter up with the Member State and if necessary bring the matter before the European Court. In a case so brought before it the Court may under Article 186 prescribe any necessary interim measures. If an order is to be made dispensing with the operation of the 1988 Act I think it much preferable that this should be made by the European Court in an action (if brought) by the Commission against the United Kingdom than by this court in this action. I take that view for two reasons:

(1) This is not a local problem confined to the United Kingdom and these applicants. It is a Community-wide problem. The Commission can make an objective appraisal of the competing interests of the various Member States and their citizens in a way in which we cannot. If the applicants' case on the law and the merits is strong, I see no reason why the Commission should hesitate to take appropriate action.

(2) If, on a preliminary consideration the Court were to conclude that the applicants have an apparently strong case. I see no reason why interim relief should be denied on application by the Commission acting as the guardian of Community interests. The Court is better placed than this court to assess whether the conditions for granting interim relief are met and whether the interests of the Community and its Member States and citizens call for the granting of such relief.

[41] For these reasons, as well as those of the Master of the Rolls (which I have had the advantage or reading in draft and with which I agree), I would allow the Secretary of State's appeal against the Divisional Court's grant or interim relief.

Mann LJ: [42] I have had the advantage of reading in draft the judgments of my Lord, the Master of the Rolls, and of my Lord, Bingham LJ I agree with them.

[43] The Merchant Shipping Act 1988, Part II, was enacted in accordance with our constitutional procedures. It was brought into force by regulations which were within the regulation-making power. This court is obliged to defer to the Sovereignty of the Queen in Parliament. We can only not so defer where legislation is inconsistent with the United Kingdom's obligations under the Treaty of Rome. I cannot in this case detect an inconsistency with the United Kingdom's obligations under the Treaty of Rome. It may be that the European Court of Justice can make such a detection. Along with Lord, [sic] the Master of the Rolls, I think that if the applicants do have a remedy it can only be provided by the European Court of Justice either in the form of a ruling in response to the reference made by the Divisional Court or in the form of interim relief in proceedings which have not yet been instituted by the Commission against Her Majesty's Government.

[44] I would allow this appeal

Appeal allowed.

EUROPEAN COURT OF JUSTICE

REGINA v SECRETARY OF STATE FOR TRANSPORT EX P FACTORTAME LTD AND OTHERS (NO 2) (Case C213/89) [1990] ECR 1-2433

1990 April 5:	President O Due
May 17:	Presidents of Chambers Sir Gordon Slynn, CN Kakouris,
June 19:	FA Shockweiler and M Zuleeg, Judges CF Mancini,
	R Joliet, JC Moitinho de Almeida,
	GC Rodriguez Iglesius, F Grevise and M de Valacso
	Advocate General C Tesauro

[HOUSE OF LORDS]

1990 July 2, 3, 4, 5, 9, 25	Lord Bridge of Harwich, Lord Brandon of Oakbrook
October 11	Lord Olive of Aylmerton, Lord Goff of Chieveley
	and Lord Jauncey of Tullichettle

...

REFERENCE by the House of Lords under Article 177 of the EEC Treaty.

The report for the hearing before the Court of Justice prepared by the Judge Reporter, Judge Kakouris, states:

I – BACKGROUND TO THE DISPUTE

1   The applicants in the main proceedings, including Factortame Ltd, were a number of companies incorporated under the laws of the United Kingdom and also the directors and shareholders or those companies, most of whom were Spanish nationals. Those Companies between them owned or managed 95 fishing vessels which were until 31 March 1989 registered as British fishing vessels under the Merchant Shipping Act 1894. Of those vessels,

53 were originally registered in Spain and flew the Spanish flag. Those 53 vessels were registered under the Act of 1894 at various dates from 1980 onwards. The remaining 42 vessels had always been British. They had been purchased by the appellants at various dates, mainly since 1983.

2   The statutory system governing the registration of British fishing vessels was radically altered by Part II of the Merchant Shipping Act 1988 and the Merchant Shipping (Registration or Fishing Vessels) Regulations 1988 (SI 1988/1926). It was common ground that the United Kingdom amended the previous legislation in order to put a stop to the practice known as 'quota hopping' whereby (according to that state) its fishing quotas were 'plundered' by fishing vessels flying the British flag but lacking any genuine link with the United Kingdom.

3   The Act of 1988 provided for the establishment of a new register of all British fishing vessels including those registered in the old register maintained under the Act of 1894. However, only fishing vessels fulfilling the conditions laid down in section 14 of the Act of 1988 could be registered in the new register.

4   Briefly the conditions laid down in section 14 of the new Act, which had to be fulfilled cumulatively, were as follows: (a) nationality: the legal title to the vessel had to be vested wholly in qualified British citizens or companies, at least 75% of the beneficial ownership of the vessel must be vested in qualified British citizens or companies; a company was 'qualified' if it was incorporated in the United Kingdom and had its principal place of business there, and if at least 75% of its shares were held by legal owners and beneficial owners who were British citizens; furthermore, at least 75% of its directors had to be British citizens, the figure of 75% may be raised provisionally to 100%, pursuant to regulations adopted under the Act of 1988; the United Kingdom had not yet availed itself of this possibility that nationality requirement also applied to a charterer or operator of the vessel, whether he was a natural person or a company; (b) residence and domicile: this is a further requirement along with nationality; (c) direction and control: the vessel must be managed, and its operations directed and controlled, from the United Kingdom.

5   The Act of 1988 and the regulations of 1988 came into force on 1 December 1988. However, under section 13 of the Act of 1988, the validity of registrations made under the previous Act had been extended for a transitional period until 31 March 1989.

6   At the time of the institution of the proceedings in which the appeal arose the 95 fishing vessels of the applicants failed to satisfy one or more of the conditions for registration under section 14(1) of the Act of 1988 and thus failed to qualify for registration. Since those vessels could no longer engage in fishing as from 1 April 1989, the companies in question sought by means of an application for judicial review to challenge the compatibility of Part II of the Act of 1988 with Community law.

7   In particular, in their application of 16 December 1988 to the High Court of Justice, Queen's Bench Division, the applicants sought: (i) a declaration that the provisions of Part II of the Act of 1988 should not 'apply to them' on the grounds that such application would be contrary to Community law, in particular Articles 7, 52, 58 and 221 of the EEC Treaty; (ii) an order prohibiting the Secretary of State from treating the existing registration of their vessels (under the Act of 1894) as having ceased from 1 April 1989; (iii) damages; and (iv) interim relief pending final determination of the issues.

8   The Divisional Court of the Queen's Bench Division gave judgment on 10 March 1989, in which it: (i) decided that it was unable to determine the issues of Community law raised in the proceedings without making a reference under Article 177 of the EEC Treaty (now Case 221/89. currently pending before the Court of Justice); and (ii) ordered that, pending final judgment or further order by the court, the operation of Part II of the Act of

1988 and of the Regulations of 1988 be disapplied and the Secretary of State should be restrained from enforcing it in respect of any of the applicants and any vessel owned (in whole or in part), managed, operated or chartered by any of them so as to enable registration of any such vessel under the Act of 1894 to continue in being.

9   On 13 March 1989 the Secretary of State appealed against the Divisional Court's order for interim relief. By judgment of 22 March 1989 the Court of Appeal held unanimously that under the British constitution the courts had no power to disapply Acts of Parliament on a temporary basis. It therefore set aside the Divisional Court's order and granted leave to appeal to the House of Lords.

II – THE HOUSE OF LORDS JUDGMENT OF 18 MAY 1989

10   In its judgment of 18 May 1989 (*Factortame Ltd v Secretary of State for Transport* [1990] 2 AC 85) the House of Lords found in the first place that the applicants' claims that they would suffer irreparable damage if the interim relief which they sought was not granted and they were successful in the main proceedings were well founded.

11   With regard to the question whether the British courts were empowered to suspend on a temporary basis the operation of an Act and to issue an interim injunction to that effect against the Secretary of State so as to protect the rights claimed by a party under directly enforceable provisions of Community law. The House of Lords found in the first place that, under national law, the British courts had no power to grant interim relief in a case such as the present. The considerations on which that finding of the House of Lords was based might be summarised as follows.

12   In the first place, the presumption that an Act of Parliament was compatible with Community law unless and until declared to be incompatible did not permit the British courts to grant interim relief suspending the operation of the Act in question. In that connection the House of Lords pointed out that an order granting the applicants the interim relief which they sought would only serve their purpose if it declared that which Parliament had enacted to be the law not to be the law until some uncertain future date. Any such order would irreversibly determine in the applicants' favour for a period of some two years rights which were necessarily uncertain until a preliminary ruling had been given by the Court of Justice.

13   Secondly, the old common law rule that a court had no jurisdiction to grant an interlocutory injunction against the Crown, that is to say against the government, also precluded the grant of interim relief in the main proceedings. The House of Lords pointed out in that connection that in *R v Secretary of State for the Home Department ex p Herbage* [1987] QB 872, the Divisional Court of the Queen's Bench Division took the view that section 31 of the Supreme Court Act 1981 (which provided that the High Court of Justice might grant interim relief, where it would be just and convenient to do so, in all cases in which an application for judicial review had been made) had removed the Crown's immunity from interim relief and that was subsequently affirmed by the Court of Appeal in *R v Licensing Authority Established under Medicines Act 1968 ex p Smith, Kline & French Laboratories Ltd (No 2)* [1990] 1 QB 574. According to the House of Lords, however, those judgments were based on an erroneous construction of the Supreme Court Act 1981. It therefore overruled them in its judgment in the present case and came to the conclusion that, as a matter of English law, the courts had no jurisdiction to grant interim injunctions against the Crown.

14   Next, the House of Lords turned to the question whether Community law empowered the national courts to grant interim relief of the kind forming the subject matter

of the main proceeding, regardless of what was laid down by national law, in order to protect rights which were defensible on serious grounds but whose existence had yet to be established and which were claimed by a party under Community law.

15   After setting out the position of the parties on that point, the House of Lords pointed out in *R v Secretary of State for Transport ex p Factortame Ltd* [1990] 2 AC 85, 151, *per* Lord Bridge of Harwich, that 'Community law embodies a principle which appears closely analogous to the principle of English law that delegated legislation must be presumed to be valid unless and until declared invalid' and referred to the Court of Justice's judgment in *Granaria BV v Hoofdproduktschap voor Akkerbouwprodukten* (Case 101/78) [1979] ECR 623. Next, it referred to paragraph 19 of the judgment in *Foto-Frost v Hauptzollamt Lubeck-Ost* (Case 314/85) [1987] ECR 4199, 4232 in which the Court of Justice stated, at paragraph 19, that 'the rule that national court may not themselves declare Community acts invalid may have to be qualified in certain circumstances in the case of proceedings relating to an application for interim measures'.

16   In those circumstances, the House of Lords considered that the dispute raised an issue concerning the interpretation of Community law and it therefore decided, pursuant to Article 177 of the EEC Treaty, to stay the proceedings until the Court of Justice had given a preliminary ruling on the following questions:

[1] Where: (i) a party before the national court claims to be entitled to rights under Community law having direct effect in national law ('the rights claimed'); (ii) a national measure in clear terms will, if applied, automatically deprive that party of the rights claimed; (iii) there are serious arguments both for and against the existence of the rights claimed and the national court has sought a preliminary ruling under Article 177 as to whether or not the rights claimed exist; (iv) the national law presumes the national measure in question to be compatible with Community law unless and until it is declared incompatible; (v) the national court has no power to give interim protection to the rights claimed by suspending the application of the national measure pending the preliminary ruling; (vi) if the preliminary ruling is in the event in favour of the rights claimed, the party entitled to those rights is likely to have suffered irremediable damage unless given such interim protection, does Community law either (a) oblige the national court to grant such interim protection of the rights claimed, or (b) give the court power to grant such interim protection of the rights claimed? [2] If question 1(a) is answered in the negative and question 1(b) in the affirmative, what are the criteria to be applied in deciding whether or not to grant such interim protection of the rights claimed?

III – COURSE OF THE PROCEDURE

17   The judgment of the House of Lords was received at the Court Registry on 10 July 1989.

18   On 4 August 1989, that is to say while the written procedure in the present case was in progress, the Commission of the European Communities brought an action before the Court of Justice under Article 169 of the EEC Treaty for a declaration that by imposing the nationality requirements laid down in section 14 of the Act of 1988, the United Kingdom had failed to fulfil its obligations under Articles 7, 52 and 221 of the EEC Treaty (Case 246/89), now pending. In a separate document, lodged at the Court Registry on the same date, the Commission applied to the Court of Justice for an interim order requiring the United Kingdom to suspend the application or those nationality requirements as regards the nationals of other Member States and in respect of fishing vessels which until 31 March 1989 were fishing under the British flag and under a British fishing licence. By order of 10 October 1989, the President of the Court of Justice granted that application. Pursuant to that order, the United Kingdom made an Order in Council amending section 14 of the Act of 1988 with effect from 2 November 1989.

19 In accordance with Article 20 of the Protocol on the Statute of the Court of Justice of the EEC, written observations were lodged on 26 October 1989 by the Commission or the European Communities, on 8 November by Ireland, on 9 November by the United Kingdom, and also on 9 November by the applicants in these proceedings.

20 In its order for reference, the House of Lords expressed the wish that the Court of Justice should give priority to the case. The President of the Court of Justice decided, in accordance with the second paragraph of Article 55(1) of the Rules of Procedure, that this case should be given priority.

21 On hearing the report of the Judge Rapporteur and the views of the Advocate General, the Court of Justice decided to open the oral procedure without any preparatory inquiry.

IV – WRITTEN OBSERVATIONS

22 The United Kingdom began by describing the judicial remedies available in the United Kingdom. It pointed out that in proceedings for judicial review, the British courts were empowered to quash the acts of public authorities on grounds including illegality arising from a breach of Community law. The effectiveness of such jurisdiction was enhanced by liberal rules as to *locus standi* and by the fact that such proceedings could be conducted expeditiously.

23 With regard to legislation, the courts did not have the right, under the British constitution, to nullify an Act of Parliament or to treat it as void or unconstitutional. It was otherwise in the case of legislation which was contrary to Community law since section 2(1) and (4) of the European Communities Act 1972 empowered the courts to uphold the primacy of rights arising from Community law. However, Parliament conferred that power on the courts only at the stage when the matter was finally determined and not for the grant of interim relief.

24 The rules of English law which in the present case precluded the grant of interim relief, namely the presumption that an Act of Parliament was compatible with community law and the immunity of the Crown from interim relief, were not discriminatory because they did not draw any distinction between rights arising under domestic law and those arising under Community law.

25 With regard to the argument put forward by the applicants in the main proceedings to the effect that, in a criminal prosecution against them, those proceedings and consequently the application of the relevant legislation were suspended in the event of a reference being made for a preliminary ruling, the United Kingdom pointed out that in those circumstances it was the proceedings initiated before the national court that were suspended and not the application of the law.

26 The impossibility of securing interim relief of the kind sought in the present case was justified by important considerations of public policy, such as compliance with the fundamental limits of the judicial function and the need for legal certainty.

27 Furthermore. in terms of Community law, individuals did not normally have *locus standi* under Article 173 of the EC Treaty to challenge Community legislation. It followed that they could not obtain from the Court of Justice the suspension of Community legislative measures, however serious the effects of such measures on their business might be. Admittedly, Community legislation could also be challenged in the national courts, but the Court of Justice had held that every regulation which was brought into force in accordance with the EEC Treaty must be presumed to be valid as long as a competent court had not

made a finding that it was invalid: see the *Granaria* case [1979] ECR 623. Although the Court of Justice had not ruled out the possibility that a national court might have jurisdiction temporarily to suspend a provision of Community law (see the *Foto-Frost* case [1987] ECR 4199 and *Zuckerfabrik Suderdithmarshen AG* (Case 143/88) now pending before the Court of Justice), the United Kingdom doubted whether it would be consistent with the principle of legal certainty to give the national courts such interim jurisdiction.

28 Following a brief survey or the laws of other Member States on interim relief, the United Kingdom found that in the majority of those countries it did not seem possible to secure, by means of an application for the grant of interim measures, an order suspending the operation of primary legislation. In the Federal Republic of Germany, the Netherlands and Portugal, where there appeared to be certain wider procedures for challenging legislation and granting interim relief, it was not clear that the courts had jurisdiction to grant a mandatory order of the kind sought in the main proceedings.

29 Next, the United Kingdom dealt with the Court of Justice's case law on national remedies for the infringement of Community law. It pointed out that, according to the Court of Justices' judgments in *Comet BV v Productschap voor Siergewassen* (Case 45/76) [1976] ECR 2043 and in *Rewe-Zentralfinanz eG v Landwirtschaftskammer für Saarland* (Case 33/76) [1976] ECR 1989, in the absence of Community harmonisation such remedies were a matter for the national legal system, provided that (a) such remedies were no less favourable than those governing domestic disputes of the same type (principle of non-discrimination), and (b) national rules of procedure did not make it impossible in practice to exercise the rights which the national courts had a duty to protect (principle of effectiveness). Furthermore, it was apparent from paragraph 12 of the judgment in *Express Dairy Foods Ltd v Intervention Board for Agricultural Produce* (Case 130/79) [1980] ECR 1887 that it was not for the Court of Justice to lay down general rules of substance or procedural provisions which only the competent institutions might adopt.

30 According to the United Kingdom, the concept of the direct effect of certain EEC Treaty provisions could not create new remedies in national law. It emphasised that this position was confirmed by the Court of Justice in its judgment in *Rewe-Handelsgesellschaft Nord mbH v Hauptzollamt Kiel* (Case 158/80) [1981] ECR 1805, 1838, at paragraph 44, according to which the EEC Treaty 'was not intended to create new remedies in the national courts to ensure the observance of Community law other than those already laid down by national law.'

31 The Court of Justice therefore acknowledged by implication that the scope of the protection of directly effective rights would vary from one member state to another, pending harmonisation by Community legislation. The only requirement of Community law was that existing remedies should not be emasculated to the point at which there was, in practice, no remedy at all. That was the effect of national legislation, particularly in *Amministrazione delle Finanze dello Stato v SpA San Giorgio* (Case 199/82) [1983] ECR 3595 and in *Les Fils de Julies Bianco SA and J Girard Fils SA v Directeur Général des Douanes et Droits Indirect* (Cases 331, 376 and 378/85) [1988] ECR 1099.

32 Finally, the principle laid down by the Court of Justice in *Amministrazione delle Finanze dello Stato v Simmenthal SpA* (Case 106/77) [1978] ECR 629, according to which a national court was under a duty to give full effect to provisions of Community law and to protect the rights which those provisions conferred on individuals, if necessary refusing of its own motion to apply any conflicting provision of national legislation, was fully recognised in United Kingdom law. In the *Simmenthal* case the rights in question were not theoretical, because they had been established by the Court of Justice in an earlier judgment (*Simmenthal SpA v Italian Minister for Finance* (Case 35/76) [1976] ECR 1871); furthermore, the

action brought by Simmenthal before an Italian court was a well-established remedy in the national legal order. The contrast with the present case was therefore striking.

33 It followed from the foregoing that the United Kingdom's position with regard to remedies was fully in accordance with Community law. None of those remedies had been withheld or fettered in the present case. In an exceptional case such as the present, the protection of individuals might be ensured by the Court of Justice's ability to expedite any reference for a preliminary ruling submitted by a national court (Article 55 of the Rules of Procedure) and by the Commission's ability to obtain interim measures under Articles 169 and 186 of the EEC Treaty, as in the present case.

34 In conclusion, the United Kingdom submitted that the answer to question 1(b) should be as follows: 'Community law does not itself confer on a national court a jurisdiction to grant an interim order to suspend national legislative measures on the basis of claimed or putative rights under Community law having direct effect, if no such remedy exists as a matter of national law.'

35 Ireland pointed out, as a preliminary remark, that what was at issue in the present case was not the enforcement of established rights enjoyed by the applicants in the main proceedings under provisions of Community law which had direct effect, but whether interim protection might or must be granted before the national court decided whether the applicants enjoyed those rights and, if so, whether such rights had been infringed.

36 Ireland went on to state that the Court of Justice had consistently been reluctant to intervene in the sphere of national remedies for the enforcement of rights conferred on individuals by Community law, even where such rights (or their infringement) had been established. Ireland referred in that regard to the judgment in the *Rewe-Zentralfinanz* case [1976] ECR 1989 in which the Court of Justice ruled that, in the absence of Community rules on remedies in the national courts, it was for the domestic legal system of each member state to ensure the protection of the rights arising from the direct effect of Community law.

37 Furthermore, the Court of Justice ruled in the *Rewe-Handelsgesellschaft* case [1981] ECR 1805 that the EEC Treaty was not intended to create new remedies in the national courts to ensure the observance of community law. The Irish Government emphasised that, if it were otherwise, there would be an unwarranted interference by the Court of Justice in the manner in which national courts applied Community law according to internal procedures.

38 According to Ireland, it did not follow from the case law of the Court of Justice concerning the principle of effectiveness (the *Comet* case [1976] ECR 2043, and *Amministrazione delle Finanze v Mireco SaS* (Case 26/79) [1980] ECR 2559) that there was a right to interim protection.

39 Finally, Ireland submitted that it would be wholly inappropriate to require the creation of new remedies in national law. Divergences between the national systems as to the right to interim protection could be removed only by legislation on the part of the Council of the European Communities. In the absence of a Community measure of that kind, any problem raised in that regard by national law might be dealt with in the context of a direct action brought by the Commission against the Member State in question.

40 In conclusion, Ireland submitted that the answer to question 1 should be as follows: '(a) Community law does not in the circumstances described in this question oblige the national courts to grant interim protection of the rights claimed where the national court has no obligation or power under national law to grant such protection, (b) Community law does not in such circumstances give the national court power to grant interim protection of the rights claimed if the national court has no power to grant such interim protection under national law.'

41   The applicants pointed out, as a preliminary remark, that they had never suggested that in the ordinary event the grant of interim protection should be mandatory. However, in the light of the specific circumstances of this case, they contended that the national court was obliged in the present case to make an appropriate protection order.

42   The applicants went on to survey the Court of Justice's case law concerning 'directly effective' provisions of Community law and the role of the national courts with regard to the rights conferred on individuals by those provisions.

43   The applicants pointed out that, according to that case law, rules of Community law which were of 'direct effect' must be uniformly applied in all the Member States from the date of their entry into force and for as long as they continued in force: see *Amministrazione delle Finanze dello Stato v Ariete SpA* (Case 811/79) [1980] ECR 2545, the *Mireco* case [1980] ECR 2559, and the *Simmenthal* case [1978] ECR 629. Those rules constituted a direct source of rights and duties for all those affected thereby (the Simmenthal case) and formed part of the citizens' legal heritage: see *NV Algemene Transport-en Expeditie Onderneming van Gend en Loos v Nederlandse Administratie der Belastingen* (Case 26/62) [1963] ECR 1. The rights arising therefrom for individual citizens were created by the provisions of Community law themselves and not by decisions of the Court of Justice which interpreted those provisions; see *Procureur de la Republic v Waterkeyn* (Cases 314/81, 315/81, 316/81, 83/82) [1982] ECR 4337.

44   It was upon the national courts that the obligation of ensuring the legal protection which individuals derived from directly effective provisions of Community law was imposed: see the *Rewe-Zentralfinanz* case [1976] ECR 1989, the *Comet* case [1976] ECR 2043, and *Amministrazione delle Finanze dello Stato v Denkavit Italiana Srl* (Case 61/79) [1980] ECR 1205. That obligation on the part of the national courts could not be diminished or avoided on the ground that the Commission was empowered to take action against a Member State under Article 169 of the EEC. Treaty or that it might, within the framework of such proceedings, obtain interim measures from the Court of Justice pursuant to Article 186 of the EEC Treaty. That followed from the Court of Justice's judgments in the *Van Gend en Loos* case and in *Molkerei-Zentrale/Westfalen Lippe GmbH v Hauptzollamt Paderborn* (Case 28/67) [1969] ECR 143.

45   The applicants emphasised that the protection afforded to individuals by the national courts must be effective (see *Bozzetti v Invernizzi SpA* (Case 179/84) [1985] ECR 2301, 2317–2318, paragraph 17) and not merely symbolic. Such protection also had to be 'direct and immediate': see *Salgoil SpA v Italian Ministry for Foreign Trade* (Case 13/68) [1968] ECR 453, 462, 463. A temporary impediment to the full effectiveness of Community law was not permitted: see the *Simmenthal* case [1978] ECR 629, 644, paragraph 23. Consequently, any provision of a national legal system and any legislative administrative or judicial practice which might impair the effectiveness of Community law by withholding from the national courts the power to give appropriate protection was itself incompatible with Community law: see the *Simmenthal* case [1978] ECR 629, *von Colson and Kamann v Land Nordrhein-Westfalen* (Case 14/83) [1984] ECR 1891, and *Johnston v Chief Constable of the Royal Ulster Constabulary* (Case 222/84) [1987] QB 129.

46   That was the case with regard to two rules of English law which precluded the grant of the interim relief sought by the applicants.

47   In particular, a reference for a preliminary ruling on the substance of the case was rendered pointless by the presumption of compatibility, because that presumption prevented the national court from safeguarding the position until such time as the Court of Justice gave judgment. Since that presumption restricted the freedom of the national courts to refer to the Court of Justice any question of Community law which needed to be resolved in order to

enable it to give judgment, it was incompatible with the principle of 'effective protection' and with the second paragraph of Article 177 of the EEC Treaty.

48 The paramount importance attributed by Community law to the protection of rights conferred on individuals by its provisions in the period between the submission of a reference for a preliminary ruling and the decision of the Court of Justice was confirmed by the judgment in the *Foto-Frost* case [1987] ECR 4199, 4232, paragraph 19.

49 With regard to the rule concerning the Crown's immunity from interim relief, the applicants pointed out that that obstacle was artificial because, if they disregarded the Act of 1988 and were prosecuted by the Crown for infringing it, the Crown would be unable to enforce that Act since the national court, by making a reference to the Court of Justice pursuant to Article 177 of the EEC Treaty, would suspend the proceedings and protect the rights claimed by the applicants.

50 In any event, the rule concerning the immunity of the Crown constituted an anomaly as regards the exercise of rights arising from provisions of Community law, in that (a) interim relief was available against all other defendants, with the exception of the Crown, although more often than not it was in fact against the authorities of the state, namely the Crown, that rights conferred by Community law had to be enforced, and (b) final relief was available against the Crown.

51 According to the applicants, Community law rendered inapplicable the two rules of English law which removed the possibility of obtaining interim relief of the kind sought in the main proceedings. They emphasised that, if it were otherwise, the United Kingdom would be able flagrantly to disregard Community law in cases such as the present, whilst at the same time taking advantage of the fact that, since a reference was likely to be made to the Court of Justice for a preliminary ruling, holders of rights conferred by Community law would be deprived of the right of exercising them in the interim period. Such deprivation of rights would in practice be permanent in cases where, as in the main proceedings, an action for damages was not available (since, as English law stood at present on the authority of *Bourgoin SA v Minister of Agriculture, Fisheries and Food* [1986] QB 716, no action for damages lay against the Crown for infringing an EEC Treaty provision, unless bad faith on the part of the Crown was established) and where the rights of applicants could never be given full retroactive protection in any other way when the final decision actually came to be made. All those considerations revealed the extent of the need, particularly in cases such as the main proceedings, for effective protection to be made available by way of interim relief.

52 Finally, the applicants pointed out that there were a number of reasons why it was entirely misplaced for the United Kingdom to rely on the Court of Justice's judgment in the *Rewe-Handelsgesellschaft* case [1981] ECR 1805 in order to justify the impossibility of obtaining interim relief. In the first place, there was no question of there being any need to create new remedies in the national courts in order to provide appropriate interim relief since the remedies which already existed under English law were perfectly adequate; it was sufficient for the two rules concerning the presumption of compatibility and Crown immunity to be disapplied. Secondly, and in any event, the *dicta* in that judgment were subject to the proviso, laid down by the Court of Justice in its judgments in the *Comet* case [1976] ECR 2043 and in the *Rewe-Zentralfinanz* case [1976] ECR 1989 and reiterated in its judgment in the *San Giorgio* case [1983] ECR 3595 and elsewhere, that in no circumstances might national measures be such as to render it impossible in practice or excessively difficult for the rights conferred on individuals by Community law to be protected. It was inconceivable that the Court of Justice would apply that proviso to cases of procedural, evidential and limitation rules, but not to a rule of *locus standi* such as that which was in issue in the *Rewe-Handelsgesellschaft* case [1981] ECR 1805.

53 In conclusion, the applicants submitted that the answer to question 1 should be that, in the circumstances referred to therein, 'Community law requires the courts of the Member States to have the duty (or at least the power) to grant such interim protection as is appropriate and to disapply to the extent necessary all national legislative measures, roles and judicial practices which constitute obstacles to the grant of effective protection to those such as the applicants in the present case, who rely on directly effective Community law rights.'

54 The Commission began with a comparative survey of Community legislation and the national legislation of the Member States on interim relief.

55 It pointed out that, in so far as Community law was concerned, Article 185 of the EEC Treaty provided, in proceedings for annulment, for the possibility of suspending a Community measure even with respect to primary legislation.

56 On the basis of its survey of national legislation, the Commission came to the conclusion that the laws of all the Member States other than Denmark and the United Kingdom empowered the courts to suspend measures which were open to challenge before them. Even in Denmark the courts had jurisdiction to grant such interim relief in certain limited classes of public law proceedings.

57 Next, the Commission referred to the case law of the Court of Justice on protection by the national courts of the rights which Community law conferred on individuals.

58 In the first place. the Court of Justice had emphasised the need for a remedy of a judicial nature against any decision of a national authority refusing to grant an individual the benefit of a right conferred by Community law: see *Union Nationale des Entraineurs et Cadres Techniques Professionnels du Football v Heylens* (Case 222/86) [1987] ECR 4097, and Johnston's case [1987] 1 QB 179.

59 Furthermore, it followed from the case law of the Court of Justice on actions brought by individuals in a national court in order to protect the rights conferred upon them by Community law (see the *Comet* case [1976] ECR 2043 and the *Rewe-Zentralfinanze* case [1976] ECR 1989) that, in the absence of Community rules, the procedures relating to such actions were governed by national law, subject to compliance with the principles of non-discrimination and effectiveness.

60 The principle of non-discrimination was not directly applicable to the present case since the British courts had no jurisdiction to grant interim relief against the Crown, even in cases involving English law alone. In contrast, the principle of effectiveness was directly relevant to the present case. The Member States were bound to observe that principle quite independently of the principle of non-discrimination. Accordingly, when a rule contravened the principle of effectiveness, it was no answer to argue that in equivalent cases involving national law alone the rule applied in exactly the same way, see the *San Giorgio* case [1983] ECR 3595.

61 According to the Commission, the most important judgment ever delivered on the scope of the principle of effectiveness was that in the *Simmenthal* case [1978] ECR 629, pp 643, 644, paragraphs 15, 16 and 21–23. That ruling made it abundantly clear that the principle of effectiveness was an immediate and inevitable consequence of the concept of direct applicability. It would be nonsense to state that certain provisions of Community law might be relied upon before the national courts if any attempts to rely on them could in fact be thwarted by national rules on remedies or procedure.

62 It followed that the national courts were required to ensure that the parties who relied in proceedings before them on provisions of Community law having direct effect had an effective remedy in national law whereby effect might be given to their rights under those

provisions. According to the Commission, the national courts must be empowered to grant interim relief, but without being required to do so in every case in which a plaintiff relied on a directly applicable provision of Community law.

63 The fact that in national law the contested national measure was presumed to be compatible with Community law unless and until it was declared incompatible constituted no logical obstacle to the grant of interim relief suspending its application. The same presumption existed in Community law (see the *Granaria* case [1979] ECR 623) but that did not prevent the Court of Justice from suspending, pursuant to article 185 of the EEC Treaty, the application of Community measures by way of interim relief. In English law also there was a presumption that measures adopted by local authorities were lawful, but that did not prevent the courts from suspending their application by the grant of interim injunctions: see *De Falco v Crawley Borough Council* [1980] QB 460, and also *R v Kensington and Chelsea Royal London Borough Council ex p Hammel* [1989] QB 518.

64 The Commission pointed out that, according to the House of Lords, the damage suffered by the applicants was likely to be irremediable unless they were granted the interim protection sought and they were successful in their main action, since they would probably have no remedy in damages in view of the judgment of the Court of Appeal in the *Bourgoin* case [1986] QB 716.

65 According to the Commission, it could be argued that the likelihood of irremediable damage necessarily implied that the only effective remedy was interim relief. If a party could neither obtain interim relief in order to prevent the damage from occurring nor recover damages *ex post facto*, the Commission submitted that on any view he was deprived of any effective remedy whereby effect might be given to his rights. That situation could not be justified by the fact that the absence of any remedy was only temporary since, according to paragraph 23 of the judgment in the *Simmenthal* case [1978] ECR 629, even the temporary absence of an effective remedy was contrary to the principle of effectiveness.

66 In conclusion, the Commission submitted that question 1 should be answered as follows: 'The obligation on national courts to apply Community law having direct effect and to protect rights which the latter confers on individuals includes the obligation to consider whether interim protection of the rights claimed against the authorities of a Member State should be granted in order to avoid irremediable damage and, where appropriate, to grant such interim relief.'

Second question

67 The United Kingdom pointed out that in view of the proposed answer to question 1(b) there was no need to answer the other questions submitted by the House of Lords.

68 Ireland submitted that the second question need not be answered in the light of the answer proposed to the first question. However, if the Court of Justice were to give an answer that question, Ireland suggested that it should be as follows: 'The conditions for the granting by a national court of such interim relief are a matter solely for national law, subject only to the qualifications that such conditions must not discriminate against Community law by comparison with national law, and must not infringe the prohibition of discrimination on grounds of nationality contained in Article 7 of the EEC Treaty.'

69 The applicants pointed out that if the Court of Justice's answer to the first question were that the national courts were empowered to grant interim relief, the answer to the second question should be that Community law left the Member States free to determine the criteria upon which that power was to be exercised, provided always that the criteria were not defined or applied in any respect (a) less favourably than would be the case if rights

under Community law were not involved, or in any event (b) so as to render protection of the rights impossible in practice or excessively difficult to achieve.

70 On that basis the appropriate criteria would be those which the English courts currently applied with regard to interim relief and which involved the court asking itself (a) whether there was a serious issue to be tried, or, in other words, whether the action had a 'real prospect of success' (in that regard the applicants referred in particular, to the decision of the House of Lords in *American Cyanamid Co v Ethicon Ltd* [1975] AC 396); (b) if so, whether damages were obtainable and, if they were, whether they constituted an adequate remedy for one side or the other; (c) if not, where the balance of convenience lay as between the parties. In considering the latter question, the court should, in particular, weigh the consequences for the applicant if interim relief were not granted against the consequences for the defendant if interim relief were granted. It could also take into account any other relevant factors such as, for example, the applicant's delay in seeking an interim remedy, or the interaction of private rights with public interests, which was pertinent to this case.

71 Next, the applicants explained in detail the reasons why they satisfied all the aforesaid criteria.

72 The Commission pointed out, as a preliminary remark, that the criteria for the grant of interim relief by the Court of Justice in accordance with Article 83(2) of the Rules of Procedure, as interpreted by the Court of Justice, were that the applicant must make out a *prima facie* case and show the existence of urgency such that interim measures were necessary to avoid serious and irreparable harm. Although Article 86(2) of the rules of procedure provided that the Court of Justice might require the applicant to lodge security as a condition for enforcing the order, the Court of Justice rarely imposed such a requirement.

73 Under English law, the criteria to be applied for the grant of interim protection were laid down in (a) the judgments in the *De Falco* case [1980] QB 460 and the *Hammel* case [1989] QB 518 concerning the grant of interim relief against public bodies other than the Crown, such as local authorities, and (b) the judgment of the House of Lords in the *American Cyanamid* case [1975] AC 396 concerning the grant of interim relief in proceedings between private individuals. The Commission stated that, according to the latter judgment, the court must first be satisfied that the applicant's claim was neither frivolous nor vexatious. If that condition was fulfilled, the matter was to be determined on a balance of convenience. Finally, if the court decided to grant the interim relief sought, the applicant was required to give a cross-undertaking as to damages.

74 Next, the Commission pointed out that there was nothing to prevent the English courts from applying the criterion already established by their case law for the grant of interim relief against local authorities.

75 In any case, the Commission submitted that, in accordance with general principles, the following matters were to be weighed up by the national courts: (i) the apparent strength of the applicant's case: it was not for Community law to determine whether the applicant must show a serious issue to be tried (see the *American Cyanamid* case) or make out a prima facie case (Article 83(2) of the Court of Justice's Rules of Procedure) or make out a strong prima facie case (the *De Falco* and *Hammel* cases); (ii) the balance of convenience, which included considerations of urgency, the risk of irreparable damage and the public interest. Where, as in this case, the applicant was deprived or his right to carry on his economic activity until the outcome of the main proceedings, great weight must be given to that factor. That was all the more so where, as in this case, he was likely to go bankrupt as a result.

76 According to the Commission, the fact that a cross-undertaking could not be required in a particular case need not constitute an obstacle to the grant of interim relief.

77 Finally, the Commission emphasised that in no case could any of the circumstances which might militate against the grant of interim relief, whether taken alone or with other such circumstances, operate as an absolute bar to such relief, since the person concerned would then be denied an effective remedy. For instance, the fact that the impugned measure constituted the straightforward application of an Act of Parliament could not automatically preclude its suspension.

78 In conclusion, the Commission submitted that question 2 should be answered as follows: 'In deciding whether to grant interim relief national courts must weigh up the interests involved in each case, without considering any particular circumstance or set of circumstances as constituting generally an absolute bar to such relief. Moreover, the criteria to be applied by national courts may not be less favourable to the individual than those applying to similar cases relating to national law alone.'

Sir Nicholas Lyell QC, SG, Christopher Bellamy, QC, Christopher Vajda and *TJG Pratt*, agent, for the United Kingdom.

James O'Reilly SC and *Louis J Dockery*, Chief State Solicitor, agent, for the Republic of Ireland.

David Vaughan QC, Gerald Darling, David Anderson and *Stephen Swabey*, solicitor, for the first to 94th applicants.

Nicholas Forwood, QC the 95th applicant, Rawlings (Trawling) Ltd.

Götz zur Hausen and Peter Oliver, agents, for the Commission of the European Communities.

17 May: **Mr Advocate General Tesauro** delivered the following opinion.

1 The reply which the Court of Justice is called upon to give to two questions referred to it by the House of Lords for a preliminary ruling in *R v The Secretary of State for Transport ex p Factortame Ltd* [1990] 2 AC 85 will rank amongst those which help to define the context of relations between national courts and Community law. And, I would add, on a point of unquestionable importance. The questions are clear. Pending a ruling by the Court of Justice on the interpretation of provisions of Community law having direct effect, and where United Kingdom law does not permit the national court to suspend, by way of interim relief, the application of the allegedly conflicting national measure and thus, provisionally, to acknowledge an individual's right claimed under Community law but denied by national law: (1) must (or may) the national court grant such relief on the basis of Community law? (2) if so, applying what criteria?

2 The dispute which gave rise to the reference for a preliminary ruling concerns a considerable number of companies operating in the fisheries sector, which are incorporated under the laws of the United Kingdom but represent Spanish interests. These undertakings contest the validity under Community law of a United Kingdom statute of 1988 (the Merchant Shipping Act 1988) which altered the requirements for registration in the register of fishing vessels, in particular as regards nationality and residence of the beneficial ownership, deliberately strengthening those requirements in the case of foreign interests (including Community interests). Relying on certain provisions of the EEC Treaty having direct effect, Factortame Ltd and others instituted proceedings for judicial review of the Act in question, seeking a declaration that the Act should not apply to them on the ground that such application would be contrary to Community law, an order prohibiting the authorities from treating the registration of the vessels under the old Act (the Merchant Shipping Act 1894) as having ceased, and interim relief pending final judgment.

3 At first instance, the Divisional Court of the Queen's Bench Division made a reference to the Court of Justice for a preliminary ruling on the interpretation of the provisions of Community law raised and, as an interim measure, ordered the Secretary of

State for Transport not to apply the new Act to the applicants pending final judgment or further order of the court.

4   The Secretary of State for Transport appealed against the order for interim relief which was set aside by the Court of Appeal on the ground that United Kingdom courts do not have the power to suspend, by way of interim relief, the application of statutes or to grant an injunction against the Crown.

5   The House of Lords, before which the matter was brought, confirmed that as a matter of English law the courts have no power to suspend the application of an Act of Parliament on the ground of its alleged, but unproved, incompatibility with Community law, and referred to the Court of Justice for a preliminary ruling the questions mentioned above, in order essentially to ascertain whether that which is not permitted by English law is required or permitted by Community law.

6   It should be stated by way of a preliminary observation that the House of Lords acknowledges that it has the power and the duty to give preference over the conflicting national statute to a provision of the EEC Treaty or a provision of secondary Community law having direct effect to the United Kingdom legal order, and that this is so when the conflict is immediately and readily discernible, either by virtue of an existing interpretation of the Community provision by the Court of Justice or by virtue of the fact that the provision itself is sufficiently 'clear' in its content. The problem arose, however, because there was no certainty as to the interpretation of the Community provisions relevant to the circumstances, but rather there were 'serious arguments both for and against the existence of the rights claimed,' which prompted the Divisional Court to ask the Court of Justice to give a preliminary ruling on the interpretation of those provisions. The questions raised form the subject matter of different proceedings (Case 221/89) which are separate from the present proceedings. Moreover, to complete the picture, I would recall that, as regards the alleged incompatibility with Community law of the same United Kingdom statute in point, the Commission of the European Communities brought proceedings under Article 169 of the EEC Treaty against the United Kingdom, but solely on the nationality aspects, likewise seeking, by way of an interim measure, the suspension of application of the Act. The Court of Justice has already made an order granting such a measure in *Commission of the European Communities v United Kingdom* (Case 246/89R) (1989) *The Times*, 28 October, and the Act has also been amended in that respect.

7   As a further preliminary matter, I think it is appropriate to point out that the problem has arisen in the context of the special proceedings by way of application for judicial review provided for by English law which were brought by the parties concerned even before the new Act on the register of shipping entered into force. On this point both the House of Lords in its order for reference and the United Kingdom in its written observations have stressed that, had the question of a conflict with Community law arisen in the course of criminal or administrative proceedings brought against those same parties for contravention of the Act on the register of shipping, the national court could well have stayed the proceedings (and even any forfeiture proceedings in respect of vessels) pending the outcome of the request for a preliminary ruling by the Court of Justice on the interpretation of the relevant Community provisions. The consequences of the Court of Justice's ruling, whether favourable or unfavourable as regards the claim made by the parties concerned, would then have been applied to them retroactively. The House of Lords infers therefrom that, in such a case, 'the prosecution or forfeiture proceedings would not be frustrated but suspended': see the order for reference.

It is not wholly clear in what perspective attention was drawn to the difference between the situation in this case (proceedings for judicial review) and that which might have arisen in ordinary proceedings of a criminal or other type instituted following the contravention of the Act. What is true, it seems to me, is that, for present purposes, the difference is not of any great importance. The mere stay of proceedings as a result of a reference to the Court of Justice pursuant to Article 177 of the EEC Treaty is not an interim measure and does not satisfy any requirements of interim protection of the rights claimed. On the contrary, it unquestionably poses in more acute terms the very problem which necessitates interim protection: whether, if stayed, the proceedings may, precisely, be 'frustrated' by the delay in giving final judgment.

Thus the question raised by the House of Lords is of importance in the same way and in the same terms with regard to both the procedural situations indicated to the Court of Justice. It would only be otherwise if, whatever the type of proceedings, the national court were entitled, where proceedings are stayed and a reference is made to the Court of Justice under Article 177, also to grant an interim measure of the type requested by the applicants in this case and if, accordingly, it had the power provisionally to allow the ships to be registered on the basis of the old Act pending final judgment; as became clear also at the hearing, this is plainly precluded whether in judicial review proceedings or any other type of proceeding.

8 On the other hand, I attach importance to the fact, stressed by the national court, that in a situation such as the one now before the Court of Justice, that is to say in the absence of interim measures, the economic damage suffered by the applicants in the course of the proceedings would remain irreparable, an action for damages being precluded by settled national case law: see the order for reference. It follows that, even were an interpretative ruling to be given by the Court of Justice, upholding the arguments of the applicants, the subsequent judgment by the national court could not award compensation for the damage suffered and the proceedings might in any event be 'frustrated'.

That is not to say that compensation for loss suffered is a decisive factor and constitutes a real alternative to interim protection, in view of the fact that, even were it provided for, it would not always and in any event be sufficient in itself to satisfy the requirement of interim protection, a requirement which arises precisely out of the inadequacy of monetary compensation from the point of view of the 'utility' of the future judgment: see, for example, the order of the Court of Justice in *Agricola Commerciale Olio Srl v Commission of the European Communities* (Case 232/81) [1981] ECR 2193, 2200, paragraph 9. Rather the fact that compensation for damages is precluded makes it by definition impossible to make good the losses suffered pending judgment in the proceedings

9 The national court has specifically identified the principles of Community law whose interpretation by way of a preliminary ruling by the Court of Justice would enable it to resolve the problem, in one way or another: the direct effect of the Community provisions relied on, the obligation to provide direct and immediate protection of individual rights, the practical efficacy of judicial remedies, the obligation to refrain from applying national measures and/or practices which render the exercise of such rights and the protection afforded to them impossible.

Similarly, the formal obstacles to the exercise by the English courts of the power to grant interim protection in proceedings of the type in question have been made clear: the presumption of validity that attaches to a statute until a final determination is made, a process which may include a ruling by the Court of Justice, and the impossibility of granting an injunction against the Crown, an impossibility which moreover relates not only to interim measures but also to final determinations: see the observations by the United Kingdom.

10 The principles of Community law which the House of Lords has stated to be relevant and on whose interpretation its decision will depend are fundamental principles enshrined

in numerous judgments of the Court of Justice. Those principles are, however, observed (and without difficulty) by the United Kingdom courts, with the sole reservation which constitutes at once the reason for and the subject of these proceedings. Are such principles also to be interpreted as meaning that the national court must (or may) grant an interim measure requiring the Crown to refrain from applying, during the proceedings on the substance of the case, a 'measure' (in this case an Act of Parliament) in respect of which there is no certainty but merely a suspicion, however serious, that it is incompatible with Community law? In other words, do the obligations which Community law imposes on the national courts concerning the protection of rights conferred directly on individuals also include the requirement to order the suspension, by way of interim protection, of the application of a national law which is alleged to be in conflict with Community law?

11 In addition to a rapid survey of the relevant principles of Community law, which are well known to the national court, the reply to this question calls for an identification of the requirement which is at the origin and is also the *raison d'être* of interim protection, a concept long established in jurisprudence and in the legal systems of the Member States.

12 The starting point for the appraisal of the problem is that, as is accepted in this case, directly effective Community provisions are involved in the now uncontested sense of measures immediately conferring on individuals enforceable legal rights which, as such, may be relied upon before national courts. It is scarcely necessary to emphasise that it is on that assumption that the questions have been referred to the Court of Justice for a preliminary ruling, irrespective of which Community provisions are involved and the correct interpretation thereof. In fact, it is not the interpretation of the individual EEC Treaty provisions relied on by the applicants in the dispute before the national court which is requested in these proceedings (merely for the sake of clarity, I would remind the Court of Justice that Articles 7, 52, 58 and 221 of the EEC Treaty are involved), but rather the interpretation of the principles of Community law mentioned above. In other words, the Court of Justice is not requested to embark upon an examination of the substance of the provisions relied on by the applicants, which is the subject of other, and separate, proceedings for a preliminary ruling, which are, I repeat, also pending before the Court of Justice (Case 221/89), but rather to give a general reply with regard to the interim protection of rights claimed by individuals by virtue of directly effective Community provisions.

13 That being so, I would recall that provisions of Community law having direct effect 'must be fully and uniformly applied in all the Member States from the date of their entry into force and for so long as they continue in force' (among other authorities, see *Amministrazione delle Finanze dello Stato v Simmenthal SpA* (Case 106/77) [1978] ECR 629, 643, paragraph 14, and *Amministrazione delle Finanze dello Stato v Ariete SpA* (Case 811/79) [1980] ECR 2545, 2552–53, paragraph 5) and that 'this consequence also concerns any national court whose task it is as an organ of a Member State to protect, in a case within its jurisdiction, the rights conferred upon individuals by Community law': see the judgment in the *Simmenthal* case [1978] ECR 629, 643, paragraph 16. And again in that judgment the Court of Justice affirmed that, in view of the supremacy of Community law, the relevant provisions having direct effect 'not only by their entry into force render automatically inapplicable any conflicting provision of current national law', but also preclude the valid adoption of new national legislative measures to the extent to which they would be incompatible with Community provisions: see the judgment in the *Simmenthal* case, p 643, paragraph 17.

It is quite clear, therefore, that a Community provision having immediate effect within the Member States confers enforceable legal rights on the individual from its entry into force and for so long as it continues in force, irrespective and even in spite of a prior or subsequent national provisions which might negate those same rights. I do not consider it useful, and even less so in this context, to enter into a sterile dialectical discussion on the theoretical basis of such a firmly established principle. What matters, in so far as is relevant in this case, is that the national court is obliged to afford judicial protection to the rights conferred by a Community provision as from the entry into force of that provision and for so long as it continues in force.

14   Equally beyond dispute, and in harmony with the principle of collaboration enshrined in Article 5 of the EEC Treaty, which is the real key to the interpretation of the whole system, is the fact that the methods and the machinery for protecting rights conferred on individuals by provisions of Community law are and remain, in the absence of a harmonised system of procedure, those provided by the domestic legal systems of the Member States. That principle, which recurs in the Court of Justice's case law, is nevertheless based on a fundamental pre-condition, which is also derived from the second paragraph of Article 5, namely that the methods and national procedures must be no less favourable than those applying to like remedies for the protection of rights founded on national provisions and must also not be such as to render impossible in practice 'the exercise of rights which the national courts are obliged to protect' see *Rewe-Zentralfinanz eG v Landwirtschaftskammer für Saarland* (Case 33/76) [1976] ECR 1989, 1997, paragraph 5; *Comet BV v Produktschap voor Siergewassen* (Case 45/76) [1976] ECR 2043, 2053, paragraphs 15, 16; the *Ariete* case [1980] ECR 2545, at p 2554, paragraph 12; *Express Dairy Foods Ltd v Intervention Board for Agricultural Produce* (Case 130/79) [1980] ECR 1887, at p 1900 paragraph 12; *Amministrazione delle Finanze delle Stato v Denkauf Italiana Srl* (Case 61/79) [1980] ECR 1205, 1226, paragraph 25; *Hans Just I/S v Danish Ministry for Fiscal Affairs* (Case 68/79) [1980] ECR 501, 522, paragraph 25: and *Amministrazione delle Finanze dello Stato v SpA San Giorgio* (Case 199/82) [1983] ECR 3595.

Moreover, in its judgment in the *Simmenthal* case [1978] ECR 629, the Court of Justice had affirmed, 644, paragraph 22:

> ... any provision of a national legal system and any legislative, administrative or judicial practice which might impair the effectiveness of Community law by withholding from the national court having jurisdiction to apply such law the power to do everything necessary at the moment of its application to set aside national legislative provisions which might prevent Community rules from having full force and effect are incompatible with those requirements which are the very essence of Community law.

(I would also cite *Commission of the European Communities v Hellenic Republic* (Case 68/88) (1990) *The Times*, 28 October, in which the Court of Justice reaffirms that 'Article 5 of the EEC Treaty required Member States to take all measures appropriate in order to guarantee the scope and effectiveness of Community law'.) In other words, the national court is to apply Community law either through the means provided for under the national legal system or, failing that, 'of its own motion': see the judgment in the *Simmenthal* case, p 644, paragraph 24.

15   It is therefore firmly established, in the light of the Court of Justice's well settled case law, which has moreover been pertinently cited by the House of Lords, that national courts are required to afford complete and effective judicial protection to individuals on whom enforceable rights are conferred under a directly effective Community provision, on condition that the Community provision governs the matter in question from the moment of its entry into force, and that from this it follows that any national provision or practice which precludes those courts from giving 'full effect' to the Community provision is incompatible with Community law.

The emphasis of this point should not appear superfluous merely because it recurs in the Court of Justice's case law, since it is precisely from this observation that I shall derive the reply which I propose that the Court of Justice should give in this case.

16 The problem which the national court has raised is a general one and is not new, even though, although it has been implicitly overcome by other courts (on more than one occasion on which a reference has been made to the Court of Justice in the context of an alleged conflict between a national provision (law or administrative act) and Community law, the national court without hesitation also granted interim measures, which in substance amounted to a provisional suspension of the application of the instrument in question: for example, a stay of execution of an expulsion order from the Netherlands was ordered in *Netherlands v Reed* (Case 59/85) [1986] ECR 1283; again, an employment relationship with the University of Venice was ordered to be maintained in *Alluè v Università degli Studi di Venezia* (Case 33/88) (1989) *The Times*, 16 June, and in another case a provisional residence permit was ordered to be issued in Belgium (Case 363/89, pending), it is submitted for the first time for the judgment of the Court of Justice, perhaps not by chance in the context of the somewhat special situation represented by the procedure for judicial review of laws provided for in the United Kingdom. The question, therefore, does not concern solely the English legal system, nor does it relate solely to the relationship between a national law and a Community provision, but rather it relates to the requirement for, and the very existence of, the interim protection of a right which is not certain but whose existence is in the course of being determined in a situation where there is a conflict between legal rules of differing rank. This is a conflict which, as regards the relationship between a national provision and a Community provision, quite apart from the theoretical or terminological choices and methods applied in the individual Member States, finds effective expression the concept of 'primauté,' that is to say the 'precedence' of the latter provision over the former.

The problem arises from the fact that in a structured and intricate context which a modern system of judicial protection demands there is a lack of contemporaneity between the two points in time which mark the course of the law, namely the point when the right comes into existence and the point (later on) when the existence of the right is (definitively) established.

17 To compensate for the fact that these two points in time do not coincide there is a first and general remedy. It is true that only the definitive establishment of the existence of the right confers on the right fullness and certainty of content in the sense of placing the right itself, and the means whereby it may be exercised, finally beyond dispute (*res judicata* in the substantive sense); but it is also true that that effect is carried back to the point in time when the right was invoked by initiating the procedure for judicial review. The effect of the establishment of the existence of the right, inappropriately but significantly described as retroactive effect, is merely the consequence of the function of the provision and of its nature and modus operandi which in fact gives rise to an enforceable legal right from the moment when the provision enters into force and for so long as it continues in force. The only possible delay is that which may occur before the right becomes fully effective and operational in cases where application to a court is needed in order to establish the existence of the right, and in particular in cases of prior review of the validity of the provision which is alleged to be applicable. And it is scarcely necessary to add that the situation would be no different if the question were examined from the opposite point of view and one were to consider the non-existence of the right and the finding to that effect.

What is important to stress is that at the time when an application is made the right already exists (or does not) and the provision which confers that right on (or denies it to) the individual is lawful or unlawful. The procedure for judicial review merely postpones the establishment of the existence of the right, that is to say its full and effective operation, to a later point in time and subject to the 'retroactivity' of the effects of the actual establishment of the right. That is plainly true both where the establishment of the right entails an appraisal of the link between the factual situation and the provision relied upon and where the national court is called upon to determine the provision applicable from between two or more provisions, which may even be in conflict. In the latter situation, too, where the existence of the right may also be established by means of a review of validity, the provision which will be determined as the one applicable (in place of another declared to be invalid or incompatible) was in reality so applicable at the time when the application was made, inasmuch as at that time what was lacking was only the establishment of the right's existence and not also its actual existence. That has been specifically emphasised also by the Court of Justice in *Amministrazione delle Finanze delle Stato v Mireco SaS* (Case 826/79) [1980] ECR 2559, when it held, p 2573, paragraph 7:

> The interpretation which, in the exercise of the jurisdiction conferred upon it by article 177, the Court of Justice gives to a rule of Community law clarifies and defines where necessary the meaning and scope of that rule as it must be or ought to have been understood and applied from the time of its coming into force.

18 The above-mentioned general remedy for the lack of contemporaneity between the establishment of the right's existence and its actual existence does not always succeed in achieving the main objective of judicial protection. Sometimes the right's existence is established too late for the right claimed to be fully and usefully exercised, which is the more likely to be the case the more structured and complex, and the more probably rich in safeguards, is the procedure culminating in the definitive establishment of the right. The result is that in such a case the utility as well as the effectiveness of judicial protection may be lost and there could be a betrayal of the principle, long established in jurisprudence, according to which the need to have recourse to legal proceedings to enforce a right should not occasion damage to the party in the right.

Interim protection has precisely that objective purpose, namely to ensure that the time needed to establish the existence of the right does not in the end have the effect of irremediably depriving the right of substance, by eliminating any possibility of exercising it; in brief, the purpose of interim protection is to achieve that fundamental objective of every legal system, the effectiveness of judicial protection. Interim protection is intended to prevent so far as possible the damage occasioned by the fact that the establishment and the existence of the right are not fully contemporaneous from prejudicing the effectiveness and the very purpose of establishing the right, which was also specifically affirmed by the Court of Justice when it linked interim protection to a requirement that, when delivered, the judgment will be fully effective (see, for example, the order in *Renckens v Commission of the European Communities* (Case 27/68) [1969] ECR 255, 274; and see also the opinion of Mr Advocate General Capotorti in *Commission of the European Communities v France* (Cases 24/80, 97/80 R) [1980] ECR 1319, 1337; further, the orders in *Gutmann v Commission of the European Communities* (Cases 18/65, 35/65) [1966] ECR 103, 135; in *Nederlandse Sigarenwinkeliers Organisatie v Commission of the European Atomic Energy Community* (Case 260/82 R) [1982] ECR 4371, 4377, 4378; in *Fabbro v Commission of the European Communities* (Case 269/84 R) [1984] ECR 4333; and in *De Compte v European Parliament* (Case 44/88 R) [1988] ECR 1669, 1670, are in substantially the same terms); or to the need to 'preserve the existing position pending a decision on the substance of the case': *CMC Cooperativa Muratori e Cementisti v Commission of the European Communities* (Case 118/83 R) [1983] ECR 2583, 2595, paragraph 37.

19 Now that the function of interim protection has been brought into focus, such protection can be seen to be a fundamental and indispensable instrument of any judicial system, which seeks to achieve, in the particular case and always in an effective manner, the objective of determining the existence of a right and more generally of giving effect to the

relevant legal provision, whenever the duration of the proceedings is likely to prejudice the attainment of this objective and therefore to nullify the effectiveness of the judgment.

The requirement for interim protection, moreover, as has already been noted, arises in the 'same terms, both where the establishment of the right's existence involves the facts and consequently, the determination of the correct provision to be applied, that is to say where the uncertainty as to the outcome of the application involves (although the expression is not perhaps a happy one) 'the facts', and where it is a question of choosing between two or more provisions which may be applicable (for example, a classification problem), irrespective of whether both are presumed to be valid or whether one is presumed to be incompatible with the other, which is of a higher order or in any event has precedence.

In particular, where, as in the case now before the Court of Justice, the determination as to the existence of the right not only involves a choice between two or more provisions which may be applicable but also involves a prior review of the validity or compatibility of one provision vis à vis another of a higher order or in any event having precedence, the difference is merely one of appearance, particularly when that review is entrusted to a court on which special jurisdiction has been conferred for the purpose. This situation, too, is fully covered by the typical function of judicial proceedings, which seek to establish the existence of and hence to give effect to the right, so that the requirement that the individual's position be protected on a provisional basis remains the same, inasmuch as it is a question of determining, interpreting and applying to the case in question the relevant (and valid) legal rules.

20 It follows that what is commonly called the presumption of validity, which attaches to laws or administrative acts no less than it does to Community acts, until such time as it is established by judicial determination that the measure in question is incompatible with a rule of law of a higher order or in any event having precedence, to the extent that such a procedure is provided for, does not constitute a formal obstacle to the interim protection of enforceable legal rights. In fact, precisely because what is concerned is a presumption, which as such may be rebutted by the final determination, it remains necessary to provide a remedy to compensate for the fact that the final ruling establishing the existence of the right may come too late and therefore be of no use to the successful party.

In fact, it is certain and undeniable that a provision, whether it is contained in an Act of Parliament or a Community act, or in an administrative act, must be presumed to be valid. But that cannot and must not mean that the courts are precluded from temporarily paralysing its effects with regard to the concrete case before them where, pending a final determination on its validity or compatibility vis à vis a provision of a higher order or having precedence, one or other of the legal rights in question is likely to be irremediably impaired and there is a suspicion (the degree of which must be established) that the final determination may entail a finding that the statute or administrative act in question is invalid.

21 In brief, the presumption that a law or an administrative act is valid may not and must not mean that the very possibility of interim protection is precluded where the measure in question may form the subject of a final judicial review of its validity.

Far from running counter to the principle of the validity of laws or administrative acts, which finds expression in a presumption that may always be rebutted by a final determination, interim protection in fact removes the risk that that presumption may lead to the perverse result, certainly not desired by any legal system, negating the function of judicial review and, in particular, of the review of the validity of laws. To take a different view would amount to denying root and branch the possibility of interim protection, not only in relation to laws, but absolutely, given that any act of a public authority, whether it is a rule-making instrument properly so called or an individual decision, is presumed to be valid until the outcome of the judicial review of its validity.

22 In a procedural situation of the type with which we are concerned here, in which one provision is alleged to be incompatible with another of a higher order or having precedence, it is essential, as has already been stressed, to bear in mind the fact that both provisions hypothetically apply to the case in question from the moment when the application is made. That is especially so since the final determination, whose consequences are made to take effect from the time of the application, creates nothing new as regards the existence (or the non-existence) of the right claimed because the provisions in point are hypothetically valid and operative in the alternative (or invalid and inoperative) and to both is attached what is commonly called a presumption of validity, whilst what is postponed, owing to the time taken by the proceedings, is merely the point in time at which the final determination is made. In the meantime, a situation prevails which may be defined precisely in terms of 'apparent law' and which is the very reason for interim measures, neither of the provisions in point giving rise to rights which are more than putative. It is therefore not a case of there being certainty (with the corresponding presumption of validity) as to one provision and uncertainty as to the other but the putative existence of both provisions. It is for the courts to assess whether the putative nature of the right claimed is such that interim protection must be granted or refused, on the basis of substantive criteria linked to the greater or lesser extent to which provision at issue appears to be valid (*prima facie* case, *fumus boni juris*, however designated) and to the possibility or otherwise that one or other of the interests in question may be prejudiced pending the final outcome of the proceedings.

23 The foregoing observations are amply confirmed by the fact that in all the legal systems of the Member States (the Danish system constitutes a partial exception), however diverse may be the forms and requirements connected with the duration of the proceedings, there is provision for the interim protection of rights denied under a lower ranking provision but claimed on the basis of a provision of a higher order.

First of all, it is beyond dispute that the application of an administrative act, which however benefits from a presumption of validity in the same way as a law, so that the bringing of an action does not suspend its operation (except in certain rare cases), may be nevertheless suspended by way of interim relief pending a definitive ruling on validity.

The provisional disapplication of primary legislation, in legal systems in which judicial review of the validity thereof is provided for, is certainly rarer.

Often the problem of the constitutionality of primary legislation is raised in the context of proceedings brought against an administrative act adopted in pursuance of the legislation in question so that the question of disapplying the legislation as such does not arise; in some systems this is the only situation possible.

In other countries, on the other hand, and in particular in those where judicial review of the (constitutional) legality of primary legislation is not generally available but is confined to a specific judicial body, provision is made, or the practice is, for provisional suspension to be ordered. For example, in Germany, the Federal Constitutional Court may provisionally suspend the application of primary legislation in a context (*Verfassungsbeschwerden*) not dissimilar to that of the English procedure for judicial review (see *Bundesverfassungsgericht*, 16 October 1977, Schleyer, *Foro Italiano*, 1978, IV, p 222; *Bundesverfassungsgericht*, 19 June 1962, BVerfGE, Vol 14, p 153); so, too, may the ordinary courts, which must then refer the matter to the Constitutional Court: see *Bundesverfassungsgericht*, 5 October 1977, BVerfGE, Vol 46, p 43.

Of particular relevance, moreover, is the case in Italy, inasmuch as not only do the ordinary courts not have the power to determine the unconstitutionality of laws and must therefore refer the matter to the Constitutional Court, but no power is expressly conferred either on the Constitutional Court or on the ordinary courts (or administrative courts) to grant interim measures (by way of suspension of the application of a law) pending the outcome of review proceedings. Notwithstanding this, many ordinary courts (Pretore, Bari, order of 4 February 1978, *Foro Italiano*, 1978, 1, p 1807; Pretore, *La Spezia*, order of 29 March 1978, *Foro Italiano* 1979, I, p 285; Pretore, Pisa, order of 30 July 1977, *Foro Italiano*, 1977, I, p 2354; Pretore, Pavia, order of 14 March 1977, Riv Giur Lav 1977, II, p 640; Pretore, Voltri, order of 1 September 1977, Riv Giur Lav, 1977, II, p 639; Pretore, La Spezia, order of 23 November 1978, *Foro Italiano* 1979. I, p 1921 *et seq*), with the support of the majority view in academic literature (see Verde, 'Considerazioni sul Procedimento d'Urgenza'. Studi Andrioli, Naples 1979, pp 446 *et seq; Mortati, Istituzioni di Diritto Pubblico*, 1976, II, p 1391; Campanile, 'Procedimento d'Urgenza e Incidente di Legittimita Costituzionale', Riv Dir Proc 1985, pp 124 *et seq*; Zagrebelsky, *'La Tutela d'Urgenza,' le Garanzie Giurisdizionali dei Diritti Fondamentali*, Padua 1988, pp 27 *et seq*; Sandulli, *Manuale di Diritto Amministrativo*, Naples 1984, II, p 1408), have taken the view that it is possible to issue interim measures suspending the application of primary legislation (obviously with regard only to the parties to the proceedings) pending a ruling by the Constitutional Court. That court, although it has never decided the specific point which is before the Court of Justice (but see, with regard to the permissibility of interim protection pending settlement of jurisdictional questions, Corte Costituzionale No 73 of 6 June 1973, *Foro Italiano* 1973, I, p 1657; and see also Corte di Cassazione, Sezioni Unite, 1 December 1978, No 5678, *Foro Italiano* 1978, I, p 2704), has not failed to affirm, on the one hand, the essential role played by interim relief in ensuring the effectiveness of the system of judicial protection (see Corte Costituzionale 27 December 1974, No 284, *Foro Italiano* 1975, I, p 263) and, on the other hand, the existence of a general principle and of a 'rule of rationality' underlying the legal system according to which it is for the courts, where the necessary preconditions are fulfilled (that is, a *prima facie* case and *periculum in mora*), to adopt such urgent measures as are appropriate for ensuring, on a provisional basis, the effect, of the final decision on the merits: Corte Costituzionale 28 June 1985 No 190, *Foro Italiano* 1985, I, 1881. See also, for some points of interest, Corte di Cassazione, Sezione Unite Civili, 1 December 1978, No 5678, Foro Italiano 1978, I, p 2704; Consiglio di Stato, 14 April 1972, No 5, *Foro Italiano* 1972, III, p 105; Consiglio di Stato, 8 October 1982, No 17, *Foro Italiano* 1983, II, p 41.

Albeit in a different context, it is also significant that the French Conseil Constitutionnel declared to be unconstitutional a law which did not empower the courts to suspend, by way of interim relief, the application of an administrative decision, and moreover described such suspension as a 'garantie essentielle des droits de la défense': see Decision No 8224 DC of 23 January 1987, JORF of 25 January 1987, p 925.

24 If attention is now turned to the relationship between national provisions and Community provisions, there is no doubt that, by means of preliminary rulings given by the Court of Justice and the 'direct' competence of national courts, machinery has been introduced which essentially consists of the review of the validity (or of compatibility, if this is preferred) of a national provision in relation to a Community provision, given that the national courts have jurisdiction to rule definitively that the former is incompatible with the latter. And if therefore the national courts may, indeed must, disapply a national law which conflicts with a Community provision having direct effect, once a definitive finding has been made to that effect (or, at any rate, must achieve that substantive result), they must also be able to disapply that law provisionally, provided that the preconditions are satisfied, where the incompatibility is not entirely certain or 'established' but may call for a preliminary ruling by the Court of Justice. Otherwise, that judicial protection of the rights conferred on individuals by the Community provision which, as has been affirmed by the Court of Justice

on numerous occasions and also specifically pointed out by the House of Lords, is the subject of a precise obligation on the part of the national courts, might be nullified.

25 This brings me back to the concrete case submitted for the consideration of the Court of Justice by way of the questions referred to it by the House of Lords. The right of the applicants in the main proceedings, which is denied by the national statute, is claimed on the basis of certain EEC Treaty provisions having direct effect, that is to say provisions which prevail over domestic law but whose interpretation in the sense contended for is not free from doubt and, consequently, requires a preliminary ruling by the Court of Justice. In the meantime, the national court finds a bar to interim protection of the rights claimed in the presumption of validity which attaches to the statute until a final determination is made.

Inasmuch as the English court, as is undisputed and as it has itself underlined, can and must give precedence, once the final determination is made, by virtue of the review which can be carried out of the compatibility of the English statute with Community law, to the 'certain' Community rule having direct effect, it must also be able, where the necessary preconditions are satisfied, to grant interim protection to the rights claimed on the basis of 'uncertain' Community rules and denied by the provisions of national law.

The problem is not one of form but of substance. The presumption of validity does not have preclusive effect in view of the fact that it may be rebutted by the final determination, as is the case in the English legal system also by virtue of the European Communities Act 1972, just as the presumption of the validity of any provision subordinate to a provision of a higher order does not preclude interim relief. And it is the national court itself which points this out in the order for reference in relation to the possibility of suspending the application of a subordinate measure which is suspected of being in conflict with a statute.

26 What I mean to say, therefore, is that this assessment must be carried out on the basis of substantive criteria and not, as suggested by the United Kingdom, on the basis of a formal criterion such as the presumption of the validity of statute.

To give priority to the national legislation merely because it has not yet been definitively established as incompatible with Community law (and thus to proceed on the basis merely of a putative compatibility) may amount to depriving the Community rules of the effective judicial protection which is to be afforded to them 'from the date of their entry into force and for so long as they continue in force.' Paradoxically, the right conferred (putatively) by the provision of Community law would as a general rule receive less, or less effective, protection than rights conferred (also putatively) by the provision of national law. That would be tantamount to saying that the right conferred by ordinary legislation may receive interim protection, whereas protection is denied to the right conferred by the Community, or in any event higher ranking, provision, on the basis of the presumption of validity in favour of that legislation; as if the same presumption, which after all is nothing other than 'putative', did not also avail the provision having precedence.

Let me be quite clear. I do not mean by this that the national court must always and in any event give priority to a right putatively conferred by Community law as opposed to a right putatively conferred by national law, but merely that it must have the power to do so where the factual and legal circumstances so require; in other words it may (and must) not find formal obstacles to any application for interim measures based on directly effective Community provisions.

27 Nor does it avail to put forward as a counter argument the presumption of validity which attaches to Community measures, a presumption stressed many times by the Court of Justice. That is an argument which ends up by demonstrating the contrary. It is scarcely necessary to recall to mind Article 185 of the EEC Treaty which expressly provides that the

Court of Justice may 'if it considers that circumstances so require, order that application of the contested act be suspended'.

But that is not all. Even in regard to a system for the review of the validity of Community measures which is rigorously centred on the Court of Justice (also as regards the preliminary rulings procedure under Article 177 of the EEC Treaty), the Court of Justice itself has not failed to stress that 'the rule that national courts may not themselves declare Community acts invalid may have to be qualified in certain circumstances in the case of proceedings relating to an application for interim measures': see *Foto-Frost v Hauptzollamt Lübeck-Ost* (Case 314/85) [1987] ECR 4199, 4232, paragraph 19.

28 Similarly, it is not at the formal but rather on the substantive level that it is necessary to assess the possibility that interim protection may be obtained (also) by way of an injunction against the Crown. By way of example, I would consider it unreasonable to think in terms of an injunction (to adopt a measure or enact primary legislation) which would amount to an interference with the discretionary powers enjoyed by the Crown or even by Parliament, whilst on the other hand I would regard it as being entirely reasonable and 'orthodox' order concrete non-discretionary action to be taken or, as in this case, the temporary suspension of application of the statute or administrative act, solely with regard to the parties to the proceedings, until such time as the court is in a position definitively to apply or to disapply one or the other.

29 In conclusion, the reply which I propose should be given by the Court of Justice to the first question put to it by the House of Lords is affirmative in the sense that, under Community law, the national court must be able to afford interim protection, where the pre-conditions are met, to rights claimed by an individual on the basis of provisions of Community law having direct effect, pending the final outcome of the proceedings, including proceedings on a reference to the Court of Justice for a preliminary ruling. And I also suggest that the Court of Justice should expressly link this power and duty of the national court to the requirement for effective judicial protection which applies in relation to provisions of Community law just as much as it does in relation to provisions of national law.

30 I need hardly add that such a reply does not amount to imposing remedies or judicial procedures different from those already provided for in the domestic law of the Member States but merely implies that such remedies or procedures must be used 'for the purpose of ensuring observance of Community provisions having direct effect, on the same conditions concerning admissibility and procedure as would apply were it a question of ensuring observance of national law': *Rewe-Handelsgesellschaft Nord mbH v Hauptzollampt Kiel* (Case 158/80) [1981] ECR 1805, 1838, paragraph 44. But I would recall once again that the principle in question, according to which the means of affording judicial protection to rights conferred by provisions of Community law remain exclusively those provided for by domestic law, does not apply if 'those rules and time limits made it impossible in practice to exercise rights which the national courts have a duty to protect': see the *Comet* case [1976] ECR 2043, 2053, paragraph 16; the *Rewe-Zentralfinanz* case [1976] ECR 1989, 1900 paragraph 15, the *Express Dairy* case [1980] ECR 1887, 1997–1998, paragraph 12, the *Denkavit* case [1980] ECR 1205, 1226, 6 paragraph 25; and the *Mireco* case [1980] ECR 2559, 2574, paragraph 13.

31 In fact, as is made clear also by the order for reference and the observations of the United Kingdom, provision is made in the United Kingdom procedural system for the interim protection of a right, pending the final determination, whenever a danger would be caused by delay (*periculum in mora*) and a *prima facie* case is made out (the Divisional Court granted the interim relief requested). Consequently, it is not a question here of a procedure which is not provided for by the national legal system, rather it is simply a question of using

the existing procedure in order to protect a right claimed on the basis of a provision of Community law having direct effect. The same may be said of the impossibility, to which reference has been made, of obtaining an injunction against the Crown, when in reality it is merely a case or ordering the provisional suspension of the application of a statute to the parties concerned, it being clearly understood that it may be the latter who will bear the risk of a final determination unfavourable to them.

If that were not the case, on the other hand, there would in any event still be a specific obligation, where the appropriate preconditions are satisfied, to afford interim protection, since otherwise we would find ourselves confronted precisely with the situation (I would again mention the *Simmenthal* case [1978] ECR 629) of a procedural system which makes it impossible in practice 'to exercise rights which the national courts have a duty to protect'. That would be all the more serious if regard were had to the fact, also mentioned in the order for reference, that under the English legal system the definitive establishment of the right claimed never entails the recovery of losses suffered in the course of the proceedings by those claiming the legal right at issue. That is something which, let me be clear, is in itself a matter for concern in the light of the obligation of national courts to give full effect to the provisions of Community law.

32 Nor does there seem to me to be any justified basis for arguing *a contrario* (as in the observations of Ireland and the United Kingdom) that individuals are afforded sufficient protection by virtue of the right of the Commission, by infringement proceedings brought under Article 169 of the EEC Treaty, to apply to the Court of Justice for interim measures, a situation which in fact has occurred in this instance in regard to the nationality requirements of the United Kingdom legislation now before the Court of Justice, as I have already indicated. In this respect may it suffice to recall the judgment in *NV Algemene Transport en Expeditie Onderneming van Gend en Loos v Nederlandse Administratie der Belastingen* (Case 26/62) [1963] ECR I, in which the Court of Justice affirmed that a restriction of the guarantees against an infringement by Member States of a Community provision having direct effect to the procedures under Articles 169 and 170 'would remove all direct legal protection of the individual rights of their nationals'.

33 The reply to the first question raised by the House of Lords, therefore, can only be in the affirmative, in the sense that the national court's duty to afford effective judicial protection to rights conferred on the individual by Community law, where the relevant requirements are satisfied, cannot fail to include the provision of interim protection for the rights claimed, pending a final determination.

Moreover, the first question is whether Community law obliges the national court to grant such interim protection or gives it the power to grant such protection, so that the second question as to the criteria which the national court should apply is dependent on a negative reply as to the obligation and an affirmative reply as to the power.

Over and above the literal formulation of the questions and the corresponding replies to be given by the Court of Justice, I consider that it is necessary to be very clear as to the substance. In the first place, it does not seem to me that we are concerned with an alternative, in the proper sense of the term, between an 'obligation' and a 'power', regard being had to the fact that what is involved is a judicial activity which the national court is called upon to carry out and which, by its very nature, is an activity involving an assessment of the factual and legal elements presented by the specific case before the national court at any given time. Consequently, it is possible to use the expression 'obligation', in accordance with the Court of Justice's case law, in the sense that the national court performs that obligation by means of an assessment on a case by case basis of the preconditions on which generally the adoption of an interim measure depends.

In this connection, I consider not only that it is for the national court, obviously, to determine whether the preconditions for interim protection are met, but also that, in the absence of Community harmonisation, those preconditions must be and must remain those provided for by the individual, national legal systems. Further, it does not seem to me that the subject matter allows much room for imagination or offers scope for revolutionary discoveries, since legal theory and positive law, including that of the United Kingdom, have long specified the *prima facie* case (however designated) and the *periculum in mora* as the two basic preconditions for interim protection. The accent may be placed on one or the other according to the legal system in question, or what is a *prima facie* case may or may not perfectly coincide with the not manifestly ill founded or the *prima facie* well founded nature of the claim and so on, or it may be that in the assessment of the *periculum in mora*, apart from the traditional and necessary balancing of the respective interests of the parties (ensuring that the interim measure does not in its turn cause irreparable damage to the other party), express consideration is also given to the public interest. All that forms part of the prudent appreciation by the national courts which, case by case, will carry out a just appraisal of the appropriateness or necessity of granting or refusing an interim measure for the interim protection of the rights claimed. And there is scarcely any need to point out that in considering whether there is a *prima facie* case the courts will take account of the possibility that the national provision may be declared incompatible with Community law.

In the result, as regards the second question in particular, I suggest that the Court of Justice should give a reply which is in conformity with the judgment in the *Comet* case [1976] ECR 2043 in the sense that 'the methods and time limits' of the interim protection are and remain, in the absence of harmonisation, those provided for by the national legal systems, provided that they are not such as to make it impossible in practice 'to exercise rights which the national courts have a duty to protect'.

Consequently, it is for the national court to draw from the above the necessary inferences as to the determination of the dispute before it on the basis of the factors set out in the statement of the grounds on which the questions are based; the Court of Justice clearly cannot make any assessment of the merits of those factors.

34 On the basis of the foregoing considerations, I therefore propose that the Court of Justice should reply as follows to the questions formulated by the House of Lords: (1) The obligation imposed by Community law on the national court to ensure the effective judicial protection of rights directly conferred on the individual by provisions of Community law includes the obligation, if the need arises and where the factual and legal preconditions are met, to afford interim and urgent protection to rights claimed on the basis of such provisions of Community law, pending a final determination and any interpretation by way of a preliminary ruling given by the Court of Justice. (2) In the absence of Community harmonisation, it is the legal system of each Member State which determines the procedural methods and the preconditions for the interim protection of rights vested in individuals by virtue of provisions of Community law having direct effect, on condition that those methods and preconditions do not make it impossible to exercise on an interim basis the rights claimed and are not less favourable than those provided to afford protection to rights founded on national provisions, any provision of national law or any national practice having such an effect being incompatible with Community law.

19 June: the following judgment was delivered in open court in Luxembourg.

1   By a judgment of 18 May 1989 in *R v Secretary of State for Transport ex p Factortame Ltd* [1990] 2 AC 85, which was received at the Court Registry on 10 July 1989, the House of Lords referred to the European Court of Justice for a preliminary ruling under Article 177 of the EEC Treaty two questions on the interpretation of Community law. Those questions concern

the extent of the power of national courts to grant interim relief where rights claimed under Community law are at issue.

2   The questions were raised in proceedings brought against the Secretary of State for Transport by Factortame Ltd and other companies incorporated under the laws of the United Kingdom, and also the directors and shareholders of those companies, most of whom are Spanish nationals (hereinafter together referred to as 'the applicants').

3   The companies in question are the owners or operators of 95 fishing vessels which were registered in the register of British vessels under the Merchant Shipping Act 1894. Of those vessels, 53 were originally registered in Spain and flew the Spanish flag, but on various dates as from 1980 they were registered in the British register. The remaining 42 vessels have always been registered in the United Kingdom, but were purchased by the companies in question on various dates, mainly since 1983.

4   The statutory system governing the registration of British fishing vessels was radically altered by Part II of the Merchant Shipping Act 1988 and the Merchant Shipping (Registration of Fishing Vessels) Regulations 1988 (SI 1988/1926). It is common ground that the United Kingdom amended the previous legislation in order to put a stop to the practice known as 'quota hopping' whereby, according to the United Kingdom, its fishing quotas were 'plundered' by vessels flying the British flag but lacking any genuine link with the United Kingdom.

5   The Act of 1988 provided for the establishment of a new register in which henceforth all British fishing vessels were to be registered, including those which were already registered in the old general register maintained under the Act of 1894. However, only fishing vessels fulfilling the conditions laid down in section 14 of the Act of 1988 could be registered in the new register.

6   Section 14(1) provides that, subject to dispensations to be determined by the Secretary of State for Transport, a fishing vessel is eligible to be registered in the new register only if:

(a) the vessel is British-owned; (b) the vessel is managed, and its operations are directed and controlled, from within the United Kingdom; and (c) any charterer, manager or operator of the vessel is a qualified person or company.

According to section 14(2), a fishing vessel is deemed to be British-owned if the legal title to the vessel is vested wholly in one or more qualified persons or companies, and if the vessel is beneficially owned by one or more qualified companies or, as to not less than 75%, by one or more qualified persons. According to section 14(7) 'qualified person' means a person who is a British citizen resident and domiciled in the United Kingdom and 'qualified company' means a company incorporated in the United Kingdom and having its principal place of business there, at least 75% of its shares being owned by one or more qualified persons or companies and at least 75% of its directors being qualified persons.

7   The Act of 1988 and the Regulations of 1988 entered into force on 1 December 1988. However, under section 13 of the Act of 1988, the validity of registrations effected under the previous Act was extended for a transitional period until 31 March 1989.

8   On 4 August 1989 the Commission of the European Communities brought an action before the Court of Justice under Article 169 of the EEC Treaty for a declaration that, by imposing the nationality requirements laid down in section 14 of the Act of 1988, the United Kingdom had failed to fulfil its obligations under Articles 7, 52 and 221 of the EEC Treaty. That action is the subject of Case 246/89, now pending before the Court of Justice. In a separate document, lodged at the Court Registry on the same date, the Commission applied to the Court of Justice for an interim order requiring the United Kingdom to suspend the

application of those nationality requirements as regards the nationals of the other Member States and in respect of fishing vessels which until 31 March 1989 had been carrying on a fishing activity under the British flag and under a British fishing licence. By an order of 10 October 1989 in *Commission of the European Communities v United Kingdom* (Case 246/89 R) (1989) *The Times*, 28 October, the President of the Court of Justice granted that application. Pursuant to that order, the United Kingdom made an Order in Council amending section 14 of the Act of 1988 with effect from 2 November 1989.

9   At the time of the institution of the proceedings in which the appeal arises, the 99 fishing vessels of the applicants failed to satisfy one or more of the conditions for registration under section 14 of the Act of 1988 and thus could not be registered in the new register.

10   Since those vessels were to be deprived of the right to engage in fishing as from 1 April 1989, the companies in question, by means of an application for judicial review, challenged the compatibility of Part II of the Act of 1988 with Community law. They also applied for the grant of interim relief until such time as final judgment was given on their application for judicial review.

11   In its judgment of 10 March 1989, the Divisional Court of the Queen's Bench Division (i) decided to stay the proceedings and to make a reference under article 177 of the EEC Treaty for a preliminary ruling on the issues of Community law raised in the proceedings; and (ii) ordered that, by way of interim relief, the application of Part II of the Act of 1988 and the Regulations of 1988 should be suspended as regards the applicants.

12   On 13 March 1989, the Secretary of State for Transport appealed against the Divisional Court's order granting interim relief. By judgment of 22 March 1989 the Court of Appeal held that under national law the courts had no power to suspend, by way of interim relief, the application of Acts of Parliament. It therefore set aside the order of the Divisional Court.

13   The House of Lords, before which the matter was brought, delivered its judgment on 18 May 1989. In its judgment it found in the first place that the claims by the applicants that they would suffer irreparable damage if the interim relief which they sought were not granted and they were successful in the main proceedings were well founded. However, it held that, under national law, the English courts had no power to grant interim relief in a case such as the one before it. More specifically, it held that the grant of such relief was precluded by the old common law rule that an interim injunction may not be granted against the Crown, that is to say against the government, in conjunction with the presumption that an Act of Parliament is in conformity with Community law until such time as a decision on its compatibility with that law has been given.

14   The House of Lords then turned to the question whether, notwithstanding that rule of national law, English courts had the power, under Community law, to grant an interim injunction against the Crown.

15   Consequently, taking the view that the dispute raised an issue concerning the interpretation of Community law, the House of Lords decided, pursuant to Article 177 of the EEC. Treaty to stay the proceedings until the Court of Justice had given a preliminary ruling on the following questions:

(1) Where: (i) a party before the national court claims to be entitled to rights under Community law having direct effect in national law ('the rights claimed'), (ii) a national measure in clear terms will, if applied, automatically deprive that party of the rights claimed, (iii) there are serious arguments both for and against the existence of the rights claimed and the national court has sought a preliminary ruling under Article 177 as to whether or not the rights claimed exist, (iv) the national law presumes the national measure in question to be compatible with

Community law unless and until it is declared incompatible, (v) the national court has no power to give interim protection to the rights claimed by suspending the application of the national measure pending the preliminary ruling, (vi) if the preliminary ruling is in the event in favour of the rights claimed, the party entitled to those rights is likely to have suffered irremediable damage unless given such interim protection, does Community law either (a) oblige the national court to grant such interim protection of the rights claimed; or (b) give the court power to grant such interim protection of the rights claimed? (2) If question 1(a) is answered in the negative and question 1(b) in the affirmative, what are the criteria to be applied in deciding whether or not to grant such interim protection of the rights claimed?

16   Reference is made to the report for the hearing for a fuller account of the facts in the proceedings before the national court, the course of the procedure before and the observations submitted to the Court of Justice, which are mentioned or discussed hereinafter only in so far as is necessary for the reasoning of the Court of Justice.

17   It is clear from the information before the Court of Justice, and in particular from the judgment making the reference and, as described above, the course taken by the proceedings in the national courts before which the case came at first and second instance, that the preliminary question raised by the House of Lords seeks essentially to ascertain whether a national court which, in a case before it concerning Community law, considers that the sole obstacle which precludes it from granting interim relief is a rule of national law, must disapply that rule.

18   For the purpose of replying to that question, it is necessary to point out that in *Amministrazione delle Finanze dello Stato v Simmenthal SpA* (Case 106/77) [1978] ECR 629 the Court of Justice held, at p 643, paragraph 14, that directly applicable rules of Community law 'must be fully and uniformly applied in all the Member States from the date of their entry into force and for so long as they continue in force' and that, p 643, paragraph 17:

> ... in accordance with the principle of the precedence of Community law, the relationship between provisions of the EEC Treaty and directly applicable measures of the institutions on the one hand and the national law of the Member States on the other is such that those provisions and measures ... by their entry into force render automatically inapplicable any conflicting provision of ... national law ...

19   In accordance with the case law of the Court of Justice, it is for the national courts, in application of the principle of co-operation laid down in Article 5 of the EEC Treaty, to ensure the legal protection which persons derive from the direct effect of provisions of Community law: see, most recently, *Amministrazione delle Finanze dello Stato v Ariete SpA* (Case 811/79) [1980] ECR 2545 and *Amministrazione delle Finanze dello Stato v MIRECO SaS* (Case 826/79) [1980] ECR 2559.

20   The Court of Justice has also held that any provision of a national legal system and any legislative, administrative or judicial practice which might impair the effectiveness of Community law by withholding from the national court having jurisdiction to apply such law the power to do everything necessary at the moment of its application to set aside national legislative provisions which might prevent, even temporarily, Community rules from having full force and effect are incompatible with those requirements. which are the very essence of Community law: see the judgment in the *Simmenthal* case [1978] ECR 629, 644, paragraphs 22 and 23.

21   It must be added that the full effectiveness of Community law would be just as much impaired if a rule of national law could prevent a court seised of a dispute governed by Community law from granting interim relief in order to ensure the full effectiveness of the judgment to be given on the existence of the rights claimed under Community law. It follows

that a court which in those circumstances would grant interim relief, if it were not for a rule of national law, is obliged to set aside that rule.

22   That interpretation is reinforced by the system established by Article 177 of the EEC Treaty whose effectiveness would be impaired if a national court, having stayed proceedings pending the reply by the Court of Justice to the question referred to it for a preliminary ruling, were not able to grant interim relief until it delivered its judgment following the reply given by the Court of Justice.

23   Consequently, the reply to the question raised should be that Community law must be interpreted as meaning that a national court which, in a case before it concerning Community law, considers that the sole obstacle which precludes it from granting interim relief is a rule of national law must set aside that rule.

Costs

24   The costs incurred by the United Kingdom, Ireland and the Commission of the European Communities, which have submitted observations to the Court of Justice, are not recoverable. Since these proceedings are, in so far as the parties to the main proceedings are concerned, in the nature of a step in the proceedings pending before the national court, the decision on costs is a matter for that court.

On those grounds, the court in reply to the question referred to it for a preliminary ruling by the House of Lords, by judgment of 18 May 1989, hereby rules: Community law must be interpreted as meaning that a national court which, in a case before it concerning Community law, considers that the sole obstacle which precludes it from granting interim relief is a rule of national law must set aside that rule.

Solicitors: Chief State Solicitor, Republic of Ireland; Treasury Solicitor; Thomas Cooper & Stibbard.

[Reported by Paul H Niekirk Esq, Barrister at Law.]

After the answers to the questions referred to the European Court of Justice had been received, the matter was reconsidered by the House of Lords.

On 9 July, their Lordships made an order for interim relief for reasons to be given later.

The facts are set out in the opinions of Lord Bridge of Harwich and Lord Goff of Chieveley.

David Vaughan QC, Gerald Barling and *David Anderson* for the first to 94th applicants.

Nicholas Forwood QC for the 95th applicant, Rawlings (Trawling) Ltd.

Sir Nicholas Lyell QC, SG, John Laws, Stephen Richards and *G Andrew Macnab* for the Secretary of State.

Their Lordships took time for consideration.

11 October: **Lord Bridge of Harwich**: My Lords, when this appeal first came before the House last year [1990] 2 AC 85, your Lordships held that, as a matter of English law, the courts had no jurisdiction to grant interim relief in terms which would involve either overturning an English statute in advance of any decision by the European Court of Justice that the statute infringed Community law or granting an injunction against the Crown. It then became necessary to seek a preliminary ruling from the European Court of Justice as to whether Community law itself invested us with such jurisdiction. In the speech I delivered on that occasion, with which your Lordships agreed, I explained the reasons which led us to those conclusions. It will be remembered that, on that occasion, the House never directed its

attention to the question how, if there were jurisdiction to grant the relief sought, discretion ought to be exercised in deciding whether or not relief should be granted.

In June of this year we received the judgment of the European Court of Justice (Case C213/89), p 852B *et seq*, replying to the questions we had posed and affirming that we had jurisdiction, in the circumstances postulated, to grant interim relief for the protection of directly enforceable rights under Community law and that no limitation on our jurisdiction imposed by any rule of national law could stand as the sole obstacle to preclude the grant of such relief. In the light of this judgment we were able to conclude the hearing of the appeal in July and unanimously decided that relief should be granted in terms of the orders which the House then made, indicating that we would give our reasons for the decision later.

My noble and learned friend, Lord Goff of Chieveley, whose speech I have had the advantage of reading in draft, has given a very full account of all the relevant circumstances arising since our decision last year in the light of which our final disposal of the appeal fell to be made. I gratefully adopt this account. I also agree with his exposition of the principles applicable in relation to the grant of interim injunctive relief where the dispute involves a conflict between private and public interests and where damages are not a remedy available to either party, leading, in the circumstances of this case, to the conclusion that it was appropriate to grant relief in terms of the orders made by the House. But I add some observations of my own in view of the importance of the subject matter.

Some public comments on the decision of the European Court of Justice, affirming the jurisdiction of the courts of Member States to override national legislation if necessary to enable interim relief to be granted in protection of rights under Community law, have suggested that this was a novel and dangerous invasion by a Community institution of the sovereignty of the United Kingdom Parliament. But such comments are based on a misconception. If the supremacy within the European Community of Community law over the national law of Member States was not always inherent in the EEC Treaty (Cmnd 5179-II) it was certainly well established in the jurisprudence of the European Court of Justice long before the United Kingdom joined the Community. Thus, whatever limitation of its sovereignty Parliament accepted when it enacted the European Communities Act 1972 was entirely voluntary. Under the terms of the Act of 1972 it has always been clear that it was the duty of a United Kingdom court, when delivering final judgment, to override any rule of national law found to be in conflict with any directly enforceable rule of Community law. Similarly, when decisions of the European Court of Justice have exposed areas of United Kingdom statute law which failed to implement Council directives, Parliament has always loyally accepted the obligation to make appropriate and prompt amendments. Thus there is nothing in any way novel in according supremacy to rules of Community law in those areas to which they apply and to insist that, in the protection of rights under Community law, national courts must not be inhibited by rules of national law from granting interim relief in appropriate cases is no more than a logical recognition of that supremacy.

Although affirming our jurisdiction, the judgment of the European Court of Justice does not fetter our discretion to determine whether an appropriate case for the grant of interim relief has been made out. While agreeing with Lord Goff's exposition of the general principles by which the discretion should be guided, I would wish to emphasise the salient features of the present case which, at the end of the argument, left me in no doubt that interim relief should be granted. A decision to grant or withhold interim relief in the protection of disputed rights at a time when the merits of the dispute cannot be finally resolved must always involve an element of risk. If, in the end, the claimant succeeds in a case where interim relief has been refused, he will have suffered an injustice. If, in the end, he fails in a case where interim relief has been granted, injustice will have been done to the other party. The objective which underlies the principles by which the discretion is to be guided must always be to ensure that the court shall choose the course which, in all the circumstances, appears to offer the best prospect that eventual injustice will be avoided or minimised. Questions as to the adequacy of an alternative remedy in damages to the party claiming injunctive relief and of a cross-undertaking in damages to the party against whom the relief is sought play a primary role in assisting the court to determine which course offers the best prospect that injustice may be avoided or minimised. But where, as here, no alternative remedy will be available to either party if the final decision does not accord with the interim decision, choosing the course which will minimise the risk presents exceptional difficulty.

If the applicants were to succeed after a refusal of interim relief, the irreparable damage they would have suffered would be very great. That is now beyond dispute. On the other hand, if they failed after a grant of interim relief, there would have been a substantial detriment to the public interest resulting from the diversion of a very significant part of the British quota of controlled stocks of fish from those who ought in law to enjoy it to others having no right to it. In either case, if the final decision did not accord with the interim decision, there would have been an undoubted injustice. But the injustices are so different in kind that I find it very difficult to weigh the one against the other.

If the matter rested there. I should be inclined to say, for the reasons indicated by Lord Goff of Chieveley, that the public interest should prevail and interim relief be refused. But the matter does not rest there. Unlike the ordinary case in which the court must decide whether or not to grant interlocutory relief at a time when disputed issues of fact remain unresolved, here the relevant facts are all ascertained and the only unresolved issues are issues of law, albeit of Community law. Now, although the final decision of such issues is the exclusive prerogative of the European Court of Justice, that does not mean that an English court may not reach an informed opinion as to how such issues are likely to be resolved. In this case we are now in a position to derive much assistance in that task from the decisions of the European Court of Justice in *R v Minister of Agriculture, Fisheries and Food ex p Agegate Ltd* (Case C3/87) [1990] 2 QB 151 and *R v Ministry of Agriculture, Fisheries and Food ex p Jaderow Ltd* (Case C216/87) [1990] 2 QB 193 and the interim decision of the President in the proceedings brought by the European Commission against the United Kingdom (*Commission of the European Communities v United Kingdom* (Case 246/89 R) (1989) *The Times*, 28 October) to which Lord Goff of Chieveley has referred. In the circumstances I believe that the most logical course in seeking a decision least likely to occasion injustice is to make the best prediction we can of the final outcome and to give to that prediction decisive weight in resolving the interlocutory issue.

It is now, I think, common ground that the quota system operated under the common fisheries policy, in order to be effective and to ensure that the quota of a member state enures to the benefit of its local fishing industry, entitles the member state to derogate from rights otherwise exercisable under Community law to the extent necessary to ensure that only fishing vessels having a genuine economic link with that industry may fish against its quota. The narrow ground on which the Secretary of State resists the applicants' claim is that the requirements of section 14 of the Merchant Shipping Act 1988 that at least 75% of the beneficial ownership of a British fishing vessel must be vested in persons resident and domiciled in the United Kingdom is necessary to ensure that the vessel has a genuine economic link with the British fishing industry. Before the decision of the European Court of Justice in *Agegate* that would have seemed to me a contention of some cogency. But in *Agegate* it was held that a licensing condition requiring 75% of the crew of a vessel fishing against the quota of a Member State to be resident within the member state could not be justified on the ground that it was 'irrelevant to the aim of the quota system': p 261. I confess that I find some difficulty in understanding the reasoning in the judgment which leads to this conclusion. But if a residence requirement relating to crew members cannot be justified as necessary to the maintenance of a genuine economic link with the local industry, it is difficult to see how residence or domicile requirements relating to beneficial owners could possibly fare any better.

The broader contention on behalf of the Secretary of State that Member States have an unfettered right to determine what ships may fly their flag raises more difficult issues. It would not be appropriate in the context of the present interlocutory decision to enter upon a detailed examination of the wide-ranging arguments bearing upon those issues. I believe the best indication that we have of the prospect of success of that contention is found in the interlocutory judgment of President Due in the case brought by the Commission against the United Kingdom. He concluded that the contention was of insufficient weight to preclude him from granting an interim order suspending the application of the nationality requirements of section 14 of the Act of 1988 to nationals of other Member States. His reasoning persuaded me that we should reach the same conclusion in relation to the residence and domicile requirements.

Lord Brandon of Oakbrook: My Lords, I have had the advantage of reading in draft the speech produced by my noble and learned friend, Lord Goff of Chieveley, and agree with it entirely.

Lord Oliver of Aylmerton: My Lords, I have had the advantage of reading in draft the speech of my noble and learned friend, Lord Goff of Chieveley. I agree with it and, for the reasons given by my noble friend, I, too, would allow this appeal.

Lord Goff of Chieveley: My Lords, this appeal was last before your Lordships' House in May 1989. The subject matter of the proceedings is an application by the applicants for judicial review, challenging the legality of certain provisions of the Merchant Shipping Act 1988, and the Merchant Shipping (Registration of Fishing Vessels) Regulations 1988 (SI 1988/1926), on the ground that they contravene provisions of European law. The matter came before a Divisional Court (Neill LJ and Hodgson J), who requested a preliminary ruling from the European Court of Justice under Article 177 of the EEC Treaty on the questions necessary to enable them finally to determine the application. They then made an order for interim relief in the form of an order that in the meanwhile Part II of the Act of 1988 and the Regulations be disapplied and the Secretary of State for Transport be restrained from enforcing the same in respect of any of the applicants and any vessel now owned (in whole or in part), managed, operated or chartered by any of them so as to enable registration of any such vessel under the Merchant Shipping Act 1894 and/or the Sea Fishing Boats (Scotland) Act 1886 to continue in being. The Court of Appeal [1989] 2 CMLR 353 allowed an appeal by the Secretary of State from the interim order of the Divisional Court [1989] 2 CMLR 353. On appeal by the applicants to your Lordships' House [1990] 2 AC 85, it was held by your Lordships that, as a matter of English law, the English courts had no power to make such an order as that made by the Divisional Court . My noble and learned friend, Lord Bridge of Harwich, said of the order for interim relief, pp 142–43:

> Any such order, unlike any form of order for interim relief known to the law, would irreversibly determine in the applicants' favour for a period of some two years rights which are necessarily uncertain until the preliminary ruling of the ECJ has been given. If the applicants fail to establish the rights they claim before the ECJ, the effect of the interim relief granted would be to have conferred upon them rights directly contrary to Parliament's sovereign will and correspondingly to have deprived British fishing vessels, as defined by Parliament, of the enjoyment of a substantial proportion of the United Kingdom quota of stocks of fish protected

by the common fisheries policy. I am clearly of the opinion that, as a matter of English law, the court has no power to make an order which has these consequences.

Your Lordships' House further held that, in any event, there was no jurisdiction in English law to grant an interim injunction against the Crown; this provided an additional reason why the order made by the Divisional Court could not be supported. Your Lordships House however sought the guidance of the European Court of Justice on the question whether, in a case such as the present, European law overrides English law. Accordingly the following questions were referred to the court:

(1) Where: (i) a party before the national court claims to be entitled to rights under Community law having direct effect in national law ('the rights claimed'), (ii) a national measure in clear terms will, if applied, automatically deprive that party of the rights claimed, (iii) there are serious arguments both for and against the existence of the rights claimed and the national court has sought a preliminary ruling under Article 177 as to whether or not the rights claimed exist, (iv) the national law presumes the national measure in question to be compatible with Community law unless and until it is declared incompatible, (v) the national court has no power to give interim protection to the rights claimed by suspending the application of the national measure pending the preliminary ruling, (vi) if the preliminary ruling is in the event in favour of the rights claimed, the party entitled to those rights is likely to have suffered irremediable damage unless given such interim protection, does Community law either (a) oblige the national court to grant such interim protection of the rights claimed; or (b) give the court power to grant such interim protection of the rights claimed? (2) If question 1(a) is answered in the negative and question 1(b) in the affirmative, what are the criteria to be applied in deciding whether or not to grant such interim protection of the rights claimed?

On 19 June 1990, in answer to the questions so referred to it, the court ruled as follows, p 856B:

Community law must be interpreted as meaning that a national court which, in a case before it concerning Community law, considers the sole obstacle which precludes it from granting interim relief is a rule of national law must set aside that rule.

Following receipt of that ruling, the applicants returned to your Lordships' House on 2 July 1990 in order to pursue further their appeal from the decision of the Court of Appeal and to seek interim relief pending the determination by the European Court of Justice of the matters referred to it by the Divisional Court. However, for reasons which will appear, they sought interim relief in a form different from that ordered by the Divisional Court. On 9 July, shortly after the conclusion of the hearing, your Lordships announced the House's decision to grant interim relief, and an order was made by your Lordships for an interim injunction in the following terms:

Pending final judgment or further order herein the Secretary of State whether by himself his servants or agents or otherwise howsoever be restrained from withholding or withdrawing registration in the register of British fishing vessels maintained by him pursuant to the Merchant Shipping (Registration of Fishing Vessels) Regulations 1988 in respect of any of the vessels specified in the first column of the schedule hereto by reason only of the following: (a) legal title or beneficial ownership of such vessel is vested in whole or in part in the person or persons listed against its name in the second column of the said schedule; and (b)(i) in the case of any natural person 'so listed, that person is resident or domiciled in a member state of the European Economic Community other than the United Kingdom; or (ii) in the case of any company so listed, (aa) 25% or more of the shares or of any class of the shares of that company. or of any company owning shares in that company, are legally or beneficially owned by a person or persons resident or domiciled in a member state of the European Economic Community other than the United Kingdom or (bb) 25% or more of the directors of that company, or of any company holding shares in that company, are resident or domiciled in a member state of the European Economic Community other than the United Kingdom.

Provision was made for liberty to apply. It was indicated that your Lordships would publish at a later date your reasons for granting such interim relief. I now set out the reasons which caused me to agree that such relief should be granted.

When your Lordships decided to make the reference to the European Court of Justice in this matter in May 1989, my noble and learned friend, Lord Bridge of Harwich, delivered a speech with which the remainder of your Lordships, including myself, agreed. In his speech on that occasion, my noble and learned friend was concerned primarily with the jurisdiction of the English courts to grant an interim injunction in a case such as the present as a matter of English law. Even so, he gave a full account of the background to the present appeal (including a reference to, and extensive quotation from, the judgment of Neill LJ in the Divisional Court, and in particular his account of the common fisheries policy); and his consideration of the question whether, as a matter of English law the court had jurisdiction in the present case to grant interim relief inevitably touched upon the question which your Lordships now have to address in the light of the ruling of the European Court of Justice. In these circumstances, it would be repetitious if I once again set out the background to the present appeal: I shall only do so to the extent necessary to set in their context certain decisions of the European Court of Justice. Furthermore I wish to stress that, in expressing my reasons why in my opinion your Lordships should grant interim relief, I have no intention of departing from anything contained in the speech of my noble and learned friend, with which I have expressed my complete agreement.

The question which arose for consideration by your Lordships, following the ruling of the European Court of Justice, concerned the appropriateness of an order for an interim injunction in a case such as the present, which is concerned with a challenge to the lawfulness of an Act of Parliament as being incompatible with European law. This inevitably raised for consideration the principles to be applied in the case of an application for such an interim injunction, and in particular the extent to which the principles stated by your Lordships' House in *American Cyanamid Co v Ethicon Ltd* [1975] AC 396 are applicable in such a case, a matter upon which my noble and learned friend made some observations in his speech upon the first hearing of the appeal. I have however to say at once that your Lordships were not concerned with the simple question whether to interfere with the exercise of discretion by the Divisional Court in favour of granting an injunction. This is for three reasons. First, after the Divisional Court made its order, as I have already indicated, circumstances occurred which rendered an order in that form inappropriate. The purpose of the order was to continue in being the registration of the applicants' fishing vessels under the Act of 1894 and/or the Act of 1886. However, during the period which elapsed since the Divisional Court made its order, the register maintained under the Act of 1894 was closed. It was for this reason that the applicants sought an injunction in a different form, directed towards restraining the Secretary of State from withholding or withdrawing registration of their vessels in the register maintained under the Act of 1988 on certain grounds which, in the applicants' submission, were incompatible with European law – an injunction which your Lordships decided to grant. Second, important legal developments had taken place since the Divisional Court's order. Two judgments were delivered by the European Court of Justice concerning the validity of certain conditions imposed by the Secretary of State on the grant of licences to fishing vessels (*R v Ministry of Agriculture, Fisheries and Food ex p Agegate Ltd* (Case C3/87) [1990] 2 QB 151 and *R v Ministry of Agriculture, Fisheries and Food ex p Jaderow Ltd* (Case C216/87) [1990] 2 QB 193), and an interim order was made by the President of the European Court of Justice, on an application by the European Commission regarding certain nationality provisions in section 14 of the Act of 1988: *Commission of the European Communities v United Kingdom* (Case 246/89) (1989) *The Times*, 28 October. The latter order was of particular relevance to the applicants' application for an interim injunction in the present case. Third, there had been certain factual developments since the last hearing before your Lordships, which were the subject of evidence. In these circumstances, it was inevitable that your Lordships' House should consider the applicants' application *de novo*, and that it should, for that purpose, consider in some depth the applicable principles.

Before turning to those applicable principles, I shall briefly summarise the effect of the intervening decisions of the European Court and of its President. The present appeal is, of course, concerned with the question whether certain provisions of the Act of 1988 are compatible with European law. The same is true of the interim order of the President, but not of the two decisions of the court. Those decisions, which I shall refer to as the *Agegate* and *Jaderow* cases, were concerned with the validity of certain conditions imposed upon the grant of licences for British fishing vessels. They are not, therefore, of such direct relevance to the present appeal as the President's interim order. They have, however, some bearing upon the present appeal, and I think it desirable to refer to them; and I propose to set them in their context, even though this may involve some repetition of matters already recorded in the speech of my noble and learned friend, Lord Bridge of Harwich.

Under the Sea Fish (Conservation) Act 1967, as subsequently amended, fishing vessels registered in the United Kingdom are required to have a licence. That Act was supplemented by certain legislation in 1983 – the British Fishing Boats Act 1983, and the British Fishing Boats Order 1983 (SI 1983/482) and the Sea Fish Licensing Order 1983 (SI 1983/1206). This legislation was passed in an attempt to meet the situation created during the previous two or three years by the registration of Spanish fishing vessels as British fishing vessels, with a view to acquiring the same rights to fish in Community waters as those to which British fishing vessels beneficially owned by British nationals were entitled. Such registration was perceived as having the effect of circumventing restrictions imposed on Spanish registered vessels under the reciprocal fishing agreement concluded by the European Community with Spain in 1981) (following the Hague resolution of 1976 (Council Regulation of 3 November 1976; Official Journal 1981 No C105/I), whereby certain Member States of the Community extended their fishing limits in the Atlantic Ocean 200 miles from the coast); under the reciprocal fishing agreement of 1981, a limited number of Spanish fishing vessels were permitted to fish only for specified quantities of hake in specified waters of Member States. It seems that the Spanish fishing vessels saw this as a substantial exclusion from fishing grounds in deep waters previously fished by them, and sought to circumvent the restriction by registering their vessels as British. It was in response to that move that the legislation of 1983 was introduced, under which a British-registered fishing boat fishing within British fishing limits was required to have a crew consisting of at least 75% of European Community nationals.

In January 1983, the system of national fish quotas was introduced by Council Regulations (EEC) Nos 170/83 and 172/83. The British authorities experienced difficulty in monitoring the catches of ex-Spanish- registered vessels, and concern about their activities was being expressed by British fishermen, especially those based in the western parts of the United Kingdom. This concern was being expressed against a background of continued activity by British-registered fishing vessels with a largely Spanish beneficial ownership operating under British registration but mainly from Spain and with only tenuous links with the United Kingdom which were believed to be making substantial inroads into the fishing opportunities allocated to the United Kingdom under the common fisheries policy in the light of this country's traditional fishing activities. Accordingly, in December 1985, new licensing conditions for British fishing vessels were announced, taking effect as from 1 January 1986. These related to crewing, social security contributions and operations. The crewing conditions required that at least 75% of the crew must be British citizens, or EEC nationals (excluding, subject to certain limited exceptions, Greek nationals until 1 January

1988, and Spanish or Portuguese nationals until 1 January 1993) ordinarily resident in the United Kingdom, the Isle of Man or the Channel Islands. The social security conditions required the skipper and all the crew to make contributions to United Kingdom national insurance, or equivalent Isle of Man or Channel Islands schemes. The operating conditions provided as follows:

> The vessel must operate from the United Kingdom, Isle of Man or Channel Islands; without prejudice to the generality of this requirement a vessel will be deemed to have been so operating if, for each six-month period in each calendar year (that is, January to June and July to December), either: (a) at least 50% by weight of the vessel's landings or transshipment of stocks to which this or any other licence in force at the relevant time relates have been landed and sold in the United Kingdom, Isle of Man or the Channel Islands or transshipped by way of sale within British fishery limits; or (b) other evidence is provided of the vessel's presence in a United Kingdom, Isle of Man or Channel Islands port on at least four occasions at intervals of at least 15 days.

The validity of the crewing and social security conditions was challenged in the *Agegate* case [1990] 2 QB 151, and in addition the validity of the operating conditions was challenged in the *Jaderow* case [1990] 2 QB 193. The Advocate General's opinion in both cases was published in November 1988, and so was available at the time of the hearing before the Divisional Court: but the judgment of the European Court of Justice in the two cases was not delivered until 14 December 1989, and differed in certain important respects from the opinion of the Advocate General. In the *Agegate* case, the court upheld the validity of the social security condition: but in respect of the crewing condition, while upholding the condition in so far as it required 75% of the crew to be nationals of Member States, the court held that Community law precluded a condition requiring 75 per cent of the crew to reside ashore in the United Kingdom. In the *Jaderow* case, the court held that Community law did not preclude a member state, in authorising one of its vessels to fish against national quotas, from laying down conditions designed to ensure that the vessel had a real economic link with that state if that link concerned only the relation between that vessel's fishing operations and the population dependent on fisheries and related industries; and, on that basis, the court broadly upheld the validity of the operating conditions imposed by the United Kingdom. These two decisions are significant in the context of the present appeal, in that they provide an indication of the nature of the economic link which the court is prepared to recognise for these purposes, a link which does not extend to include a residence requirement imposed upon 75% of the vessels crew.

Meanwhile the United Kingdom Government had come to the conclusion that there was substantial non-compliance with these conditions. Furthermore, the number of largely foreign beneficially owned vessels on the United Kingdom register continued to grow, mainly through the acquisition by Spanish interests of British fishing vessels; Spanish interests were also able to increase the number of licences held by them by acquiring vessel's already holding United Kingdom licences. As a result, the problem was considered at a more fundamental level, by looking at the arrangements for registration of United Kingdom fishing vessels; and it was decided to introduce fresh legislation which, it was thought, would bring United Kingdom fishing vessel registration requirements 'broadly into line with arrangements in a number of other Member States' (see the first affidavit of Mr Noble of the Ministry of Agriculture, Fisheries and Food) and to require fishing vessels on the United Kingdom register to be substantially owned by British interests. Hence the provisions of Part II of the Act of 1988.

The interim order of the President (Case 246/89 R) (1989) *The Times*, 28 October, related to certain provisions of section 14 of the Act of 1988. Other provisions of that section formed the basis of the applicants' application for interim relief before your Lordships' House, and I think it desirable that I should set out the relevant parts of the section. Section 14(1), (2) and (7) provide as follows:

> (1) Subject to subsections (3) and (4), a fishing vessel shall only be eligible to be registered as a British fishing vessel if – (a) the vessel is British-owned; (b) the vessel is managed, and its operations are directed and controlled, from within the United Kingdom; and (c) any charterer, manager or operator of the vessel is a qualified person or company. (2) For the purposes of subsection (1)(a) a fishing vessel is British owned if – (a) the legal title to the vessel is vested wholly in one or more qualified persons or companies; and (b) the vessel is beneficially owned – (i) as to not less than the relevant percentage of the property in the vessel, by one or more qualified persons, or (ii) wholly by a qualified company or companies, or (iii) by one or more qualified companies and, as to not less than the relevant percentage of the remainder of the property in the vessel, by one or more qualified persons ... (7) In this section 'qualified company' means a company which satisfies the following conditions, namely – (a) it is incorporated in the United Kingdom and has its principal place of business there; (b) at least the relevant percentage of its shares (taken as a whole), and of each class of its shares, is legally and beneficially owned by one or more qualified persons or Companies; and (c) at least the relevant percentage of its directors are qualified persons; 'qualified person' means – (a) a person who is a British citizen resident and domiciled in the United Kingdom or (b) a local authority in the United Kingdom; and 'the relevant percentage' means 75% or such greater percentage (which may be 100%) as may for the time being be prescribed.

The interim order of the President (Case 246/89 R) (1989) *The Times*, 28 October, was made upon an application to him by the European Commission. The Commission brought an action under Article 169 of the Treaty for a declaration that, by imposing the nationality requirements enshrined in sections 13 and 14 of the Act of 1988, the United Kingdom had failed to fulfil its obligations under Articles 7, 52 and 221 of the Treaty. The Commission further applied under Article 186 of the Treaty and Article 83 of the Rules of Procedure for an order requiring the United Kingdom to suspend the application of the nationality requirements enshrined in section 14(1)(a) and (c) of the Act, read in conjunction with paragraphs (2) and (7) of the section, as regards the nationals of other Member States and in respect of fishing vessels which until 31 March 1989 were pursuing a fishing activity under the British flag and under a British fishing licence. Under Article 83(2) of the Rules of Procedure, interim measures such as those requested may not be ordered unless there are circumstances giving rise to urgency and factual and legal grounds establishing a *prima facie* case for the measures applied for.

The President granted the interim order asked for by the Commission. With regard to the issue whether a *prima facie* case had been established, he said:

> 25   The United Kingdom further considers that the nationality requirements introduced by the Act of 1988 are justified by the present Community legislation on fisheries; that legislation, although it establishes a common system, is based on a principle of nationality for the purposes of the distribution of fishing quotas. Under Article 5(2) of Council Regulation 170/83 it is for the Member States to determine the detailed rules for the utilisation of the quotas allocated to them and thus to lay down the conditions which the vessels authorised to fish from these quotas must satisfy.

> 26   It must be observed that the system of national quotas established by Council Regulation 170/83 constitutes, as the United Kingdom contends, a derogation from the principle of equal access for Community fishermen to fishing grounds and the exploitation thereof in waters coming within the jurisdiction of the Member States, which is itself a specific expression of the principle of non-discrimination laid down in Article 40(3) of the EEC Treaty.

> 27   That derogation is justified, according to the recitals in the preamble to Regulation No 170/83, by the need, in a situation where there is a dearth of fishery resources, to ensure a relative stability in regard to fishing activities in order to safeguard the particular need of regions where local populations are especially dependent on fisheries and related industries.

28   The possibility cannot therefore be excluded that in their legislation concerning in particular the registration of fishing vessels and access to fishing activities the Member States may be led to introduce requirements whose compatibility with Community law can be justified only by the necessity to attain the objectives of the Community system of fishing quotas. As the Commission itself has admitted in these proceedings, such requirements may be necessary in order to ensure that there is a genuine link with the fishing industry of the Member State against whose quota the vessel may fish.

29   However, there is nothing which would *prima facie* warrant the conclusion that such requirements may derogate from the prohibition of discrimination on grounds of nationality contained in Articles 52 and 221 of the EEC Treaty regarding, respectively, the right of establishment and the right to participate in the capital of companies or firms within the meaning of Article 58.

30   The rights deriving from the above mentioned provisions of the Treaty include not only the rights of establishment and of participation in the capital of companies or firms but also the right to pursue an economic activity, as the case may be through a company, under the conditions laid down by the legislation of the country of establishment for its own nationals.

31   These rights *prima facie* also include the right to incorporate and manage a company whose object is to operate a fishing vessel registered in the state of establishment under the same conditions as a company controlled by nationals of that state.

32   As regards the United Kingdom's first submission based on its obligations under international law, it is sufficient to note, at this stage, that in this respect nothing has been put forward which at first sight could necessitate any derogation from the above-mentioned rights under Community law in order to ensure the effective exercise of British jurisdiction and control over the vessels in question.

33   It must therefore be held that, at the stage of these proceedings for the grant of interim relief, the application of the main proceedings does not appear to be without foundation and that the requirement of a *prima facie* case is thus satisfied.

The President went on to hold that sufficient urgency had also been established; in particular, for fishing vessels hitherto flying the British flag, cessation of their activities could cause serious damage. As regards the balance of interests he had this to say:

39   Finally, as regards the balance of interests, it is not established that the interim measures applied for may jeopardise the objective pursued by the British legislation at issue, namely to ensure the existence of a genuine link between the vessels fishing against the British quotas and the British fishing industry.

40   It appears *prima facie* that the registration requirements laid down by the new legislation, other than those relating to nationality and the measures adopted by the United Kingdom authorities in 1983 and 1986 would be sufficient to ensure the existence of such a link. The United Kingdom itself considers that the Anglo-Spanish vessels, which do not have that link with the United Kingdom, will not be able to satisfy the aforesaid requirements.

Following the President's order, section 14 of the Act of 1988 was amended (by the Merchant Shipping Act 1988 (Amendment) Order 1989 (SI 1989/2006)) with effect from 2 November 1989 to give effect to his order until after the final determination of the issue which was the subject of the Commission's substantive application. In section 14(1)(a) and (2), the expression 'Community-owned' was substituted for 'British-owned'; in section 14(7)(a), the words 'or another state of the European Community' were added after the words 'United Kingdom', and in (7)(c) the words 'or a citizen of a Community state' were added after the words 'British citizen.' These changes have the effect that the nationality issue ceases to be relevant for the purposes – of the present appeal, though the issue is, your Lordships were told, still being vigorously contested by the United Kingdom before the European Court of Justice on the substantive reference by the Divisional Court.

The applicants nevertheless pursued their application for an interim injunction before your Lordships' House, but their complaint was restricted to other matters in section 14. They did not object, for the purposes of the present application, to the requirement, in section 14(1)(b), that a vessel should be managed and its operations directed and controlled from within the United Kingdom, they stated that they were able to comply with these requirements. Their complaint was directed towards the requirements for domicile and residence in the United Kingdom contained in the definition of 'qualified person' in section 14(7), which apply both to beneficial owners of vessels and, in the case of vessels beneficially owned by companies, both to shareholders and to directors (under section 14(7)(b) and (c) respectively), with the effect that 75% of the relevant shareholders and directors are required to be resident and domiciled in the United Kingdom. This, they submitted, is contrary to the right of establishment under Article 52 of the Treaty, and the right to participate in capital under Article 221. In answer, the Secretary of State submitted that Articles 52 and 221 of the Treaty cannot be taken to apply in their full rigour to the fisheries sector. If these articles, and Article 7, were so to apply, it would be impossible to prevent fishing interests in one member state registering vessels in another member state in which event it would be impossible (*inter alia*) to prevent such vessels fishing against the quotas of the latter Member State, to the detriment of that Member State's fishing community and allied industries (who were intended to be protected by the quota system), and also to prevent Spanish vessels avoiding provisions of the Act of Accession of 1985 (Act of Accession of Spain and Portugal, Official Journal 1985 No L302).

It was further submitted by the applicants that the effect of the provisions relating to residence and domicile in section 14, whether or not coupled with the nationality provisions, was to render it impossible for many of the applicants' vessels to register as British fishing vessels on the register now maintained under the Act of 1988, with possibly catastrophic financial results for their owners. They relied upon the conclusion of Neill LJ in the Divisional Court that he was not persuaded on the evidence before him that there were identifiable persons or communities whose activities or livelihood were being so seriously damaged, or would be so seriously damaged, as to outweigh the very obvious and immediate damage which would be caused by these new provisions if no interim relief were granted to the applicants. They submitted fresh evidence to your Lordships as showing that such damage was already being suffered; and they referred to the fact that, on the law as it stands at present (*Bourgoin SA v Ministry of Agriculture, Fisheries and Food* [1986] QB 716), the applicants would have no remedy in damages for loss or damage suffered by them by reason of the enforcement against them of provisions of the Act of 1988 if subsequently held to be incompatible with European law. Finally, it was stated that the judgment of the European Court of Justice on the substantive reference from the Divisional Court was expected in about a year's time, and that it would therefore be for no longer than that period that interim relief was required.

I turn now to the applicable principles in cases in which an interim injunction is sought, with particular reference to a case such as the present, in which the public interest is involved.

The jurisdiction of courts to grant interim injunctions is to be found in section 37 of the Supreme Court Act 1981, under which the court has power to grant an injunction in all cases in which it appears to it to be just or convenient so to do, and has power to do so on such terms and conditions as it thinks fit. Guidelines for the exercise of the court's jurisdiction to grant interim injunctions were laid down by your Lordships' House in *American Cyanamid Co v Ethicon Ltd* [1975] AC 316, in the speech of Lord Diplock in that case, with which the remainder of their Lordships concurred. I use the word 'guidelines' advisedly, because I do not read Lord Diplock's speech as intended to fetter the broad discretion conferred on the courts by section 37 of the Supreme Court Act 1981; on the contrary, a prime purpose of the guidelines established in the *Cyanamid* case was to remove a fetter which appeared to have been imposed in certain previous cases, viz, that a party seeking an interlocutory injunction had to establish a *prima facie* case for substantive relief. It is now clear that it is enough if he can show that there is a serious case to be tried. If he can establish that, then he has, so to speak, crossed the threshold; and the court can then address itself to the question whether it is just or convenient to grant an injunction.

Nothing which I say is intended to qualify the guidelines laid down in Lord Diplock's speech. But, before I turn to the question of public interest, which lies at the heart of the rival submissions in the present case, I must advert to the fact that Lord Diplock approached the matter in two stages. First, he considered the relevance of the availability of an adequate remedy in damages, either to the plaintiff seeking the injunction, or to the defendant in the event that an injunction is granted against him. As far as the plaintiff is concerned, the availability to him of such a remedy will normally preclude the grant to him of an interim injunction. If that is not so, then the court should consider whether, if an injunction is granted against the defendant, there will be an adequate remedy in damages available to him under the plaintiffs undertaking in damages; if so, there will be no reason on this ground to refuse to grant the plaintiff an interim injunction.

At this stage of the court's consideration of the case (which I will for convenience call the first stage) many applications for interim injunctions can well be decided. But if there is doubt as to the adequacy of either or both of the respective remedies in damages, then the court proceeds to what is usually called the balance of convenience, and for that purpose will consider all the circumstances of the case. I will call this the second stage. Again, I stress that I do not wish to place any gloss upon what Lord Diplock said about this stage. I wish only to record his statement, p 408, that:

> ... It would be unwise to attempt even to list all the various matters which may need to be taken into consideration in deciding where the balance lies, let alone to suggest the relevant weight to be attached to them. These will vary from case to case.

and his further statement, at p 409 (after referring to particular factors) that 'there may be many other special factors to be taken into consideration in the particular circumstances of individual cases'.

I turn to consider the impact upon these guidelines of the public interest, with particular reference to cases in which a public authority is seeking to enforce the law against some person, and either the authority seeks an interim injunction to restrain that person from acting contrary to the law, and that person claims that no such injunction should be granted on the ground that the relevant law is, for some reason, invalid; or that other person seeks an interim injunction to restrain the action of the authority, on the same ground.

I take the first stage. This may be affected in a number of ways. For example, where the Crown is seeking to enforce the law, it may not be thought right to impose upon the Crown the usual undertaking in damages as a condition of the grant of an injunction: see *Hoffmann-La Roche & Co AG v Secretary of State for Trade and Industry* [1975] AC 295. Again, in this country there is no general right to indemnity by reason of damage suffered through invalid administrative action; in particular, on the law as it now stands, there would be no remedy in damages available to the applicants in the present case for loss suffered by them by reason of the enforcement of the Act of 1988 against them, if the relevant part of the Act should prove to be incompatible with European law: see *Bourgoin SA v Ministry of Agriculture, Fisheries and Food* [1986] QB 716. Conversely, an authority acting in the public interest cannot normally be protected by a remedy in damages because it will itself have suffered none. It follows that, as a general rule, in cases of this kind involving the public interest, the problem cannot be solved at the first stage, and it will be necessary for the court to proceed to the second stage, concerned with the balance of convenience.

Turning then to the balance of convenience it is necessary in cases in which a party is a public authority performing duties to the public that 'one must look at the balance of convenience more widely, and take into account the interests of the public in general to whom these duties are owed': see *Smith v Inner London Education Authority* [1978] 1 All ER 411, p 22, *per* Browne LJ, and see also *Sierbein v Westminster City Council* [1987] 86 LGR 431. Like Browne LJ, I incline to the opinion that this can be treated as one of the special factors referred to by Lord Diplock in the passage from his speech which I have quoted. In this context, particular stress should be placed upon the importance of upholding the law of the land, in the public interest, bearing in mind the need for stability in our society, and the duty placed upon certain authorities to enforce the law in the public interest. This is of itself an important factor to be weighed in the balance when assessing the balance of convenience. So if a public authority seeks to force what is on its face the law of the land, and the person against whom such action is taken challenges the validity of that law, matters of considerable weight have to be put into the balance to outweigh the desirability of enforcing, in the public interest, what is on its face the law, and so to justify the refusal of an interim injunction in favour of the authority, or to render it just or convenient to restrain the authority for the time being from enforcing the law. This was expressed in a number of different ways by members of the Appellate Committee in the *Hoffmann-La Roche* case [1975] AC 295. Lord Reid said, at p 341, that:

> ... it is for the person against whom the interim injunction is sought to show special reason why justice requires that the injunction should not be granted or should only be granted on terms.

Lord Morris of Borth-y-Gest, pp 352, 353, stressed that all considerations appertaining to the justice of the matter become within the purview of the court; but he also stated that, in a case where the defendant attacks the validity of what appears to be an authentic law, the measure of the strength of this attack must inevitably call for some consideration. Lord Diplock, p 367, asserted that *prima facie* the Crown is entitled as of right to an interim injunction to enforce obedience to the law; and that:

> To displace this right or to fetter it by the imposition of conditions it is for the defendant to show a strong *prima facie* case that the statutory instrument is *ultra vires*.

Lord Cross of Chelsea did not expressly address the point. Lord Wilberforce, in a dissenting speech, stressed, p 358, that, in the last resort, the matter is one for the discretion of the judge; in particular, he rejected a suggestion that the presumption of validity of subordinate legislation required the court to enforce such legislation, by an interlocutory injunction, against the party who was calling the validity of such legislation in question.

I myself am of the opinion that in these cases, as in others, the discretion conferred upon the court cannot be fettered by a rule; I respectfully doubt whether there is any rule that, in cases such as these, a party challenging the validity of a law must – to resist an application for an interim injunction against him, or to obtain an interim injunction restraining the enforcement of the law – show a strong *prima facie* case that the law is invalid. It is impossible to foresee what case; may yet come before the courts; I cannot dismiss from my mind the possibility (no doubt remote) that such a party may suffer such serious and irreparable harm in the event of the law being enforced against him that it may be just or convenient to restrain its enforcement by an interim injunction even though so heavy a burden has not been discharged by him. In the end, the matter is one for the discretion of the court, taking into account all the circumstances of the case. Even so, the court should not restrain a public authority by interim injunction from enforcing an apparently authentic law unless it is satisfied, having regard to all the circumstances, that the challenge to the validity of the law is, *prima facie*, so firmly based as to justify so exceptional a course being taken.

With these principles in mind, I come to the facts of the present case. There can be no question of the present application being decided at the first stage of Lord Diplock's approach, and it is necessary to proceed at once to the second stage.

Your Lordships heard submissions from both parties about the strength of the applicants' challenge to the relevant provisions of section 14 of the Act of 1988. It is plain that the United Kingdom will, before the European Court of Justice, be resisting most strongly arguments by the applicants that any provision in section 14 is incompatible with European law, whether in respect of nationality (despite the recent decision of the President to grant interim relief), or in respect of domicile and residence of beneficial owners, shareholders and directors. It is unnecessary, and perhaps undesirable, for your Lordships now to analyse these arguments. They are set out in detail in the written observations already submitted by the United Kingdom and by the applicants to the European Court of Justice on the substantive reference by the Divisional Court, copies of which have been made available to your Lordships. There are, however, certain reasons which persuaded me to conclude, for present purposes, that, *prima facie*, the applicants had strong grounds for challenging the validity of the provisions relating to residence and domicile. First, a central element in the argument of the United Kingdom, in seeking to uphold the validity of section 14, is that Articles 7, 52 and 221 of the Treaty should not be interpreted as affecting the nationality of vessels, or the grant of flags, in respect of which competence remains in principle with the Member States. It has to be said, however, that an argument on these lines does not appear to have found favour with the President on the Commission's application for interim relief: *Commission of the European Communities v United Kingdom* (Case 246/89 R) (1989) *The Times*, 28 October. Second, although in the *Jaderow* case [1990] 2 QB 193 the European Court accepted that a member state, in authorising a vessel to fish against national quotas, might lay down conditions designed to ensure that it had a real economic link with the state if that link concerned only the relation between that vessel's fishing operations and the populations dependent on fisheries and related industries, yet in the *Agegate* case [1990] 2 QB 151 the court rejected as invalid a condition requiring residence in the Member State of 75% of the vessel's crew. If such a residence qualification is rejected in respect of the crew, as a condition of the grant of a vessel's licence, it may well be difficult to persuade the court to adopt a residence qualification relating to beneficial owners, or to 75% of shareholders in or directors of a company which beneficially owns a vessel, as a condition of registration of a fishing vessel under the Act of 1988: *a fortiori* must the same be true of a condition relating to domicile. As to the final outcome on these issues after consideration by the Court, your Lordships can of course express no opinion; but these two points alone led me to conclude that the applicants' challenge is, *prima facie*, a strong one.

It is on that basis that I turn to consider the balance of convenience as a whole. I have already referred to the view formed by Neill LJ, when the matter was before the Divisional Court [1989] CMLR 353, that serious damage may be caused to the applicants if no interim relief is granted. Your Lordships were furnished with up to date evidence in the form of answers to a questionnaire sent to owners of 62 vessels during the recent hearing. None of the answers to the questionnaire was on oath; and it was not in the circumstances possible for the Secretary of State to test the answers. or indeed to check their accuracy. However, no objection was made to this material being placed before your Lordships.

The answers to the questionnaire were not complete. However, from the answers received it was possible to derive the following basic information. All 62 vessels ceased to be on the United Kingdom register after the lapse of the old register on 1 April 1989. Twenty four of the vessels have not fished since their registration lapsed; of the remainder, 33 have fished but only outside EEC waters, in some cases for very short periods and in most cases after being laid up for a considerable time. Twenty four vessels have succeeded in obtaining registration under the Act of 1988, but always for special reasons, 14 of them because shares in the owning company had been sold to qualified persons or companies. Thirty owners have tried to sell their vessels, but none of them has received an acceptable offer. Many owners claim to have suffered damages to date of well over £100,000; some fear imminent bankruptcy.

Your Lordships also had the benefit of a fourth affidavit sworn by Mr Noble of the Ministry of Agriculture, Fisheries and Food. Apart from specific comments on particular vessels in the ownership of the applicants, he placed evidence before your Lordships to the effect that, as a result of the introduction of the new register, a number of British fishing vessels other than those owned by Spanish interests had been able to take up the opportunities now available to them, taking increased catches, employing extra crew, investing in new vessels to take advantage of the new opportunities, and generating increased activity on shore. He considered that, if the applicants' vessels returned to the British fleet and resumed their previous activities, the owners of these British fishing vessels would suffer serious losses; and he anticipated that the re-introduction of stiff quota restrictions would be required. However, even taking this evidence fully into account, I have, on all the material available to your Lordships, formed the same opinion as that formed by Neill LJ in the Divisional Court on the material then before him, that there was not sufficient to outweigh the obvious and immediate damage which would continue to be caused if no interim relief were granted to the applicants.

It was for these reasons that, in agreement with the remainder of your Lordships, I concluded that the appeal should be allowed and interim relief granted in the terms of the order made.

Lord Jauncey of Tullichettle: My Lords, I have had the advantage or reading in draft the speech to be delivered by my noble and learned friend Lord Goff of Chieveley. I agree with the conclusion at which he has arrived and I gratefully adopt his detailed account of the circumstances giving rise to the present appeal. It is only because of the importance and novelty of the principal question to be considered that I venture to add a few observations thereanent.

The European Court of Justice has ruled, p 856B, that:

Community law must be interpreted as meaning that a national court which, in a case before it concerning Community law, considers that the sole obstacle which precludes it from granting interim relief is a rule of national law must set aside that rule.

This House is accordingly now faced with the wholly novel situation of determining whether in the circumstances of this appeal interim relief against the application of primary legislation should be granted to the applicants, pending the decision of the European Court of Justice on the reference by the Divisional Court of 10 March 1989. In reaching a conclusion the following matters have to be addressed, namely: (1) the threshold which must be crossed by the applicants before this House will consider intervening, (2) whether they have crossed that threshold, and (3) if they have, whether the balance of convenience favours the granting of interim relief.

(1) The threshold

When this appeal was last before your Lordships' House [1990] 2 AC 85 my noble and learned friend, Lord Bridge of Harwich, referred to the familiar situation in which a plaintiff seeks an interim injunction to protect a right when the material facts are in dispute and continued, p 139:

> In this situation the court has a discretion to grant or withhold interim relief which it exercises in accordance with the principles laid down by your Lordships' House in *American Cyanamid Co v Ethicon Ltd* [1975] AC 396. In deciding on a balance of convenience whether or not to make an interim injunction the court is essentially engaged in an exercise of holding the ring.

American Cyanamid concerned a claim for alleged infringement of patent and an application for interim injunction was made upon contested facts. Lord Diplock referred, p 407, to:

> the supposed rule that the court is not entitled to take any account of the balance of convenience unless it has first been satisfied that if the case went to trial upon no other evidence than is before the court at the hearing of the application the plaintiff would be entitled to judgment for a permanent injunction in the same terms as the interlocutory injunction sought ...

and continued:

> Your Lordships should in my view take this opportunity of declaring that there is no such rule. The use of such expressions as 'a probability', 'a *prima facie* case', or 'a strong *prima facie* case' in the context of the exercise of a discretionary power to grant an interlocutory injunction leads to confusion as to the object' sought to be achieved by this form of temporary relief. The court no doubt must be satisfied that the claim is not frivolous or vexatious; in other words, that there is a serious question to be tried. It is no part of the court's function at this stage of the litigation to try to resolve conflicts of evidence on affidavit as to facts on which the claims of either party may ultimately depend nor to decide difficult questions of law which call for detailed argument and mature considerations. These are matters to be dealt with at the trial.

As I understand it Lord Diplock in that passage was saying that the court must be satisfied that there is a serious question to be tried before it considers the balance of convenience. Indeed, this must be so since it would be quite wrong that a plaintiff should obtain interim relief on the basis of a claim which was groundless. I agree that it is not the function of the court to try to resolve conflicts of evidence at an interlocutory stage but I would demur to any suggestion that in no circumstances would it be appropriate to decide questions of law. If the only question at issue between the parties is one of law it may be possible in many cases to decide this at the stage of a contested application for an interim injunction. For example, where an employer seeks to enforce a restrictive covenant in a former employee's contract of employment and the only defence is that the covenant by reason of its wide terms is unenforceable, it would be wholly illogical to grant to the employer an interim injunction on the basis that there was a serious question to be tried when the question could at the same time be resolved as matter of law in favour of the employee.

However, while the test of a serious question to be tried is appropriate to proceedings between private parties where no presumption favours the position of one party as against the other it does not follow that the same considerations apply when primary legislation and the public interest are involved. Indeed, my noble and learned friend, Lord Bridge of Harwich (*R v Secretary of State for Transport ex p Factortame Ltd* [1990] 2 AC 85, p 140). remarked upon the fundamental distinction between the familiar situation and that which arises in this appeal. In *Hoffmann-La Roche & Co AC v Secretary of State for Trade and Industry* [1975] AC 299, the Secretary of State having sought by interim injunction to enforce a statutory instrument approved by both Houses of Parliament the defenders maintained that the instrument was *ultra vires*. Lord Reid said, p 341, that:

> ... it is for the person against whom the interim injunction is sought to show special reason why justice requires that the injunction should not be granted or should only be granted on terms

and Lord Morris of Borth-y-Gest, p 353, pointed out that the measure of the strength of the attack upon the statutory instrument must inevitably call for some consideration. Lord Diplock said, p 366:

> All that can usefully be said is that the presumption that subordinate legislation is *intra vires* prevails in the absence of rebuttal, and that it cannot be rebutted except by a party to legal proceedings in a court of competent jurisdiction who has *locus standi* to challenge the validity of the subordinate legislation in question.

He said, p 367:

> So in this type of law enforcement action it the only defence is an attack on the validity of the statutory instrument sought to be enforced the ordinary position of the parties as respects the grant of interim injunctions is reversed, the duty of the Crown to see that the law declared by the statutory instrument is obeyed is not suspended by the commencement of proceedings in which the validity of the instrument is challenged. *Prima facie* the Crown is entitled as of right to an interim injunction to enforce obedience to it. To displace this right or to fetter it by the imposition of conditions it is for the defendant to show a strong *prima facie* case that the statutory instrument is *ultra vires*.

These observations, in my view, apply not only where a defendant is seeking to resist an attempt by the Crown to enforce secondary legislation but also where a plaintiff is seeking to restrict the Crown in its operation of such legislation. They must be equally appropriate to a challenge to primary legislation as they are to a challenge to secondary legislation. Indeed, when this appeal was last before this House, Lord Bridge said, p 142:

> In this situation the difficulty which confronts the application is that the presumption that an Act of Parliament is compatible with Community law unless and until declared to be incompatible must be at least as strong as the presumption that delegated legislation is valid unless and until declared invalid.

Given this presumption it follows from the above observations of Lord Diplock that it is for the Crown to enforce the provisions of the Act of 1988 and that anyone, whether a plaintiff or defendant, who seeks to challenge the validity thereof must at least show a strong *prima facie* case of incompatibility with Community law. It is the presumption in favour of the legislation being challenged which in my view makes the *American Cyanamid* test of a serious question to be tried inappropriate in a case such as the present. In expressing this opinion I must emphasise that I am in no way criticising the appropriateness of the *American Cyanamid* test for cases where primary or secondary legislation is not being challenged nor am I suggesting that Lord Diplock's approach to the balance of convenience is not appropriate in this case.

My Lords, I have considered anxiously whether other factors such as relative hardship or injustice should play any part in determining the appropriate threshold which an applicant for relief in circumstances such as the present should cross. Given the wide discretion conferred upon the courts by section 37 of the Supreme Court Act 1981 I would not wish to lay down any rules which might unduly inhibit that discretion in unforeseen circumstances in the future. Suffice it to say that as at present advised it would only be in the most exceptional circumstances that I can foresee the threshold being lowered by factors not directly related to the invalidity of the legislation under challenge. In the normal case other factors would be considered in relation to the balance of convenience. If an applicant seeking an injunction against primary or secondary legislation cannot show a strong *prima facie* ground of challenge it will in the absence of quite exceptional circumstances avail him nought that a refusal of an injunction would result in greater injustice to him should he succeed at trial than would result to the other party if the injunction was granted and he failed at trial.

I therefore conclude that the applicants will only cross the threshold if they demonstrate that there is a strong *prima facie* case that section 14 of the Act of 1988 is incompatible with Community law, which failing that exceptional circumstances exist would justify lowering the threshold.

(2) Have the applicants crossed the threshold?

Section 14(1) provides that a fishing vessel shall only be eligible to be registered as a British fishing vessel if *inter alia* 'the vessel is British-owned'. Section 14(2) provides that a fishing vessel is British-owned if the legal title is vested wholly in one or more qualified persons or companies and section 14(7) provides that a qualified company is one which is incorporated in the United Kingdom with 75% of the shares held by and 75% of its directors being qualified persons. Qualified person is defined in section 14(7) as 'a person who is a British citizen resident and domiciled in the United Kingdom'. It is to this latter definition that Mr Vaughan confined his attack on the ground that such a restriction in ownership was incompatible with Community law.

Since the appeal was last before this House in 1989 certain important events have taken place in the European Court. On 4 August 1989 (*Commission of the European Communities v United Kingdom* (Case 246/89 R) (1989) *The Times*, 28 October), the Commission sought a declaration that the nationality requirements in section 14 of the Act of 1988 constituted a failure by the United Kingdom to fulfil certain of its Treaty obligations. On 10 October 1989 the President of the court made the following order:

> Pending delivery of the judgment in the main proceedings the United Kingdom shall suspend the application of the nationality requirements laid down in section 14(1)(a) and (c) of the Merchant Shipping Act 1988, read in conjunction with paragraphs (2) and (7) of that section, as regards the nationals of other Member States and in respect of fishing vessels which, until 31 March 1989, were pursuing a fishing activity under the British flag and under a British fishing licence.

Effect was given to this order by the Merchant Shipping Act 1988 (Amendment) Order 1989 which, in relation to the fishing vessels in question, amended section 14 by substituting 'Community-owned' for 'British owned' in subsection 1 and by amending the definition of the 'qualified person' to read 'a person who is a British citizen or a national of a member state other than the United Kingdom and is either resident 'and domiciled in the United Kingdom'.

It will be noted that the Commission did not seek to challenge the residence and domicile qualification which is now challenged by Mr Vaughan. On 14 December 1989 the European Court similarly constituted gave judgment in two cases which may for convenience be called *Agegate* [1990] 2 QB 151 and *Jaderow* [1991] 2 QB 193. Both cases concerned the grant to British-registered fishing vessels with strong Spanish connections of fishing licences which contained crewing conditions to the effect that: (1) at least 75% of the crew must be British citizens or EEC nationals (excluding until 1 January 1993 Spanish nationals), and (2) the skipper and all the crew must be making contributions to United Kingdom national insurance. In the course of the *Agegate* judgment the following observations on the quota system were made, [1991] 2 QB 151, 188:

24   It follows from the foregoing that the aim of the quotas is to assure to each member state a share of the Community's total allowable catch, determined essentially on the basis of the catches from which traditional fishing activities, the local populations dependent on fisheries and related industries of the Member State benefited before the quota system was established.

25   In that context a residence requirement such as the one in point in this case is irrelevant to the aim of the quota system and cannot therefore be justified by that aim.

And the court ruled, *inter alia*, at p 192:

2   Community law precludes a member state from requiring, as a condition for authorising one of its vessels to fish against its quotas, That 5% of the crew of the vessel in question must reside ashore in that Member State.

3   Save in those cases where Council Regulation (EEC) No 1408/71 otherwise provides, Community law does not preclude a Member State from requiring, as a condition for authorising one of its vessels to fish against its quotas, that the skipper and all the crew of the vessel must be making contributions to the social security scheme of that Member State.

In the *Jaderow* judgment [1990] 2 QB 193 the court recognised that the aim of national quotas derived from the common fisheries policy might justify conditions designed to ensure that there was a real economic link between the vessel and the Member State in question if the purpose of such conditions was that the populations dependent on fisheries and related industries should benefit from them. The court ruled, *inter alia*, p 226, that Community law as it now stands:

(1) does not preclude a member state, in authorising one of its vessels to fish against national quotas, from laying down conditions designed to ensure that the vessel has a real economic link with that state if that link concerns only the relations between that vessel's fishing operations and the populations dependent on fisheries and related industries; (2) does not preclude a Member State, in authorising one of its vessels to fish against national quotas from laying down the condition, in order to ensure that there is a real economic link as defined above, that the vessel is to operate from national ports, if that condition does not involve an obligation for the vessel to depart from a national port on all its fishing trips ...

It is to my mind implicit in these two decisions that the court did not consider that residence and domicile of a specified percentage of the crew was justified as a condition designed to ensure the existence of a real economic link between the vessel and the Member State.

Had the court so considered *Agegate* [1990] 2 QB 151 must have been decided differently. If residence of the crew is not relevant to ensure the existent of a real economic link between vessel and member state what is the position in relation to the residence of shareholders and directors of an owning company? The role of this House is not to give an answer to that question but rather to assess the prospects of the European Court giving an answer which is favourable to the applicants. Directors and shareholders are further removed from any link between a vessel and a member state than are members of the crew and the European Court having decided that residence of the latter is not relevant to ensure the existence of a real economic link there must at least be a strong probability that the court will take a similar view in relation to the former. Upon that assumption it would appear that the applicants can show a strong *prima facie* ground of challenge to the relevant statutory provision. However, there remains for consideration the argument of the Crown that Community law does not affect the sovereign right of a Member State to lay down the conditions for the grant of its flag to ships. Customary international law, as expressed in Article 5(1) of the Geneva Convention on the High Seas, requires that there should be a genuine link between a vessel and the state of her flag. Article 94 of the 1982 Convention of the Law on the Sea sets out the important legal and international obligations incurred by a state in relation to a vessel to whom the flag of the state has been granted. In the absence of any express provision it should not be presumed that the Treaty interferes with the exercise by a Member State of its sovereign powers. I was initially attracted by these submissions and in some doubt as to whether they should not be given effect to. However, on further consideration of the President's ruling of 10 October 1989, I have come to the conclusion that the applicants can show that they are very likely to be rejected by the European Court. In the context of legislative requirements introduced by Member States to obtain the objective of the Community system of fishing quotas the President said:

> 29   However there is nothing which would *prima facie* warrant the conclusion that such requirements may derogate from the prohibition of discrimination on grounds of nationality contained in Articles 52 and 221 of the EEC Treaty regarding, respectively, the right of establishment and the right to participate in the capital of companies or firms within the meaning of Article 58.
>
> 30   The rights deriving from the above mentioned provisions of the Treaty include not only the rights of establishment and of participation in the capital of companies or firms but also the right to pursue an economic activity, as the case may be through a company, under the conditions laid down by the legislation of the country of establishment for its own nationals.
>
> 31   These rights *prima facie* also include the right to incorporate and manage a company whose object is to operate a fishing vessel registered in the state of establishment under the same conditions as a company controlled by nationals of that state.
>
> 32   As regards the United Kingdom's first submission based on its obligations under international law, it is sufficient to note, at this stage, that in this respect nothing has been put forward which at first sight could necessitate any derogation from the above-mentioned rights under Community law in order to ensure the effective exercise of British jurisdiction and control over the vessels in question.
>
> 33   It must therefore be held that, at the stage of these proceedings for the grant of interim relief, the application of the main proceedings does not appear to be without foundation and that the requirement of a *prima facie* case is thus satisfied.

Given the foregoing observations of the President it would appear that the applicants have a strong chance of successfully arguing before the European Court that international law does not justify derogation from the prohibition of discrimination on grounds of nationality contained in Articles 52 and 221 of the Treaty.

In all these circumstances I consider that the applicants have crossed the threshold in relation to section 14 of the Act of 1988. It is therefore unnecessary to consider whether such exceptional circumstances exist as will justify lowering that threshold.

(3) Balance of convenience

In *Films Rover International Ltd v Cannon Film Sales Ltd* [1987] 1 WLR 670, Hoffmann J in considering an application for an interlocutory mandatory injunction implicitly acknowledged that there was a serious question to be tried and said, p 680:

> The principal dilemma about the grant of interlocutory injunctions, whether prohibitory or mandatory, is that there is by definition a risk that the court may make the 'wrong' decision, in the sense of granting an injunction to a party who succeeds (or would succeed) at trial. A fundamental principle is therefore that the court should take whichever course appears to carry the lower risk of injustice if it should turn out to have been 'wrong' in the sense I have described. The guidelines for the grant of both kinds of interlocutory injunctions are derived from this principle.

I find this approach of assistance in the present case.

If the applicants are successful in the end of the day but are afforded no interim relief they will, standing the law as laid down in *Bourgoin SA v Ministry of Agriculture, Fisheries and Food* [1986] QB 716, suffer very severe and irrecoverable damage. If they are ultimately unsuccessful but are afforded interim relief, the loss suffered by the British fishing industry as a whole and by individual members thereof during the period of interim relief will be relatively minor. Beyond this I cannot usefully add anything to what has already been said on the matter by my noble and learned friend Lord Goff of Chieveley. It follows that, the applicants having crossed the threshold, the balance of convenience favours the granting to them of interim relief.

Order accordingly.

Solicitors: Thomas Cooper & Stibbard; Treasury Solicitor.

(2) TILLOTSON, J, *EUROPEAN COMMUNITY LAW: TEXT, CASES AND MATERIALS*, 2ND EDN, 1996 (4TH EDN, 2003), LONDON: CAVENDISH PUBLISHING, PP 56–59; 78–87; 479–82

TRANSFERS OF SOVEREIGNTY AND PARLIAMENTARY SOVEREIGNTY

Sovereignty is a word of many meanings. In the United Kingdom, the expression *parliamentary* sovereignty refers to the constitutional doctrine that there are no legal limits to the legislative power of Parliament except that Parliament cannot limit its own powers for the future. Thus, in national law there is nothing that a statute properly enacted cannot do and therefore no act is irreversible. Now, as Collins points out:

> It is only in the sense last mentioned that the word has any useful meaning in relation to the national law of the United Kingdom. In the international sphere and in the political sphere there may have been a limitation of sovereignty but there is no reason to believe that there has yet been any limitation on the sovereignty of the United Kingdom Parliament [Collins, *European Community Law in the United Kingdom*, 1990].

... Therefore, as regards transfers of *national* sovereignty ... it is agreed that whereas this involves the removal of legislative powers from the United Kingdom Parliament by limiting its authority, such transfers do not amount (at least in theory) to an encroachment upon the doctrine of parliamentary sovereignty:

> The stage has now been reached where the current legal and political reality is that there has been a transfer of powers to the Community. It has already been suggested that the traditional rule that Parliament may not bind its successors is not necessarily irreconcilable with the concept of a transfer of powers to another authority. It may further be suggested that whilst the political reality remains membership of the Community, such powers are unlikely in practice to be recovered, and at least to that extent the transfer can be regarded as irreversible [Usher, 1981].

For an international treaty to be binding and enforceable at the domestic level, UK law, which regards international law and domestic law as separate systems of law, requires the treaty to be incorporated into the national legal system by means of an enabling act. The European Communities Act 1972, which provides for the incorporation of Community law into the law of the UK, whilst recognising in ss 2 and 3 the supremacy of Community law (as established by the European Court of Justice), also lays down a rule of interpretation to the effect that Parliament is to be presumed not to intend any statute to override Community law. Community law will therefore always prevail over national law unless Parliament expressly states in a future Act that it is to override Community law.

In this way, the remote possibility that Parliament might some day wish to repeal the 1972 Act is not excluded and the ultimate sovereignty of Parliament is upheld:

> We have all been brought up to believe that, in legal theory, one Parliament cannot bind another and that no Act is irreversible. But legal theory does not always march alongside political reality ... What are the realities here? If Her Majesty's Ministers sign this Treaty and Parliament enacts provisions to implement it [the 1972 Act], I do not envisage that Parliament would afterwards go back on it and try to withdraw from it. But if Parliament should do so, then I say we will consider that event when it happens [Lord Denning in *Blackburn v Attorney General* (1971)].

Lord Denning is here referring to the unlikely eventuality of this country withdrawing from the Community. (The Treaty contains no provisions for withdrawal.)

The reality, therefore, is that while the United Kingdom is a member of the Community, the constitutional doctrine of Parliamentary sovereignty cannot be relied upon in the face of directly enforceable rules of Community law. Although in 1983, Sir Robert Megarry VC stated in *Manuel v Attorney General* that 'once an instrument is recognised as being an Act of Parliament, no English court can refuse to obey it or question its validity', this statement must certainly now be modified to read '... once an instrument is recognised as being an Act of Parliament and is compatible with enforceable Community law, no English court can refuse to obey it or question its validity'. That this is the present state of the law in this country was expressed in the clearest terms and on the highest judicial authority by Lord Bridge in the *Factortame (No 2)* case ...:

> Some public comments on the decision of the European Court of Justice, affirming the jurisdiction of the courts of Member States to override national legislation if necessary to enable interim relief to be granted in protection of rights under Community law, have suggested that this was a novel and dangerous invasion by a Community institution of the sovereignty of the United Kingdom Parliament. But such comments are based on a misconception. If the supremacy within the European Community of Community law over the national law of Member States was not always inherent in the EEC Treaty it was certainly well-established in the jurisprudence of the European Court of Justice long before the United Kingdom joined the Community. Thus, whatever limitation of its sovereignty Parliament accepted when it enacted the European Communities Act 1972 was entirely voluntary. Under the terms of the Act of 1972 it has always been clear that it was the duty of a United Kingdom court, when delivering final judgment, to override any rule of national law found to be in conflict with any directly enforceable rule of Community law ... Thus, there is nothing in any way novel in according supremacy to rules of Community law in those areas to which they apply and to insist that, in the protection of rights under Community law, national courts must not be inhibited by rules of national law from granting interim relief in appropriate cases is no more than a logical recognition of that supremacy.

The *Factortame* litigation involved the disapplication of certain provisions of an Act of Parliament pending a decision by the Court of Justice on the question of whether the legislation was in breach of Community law and the directly enforceable Treaty rights of a number of private parties. The Court later held that the statute did infringe Community law and the private parties concerned brought an action for damages against the government department responsible for the legislation on the basis of what is known as the Francovich principle of State liability ... This case, one half of joined cases Case 46 and Case 48/93 *Brasserie du Pêcheur/Factortame*, has yet to be finally decided at national level but the following passages from the Advocate General's Opinion is of particular relevance in the context of the continuing developing relationship between Community law and national law:

> It is beyond argument that the State should not incur liability for legislative action except in exceptional circumstances. The freedom of the legislature must not be trammelled by the prospect of actions for damages ... The 'power to express the sovereignty of the people' justifies the legislature's immunity in relation to the general rule of liability ...
>
> State liability for breach of Community law and State liability in domestic law for legislative action do not have the same basis. The first type of liability is necessarily founded on illegality: breach of a higher ranking rule of law and therefore of the principle of primacy ...
>
> Respect for primacy requires not only that legislation contrary to Community law should be disapplied. It requires also that damage resulting from its application in the past should be made good ...
>
> Refuge can no longer be taken behind the supremacy or unchallengeability of legislation ... the bringing of an action for damages against the State for the legislatures' failure to act is perfectly permissible where the State's liability is based on a breach of Community law, as *Francovich* shows, whereas refuge can no longer be taken behind the supremacy or unchallengeability of

legislation ... the bringing of an action for damages against the State for the legislatures' failure to act is perfectly permissible where the State's liability is based on a breach of Community law, as *Francovich* shows, whereas this is hardly conceivable in domestic law.

As Lord Bridge explained in the judgment delivered after the Court had given its judgment in *Factortame (No 2)*, by ratifying the Treaty of Rome (or, in the United Kingdom's case, by adopting the 1972 European Communities Act), the Member States accepted that the legislative sovereignty of their Parliaments was limited by the principle of the primacy of Community law [pp 56–59].

Direct applicability, which strictly speaking only applies to Regulations, relates to *how* provisions of Community law enter the legal order of the Member States. The principle of *direct effect* on the other hand concerns the effectiveness of provisions of Community law once they enter the national legal systems. Although closely related, the two principles should be considered separately.

In *Costa v ENEL*, the Court of Justice stated that Community law binds both Member States and individuals and also that the national courts of the Member States are bound to apply Community law. As we have seen when examining the definitions of the binding Community acts in Art 189, such acts may well create rights for individuals which may be relied upon by them in national courts. And, if this is so as regards Community legislation (a secondary source), then, although the Treaty does not state as such, it must also be the case as regards Treaty provisions themselves (a primary source).

In the famous *Van Gend en Loos* case in 1963, the principle of direct effect, the clearest legal indicator of supranationality, was fully explained by the Court of Justice. In the course of answering questions regarding the nature and effect of one of the Treaty's customs union rules (Art 12), put to it by a Dutch court called upon to decide a case brought by a Dutch company against the national customs authorities, the Court ruled that this provision of Community law 'produces direct effects and creates individual rights which national courts must protect'. The Court stressed the constitutional nature of the Treaty – 'this Treaty is more than an agreement which merely creates mutual obligations between the contracting states' – and thus, a consequent need to provide 'direct legal protection of the individual rights of ... nationals'. These rights find their Community law corollary in *obligations* which rest upon others – in this case the Dutch State. Because the article in question was 'ideally adapted to produce direct effects in the legal relationship between Member States and their subjects', it enabled the plaintiff company, threatened by the breach of its Treaty obligations by the Dutch state, to assert its rights before the national court.

As Brown and Jacobs have explained:

> The notion of the direct effect of Community law, coupled with the jurisdiction of the Court to give preliminary rulings and so to determine the scope of the individual's rights and obligations, is a more powerful weapon than Arts 169 and 170. The individual has no direct remedy, before the Court, against the default of a State. The remedy lies with the national court, with the use of Art 177 where necessary. In this way the national courts enforce, if necessary against their own State, the rights conferred on the individual by the Treaty.

VAN GEND EN LOOS (CASE 26/62)

In September 1960, VG imported into the Netherlands from West Germany a quantity of a chemical product known as ureaformaldehyde.

In December 1959, a Dutch statute had been passed which brought into force modifications of the Benelux tariff system as a result of acceptance of the Brussels Nomenclature, a measure designed to secure international unification of the classification of goods for customs purposes. Regrouping of goods under the nomenclature resulted in an increase in the amount of duty payable on ureaformaldehyde to 8% on an *ad valorem* basis.

However, Art 12, EEC had come into force as regards intra-Community trade on January 1958.

Article 12: Member States shall refrain from introducing between themselves any new customs duties on imports or exports or any charges having equivalent effect, and from increasing those which they already apply in their trade with each other.

VG contended that on 1 January 1958 the duty payable under Dutch law on the product in question was 3% and they objected to paying the additional 5%.

The Customs Inspector having rejected their claim, VG appealed to the Dutch Tariefcommissie (Customs Court) in Amsterdam. Under Art 177, the Tariefcommissie certified two questions to the Court of Justice in Luxembourg regarding the nature of Art 12:

1   Does Art 12 have the effect of national law as claimed by VG, and may individuals derive rights from it which a national court must protect?

2   If the answer is affirmative, has there been an unlawful increase in customs duties or merely a reasonable modification of the duties which, although bringing about an increase, is not prohibited by Art 12?

The Governments of Belgium, West Germany and the Netherlands, and the EC Commission filed additional memoranda with the Court. All three Governments argued that Art 12 merely created obligations for Member States and did not therefore create rights for individuals. A claim might be brought against a Member State which broke its Treaty obligations under EEC Art 169 or 170.

The Court ruled as follows:

The first question of the Tariefcommissie is whether Art 12 of the Treaty has direct application in national law in the sense that the nationals of Member States may on the bask of this Article lay claim to rights which the national court must protect.

To ascertain whether the provisions of an international treaty extend so far in their effects it is necessary to consider the spirit, the general scheme and the wording of those provisions.

The objective of the EEC Treaty, which is to establish a Common Market, the functioning of which is of direct concern to interested parties in the Community, implies that this Treaty is more than an agreement which merely creates mutual obligations between the contracting states. This view is confirmed by the preamble to the Treaty which refers not only to governments but to peoples. It is also confirmed more specifically by the establishment of institutions endowed with sovereign rights, the exercise of which affects Member States and also their citizens. Furthermore, it must be noted that the nationals of the states brought together in the Community are called upon to co-operate in the functioning of this Community through the intermediary of the European Parliament and the Economic and Social Committee.

In addition, the task assigned to the Court of Justice under Art 177, the object of which is to secure uniform interpretation of the Treaty by national courts and tribunals, confirms that the States have acknowledged that Community law has an authority which can be invoked by their nationals before those courts and tribunals.

The conclusion to be drawn from this is that the Community constitutes a new legal order of international law for the benefit of which the Sates have limited their sovereign rights, albeit within limited fields, and the subjects of which comprise not only Member States but also their nationals. Independently of the legislation of Member States, Community law therefore not only imposes obligations on individuals but is also intended to confer upon them rights which become part of their legal heritage. These rights arise not only where they are expressly granted by the Treaty, but also by reason of obligations which the Treaty imposes in a clearly defined way upon individuals as well as upon the Member States and upon the institutions of the Community.

With regard to the general scheme of the Treaty as it relates to customs duties and charges having equivalent effect it must be emphasised that Art 9, which bases the Community upon a customs union, includes as an essential provision the prohibition of customs duties and charges. This provision is found at the beginning of the part of the Treaty which defines the 'Foundations of the Community'. It is applied and explained by Art 12.

The wording of Art 12 contains a clear and unconditional prohibition which is not a positive but a negative obligation. This obligation, moreover, is not qualified by any reservation on the part of States which would make its implementation conditional upon a positive legislative measure enacted under national law. The very nature of this prohibition makes it ideally adapted to produce direct effects in the legal relationship between Member States and their subjects.

The implementation of Art 12 does not require any legislative intervention on the part of the States. The fact that under this article it is the Member States who are made the subject of the negative obligation does not imply that their nationals cannot benefit from this obligation.

In addition the argument based on Arts 169 and 170 of the Treaty put forward by the three Governments which have submitted observations to the Court in their statements of the case is misconceived. The fact that these Articles of the Treaty enable the Commission and the Member States to bring before the Court a State which has not fulfilled its obligations doff not mean that individuals cannot plead these obligations, should the occasion arise, before a national court, any more than the fact that the Treaty places at the disposal of the Commission ways of ensuring that obligations imposed upon those subject to the Treaty are observed, precludes the possibility, in actions between individuals before a national court, of pleading infringements of these obligations.

A restriction of the guarantees against an infringement of Art 12 by Member States to the procedures under Arts 169 and 170 would remove all direct legal protection of the individual rights of their nationals. There is the risk that recourse to the procedure under these articles would be ineffective if it were to occur after the implementation of a national decision taken contrary to the provisions of the Treaty.

The vigilance of individuals concerned to protect their rights amounts to an effective supervision in addition to the supervision entrusted by Arts 169 and 170 to the diligence of the Commission and of the Member States.

It follows from the foregoing considerations that, according to the spirit, the general scheme and the wording of the Treaty, Art 12 must be interpreted as producing direct effects and creating individual rights which national courts must protect.

It follows from the wording and the general scheme of Art 12 of the Treaty that, in order to ascertain whether customs duties or charges having equivalent effect have been increased contrary to the prohibition contained in the said article, regard must be had to the customs duties and charges actually applied at the date of the entry into force of the Treaty.

Further, with regard to the prohibition in Art 12 of the Treaty, such an illegal increase may arise from a re-arrangement of the tariff resulting in the classification of the product under a more highly taxed heading and from an actual increase in the rate of customs duty.

It is of little importance how the increase in customs duties occurred when, after the Treaty entered into force, the same product in the same Member State was subjected to a higher rate of duty.

The application of Art 12, in accordance with the interpretation given above, comes within the jurisdiction of the national court which must enquire whether the dutiable product, in this case ureaformaldehyde originating in the Federal Republic of Germany, is charged under the customs measures brought into force in the Netherlands with an import duty higher than that with which it was charged on 1 January 1958.

The Court has no jurisdiction to check the validity of the conflicting views on this subject which have been submitted to it during the proceedings but must leave them to be determined by the national courts ...

The costs incurred by the Commission of the EEC and the Member States which have submitted their observations to the Court are not recoverable, and as these proceedings are, in so far as the parties to the main action are concerned, a step in the action pending before the Tariefcommissie, the decision as to costs is a matter for that court.

On those grounds;

Upon reading the pleadings;

Upon hearing the report of the Judge-Rapporteur;

Upon hearing the opinion of the Advocate-General;

Having regard to Arts 9, 12, 14, 169, 170 and 177 of the Treaty establishing the European Economic Community;

Having regard to the Rules of Procedure of the Court of Justice of the European Communities;

The Court in answer to the questions referred to it for a preliminary ruling by the Tariefcommissie by decision of 16 August 1962, hereby rules:

1   Article 12 of the Treaty establishing the European Economic Community produces direct effects and creates individual rights which national courts must protect.

2   In order to ascertain whether customs duties or charges having equivalent effect have been increased contrary to the prohibition contained in Art 12 of the Treaty, regard must be had to the duties and charges actually applied by the Member State in question at the date of the entry into force of the Treaty.

Such an increase can arise both from a re-arrangement of the tariff resulting in the classification of the product under a more highly taxed heading and from an increase in the rate of customs duty applied.

3   The decision as to costs in these proceedings is a matter for the Tariefcommissie.

The decision in *Van Gend en Loos* dramatically increased the impact of Community law in the Member States. It is a decision which ultimately rests on two related factors: first, on the Court's perception of the federal and constitutional (as opposed to international) nature of the Treaty, key provisions of which bear directly upon the individual and, secondly, on the Court's clear appreciation that the establishment of the customs union was a key element of negative integration within the Community – and that Community law must be fully effective in that respect. It is 'undoubtedly the richest and most creative of all Community cases, and one in which virtually every later development can – at least with hindsight – be seen to have its germ' (Rudden).

Thus, the case law of the Court of Justice clearly shows that a *directly effective* provision of Community law, whether of the Treaty or a legally binding secondary act, always prevails (takes precedence) over a conflicting provision of national law. In such cases, individual Community rights must be protected irrespective of whether the Community provision takes effect before, or after, the national provision. The case which follows concerns the impact of a Community Regulation within Italian national law. A Regulation, as we have seen, is directly applicable. The Court of Justice assumes that it is therefore 'a direct source of rights and duties for all those affected thereby', that is, that direct effect is the norm for Regulations. (On this point and possible confusion between direct applicability and direct effect, see Chapter 8.)

AMMINISTRAZIONE DELLE FINANZE v SIMMENTHAL (CASE 106/77)

S imported a consignment of beef from France into Italy. In accordance with an Italian statute of 1970, the company was charged fees for veterinary and public health inspections made at the frontier. S sued for the return of their money in the Italian courts, pleading that the charges were contrary to EEC law. Following an Art 177 reference, the Court of Justice held that the inspections were contrary to Art 30, being measures having an equivalent effect to a quantitative restriction, and the fees were contrary to Art 12 being charges equivalent to customs duties. The Court also held that this question of animal and public health had been governed by EC Regulations since 1964 and 1968.

In consequence the national court ordered the Italian Finance Ministry to repay the fees charged. The Ministry, however, pleaded the national statute of 1970 and argued that, under the Italian Constitution, this bound them until such time as it was set aside by the Constitutional Court. Following a further reference, the Court held:

The main purpose of the first question is to ascertain what consequences flow from the direct applicability of a provision of Community law in the event of incompatibility with a subsequent legislative provision of a Member State.

Direct applicability in such circumstances means that rules of Community law must be fully and uniformly applied in all Member States from the date of their entry into force and for so long as they continue in force.

These provisions are therefore a direct source of rights and duties for all those affected thereby, whether Member States or individuals, who are parties to legal relationships under Community law.

This consequence also concerns any national court whose task it is as an organ of a Member State to protect, in a case within its jurisdiction, the rights conferred upon individuals by Community law.

Furthermore, in accordance with the principle of the precedence of Community law, the relationship between provisions of the Treaty and directly applicable measures of the institutions on the one hand and the national law of the Member States on the other is such that those provisions and measures not only by their entry into force render automatically inapplicable any conflicting provision of current national law but – in so far as they are an integral part of, and take precedence in, the legal order applicable in the territory of each of the Member States – also preclude the valid adoption of new national legislative measures to the extent to which they would be incompatible with Community provisions.

Indeed, any recognition that national legislative measures which encroach upon the field within which the Community exercises its legislative power or which are otherwise incompatible with the provisions of Community law had any legal effect would amount to a corresponding denial of the effectiveness of obligations undertaken unconditionally and irrevocably by Member States pursuant to the Treaty and would thus imperil the very foundations of the Community.

The same conclusion emerges from the structure of Art 177 of the Treaty which provides that any court or tribunal of a Member State is enticed to make a reference to the Court whenever it considers that a preliminary ruling on a question of interpretation or validity relating to Community law is necessary to enable it to give judgment.

The effectiveness of that provision would be impaired if the national court were prevented from forthwith applying Community law in accordance with the decision or the case law of the Court.

It follows from the foregoing that every national court must, in a case within its jurisdiction, apply Community law in its entirety and protect rights which the latter confers on individuals and must accordingly set aside any provision of national law which may conflict with it, whether prior or subsequent to the Community rule.

Accordingly any provision of a national legal system and any legislative, administrative, or judicial practice which might impair the effectiveness of Community law by withholding from the national court having jurisdiction to apply such law the power to do everything necessary at the moment of its application to set aside national legislative provisions which might prevent Community rules from having full force and effect are incompatible with those requirements which are the very essence of Community law.

This would be the case in the event of a conflict between a provision of Community law and a subsequent national law if the solution of the conflict were to be reserved for an authority with a discretion of its own, other than the court called upon to apply Community law, even if such an impediment to the full effectiveness of Community law were only temporary.

The first question should therefore be answered to the effect that a national court which is called upon, within the limits of its jurisdiction, to apply provisions of Community law is under a duty to give full effect to those provisions, if necessary refusing of its own motion to apply any conflicting provision of national legislation, even if adopted subsequently, and it is not necessary for the court to request or await the prior setting aside of such provision by legislation or other constitutional means ...

It follows from the answer to the first question that national courts must protect rights conferred by provisions of the Community legal order and chat it is not necessary for such courts to request or await the actual setting aside by the national authorities empowered so to act of any national measures which might impede the direct and immediate application of Community rules ...

On those grounds the court hereby rules:

A national court which is called upon, within the limits of its jurisdiction, to apply provisions of Community law is under a duty to give full effect to those provisions, if necessary refusing of its own motion to apply any conflicting provisions of national legislation, even if adopted subsequently, and it is not necessary for the court to request or await the prior seeing aside of such provisions by legislative or other constitutional means.

The need for national courts to set aside the law of their own country when it is found to conflict with directly effective Community law is a point which will be seen to arise in many of the cases which follow, for example, *Factortame (No 2)*, see Chapters 2 and 20. Such national law must be repealed by the national legislature and the failure to do so amounts to a breach of Art 5 of the Treaty.

Reaction in the Member States

As these cases illustrate, some Member States, at least initially, encountered difficulties in accepting the supremacy of directly effective Community law in their courts. That the Court of Justice would brook no interference with the requirement that Community rules be uniformly applied by national courts throughout the Member States is thrown into sharp relief in the following German case. It concerns the question of a possible conflict between a provision of a Regulation (secondary Community law) and fundamental human rights provisions of the West German Constitution. The case also illustrates the point that the validity of Community law may not be tested against provisions of national law.

INTERNATIONALE HANDELSGESELLSCHAFT (CASE 11/70)

In order to export certain agricultural products an export licence was required. If the products were not exported during the period of the licence's validity, the exporter forfeited a deposit. The company, having lost a deposit of DM 17,000, claimed that this Community system, based on two Community Regulations and operated through the West German National Cereals Intervention Agency, was contrary to the fundamental human rights provisions of the German Constitution. In particular it was in breach of the principle of proportionality: it imposed obligations (relating to deposits) on individuals that were not necessary for the attainment of the intended objective (the regulation of the cereals market).

The question of the validity of one of the Regulations was referred to the Court of Justice under Art 177(1)(b) by the Frankfurt Administrative Court. The Court stated that the validity of Community measures could not be judged according to the principles of national law; Community criteria only might be applied.

The Court continued:

Recourse to the legal rules or concepts of national law in order to judge the validity of measures adopted by the institutions of the Community would have an adverse effect on the uniformity and efficiency of Community law. The validity of such measures can only be judged in the light of Community law. In fact, the law stemming from the Treaty, an independent source of law, cannot because of its very nature be overridden by rules of national law, however framed,

without being deprived of its character as Community law and without the legal basis of the
Community itself being called in question. Therefore the validity of a Community measure or
its effect within a Member State cannot be affected by allegations that it runs counter to either
fundamental rights as formulated by the constitution of that State or the principles of a national
constitutional structure.

However, an examination should be made as to whether or not any analogous guarantee
inherent in Community law has been disregarded. In fact, respect for fundamental rights forms
an integral part of the general principles of law protected by the Court of Justice.

The protection of such rights, whilst inspired by the constitutional traditions common to the
Member States, must be ensured within the framework of the structure and objectives of the
Community. It must therefore be ascertained, in the light of the doubts expressed by the
Verwaltungsgericht, whether the system of deposits has infringed rights of a fundamental
nature, respect for which must be ensured in the Community legal system ...

It follows from all these considerations that the system of licences involving an undertaking, by
those who apply for them, to import or export, guaranteed by a deposit, does not violate any
right of a fundamental nature. The machinery of deposits constitutes an appropriate method,
for the purposes of Art 40(3) of the Treaty, for carrying out the common organisation of the
agricultural markets and also conforms to the requirements of Art 43.

However, the referring Frankfurt court *did not apply* the Court's ruling that the Regulation
did not contravene the Community concept of human rights. Instead it made a reference to
the West German Federal Constitutional Court which, drawing attention to the absence of a
'codified catalogue of human rights' at Community level, allowed the reference and held
that Community measures were *subject to the fundamental rights provisions of the German
Constitution*. Nevertheless, it ruled that the Community Regulation in issue was not contrary
to the Constitution. Thus, although the Federal Constitutional Court refused to acknowledge
the absolute supremacy of Community law, an open rift with the Court of Justice was
averted.

By 1986, however, the Federal Constitutional Court felt sufficiently confident regarding
the protection of human rights at Community level that in *Wünsche Handelsgesellschaft* it
reversed its previous decision in the following terms:

Since 1974, the Community has advanced convincingly in the protection of human rights both
in the adoption in a legally significant manner of texts whereby the institutions agree to be
guided as a legal duty by respect for fundamental rights and by the development of case law
by the European Court. The consequent connection of human rights guarantees in the national
constitutions and European Convention on Human Rights on the one hand and the general
principles of Community law on the other obviates the continuing need for a catalogue of
fundamental rights. In view of these developments, it is now the position that, so long as the
European Communities and particularly the case law of the European Court generally ensure
an effective protection of fundamental rights as against the sovereign powers of the
Community which is to be regarded as substantially similar to the protection required
unconditionally by the German Constitution, and in so far as they generally safeguard the
essential content of fundamental rights, the German Federal Constitutional Court will no
longer exercise its jurisdiction to decide on the applicability of secondary Community law cited
as the legal basis for any acts of German courts or authorities within the sovereign jurisdiction
of the Federal Republic of Germany; and it will no longer review such legislation by the
standard of the fundamental rights contained in the German Constitution. References to the
Constitutional Court under Art 100(1) of the Constitution for that purpose are therefore
inadmissible.

On the strength of this development, together with similar ones in other Member States, it is
possible to say that the courts (if not some politicians) of the Member States have now
accepted the doctrine of the supremacy of directly effective Community law. Following the
Factortame (No 2) decision, the Master of the Rolls, Sir Thomas Bingham, stated that: '... The

supremacy of Community law has been accepted by the English courts with a readiness, and applied with a loyalty, which, if equalled in one or two other Member States, has probably been exceeded in none'.

In the light of these (at one time) controversial cases on direct effect, it is important to consider the attention they direct towards the role of the Member States in the development of the Community and the duty of solidarity which rests on them by virtue of Art 5 of the Treaty.

The Community, principally through the exercise of its Treaty powers by the Commission, is concerned to achieve full and effective implementation of the policies within its competence. However, in many cases the Commission must, in order to achieve its aims, work with and through one of a variety of national authorities (government departments, customs authorities, agricultural intervention agencies, etc). Within this working relationship, Member States and their agencies are required to adopt certain courses of action or to refrain from doing so. This can involve an obligation to adopt new legislation (or secondary legislation), to revise existing legislation, or to repeal existing legislation.

Similarly, national courts, often in co-operation with the Court of Justice through the medium of the preliminary rulings procedure of Art 177, have a duty, based again on Art 5, to ensure the full effectiveness of Community law within the scope of their jurisdictions. Where there is a Community dimension to a case, national courts and tribunals are obliged to interpret Community law (or request an interpretation from the Court of Justice), to apply Community law and to enforce it.

Interpretations of Community law by the Court of Justice are definitive in the courts and tribunals of the Member States. It may also be called upon to assess the validity of the acts of the Community institutions. It may not exceed its powers as laid down in the Treaty but it does not look to a Parliament as supreme law-maker. It is not bound by its own decisions but frequently cites such decisions to indicate a consistent line of reasoning. Its crucial role in the development of the Community will become increasingly apparent in succeeding chapters.

At national level again, in Art 177(1)(b) cases, a court may grant interim relief against the application of a national measure based on a disputed Community act (*Zuckerfabrik Süderdithmarschen*) and, in similar circumstances and under the same conditions, grant interim relief which in effect suspends the disputed Community act itself (Atlanta): both cases discussed in the previous chapter.

In the next section, it will be seen that a national court also has the power to grant interim relief against the application of national law alleged to be in violation of Community rules: *R v Secretary of State for Transport ex p Factortame Ltd* (Case 213/89). The aim of the Court of Justice is to achieve balance and coherence as regards enforcement and remedies.

SUPERVISION AT NATIONAL LEVEL: RIGHTS AND REMEDIES IN NATIONAL COURTS

The 'quota hopping' litigation (generally known as *Factortame*) not only involved the Commission's actions under Arts 169 and 186 but claims at the national level as well: see diagram ... The compatibility of the Merchant Shipping Act 1988 with Community law was the subject of challenge by Factortame Ltd and other members of the 'Anglo-Spanish' fishing fleet in the English courts. This challenge was similarly double-edged.

Factortame claimed that the Act's new registration requirements were in violation of their directly enforceable Community right not to be discriminated against on grounds of nationality under Art 7, in conjunction with their similar rights of establishment under Arts 52 and 58 of the Treaty. These claims became the subject of an Art 177 reference from the Divisional Court of the QBD for a interpretive ruling. However, before examining this claim, or the second aspect of the case, Factortame's application for the relevant parts of the 1988 Act to be suspended by the national court pending a determination of their compatibility with Community law by the Court of Justice, it is important to recall the relationship between the first, substantive issue (concerning directly effective rights) and an enforcement action brought by the Commission under Art 169.

As we have seen on numerous occasions, on the basis of the twin principles of supremacy and the direct effect of Community law, an infringement of Community law by a Member State may be challenged by private parties at national level. Returning to the Court's landmark decision in *Van Gend en Loos* (Case 26/62) regarding the standstill on customs duties in Art 12, following a reference from the Dutch customs court under Art 177, the Court stated in clear terms that:

> A restriction of the guarantees against an infringement of Art 12 by Member States to the procedures under Arts 169 and 170 would remove all direct legal protection of the individual rights of their nationals ... The vigilance of individuals concerned to protect their rights amounts to an effective supervision in addition to the supervision entrusted by Arts 169 and 170 to the diligence of the Commission and of the Member States.

THE FACTORTAME 'ANGLO-SPANISH' FISHING FLEET LITIGATION

Was an amendment of United Kingdom national law, designed to counter 'quota hopping', in breach of the directly effective Community rights of Spanish business interests?

It will be recalled that in this case the importer successfully argued that he could resist the application of national law (and a higher rate of duty) as it conflicted with his rights under the Treaty (to pay a lower rate). In another important decision, in the case of *Defrenne v Sabena (No 2)*, the effect of the Court's ruling was that compensation must be paid by any employer who discriminates against his employees in terms of pay. The equal treatment case of *Marshall* and *Van Colson* each in their different ways established the plaintiff's right to compensation. In the latter, we have seen how national law was interpreted so as to provide damages beyond the merely nominal.

All these Art 177 rulings of the Court of Justice (and many others of course) were resumed to the originating national court or tribunal to be applied. An inquiry into the eventual outcome raises the important general question of the effectiveness of Community rights in national courts or tribunals in terms of the remedies available. For example, upon what terms did English law provide for compensation for Miss Marshall? What remedies were available for Factortame and the other members of the 'Anglo-Spanish' fishing fleet should their claims in the national courts succeed?

The general trend in the development of the law in this respect shows a gradual change of emphasis from the creation of Community law rights for private parties to the provision of effective remedies for such individuals in their national courts.

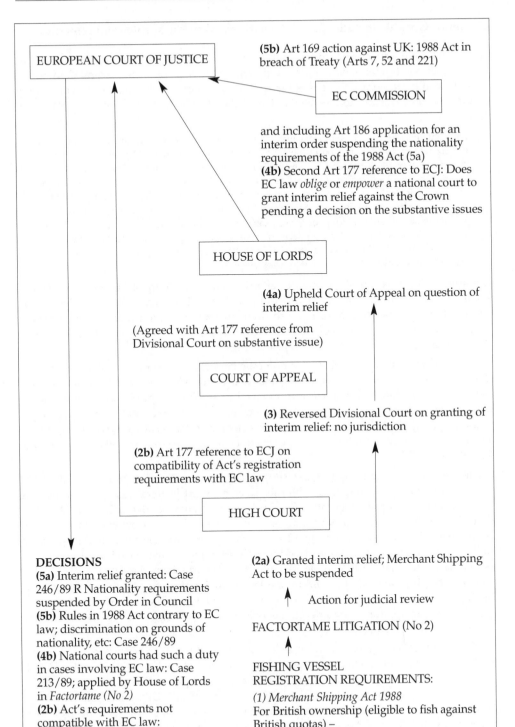

EUROPEAN COURT OF JUSTICE

(5b) Art 169 action against UK: 1988 Act in breach of Treaty (Arts 7, 52 and 221)

EC COMMISSION

and including Art 186 application for an interim order suspending the nationality requirements of the 1988 Act (5a)
(4b) Second Art 177 reference to ECJ: Does EC law *oblige* or *empower* a national court to grant interim relief against the Crown pending a decision on the substantive issues

HOUSE OF LORDS

(4a) Upheld Court of Appeal on question of interim relief

(Agreed with Art 177 reference from Divisional Court on substantive issue)

COURT OF APPEAL

(3) Reversed Divisional Court on granting of interim relief: no jurisdiction

(2b) Art 177 reference to ECJ on compatibility of Act's registration requirements with EC law

HIGH COURT

DECISIONS
(5a) Interim relief granted: Case 246/89 R Nationality requirements suspended by Order in Council
(5b) Rules in 1988 Act contrary to EC law; discrimination on grounds of nationality, etc: Case 246/89
(4b) National courts had such a duty in cases involving EC law: Case 213/89; applied by House of Lords in *Factortame (No 2)*
(2b) Act's requirements not compatible with EC law: Factortame's directly effected rights upheld and prevail over national law: Case 221/89

(2a) Granted interim relief; Merchant Shipping Act to be suspended

Action for judicial review

FACTORTAME LITIGATION (No 2)

FISHING VESSEL REGISTRATION REQUIREMENTS:

(1) Merchant Shipping Act 1988
For British ownership (eligible to fish against British quotas) –

NATIONALITY REQUIREMENTS;
RESIDENCE REQUIREMENTS;
MANAGEMENT AND CONTROL FROM UK.

Community rights in national courts: national procedural rules and remedies

Although Community law has increasingly established substantive rights for individuals, as regards their vindication it has, until recently, and in the absence of any general Community rules, tended to leave the questions of the appropriate court, the *procedural rules* which apply and the *remedies* available to the national law of the Member States. As Steiner explained in 1987:

> The growing acceptance by national courts of the principle of directly effective Community law has brought in its wake a second problem. If EEC law may be invoked by individuals before their national courts, what remedies are available for its breach? It has long been clear that EEC law may be invoked as a shield, whether in civil or criminal proceedings, or to provide the basis for an action in restitution, for example, for money paid in breach of Community law It is less clear to what extent, and in what action, it may be invoked by an individual in order to prevent damage from occurring, or to seek compensation for damage already suffered. When, if at all, will a breach of EEC law give rise to a remedy in damages? When will an injunction be more appropriate? When a declaration? Where the defendant is a public body, should the plaintiff proceed by writ or by way of judicial review?

It might be asked why, in the pursuit of effective remedies, Bourgoin did not seek interim relief as soon as the embargo took effect in late 1981. The answer must be that it was accepted at the time that, despite a requirement that effective protection be afforded Community rights, interim relief was not available against the Crown: s 21 of the Crown Proceedings Act 1947 in relation to civil proceedings.

The non-availability (as a matter of domestic law) of an interlocutory injunction against the Crown or an officer of the Crown, together with serious doubts, following *Bourgoin*, as to any other than limited avenues to damages in tort against public authorities is the background against which to examine the claims at national level in the Factortame 'quota-hopping' affair, discussed earlier in this chapter in the section on the supervision of Member States at Community level: see *Commission v UK (Re Merchant Shipping Rules)* (Case 246/89 R).

In the Divisional Court of the QBD (see the diagram on p 469), Factortame and the other members of the 'Anglo-Spanish' fishing fleet brought judicial review proceedings challenging the nationality (and other residence and domicile) requirements of the Merchant Shipping Act 1988 on the ground that, as in the case at Community level, they were in contravention of their directly effective Treaty rights, particularly their right of establishment under Art 52. This question was referred to the Court of Justice by the Divisional Court for a preliminary interpretive ruling under Art 177. As it would take perhaps two years for that ruling to be given and as in the meantime Factortame, not being able to fish against UK fishing quotas (or Spanish quotas either), claimed to be incurring heavy and irreparable financial loss, an application for interim relief pending final determination of the substantive issue was made to the court.

This application required the relevant section of the 1988 Act to be suspended to enable Factortame and the others to continue to operate their vessels as if duly registered as British ships. (It was also considered on the facts that in the light of Bourgoin no remedy in damages would be available.) On the basis of recent case law, the Divisional Court felt that it possessed the power in these circumstances to grant the application. This decision was reversed by the Court of Appeal, at which stage the Commission's application for interim relief under Art 186 with respect to the Act's nationality requirements was made and, as we have seen, was granted by the Court of Justice. Compliance was achieved by means of the Merchant Shipping Act 1988 (Amendment) Order 1989.

In the national courts, following a further appeal, the House of Lords held that, under *national* law, the English courts had no power to grant interim relief by way of an order suspending the operation of a statute pending a determination of its validity by the Court of Justice, nor had they the power to grant an interim injunction restraining the Secretary of State from enforcing the Act. Their Lordships, however, asked the Court for a preliminary ruling as to whether there was an overriding principle of Community law that a national court was under an obligation or had the power to provide an effective interlocutory remedy to protect directly effective rights where a seriously arguable claim to such rights had been advanced and irremediable loss was at stake.

Just over a year later, in June 1990, in response to this Art 177 reference, the Court, having drawn attention to the *Simmenthal* principle of the primacy of Community law and to the principle of co-operation in Art 5 of the Treaty, designed to ensure the legal protection which persons derived from the direct effect of Community law, ruled that: Community law was to be interpreted as meaning that a national court which, in a case before at concerning Community law, considers that the sole obstacle precluding it from granting interim relief is a rule of national law, must set aside that rule: *R v Secretary of State for Transport ex p Factortame Ltd* (Case 213/89).

Amid considerable controversy regarding what was perceived by some in the UK as an unacceptable intrusion on UK sovereignty, the House of Lords just a month later applied the Court's ruling. This was on the basis of the facts before it and pending final judgment by the Court of Justice on the validity of the 1988 Act in the face of Factortame's putative rights under the Treaty.

R v SECRETARY OF STATE FOR TRANSPORT EX P FACTORTAME LTD (NO 2) (1991)

In July 1990, the House of Lords, using the powers established by the ruling of the Court of Justice, allowed Factortame's appeal and granted an interim injunction restraining the Government from withholding or withdrawing registration under the 1988 Act to named fishing vessels on grounds of residence or domicile abroad. (It will be recalled that the Act's nationality requirements had previously been suspended by an amendment to the Act following a ruling by the President of the Court of Justice, see above.) The position was summed up by Lord Bridge as follows:

> Some public comments on the decision of the European Court of Justice, affirming the jurisdiction of the courts of Member States to override national legislation if necessary to enable interim relief to be granted in protection of rights under Community law, have suggested that this was a novel and dangerous invasion by a Community institution of the sovereignty of the United Kingdom Parliament. But such comments are based on a misconception.
>
> If the supremacy within the European Community of Community law over the national law of Member States was not always inherent in the EEC Treaty it was certainly well-established in the jurisprudence of the European Court of Justice long before the UK joined the Community. Thus, whatever limitation of its sovereignty Parliament accepted when it enacted the European Communities Act 1972 it was entirely voluntary. Under the terms of the Act of 1972 it has always been clear that it was the duty of a UK court, when delivering final judgment, to override any rule of national law found to be in conflict with any directly enforceable rule of Community law.
>
> Similarly, when decisions of the European Court of Justice have exposed areas of United Kingdom statute law which failed to implement Community directive, Parliament has always loyally accepted the obligation to make appropriate and prompt amendments. Thus there is nothing in any way novel in according supremacy to rule of Community law in those areas to which they apply and to insist chat, in the

protection of rights under Community law, national courts must not be inhibited by rule of national law from granting interim relief in appropriate cases is no more than a logical recognition of that supremacy.

When considering its decision, the House of Lords had available to it unsworn evidence indicating that many of the owners of the 95 vessels involved (the 'Anglo-Spanish' fleet) had already suffered losses well in excess of £100,000 and that some feared imminent bankruptcy.

In reaching their unanimous decision, their Lordships took account of the two-stage guidelines for the exercise of the court's discretionary jurisdiction to grant interim injunctions as laid down by the House in *American Cyanamid v Ethicon* in 1975. Such jurisdiction concerns the power to grant an injunction where it is just or convenient on such terms and conditions as the court thinks fit: s 37 of the Supreme Court Act 1981. Their Lordships also considered that on the basis of the decision in *Bourgoin*, the applicants would be unable to recover damages from the Crown if the Act were ultimately found to be contrary to the Treaty (their being unable to establish wrongful conduct on the part of the Secretary of State). It was therefore agreed that the application for an interim injunction against the Crown should go directly to the second stage of consideration, regarding the balance of convenience, and need not pass through the first stage, regarding whether damages were an adequate remedy.

On the question of the balance of convenience (the balance of interests in Community law), it was stressed that matters of considerable weight had to be put in the balance to outweigh the desirability of enforcing, in the public interest, what was on its face the law of the land. Each case was to be considered in the light of its circumstances. There was no rule that it was necessary to show a *prima facie* case that the law was invalid; it was enough if the applicant could show that there was a serious case to be tried.

In this respect, it is noteworthy that in *La Cinq v Commission* (Case T-44/90) the Court of First Instance annulled a Commission refusal to order interim measures (see, also, *Camera Car* Case 792/79 R in Chapter 17), stating that the complainant company need not show a clear and flagrant breach of the competition rules by another party, merely a *prima facie* case. On the question of damage to La Cinq, if the interim measures were not ordered and the company had to await the outcome of the Commission's final decision, the Court stated that all the company's circumstances must be taken into account. Although the Court of Justice had held in *Cargill v Commission* (Case 229/88 R) that damage is not serious and irreparable (a necessary requirement for the ordering of interim measures) if it is purely financial and can, if the complainant is successful in the main action, be fully recovered, La Cinq's position was that it ran the risk of going out of business altogether in the interim (cf the position of Factortame and the others) and suffering serious and irreparable damage whatever the outcome of the final decision.

It is important to recognise that the granting of interim relief in *Factortame* meant that a new remedy had been created by the national court in order to ensure the effectiveness of Community law. This case therefore marks a significant development from previous rulings on supremacy and direct effect and a change of stance on the part of the Court of Justice which, in *Rewe v HZA* (Case 158/80) (see above) had stated that 'it was not intended to create new remedies in the national courts to ensure the observance of Community law other then those already laid down by national law'. The House of Lords had stated that interim relief against the Crown was not available under national law. Nevertheless, this was a rule governing the grant of remedies which, according to other previous rulings of the Court, precluded the grant of an appropriate remedy. Accordingly, it was to be set aside. (Since *Factortame*, the House of Lords has changed its position concerning interim injunctions as a matter of English law irrespective of a Community dimension: see *M v Home Office* (1993), in which, in the Court of Appeal, Lord Donaldson MR stated that it would be 'anomalous and wrong in principle' if the courts' powers were limited in domestic law matters when the limitations had been removed by Community law in disputes concerning rights under that law. *M* is therefore authority for the availability of interim injunctions against ministers of the Crown as a matter of English law.)

That the applicant in *Factortame* had a serious case to be tried was later confirmed by the Court of Justice in response to the original Art 177 reference from the Divisional Court of the Queen's Bench Division. The Court ruled that the nationality, residence and domicile requirements of the 1988 Act were contrary to Community law, in particular Art 52 concerning the applicant's directly effective right of establishment: *R v Secretary of State for Transport ex p Factortame Ltd* (Case C221/89). As in the case brought by the Commission, the Court stated that the system of national quotas under the Common Fisheries Policy did not affect the decision. However, although introduced on sound, conservational grounds, the national quota system does appear to lie at the heart of this problem. Nonetheless, as Lord Bridge had stated earlier in these proceedings:

> ... it is common ground, that in so far as the applicants succeed before the ECJ in obtaining a ruling in support of the Community rights which they claim, those rights will prevail over the restrictions imposed on registration of British fishing vessels by Part II of the Act of 1988 and the Divisional Court will, in the final determination of the application for judicial review be obliged to make appropriate declarations to give effect to those rights.

As regards a further action for damages brought by Factortame and the other members of the 'Anglo-Spanish' fishing fleet against the British government, see the final part of this chapter.

Further difficulties have arisen in the UK regarding remedies despite the fact that the situation in question involved loss suffered as the result of a breach of an individual's directly effective rights and that damages to compensate for losses of the type in question were provided for under the relevant provisions of national law.

BIBLIOGRAPHY

Anderson, R, *The Power and the Word*, 1988, London: Paladin.

Anderson, T and Twining, W, *Analysis of Evidence*, 1991, London: Butterworths.

Bailey, SH and Gunn, M, *Smith, Bailey and Gunn on the Modern English Legal System*, 4th edn, 2002, London: Sweet & Maxwell.

Barrass, R, *Students Must Write*, 1998, London: Routledge.

Berger, J, *Ways of Seeing*, 1990, London: Penguin.

Brookfield, S, *Developing Critical Thinkers*, 1987, Milton Keynes: OU Press.

Clinch, P, *Using a Law Library: A Students Guide to Legal Research Skills*, 2nd edn, 2001, London: Blackstone.

Coates, J, *Women, Men and Language: A Sociolinguistic Account of Gender Differences in Language*, 2003, London: Longman.

Costanzo, M, *Problem Solving*, 1994, London: Cavendish Publishing.

Cross, R and Harris, JW, *Precedent in English Law*, 4th edn, 1991, Oxford: Clarendon.

Fairclough, N, *Language and Power*, 2nd edn, 2001, London: Longman.

Fox, M and Bell, C, *Learning Legal Skills*, 3rd edn, 1999, London: Blackstone.

French, D, *How to Cite Legal Authorities*, 1996, London: Blackstone.

Goodrich, P, *Languages of Law from the Logics of Memory to Nomadic Masks*, 1990, London: Weidenfeld & Nicolson.

Hargie, O, *A Handbook of Communication Skills*, 1996, London: Routledge.

Hartley, TC, *The Foundations of European Community Law*, 2003, Oxford: OUP.

Hawkins, L, Hudson, M and Cornall, R, *The Legal Negotiator*, 1991, London: Sweet & Maxwell.

Holland, JA and Webb, J, *Learning Legal Rules*, 1991, London: Blackstone; 5th edn, 2003, Oxford: OUP.

Honey, P, *Does Accent Matter?*, 1991, London: Faber & Faber.

Honey, P, *Improve Your People Skills*, 1989, Oxford: Blackwells.

Maughan, C and Webb, J, *Lawyering Skills and the Legal Process*, 1995, London: Butterworths.

McGovern, D, Matthews, M and Mackay, S, *Reading*, 1994, Hemel Hempstead: Prentice Hall.

Nash, W, *Rhetoric: The Wit of Persuasion*, 1992, Oxford: Blackwell.

Northledge, A, *The Good Study Guide*, 1995, Milton Keynes: OU Press.

Riley, A, *English for Law*, 1995, Hemel Hampstead: Prentice Hall.

Russell, F and Locke, C, *English Law and Language*, 1995, Hemel Hempstead: Phoenix ELT.

Scherr, A, *Client Interviewing for Lawyers: An Analaysis and Guide*, 1986, London: Sweet & Maxwell.

Sychin, C, Legal Method, 1999, London: Sweet & Maxwell.

Tillotson, J, *European Community Law: Text, Cases and Materials*, 2nd edn, 1996 (4th edn, 2003), London: Cavendish Publishing.

Trzeciak, J and Mackey, SE, *Study Skills for Academic Writing*, 1994, Hemel Hempstead: Prentice Hall.

Twining, W and Miers, D, *How to do Things with Rules*, 1991, London: Weidenfeld & Nicolson; 4th edn, 1999, London: Butterworths.

White, R and McGovern, D, *Writing*, 1994, Hemel Hempstead: Prentice Hall.

Wigmore, JH, '*The problem of proof*' (1913) 8 Illinois Law Review 77.

Zander, M, *The Law Making Process*, 5th edn, 1999, London: Butterworths.

Zander, M, *Cases and Materials on the English Legal System*, 9th edn, 2003, London: Butterworths.

INDEX

UNIVERSITY OF
PORTSMOUTH
LIBRARY